Compliments of
A. W. Bishop,
Adjt. Gen'l, Ark.

REPORT

OF

THE ADJUTANT GENERAL OF ARKANSAS,

FOR THE

PERIOD OF THE LATE REBELLION, AND TO NOVEMBER 1, 1866.

WASHINGTON:
GOVERNMENT PRINTING OFFICE
1867.

Notice

In many older books, foxing (or discoloration) occurs and, in some instances, print lightens with wear and age. Reprinted books, such as this, often duplicate these flaws, notwithstanding efforts to reduce or eliminate them. The pages of this reprint have been digitally enhanced and, where possible, the flaws eliminated in order to provide clarity of content and a pleasant reading experience.

Originally published:
Washington: 1867

Reprinted:
Janaway Publishing, Inc.
2012

Janaway Publishing, Inc.
732 Kelsey Ct.
Santa Maria, California 93454
(805) 925-1038
www.janawaygenealogy.com

ISBN: 978-1-59641-259-0

Made in the United States of America

ERRATA.

Page 6, for "1855," in last paragraph, read "1865."
Page 7, for "July 26, 1866," in paragraph next to last, read "July 28, 1866."
Page 10, for "Sept. 27, 1861," date of enlistment of M. LaRue Harrison, read "Sept. 24, 1861."
Page 12, for date of enlistment of M. LaRue Harrison, read "Sept. 24, 1861," and for date of rank "July 3, 1862;" also, for the word "infantry," after the word "entered," in same line," read "regiment."
Page 51, for date of enlistment of William S. Johnson read "April 10, 1861."
Page 56, for "October," in line 42, read "November."
Page 166, for "Jan. 25, 1865," date of rank of William J. Hunter, read "June 20, 1865."
Page 169, under the head of remarks for James M. Johnson, add "brevetted brigadier general of volunteers April, 10, 1867, with rank from March 13, 1865."
Page 225, for company "F," in remarks opposite name of Ira D. Bronson, read company "K."
Page 229, under head of remarks for James M. Bethel, captain company "K," read also "mustered out with regiment."
Page 251, for "Aug. 15, 1863," date of enlistment of Denton D. Stark, read "Aug. 15, 1861."
Page 255, in historical memoranda, read "Robert Thompson" for "Robert V. Thompson," and "Aug. 10, 1865," for "Aug. 30, 1865," as date of muster out of battery.
Page 256, under the head of enlisted men deserted in 1st Arkansas battery, insert the figures "24."
Page 265, in line 39, for "Hon. John T. Henderson" read "Hon. John B. Henderson."
Page 272, for "William Shreve" read "Wilson Shreve."
Page 273, for "James F. Clean" read "James F. Clure."

REPORT

OF THE

ADJUTANT GENERAL OF THE STATE OF ARKANSAS,

FOR

The period of the late rebellion, and to November 1, 1866.

NOTE.

In November last the following report was submitted, in manuscript, to the legislature of the State of Arkansas, as a document accompanying the governor's message. That body, however, disregarding the governor's recommendation that by their order it should be printed, and having otherwise shown their hostility to the efficient management of the adjutant general's office, my petition to Congress for the publication of this report, in order that some record might be preserved of the loyal soldiery of a rebellious State, was, on the 25th ultimo, presented by Hon. Henry Wilson, chairman of the Senate Committee on Military Affairs. Subsequently the following proceedings were had:

"IN SENATE, *Friday, February* 15, 1867.

* * * * * * * * * * *

"ARKANSAS LOYAL TROOPS.

"Mr. ANTHONY. The Committee on Printing, to whom was referred a memorial of Albert W. Bishop, adjutant general of Arkansas, praying that an appropriation be made for the publication of his report presented to the legislature of that State, have instructed me to report a resolution in conformity with the prayer of the memorialist; and, if the Senate will now indulge me, I will state the object of the resolution, and ask for its present consideration, if no one objects, because as the Senate nearly always indulges the Committee on Printing with the present consideration of their resolutions, I do not wish to ask for it unless it is necessary for the public service. All the loyal States have prepared rosters of the men who served in the loyal army, and they have been published, with the reports of the adjutants general of the various States.

"The State of Arkansas furnished over ten thousand men to the loyal army. The adjutant general presented his report, with a roster of those names, to the legislature of that State, which is now under disloyal control, and they have refused to publish it, so that there is no record whatever of the services of these gallant men. It seemed to the committee that it was due to them that this dereliction on the part of their own State should be made up by Congress. They have also received a letter from General Grant, strongly urging the publication of the report. Now, if no senator objects, I ask for the present consideration of the resolution.

"By unanimous consent the Senate proceeded to consider the following resolution:

"*Resolved*, That the report of Albert W. Bishop, adjutant general of Arkansas, be printed for the use of the Senate, and that one thousand extra copies be printed for the use of the adjutant general of Arkansas, to be distributed among the loyal officers of that State mentioned therein.

"The resolution was agreed to."

For this recognition of their military services in sustaining the national flag and defending the honor of a common country, the Union men of Arkansas are profoundly grateful to the Senate of the United States and General Grant.

ALBERT W. BISHOP,
Adjutant General of Arkansas.

WASHINGTON, D. C., *February* 1867.

HEADQUARTERS STATE OF ARKANSAS,
ADJUTANT GENERAL'S OFFICE,
Little Rock, November 1, 1866.

GOVERNOR: I have the honor to transmit herewith my report of the organization and operations of the loyal troops of the State during the late rebellion, and the transactions of this department since the establishment of the present State government.

I am, very respectfully, your obedient servant,

ALBERT W. BISHOP,
Adjutant General.

His Excellency ISAAC MURPHY,
Governor of Arkansas.

REPORT.

The gathering storm of 1860 was nowhere more sincerely regretted than by thousands in the south. In this State there was sincere devotion to the Union, but her power was mainly wielded by open or concealed enemies of the general government, and it was impossible to stay the tide that swept her into rebellion.

On the 6th day of May, 1861, the State assumed to secede. Union men who were members of the convention, and even signed the ordinance of secession, and those who sympathized with them throughout the State, were for many months powerless in council and the field, and some, indeed, never threw off their enforced adhesion to the southern confederacy until the war had ceased, and the confederacy itself was hopelessly shattered. For nearly a year, in fact, after this attempted secession of the State, there was a substantial want of concert of action among Union men, and they quietly submitted to what they could not prevent, or fled for security to the caves and hills. Thus wore away the first year of the war.

After the battle of Pea Ridge, in March, 1862, and while General Curtis was traversing the northern portion of the State from the Upper White river to Helena, on the Mississippi, the Union men of Arkansas began to appear within the federal lines, and efforts for their military organization were promptly made. Some of them, meantime, participated in the battle referred to, fighting with whatever regiment they fell in with; and when General Curtis arrived at Batesville, he found several hundred men ready to enter the service of the United States. For weeks they had been partly organized, and were only waiting a favorable opportunity to identify themselves more efficiently with the Union cause. Accompanying the army to Helena, they entered the service as mounted infantry. For an account of their organization and services, attention is called to Appendix A.

The successful issue of the battle of Pea Ridge was the signal for loyal citizens, especially in northwestern Arkansas, to leave their homes for the federal lines. Many came, also, from the woods where for months they had secreted themselves, and shortly there assembled at Cassville, Missouri, a number sufficient to warrant the organization of a company. M. La Rue Harrison, of the thirty-sixth Illinois infantry volunteers, then post quartermaster at the place last mentioned, conceived the idea of effecting this organization, and with great assiduity immediately set about the accomplishment of his purpose. A company was promptly organized, with himself as captain, and attached to the sixth Missouri cavalry volunteers, then commanded by Colonel Clark Wright.

Loyal Arkansians, however, continuing still to cross the border, Colonel

Harrison (as he afterwards became) now determined to raise a regiment, and one to be known distinctively as an Arkansas organization. Without delay he applied to the Secretary of War for authority to raise the first regiment of Arkansas cavalry volunteers. Hon. John S. Phelps, of Missouri, then in Washington, heartily seconded his efforts, and by dint of no little persistency succeeded in obtaining a special order to raise the regiment. At first the department was averse to granting the order, but the loyalty of these men admitted of no doubt, and on the 16th day of June, 1862, the order was issued.

As will more fully appear from Appendix A, the raising of this regiment gave great encouragement to loyal citizens of the State, especially in the northwest, and was followed, as soon as circumstances would allow, by the organization and muster in for three years or during the war of the first and second regiments of Arkansas infantry, the second Arkansas cavalry, and battery A, first Arkansas light artillery. To the commanders of these and all other organizations sent by Arkansas into the field to maintain the integrity of the Union, great credit is due for the prosecution of their labors under circumstances both extraordinary and anomalous.

A large proportion of the population of the State had in one form or another identified themselves with the rebellion. Public sentiment was disloyal, and a citizen of the State could do no act so odious to the majority as enlisting in the federal army. It was regarded as the clearest evidence of treason, and for a time there was a strong disposition not to accord to "Arkansas federals," as they were termed, the rights of prisoners of war. Happily, however, wiser counsels prevailed, and this feature in warfare, which at first seemed to be culminating in the worst form of retaliation, was no longer observable.

After the occupation of Helena by the United States forces in the summer of 1862, it was thought advisable that a military governor for the State should be created, and a commission was accordingly issued to Hon. John S. Phelps, to whom the following instructions were given:

War Department,
Washington City, July 19, 1862.

Sir: The commission you have received expresses on its face the nature and extent of the duties and power devolved on you by the appointment of military governor of Arkansas.

Instructions have been given to Major General Butler to aid you in the performance of your duty and the exercise of your authority. He has also been instructed to detail an adequate military force for the special purpose of a governor's guard, and to act under your directions.

It is obvious to you that the great purpose of your appointment is to reestablish the authority of the federal government in the State of Arkansas, and to provide the means of maintaining peace and security to the loyal inhabitants of that State, until they shall be able to re-establish a civil government. Upon your wisdom and energetic action much will depend in accomplishing that result. It is not deemed necessary to give any specific instructions, but rather to confide in your sound discretion to adopt such measures as circumstances may demand. Specific instructions will be given when requested. You may rely upon the perfect confidence and full support of the department in the performance of your duties.

With respect, I am, your obedient servant,
EDWIN M. STANTON,
Secretary of War.

Hon. John S. Phelps,
Military Governor of Arkansas.

Establishing his headquarters at Helena, Governor Phelps discharged the duties of his position as the exigency of the times allowed, organizing the second Arkansas cavalry, and commissioning various officers in other State organizations, until July, 1863, when the maintenance of a military governorship being no longer considered necessary, the following order was promulgated:

[General Orders No. 211.]

WAR DEPARTMENT, ADJUTANT GENERAL'S OFFICE,
Washington, July 9, 1863.

Order abolishing military governorship of Arkansas.

Ordered, That the appointment of John S. Phelps, as military governor of the State of Arkansas, and of Amos F. Eno, as secretary, be revoked, and the office of military governor in said State is abolished, and that all authority, appointments, and power heretofore granted to and exercised by them, or either of them, as military governor or secretary, or by any person or persons appointed by or acting under them, is hereby revoked and annulled.

By order of the President:

E. D. TOWNSEND,
Assistant Adjutant General.

Though the powers conferred upon Governor Phelps were, by the terms of this order, "revoked and annulled," the commissions issued by him to officers of Arkansas regiments were not invalidated, and in every respect the operations of these troops continued as before, the War Department having always in fact had substantial control over them.

After the occupation of Little Rock by the army of Arkansas in September, 1863, Major General F. Steele commanding, authority was given by him to raise the 3d and 4th regiments of Arkansas cavalry volunteers and the 4th regiment of Arkansas mounted infantry, which was done, wholly as to the first two commands, and partly as to the last, and all of which entered upon active duty. For a sketch of their organization and services, attention is called to the memoranda accompanying rosters in Appendix A.

On the organization of the provisional government of the State in January, 1864, Captain C. A. Henry, assistant quartermaster United States volunteers, was appointed provisional adjutant general; and on the establishment of the present State government in April of the same year, F. M. Sams, then adjutant of the 1st Arkansas infantry volunteers, was duly commissioned as adjutant general of the State. Meantime, although the present State government had not been fully recognized at Washington by the admission of members of Congress, your excellency had issued a large number of commissions to officers in Arkansas regiments, upon which they were duly mustered into the service. In September of the same year I was commissioned adjutant general, and entered on duty November 15.

On the 13th day of December General Steele, then commanding the department of Arkansas, received an order from the commanding general of the division of West Mississippi directing the immediate evacuation of Fort Smith and its dependencies. The execution of this order being considered by your excellency disastrous to the State, you directed me to proceed at once to Washington to do what I could to procure its countermand. For the particulars of the mission, and its ultimate accomplishment, your attention is called to the documents herewith transmitted, marked Appendix B.

In February, 1865, under the supervision of Major General J. J. Reynolds, commanding the department of Arkansas, the organization of a local militia, without expense to the State, and for the double purpose of protection and the cultivation of the soil, was begun. During that and the present year, sixty-three commissions have been issued to captains of companies, the most of them in the spring and summer of 1865; but the peculiar exigency for the organization of these companies having in most localities passed away, very few of them are now existing.

Commanding officers were instructed to enlist their men for mutual protection and the defence of their homes and property; they were to report to and be governed by the orders of the nearest military post commandant in all that pertained to the equipment and military discipline of their commands, furnishing such commandants with company rolls, and such statistical returns as they might require, and in the general administration of affairs were to be governed by the letter of instructions of which the following is a copy:

EXECUTIVE OFFICE, STATE OF ARKANSAS,
Little Rock, 1865.

In issuing the attached authority, especial confidence is reposed in your integrity and ability to command; the measure of your success will determine the wisdom of the selection. You are encouraged to expect aid from the commander of the military department, who will cause arms and ammunition to be furnished for your defence, and will render such other assistance as your necessities may require until you have means for self-support.

It is expected that you will impress those enlisted under you that they are not organized as soldiers, but as farmers, mutually pledged to protect each other from the depredations of outlaws who infest the State. The main object of all must be the raising of such crops as will secure subsistence to families dependent upon them for support. The magnitude of your agricultural operations will be the full capacity of manual labor at your command, as the combined strength of the productive labor of the State is demanded in the impending emergency to prevent starvation of citizens.

Idlers should not be permitted to domicile in your colony; their influence is mischievous, and they consume means which should be contributed to the helpless.

All able-bodied male persons in your community should be identified with your organization, there being mutual obligations for self-protection, and none should be defended who refuse to join in the common cause.

Monthly reports in detail of all that pertains to appropriation of labor, prospects for crops, and the general administration of affairs, will be made by you to this office.

Very respectfully, &c.,

ISAAC MURPHY,
Governor of Arkansas.

To ——— ———,
Commanding Company of Militia, ——— *County, Arkansas.*

The surrender of Lieutenant General E. Kirby Smith, commanding the Trans-Mississippi department of the Confederate States, May 26, 1865, did away, to a very great extent, with the necessity for these companies. Quite a number of block-houses had, however, been previously built, and the loyally disposed portion of the farming population of the State were at work in communities, some of the members standing guard, while others held the plough. In northwestern Arkansas especially was this system pursued, and great material good resulted to the several counties constituting this portion of the State. Crops were planted that otherwise would not have been, and much anticipated suffering and want were thereby avoided.

An occasional company is still organized, and it is gratifying to know that the policy heretofore pursued in this regard meets the approval of Major General

Ord, now commanding the department of the Arkansas, and will be carried out by him so far as it may be considered advisable to do so. For roster of officers your attention is called to Appendix C.

The principal object of these companies being to preserve peace and good order in neighborhoods where disturbances are known to have happened, or there is good reason to apprehend them, and where it is not considered necessary to station United States troops, they have been organized of men who are believed to be quiet and well-disposed citizens of the United States government, and no restriction is placed upon the enrolling of those who, during the late war, attached their fortunes to the southern confederacy, if they are now really desirous of living in peace with those with whom they were then at variance, and will aid in suppressing violence of persons and depredations upon property.

I do not regard it advisable, at present, to put any other militia system in practical operation, and I have, therefore, in this report, no suggestions to make with reference to that revision of the militia laws of the State which, in the progress of events, may become necessary.*

During the rebellion several organizations of local militia became necessary, but expired with the emergency that gave them rise. Created under department and district orders, their records have never been on file in this office, but their duties were at times quite arduous, and the services rendered by them were efficient.

In accordance with orders from headquarters of the military division of West Mississippi, a draft was undertaken in the State, in the latter part of the year 1864, but the course pursued was not approved by the Provost Marshal General of the United States, and no drafted men from Arkansas entered the service, although a regiment was partially organized, of which John B. Kirkwood, of Little Rock, was appointed lieutenant colonel, by General Steele, then commanding the department of Arkansas. To quite a considerable extent, citizens of Arkansas were enlisted during the war in Missouri, Kansas, Iowa, Indiana, and Illinois regiments, while on duty in the State, but their number and military history I am unable to give. Of the following case, however, I am able and deem it proper to make special mention. Early in 1861 George G. Shumard, M. D., then a resident of Fort Smith, was compelled to leave the State. In April of that year he was appointed surgeon general of Ohio, and subsequently served with distinction as a medical officer, contributing largely to the efficiency of the army in the campaigns of that year in Virginia, Kentucky, and Tennessee.

In August, 1861, he was appointed a surgeon of volunteers, and afterwards became medical director of the district of Kentucky. In 1864 he was a prominent candidate for the surgeon generalship of the army, receiving recommendations from Governors Yates, Morton, Andrews, and Brough, Hon. James Speed, Attorney General, Hon. Joseph Holt, Judge Advocate General, Senators King of New York, and Lane of Indiana, Hon. Schuyler Colfax, Speaker of the House of Representatives, and other prominent men of the nation. Though failing to obtain this appointment, he otherwise served during the war. There was, also, enlisted in the State a large number of colored troops, for what were at first known as Arkansas organizations, and many of their muster-in rolls are now on file in this office. Their designations, however, were subsequently changed; copies of muster-in rolls ceased to be filed as indicated, and the control of these troops passed beyond the official knowledge of this office.

In July, 1855, a convention of adjutants general of States was held at Boston, Massachusetts, which, by your order, I attended, though I arrived too late to participate in the principal deliberations of the body. Nevertheless I had ample communication with most of its members, and was received with generous cour-

---

* The protection of the loyal citizens of the State is still entrusted in a great measure to United States forces, and until civil government is re-established upon a thoroughly loyal basis, this element of strength and security cannot safely be dispensed with.

tesy, the anomalous relations of our State to the Union being no restriction upon the full exercise of the privilege of representation.

Among the subjects discussed in the convention, and in which Arkansas has an interest, was the propriety of the enactment by Congress of a general militia law, and when the convention adjourned, it was to reassemble at Washington, in March, 1866, where this subject was further to be considered. I did not attend the adjourned session, and such a law as was had under discussion has not yet been enacted.

On the return of the State archives, in the summer of 1865, I received a large number of muster-rolls and other documents belonging to the office of the confederate adjutant general of the State, which have been carefully preserved, and are now in this office.

By section six of an act of the legislature, entitled "An act amendatory of the militia laws of the State of Arkansas," approved January 21, 1861, the staff of the governor is made to consist of one adjutant general, one quartermaster general, one commissary general, one paymaster general, one inspector general, one judge advocate, one surgeon general, and such aides-de-camp as he may think proper to appoint. I respectfully suggest for your consideration, and any legislative action in the premises that you may think proper to recommend, that at least four of these offices should be consolidated, the adjutant general to be made *ex officio* quartermaster, commissary, and inspector general of the State. This is the case in some other States in the Union, and it is believed that similar legislation can with propriety be resorted to in Arkansas.

In fact, the offices of quartermaster, commissary, and inspector general have been nominal only since the organization of the existing State government, the former two not even having been filled. In this office, which you tendered to me in October, 1864, there have been constant duties to perform. Aside from the organization of the militia referred to, my necessary communication with departments at Washington has been frequent, and especially so since, by order of the Secretary of War, copies of the muster-out rolls of our regiments were placed on file in this office. I am constantly in receipt of applications from the Surgeon General of the army and the Commissioner of Pensions for official certificates of the enrolment, muster, duty, death, and cause of death of our deceased soldiers, to comply with which involves no trifling labor.

The adjustment of the claims of our soldiers for bounty, under the act of Congress of July 26, 1866, will also require consultation with this office, and the duties thus imposed upon me must be performed. By the Adjutant General of the army and many of the adjutants general of States, I have been asked to send them my report of the organization and operations of our troops during the war, and could only reply that I had not yet had an opportunity to make it.

For the disbursements of this department since my connection with it, aside from clerk hire which I have been compelled to pay from my own salary, your attention is called to the statement herewith submitted, marked Appendix D. For several months, however, after my acceptance of this office, when there was no money in the treasury, and State warrants had scarcely more than a nominal value, I paid all the expenses of the office, with the exception of a single small item, and could only dispose of the warrants issued to me for my own services at a sacrifice of from sixty to seventy-five per cent. But this period of stringency has passed, and it cannot but be a source of gratification to every one interested in the welfare of the State, that neither for this nor any other of the departments of its present government has any money been borrowed since the government itself went into operation.

ALBERT W. BISHOP,
Adjutant General.

APPENDIX A.

ROSTER

OF

ARKANSAS VOLUNTEERS,

ACCOMPANYING

REPORT OF ADJUTANT GENERAL,

WITH HISTORICAL MEMORANDA ANNEXED.

First regiment Arkansas cavalry volunteers. Mustered into service August 7, 1862 (three years;) mustered out August 23, 1865.

FIELD AND STAFF.

Names.	Rank.	Enlistment.	Date of rank.	Remarks.
M. LaRue Harrison	Colonel	Sept. 27, 1861	Aug. 7, 1862	Promoted from captain of company A to fill original vacancy; mustered out August 23, 1865. Brevetted brigadier general for gallant and meritorious services during the war, with rank from March 13, 1865.
Albert W. Bishop	Lieutenant colonel	Aug. 21, 1861	July 10, 1862	Promoted from captain of company B, 2d Wisconsin cavalry, July 10, 1862, to fill original vacancy; mustered out February 22, 1865, to accept commission as adjutant general of Arkansas.
Thomas J. Hunt	...do	July 3, 1862	April 29, 1865	Promoted from captain of company B to major, August 7, 1862, to fill original vacancy; promoted lieutenant colonel, vice A. W. Bishop, promoted; mustered out August 23, 1865.
James J. Johnson	Major	—, 1861	Aug. 8, 1862	Promoted from 1st lieutenant of company A to fill original vacancy; resigned December 1, 1863.
Ezra Fitch	...do	July 31, 1862	Oct. 2, 1862	Promoted from captain of company C to fill original vacancy; resigned November 24, 1864.
Charles Galloway	...do	July 10, 1862	Mar. 2, 1864	Promoted from captain of company E, vice J. J. Johnson, resigned; resigned March 1, 1865.
John I. Worthington	...do	Aug. 7, 1862	Feb. 28, 1865	Promoted from captain of company H, vice Ezra Fitch, resigned; killed in action March 11, 1865.
Richard H. Wimpy	...do	June 15, 1862	May 1, 1865	Promoted from captain of company F, vice John I. Worthington, killed; mustered out August 23, 1865.
Hugo C. C. Botefuhr	...do	Aug. 7, 1862	June 4, 1865	Promoted from captain of company B, vice T. J. Hunt, promoted; mustered out August 23, 1865.
Frank Strong	...do	Nov. 18, 1861	June 4, 1865	Promoted from captain of company L, vice Charles Galloway, resigned; mustered out August 23, 1865.
Henry J. Maynard	Surgeon	—, 1861	Sept. 27, 1862	Promoted from assistant surgeon, 59th Illinois infantry, to fill original vacancy; mustered out August 23, 1865.
William Hunter	Assistant surgeon		Aug. 8, 1862	Promoted from 1st lieutenant of company B to fill original vacancy; resigned January 31, 1863.
Amos H. Caffee	...do	Oct. 1, 1862	Jan. 12, 1863	Appointed from hospital steward to fill original vacancy; mustered out to accept commission as surgeon 13th Kansas infantry, February 22, 1865.
Jonathan E. Tefft	...do	Feb. 25, 1863	Feb. 25, 1863	Appointed from civil life, vice William Hunter, resigned; resigned January 22, 1865.
Reuben North	Chaplain	—, 1861	Feb. 17, 1863	Appointed from private company G, 2d Wisconsin cavalry, to fill original vacancy; mustered out August 23, 1865.
Denton D. Stark	Adjutant	Aug. 15, 1861	Oct. 2, 1862	Promoted from 2d lieutenant company B to fill original vacancy; promoted to captain battery A, 1st Arkansas light artillery, April 1, 1863.
Henry M. Kidder	...do	April 1, 1863	July 1, 1863	Promoted from 2d lieutenant company K, vice D. D. Stark, promoted; mustered out to accept commission as major 5th United States colored cavalry, March 15, 1865.
Elizur B. Harrison	Adjutant, 1st battalion	Aug. 7, 1862	Aug. 7, 1862	Appointed from civil life to fill original vacancy; mustered out at St. Louis, Mo., September 20, 1862, by order of War Department.
Frank Strong	Adjutant, 2d battalion	Nov. 18, 1861	Aug. 7, 1862	Appointed from hospital steward, 2d Wisconsin cavalry, to fill original vacancy; mustered out at St. Louis, Mo., September 20, 1862, by order of War Department.
James H. Wilson	Regimental quartermaster	Aug. 15, 1861	Nov. 1, 1862	Promoted from 1st lieutenant of company D to fill original vacancy; resigned January 12, 1864.

REPORT OF THE ADJUTANT GENERAL OF ARKANSAS.

Name	Rank	Date	Date	Remarks
John M. Bigger	......do......	Aug. 15, 1862	Mar. 1, 1864	Appointed from quartermaster sergeant, *vice* J. H. Wilson, resigned; resigned March 11, 1865.
Thomas J. Rice	Regimental commissary of subsistence.	Sept. 22, 1862	Oct. 1, 1862	Promoted from 2d lieutenant of company M to fill original vacancy; resigned April 6, 1863.
John A. Maxwell	......do......	—, 1861	April 7, 1863	Appointed from private of company K, 26th Indiana infantry, *vice* T. J. Rice, resigned; mustered out August 23, 1865.

NON-COMMISSIONED STAFF.

Name	Rank	Date	Date	Remarks
Robert Thompson	Sergeant major		July 10, 1862	Appointed from private of company F to fill original vacancy; appointed 1st lieutenant battery A, 1st Arkansas light artillery, April 1, 1863.
Thomas Brooks	......do......	July 5, 1862	April 1, 1863	Appointed from private of company B, *vice* R. Thompson, promoted, to 2d lieutenant company L, February 8, 1864.
Warren W. Munday	......do......	Aug. 16, 1862	Feb. 8, 1864	Appointed from sergeant of company L, *vice* Brooks, promoted; appointed 2d lieutenant of company H, July 14, 1864.
Simeon A. Baker	......do......	Sept. 4, 1862	July 14, 1864	Appointed from sergeant of company L, *vice* Munday, promoted; appointed 2d lieutenant of company L March 1, 1865.
Jonathan Douglass	......do......	July 21, 1862	Mar. 1, 1865	Appointed from sergeant of company F; mustered out August 23, 1865.
John M. Bigger	Regimental quartermaster sergeant.	Aug. 15, 1862	Nov. 6, 1862	Appointed from private of company M to fill original vacancy; appointed regimental quartermaster March 1, 1864.
James C. Summers	......do......	Aug. 8, 1862	Mar. 1, 1864	Appointed from sergeant of company E, *vice* Bigger, promoted; mustered out August 23, 1865.
Thomas H. Scott	Regimental commissary sergeant.	July 24, 1862	Nov. 1, 1862	Appointed from private of company C to fill original vacancy; appointed 2d lieutenant of company B, 1st Arkansas infantry, February 23, 1863.
Jeremiah B. Hale	......do......	Dec. 10, 1862	April 7, 1863	Appointed from private of company L, *vice* Scott, promoted; mustered out August 23, 1865.
Amos H. Caffee	Hospital steward	Oct. 1, 1862	Oct. 2, 1862	Appointed from private of company L to fill original vacancy; appointed assistant surgeon January 12, 1863.
Willis E. Maynard	......do......	Jan. 22, 1863	Aug. 31, 1863	Appointed from civil life to fill original vacancy; appointed 2d lieutenant of company I July 15, 1864.
Melancthon Hilbert	......do......	July 19, 1863	Aug. 15, 1863	Appointed from private of company L, *vice* Caffee, promoted; promoted to 2d lieutenant of company H January 1, 1865.
Thomas J. McCord	......do......	Aug. 4, 1862	July 15, 1864	Appointed from private of company G, *vice* Maynard, promoted; mustered out August 23, 1865.
Samuel W. Chism	......do......	—, 1862		Appointed from corporal of company A, *vice* Hilbert, promoted; mustered out August 23, 1865.
John Pool	Chief trumpeter	Nov. 1, 1862	July 1, 1865	Appointed from bugler of company B, *vice* Lusk, reduced to the ranks; mustered out August 25, 1865.
Oren A. Whitcomb	......do......		Aug. 31, 1863	Appointed from private of 37th Illinois infantry to fill original vacancy; appointed 2d lieutenant of company B July 14, 1864.
James Lusk	......do......	Aug. 4, 1862	July 14, 1864	Appointed from bugler of company G, *vice* Whitcomb, promoted; reduced to the ranks May 28, 1865.
William Hunt	Veterinary surgeon	Nov. 1, 1863	Jan. 12, 1864	Appointed from civil life to fill original vacancy; mustered out August 23, 1865.
Jacob Q. Johnson	Chief farrier	June 23, 1862	Aug. 7, 1862	Appointed from farrier of company B to fill original vacancy; reduced to the ranks January 6, 1863.

First regiment Arkansas cavalry volunteers. Mustered into service August 7, 1862, (three years;) mustered out August 23, 1865.

COMPANY A.

Names.	Rank.	Enlistment.	Date of rank.	Remarks.
M. LaRue Harrison	Captain	—, 1861	June 16, 1862	Entered infantry from 36th Illinois infantry March 31, 1862. Promoted to colonel August 7, 1862.
Steward H. Carlile	do	Aug. 7, 1862	Aug. 8, 1862	Appointed from civil life, vice Harrison, promoted. Resigned December 5, 1862.
Joshua S. Dudley	do	—, 1861	Dec. 5, 1862	Promoted from 1st lieutenant company G, vice Carlile, resigned; mustered out with regiment.
James J. Johnson	1st lieutenant	—, 1861	July 10, 1862	Entered regiment from sergeant 36th Illinois infantry March 31, 1862. Promoted to major August 8, 1862.
Thomas J. Gilstrap	do	May 10, 1862	Aug. 8, 1862	Appointed 2d lieutenant July 3, 1862. Died November 1, 1862, near Cross Hollows, Arkansas.
William J. Patton	do	May 18, 1862	Nov. 1, 1862	Entered the service as a scout July 5, 1861; appointed 2d lieutenant August 8, 1862. Promoted captain company K, 4th Arkansas cavalry, April 1, 1865.
Frederick Kise	do	May 18, 1862	June 4, 1865	Appointed corporal July 3, 1862; sergeant, January 1, 1863; 1st sergeant, May 1, 1863; mustered out with regiment.
Charles F. Eichacker	2d lieutenant	Nov. 3, 1862	Dec. 5, 1862	Appointed 2d lieutenant December 5, 1862; discharged January 31, 1864, to accept appointment as captain 22d U. S. colored troops, February 1, 1864.
Brannick, Elias	Sergeant	Mar. 3, 1862	July 3, 1862	No discharge given at muster out of regiment.
Quinton, Jefferson	do	May 14, 1862	Jan. 1, 1863	Appointed corporal July 3, 1862; mustered out with regiment.
Holmesly, Sidney E	do	June 26, 1862	Dec. 8, 1863	Appointed corporal January 1, 1863; mustered out with regiment.
Bradford, John	do	May 14, 1862	June 1, 1864	Appointed corporal May 1, 1863; mustered out with regiment.
Edwards, John F	do	June 23, 1862	Dec. 26, 1863	Do.
Kimes, Francis M	do	May 14, 1862	Jan. 1, 1863	Appointed corporal July 3, 1862; mustered out with regiment.
Robinson, Perry G	do	June 28, 1862	Jan. 1, 1863	Appointed corporal _____, _____; mustered out with regiment.
Council, James J	Corporal	June 21, 1862	Dec. 8, 1862	Mustered out with regiment.
Fears, Josiah	do	June 21, 1862	Jan. 1, 1863	Do.
Miller, Marion J	do	June 15, 1862	Jan. 1, 1863	Do.
Bird, John H	do	Nov. 12, 1862	Dec. 8, 1863	Do.
Van Zandt, Elijah	do	Feb. 2, 1863	May 1, 1864	Do.
Sanders, Anderson	do	June 28, 1862	Jan. 6, 1864	Do.
Martin, Baron De K	do	Nov. 5, 1862	Dec. 31, 1864	Do.
Smith, John W	Trumpeter	May 10, 1862	July 3, 1863	Do.
Zimmerman, William	Farrier	May 13, 1862	July 3, 1862	Do.
Reed, William	do	May 10, 1862	Sept. 25, 1862	Do.
			Muster.	
Anderson, William	Private	Sept. 16, 1862	Oct. 16, 1862	Mustered out with regiment.
Bullard, Spencer	do	May 4, 1864	June 30, 1864	Do.
Cravens, Robert D	do	May 14, 1862	July 3, 1862	Do.
Caughman, Nathan	do	May 14, 1862	July 3, 1862	Do.
Caughman, Seaburn	do	June 16, 1862	July 3, 1862	Do.
Casey, Alfred	do	Nov. 12, 1862	Sept. 23, 1863	Do.
Cornwall, George	do	June 6, 1862	July 3, 1862	Do.

REPORT OF THE ADJUTANT GENERAL OF ARKANSAS. 13

Name		Enlisted	Mustered	Remarks
Cartwright, Samuel		Nov. 2, 1862	Aug. 14, 1863	Do.
Clark, William	do	June 23, 1862	July 3, 1862	Do.
Douglass, William	do	June 23, 1862	July 3, 1862	Do.
Ennis, William	do	Nov. 6, 1862	Aug. 14, 1863	Do.
Elkins, Furiben	do	May 10, 1863	July 3, 1862	Do.
Elkins, Leander	do	May 14, 1864	June 30, 1864	Do.
Fears, Ebenezer	do	June 12, 1864	Nov. 30, 1864	Do.
Fears, James	do	June 23, 1862	July 3, 1862	Do.
Fears, William A	do	June 23, 1862	July 3, 1862	Do.
Hayes, Joseph	do	Nov. 12, 1862	Aug. 14, 1863	Do.
Harp, John	do	Nov. 6, 1862	Sept. 6, 1863	Do.
Harp, William	do	Nov. 6, 1862	Aug. 14, 1863	Do.
Harp, Talbot	do	Aug. 8, 1862	Aug. 14, 1863	Do.
Holmesly, Marion F	do	June 25, 1862	July 3, 1862	Do.
Johnson, James W	do	Nov. 15, 1862	Aug. 14, 1863	Do.
Johnson, Herrod	do	Nov. 8, 1862	Aug. 14, 1863	Do.
Kimes, David G	do	May 14, 1862	July 3, 1862	Do.
Kessee, Eli H	do	June 25, 1862	July 3, 1862	Do.
Killian, William	do	Sept. 28, 1862	Oct. 14, 1862	Do.
Lynch, Jesse	do	Aug. 7, 1864	Aug. 20, 1864	Do.
Lewis, Elijah	do	Nov. 12, 1862	Aug. 14, 1863	Do.
Meadows, Austin	do	Nov. 20, 1864	Nov. 20, 1864	Do.
Meadows, William P	do	Nov. 20, 1864	Nov. 20, 1863	Do.
Morrow, John H	do	July 16, 1863	Aug. 14, 1863	Do.
Mackey, Andrew J	do	Nov. 22, 1862	Aug. 14, 1863	Do.
Nail, Thomas	do	June 10, 1862	July 3, 1862	Do.
Reed, John R	do	June 10, 1862	July 3, 1862	Do.
Reed, Joseph P	do	May 10, 1862	July 3, 1862	Was taken prisoner October 28, 1864. Returned January 23, 1865; mustered out with regiment.
Roburn, William C	do	July 2, 1864	July 31, 1864	Mustered out with regiment.
Riddle, Jefferson	do	Nov. 12, 1862	Aug. 14, 1863	Do.
Riddle, Lewis F	do	Nov. 12, 1862	Aug. 14, 1863	Do.
Ritchie, Henry C	do	Nov. 12, 1862	Aug. 14, 1863	Do.
Ritchie, Gabriel H	do	July 2, 1864	July 31, 1864	Do.
Sanderson, John S	do	Dec. 31, 1862	Aug. 14, 1863	Do.
Seratt, George	do	June 20, 1862	July 3, 1862	Do.
Shelby, Levi	do	June 23, 1862	July 3, 1862	Do.
Sparks, John	do	Sept. 23, 1863	Nov. 4, 1863	Do.
Trease, John	do	Oct. 15, 1862	Aug. 14, 1863	Do.
Trewhitt, William, jr	do	June 23, 1862	July 3, 1862	Do.
Trewhitt, William, sr	do	May 14, 1864	June 30, 1864	Do.
Taylor, John S	do	June 4, 1864	June 30, 1864	Do.
Vaughan, Jesse	do	June 22, 1862	July 3, 1862	Do.
Vaughan, William	do			Was taken prisoner October 28, 1864. Returned January 23, 1865; mustered out with regiment.
Vance, Harris	do	Nov. 28, 1863	Aug. 14, 1863	Do.
Wilson, Hosea	do	May 14, 1862	July 3, 1862	Do.
Wheeler, Fantleroy	do	June 2, 1862	July 3, 1862	Do.
Whinery, William	do	June 23, 1864	July 2, 1864	Do.
Whinery, Mark R	do	Nov. 4, 1864	Nov. 24, 1864	Do.
Wilson, Madison M	do	June 12, 1864	Nov. 30, 1864	Do.

First regiment Arkansas cavalry volunteers. Mustered into service August 7, 1862, (three years;) mustered out August 23, 1865.

COMPANY A.—Continued.

Names.	Rank.	Enlistment.	Muster.	Remarks.
Killed.				
Burrows, Reuben B.	Private	May 10, 1862	July 3, 1862	Killed in action at battle of Fayetteville, Arkansas, April 18, 1863.
Caughman, Nelson	do	Oct. 31, 1862	Aug. 14, 1863	Killed in action in Washington county, Arkansas, April 7, 1864.
Coomer, Richard W.	do	Feb. 18, 1863	Aug. 14, 1863	Killed in action in Benton county, Arkansas, September 4, 1863.
Day, Joshua W.	do	Nov. 2, 1862	Nov. 2, 1862	Shot at Fort Smith, Ark., while a prisoner of war, by order of Major Gen. Hindman.
Echols, James	do	Nov. 2, 1862	Nov. 2, 1862	Shot at Fort Smith, Ark., while a prisoner of war, by order of Major Gen. Hindman.
Heridon, George	do	June 23, 1862	July 3, 1862	Killed by guerillas in Washington county, Arkansas, April 7, 1864.
Hixon, George	do	June 15, 1862	July 3, 1862	Killed by guerillas in Washington county, Arkansas, April 7, 1864.
Holmesly, Randolph L.	do	June 25, 1862	July 3, 1862	Killed in action in Searcy county, Arkansas, December 25, 1863.
Jack, James	do	Nov. 12, 1862	Aug. 14, 1863	Killed by guerilas in Washington county, Arkansas, August 27, 1864.
Kessee, Thomas	do	June 5, 1864	June 30, 1864	Killed in battle at Fayetteville, Arkansas, November 6, 1864.
Littrell, William T.	do	Sept. 23, 1863	Nov. 4, 1863	Killed by guerillas at Huntsville, Arkansas, January 6, 1865.
Marshall, William T.	do	May 15, 1864	June 30, 1864	Killed by guerillas in Washington county, Arkansas, October 8, 1864.
Nelson, George W.	do	May 14, 1862	July 3, 1862	Promoted to corporal July 3, 1862. Killed at battle of Prairie Grove, Dec. 7, 1862.
Poor, William H.	do	June 16, 1862	July 3, 1862	Killed by guerillas in Washington county, Arkansas, April 7, 1864.
Riddell, Jonas	do	Nov. 2, 1862	Nov. 2, 1862	Killed at battle of Fayetteville, Arkansas, April 18, 1863.
Shibley, James W.	do	Feb. 18, 1863	Aug. 14, 1863	Killed by guerillas in Washington county, Arkansas, April 7, 1864.
Died.				
Asbell, Thomas	Sergeant	June 22, 1862	July 3, 1862	Appointed sergeant July 3, 1862. Died of measles at Mount Vernon, Missouri, August 31, 1862.
Brown, James W.	Private	Nov. 14, 1862	Aug. 14, 1863	Died of dropsy in regimental hospital, Fayetteville, Arkansas, July 3, 1864.
Brooks, William M.	do	May 14, 1862	July 3, 1862	Died at Elkhorn tavern, Arkansas, October 18, 1862.
Cardin, Robert G.	do	June 21, 1862	July 3, 1862	Died at Mount Vernon, Missouri, September 28, 1862.
Cornwall, James	do	June 6, 1862	July 3, 1862	Died at regimental hospital, Fayetteville, Arkansas, February 21, 1863.
Cox, John	do	Nov. 12, 1862	Nov. 12, 1862	Died at regimental hospital, Fayetteville, Arkansas, January 17, 1863.
Eaton, William	do	May 14, 1862		Died at Forsyth, Missouri, June 2, 1862.
Elkins, Kelly	Corporal	May 10, 1862	July 3, 1862	Appointed corporal July 3, 1862; died at Springfield, Missouri, July 28, 1862.
Faulkner, Albert	Private	Aug. 14, 1862	July 3, 1862	Died in regimental hospital, Fayetteville, Arkansas, March 22, 1863.
Flinn, Thomas	Sergeant	Nov. 12, 1862	Nov. 12, 1862	Died in regimental hospital, Fayetteville, Arkansas, February 26, 1863.
Hodge, George W.	Private	June 27, 1862	July 3, 1862	Appointed sergeant October 1, 1862; 1st sergeant January 1, 1863; died at Fayetteville, Arkansas, March 22, 1863.
Hixon, William T.	do	June 15, 1862	July 3, 1862	Died of wounds received in action in Benton county, Arkansas, August 26, 1864.
Hayes, James	do	Nov. 12, 1862	Nov. 12, 1862	Died in regimental hospital, Fayetteville, Arkansas, January 1, 1863.
Henderson, Jonas	do	Nov. 12, 1862	Nov. 12, 1862	Died in regimental hospital, Fayetteville, Arkansas, February 21, 1863.
Harp, William, sr.	do	June 24, 1862	July 10, 1862	Died at Flat Creek, Missouri, August 12, 1862.
Helmvick, James	do	June 15, 1862	July 3, 1862	Died at Wilson's Creek, Missouri, September 19, 1862.
Jones, John	do	Feb. 6, 1863	Aug. 14, 1863	Died of wounds received in action in Washington county, Arkansas, April 30, 1864.
Mackey, Abram S.	do	Nov. 12, 1862	Nov. 23, 1862	Died in regimental hospital, Fayetteville, Arkansas, January 18, 1863.
Nail, Robert	do	June 10, 1862	July 3, 1862	Died at Springfield, Missouri, October 16, 1862.
Pollard, Moses G.	do	May 14, 1862	July 3, 1862	Died in regimental hospital, Fayetteville, Arkansas, April 19, 1863.

REPORT OF THE ADJUTANT GENERAL OF ARKANSAS. 15

Name	Rank	Date of rank		Remarks
Reed, John B.	Private	May 10, 1862	July 3, 1862	Died in regimental hospital, Fayetteville, Arkansas, February 19, 1864.
Simpkins, William	do	Nov. 16, 1862	Dec. 3, 1862	Died in Crawford county, Arkansas, while on a scout, February 7, 1863.
Serat, Calvin	do	June 14, 1862	July 3, 1862	Died in regimental hospital, Fayetteville, Arkansas, January 4, 1863.
Vaughan, Benjamin	do	June 25, 1862	July 3, 1862	Died in regimental hospital, Fayetteville, Arkansas, January 4, 1863.
Whinery, Wallace W.	do	Nov. 2, 1862	Nov. 2, 1862	Died in regimental hospital, Fayetteville, Arkansas, May 18, 1863.

Discharged.

Name	Rank	Date of rank		Remarks
Blevins, Elias	Sergeant	Aug. 7, 1862	Aug. 7, 1862	Appointed corporal September 1, 1862, sergeant April 20, 1863; discharged at Springfield, Missouri, for wounds received in action, May 1, 1864.
Caughman, Alfred	Private	May 14, 1862	July 3, 1862	Discharged for disability, at Fayetteville, Arkansas, April 2, 1863.
Carter, Samuel B.	do	Nov. 28, 1862	Dec. 31, 1862	Discharged for disability, at Fayetteville, Arkansas, April 2, 1863.
Easby, George A.	do	May 14, 1862	July 3, 1862	Discharged for disability, at Fayetteville, Arkansas, April 2, 1863.
Hayes, John	do	Nov. 12, 1862	Nov. 12, 1862	Discharged for woutnds received in action, at Springfield, Mo., October 16, 1863.
McKnight, Thomas	do	June 23, 1862	July 3, 1862	Discharged at Fayetteville, Arkansas, for disability, April 2, 1863.
Neal, John	do	June 18, 1862	July 3, 1862	Discharged for disability, at Fayetteville, Arkansas, January 17, 1863.
Perry, James O. K.	do	Nov. 12, 1862	Nov. 12, 1862	Discharged for disability, at Fayetteville, Arkansas, January 17, 1863.
Taylor, Hiram	do	May 14, 1862	July 3, 1862	Discharged for disability, at Fayetteville, Arkansas, January 17, 1863.
Wilson, Wesley W.	do	May 14, 1862	July 3, 1862	Discharged for disability, at Fayetteville, Arkansas, January 17, 1863.

Deserted.

Name	Rank	Date of rank		Remarks
Farmer, William B.	Private	Nov. 6, 1863	Nov. 11, 1863	Deserted at Fayetteville, Arkansas, April 7, 1864.
Milsap, John	do	Nov. 19, 1862	Oct. 3, 1863	Deserted at Fayetteville, Arkansas, April 30, 1863.
Nail, Jesse	do	June 10, 1862	July 3, 1862	Deserted at Fayetteville, Arkansas, April 7, 1864.

COMPANY B.

Name	Rank		Date of rank	Remarks
Thomas J. Hunt	Captain	July 3, 1862	July 3, 1862	Promoted to major August 7, 1862.
Bracken Lewis	do		Aug. 7, 1862	Resigned March 30, 1863.
Hugo C. C. Boteführ	do		April 1, 1863	Promoted from 1st lieutenant company H. Promoted to major June 4, 1865.
William Hunter	1st lieutenant	Aug. 7, 1862	Aug. 7, 1862	Promoted from private August 7, 1862.
Denton D. Stark	do	Aug. 15, 1861	July 3, 1862	Entered regiment from 37th Illinois infantry as 1st lieutenant; promoted to regimental adjutant October 2, 1862.
Thomas Wilhite	do	May 14, 1862	Nov. 1, 1862	Dismissed January 7, 1864.
Gustavus F. Hottenhauer	do		March 2, 1864	Mustered out with regiment.
Crittenden C. Wells	2d lieutenant	June 23, 1862	July 31, 1862	Promoted to regimental quartermaster 1st Arkansas infantry March 25, 1863.
Oren A. Whitecomb	do		July 14, 1864	Appointed from chief trumpeter; mustered out with regiment.
Lafayette Brooks	1st sergeant	June 24, 1862	July 25, 1864	Appointed sergeant July 3, 1862.
Isaac H. A. Daniel	Commissary sergeant	June 24, 1862	Jan. 18, 1863	Appointed sergeant July 3, 1862.
Benjamin Ramey	Quartermaster sergeant	June 24, 1862	Jan. 29, 1864	Appointed sergeant July 3, 1862.
Lewis Farris	Sergeant	July 1, 1862	Jan. 18, 1863	Mustered out with the regiment.
Rasha G. Daniel	do	June 23, 1862	Jan. 18, 1863	Do.
Joel M. Ferguson	do	June 24, 1862	July 1, 1862	Do.
William H. Lemaster	do	June 23, 1862	July 24, 1862	Do.
William M. Craig	do	June 24, 1862	Aug. 1, 1864	Do.
Abraham Lancaster	Corporal	June 24, 1862	April 4, 1863	Do.
Thomas Paschal	do	Oct. 31, 1862	May 7, 1863	Do.
Henry Williford	do	Feb. 18, 1863	June 20, 1863	Do.

First regiment Arkansas cavalry volunteers. Mustered into service August 7, 1862, (three years;) mustered out August 23, 1865.

COMPANY B—Continued.

Names.	Rank.	Enlistment.	Date of rank.	Remarks.
James M. Rainey	Corporal	June 25, 1862	Mar. 31, 1863	Mustered out with the regiment.
William J. Gilliland	do	June 23, 1862	July 12, 1862	Do.
Charles L. Bradshaw	do	June 14, 1862	Nov. 6, 1863	Do.
Pleasant Miller	do	June 24, 1862	Aug. 10, 1864	Do.
William Fincher	do	Feb. 2, 1863	May 1, 1865	Do.
Jacob Q. Johnson	Farrier	June 23, 1862	June 23, 1862	Do.
Alexander White	do	June 23, 1862	June 23, 1862	Do.
Robert Reed	Bugler	Nov. 5, 1862	Aug. 14, 1863	Do.
			Muster.	
Adams, Jesse	Private	Feb. 1, 1864	Feb. 22, 1864	Mustered out with the regiment.
Adams, John M	do	Feb. 1, 1864	Feb. 22, 1864	Do.
Adams, George W	do	Feb. 1, 1864	Feb. 22, 1864	Do.
Bassett, John N	do	June 22, 1862	July 3, 1862	Do.
Baskett, William	do	June 22, 1862	July 3, 1862	Do.
Baskett, James	do	Oct. 12, 1863	Oct. 31, 1863	Do.
Bardine, Nathaniel	do	Sept. 27, 1862	Sept. 30, 1862	Do.
Boswell, John	do	Aug. 3, 1863	Sept. 4, 1863	Do.
Brinley, Levi	do	Oct. 1, 1863	Oct. 5, 1863	Do.
Cross, John	do	June 5, 1862	July 3, 1862	Do.
Carrigan, James M	do	Sept. 27, 1863	Oct. 5, 1863	Do.
Cook, Christopher M	do	July 27, 1862	July 28, 1862	Do.
Cox, Zachariah	do	Aug. 7, 1863	Oct. 31, 1863	Do.
Davis, William	do	June 2, 1862	July 3, 1862	Do.
Dye, William R	do	July 18, 1862	Aug. 14, 1863	Do.
Edson, Luther	do	July 5, 1862	July 8, 1862	Do.
Fincher, John	do	Jan. 1, 1863	Aug. 14, 1863	Do.
Fillingim, David	do	July 8, 1862	July 8, 1862	Do.
Ferguson, Henry H	do	June 24, 1862	July 3, 1862	Do.
Glazebrook, John	do	Dec. 3, 1862	Aug. 14, 1863	Do.
Glazebrook, Richard	do	June 2, 1862	July 3, 1862	Do.
Glazebrook, William	do	June 2, 1862	July 3, 1862	Do.
Gordinier, Jacob	do	Oct. 1, 1862	Oct. 5, 1863	Do.
Harden, William	do	Dec. 7, 1863	Dec. 7, 1862	Do.
Hughes, Joseph	do	June 24, 1862	July 3, 1862	Do.
Hanna, William	do	June 23, 1862	July 3, 1862	Do.
Harris, William	do	Oct. 3, 1862	Oct. 5, 1863	Do.
Harris, Henry	do	Sept. 25, 1863	Oct. 5, 1863	Do.
Jones, Charles M	do	Oct. 1, 1862	Aug. 14, 1863	Do.
Jones, Joel W	do	Sept. 30, 1863	Oct. 3, 1863	Do.
Jackson, Smith	do	June 24, 1862	July 3, 1862	Do.
Johnson, Andrew J	do	Sept. 24, 1863	Oct. 5, 1863	Do.

REPORT OF THE ADJUTANT GENERAL OF ARKANSAS.

Name	Rank	Date	Date	Remarks
Johnson, James	do	Dec. 4, 1863	Feb. 28, 1864	Ex.
Keaton, Daniel	do	Oct. 4, 1862	Aug. 24, 1863	Do.
Lee, James J	do	Dec. 3, 1862	Aug. 14, 1863	Do.
Lail, William	do	Oct. 1, 1863	Oct. 31, 1863	Do.
Lewis, Daniel	do	Sept. 25, 1863	Oct. 5, 1863	Do.
Lewis, Zachariah	do	Dec. 6, 1863	Dec. 6, 1863	Do.
Mustin, James B	do	June 24, 1862	July 3, 1862	Do.
Mathews, Abraham	do	June 24, 1862	July 3, 1862	Do.
Mullinix, EN	do		Oct. 3, 1862	Do.
Maladon, Jacob	do	June 20, 1862	July 3, 1862	Do.
Morgan, Doctor M	do	July 4, 1862	July 22, 1862	Do.
Morgan, Henry	do	July 1, 1862	July 3, 1862	Do.
Malone, William J	do	Oct. 26, 1862	Oct. 31, 1862	Do.
Mahurin, William R	do	Dec. 15, 1863	Dec. 15, 1863	Do.
Phipps, Thomas J	do	June 24, 1862	July 3, 1862	Do.
Prewett, Peter O	do	Aug. 10, 1862	Aug. 16, 1862	Do.
Pool, James M	do	Jan. 1, 1863	Aug. 14, 1863	Do.
Paschal, Thomas	do	Feb. 15, 1863	Feb. 15, 1863	Do.
Parks, William	do	Feb. 1, 1864	Feb. 12, 1864	Do.
Reed, Adam J	do	Nov. 6, 1862	Aug. 14, 1863	Do.
Rutherford, John	do	June 23, 1862	July 3, 1862	Do.
Smith, George W	do	June 24, 1862	July 3, 1862	Do.
Sutton, William H	do	June 1, 1862	July 3, 1862	Do.
Spurlock, George	do	June 15, 1862	July 3, 1862	Do.
Steward, Thomas	do	June 23, 1862	July 3, 1862	Do.
Sehrader, John	do	Dec. 7, 1863	Dec. 7, 1863	Do.
Skaggs, Hannibal	do	Feb. 10, 1863	Aug. 14, 1863	Do.
Thurber, James	do	Oct. 12, 1863	Feb. 24, 1864	Do.
Thompson, Cyrus	do	June 24, 1862	July 3, 1862	Do.
Vanderpool, John A	do	June 24, 1862	July 3, 1862	Do.
Williams, John C	do	June 24, 1862	July 3, 1862	Do.
Williams, John	do	June 20, 1862	July 3, 1862	Do.
Whinkler, Henry	do	June 23, 1862	July 3, 1862	Do.
Watts, James	do	Sept. 26, 1863	Oct. 5, 1863	Do.
Williford, Seneca	do	Sept. 25, 1863	Oct. 5, 1863	Do.
Wood, Henry	do	Nov. 23, 1863	Nov. 24, 1863	Do.
White, John	do	Oct. 5, 1863	Oct. 5, 1863	Do.
Younger, John L	do	Feb. 1, 1864	Feb. 22, 1864	Do.
Young, James M	do	Aug. 2, 1862	Aug. 12, 1862	Do.

Killed.

Carrigan, James C	Private	June 24, 1862	July 3, 1862	Killed in Washington county, Arkansas, February 19, 1865.
Fraley, John	do	Sept. 25, 1863	Oct. 5, 1863	Killed at Freyschlag's Mills, Washington county, Arkansas, January 2, 1865.
Hughes, James	do	June 23, 1862	July 3, 1862	Killed in Washington county, Arkansas, March 30, 1863.
Jones, Riley	do	Nov. 1, 1862		Killed in Washington county, Arkansas, November 29, 1862.
Mills, Enos	do	July 7, 1862	July 12, 1862	Killed in Washington county, Arkansas, September 15, 1863.

Died.

Cooper, Moses	Private	June 15, 1862	July 3, 1862	Died November 7, 1862.
Carrigan, John C	do	Oct. 1, 1862	Oct. 31, 1862	Died of wounds received in Washington county, Arkansas, April 10, 1863.

Mis. Doc. 53——2

First regiment Arkansas cavalry volunteers. Mustered into service August 7, 1862, (three years;) mustered out August 23, 1865.

COMPANY B—Continued.

Names.	Rank.	Enlistment.	Muster.	Remarks.
Daniel, Reuben	Private	June 24, 1862	July 3, 1862	Died of wounds received in Washington county, Arkansas, April 3, 1863.
David, John, 2d	do	June 21, 1862	July 3, 1862	Died February 28, 1863.
Hatfield, Thomas J	do	No record.	Never	Died February 8, 1863, of measles, at Fayetteville, Arkansas.
Hughes, George	do	June 24, 1862	July 3, 1862	Died December 30, 1862, of wounds, at Fayetteville, Arkansas.
Jones, Abraham	do	July 18, 1862	July 28, 1862	Died fall of 1862; date not known, at Elkhorn Tavern, Arkansas.
Jones, Anderson	do	June 24, 1862	July 3, 1862	Died September 15, 1862, in hospital, at Springfield, Missouri.
Jones, Daniel	Sergeant	June 23, 1862	July 3, 1862	Died November 30, 1862, of wounds.
Jones, Samuel	Private	June 24, 1862	July 3, 1862	Died September 3, 1864, at Fayetteville, Arkansas.
Johnson, Hugh L. W	do	June 23, 1862	July 3, 1862	Died July 11, 1863, in Washington county, Arkansas.
Lemaster, John F	do	July 3, 1862	July 31, 1862	Died December 6, 1862, at Elkhorn Tavern, Arkansas.
Link, Paulus	do	June 25, 1862	July 3, 1862	Died fall of 1862; date not known, Springfield, Missouri.
Long, Jesse	do	June 24, 1862	Never	Died July 1, 1862, of wounds; accidentally shot.
Morgan, Joseph	do	July 21, 1862	July 24, 1862	Died June 1, 1863, of small pox, at Rolla, Missouri.
Paschal, William H. H	Corporal	June 23, 1862	July 3, 1862	Died February —, 1863, of measles.
Phipps, William H. H	Private	June 24, 1862	July 3, 1862	Died January 18, 1863.
Robertson, La Fayette	do	July 3, 1862	July 10, 1862	Died; date not known, in hospital, at Springfield, Missouri.
White, Willis	do	July 3, 1862	July 3, 1862	Died December 6, 1862, on the road to Prairie Grove.
Young, Jasper M	do	July 3, 1862	July 8, 1862	Died November —, 1862, at Elkhorn Tavern, Arkansas.
Deserted.				
Cavin, James	Private	Sept. 25, 1862	Never	Deserted November 9, 1862, from a scout on White river, Arkansas.
Dickerson, Robert	do	Feb. 1, 1864	Feb. 28, 1864	Deserted August 14, 1864, at Fayetteville, Arkansas.
Davis, John, 1st	do	June 21, 1862	July 3, 1862	Deserted May 26, 1865, escaped from prison, Fayetteville, Arkansas.
Jones, John W	do	Oct. 1, 1862	Never	Deserted November 9, 1862, from a scout on White river, Arkansas.
Pearson, William	do	Oct. 2, 1862	Aug. 14, 1863	Deserted January 11, 1865, at Fayetteville, Arkansas.
Story, Samuel T	do	June 2, 1862		Deserted January 1, 1863, at Fayetteville, Arkansas.
Discharged.				
Bradshaw, Jacob N	Private	June 24, 1862	July 3, 1862	Discharged April 6, 1863, for disability, Fayetteville, Arkansas.
Bradshaw, Elias	do	July 3, 1862	July 3, 1862	Discharged July 5, 1863, for disability, Fayetteville, Arkansas.
Brotherton, Henry	do	Nov. 20, 1862	Never	Discharged July 1, 1867, for disability, Cassville, Missouri.
Chandler, William	do	July 3, 1862	July 19, 1862	Discharged March 3, 1863, for disability, Fayetteville, Arkansas.
Campbell, William H	do	Oct. 12, 1862	Aug. 14, 1862	Discharged June 19, 1865, by sentence of G. C. M., at Fayetteville, Arkansas.
Hobbs, Jesse H	do	June 24, 1862	July 3, 1862	Discharged March 31, 1863, for disability, Fayetteville, Arkansas.
Hutchinson, William	do	July 18, 1862	July 28, 1862	Discharged March 31, 1863, for disability, Fayetteville, Arkansas.
Jackson, John B	do	June 24, 1862	July 3, 1862	Discharged April 4, 1863, for disability, Springfield, Missouri.
Lemaster, Eleazer	do	July 31, 1862	Aug. 7, 1862	Discharged July 5, 1863, for disability, Fayetteville, Arkansas.
McNealy, Philip	do	June 21, 1862	July 3, 1862	Discharged December 22, 1863, for disability, Fayetteville, Arkansas.
Moon, Jacob	do	Aug. 29, 1862	Sept. 3, 1862	Discharged April 6, 1863, for disability, Fayetteville, Arkansas.
Newberry, Stephen C	do	July 1, 1862	July 24, 1862	Discharged June 23, 1865.
Strickler, Jacob	do	July 18, 1862	Aug. 14, 1863	Discharged December 22, 1863, to accept promotion as captain of 1st infantry.

REPORT OF THE ADJUTANT GENERAL OF ARKANSAS. 19

Name	Rank	Date of enlistment	Date of muster	Remarks
Vanderpool, James R.	do	June 21, 1862	July 3, 1862	Discharged February 27, 1863, to accept promotion as captain of company C, 1st infantry.
Wood, Joseph P.	do	June 24, 1862	July 3, 1862	Discharged April 6, 1863.
Weldon, James H.	do	June 24, 1862	July 3, 1862	Discharged October 15, 1863, Springfield, Missouri.
Cross, William	do	June 21, 1862	July 3, 1862	Discharged ——, 1863, to accept promotion, 1st Arkansas Infantry.
Brooks, Thomas	do	July 5, 1862	July 8, 1862	Discharged to accept promotion as sergeant major.
Brazil, Elijah	do	June 23, 1862	July 7, 1862	Discharged ——, 1863, on recommendation for invalid corps.
Risley, Wilson	do	Nov. 6, 1862	Aug. 14, 1863	Discharged by order of Major General Reynolds, commanding department of Arkansas, having been elected member of State legislature.

COMPANY C.

Name	Rank	Date of enlistment	Date of rank	Remarks
Ezra Fitch	Captain	——, 1861	July 31, 1862	Promoted to major, October 2, 1862, to fill original vacancy.
Charles C. Moss	do	Aug. 7, 1862	Oct. 2, 1862	Promoted from 1st lieutenant; mustered out January 10, 1864.
Elizar B. Harrison	do		April 7, 1864	Appointed from private company L to 2d lieutenant, October 2, 1862; promoted to captain, vice Moss, mustered out; mustered out with regiment.
Samuel W. Chism	1st lieutenant	——, 1862	Oct. 2, 1862	Appointed 2d lieutenant on organization of company; promoted to 1st lieutenant October 2, 1862; mustered out January 9, 1864.
James R. Ivie	do	Mar. 29, 1863	July 14, 1864	Appointed 2d lieutenant April 15, 1864, from sergeant company M; mustered out with regiment.
Philip McGuire	2d lieutenant		July 14, 1864	Appointed sergeant April 1, 1863; 1st sergeant October 1, 1863; mustered out with regiment.
Oscar D. Johnson	1st sergeant	Nov. 29, 1862	July 15, 1864	Appointed sergeant January 10, 1864; mustered out with regiment.
James T. Counts	Quartermaster sergeant	July 28, 1862	July 11, 1864	Appointed sergeant July 31, 1862; mustered out with regiment.
Jasper J. Eubanks	Commissary sergeant	July 28, 1862	July 1, 1863	Appointed sergeant January 25, 1863; mustered out with regiment.
William H. Ladd	Sergeant	June 2, 1862	July 3, 1862	Mustered out with regiment.
Clinton H. Duval	do	June 2, 1862	July 3, 1862	Do.
John M. Fine	do	Aug. 13, 1862	Oct. 1, 1863	Do.
Isam Amas	do	July 1, 1862	Oct. 1, 1863	Do.
James M. Duncan	do	July 24, 1862	Sept. 14, 1864	Appointed corporal July 31, 1862; mustered out with regiment.
Noah Johnson	Corporal	Nov. 20, 1862	Jan. 17, 1863	Appointed corporal September 1, 1862; mustered out with regiment.
Richmond Johnson	do	Nov. 20, 1862	Feb. 1, 1863	Mustered out with regiment.
Joshua J. Dodd	do	Oct. 29, 1862	Sept. 1, 1863	Do.
William H. Harper	do	Dec. 30, 1862	Oct. 1, 1863	Do.
Jacob T. Glenn	do	Aug. 11, 1863	Mar. 1, 1864	Do.
William O. Harper	do	Dec. 31, 1862	July 14, 1863	Do.
William P. Ferry	do	Jan. 10, 1863	Sept. 14, 1864	Do.
John O. Brown	do	Oct. 25, 1862	Nov. 1, 1864	Do.
William J. Wallis	do	Aug. 12, 1863	Aug. 12, 1863	Do.
John Kimball	Farrier	July 12, 1862	July 12, 1862	Do.
John Painter	Trumpeter	Sept. 2, 1863	Sept. 2, 1863	Do.
Thomas J. Reardon	do	July 3, 1862	July 3, 1862	Do.
Harding Trammell	Wagoner	Aug. 6, 1862	Aug. 6, 1862	Do.

First regiment Arkansas cavalry volunteers. Mustered into service August 7, 1862, (three years;) mustered out August 23, 1865.

COMPANY G—Continued.

Names.	Rank.	Enlistment.	Muster.	Remarks.
Allen, Alexander	Private	May 3, 1862	July 15, 1862	Mustered out with regiment.
Baker, Thomas	do	June 30, 1862	July 24, 1862	Do.
Block, Lewis	do	Sept. 11, 1863	Oct. 5, 1863	Do.
Brown, James	do	July 10, 1862	July 18, 1862	Do.
Counts, Rufus B	do	July 28, 1862	July 28, 1862	Do.
Coker, Joel C	do	Oct. 29, 1863	Aug. 31, 1863	Do.
Carney, George	do	May 3, 1864	June 30, 1864	Do.
Coombs, Benjamin F	do	May 5, 1864	June 30, 1864	Do.
Duncan, Andrew J	do	July 24, 1862	July 28, 1862	Do.
Dening, Elihu	do	May 11, 1864	June 12, 1864	Do.
Daugherty, James T	do	Nov. 20, 1862	Aug. 31, 1863	Do.
Evans, Drury	do	July 2, 1862	July 28, 1864	Do.
Evans, Benjamin F	do	July 2, 1862	July 28, 1864	Do.
Elam, George F	do	Feb. 16, 1864	July 28, 1864	Do.
Exendine, Francis M	do	June 28, 1862	July 10, 1862	Do.
Eubanks, William	do	Nov. 24, 1863	Dec. 4, 1863	Do.
Ferguson, John W	do	July 14, 1862	July 21, 1862	Do.
Frazier, Eli	do	July 7, 1862	July 18, 1862	Do.
Gates, Joshua	do	Dec. 23, 1862	Aug. 31, 1863	Do.
Nichols	do	Jan. 8, 1863	Aug. 31, 1863	Do.
Harper, James M	do	Dec. 31, 1862	Aug. 31, 1863	Do.
Ham, John N	do	Jan. 2, 1863	May 31, 1863	Do.
Ham, William M	do	July 28, 1862	July 28, 1862	Do.
Harrison, George W	do	Feb. 1, 1863	Oct. 31, 1863	Do.
Holcomb, George P	do	Nov. 24, 1864	Jan. 28, 1865	Do.
Jones, James W	do	July 28, 1862	July 30, 1862	Do.
Jones, John A	do	Aug. 6, 1862	Aug. 10, 1862	Do.
Jones, Charles M	do	Aug. 10, 1862	Aug. 10, 1862	Do.
Jones, William A	do	July 20, 1862	July 30, 1862	Do.
Jones, Robert	do	Nov. 27, 1863	Dec. 21, 1863	Do.
Johnson, Emerson	do	April 1, 1864	April 30, 1864	Do.
Jackson, James	do	April 19, 1864	April 20, 1864	Do.
Keeling, Campbell W	do	July 10, 1864	July 14, 1864	Do.
Logue, William	do	Feb. 1, 1863	Oct. 31, 1863	Do.
Logue, James C	do	Feb. 1, 1864	Feb. 8, 1864	Do.
Mentor, Joseph G	do	June 8, 1863	June 30, 1864	Do.
Murphy, Joseph W	do	Jan. 8, 1863	Oct. 31, 1864	Do.
Martin, Felix	do	Feb. 16, 1864	Feb. 28, 1864	Do.
McDougall, Alex	do	Nov. 24, 1863	Dec. 31, 1863	Do.
Logue, Robert B	do	Feb. 1, 1863	Aug. 31, 1863	Do.
Mallicoat, Nelson	do	Nov. 21, 1863	Dec. 31, 1863	Do.
Miller, John	do	July 9, 1862	July 10, 1862	Do.

REPORT OF THE ADJUTANT GENERAL OF ARKANSAS. 21

Name	Rank	Enlisted	Discharged	Remarks
Overstreet, George	do	July 2, 1862	July 28, 1862	Do.
Prewett, Elijah	do	July 20, 1862	July 28, 1862	Do.
Prewett, jr., David	do	Aug. 6, 1862	Aug. 6, 1862	Do.
Parks, Thos. B	do	Feb. 16, 1864	Feb. 28, 1864	Do.
Parks, Calvin	do	May 24, 1864	June 3, 1864	Do.
Pratt, Joel	do	Aug. 11, 1863	Aug. 31, 1863	Do.
Parshall, Wm. H	do	July 25, 1863	July 28, 1863	Do.
Ruckman, Amos	do	Sept. 2, 1863	Sept. 2, 1863	Do.
Rooman, Richard	do	Oct. 2, 1863	Oct. 30, 1863	Do.
Ryals, Chas. C	do	July 28, 1862	July 28, 1862	Do.
Spurlock, David	do	Aug. 6, 1862	Aug. 7, 1862	Do.
Skidmore, John O	do	Feb. 11, 1864	Feb. 28, 1864	Do.
Sanders, Washington J	do	April 19, 1864	April 30, 1864	Do.
Spencer, Christopher L	do	March 1, 1863	Aug. 31, 1863	Do.
Stinson, Willis H	do	Sept. 26, 1863	Oct. 3, 1863	Do.
Stinson, Richard C	do	June 23, 1862	Oct. 15, 1862	Do.
Stinson, Wm. C	do	Nov. 12, 1863	Dec. 31, 1863	Do.
Sutton, Andrew J	do	June 18, 1862	July 10, 1862	Do.
Sutton, Joshua P	do	June 18, 1862	July 10, 1862	Do.
Thurman, John	do	June 4, 1864	June 30, 1864	Do.
Trammell, Jas. B	do	Aug. 6, 1862	Aug. 7, 1862	Do.
Trammell, Samuel	do	Aug. 28, 1863	Aug. 31, 1863	Do.
Todd, James C	do	Dec. 23, 1862	Dec. 31, 1862	Do.
Todd, Wm. A	do	April 1, 1864	April 30, 1864	Do.
Torix, John L	do	Jan. 20, 1864	Feb. 28, 1864	Do.
Torix, Peter	do	Jan. 20, 1864	Feb. 28, 1864	Do.
Woodworth, Wm. D	do	June 18, 1862	July 8, 1862	Do.
Williams, William	do	Oct. 29, 1862	Aug. 31, 1863	Do.
Wooten, George W	do	Dec. 20, 1862	Aug. 31, 1863	Do.
Wooten, Wm. W	do	July 28, 1862	July 28, 1862	Do.
Young, James M	do	July 28, 1862	Aug. 3, 1862	Do.

Discharged.

Name	Rank	Enlisted	Discharged	Remarks
Brown, Anderson	Private	July 10, 1862	July 10, 1862	Discharged for disability March 20, 1863.
Counts, Bethel	do	July 28, 1862	July 28, 1862	Discharged for disability March 1, 1864.
Duncan, Lemuel J	do	July 24, 1862	July 28, 1862	Discharged for disability March 26, 1863.
Jones, Stephen	do	Aug. 6, 1862	Aug. 7, 1862	Discharged for disability January 10, 1864.
Keller,	do	June 10, 1862	July 3, 1862	Discharged for disability August 14, 1863.
Kimball, sr., Basil	do	July 2, 1862	July 10, 1862	Discharged for disability March 26, 1863.
Kimball, jr., Basil	do	July 2, 1862	July 10, 1862	Discharged for disability March 26, 1863.
McWhorter, Prater	do	July 25, 1862	July 28, 1862	Discharged, by order, by reason of being a minor August 20, 1862.
Martin, George	do	Sept. 1, 1862	Sept. 1, 1862	Discharged for disability March 26, 1863.
Painter, Lemuel D	do	July 15, 1862	Sept. 1, 1862	Discharged, by order, by reason of being a minor September 1, 1862.
Robertson, Ezekiel J	do	June 26, 1862	July 5, 1862	Discharged by G. C. M. January 8, 1864.
Robertson, Wm. F	do	June 26, 1862	July 3, 1862	Discharged by G. C. M. January 8, 1864.
Rose, William	do	June 23, 1862	July 3, 1862	Discharged by G. C. M. January 8, 1864.
Ship, Carter	do	July 24, 1862	July 31, 1862	Discharged for disability March 26, 1863.
Sallee, John K	do	Sept. 17, 1862	Sept. 28, 1862	Discharged for disability March 26, 1863.
Sharp, John	do	July 2, 1862	Sept. 18, 1862	Drummed out of service, by order of Brig. Gen. E. B. Brown, August 22, 1863.
Terry, Aaron C	Commissary sergeant	July 21, 1862	July 23, 1862	Appointed commissary sergeant November 1, 1863; discharged to accept promotion in 1st Arkansas infantry, March 20, 1863.

First regiment Arkansas cavalry volunteers. Mustered into service August 7, 1862, (three years;) mustered out August 23, 1865.

COMPANY C—Continued.

Names.	Rank.	Enlistment.	Muster.	Remarks.
Vaughan, John	1st sergeant	July 2, 1862	July 3, 1862	Appointed 1st sergeant July 31, 1862; discharged, to accept promotion as 2d lieutenant of company I, November 28, 1862.
Clark, Tilman	Private	July 15, 1862	July 18, 1862	Discharged, by order of Gen. Brown by reason of being a minor, August 1, 1862.
Jernegan, Lawson D	do	Aug. 3, 1862	Aug. 5, 1862	Appointed sergeant September 1, 1862; discharged, to accept appointment as 2d lieutenant of company H, April 1, 1863.
O'Brien, Martin E	do	June 3, 1862	July 3, 1862	Appointed sergeant July 31, 1862; discharged, to accept appointment as captain of company G, 2d Arkansas cavalry, October 5, 1863.
Scott, Thomas H	do	July 24, 1862	July 28, 1862	Appointed battalion commissary sergeant July 31, 1862; regimental commissary sergeant November 1, 1862; discharged to accept appointment as 2d lieutenant of company B, 1st Arkansas infantry, February 23, 1863.
Died.				
Adkins, William	Private	Sept. 18, 1862	Sept. 18, 1862	Died at Crane Creek, Missouri, November 17, 1862.
Bolinger, Samuel M	do	July 24, 1862	July 28, 1862	Died at Springfield, Missouri, September 1, 1862.
Bridges, John S	Farrier	July 24, 1862	July 24, 1862	Killed at Elm Springs, Arkansas, April 26, 1863.
Byrd, George T	Private	Aug. 1, 1863	Aug. 31, 1863	Killed at Beaver Pond, Arkansas, August 10, 1864.
Brown, Owen	do	July 28, 1862	July 28, 1862	Died of fever at Cassville, Missouri, December 8, 1862.
Crawford, John B	do	July 28, 1862	July 28, 1862	Killed in Searcy county, Arkansas, December 25, 1863.
Crawford, Thos. J	Corporal	Oct. 28, 1862	Oct. 28, 1862	Appointed corporal July, 1, 1863; killed in Benton county, Arkansas, April 27, 1864.
Crawford, Wm. H	Sergeant	July 26, 1862	July 28, 1862	Appointed corporal September 1, 1862; sergeant February 8, 1863; died at Fayetteville, Arkansas, February 28, 1863.
Duncan, Wm. M	Private	July 24, 1862	July 28, 1862	Died of brain fever at Fayetteville, Arkansas, January 1, 1864.
Downey, John R	do	July 21, 1862	July 28, 1862	Killed in Benton county, Arkansas, January 24, 1864.
Exendine, Johnson M	do	June 28, 1862	July 10, 1862	Died of brain fever at Fayetteville, Arkansas, February 15, 1863.
Ferguson, Joel M	do	Aug. 4, 1862	Aug. 7, 1862	Died at Springfield, Missouri, November 25, 1862.
Horn, Harmon	Quartermaster sergeant	July 10, 1862	July 10, 1862	Promoted to quartermaster sergeant July 31, 1862; died of brain fever January 26, 1863.
Lawson, David	Private	July 28, 1862	July 28, 1862	Died of lung fever at Cassville, Missouri, December 2, 1863.
Mains, Thomas	do	April 1, 1864	April 30, 1864	Died of measles at Rolla, Missouri, February —, 1865.
Neal, Sylvanus B	do	July 10, 1862	July 28, 1862	Died of consumption at Springfield, Missouri, July —, 1863.
Neal, Peter J, M. T. D	do	July 28, 1862	July 28, 1862	Died of brain fever at Cassville, Missouri, December —, 1862.
Prewett, sr., David	do	Aug. 5, 1862	Aug. 5, 1862	Died of chronic diarrhœa at Fayetteville, Arkansas, February 20, 1863.
Prior, Francis M	do	July 16, 1862	July 28, 1862	Died at Springfield, Missouri, October —, 1862.
Reaves, Colonel T	do	July 27, 1862	July 28, 1862	Died of consumption at Fayetteville, Arkansas, February 4, 1863.
Redman, Daniel R	do	June 23, 1862	July 3, 1862	Died at Springfield, Missouri, November 24, 1862.
Redman, Daniel L	do	June 23, 1862	July 3, 1862	Died at Springfield, Missouri, December 1, 1862.
Redman, Edmond G	do	June 23, 1862	July 3, 1862	Died at Springfield, Missouri, November 23, 1862.
Rose, Andrew	do	June 23, 1862	July 3, 1862	Killed in Green county, Missouri, December —, 1862.
Ragsdale, William	do	Nov. 20, 1863	Dec. 31, 1863	Killed in Madison county, Arkansas, January 16, 1865.
Sharp, William	do	July 7, 1862	July 10, 1862	Died at Cassville, Missouri, November 1, 1862.
Thompson, James	do	Aug. 18, 1862	Aug. 30, 1862	Died at Fayetteville, Arkansas, February 18, 1863.
Trammell, William	do	Oct. 28, 1862	Oct. 28, 1862	Died at Fayetteville, Arkansas, February —, 1863.
Tucker, John M	do	July 24, 1862	July 28, 1862	Died at Cassville, Missouri, December 6, 1862.
Willis, Jacob J	do	July 10, 1862	July 20, 1862	Killed in Benton county, Arkansas, April 22, 1864.

REPORT OF THE ADJUTANT GENERAL OF ARKANSAS. 23

Name	Rank	Date	Remarks
Wilburn, Francis D	do	Aug. 1, 1862	Killed in battle at Fayetteville, Arkansas, October 28, 1864.
Williams, Daniel R	do	Oct. 29, 1862	Died of consumption at Fayetteville, Arkansas, December 25, 1862.
Whitson, Nephi J	do	July 1, 1863	Died of brain fever at Fayetteville, Arkansas, December 1, 1863.

Deserted.

Name	Rank	Date	Remarks
Beach, George W	Private	Oct. 28, 1863	Deserted at Fayetteville, Arkansas, April 30, 1865.
Dram, John W	do	Dec. 4, 1863	Deserted at Fayetteville, Arkansas, May 4, 1864.
Matthews, Robert H	Corporal	June 5, 1862	Promoted to corporal September 1, 1862; deserted at Springfield, Missouri, January —, 1863.
Mavry, Joseph G	Private	Aug. 7, 1863	Deserted at Cassville, Missouri, September 20, 1863.
——, David	do	July 7, 1862	Deserted at Fayetteville, Arkansas, February 18, 1863.
Oliver, Isaac A	Sergeant	July 15, 1862	Deserted at Crane creek, Missouri, July 1, 1863.
Rodgers, Cicero F	Private	Dec. 20, 1863	Deserted at Fayetteville, Arkansas, June 16, 1864.
Rose, Hiram	do	June 23, 1862	Deserted at Fayetteville, Arkansas, March —, 1863.

COMPANY D.

Name	Rank	Date	Date of rank	Remarks
Jesse M. Gilstrap	Captain	May 14, 1862	July 3, 1862	Dismissed December 21, 1862.
William L. Messenger	do	June 16, 1862	Feb. 6, 1864	Appointed from private of company L 2d lieutenant November 1, 1862; promoted to 1st lieutenant February 17, 1863; dismissed January 13, 1865.
James Allison	do	Oct. 16, 1862	May 3, 1865	Appointed from 1st sergeant company F to 1st lieutenant January 26, 1864; mustered out with regiment.
James H. Wilson	1st lieutenant	Aug. 15, 1861	June 23, 1862	Appointed 1st lieutenant from private company H, 37th Illinois infantry volunteers; promoted to regimental quartermaster November 1, 1862.
George W. M. Reid	do	June 23, 1862	Nov. 1, 1862	2d lieutenant from organization of company to November 1, 1862; resigned January 16, 1863.
William P. Clark	do	June 5, 1862	May 5, 1865	Appointed from 1st sergeant to 2d lieutenant May 22, 1864; mustered out with regiment.
Jacob H. Keiser	2d lieutenant	Feb. 2, 1863	Feb. 17, 1863	Appointed from private; dismissed April 28, 1864.
George W. Webb	1st sergeant	June 14, 1862	May 22, 1864	Appointed corporal July 3, 1862; sergeant Jan. 1, 1863; mustered out with regiment.
William H. H. Nott	Commissary sergeant	July 29, 1862	Nov. 1, 1862	Mustered out with regiment.
Reuben A. Haley	Quartermaster sergeant	May 14, 1862	Oct. 3, 1862	Do.
John M Caldwell	Sergeant	June 20, 1862	July 1, 1863	Appointed corporal July 3, 1862; sergeant July 1, 1863; mustered out with regiment.
Jacob Yows	do	June 23, 1862	Nov. 1, 1862	Mustered out with regiment.
Benjamin F. Little	do	June 23, 1862	June 1, 1864	Appointed corporal July 1, 1863; mustered out with regiment.
Alfred A. Lockhart	do	May 14, 1862	June 1, 1864	Appointed corporal July 5, 1863; mustered out with regiment.
Benjamin F. Johnson	do	July 29, 1862	Aug. 1, 1864	Appointed farrier Aug. 1, 1862; sergeant Aug. 1, 1864; mustered out with regiment.
Alexander C. Robinson	Corporal	June 24, 1862	July 3, 1862	Mustered out with regiment.
Alfred R. Quinton	do	June 23, 1862	June 1, 1863	Do.
William H. Caughman	do	May 14, 1862	Dec. 1, 1863	Do.
John T. Little	do	June 23, 1862	July 1, 1863	Do.
James A. Males	do	June 23, 1862	June 1, 1864	Do.
William C. Lichlyter	do	Nov. 1, 1863	June 1, 1864	Do.
Stephen D. Gilbreath	do	Aug. 2, 1863	June 1, 1864	Do.
John Reed	do	July 28, 1862	Jan. 1, 1865	Do.
Roderick A. Caldwell	Trumpeter	June 23, 1862	June 1, 1864	Do.

24   REPORT OF THE ADJUTANT GENERAL OF ARKANSAS.

First regiment Arkansas cavalry volunteers. Mustered into service August 7, 1862, (three years;) mustered out August 23, 1865.

COMPANY D—Continued.

Names.	Rank.	Enlistment.	Date of rank.	Remarks.
			Muster.	
Abram C. Males	Saddler	Aug. 4, 1862	Jan. 1, 1863	Mustered out with the regiment.
Robert McCaslin	Farrier	June 25, 1862	Jan. 1, 1865	Do.
Asbell, John	Private	June 22, 1862	July 3, 1862	Do.
Aiken, James	do	April 2, 1863	Aug. 14, 1863	Do.
Bloyed, William	do	June 26, 1862	July 3, 1862	Do.
Baker, Richmond	do	July 3, 1862	July 3, 1862	Do.
Bievins, Jasper	do	July 3, 1862	July 3, 1862	Do.
Center, William R.	do	June 14, 1862	July 3, 1862	Do.
Center, Amos N.	do	June 14, 1862	July 3, 1862	Do.
Coatney, James F.	do	June 14, 1862	July 3, 1862	Do.
Coatney, William T.	do	June 14, 1862	July 3, 1862	Do.
Cartwright, Joseph	do	June 21, 1862	July 3, 1862	Do.
Cartwright, Sylvanus	do	Nov. 9, 1862	Aug. 14, 1863	Do.
Cradduck, Moses M.	do	Nov. 19, 1862	Aug. 14, 1863	Do.
Currey, Mark H.	do	Jan. 15, 1863	Aug. 14, 1863	Do.
Currey, William E.	do	Jan. 15, 1863	Aug. 14, 1863	Do.
Conley, James	do	Jan. 18, 1863	Aug. 14, 1863	Do.
Carter, Adam	do	Feb. 21, 1863	Oct. 31, 1863	Do.
Carney, William J.	do	Sept. 12, 1863	Oct. 31, 1863	Do.
Carney, Arthur E.	do	Oct. 31, 1863	Oct. 31, 1863	Do.
Dill, Francis M.	do	July 2, 1862	July 3, 1862	Do.
Dye, Thomas H.	do	June 23, 1862	July 3, 1862	Do.
Fine, Thomas J.	do	June 28, 1862	July 3, 1862	Do.
Gilbreath, Henderson W.	do	July 21, 1862	Aug. 9, 1862	Do.
Gilstrap, Wesley H.	do	July 21, 1862	Aug. 9, 1862	Do.
Hobaugh, Andrew J.	do	Nov. 14, 1862	Aug. 14, 1863	Do.
Henderson, John H.	do	July 3, 1862	July 10, 1862	Do.
Henderson, William J.	do	July 5, 1862	July 10, 1862	Do.
Hulse, Isaac N.	do	July 15, 1862	Dec. 24, 1862	Do.
Hurst, Harrison	do	Sept. 14, 1862	Feb. 24, 1863	Do.
Hodges, Roland E.	do	Nov. 4, 1862	Aug. 14, 1863	Do.
Horseman, Lewis J.	do	Oct. 4, 1862	Aug. 14, 1863	Do.
Haley, William M.	do	June 14, 1862	June 3, 1862	Do.
Head, Harvey T.	do	May 20, 1864	May 25, 1864	Do.
Jackson, William H.	do	July 5, 1862	July 10, 1862	Do.
Jones, Thomas	do	Nov. 10, 1864	Nov. 16, 1864	Do.
Lane, Fidelo P.	do	May 14, 1862	July 3, 1862	Do.
Lane, Charles M.	do	Nov. 9, 1862	Aug. 14, 1863	Do.
Lofton, Giles	do	June 23, 1862	July 3, 1862	Do.
Lofton, Meredith	do	June 23, 1862	July 3, 1862	Do.

REPORT OF THE ADJUTANT GENERAL OF ARKANSAS. 25

Name	Rank	Date	Date	Remarks
Little, Angus	do	June 23, 1862	July 3, 1862	Do.
Lingo, William B	do	July 4, 1862	July 10, 1862	Do.
Lawrence, Joseph	do	Oct. 6, 1863	Oct. 31, 1863	Do.
Lewis, Henry C	do	June 14, 1862	July 3, 1862	Do.
McCaslin, James	do	June 13, 1862	July 3, 1862	Do.
McCaslin, John W	do	June 29, 1862	July 3, 1862	Do.
McCaslin, William	do	June 23, 1862	July 3, 1862	Do.
McCaslin, George W	do	May 23, 1863	Aug. 14, 1863	Do.
Mullins, Andrew J	do	June 23, 1862	July 3, 1862	Do.
Mannon, Francis M	do	June 14, 1862	July 3, 1862	Do.
Manney, Ira W	do	June 10, 1862	July 3, 1862	Do.
Marshal, Jos. E	do	June 2, 1863	Aug. 14, 1863	Do.
Murvin, Allison E	do	May 23, 1864	May 24, 1864	Do.
Miller, William H	do	June 10, 1862	July 3, 1862	Do.
Nailor, Alexander T	do	Oct. 6, 1863	Oct. 31, 1863	Do.
Pearson, Daniel L	do	June 23, 1862	July 3, 1862	Do.
Pearson, John A	do	Aug. 2, 1863	Aug. 14, 1863	Do.
Phelan, John W	do	June 23, 1862	July 3, 1862	Do.
Perry, Henry	do	June 23, 1862	July 3, 1862	Do.
Patton, James	do	Aug. 10, 1863	April 2, 1864	Do.
Ripley, Manson M	do	July 28, 1863	Aug. 14, 1863	Do.
Reese, John	do	Nov. 3, 1862	Aug. 14, 1863	Do.
Sherry, John C	do	June 23, 1862	July 3, 1862	Do.
Strickland, Charles	do	May 23, 1864	May 23, 1864	Do.
Skelton, Robert	do	June 24, 1862	July 3, 1862	Do.
Sawyers, Alonzo	do	Aug. 25, 1864	Aug. 31, 1864	Do.
Temple, Francis M	do	July 3, 1862	July 3, 1862	Do.
Temple, William	do	July 1, 1862	July 3, 1862	Do.
Toon, Asbury	do	Nov. 2, 1862	Aug. 14, 1863	Do.
Taylor, William M	do	July 28, 1863	Aug. 9, 1863	Do.
T——, Campbell G	do	Nov. 16, 1864	Nov. 16, 1864	Do.
Walkup, Finley	do	June 28, 1862	July 3, 1862	Do.
Wood, Joel	do	June 26, 1862	July 3, 1862	Do.
Winn, Zadock	do	Sept. 12, 1863	Oct. 9, 1863	Do.
Winn, Zadock C	do	Oct. 6, 1863	Oct. 31, 1863	Do.
Yows, James K	do	June 27, 1862	July 10, 1862	Do.

Killed.

Covington, Van Buren	Corporal	May 14, 1862	Aug. 14, 1863	Appointed corporal August 1, 1864; killed by guerillas October 12, 1864.
Daniels, James	Private	June 23, 1862	July 3, 1862	Killed by guerillas July 10, 1862.
Norris, Jesse G	Sergeant	June 14, 1862	July 3.	Appointed corporal July 3, 1862; sergeant June 1, 1863; killed by guerillas July 4, 1863.
Parker, Elijah	Private	Aug. 2, 1863	Aug. 14, 1863	Killed by guerillas August 1, 1864.
Rutherford, Noel G	Corporal	June 24, 1862	July 3, 1862	Appointed corporal July 3, 1862; killed in action at Vine Prairie Lake, Arkansas, February 21, 1863.
Strickland, Levi	Trumpeter	June 24, 1862	July 3, 1862	Appointed trumpeter February 1, 1863; killed in action September 4, 1864.

Died.

| Coombs, Alfred B | Private | July 3, 1862 | July 10, 1862 | Died at Fayetteville, Arkansas, May 31, 1864. |
| Cradduck, Elbert | do | Nov. 9, 1862 | Never | Died at Elkhorn, Arkansas, November 23, 1862. |

REPORT OF THE ADJUTANT GENERAL OF ARKANSAS.

First regiment Arkansas cavalry volunteers. Mustered into service August 7, 1862, (three years;) mustered out August 23, 1865.

COMPANY D.—Continued.

Names.	Rank.	Enlistment.	Muster.	Remarks.
Dye, John W	Private	Aug. 5, 1862	Aug. 10, 1862	Died near Fayetteville, Arkansas, January 4, 1863.
Gilstrap, Benjamin P	do	July 20, 1862	Aug. 7, 1862	Appointed corporal November 1, 1862. Died January 10, 1863.
Hodges, Anson	do	Nov. 4, 1862	Never	Taken prisoner at Prairie Grove, Arkansas, December 7, 1862. Died in hands of enemy.
Hutton, Moses	do	June 25, 1862	July 3, 1862	Died near Fayetteville, Arkansas, February 23, 1863.
Jett, James	do	June 23, 1862	July 3, 1862	Died in Washington county, Arkansas, January 9, 1863.
Males, William N	do	June 23, 1862	July 3, 1862	Died near Fayetteville, Arkansas, February 21, 1863.
Quinton, William J	do	June 23, 1862	July 3, 1862	Died near Fayetteville, Arkansas, January 10, 1865.
Reed, James W	do	June 24, 1862	July 3, 1862	Died near Fayetteville, Arkansas, January 4, 1863.
Reed, William D	do	Nov. 7, 1862	Aug. 14, 1863	Died near Fayetteville, Arkansas, July 12, 1864.
Ritchie, James A	do	June 23, 1862	July 3, 1862	Died near Fayetteville, Arkansas, February 4, 1863.
Rains, John M	do	June 14, 1862	July 3, 1862	Died near Elkhorn, Arkansas, December 25, 1862.
Strickland, William M	do	June 14, 1862	July 3, 1862	Died near Fayetteville, Arkansas, February 4, 1862.
Waters, Samuel C	do	June 23, 1862	July 3, 1862	Died at Elkhorn, Arkansas, December 4, 1862.
Discharged.				
Bloyed, James	Private	June 22, 1862	July 3, 1862	Discharged for disability at Fayetteville, Arkansas, March 12, 1864.
Center, Guilford	do	June 14, 1862	July 3, 1862	Discharged for disability at Fayetteville, Arkansas, February 1, 1863.
Covington, William	do	June 14, 1862	July 3, 1862	Discharged for disability at Fayetteville, Arkansas, February 1, 1863.
Caldwell, William H	do	June 23, 1862	July 3, 1862	Discharged for disability at Fayetteville, Arkansas, February 1, 1863.
Eaton, John	do	June 14, 1862	July 3, 1862	Discharged for disability at Fayetteville, Arkansas, January 13, 1865.
Lane, Samuel P	do	May 14, 1862	July 3, 1862	Discharged for disability at Fayetteville, Arkansas, January 20, 1863.
Loftin, Stephen	do	June 23, 1862	July 3, 1862	Discharged for disability at Fayetteville, Arkansas, February 1, 1863.
Millicon, David G	do	June 14, 1862	July 3, 1862	Discharged for disability at Fayetteville, Arkansas, December 15, 1863.
Neal, William T	do	June 20, 1862	July 3, 1862	Discharged for disability at Fayetteville, Arkansas, February 1, 1863.
Rutherford, William M	do	June 24, 1862	July 3, 1862	Discharged for disability at Fayetteville, Arkansas, January 15, 1865.
Roberts, Elijah	do	July 28, 1862	Aug. 10, 1862	Discharged for disability at Fayetteville, Arkansas, February 1, 1863.
Seagraves, Gabriel	do	July 3, 1862		Discharged for disability at Fayetteville, Arkansas, February 1, 1863.
Toon, Charles	do	June 23, 1862		Discharged for disability at Fayetteville, Arkansas, February 1, 1863.

COMPANY E.

		Date of rank.	
Charles Galloway	Captain	July 10, 1862	Appointed from civil life; promoted to major March 2, 1864.
George R. King	do	July 10, 1862	Appointed 1st sergeant August 1, 1862; 2d lieutenant January 1, 1863; mustered out with regiment.
Philip M. Slaughter	1st lieutenant	July 7, 1862	Resigned November 27, 1862.

REPORT OF THE ADJUTANT GENERAL OF ARKANSAS. 27

Name	Rank			Remarks
		July 10, 1862	Nov. 27, 1862	
Elam O. Kincaid	do	July 10, 1862	Nov. 27, 1862	2d lieutenant from organization of company to November 27, 1862; dismissed May 28, 1864.
George W. Rowe	do	Sept. 14, 1862	July 14, 1864	Appointed sergeant October 1, 1862; 2d lieutenant March 2, 1864; dismissed June 10, 1865.
George A. Purdy	2d lieutenant	July 7, 1864	Jan. 1, 1865	Appointed from 1st sergeant company G; mustered out with regiment.
John Dougherty	1st sergeant	Aug. 9, 1862	May 1, 1863	Appointed corporal October 1, 1862; mustered out with regiment.
Charles R. Cummings	Quartermaster sergeant	Aug. 18, 1862	July 1, 1864	Appointed corporal October 1, 1862; mustered out with regiment.
Alfred H. Fesperman	Commissary sergeant	Sept. 26, 1862	Nov. 1, 1862	Mustered out with regiment.
Noah F. Wade	Sergeant	Jan. 31, 1863	Aug. 26, 1863	Appointed corporal April 1, 1863; mustered out with regiment.
John Miles	do	Aug. 8, 1862	April 15, 1864	Appointed corporal September 1, 1862; mustered out with regiment.
George W. Barnes	do	Jan. 3, 1863	April 15, 1864	Appointed corporal March 1, 1863; mustered out with regiment.
Charles C. Coones	do	Aug. 7, 1862	July 1, 1864	Appointed corporal April 1, 1863; mustered out with regiment.
Price Summers	do	Aug. 8, 1862	Nov. 1, 1864	Appointed corporal August 26, 1863; mustered out with regiment.
Lewis Harp	Corporal	June 24, 1862	Aug. 26, 1863	Mustered out with regiment.
William Johnson	do	June 15, 1862	Aug. 25, 1863	Do.
Andrew J. Moore	do	July 4, 1862	April 15, 1864	Do.
John S. Lee	do	July 4, 1862	July 1, 1864	Do.
Andrew J. Patrick	do	Jan. 7, 1863	Nov. 1, 1864	Do.
Pleasant H. Ripley	do	July 4, 1862	Nov. 1, 1864	Do.
Peter Dennis	do	July 22, 1862	July 22, 1862	Do.
George W. Hoyal	do	Aug. 15, 1862	Aug. 15, 1862	Do.
James W. Quick	do	June 16, 1863	June 16, 1863	Do.
John Shirley	do	July 1, 1862	July 1, 1862	Do.
James L. Payne	Sadler	Aug. 1, 1863	Aug. 1, 1863	Do.
			Muster.	
Baze, Abednego P	Private	June 12, 1862	July 10, 1862	Do.
Baze, John P	do	June 9, 1862	July 10, 1862	Do.
Burke, Elijah	do	July 1, 1862	July 10, 1862	Do.
Barnard, Gilbert	do	Aug. 3, 1862	Aug. 9, 1862	Do.
Clemens, Jas. T	do	June 15, 1862	July 22, 1862	Do.
Cummings, Robert H	do	July 11, 1862	July 12, 1862	Do.
Clarke, Thomas	do	June 24, 1862	July 3, 1862	Do.
Clarke, Elijah	do	June 3, 1862	July 22, 1862	Do.
Campbell, John A	do	Aug. 15, 1862	Aug. 25, 1862	Do.
Castile, John	do	Feb. 3, 1864	Feb. 28, 1864	Do.
Dryden, Jas. N	do	Sept. 2, 1863	Sept. 25, 1863	Do.
Eden, Jonathan	do	Aug. 3, 1862	Aug. 3, 1862	Do.
Eden, Bolen G	do	June 25, 1862	July 22, 1862	Do.
Edwards, James	do	Aug. 15, 1862	Aug. 15, 1862	Do.
Galloway, Melvin	do	Aug. 1, 1862	Aug. 15, 1862	Do.
Galloway, Francis M	do	July 14, 1863	Aug. 14, 1863	Do.
Grubb, John A	do	June 16, 1862	July 10, 1862	Do.
Hayes, Lewis C	do	Oct. 6, 1862	Aug. 14, 1863	Do.
Hayes, James A	do	Aug. 12, 1862	Aug. 18, 1862	Do.
Hayes, Joseph W	do	Aug. 22, 1862	Aug. 26, 1862	Do.
Hill, William	do	Aug. 1, 1863	Aug. 14, 1863	Do.
Howard, Nicholas W	do	May 10, 1862	July 8, 1862	Do.
Hudson, John B	do	June 12, 1862	July 10, 1862	Do.
Harp, James	do	June 24, 1862	July 3, 1862	Do.
Irby, James	do	Aug. 18, 1862	Aug. 18, 1862	Do.

28   REPORT OF THE ADJUTANT GENERAL OF ARKANSAS.

First regiment Arkansas cavalry volunteers. Mustered into service August 7, 1862, (three years;) mustered out August 23, 1865.

COMPANY E—Continued.

Names.	Rank.	Enlistment.	Muster.	Remarks.
Johnson, Levi	Private	Jan. 7, 1863	Oct. 31, 1863	Mustered out with regiment.
Johnson, Micajah	do	Aug. 21, 1862	Aug. 22, 1862	Do.
Johnston, Jas. H	do	July 26, 1862	Aug. 5, 1862	Do.
Lee, Levastus M	do	July 4, 1862	July 10, 1862	Do.
Lensing, Joel	do	April 19, 1864	April 29, 1864	Do.
Lynch, Wilson	do	Feb. 23, 1864	Feb. 28, 1864	Do.
Messenger, Daniel	do	June 18, 1862	July 18, 1862	Do.
McCay, John	do	Aug. 1, 1863	Aug. 14, 1863	Do.
McCay, Fielden	do	Feb. 1, 1864	Feb. 28, 1864	Do.
Mayberry, Robert	do	Oct. 28, 1863	Oct. 31, 1863	Do.
Pryor, William J	do	Aug. 3, 1862	Aug. 8, 1862	Do.
Poe, Lewis	do	July 24, 1863	Aug. 14, 1863	Do.
Payne, George J	do	Aug. 1, 1863	Aug. 14, 1863	Do.
Patrick, Samuel	do	May 1, 1864	June 30, 1864	Do.
Phillips, Andrew J	do	Aug. 12, 1862	Aug. 14, 1863	Do.
Russell, Allen	do	Sept. 1, 1863	Sept. 5, 1863	Do.
Ross, John A	do	Aug. 3, 1862	Aug. 8, 1862	Do.
Ricketts, Joel	do	July 3, 1862	Feb. 1, 1864	Do.
Stockton, John J	do	Aug. 3, 1862	Oct. 28, 1863	Do.
Stockton, Samuel M	do	July 10, 1862	Aug. 3, 1862	Do.
Stockton, George M	do	July 10, 1862	July 24, 1863	Do.
Springfield, John	do	Aug. 1, 1863	Dec. 31, 1863	Do.
Stone, Little B	do	Feb. 28, 1864	May 1, 1864	Do.
Solomon, George W	do	July 22, 1862	Sept. 11, 1862	Do.
Solomon, John	do	Sept. 11, 1862	July 10, 1862	Do.
Stout, Jacob	do	July 1, 1862	Aug. 14, 1863	Do.
Smith, Rufus H	do	June 12, 1863	Oct. 31, 1863	Do.
Stokes, Thomas P	do	Oct. 2, 1863	Aug. 8, 1862	Do.
Taylor, Jordan	do	Aug. 1, 1862	Aug. 15, 1862	Do.
Taylor, James	do	Aug. 1, 1862	Sept. 17, 1862	Do.
Taylor, Samuel	do	Aug. 29, 1862	Aug. 14, 1863	Do.
Vickery, Jabel	do	Jan. 25, 1863	Aug. 14, 1863	Do.
Watkins, Samuel	do	Jan. 7, 1863	Jan. 2, 1864	Do.
Watkins, William	do	Jan. 1, 1864		Do.
Killed.				
Bodine, Isaac N	Private	Feb. 1, 1864	Feb. 28, 1864	Killed by guerillas January 1, 1865.
Brooman, William	do	Mar. 12, 1864	Never	Killed in action April 7, 1864.
McGlothlin, Burley	do	Feb. 1, 1864	Feb. 28, 1864	Do.
McGuire, Moses H	do	Sept. 16, 1863	Sept. 25, 1863	Killed in attempt to escape from rebel prison at Little Rock May 25, 1863.
Patrick, William	do	Jan. 7, 1863	Never	Killed by guerillas January 1, 1865.
Ross, Hiram	do	June 6, 1862	July 3, 1862	

REPORT OF THE ADJUTANT GENERAL OF ARKANSAS. 29

Name	Rank	Enlisted	Mustered	Remarks
Rainey, John E	Corporal	Feb. 1, 1864	Feb. 28, 1864	Killed by guerillas October 8, 1864.
Stockton, David C	Private	June 24, 1862	July 22, 1862	Killed by guerillas October 12, 1864.
Tucker, John R	do	Dec. 20, 1863	Dec. 30, 1863	Do.
Watkins, Isaac	do	Oct. 2, 1863	Oct. 31, 1863	Killed by guerillas May 16, 1865.

Died.

Name	Rank	Enlisted	Mustered	Remarks
Armstrong, Quinton	Private	Nov. 14, 1862	Never	Died March 14, 1863.
Burrow, William	1st sergeant	July 24, 1862	Aug. 3, 1862	Appointed 1st sergeant January 1, 1863; died of wounds received in battle at Fayetteville, April 26, 1863.
Bryant, William	Private	May 10, 1862	July 3, 1862	Died April 21, 1863.
Begley, Hiram	do	Aug. 15, 1862	Aug. 15, 1862	Died November 15, 1862.
Boatman, William	do	Aug. 7, 1862	Aug. 7, 1862	Died December 21, 1862.
Cassidy, Clinton	Corporal	Dec. 2, 1862	Aug. 14, 1863	Appointed corporal January 1, 1863; died August 27, 1863.
Eden, John	Private	Aug. 3, 1862	Aug. 3, 1862	Died December 16, 1862.
Elsasman, Gottlieb	do	June 18, 1862	July 10, 1862	Died September 26, 1862.
Farley, George W	do	May 10, 1862	July 3, 1862	Died July 7, 1863.
Fisher, Enoch G	do	Feb. 4, 1863	Never	Died April 1, 1863.
Gamblin, Reuben	do	July 3, 1862	July 31, 1862	Died January 1, 1863.
Henderson, Joseph	do	Dec. 16, 1862	Aug. 14, 1863	Died May 12, 1864.
Hobbs, Nathan	do	Oct. 6, 1863	Never	Died March 5, 1863.
Kimbrough, James	do	June 16, 1862	July 10, 1862	Died April 8, 1863.
Keeney, Calvin L	do	Sept. 1, 1863	Sept. 25, 1863	Died March 5, 1864.
Lee, Lansden W	do	July 4, 1862	July 10, 1862	Died November 24, 1862.
Lee, James N	Sergeant	Aug. 15, 1862	Aug. 15, 1862	Died September 26, 1862.
Moore, John M	Private	July 4, 1862	July 10, 1862	Appointed quartermaster sergeant July 10, 1862; died December 19, 1862.
Moore, Richard W	do	Sept. 7, 1863	Sept. 1, 1863	Died December 23, 1862.
Prater, Robert	do	Jan. 1, 1863	Never	Died February 28, 1863.
Pitts, William	do	July 13, 1862	July 22, 1862	Died March 5, 1863.
Patrick, John	do	Jan. 1, 1863	Never	Died May 10, 1863, in rebel prison at Little Rock, Arkansas.
Rice, Thomas A	do	July 4, 1862	July 10, 1862	Died October 2, 1863, of wounds received in action.
Ripley, Francis S	Corporal	Feb. 12, 1863	Never	Promoted corporal July 10, 1862; died December 1, 1862.
Steward, Henry	Private	Aug. 29, 1862	Sept. 17, 1862	Died June 1, 1863.
Taylor, John	do	July 4, 1862	July 10, 1862	Died January 25, 1863.
White, Elias H	do	July 4, 1862	July 22, 1862	Died April 1, 1863.
Wilson, Julius	do	Aug. 1, 1863	Aug. 14, 1863	Died December 15, 1862.
Woodward, James	do	April 1, 1862	Never	Died May 12, 1864.
White, William G	do	July 4, 1862	July 10, 1862	Died April 9, 1863.
Youngblood, Pleasant	Corporal			Appointed corporal August 6, 1862; died January 1, 1863.

Discharged.

Name	Rank	Enlisted	Mustered	Remarks
Baker, John	Private	Oct. 16, 1862	Never	Discharged for disability June 5, 1863.
Berry, Patrick C	do	July 10, 1862	July 22, 1862	Discharged for disability January 23, 1865.
Galloway, Alexander	do	Aug. 6, 1862	Aug. 15, 1862	Discharged for disability March 25, 1863.
Kirk, Henry J	do	Aug. 1, 1862	July 10, 1862	Discharged for disability March 23, 1863.
Lee, Samuel J	do	July 1, 1862-	Aug. 15, 1862	Discharged for disability February 1, 1863.
Lee, Sir W	do	Aug. 15, 1863	Aug. 15, 1862	Do.
Moore, John	Quartermaster sergeant	Sept. 10, 1862	Sept. 10, 1862	Discharged for disability December 25, 1863.
Miles, John C	Farrier	Sept. 25, 1862	Sept. 25, 1862	Discharged for promotion April 1, 1863.
Plumlee, John W	Sergeant	Jan. 20, 1863	Aug. 14, 1863	Discharged for promotion June 10, 1864.
Parker, William C	Private	July 3, 1862	July 10, 1862	Discharged for promotion April 1, 1863.

First regiment Arkansas cavalry volunteers. Mustered into service August 7, 1862, (three years;) mustered out August 23, 1865.

COMPANY E—Continued.

Names.	Rank.	Enlistment.	Muster.	Remarks.
Rhodes, Ransom R	Sergeant	June 18, 1862	July 22, 1862	Discharged for promotion March 1, 1863.
Riddle, George W	do	Aug. 3, 1862	Aug. 3, 1862	Discharged for disability March 25, 1863.
Taylor, James, 1st	Private	Aug. 3, 1862	Aug. 3, 1862	Discharged for disability March 21, 1863.
Taylor, James, 2d	do	Aug. 1, 1862	Aug. 15, 1862	Discharged for disability March 30, 1863.
Taylor, Henry D	do	Aug. 2, 1862	Aug. 15, 1862	Discharged for disability January 31, 1863.
Taylor, Benjamin	do	Aug. 29, 1862	Sept. 17, 1862	Discharged for disability February 3, 1863.
Todd, Leroy C	do	Oct. 24, 1862	Never	Discharged for disability January 31, 1863.
White, George A	do	July 1, 1862	July 10, 1862	Discharged for promotion December 13, 1863.
Wilson, Daniel	do	Aug. 7, 1862	Oct. 1, 1862	Discharged for disability March 21, 1863.
Somers, James C	Quartermaster sergeant	Aug. 8, 1862	Aug. 8, 1862	Discharged for promotion May 1, 1864.
Lucius, Raphael	Private	May 28, 1864	June 30, 1864	Discharged, by sentence of G. C. M., July 10, 1865.
Deserted.				
Hobbs, James	Private	Oct. 17, 1862	Aug. 14, 1863	Deserted at Fayetteville, Arkansas, December 24, 1864.
Trammell, John	do	Nov. 6, 1863	Nov. 8, 1863	Deserted at Fayetteville, Arkansas, November 12, 1863.
White, Henry C	do	July 4, 1862	July 10, 1862	Deserted at Fayetteville, Arkansas, December 1, 1863.
White, John B	do	April 29, 1863	Never	Do.

COMPANY F.

Names.	Rank.	Enlistment.	Date of rank.	Remarks.
Richard H. Wimpy	Captain	June 15, 1862	Aug. 11, 1862	Promoted to Major May 1, 1865.
John A. Dienst	do	July 31, 1862	May 16, 1865	Appointed sergeant October 1, 1862; 1st sergeant November 1, 1862; 2d lieutenant August 5, 1863; promoted 1st lieutenant June 18, 1864; mustered out with reg't.
Frederick Ohlemacher	1st lieutenant	Aug. 7, 1862	Aug. 11, 1862	Resigned October 29, 1862.
Robert N. Thompson	do	Aug. 7, 1862	Oct. 29, 1862	Resigned January 30, 1864.
Isaac A. Copeland	do	July 21, 1862	May 16, 1865	Appointed sergeant July 16, 1863; 1st sergeant March 1, 1864; 2d lieutenant June 18, 1864; mustered out with regiment.
Alfred M. Hutchinson	2d lieutenant		Oct. 29, 1862	Dismissed.
John P. Todd	do	Oct. 14, 1862	June 4, 1865	Appointed from sergeant company M; mustered out with regiment.
Martin M. Tygert	1st sergeant	July 16, 1862	June 18, 1864	Appointed sergeant August 11, 1863; mustered out with regiment.
John B. Stack	Quartermaster sergeant	Dec. 10, 1862	Aug. 16, 1863	Appointed sergeant April 4, 1863; mustered out with regiment.
John W. Kimbrough	Commissary sergeant	June 18, 1862	Aug. 5, 1863	Appointed corporal March 1, 1863; mustered out with regiment.
Wm. G. Wingfield	Sergeant	June 29, 1862	Dec. 21, 1862	Mustered out with regiment.
Josiah Souther	do	July 14, 1862	Dec. 21, 1862	Mustered out with regiment.
Mark B. Wilson	do	Nov. 15, 1862	Mar. 22, 1863	Appointed corporal September 16, 1862; mustered out with regiment.
Ephraim M. Thomason	do	July 21, 1862	Mar. 18, 1864	Appointed corporal August 1, 1863; mustered out with regiment.
William J. Hutchinson	do	Nov. 15, 1862	Mar. 1, 1865	Mustered out with regiment.
Samuel Cautrell	Corporal	Nov. 15, 1862	Mar. 1, 1863	Do.

REPORT OF THE ADJUTANT GENERAL OF ARKANSAS. 31

				Muster.	
John P. Truesdale	do	Dec. 27, 1862	Mar. 1, 1864		Do.
Samuel H. Hughes	do	Jan. 1, 1863	April 10, 1864		Do.
John H. Cook	do	Nov. 18, 1863	April 10, 1864		Do.
John M. James	do	Nov. 19, 1863	May 1, 1864		Do.
John M. Jones	do	Dec. 4, 1862	June 1, 1864		Do.
King R. Goddard	do	May 30, 1864	May 1, 1865		Do.
Joseph Huff	do	Nov. 3, 1863	May 1, 1865		Do.
Alexander Copeland	Farrier	July 21, 1862	July 16, 1863		Do.
Wesley Lewis		Mar. 1, 1863	Aug. 11, 1862		Do.
John M. Wyatt	Trumpeter	Jan. 10, 1863	July 16, 1863		Do.
Edward M. Harrison	do	June 1, 1862	Aug. 11, 1862		Do.
Abbott, Henry	Private	Jan. 1, 1863	Oct. 31, 1863		Do.
Adkins, Stephen J	do	Oct. 2, 1863	Oct. 31, 1863		Do.
Baker, James C	do	Dec. 29, 1862	Aug. 31, 1863		Do.
—, Samuel	do	Nov. 29, 1864			Do.
Bell, George J	do	Jan. 1, 1863	Sept. 22, 1863		Do.
Bradshaw, James	do	July 21, 1862	July 21, 1862		Do.
Carter, Josiah	do	July 21, 1862	July 21, 1862		Do.
Cantrell, Shadrach	do	Dec. 10, 1862	Sept. 22, 1863		Do.
Cavin, Alex	do	Dec. 7, 1863	Dec. 31, 1863		Do.
Cate, James	do	May 15, 1864	Aug. 31, 1864		Do.
Chambers, John P	do	Mar. 31, 1864	April 30, 1864		Do.
Colwell, Abiram	do	Nov. 15, 1863	Dec. 31, 1863		Do.
Copeland, Seaburn	do	July 21, 1862	July 21, 1862		Do.
Cooper, Martin F	do	Oct. 31, 1863	Oct. 31, 1863		Do.
Cook, Robert W	do	July 21, 1862	July 21, 1862		Do.
Davis, Elihu	do	July 16, 1862	July 16, 1862		Do.
Davis, James R	do	July 26, 1862	July 26, 1862		Do.
De Priest, Thomas J	do	July 21, 1862	July 21, 1862		Do.
De Priest, John A	do	July 21, 1862	July 21, 1862		Do.
Denton, William	do	Nov. 8, 1863	Dec. 31, 1863		Do.
Dodd, William	do	June 27, 1863	Aug. 3, 1863		Do.
Doke, Robert	do	July 18, 1862	July 18, 1862		Do.
Doke, Nathaniel	do	July 18, 1862	July 18, 1862		Do.
Doke, Samuel	do	July 18, 1862	July 18, 1862		Do.
Doke, James	do	May 2, 1964	Aug. 31, 1864		Do.
Edwards, George W	do	July 16, 1862	July 16, 1862		Do.
Fallin, Robert R	do	Dec. 17, 1862	Aug. 13, 1863		Do.
Freeze, Wm	do	Nov. 30, 1863	Dec. 31, 1863		Do.
Freeze, Lewis A	do	April 18, 1864	April 30, 1864		Do.
Guttery, Thomas H	do	July 21, 1862	July 21, 1862		Do.
Hall, Elisha	do	July 3, 1862	July 3, 1862		Do.
Hall, Allen	do	Aug. 4, 1863	Aug. 31, 1863		Do.
Huff, Henderson	do	April 15, 1864	April 30, 1864		Do.
Hutchinson, Wm	do	Dec. 21, 1862	Aug. 31, 1863		Do.
Huckaby, Robert G	do	Feb. 23, 1864	Feb. 28, 1864		Do.
January, Thomas B	do	July 16, 1862	July 16, 1862		Do.
Jeffreys, Samuel S	do	July 21, 1862	July 21, 1862		Do.
Jeffreys, Marmaduke	do	Feb. 6, 1863	Aug. 31, 1863		Do.

First regiment Arkansas cavalry volunteers. Mustered into service August 7, 1862, (three years;) mustered out August 23, 1865.

COMPANY F—Continued.

Names.	Rank.	Enlistment.	Muster.	Remarks.
Kidwell, John F	Private	July 21, 1862	July 21, 1862	Mustered out with regiment.
Larimore, James J	do	Dec. 16, 1862	Aug. 21, 1863	Do.
Lewis, Amos G	do	Dec. 16, 1862	Aug. 31, 1863	Do.
Mathews, Ansel	do	Nov. 16, 1862	Sept. 22, 1863	Do.
Martin, Abner	do	Nov. 20, 1862	Sept. 22, 1863	Do.
Magnus, Marday	do	Aug. 5, 1863	Aug. 31, 1863	Do.
Mack, Benjamin J. J	do	Aug. 14, 1862	Aug. 14, 1862	Do.
Mason, David	do	Nov. 30, 1863	Dec. 31, 1863	Do.
———, Josiah D	do	Feb. 1, 1864	Feb. 28, 1864	Do.
McClenedon, James F	do	Feb. 1, 1863	Aug. 31, 1863	Do.
Medden, Samuel	do	Nov. 15, 1862	Aug. 31, 1863	Do.
Noe, Isaac B	do	July 21, 1862	July 21, 1862	Do.
Norwood, Thomas W	do	Feb. 1, 1863	Sept. 22, 1863	Do.
Oaks, Alexander	do	Aug. 24, 1863	Aug. 31, 1863	Do.
Odle, Samuel	do	Dec. 14, 1862	Sept. 22, 1863	Do.
Odle, John	do	Dec. 14, 1862	Sept. 22, 1863	Do.
Ponts, William T	do	July 21, 1862	July 21, 1862	Do.
Reed, Samuel K	do	Nov. 17, 1862	Aug. 31, 1863	Do.
———, James	do	Aug. 18, 1862	Aug. 31, 1863	Do.
Roberts, Isaac G	do	Dec. 21, 1862	Sept. 21, 1863	Do.
Riley, Seth K	do	July 14, 1862	July 14, 1862	Do.
Sisemore, James	do	Oct. 2, 1863	Oct. 31, 1863	Do.
Stark, Thomas A	do	Dec. 16, 1862	Sept. 22, 1863	Do.
Smith, Enoch	do	Oct. 24, 1863	Oct. 31, 1863	Do.
Taylor, Andrew J	do	Jan. 27, 1863	Aug. 31, 1863	Do.
Thomason, Milton M	do	July 21, 1862	July 21, 1862	Do.
Thomason, John C	do	July 21, 1862	July 21, 1862	Do.
Thurman, Daniel	do	May 1, 1863	Sept. 22, 1863	Do.
Wells, Thomas J	do	June 18, 1862	June 18, 1862	Do.
———, Henry	do	June 1, 1863	Sept. 1, 1863	Do.
———, Francis M	do	June 6, 1863	Sept. 1, 1863	Do.
Wilson, Theodore	do	—, 1862		
Yarberry, William	do	—, 1862		
Killed.				
Cooper, Benjamin F	Private	Dec. 21, 1863		Killed near Fayetteville, Arkansas, August 9, 1864.
Jeffreys, Osborn	do	July —, 1862		Killed near Fayetteville, Arkansas, November 3, 1864.
Watkins, Daniel	do	—, 1862		Killed in Benton county, Arkansas, March 15, 1863.
Williams, Ira B	Corporal	Dec. 4, 1862	Sept. 22, 1863	Wounded in action and died near Bentonville, Arkansas, April 12, 1865.

REPORT OF THE ADJUTANT GENERAL OF ARKANSAS. 33

Died.

Name	Rank	Enlisted	Died	Remarks
Autry, Benjamin F	Private	July 21, 1862	July 21, 1862	Died at Fayetteville, Arkansas, March 1, 1863.
Carter, Columbus C	do	July 21, 1862	July 21, 1862	Died in Benton county, Arkansas, November 24, 1862.
Davis, Anderson	do	June 14, 1862	June 14, 1862	Died at Springfield, Missouri, September 28, 1862.
Davidson, Alexander	do	Nov. 19, 1862		Died at Fayetteville, Arkansas, March 3, 1863.
Douglass, Marion F	Corporal	July 21, 1862	July 21, 1862	Died at Springfield, Missouri, October 20, 1863; appointed corporal August 11, 1862.
Edwards, Thomas J	do	July 16, 1862	July 21, 1862	Died at Fayetteville, Arkansas, January 13, 1863; promoted corporal Aug. 11, 1862.
Graves, Leonard	Private	—, 1862	June 27, 1862	Died at Elkhorn, Arkansas, December 13, 1862.
Grison, John J	do	June 17, 1862		Died at Fayetteville, Arkansas, February 14, 1863.
Gutery, Joseph	Sergeant	July 21, 1862	July 21, 1862	Died at Fayetteville, Arkansas, April 4, 1863; appointed corporal August 11, 1862; sergeant December 21, 1862.
Guttery, Samuel	do	July 21, 1862	July 21, 1862	Died at Fayetteville, Arkansas, March 22, 1863; appointed sergeant Dec. 21, 1862.
Hagins, Moses	Private	Dec. 14, 1862		Died at Fayetteville, Arkansas, March 21, 1863.
Jobe, Thomas	do	June 6, 1862	June 6, 1862	Died at Fayetteville, Arkansas, February 24, 1863.
Keller, Jesse E	Farrier	Nov. 11, 1862		Died in Benton county, Arkansas, February 25, 1863.
Mathews, Jacob	Private	Nov. 20, 1862		Died at Fayetteville, Arkansas, February 3, 1863.
Mitchell, M. D. F	do	Nov. 17, 1862		Died at Fayetteville, Arkansas, February 20, 1863.
Roach, John M	do	Dec. 19, 1862		Died at Fayetteville, Arkansas, February 14, 1863.
Rodgers, John W	do	July 18, 1862	July 18, 1862	Died at Fayetteville, Arkansas, February 28, 1863.
Rodgers, James S	do	July 18, 1862	July 18, 1862	Died at Fayetteville, Arkansas, March 17, 1863.
William, Thomas M	do	—, 1862		Died at Springfield, Missouri, September 30, 1862.
Whitson, Charles T	do	—, 1862		Died in Washington county, Arkansas, December 25, 1862.
Wimpy, Alfred	1st sergeant	June 6, 1862	June 6, 1862	Died at Springfield, Missouri, November 6, 1862; appointed 1st sergeant August 11, 1862.
Wimpy, William	Quartermaster sergeant	June 30, 1862	June 30, 1862	Died at Fayetteville, Arkansas, April 25, 1863; appointed quartermaster sergeant August 11, 1862.
Wallace, Yancey	Corporal	July 21, 1862	July 21, 1862	Died at Springfield, Missouri, September 16, 1862; appointed corporal Aug. 11, 1862.

Discharged.

Name	Rank	Enlisted	Discharged	Remarks
Allen, George W	Private	Sept. 10, 1862		Discharged for disability, April 10, 1863.
Allison, James	1st sergeant	Dec. 8, 1862	Aug. 31, 1863	Discharged to accept promotion, January 26, 1864.
Davis, Hezekiah	Private	July 3, 1862	July 3, 1862	Discharged for disability, December 25, 1863.
Douglass, Joseph M	Commissary sergeant	Aug. 21, 1862	Aug. 26, 1862	Discharged for disability, March 20, 1863.
Douglass, Jonathan	Sergeant	July 21, 1862	July 21, 1862	Discharged by order, March 1, 1864.
Edwards, John A	Private	July 16, 1862	July 16, 1862	Discharged to accept promotion, April 11, 1864.
Ridewell, Dudley P	do	July 21, 1862	July 21, 1862	Discharged for disability, April 10, 1863.
Powell, James L	do	June 11, 1862	June 11, 1862	Discharged to accept appointment as captain company F, 2d Arkansas cavalry.
Roberts, Rezin	do	—, 1862		Discharged for disability, February 24, 1863.
Spradling, John S	do	—, 1862		Discharged to accept promotion.
Townsend, Solomon	do			Discharged for disability, June 4, 1863.
Vaughan, Matthew	Corporal	Dec. 5, 1862	Sept. 1, 1863	Discharged for disability, December —, 1862.
Thompson, Robert	Commissary sergeant	—, 1862		Discharged to accept appointment as 1st lieutenant battery A, 1st Ark. light artillery.
Baker, William S	Private	July 16, 1862	July 16, 1862	Discharged by order to accept civil office.

Deserted.

Name	Rank	Enlisted	Deserted	Remarks
Brown, William C	Private	Sept. 5, 1862		Deserted at Fayetteville, Arkansas, December 31, 1862.
Denton, James W	do	—, 1862		Deserted at Springfield, Missouri, October 1, 1862.
Downum, Thomas J	do	Feb. 16, 1863		Deserted at Fayetteville, Arkansas, April 5, 1863.

First regiment Arkansas cavalry volunteers. Mustered into service August 7, 1863, (three years;) mustered out August 23, 1865.

COMPANY F.—Continued.

Names.	Rank.	Enlistment.	Muster.	Remarks.
Kirby, Albert A.	Private.	Oct. 29, 1863	—, 1863	Deserted at Fayetteville, Arkansas, April 5, 1863.
Lee, Francis M.	do.	Dec. 11, 1863		Deserted at Elkhorn, Arkansas, December 22, 1862.
Lefors, William S.	do.	July 16, 1862	—, 1862	Deserted at Fayetteville, Arkansas, March 1, 1863.
Matthews, Commodore	do.	Oct. 8, 1862	Oct. 31, 1863	Deserted at Fayetteville, Arkansas, March 28, 1864.
Mitchell, George C.	do.			Deserted at Springfield, Missouri, October 1, 1862.
Montgomery, Samuel	do.	Feb. 2, 1864	Feb. 28, 1864	Deserted at Fayetteville, Arkansas, November 4, 1864.
Odle, James S.	do.	Dec. 14, 1862		Deserted at Fayetteville, Arkansas, March 17, 1863.
Shipman, William K.	do.	Aug. 27, 1863	Aug. 31, 1863	Deserted at Fayetteville, Arkansas, January 4, 1864.

COMPANY G.

Names.	Rank.	Enlistment.	Date of rank.	Remarks.
Rowan E. M. Mack	Captain	Aug. 6, 1862	Aug. 6, 1862	Killed in action, Washington county, Arkansas, May 28, 1864.
Francis M. Ward	do.	Jan. 30, 1864	July 14, 1864	Appointed from sergeant company I, vice Mack, killed in action; mustered out with regiment.
Joshua S. Dudley	1st lieutenant	—, 1861	July 31, 1862	Appointed from 37th Illinois infantry; promoted to captain company A December 5, 1862.
Robert B. Mack	do.	July 31, 1862	Dec. 5, 1862	Promoted from 2d lieutenant; resigned December 6, 1863.
Washington W. Davis	do.	July 31, 1862	July 14, 1864	Appointed 1st sergeant December 5, 1862; 2d lieutenant June 18, 1864; mustered out with regiment.
Matthew W. Hilbert	2d lieutenant	Mar. 3, 1863	Mar. 3, 1863	Resigned February 15, 1864.
William J. O'Neal	1st sergeant	July 7, 1862	Mar. 1, 1865	Appointed corporal August 6, 1862; commissary sergeant November 1, 1862; mustered out with regiment.
Hiram S. Shalian	Quartermaster sergeant	July 7, 1862	May 23, 1865	Appointed corporal September 16, 1862; mustered out with regiment.
Hiram H. Jones	Commissary sergeant	Aug. 22, 1862	May 23, 1865	Appointed corporal November 1, 1862; sergeant May 25, 1865; mustered out with regiment.
Joseph Standlee	Sergeant	July 10, 1862	July 31, 1862	Mustered out with regiment.
George W. Morris	do.	Aug. 2, 1862	Jan. 1, 1864	Appointed corporal January 1, 1863; was wounded at battle of Fayetteville April 18, 1863; mustered out with regiment.
William Glidewell	do.	July 31, 1862	Mar. 1, 1865	Appointed corporal April 1, 1863; mustered out with regiment.
Samuel D. L. D. Scott	do.	Aug. 21, 1862	May 23, 1865	Appointed corporal June 15, 1863; mustered out with regiment.
Ervin M. Davis	do.	Nov. 14, 1862	May 23, 1865	Appointed corporal June 15, 1863; mustered out with regiment.
Allen Jones	Corporal	July 31, 1862	Oct. 29, 1863	Mustered out with regiment.
Dewitt C. Carr	do.	July 30, 1862	Jan. 1, 1864	Do.
John W. Reed	do.	Aug. 10, 1862	July 1, 1864	Do.
George W. O'Neal	do.	June 15, 1862	Sept. 20, 1864	Do.
Lewis Jones	do.	July 23, 1862	Sept. 20, 1864	Do.
William Aikin	do.	Oct. 5, 1863	Mar. 1, 1865	Do.

REPORT OF THE ADJUTANT GENERAL OF ARKANSAS. 35

Name	Rank	Enlisted	Muster
John O. Crabaugh	do	Mar. 1, 1864	May 23, 1865
Caleb Sill	do	July 17, 1862	May 23, 1862
James W. Butler	Trumpeter	July 31, 1862	Aug. 1, 1863
Elias O. Hall	Farrier	July 28, 1862	Mar. 1, 1865
John L. Standlee	do	Aug. 7, 1862	Sept. 1, 1864
Bledsoe, Charles	Private	July 7, 1862	July 18, 1862
Butler, Richard	do	Dec. 17, 1863	Dec. 22, 1863
Call, William C	do	Sept. 12, 1862	Sept. 13, 1862
Crabaugh, Isaac	do	July 25, 1862	July 25, 1862
			Muster.
Davis, Thomas D	do	Aug. 1, 1864	Aug. 6, 1864
Eubanks, Spencer	do	Aug. 6, 1862	Aug. 7, 1862
Fanning, Samuel	do	Feb. 2, 1863	Aug. 14, 1863
Fanning, Joseph	do	Nov. 24, 1863	Nov. 24, 1863
Fanning, Abraham	do	Mar. 1, 1864	Mar. 1, 1864
Guy, Albert J	do	Sept. 10, 1862	Sept. 10, 1862
Harper, David	do	July 30, 1862	July 31, 1862
Harper, John	do	July 31, 1862	July 31, 1862
Hembree, William	do	Aug. 16, 1862	Aug. 16, 1862
Hayhurst, William	do	Aug. 21, 1862	Aug. 25, 1862
Hayhurst, Michael	do	Aug. 22, 1862	Aug. 22, 1862
High, Elisha	do	Aug. 16, 1862	Aug. 17, 1862
High, George W	do	Aug. 16, 1862	Aug. 22, 1862
Haynes, Lazarus	do	Aug. 5, 1862	Aug. 6, 1862
Huff, John A. J	do	Aug. 2, 1862	Aug. 3, 1862
Hurd, Richard	do	Aug. 23, 1862	Aug. 14, 1863
Jones, Isaac N	do	Dec. 8, 1862	Aug. 9, 1862
Kerr, Thomas S	do	Jan. 12, 1863	Aug. 14, 1862
Lucas, Jesse	do	June 21, 1862	Aug. 22, 1862
Lusk, James M	do	Aug. 4, 1862	July 5, 1863
Littrell, Samuel	do	July 7, 1862	July 12, 1862
Littrell, Jesse	do	July 7, 1862	July 12, 1862
Littrell, Joseph G	do	July 7, 1862	July 12, 1862
Littrell, James	do	Nov. 6, 1862	Aug. 14, 1863
Leach, William	do	June 19, 1862	Aug. 20, 1862
Leach, Jeremiah	do	June 19, 1862	Aug. 20, 1862
Leach, Hiram	do	July 3, 1862	Aug. 14, 1863
Lockport, Isaac	do	June 7, 1862	July 12, 1862
McDowell, William E	do	Aug. 10, 1862	Aug. 10, 1862
Merritt, Joseph P	do	July 31, 1862	July 31, 1862
Meek, Samuel B	do	Jan. 13, 1864	Sept. 14, 1864
Rhodes, Riley R	do	June 14, 1862	July 12, 1862
Rogers, John W	do	Aug. 22, 1863	Aug. 31, 1863
Rogers, Franklin M	do	Aug. 22, 1863	Aug. 31, 1863
Sutton, George W	do	July 8, 1862	Aug. 9, 1862
Sutton, John	do	July 8, 1862	Aug. 18, 1862
Shelton, William	do	July 31, 1862	July 31, 1862
Standlee, James	do	Aug. 20, 1862	Aug. 23, 1862
Standlee, Joseph	do	Aug. 8, 1862	Aug. 8, 1862
Standlee, David	do	Sept. 22, 1863	Nov. 23, 1863

First regiment Arkansas cavalry volunteers. Mustered into service August 7, 1862, (three years;) mustered out August 23, 1865.

COMPANY G.—Continued.

Names.	Rank.	Enlistment.	Muster.	Remarks.
Sill, Samuel C	Private	July 17, 1862	July 22, 1862	Mustered out with regiment.
Teagne, John H	do	June 15, 1862	July 14, 1862	Do.
Torrance, Jennison P	do	July 30, 1862	July 31, 1862	Do.
Wise, Francis M	do	Aug. 2, 1862	Aug. 4, 1862	Do.
Wilson, James	do	July 31, 1862	July 31, 1862	Do.
Wilson, Ezekiel	do	Sept. 23, 1863	Sept. 28, 1863	Do.
Wright, Brantley	do	Oct. 26, 1863	Oct. 31, 1863	Do.

Killed.

Names.	Rank.	Enlistment.	Muster.	Remarks.
Scott, Robert J	Sergeant	Aug. 7, 1862	Aug. 7, 1862	Appointed corporal September 4, 1862; sergeant November 15, 1863. Killed in action in Washington county, Arkansas, May 28, 1864.
O'Neal, Charles B	Corporal	July 25, 1862	July 27, 1862	Appointed corporal November 1, 1862; taken prisoner December 7, 1862; shot December 24, 1862.
Miles, Frederick	Trumpeter	July 21, 1862	July 21, 1862	Taken prisoner December 7, 1862; died in prison.
Littrell, Joseph N	Private	July 7, 1862	July 12, 1862	Killed in action in Carroll county, Arkansas, March 13, 1864.
Russell, George W	do	July 16, 1862	July 18, 1862	Captured by bushwhackers April 18, 1863, and found dead.
Weaver, Henry E	do	Nov. 24, 1863	Nov. 24, 1863	Killed in action in Crawford county, Arkansas, October 19, 1864.

Died.

Names.	Rank.	Enlistment.	Muster.	Remarks.
Hall, Elisha B	Quartermaster sergeant	Aug. 23, 1862	Aug. 23, 1862	Appointed quartermaster sergeant November 25, 1862; died April 25, 1865.
Hall, James M	Sergeant	July 25, 1862	July 27, 1862	Appointed sergeant July 1, 1864; died May 22, 1865.
Frazier, John L	Corporal	July 31, 1862	July 31, 1862	Appointed corporal ———; died November 14, 1862.
Leonard, George R	do	Aug. 8, 1862	Aug. 10, 1862	Appointed corporal September 16, 1862; died February 7, 1863.
Mason, Henry H	do	July 18, 1862	July 18, 1862	Appointed corporal January 1, 1864; died May 13, 1864.
Rhodes, John	do	July 2, 1862	July 8, 1862	Appointed corporal December 1, 1862; died March 19, 1863.
Ashmore, Harvey W	do	July 16, 1862	July 31, 1862	Appointed corporal ———; died December 22, 1862.
Russell, James W	Private	July 31, 1862	July 31, 1862	
Boren, John	do	Sept. 11, 1863	Sept. 19, 1863	Died April 22, 1865.
Bridges, Franklin	do	July 18, 1862	July 18, 1862	Died January 22, 1865.
Dean, Burrell	do	Nov. 1, 1862	Never	Died August 17, 1862.
Davis, John S	do	Nov. 10, 1862	Never	Died January 9, 1863.
Gaddy, Winship N	do	July 8, 1862	July 8, 1862	Died March 18, 1863.
Hall, Benjamin F	do	June 15, 1862	July 12, 1862	Died January 22, 1863.
Harbert, James C	do	Aug. 16, 1862	Aug. 18, 1862	Died October 7, 1862.
High, Oliver	do	July 25, 1862	July 27, 1862	Died December 7, 1862.
O'Neal, Isaac M	do	Aug. 1, 1862	Never	Died January 19, 1863.
Price, Francis M	do	Aug. 8, 1862	Aug. 10, 1862	Died April 22, 1863.
Plumlee, John	do	Dec. 19, 1863	Dec. 31, 1863	Died, date unknown.
Roberts, Francis M	do	June 22, 1862	July 12, 1862	Died March 2, 1863.
Riddle, John E	do	July 17, 1862	July 22, 1862	Died April 5, 1865.
Sill, Oty	do			Died January 13, 1863.
				Died February 11, 1863.

Discharged.

Name	Rank	Date	Remarks
Carr, Wm. A.	Quartermaster sergeant	July 31, 1862	Discharged for disability March 22, 1863.
Carr, Francis M.	Private	July 31, 1862	Discharged for disability September 17, 1862.
Davis, Wm. F.	do	Nov. 14, 1862	Wounded in battle of Fayetteville, Arkansas, April 18, 1863; discharged for disability January 28, 1864.
Frazier, Thomas J.	do	July 31, 1862	Discharged for disability March 25, 1863.
Freeman, Jesse W.	do	Jan. 15, 1863	Wounded in action in Carroll county, Arkansas; discharged for disability November 25, 1864.
Hedgepath, Emanuel	do	July 31, 1862	Discharged for disability April 25, 1864.
Harbert, Francis M	do	June 1, 1862	Discharged for disability April 8, 1863.
McCord, Thos. J	do	Aug. 4, 1862	Discharged for disability July 15, 1864.
McGuire, Bill J.	do	Nov. 18, 1862	Discharged for disability August 23, 1863.
Owen, Samuel	do	July 31, 1862	Discharged for disability March 24, 1863.
Standlee, Joseph	Farrier	Aug. 7, 1862	Discharged for disability March 24, 1863.
Shelton, Robert R.	Private	Aug. 14, 1863	Discharged for disability April 24, 1863.
Henry, Alexander	do	Mar. 21, 1864	Discharged for disability July 2, 1864.
Purdy, George A.	1st sergeant	July 7, 1864	Discharged to accept promotion January 1, 1865.

Deserted.

Name	Rank	Date	Remarks
Carpenter, Wm.	Farrier	July 31, 1862	Deserted December 5, 1862.
Denny, James J.	Private	Nov. 24, 1863	Deserted July 18, 1864.
Denny, Malachi A.	do	Nov. 24, 1863	Deserted July 18, 1864.
Hedgepath, James M	do	Sept. 30, 1862	Deserted December 5, 1862.
Martin, Daniel H.	do	July 28, 1862	Deserted November 1, 1863.
Nance, Elisha B	do	June 4, 1862	Deserted June 15, 1863.
Pitts, Alfred	do	July 28, 1862	Deserted March 31, 1864.
Sims, Matthew	do		Deserted August 6, 1862.
Fanning, James	do	Aug. 7, 1863	Deserted July 25, 1864.

COMPANY H.

Name	Rank	Date of rank.	Remarks
John I. Worthington	Captain	—, 1861	Appointed from civil life to fill original vacancy, but was previously sergeant 6th Kansas cavalry; promoted to major February 28, 1865.
Lawson L. Jernegan	do	Aug. 3, 1862	Appointed from sergeant company C to 2d lieutenant April 1, 1863; promoted to 1st lieutenant January 6, 1864; mustered out with regiment.
John W. Morris	1st lieutenant	July 23, 1862	Appointed from civil life to fill original vacancy; resigned February 2, 1863.
Hugo C. C. Boteführ	do	—, 1861	Appointed 2d lieutenant from 1st Missouri cavalry August 7, 1862; promoted to captain company B April 1, 1863.
James G. Robertson	do	—, 1862	Appointed sergeant August 7, 1862; killed in action October 26, 1863.
Warren W. Munday	do	Aug. 16, 1862	Appointed from sergeant major to 2d lieutenant July 14, 1863; mustered out with regiment.
Melancthon Hilbert	2d lieutenant	July 19, 1863	Appointed from hospital steward; mustered out with regiment.
Benjamin P. Hensley	1st sergeant	July 28, 1862	Appointed commissary sergeant August 7, 1862; mustered out with regiment.
John G. Black	Quartermaster sergeant	July 28, 1862	Appointed sergeant August 7, 1862; mustered out with regiment.
Isaac J. Mills	Commissary sergeant	July 30, 1862	Appointed corporal August 7, 1862; sergeant November 1, 1862; mustered out with regiment.

First regiment Arkansas cavalry volunteers. Mustered into service August 7, 1862, (three years;) mustered out August 23, 1865.

COMPANY H—Continued.

Names.	Rank.	Enlistment.	Date of rank.	Remarks.
John H. Ruff	Sergeant	July 30, 1862	Aug. 7, 1862	Mustered out with regiment.
John W. McDaniel	do	Aug. 2, 1862	April 1, 1863	Appointed corporal August 7, 1862; mustered out with regiment.
Harmon W. Hodges	do	July 2, 1862	June 1, 1863	Appointed corporal August 7, 1862; mustered out with regiment.
Jonathan F. Smith	do	July 31, 1862	Mar. 1, 1865	Appointed corporal September 1, 1863; mustered out with regiment.
John A. Strickland	do	July 30, 1862	July 1, 1865	Appointed corporal November 1, 1862; mustered out with regiment.
William G. Goodnight	Corporal	Aug. 8, 1862	Aug. 11, 1862	Mustered out with regiment.
William V. Robertson	do	July 21, 1862	Nov. 1, 1862	Do.
James F. H. Christy	do	Sept. 10, 1862	Feb. 1, 1863	Do.
James F. Winchester	do	July 31, 1862	April 1, 1863	Do.
John W. Robertson	do	July 31, 1862	Feb. 1, 1863	Do.
Jeptha Kite	do	Aug. 5, 1862	June 1, 1863	Do.
James H. Reed	do	Aug. 1, 1862	Mar. 1, 1865	Do.
Wayne McBride	do	July 12, 1862	July 1, 1865	Do.
Archibald Autry	Farrier	Jan. 2, 1863	Jan. 2, 1863	Do.
Washington Leadford	do	May 7, 1864	Aug. 7, 1864	Do.
John P. Stills	Wagoner	Aug. 10, 1862	Aug. 11, 1864	Do.
John King	Saddler	Aug. 11, 1862	Mar. 1, 1865	Do.
Marion F. Evans	Trumpeter	Feb. 1, 1864	Mar. 1, 1865	Do.
Calvin H. Burns	do	July 28, 1862		Do.
			Muster.	
Ballard, Andrew	Private	Aug. 5, 1862	Aug. 8, 1862	Do.
Ballard, John M	do	Aug. 10, 1862	Aug. 13, 1862	Do.
Burger, Henry	do	Aug. 5, 1862	Aug. 10, 1862	Do.
Beek, James	do	Aug. 11, 1863	Aug. 14, 1863	Do.
Blair, Joseph W	do	Aug. 27, 1863	Sept. 4, 1863	Do.
Blares, Henry	do	April 15, 1864	April 29, 1864	Do.
Blares, William T	do	Mar. 21, 1865	Mar. 21, 1865	Do.
Brixey, James	do	Mar. 1, 1865	Mar. 1, 1865	Do.
Cooper, William B	do	July 21, 1862	Aug. 9, 1862	Do.
Denton, Commodore P	do	Aug. 21, 1862	Aug. 28, 1862	Do.
Denton, William J	do	Oct. 6, 1862	Aug. 14, 1863	Do.
Duncan, John C	do	Aug. 1, 1862	Aug. 7, 1862	Do.
Dunbar, William	do	July 7, 1862	Aug. 15, 1862	Do.
Edwards, William	do	Aug. 6, 1862	Aug. 8, 1862	Do.
Evans, William J	do	Mar. 11, 1865	Mar. 11, 1865	Do.
Farmer, Aquilla	do	May 14, 1862	May 20, 1862	Do.
Finn, James	do	July 1, 1862	Aug. 5, 1862	Do.
Gillihan, Thomas J	do	Aug. 1, 1862	Aug. 1, 1863	Do.
Green, Martin	do	Dec. 1, 1862	Aug. 14, 1863	Do.
Glenn, Josiah P	do	July 31, 1862	Aug. 2, 1862	Do.
Hall, John	do	Aug. 15, 1862	Aug. 26, 1862	Do.

REPORT OF THE ADJUTANT GENERAL OF ARKANSAS. 39

Name	Rank	Enlisted		Remarks
Holland, Samuel	do	July 30, 1862	July 30, 1862	Do.
Hendricks, Thomas J	do	Aug. 28, 1863	Aug. 28, 1863	Do.
Hutson, Dyer	do	Feb. 13, 1864	April 29, 1864	Wounded in action; mustered out with regiment.
Johnson, Jeptha	do	Aug. 22, 1862	Aug. 24, 1862	
Johnson, Isaac N. E	do	Aug. 22, 1862	Aug. 24, 1862	Mustered out with regiment.
James, Francis A	do	Aug. 13, 1862	Aug. 15, 1862	Do.
James, Dempsey	do	Aug. 13, 1862	Sept. 14, 1862	Do.
Jettor, Thomas	do	Sept. 10, 1862	Oct. 11, 1862	Do.
Jenkins, John T	do	Oct. 10, 1862	Sept. 14, 1863	Do.
Jay, Robert	do	Aug. 28, 1863	April 29, 1864	Do.
Jackson, William	do	Feb. 12, 1864	Aug. 1, 1862	Do.
King, Bryant	do	July 21, 1862	Aug. 1, 1862	Do.
King, Allen	do	July 21, 1862	Aug. 28, 1862	Do.
Kilburn, John D	do	Aug. 21, 1862	April 29, 1864	Do.
Kilgore, Reuben S	do	Jan. 27, 1864	April 28, 1864	Do.
Kirk, James	do	Feb. 14, 1864	Sept. 4, 1863	Do.
Knight, Jackson	do	Aug. 27, 1863	Aug. 14, 1863	Do.
Mode, Albert	do	Mar. 2, 1863	July 12, 1862	Do.
Mackey, Henderson P	do	July 12, 1862	April 29, 1864	Do.
Moton, Theodore	do	Dec. 11, 1863	Aug. 14, 1863	Do.
Owen, Willis	do	Dec. 27, 1862	Sept. 4, 1863	Do.
O'Neal, Richard	do	Jan. 2, 1863	Aug. 7, 1862	Do.
Robertson, James	do	Aug. 4, 1862	Aug. 7, 1862	Do.
Rush, Benjamin F	do	July 4, 1862	Aug. 14, 1863	Do.
Roth, Stephen	do	Dec. 1, 1862	July 30, 1862	Do.
Roberts, Wesley	do	Aug. 27, 1863	July 18, 1862	Do.
Stephenson, Mattison	do	July 28, 1862	July 18, 1862	Do.
Shaw, Ambrose	do	July 16, 1862	Aug. 14, 1863	Do.
Shaw, Lewellen	do	July 11, 1862	Aug. 14, 1863	Do.
Sinclair, James	do	Oct. 11, 1862	Sept. 4, 1863	Do.
Skelton, Isaac S	do	Feb. 1, 1863	Sept. 4, 1863	Do.
Smith, John H	do	Aug. 27, 1863	Sept. 2, 1863	Do.
Smith, Irvin	do	Aug. 14, 1863	April 29, 1864	Do.
Smith, Joseph	do	Feb. 17, 1863	June 29, 1864	Do.
Simmons, Wesley	do	Jan. 6, 1864	Sept. 4, 1863	Do.
Strickland, James W	do	June 1, 1864	Sept. 4, 1863	Do.
Shelly, Thomas	do	Aug. 27, 1863	Aug. 14, 1863	Do.
Smith, Claiborne M	do	Aug. 27, 1863	Sept. 4, 1863	Do.
True, Davier	do	Oct. 30, 1862	Aug. 14, 1863	Do.
True, Irvin	do	Oct. 30, 1862	Sept. 4, 1863	Do.
Thacher, William J	do	Aug. 27, 1863	Aug. 2, 1862	Do.
Winchester, William F	do	July 31, 1862	April 25, 1864	Do.
Wishon, Isaac	do	Jan. 2, 1864	April 29, 1864	Do.
Wishon, Thomas	do	Feb. 15, 1864		Do.

Killed.

Name	Rank	Enlisted		Remarks
Arbaugh, Jacob M	Private	Aug. 2, 1862	Aug. 5, 1862	Killed on a scout in Franklin county, Arkansas, October 2, 1863.
Amos, Lucien	do	June 9, 1862	July 12, 1862	Killed on picket at Fayetteville, Arkansas, April 18, 1863.
Dunfield, Ahaz	do	Aug. 15, 1862	Aug. 28, 1862	Killed on mail escort near Cassville, Missouri, September 17, 1862.
Davis, George W	do	Aug. 5, 1862	Aug. 9, 1862	Killed in action at Fayetteville, Arkansas, April 18, 1863.
Forehand, John	do	July 25, 1862	July 31, 1862	Killed in action in Searcy county, Arkansas, December 25, 1863.
Mears, William	do	July 20, 1862	Aug. 1, 1862	Killed in action in Searcy county, Arkansas, February 7, 1864.

First regiment Arkansas cavalry volunteers. Mustered into service August 7, 1862, (three years;) mustered out August 23, 1865.

COMPANY H—Continued.

Names.	Rank.	Enlistment.	Muster.	Remarks.
Died.				
Reed, G. K. L.	Corporal	Aug. 4, 1862	Aug. 7, 1862	Died at Springfield, Missouri, May 5, 1863.
Slay, Benjamin F.	...do...	July 23, 1862	Aug. 2, 1862	Died at Fayetteville, Arkansas, March 1, 1863.
Burns, John F.	Trumpeter	July 21, 1862	Aug. 25, 1862	Died at Cassville, Missouri, December 10, 1862.
Brown, Robert	Private			Died at Springfield, Missouri, December 3, 1862.
Baker, Jesse C.	...do...	July 14, 1862	July 21, 1862	Died at Elkhorn, Arkansas, October 24, 1862.
Brooks, George W.	...do...			Died at Fayetteville, Arkansas, March 19, 1863.
Burks, James H.	...do...	Aug. 2, 1862	Aug. 8, 1862	Died at Cassville, Arkansas, October 16, 1863.
Conness, Jacob	...do...	Aug. 27, 1863	Sept. 4, 1863	Died at Fayetteville, Arkansas, December 10, 1863.
Hughes, Henry C.	...do...			Died at Springfield, Missouri, September 15, 1862.
Hughes, Enoch	...do...	Aug. 2, 1862	Aug. 5, 1862	Died at Elkhorn, Arkansas, December 27, 1862.
Hindricks, Larkin	...do...	Aug. 28, 1862	Sept. 4, 1862	Died of wounds received in action, in Searcy county, Arkansas, January 10, 1864.
Jennings, James A.	...do...	Aug. 27, 1862	Aug. 29, 1862	Died at Fayetteville, Arkansas, February 16, 1863.
Jetton, James	...do...	Aug. 4, 1862	Aug. 5, 1862	Died at Fayetteville, Arkansas, March 3, 1863.
Leonard, William H.	...do...	Aug. 5, 1862	Aug. 8, 1862	Died at Fayetteville, Arkansas, February 6, 1863.
Leonard, Benjamin F.	...do...	Aug. 5, 1862	Aug. 8, 1862	Died at Fayetteville, Arkansas, February 6, 1863.
Leonard, Joseph W.	...do...	Aug. 5, 1862	Aug. 8, 1862	Died at Fayetteville, Arkansas, February 5, 1863.
Long, Samuel	...do...	July 31, 1862	Aug. 2, 1862	Died in Lawrence county, Missouri, December 2, 1862.
McDaniel, Isaac	...do...	July 28, 1862	Aug. 2, 1862	Died at Elkhorn, Arkansas, November 29, 1862.
Mullens, Elijah	...do...	Aug. 5, 1862	Aug. 15, 1862	Died at Fayetteville, Arkansas, November 4, 1863.
Martin, Ransom	...do...	July 31, 1862	Aug. 2, 1862	Died in Lawrence county, Missouri, November 30, 1862.
Reynolds, David	...do...	July 22, 1862	July 22, 1862	Died at Springfield, Missouri, October 21, 1862.
Stockton, Lewis W.	...do...	July 23, 1862	Aug. 2, 1862	Died while a prisoner in the hands of the enemy, January 7, 1863.
Strickland, Eli F.	...co...	July 30, 1862	Aug. 2, 1862	Died at Fayetteville, Arkansas, January 28, 1863.
Slay, Levi G.	...do...	July 21, 1862	Aug. 2, 1862	Died at Fayetteville, Arkansas, February 2, 1863.
Slay, Thomas	...do...	Aug. 4, 1862	Aug. 2, 1862	Died at Fayetteville, Arkansas, February 3, 1863.
Slay, Cornelius D.	...do...	July 21, 1862	Aug. 2, 1862	Died at Fayetteville, Arkansas, from accidental wound, April 27, 1863.
Slay, William H.	...do...	July 21, 1862	Aug. 2, 1862	Died at Fayetteville, Arkansas, February 23, 1863.
Stanley, Joseph	...do...	Dec. 10, 1863	Feb. 28, 1864	Died at Fayetteville, Arkansas, of wounds received in action, April 19, 1861.
Stockton, Elkanah	...do...	July 22, 1862	July 22, 1862	Died at Fayetteville, Arkansas, September 30, 1864.
Willison, William	...do...	July 23, 1863	Sept. 2, 1863	Died at Cassville, Missouri, August 29, 1863.
Deserted.				
Brown, Amos	Private	Feb. 11, 1863	Never.	Deserted at Fayetteville, Arkansas, March 30, 1863.
Bar, Franklin B.	...do...	Aug. 28, 1863	Sept. 4, 1863	Deserted on a scout in Benton county, Arkansas, September 19, 1863.
Carter, Thomas	...do...	Dec. 1, 1863	Dec. 1, 1863	Deserted at Springfield, Missouri, June 10, 1861.
Green, William	...do...	Aug. 28, 1863	Sept. 4, 1863	Deserted from picket at Springfield, Missouri, September 4, 1863.
Harris, George D.	...do...	Feb. 6, 1865	Feb. 28, 1865	Deserted near Fayetteville, Arkansas, April 4, 1865.
Lumpkins, Henry	...do...	Aug. 28, 1863	Sept. 4, 1863	Deserted at Cassville, Missouri, September 10, 1863.
Owen, Owen J.	...do...	Jan. 5, 1863	Aug. 14, 1863	Deserted at Cassville, Missouri, August 10, 1863.
Pollock, James R.	...do...	Aug. 6, 1864	Aug. 6, 1864	Deserted at Fayetteville, Arkansas, October 30, 1864.

REPORT OF THE ADJUTANT GENERAL OF ARKANSAS. 41

Name	Rank	Date	Date	Remarks
Rose, William	do	Aug. 28, 1863	Sept. 4, 1863	Deserted at Cassville, Missouri, September 10, 1863.
Trout, George	do	July 31, 1862	Aug. 2, 1862	Deserted October 1, 1862.
Ward, Elijah N	do	April 10, 1864	April 30, 1864	Deserted at Fayetteville, Arkansas, August 7, 1864.

Discharged.

Name	Rank	Date	Date	Remarks
Jameson, Lorenzo D	1st sergeant	Aug. 5, 1862	Aug. 7, 1862	Discharged by order.
Farrell, Thomas	Sergeant	July 7, 1862	Aug. 2, 1862	Discharged for disability, August 11, 1863.
Winchester, Lewis K	do	Aug. 2, 1862	Aug. 5, 1862	Discharged for disability, August 27, 1865.
Burns, Ransom S	Private	Aug. 5, 1862	Aug. 8, 1862	Discharged for disability, December 10, 1863.
Garrett, Laban N	do	April 1, 1863	Never	Discharged to accept promotion in 2d Arkansas cavalry.
Greathouse, John W	do	Aug. 28, 1862	Aug. 28, 1862	Discharged for disability, May 1, 1864.
James, Calvin	do	Aug. 13, 1862	Aug. 15, 1862	Discharged for disability, February —, 1863.
Napier, Isaac C	do	Oct. 9, 1862	Oct. 11, 1862	Discharged to accept promotion in 3d Arkansas cavalry, February 26, 1864.
O'Brien, John	do	July 7, 1862	Aug. 6, 1862	Discharged for disability, at Fort Smith, Arkansas, June 22, 1865.
Pound, William	do	Aug. 28, 1862	Aug. 28, 1862	Discharged for disability, March —, 1864.
Smith, Doctor R	do	Aug. 14, 1862	Aug. 16, 1862	Discharged for disability, March —, 1863.
Smith, John N	do	Aug. 14, 1862	Aug. 16, 1862	Discharged for disability, March —, 1863.
Stockton, Gibson W	do	July 22, 1862	July 22, 1862	Discharged for disability, at Springfield, Missouri, June 22, 1865.
Walker, John M	do	Aug. 7, 1862	Aug. 7, 1862	Discharged for disability, June —, 1863.
York, William J	do	Nov. 30, 1862	Aug. 31, 1863	Discharged for disability, September 12, 1863.

COMPANY I.

Name	Rank		Date of rank.	Remarks
De Witt C. Hopkins	Captain		Sept. 10, 1862	Appointed from 1st sergeant company A to fill original vacancy; mustered out with regiment.
Jacob J. Reel	1st lieutenant		Aug. 21, 1862	Appointed from corporal 4th Iowa infantry to fill original vacancy. Died November 28, 1862.
Henry W. Gildemeister	do	—, 1861	Nov. 28, 1862	Appointed from corporal 1st Missouri cavalry to 2d lieutenant company I August 4, 1862; resigned January 3, 1864.
John Vaughan	do	July 2, 1862	July 14, 1864	Appointed from 1st sergeant company C; 2d lieutenant company I November 28, 1862; mustered out with regiment.
Willis E. Maynard	2d lieutenant	Jan. 22, 1863	July 15, 1864	Appointed from hospital steward; mustered out with regiment.
James Hardin	1st sergeant	Aug. 18, 1862	Sept. 10, 1862	Mustered out with regiment.
Washington F. Wilcox	Quartermaster sergeant	Sept. 20, 1863	July 15, 1864	Do.
John F. McGuire	Commissary sergeant	Feb. 2, 1863	June 1, 1864	Promoted to corporal May 1, 1863; mustered out with regiment.
Fountain A. Parish	Sergeant	Sept. 9, 1862	May 1, 1863	Promoted to corporal September 10, 1862; mustered out with regiment.
John Seizemore	do	Aug. 13, 1862	Sept. 10, 1862	Mustered out with regiment.
Bennett B. Bailey	do	Aug. 28, 1862	Sept. 10, 1862	Do.
Henry Glasscock	do	Sept. 9, 1862	Jan. 1, 1865	Promoted to corporal October 1, 1862; mustered out with regiment.
William J. Farley	Corporal	Dec. 25, 1862	Jan. 1, 1863	Mustered out with regiment.
Aaron Woods	do	Aug. 10, 1862	Feb. 1, 1863	Do.
Jasper B. Davis	do	Feb. 10, 1863	May 1, 1863	Do.
Daniel Blythe	do	Nov. 20, 1862	July 12, 1864	Do.
John Harrison	do	Jan. 7, 1863	Jan. 1, 1865	Do.
Samuel Prater	do	Sept. 9, 1862	Feb. 1, 1865	Do.
Edward J. Forbes	do			Do.

First regiment Arkansas cavalry volunteers. Mustered into service August 7, 1862: (three years;) mustered out August 23, 1865.

COMPANY I—Continued.

Names.	Rank.	Enlistment.	Date of rank.	Remarks.
Jonathan Jamison	Corporal	Sept. 20, 1863	Feb. 1, 1865	Mustered out with regiment.
John Truelove	Farrier	Sept. 9, 1863	Sept. 10, 1862	Do.
Guilford Thomas	do	Dec. 9, 1862	Jan. 14, 1863	Do.
John R. Ward	Trumpeter	May 1, 1864	May 1, 1864	Do.
Darius Thomas	do	Oct. 1, 1862	Feb. 1, 1865	Do.
			Muster.	
Adair, James M.	Private	Aug. 18, 1862	Sept. 10, 1862	Do.
Austin, John K.	do	Dec. 9, 1862	Aug. 31, 1862	Do.
Aldridge, Milton	do	Sept. 20, 1863	Oct. 5, 1863	Do.
Aldridge, Alfred	do	Sept. 20, 1863	Oct. 5, 1863	Do.
Ash, William D.	do	Sept. 20, 1863	Oct. 5, 1863	Do.
Blares, John	do	Jan. 5, 1863	Aug. 31, 1863	Do.
Blythe, James	do	Feb. 10, 1863	Feb. 10, 1863	Do.
Bennett, John	do	Sept. 20, 1863	Oct. 5, 1863	Do.
Burt, Monta Z.	do	Sept. 20, 1863	Oct. 5, 1863	Do.
Ball, Enoch	do	Oct. 5, 1863	Oct. 16, 1863	Do.
Brooks, Anderson	do	Oct. 5, 1863	Oct. 20, 1863	Do.
Cranse, George	do	Feb. 6, 1863	Aug. 31, 1863	Do.
Cook, George	do	Aug. 15, 1863	Aug. 31, 1863	Do.
Carmack, Absalom	do	Sept. 1, 1863	Sept. 1, 1863	Do.
Calico, Josiah	do	Nov. 25, 1862	Feb. 20, 1864	Do.
Calico, James	do	Feb. 5, 1863	Feb. 20, 1864	Do.
Deurnell, Chas.	do	Aug. 8, 1862	Aug. 20, 1862	Do.
Evans, James M.	do	Dec. 1, 1863	Feb. 27, 1864	Do.
Fulbright, Thomas	do	Aug. 14, 1863	Aug. 31, 1863	Do.
Gardner, Lewis J.	do	Aug. 3, 1862	Aug. 20, 1862	Do.
Gardner, Eli	do	Aug. 13, 1862	Aug. 20, 1862	Do.
Gilbert, Isaac T.	do	Aug. 20, 1862	Aug. 20, 1862	Do.
Gibson, John	do	Jan. 3, 1863	Aug. 31, 1863	Do.
Gibson, Moses	do	Feb. 7, 1863	Aug. 31, 1863	Do.
Gibson, James	do	Feb. 7, 1863	Aug. 31, 1863	Do.
Howard, Lemuel	do	Feb. 10, 1863	Aug. 13, 1863	Do.
Henson, Thos. A.	do	Sept. 20, 1863	Oct. 5, 1863	Do.
Harp, Wm. A.	do	Nov. 13, 1863	Feb. 27, 1864	Do.
Hall, Robert	do	Aug. 10, 1862	Aug. 20, 1862	Do.
Hall, Elijah	do	Aug. 10, 1862	Aug. 20, 1862	Do.
Jones, Andrew J.	do	Feb. 3, 1864	Feb. 27, 1864	Do.
Long, John P.	do	Sept. 5, 1862	Sept. 8, 1862	Do.
McNatt, Gilbert E.	do	Nov. 11, 1862	Nov. 12, 1862	Do.
Morris, Hamilton	do	Aug. 7, 1863	Aug. 31, 1863	Do.
Morris, John	do	Oct. 24, 1863	Oct. 31, 1863	Do.

REPORT OF THE ADJUTANT GENERAL OF ARKANSAS. 43

Name	Rank	Date	Date	Remarks
Murphy, John A	do	Jan. 6, 1863	Aug. 31, 1863	Do.
Meeks, Thos. J	do	June 6, 1863	Aug. 31, 1863	Do.
Meeks, Squire	do	June 6, 1863	Aug. 31, 1863	Do.
Manns, Jesse R	do	Dec. 7, 1862	Jan. 27, 1864	Do.
Montgomery, Lee S	do	Oct. 16, 1863	Oct. 31, 1863	Do.
Muckler, Ebenezer	do	Dec. 20, 1872	Aug. 31, 1863	Do.
Muckles, Benjamin	do	Jan. 7, 1863	Aug. 31, 1863	Do.
Pennington, Daniel	do	Sept. 1, 1862	Sept. 1, 1862	Do.
Pennington, Wesley	do	Sept. 1, 1862	Sept. 1, 1863	Do.
Patrick, Meredith	do	Jan. 7, 1863	Aug. 31, 1863	Do.
Patrick, George W	do	Jan. 12, 1863	Oct. 31, 1863	Do.
Prater, Wiley	do	Apr. 13, 1863	Aug. 13, 1863	Do.
Parker, Nelson S	do	Sept. 1, 1863	Sept. 1, 1863	Do.
Pointer, George W	do	Oct. 16, 1863	Feb. 27, 1864	Do.
Russell, John J	do	Jan. 6, 1863	Aug. 10, 1863	Do.
Rush, Jackson R	do	Jan. 8, 1863	Sept. 1, 1863	Do.
Ramsey, Samuel	do	Oct. 16, 1863	Oct. 31, 1863	Do.
Reed, James	do	Dec. 25, 1862	Aug. 31, 1863	Do.
Stufflebeam, Jacob	do	Jan. 7, 1863	Aug. 31, 1863	Do.
Stufflebeam, John	do	Jan. 15, 1864	Feb. 27, 1864	Do.
Stephens, John	do	Aug. 18, 1862	Sept. 4, 1862	Do.
Smith, David A	do	Feb. 6, 1863	Aug. 31, 1863	Do.
Shults, Wiley	do	Nov. 1, 1862	Nov. 12, 1862	Do.
Sizemore, George W	do	Jan. 10, 1863	Aug. 31, 1864	Do.
Sparkman, Madison	do	Jan. 30, 1863	Aug. 20, 1863	Do.
Turner, Miles H	do	Nov. 21, 1862	Aug. 31, 1863	Do.
Templeton, Thomas	do	Jan. 26, 1863	Sept. 1, 1863	Do.
Thomas, Thomas W	do	Oct. 18, 1863	Oct. 31, 1863	Do.
Tucker, Washington	do	Oct. 21, 1862	Oct. 31, 1863	Do.
Tucker, Thomas	do	Nov. 21, 1862	Feb. 7, 1864	Do.
Woods, John D	do	Dec. 25, 1862	Sept. 20, 1863	Do.
Woods, George	do	Feb. 10, 1863	Aug. 31, 1863	Do.
Wetherby, Worthington	do	April 4, 1863	Oct. 31, 1863	Do.
Wilcox, Jeremiah W	do	Sept. 20, 1863	Oct. 5, 1863	Do.
Ward, William F	do	Sept. 20, 1863	Oct. 5, 1863	Do.
West, James D	do	Oct. 24, 1863	Oct. 31, 1863	Do.
Young, Isaac L. F	do	Mar. 9, 1863	Oct. 31, 1863	Do.

Killed.

Name	Rank	Date	Date	Remarks
Bell, James D	Private	Jan. 8, 1863	Jan. 9, 1863	Killed in battle of Fayetteville, Ark., April 18, 1863.
Clark, Jackson C	Sergeant	Aug. 13, 1862	Aug. 20, 1862	Killed accidentally at Mount Vernon, Mo., October 27, 1862.
Cornelius, Henry	Private	Jan. 9, 1863	Sept. 1, 1863	Killed by guerillas near Fort Smith, Ark., December 24, 1863.
Kelly, Robert	Sergeant	Sept. 9, 1862	Sept. 10, 1862	Killed by guerillas near Cross Hollows, Ark., March 30, 1863.
McDonough, Francis M	Corporal	Feb. 4, 1863	Aug. 31, 1863	Killed by guerillas near Fayetteville, Ark., January 24, 1865.
Manon, William C	Sergeant	Sept. 8, 1862	Sept. 10, 1862	Killed by guerillas in Franklin county, Ark., April 4, 1864.
Smith, Richard	Corporal	Sept. 20, 1862	Oct. 5, 1863	Killed by guerillas near Fayetteville, Ark., January 24, 1865.
Smith, Calvin	Private	Feb. 3, 1862	Jan. 7, 1863	Killed by guerillas near Fayetteville, Ark., January 24, 1865.
Stewart, Marion	do	Sept. 20, 1863	Jan. 7, 1863	Killed at Crane Creek, Mo., accidentally, May 17, 1863.
Stewart, Joshua	do	Jan. 7, 1863	Jan. 7, 1863	Killed by guerillas at Mudtown, Ark., April 18, 1863.
Strohan, John	do	Nov. 1, 1862	Nov. 12, 1862	Killed in battle of Prairie Grove December 7, 1862.

First regiment Arkansas cavalry volunteers. Mustered into service August 7, 1862, (three years,) mustered out August 23, 1865.

COMPANY I—Continued.

Names.	Rank.	Enlistment.	Muster.	Remarks.
Died.				
Adair, Joseph	Private	Aug. 7, 1862	Aug. 8, 1862	Died at Cassville, Mo., November 29, 1862.
Austin, Thomas	do	Jan. 1, 1863	Jan. 1, 1863	Died at Cassville, Mo., January 19, 1863.
Buis, Irvin	Corporal	Sept. 9, 1862	Sept. 10, 1862	Died at Springfield, Mo., January 12, 1863.
Canter, George W	do	Sept. 9, 1862	Sept. 10, 1862	Died at Fayetteville, Ark., July 12, 1864.
Dunning, Cordy C	Private	Aug. 16, 1862	Aug. 20, 1862	Died at Fayetteville, Ark., January 21, 1863.
Foster, James W	Corporal	Aug. 13, 1862	Aug. 20, 1862	Died en route from Springfield to Rolla, Mo., November 13, 1862.
Gentry, William W	Private	Sept. 9, 1862	Sept. 10, 1862	Died at Springfield, Mo., November 23, 1862.
Goddard, Albert B	do	Dec. 23, 1862	Dec. 25, 1862	Died at Cassville, Mo., May 11, 1863.
Haley, Joel	do	Jan. 30, 1863	Aug. 31, 1863	Died at Springfield, Mo., October 1, 1863.
Roberts, Richard	do	Oct. 10, 1862	Oct. 10, 1862	Died at Springfield, Mo., January 14, 1863.
Stufflebeam, William A	do	Jan. 7, 1863	Feb. 7, 1863	Died at Fayetteville, Ark., February 22, 1863.
Thomas, Lorenzo	do	Aug. 13, 1862	Aug. 19, 1862	Died en route from Springfield, Mo., to Rolla, Mo., December 3, 1862.
Thomas, William	do	Dec. 9, 1862	Dec. 25, 1862	Died at Fayetteville, Ark., February 1, 1863.
Discharged.				
Bell, Joseph	Private	Sept. 9, 1862	Sept. 10, 1862	Discharged for disability at Fayetteville, Ark., May 7, 1864.
Dixon, Henry W	Sergeant	Sept. 9, 1862	Sept. 10, 1862	Discharged to accept promotion in 3d Arkansas infantry.
Hogan, Anthony	Private	Sept. 9, 1862	Sept. 10, 1862	Discharged for disability at Fayetteville, Ark., February 27, 1863.
Anderson, Robert	Corporal	Sept. 9, 1862	Sept. 18, 1862	Discharged for disability at Fayetteville, Ark., February 28, 1863.
Hall, Wm	Private	Sept. 9, 1862	Sept. 10, 1862	Discharged for disability at Fayetteville, Ark., February 1, 1863.
Johnson, James M	do	Aug. 13, 1862	Aug. 18, 1862	Discharged for disability at Fayetteville, Ark., February 28, 1863.
Murrell, Mitchell	do	Aug. 15, 1862	Aug. 18, 1862	Discharged, by order, at Fort Smith, Ark., April 23, 1864.
McNatt, Malcolm G	do	Nov. 1, 1862	Nov. 12, 1862	Discharged for disability at Fayetteville, Ark., April 20, 1864.
Ward, Francis M	Sergeant	Jan. 30, 1863	Aug. 13, 1863	Discharged to accept promotion as captain of company G, July 14, 1864.
Deserted.				
Adair, Stephen C	Private	Aug. 28, 1862	Sept. 1, 1862	Deserted at Springfield, Mo., January 1, 1863.
Brooks, John F	do	Nov. 3, 1862	Dec. 21, 1862	Deserted at Fayetteville, Ark., January 3, 1863.
Cooper, Jeremiah	do	Dec. 28, 1862	Dec. 28, 1862	Deserted at Fayetteville, Ark., April 1, 1863.
Farley, Samuel A	do	July 29, 1863	Aug. 1, 1863	Deserted at Ironton, Mo., September 1, 1864.
Gregg, Allen C	do	Jan. 9, 1863	Feb. 3, 1863	Deserted at Fayetteville, Ark., April 18, 1863.
High, Oliver	do	Aug. 17, 1862	Aug. 25, 1862	Deserted at Springfield, Mo., January 5, 1863.
Long, George W	do	Aug. 21, 1862	Aug. 25, 1862	Deserted at Springfield, Mo., December 7, 1862.
Long, William B	do	Aug. 20, 1862	Aug. 25, 1862	Deserted at Fayetteville, Ark., October 12, 1863.
Long, Marcellus H	do	Sept. 1, 1862	Sept. 1, 1862	Deserted at Fayetteville, Ark., November 1, 1863.
Lawrence, James P	do	Aug. 13, 1862	Sept. 10, 1862	Deserted at Fayetteville, Mo., February 1, 1863.
Miser, Michael	do	Sept. 9, 1862	Sept. 10, 1862	Deserted at Cassville, Mo., December 1, 1862.
Oxford, Jacob J	do	Feb. 3, 1863	Feb. 3, 1863	Deserted at Fayetteville, Ark., April 8, 1863.
Perkins, Richard	do	Feb. 21, 1863	Aug. 30, 1863	Deserted at Springfield, Mo., August 5, 1863.
Manus, George W	Sergeant	Jan. 7, 1863	Aug. 31, 1863	Deserted at Fayetteville, Ark., June 5, 1865.

Name	Rank	Muster	Date of rank	Remarks
Theodoric B. Youngblood	Captain	July 19, 1862	Aug. 7, 1862	Resigned March 10, 1863, for disability.
Albert Pearson	do	—, 1861	Mar. 25, 1863	Appointed from chief trumpeter 2d Wisconsin cavalry 2d lieutenant August 7, 1862; resigned July 17, 1865.
Doctor F. Yr'ungblood	1st lieutenant	July 19, 1862	July 25, 1862	Mustered out with regiment.
Henry M. Kidder	2d lieutenant	Apr. 1, 1863	Apr. 1, 1863	Appointed from civil life; promoted to regimental adjutant July 1, 1863.
William S. Woodbridge	do	Sept. 13, 1862	July 1, 1863	Appointed from commissary sergeant company M; mustered out with regiment.
Permenitus T. Rose	1st sergeant	Aug. 1, 1862	Jan. 1, 1864	Appointed sergeant August 7, 1862; mustered out with regiment.
John R. Byrns	Quartermaster sergeant	Aug. 10, 1862	Mar. 1, 1864	Appointed farrier November 1, 1862; mustered out with regiment.
James P. Youngblood	Commissary sergeant	July 19, 1862	Apr. 15, 1863	Mustered out with regiment.
Williams L. Majors	Sergeant	July 21, 1862	Aug. 7, 1862	Do.
Jefferson A. Johnson	do	Aug. 4, 1862	Aug. 7, 1862	Do.
George W. Buckner	do	July 19, 1862	Mar. 1, 1863	Appointed corporal August 7, 1862; mustered out with regiment.
Thomas P. Wilson	do	July 30, 1862	Sept. 30, 1863	Appointed corporal August 7, 1862; mustered out with regiment.
Jefferson L. Butler	do	July 25, 1862	July 1, 1864	Appointed corporal May 1, 1863; mustered out with regiment.
Reuben C. Taylor	Corporal	Aug. 5, 1862	Sept. 20, 1863	Mustered out with regiment.
Anderson Weese	do	Aug. 6, 1862	Sept. 1, 1863	Do.
Jackson Blevins	do	July 19, 1862	Sept. 1, 1864	Do.
John C. McAffee	do	July 21, 1862	Jan. 1, 1864	Do.
Jonathan A. Burleson	do	Aug. 11, 1862	July 1, 1864	Do.
Pleasant Snow	do	Dec. 1, 1862	Dec. 1, 1864	Do.
John M. Fraim	do	July 28, 1862	Dec. 1, 1864	Do.
Green S. Wilson	do	Oct. 18, 1862	Apr. 1, 1865	Do.
Benjamin F. Warick	Farrier	Nov. 29, 1862	Sept. 1, 1863	Do.
William Youngblood	do	July 19, 1862	June 1, 1864	Do.
Lycurgus M. Butler	Trumpeter	July 25, 1862	Sept. 1, 1863	Do.
James J. Reeves	do	Oct. 28, 1862	Apr. 1, 1865	Do.
		Muster.		
Albred, Henry	Private	Sept. 1, 1863	Oct. 1, 1862	Do.
Albred, Gamblin M	do	May 24, 1864	May 31, 1864	Do.
Askins, John W	do	Dec. 25, 1862	Feb. 28, 1864	Do.
Ayres, Alvin	do	July 9, 1863	July 14, 1862	Do.
Barbee, Lewis W	do	Nov. 6, 1863	Aug. 31, 1863	Do.
Battenfield, Alexander	do	Oct. 23, 1862	Aug. 31, 1863	Do.
Battenfield, Philip	do	Aug. 1, 1862	Aug. 31, 1863	Do.
Blevins, James M	do	Nov. 1, 1862	Aug. 31, 1863	Do.
Boyd, James A	do	Feb. 8, 1864	Feb. 28, 1864	Do.
Buckner, Jesse F	do	July 13, 1862	July 15, 1862	Do.
Cameron, James	do	July 28, 1862	July 28, 1862	Do.
Cooper, Joseph B	do	June 15, 1862	July 21, 1862	Do.
Dunlap, Oscar L	do	July 19, 1862	July 24, 1862	Do.
Dunlap, James H	do	July 14, 1863	Aug. 31, 1863	Do.
Ewen, Givin	do	July 26, 1862	Aug. 31, 1862	Do.
Flood, John	do	June 4, 1862	July 9, 1862	Do.
Flood, George W	do	June 21, 1862	July 26, 1862	Do.
Gaddy, Milton F	do	Aug. 1, 1863	Aug. 31, 1863	Do.

First regiment Arkansas cavalry volunteers. Mustered into service August 7, 1862, (three years;) mustered out August 23, 1865.

COMPANY K—Continued.

Names.	Rank.	Enlistment.	Muster.	Remarks.
Gregory, W. H. H.	Private	Dec. 22, 1863	Dec. 31, 1863	Mustered out with regiment.
Holt, Francis M.	do	July 26, 1862	July 31, 1862	Do.
Hutchinson, Shelby N.	do	Aug. 4, 1862	Aug. 7, 1862	Do.
Harp, John A.	do	July 1, 1862	July 3, 1862	Do.
Huey, Charles	do	Mar. 14, 1864	Apr. 30, 1864	Do.
Inman, Henry	do	June 14, 1863	Aug. 31, 1863	Do.
James, Caleb M.	do	June 29, 1864	June 30, 1864	Do.
Layton, William J.	do	July 19, 1862	July 24, 1862	Do.
Lowe, William	do	July 29, 1862	Aug. 2, 1862	Do.
Lee, John A.	do	Aug. 1, 1862	Aug. 4, 1862	Do.
Lee, William T.	do	Aug. 1, 1862	Aug. 4, 1862	Do.
Long, Thomas	do	Aug. 1, 1862	Aug. 4, 1862	Do.
Lorette, George M. D.	do	May 22, 1862	Aug. 31, 1863	Do.
Matthews, Marcus H.	do	Jan. 25, 1864	Jan. 28, 1864	Do.
Mead, Benjamin Y.	do	July 28, 1862	July 31, 1862	Do.
Pierce, Joseph	do	June 17, 1862	July 24, 1862	Do.
Patton, Laban	do	July 17, 1862	July 24, 1862	Do.
Roberts, John W.	do	July 19, 1862	July 25, 1862	Do.
Sharp, Calvin T.	do	Dec. 25, 1863	Feb. 28, 1864	Do.
Shelton, Richard	do	Feb. 8, 1864	Feb. 28, 1864	Do.
Smith, Jesse W.	do	Aug. 5, 1862	Aug. 9, 1862	Do.
Smith, William L.	do	Aug. 28, 1862	Sept. 4, 1862	Do.
Steele, George W.	do	May 1, 1863	Aug. 31, 1863	Do.
Storey, Charles	do	July 28, 1864	Aug. 20, 1864	Do.
Swift, James	do	Feb. 8, 1864	Feb. 8, 1864	Do.
Swift, Leander	do	Mar. 14, 1864	Apr. 30, 1864	Do.
Taylor, Wm. F.	do	Sept. 9, 1862	Sept. 14, 1862	Do.
Taylor, Joel T.	do	Aug. 5, 1862	Aug. 9, 1862	Do.
Taylor, George W.	do	Sept. 9, 1862	Sept. 14, 1862	Do.
Tennis, Wm.	do	Aug. 28, 1862	Sept. 2, 1862	Do.
Thomas, John A.	do	Nov. 5, 1862	Sept. 18, 1863	Do.
Towns, Richard T.	do	June 1, 1863	Aug. 31, 1863	Do.
Vaughan, John C.	do	July 12, 1862	July 13, 1862	Do.
Watkins, Wm.	do	May 11, 1862	Aug. 14, 1862	Do.
Watson, Perry	do	Nov. 19, 1864	June 24, 1865	Do.
Weese, John	do	Aug. 6, 1862	Aug. 11, 1862	Do.
Wilson, George W.	do	Jan. 9, 1863	Feb. 14, 1863	Do.
Youngblood, Geo. Q.	do	July 19, 1862	July 25, 1862	Do.
Youngblood, John	do	July 19, 1862	July 25, 1862	Do.
Youngblood, sr., Wm.	do	July 19, 1862	July 25, 1862	Do.
Youngblood, Jeremiah M. C.	do	July 19, 1862	July 24, 1862	Do.
Youngblood, Benj. F.	do	July 19, 1862	July 25, 1862	Do.

REPORT OF THE ADJUTANT GENERAL OF ARKANSAS. 47

Name	Rank			Remarks
Youngblood, Wm. J	do	July 24, 1863	Aug. 31, 1863	Do.
Killed.				
Hood, Samuel	Corporal	Nov. 5, 1862	Dec. 31, 1863	Killed in action in Washington county, Arkansas, March 17, 1865.
Hubbard, Thomas W	Private	Dec. 30, 1862	Never	Killed in action at Richland, Arkansas, December 25, 1863.
Moore, Curney C	do	Nov. 2, 1862	Never	Killed in action at Prairie Grove, Arkansas, December 7, 1862.
Phillips, Luther P	do	July 25, 1862	July 30, 1862	Killed in action at Yokum Creek, Arkansas, November 15, 1862.
Rose, Jesse M	Sergeant	Aug. 1, 1862	Aug. 4, 1862	Killed in action at Richland, Arkansas, December 25, 1863.
Simpson, Wm. T	Private	Oct. 28, 1862	Aug. 31, 1863	Killed in action in Carroll county, Arkansas, February 17, 1865.
Snow, Larkin	Corporal	Dec. 1, 1862	Aug. 31, 1863	Killed accidentally at Springfield, Missouri, September 2, 1863.
Taylor, James R	Private	Sept. 7, 1862	Sept. 14, 1862	Killed in action in Carroll county, Arkansas, February 17, 1865.
Watkins, Isaac	do	July 28, 1862	July 28, 1862	Killed in action at Richland, Arkansas, December 25, 1863.
Wikle, Jared B	Sergeant	July 17, 1862	July 21, 1862	Killed in action at White Oak, Arkansas, September 1, 1863.
Died.				
Evans, John W	Private	July 28, 1862	July 28, 1862	Died at Fort Scott, Kansas, November 30, 1862.
Hutchinson, Sergeant	Sergeant	Aug. 4, 1862	Aug. 6, 1862	Died at Fort Smith, Arkansas, June 11, 1864.
Justice, Washington E	Private	July 19, 1862	July 25, 1862	Died by drowning, in Arkansas river, February 9, 1863.
Lee, James J	do	Aug. 1, 1862	Aug. 4, 1862	Died at Springfield, Missouri, February 25, 1863.
Lee, Samuel B	do	Aug. 1, 1862	Aug. 1, 1862	Died at Fayetteville, Arkansas, January 29, 1863.
Moseley, Wm	do	July 28, 1862	Aug. 2, 1862	Died at Mount Vernon, Missouri, October 15, 1862.
Rhodes, Monroe	do	July 31, 1862	July 31, 1862	Died at Springfield, Missouri, November 25, 1862.
Terrell, Eli	do	July 20, 1862	July 25, 1862	Died at Springfield, Missouri, September 1, 1862.
Terrell, Jesse	do	July 22, 1862	Aug. 22, 1862	Died at Springfield, Missouri, September 1, 1862.
Weese, Josiah	do	Aug. 4, 1862	Aug. 6, 1862	Died at Springfield, Missouri, October 10, 1862.
Wilburn, Jos. B	Sergeant	Aug. 1, 1862	Aug. 4, 1862	Died at Springfield, Missouri, February 4, 1863.
Deserted.				
Cobb, Daniel	Private	Nov. 15, 1862	Never	Deserted at Fayetteville, Arkansas, March 20, 1863.
Flood, Wm. R	do	July 31, 1862	Aug. 1, 1862	Deserted at Cassville, Missouri, September 13, 1863.
Keeling, Elijah	do	Aug. 5, 1862	Aug. 9, 1862	Deserted at Huntsville, Arkansas, March 21, 1863.
Keeling, Leonard	do	Aug. 5, 1862	Aug. 5, 1862	Deserted at Forsyth, Missouri, March 21, 1863.
Langley, Marcus L	do	Aug. 1, 1863	Aug. 5, 1862	Deserted at Easley's Ferry, Arkansas, February 1, 1863.
Lee, Wm. R	do	July 1, 1862	Aug. 4, 1862	Deserted at Springfield, Missouri, October 10, 1863.
Pierce, William	do	Feb. 13, 1863	Feb. 13, 1863	Deserted at Cassville, Missouri, September 13, 1863.
Smith, Levi	do	Dec. 27, 1863	Feb. 28, 1864	Deserted at Fayetteville, Arkansas, February 29, 1864.
Smith, John	do	Aug. 25, 1862	Aug. 25, 1865	Deserted at Osage Springs, Arkansas, October 3, 1862.
Taylor, John	do	Oct. 25, 1864	Feb. 25, 1862	Deserted at Cassville, Missouri, March 29, 1865.
Taylor, John A	do	Sept. 9, 1863	Sept. 14, 1862	Deserted at Huntsville, Arkansas, March 4, 1863.
Teague, Hiram	do	Aug. 1, 1862	Aug. 25, 1862	Deserted at Flat Creek, Missouri, March 1, 1863.
Discharged.				
Fesperman, John F	Private	June 21, 1862	July 26, 1862	Discharged for promotion in 1st Arkansas infantry March 10, 1863.
Griffith, Green L	do	Nov. 29, 1862	Never	Discharged for disability at Fayetteville, Arkansas, March 25, 1863.
Horn, George H	do	July 28, 1862	July 28, 1862	Discharged for disability at Fayetteville, Arkansas, April 1, 1863.
Justice, Robert M	do	July 19, 1862	July 25, 1862	Discharged for disability at Fayetteville, Arkansas, March 26, 1863.
McHughes, Geo. W	do	June 26, 1862	July 21, 1862	Discharged for disability at St. Louis, Missouri, February 16, 1864.
Neal, John	do	July 20, 1862	July 25, 1862	Discharged for disability at Fayetteville, Arkansas, January 30, 1863.

First regiment Arkansas cavalry volunteers. Mustered into service August 7, 1862, (three years;) mustered out August 23, 1865.

COMPANY K—Continued.

Names.	Rank.	Enlistment.	Muster.	Remarks.
Rose, John	Private	Aug. 11, 1862	Aug. 16, 1862	Discharged for disability at Fayetteville, Arkansas, March 26, 1863.
Smith, James	do	Aug. 5, 1862	Aug. 9, 1862	Discharged for promotion September 21, 1864.
Wade, Pleasant C	do	Aug. 28, 1862	Sept. 12, 1862	Discharged for disability at Fayetteville, Arkansas, February 5, 1864.
Wikle, Samuel B	Sergeant	Sept. 17, 1862	Sept. 21, 1862	Discharged for disability at Crane creek, Missouri, March 26, 1863.
Youngblood, Francis M	Private	July 19, 1862	July 24, 1862	Discharged for disability at Fayetteville, Arkansas, February 5, 1864.

COMPANY L.

Names.	Rank.	Enlistment.	Date of rank.	Remarks.
John Bonine	Captain	——, 1861	Oct. 2, 1862	Appointed from private of company E, 4th Iowa infantry, to fill original vacancy; dismissed April 19, 1863.
Joseph S. Robb	do	——, 1861	May 18, 1863	Appointed from private of company E, 4th Iowa infantry, to fill original vacancy of 1st lieutenant; died of accidental gun-shot wound January 20, 1864.
Frank Strong	do	Nov. 18, 1861	Feb. 5, 1864	Appointed from hospital steward 2d Wisconsin cavalry to battalion adjutant August 7, 1862; mustered out September 20, 1862; re-enlisted in company L and appointed 2d lieutenant; promoted to 1st lieutenant May 1, 1863; to major June 4, 1865.
George S. Albright	1st lieutenant	Jan. 7, 1864	Feb. 8, 1864	Appointed from civil life to 2d lieutenant January 7, 1864; resigned December 31, 1864.
Thomas Brooks	do	July 5, 1862	Jan. 11, 1865	Appointed 2d lieutenant from sergeant major February 8, 1864; mustered out with regiment.
Simeon A. Baker	2d lieutenant	Sept. 4, 1862	Mar. 1, 1865	Appointed from sergeant major; mustered out with regiment.
Harrison Horine	1st sergeant	Aug. 16, 1862	Nov. 16, 1864	Appointed sergeant October 2, 1862; mustered out with regiment.
Walter W. Brashear	Quartermaster sergeant	Sept. 11, 1862	Aug. 1, 1864	Appointed corporal February 12, 1864; mustered out with regiment.
Benjamin K. Graham	Commissary sergeant	Aug. 16, 1862	Nov. 4, 1862	Mustered out with regiment.
William G. Farr	Sergeant	Aug. 15, 1862	Oct. 2, 1862	Do.
William R. Wilkes	do	Aug. 15, 1862	Jan. 1, 1863	Do.
James A. Irvin	do	Sept. 12, 1862	Apr. 21, 1863	Appointed corporal October 2, 1862; mustered out with regiment.
Benjamin Brannon	do	Aug. 15, 1862	Aug. 1, 1864	Appointed quartermaster sergeant October 2, 1862, reduced at his own request to sergeant August 1, 1864; mustered out with regiment.
Daniel F. Thomas	Corporal	Aug. 15, 1862	Oct. 2, 1862	Mustered out with regiment.
William M. Carlin	do	Aug. 12, 1862	Oct. 1, 1863	Do.
Charles F. Cole	do	Aug. 26, 1862	Oct. 2, 1862	Do.
John W. Brashear	do	Sept. 11, 1862	Aug. 1, 1864	Do.
Joseph M. Cole	do	Aug. 26, 1862	Nov. 16, 1864	Do.
William W. Brock	do	Aug. 16, 1862	Jan. 1, 1865	Do.
Allison Boyd	do	Nov. 26, 1862	July 25, 1864	Do.
Isaac Hodson	Trumpeter	Aug. 28, 1862	Aug. 28, 1862	Do.
John Holley	do	Aug. 28, 1862	Jan. 1, 1865	Do.

REPORT OF THE ADJUTANT GENERAL OF ARKANSAS. 49

Name	Rank	Enlisted	Muster	
George Irby	Farrier	Aug. 12, 1862	Oct. 2, 1862	Do.
Ewing G. Suttle	...do...	Nov. 4, 1863	July 1, 1864	Do.
Edward Clauton	Wagoner	Aug. 16, 1862	Oct. 2, 1862	Do.
Allmon, William	Private	Aug. 21, 1862	Aug. 28, 1862	Do.
Buist, Elbert	...do...	Aug. 16, 1862	Aug. 21, 1862	Do.
Brown, Ptolemy P.	...do...	Aug. 18, 1862	Aug. 21, 1862	Do.
Barrett, James	...do...	Aug. 16, 1862	Aug. 21, 1862	Do.
Ball, James	...do...	Feb. 17, 1863	Aug. 14, 1863	Do.
Brandon, Columbus	...do...	Oct. 27, 1863	D-c. 30, 1863	Do.
Beatie, Frank	...do...	Apr. 18, 1864	Apr. 29, 1864	Do.
Bledsoe, John	...do...	Sept. 10, 1862	Sept. 12, 1862	Do.
Barber, Cyrus	...do...	Aug. 16, 1862	Aug. 26, 1862	Do.
Cook, Meredith	...do...	Nov. 5, 1862	Aug. 14, 1863	Do.
Cook, Hugh	...do...	Nov. 5, 1862	Aug. 14, 1863	Do.
Cook, William	...do...	Apr. 1, 1863	Aug. 14, 1863	Do.
Cornelison, George W.	...do...	Oct. 1, 1863	Dec. 31, 1863	Do.
Carter, James C	...do...	July 21, 1864	July 31, 1864	Do.
Drury, Patton	...do...	Aug. 27, 1863	Sept. 5, 1863	Do.
Dunaway, Andrew	...do...	Oct. 27, 1863	Dec. 30, 1863	Do.
Davis, Andrew	...do...	Sept. 19, 1862	Sept. 21, 1862	Do.
Davis, Thomas	...do...	Apr. 25, 1864	Apr. 29, 1864	Do.
Edwards, Alva	...do...	May 25, 1864	May 31, 1864	Do.
Gordan, Noah	...do...	Oct. 1, 1862	Oct. 9, 1862	Do.
Graham, Isaac	...do...	Oct. 25, 1863	Dec. 31, 1863	Do.
Gwinn, John	...do...	Oct. 25, 1863	Dec. 31, 1863	Do.
Hogue, John	...do...	Oct. 25, 1863	Dec. 31, 1863	Do.
Hillis, Francis M	...do...	Jan. 10, 1863	Apr. 14, 1863	Do.
Holt, DeKalb	...do...	Aug. 26, 1862	Aug. 26, 1862	Do.
Haynes, Elijah	...do...	July 1, 1863	Aug. 14, 1863	Do.
Haynes, John M	...do...	Feb. 23, 1864	Feb. 28, 1864	Do.
Hale, Dewitt C	...do...	Nov. 20, 1864	Jan. 24, 1865	Do.
Jackson, George W	...do...	Aug. 16, 1862	Sept. 21, 1862	Do.
Jones, William A	...do...	Sept. 11, 1862	Sept. 21, 1862	Do.
Johnson, John A	...do...	May 20, 1864	May 21, 1864	Do.
Johnson, William H	...do...	May 20, 1864	May 21, 1864	Do.
Keaton, James	...do...	Nov. 15, 1863	Aug. 14, 1863	Do.
King, Hiram	...do...	Apr. 28, 1864	Apr. 29, 1864	Do.
Luper, Jordan	...do...	Aug. 27, 1863	Sept. 5, 1863	Do.
Luper, Gilbert	...do...	Aug. 27, 1863	Sept. 5, 1863	Do.
Laffor, James	...do...	Oct. 25, 1863	Dec. 30, 1863	Do.
Leningham, William A	...do...	Feb. 1, 1864	Feb. 28, 1864	Do.
Ledbetter, Josiah	...do...	Apr. 14, 1864	Apr. 29, 1864	Do.
Lewis, Abner	...do...	Jan. 18, 1865	Jan. 21, 1865	Do.
Morris, Chelsey	...do...	Oct. 27, 1863	Dec. 30, 1863	Do.
McMillan, Andrew J	...do...	Dec. 10, 1862	Aug. 14, 1863	Do.
McMillan, John A	...do...	Sept. 13, 1864	Sept. 13, 1864	Do.
Nott, John A	...do...	May 23, 1864	May 31, 1864	Do.
Officer, Robert	...do...	April 20, 1864	April 29, 1864	Do.
Olinger, John	...do...	Sept. 25, 1862	Oct. 1, 1862	Do.

Mis. Doc. 53——4

First regiment Arkansas cavalry volunteers. Mustered into service August 7, 1862, (three years;) mustered out August 23, 1865.

COMPANY I—Continued.

Names.	Rank.	Enlistment.	Muster.	Remarks.
Phillips, William H	Private	Oct. 27, 1863	Dec. 30, 1863	Mustered out with regiment.
Qualls, William J	do	Oct. 29, 1863	Dec. 30, 1863	Do.
Ryker, Jacob	do	May 1, 1863	Aug. 4, 1863	Do.
Ryker, James M	do	Aug. 16, 1862	Aug. 21, 1862	Do.
Sharp, William S	do	Dec. 25, 1862	Aug. 14, 1863	Do.
Stubblefield, Edward	do	Aug. 14, 1862	Aug. 21, 1862	Do.
Stubblefield, John	do	Aug. 15, 1862	Aug. 21, 1862	Do.
Stout, Isaac B	do	Oct. 27, 1863	Dec. 30, 1863	Do.
Smith, Francis M	do	Dec. 8, 1862	Aug. 14, 1863	Do.
Smith, George W	do	Dec. 8, 1862	Aug. 14, 1863	Do.
Stevens, William	do	July 1, 1863	Aug. 14, 1863	Do.
Skelton, Jacob	do	May 11, 1864	May 31, 1864	Do.
Suttle, John F	do	Aug. 12, 1862	Aug. 21, 1862	Do.
Teall, Robert	do	Aug. 27, 1863	Sept. 5, 1863	Do.
Teall, Hiram	do	Aug. 27, 1863	Sept. 5, 1863	Do.
Thomas, Doctor D	do	Aug. 12, 1862	Aug. 26, 1862	Do.
Thomas, William F	do	Aug. 28, 1862	Aug. 30, 1862	Do.
Thomas, Carey	do	Aug. 12, 1862	Aug. 26, 1862	Do.
Thomas, Joshua	do	May 1, 1863	Aug. 14, 1863	Do.
Thomas, William	do	Oct. 27, 1863	Dec. 30, 1863	Do.
Taylor, John L	do	Oct. 1, 1863	Oct. 3, 1863	Do.
West, John H	do	Oct. 27, 1863	Dec. 30, 1863	Do.
Killed.				
Dotson, Bloomington I	Private	Mar. 18, 1864	April 29, 1864	Killed while carrying mail to Fort Smith August 15, 1864.
Evans, James A	do	Oct. 4, 1862	Oct. 7, 1862	Shot himself accidentally January 5, 1864.
Keaton, Andrew J	do	Oct. 26, 1862	Aug. 14, 1863	Killed while on furlough in Missouri October 18, 1864.
Stacy, James	do	June 12, 1863	Aug. 14, 1863	Shot himself accidentally May 19, 1864.
Weaver, Micajah	do	Sept. 11, 1862	Sept. 15, 1862	Shot himself accidentally June 15, 1865.
Died.				
Clanton, Harrison	Private	Aug. 15, 1862	Aug. 26, 1862	Died in regimental hospital at Fayetteville, Arkansas.
Estes, James H	do	Sept. 11, 1862	Sept. 2, 1862	Do.
Jones, Thomas J	do	Sept. 11, 1862	Sept. 2, 1862	Do.
Reeves, David	do	Aug. 28, 1862	Aug. 30, 1862	Died in regimental hospital at Springfield, Missouri.
Sisk, James	do	Aug. 16, 1862	Aug. 21, 1862	Died in regimental hospital at Fayetteville, Arkansas.
Suttle, Leroy	Sergeant	Sept. 28, 1862	Oct. 1, 1862	Died as prisoner of war at Fort Smith, Arkansas, December 20, 1864.
Scritchfield, Jacob K	Private	Oct. 26, 1862		Died in regimental hospital at Fayetteville, Arkansas, March 25, 1863.
Scritchfield, James	do	Aug. 15, 1862	Aug. 21, 1862	Died at Fayetteville, Arkansas, February 7, 1863.
Wood, James	do	Aug. 15, 1862	Aug. 21, 1862	Died at Cassville, Missouri, February 6, 1863.
Tokmun, Solomon	do	Aug. 16, 1863	Aug. 21, 1862	Died at Cassville, Missouri, June 29, 1863.

REPORT OF THE ADJUTANT GENERAL OF ARKANSAS.   51

Deserted.

Name	Rank	Date	Remarks
Bivens, St. George	Private	Aug. 27, 1863	Deserted at Fayetteville, Arkansas, November 15, 1863.
Cook, Isam	do	Nov. 5, 1862	Deserted at Cassville, Missouri, July 19, 1864.
Daniels, James	do	Aug. 28, 1862	Deserted from stockade at Fayetteville, Arkansas, March 13, 1864.
Hanna, Ebenezer	do	Aug. 12, 1864	Deserted at Fayetteville, Arkansas, June 7, 1864.
Stout, James	do	Aug. 27, 1862	Deserted from stockade at Fayetteville, Ark., March 13, 1864; confined for murder.

Discharged.

Name	Rank	Date	Remarks
Brashear, Alva S	Corporal	Sept. 11, 1862	Discharged for disability at Fayetteville, Arkansas, March 25, 1863.
Brannon, James L	Private	Aug. 16, 1862	Discharged for disability at Fayetteville, Arkansas, January 28, 1864.
Brannon, John	do	Aug. 16, 1862	Do.
Clark, Reuben D	do	Oct. 26, 1862	Discharged for disability at Fayetteville, Arkansas, March 12, 1864.
Davis, Maxfield B	do	Aug. 15, 1862	Discharged by order at Fort Smith, Arkansas, June 22, 1865.
Garris, John W	do	Sept. 28, 1862	Discharged for disability at Fayetteville, Askansas, February 28, 1863.
Glenn, Benjamin F	do	Oct. 1, 1862	Discharged for disability at Fayetteville, Arkansas, March 8, 1864.
Hembree, Ephraim T	do	Nov. 26, 1863	Discharged for disability at Fayetteville, Arkansas, March 25, 1863.
Hank, Alexander T	do	Aug. 16, 1862	Discharged for disability at Fayetteville, Arkansas, December 5, 1864.
Harrison, Eliznr B	Corporal	Aug. 28, 1862	Discharged to accept promotion October 2, 1862.
McGinnis, Elisha	Private	July 10, 1862	Discharged for disability at Fayetteville, Arkansas, March 12, 1864.
Ross, James	do	Dec. 10, 1862	Discharged for disability at Fayetteville, Arkansas, March 25, 1863.
Reeves, James	do	Aug. 15, 1863	Do.
Riddle, James	do	Aug. 28, 1862	Do.
Reeves, Jasper	do	Sept. 12, 1862	Discharged for disability at Fayetteville, Arkansas, April 30, 1864.
Stout, Joseph	do	Aug. 15, 1862	Discharged for disability at Fayetteville, Arkansas, March 25, 1863.
Stringer, James	do	Aug. 15, 1862	Discharged by order at Springfield, Mo., on account of being a minor, Aug. 18, 1863.
Wooten, William	do	Aug. 15, 1862	Discharged for disability at Fayetteville, Arkansas, June 30, 1864.
Zinn, William H	do	Oct. 7, 1862	Discharged for disability at Fayetteville, Arkansas, March 21, 1863.
Zinn, George W	do	Aug. 15, 1862	Discharged for disability at Fayetteville, Arkansas, March 28, 1863.

Transferred.

Name	Rank	Date	Remarks
Baker, Simeon A	Sergeant	Sept. 4, 1862	Transferred to non-commissioned staff as sergeant major.
Caffee, Amos H	Private	Oct. 1, 1862	Transferred to non-commissioned staff as hospital steward.
Hall, Jeremiah B	do	Dec. 10, 1862	Transferred to non-commissioned staff as regimental commissary sergeant.
Hilbert, Melanchton	do	July 19, 1863	Transferred to non-commissioned staff as hospital steward.
Munfay, Warren W	do	Aug. 16, 1863	Transferred to non-commissioned staff as sergeant major.
Merrill, John W	Sergeant	Aug. 15, 1862	Discharged for disability March 25, 1863.

COMPANY M.

Name	Rank	Date of rank.	Remarks
Robert E. Travis	Captain	Sept. 22, 1862	Appointed from private of company A to fill original vacancy; mortally wounded in skirmish near Arkansas river, February 3, 1863; died, February 4, 1863.
William S. Johnson	do	Feb. 5, 1863	Was in three months service at Washington city; appointed 1st lieutenant from civil life to fill original vacancy; discharged on account of wounds received in action, July 21, 1864.

First regiment Arkansas cavalry volunteers. Mustered into service August 7, 1862, (three years;) mustered out August 23, 1865.

COMPANY M—Continued.

Names.	Rank.	Enlistment.	Date of rank.	Remarks.
John B. C. Turman	Captain	—, 1862	Jan. 1, 1865	Appointed from sergeant, company D, to 2d lieutenant, February 1, 1863; mustered out with regiment.
James Roseman	1st lieutenant	—, 1861	Feb. 5, 1863	Appointed from regimental quartermaster sergeant, 36th Illinois infantry, to 2d lieutenant, November 1, 1862; murdered June 28, 1864, on Frog bayou, Arkansas, by Jos. R. Wisdom, a private of the same company.
Alvin D. Norris	do	July 9, 1862	Mar. 22, 1865	Appointed sergeant, January 8, 1863; 1st sergeant, September 1, 1863; mustered out with regiment.
Thomas J. Rice	2d lieutenant	Sept. 22, 1862	Sept. 22, 1862	Appointed from civil life to fill original vacancy; promoted to R. C. S., Oct. 1, 1862.
Axiey Mitchell	1st sergeant	Oct. 16, 1862	April 1, 1865	Appointed quartermaster sergeant, November 1, 1862; mustered out with regiment.
George Luttrell	Quartermaster sergeant	Oct. 16, 1862	April 1, 1865	Appointed corporal, December 1, 1862; sergeant, February 1, 1865; mustered out with regiment.
Marcus B. Calmes	Sergeant	Oct. 29, 1862	Jan. 1, 1864	Appointed corporal, December 1, 1862; mustered out with regiment.
Jeremiah P. Packer	do	Nov. 20, 1862	June 1, 1864	Appointed corporal, January 8, 1863; mustered out with regiment.
Thomas J. Johnson	do	Aug. 12, 1862	Dec. 1, 1864	Appointed corporal, September 22, 1862; mustered out with regiment.
William H. Shaver	do	Mar. 16, 1862	April 1, 1865	Appointed corporal, June 5, 1863; mustered out with regiment.
Francis M. Steel	Corporal	Nov. 7, 1863	Mar. 1, 1864	Mustered out with regiment.
Randolph D. Boydston	do	Aug. 29, 1863	Mar. 3, 1864	Do.
James T. Mullin	do	Nov. 21, 1863	Mar. 1, 1865	Do.
Benjamin F. Boydston	do	Aug. 29, 1863	April 1, 1865	Do.
Henderson Hood	do	Jan. 11, 1864	April 1, 1865	Do.
Lewis Hawkins	do	May 14, 1864	April 1, 1865	Do.
William H. Washburn	do	Feb. 5, 1864	April 1, 1865	Do.
Charles H. Hyatt	Trumpeter	Feb. 12, 1863	Sept. 1, 1864	Do.
John M. Thomason	Farrier	Sept. 1, 1862	Jan. 1, 1865	Do.
Moses Dutton	do	Feb. 2, 1863	May 1, 1863	Do.
Sylvester Workman	Wagoner		Jan. 15, 1865	Do.
			Muster.	
Bohn, Samuel	Private	Feb. 23, 1863	Aug. 31, 1863	Do.
Blanton, John C	do	Sept. 7, 1862	Aug. 31, 1863	Do.
Bridges, Willis	do	Nov. 29, 1862	Aug. 31, 1863	Do.
Crabtree, Rees	do	Aug. 12, 1862	Oct. 1, 1862	Do.
Chyle, Davis	do	Aug. 23, 1862	Oct. 1, 1862	Do.
Dutton, Andrew J	do	Feb. 11, 1863	Oct. 1, 1862	Do.
Eason, Theodore G	do	Oct. 1, 1862	Oct. 1, 1862	On duty with Major General Herron since October 11, 1862; no discharge given on muster out of company.
Fatemore, Philip	do	Sept. 18, 1862	Oct. 1, 1862	Mustered out with regiment.
Gready, Jasper P	do	Mar. 16, 1863	Aug. 31, 1863	Do.
Grassfenner, William	do	Dec. 7, 1862	Oct. 7, 1863	Do.
Hunter, John	do	Feb. 23, 1863	Aug. 31, 1863	Do.
Hunter, John R	do	Dec. 1, 1863	Dec. 1, 1863	Do.
Hawkins, James S	do	Nov. 1, 1863	Dec. 7, 1863	Prisoner in hands of enemy since September 15, 1864; no discharge given on muster out of company.

REPORT OF THE ADJUTANT GENERAL OF ARKANSAS.   53

Name	Rank	Date	Date	Remarks
Hawkins, Elijah	do	Feb. 9, 1864	May 4, 1864	Mustered out with regiment.
Hood, William	do	Sept. 4, 1862	Oct. 1, 1862	Do.
Hood, Allen	do	Jan. 11, 1864	May 4, 1864	Do.
Irvie, Joseph G	do	Mar. 20, 1863	Aug. 31, 1863	Do.
Jones, John	do	Feb. 2, 1863	Aug. 31, 1863	Do.
Johnson, Andrew J	do	Aug. 12, 1862	Oct. 1, 1862	Do.
Johnson, Francis M	do	Oct. 18, 1862	Aug. 31, 1863	Do.
Lund, John T	do	Aug. 23, 1862	Oct. 1, 1862	Do.
Lund, James F	do	Aug. 23, 1862	Oct. 1, 1862	Do.
Lane, Elias R	do	Feb. 23, 1863	Aug. 31, 1863	Do.
Locklin, Wesley	do	Mar. 20, 1863	Aug. 31, 1863	Do.
Meek, Moses	do	Oct. 21, 1864	Oct. 21, 1864	Do.
Mullen, Benjamin H	do	Mar. 21, 1864	May 4, 1864	Do.
Moody, Joseph A	do	Mar. 20, 1863	Aug. 31, 1863	Do.
McCabe, William	do	Sept. 18, 1862	Oct. 1, 1862	Do.
Pitts, John	do	Aug. 4, 1863	Aug. 31, 1863	Do.
Pitts, Martin V	do	Dec. 21, 1863	Aug. 31, 1863	Do.
Rush, Clemons	do	Jan. 7, 1863	Aug. 31, 1863	Do.
Rush, Jesse	do	Aug. 23, 1862	Oct. 1, 1862	Do.
Sander, Jesse R	do	Mar. 21, 1863	Aug. 31, 1863	Do.
Smith, Samuel	do	Sept. 10, 1862	Oct. 1, 1862	Do.
Shears, Henry	do	July 27, 1863	Aug. 31, 1863	Do.
Shears, William	do	July 23, 1863	Aug. 31, 1863	Do.
Teague, William S	do	Aug. 28, 1862	Oct. 7, 1862	Do.
Tomlinson, Joseph	do	Sept. 28, 1862	Aug. 31, 1863	Do.
Trammell, Jarrett	do	July 25, 1863	Aug. 31, 1863	Do.
Workman, John	do	Aug. 23, 1862	Oct. 1, 1862	Do.
Wagoner, Benjamin	do	Jan. 1, 1863	Aug. 31, 1863	Do.
Wice, James	do	June 20, 1864	Oct. 31, 1864	Do.
Young, John W	do	Dec. 24, 1862	Aug. 31, 1863	Do.
Yokum, John	do	Sept. 15, 1862	Oct. 1, 1862	Do.

Killed.

Name	Rank	Date	Date	Remarks
Bell, Eli	Private	Nov. 7, 1863	Dec. 7, 1863	Killed near Van Buren, Arkansas, July 7, 1864.
Bowman, George W	do	July 25, 1863	Aug. 31, 1863	Killed by guerillas near Van Buren, Arkansas, October 21, 1864.
Dillingham, George W	do	July 27, 1863	Aug. 31, 1863	Killed on picket at Cross Timbers, Arkansas, October 15, 1863.
Hurst, Thomas J	do	Aug. 4, 1863	Aug. 31, 1863	Killed in Stone county, Missouri, April 1, 1865.
Johnson, John T	do	Aug. 12, 1862	Oct. 1, 1862	Killed in action near White River, Arkansas, February 17, 1864.
McLaughlin, William H	do	Feb. 26, 1864	May 4, 1864	Killed by guerillas in Franklin county, Arkansas, May 21, 1864.
Peters, Michael	do	Nov. 7, 1863	Dec. 7, 1863	Killed in action near Van Buren, Arkansas, August 7, 1864.
Vice, George W	Sergeant	Oct. 18, 1862	Aug. 31, 1863	Killed on picket at Cross Timbers, Missouri, October 15, 1863.
Wisdom, Creed T	Private	Mar. 16, 1863	Aug. 31, 1863	Killed at Van Buren, Arkansas, September 10, 1864.
Young, William	do	Dec. 24, 1862	Aug. 31, 1863	Killed by guerillas near Fayetteville, Arkansas, September 1, 1864.

Died.

Name	Rank	Date	Date	Remarks
Adkins, William	Private	Sept. 2, 1862	Oct. 1, 1862	Died at Crane creek, Missouri, November 30, 1862.
Brown, Francis M	do	Nov. 20, 1862	Dec. 24, 1862	Died in Washington county, Arkansas, July 15, 1863.
Boggs, John R	do	Dec. 8, 1862	Dec. 29, 1862	Died at Fayetteville, Arkansas, March 25, 1863.
Ferrell, Morgan B	do	Sept. 19, 1862	Oct. 1, 1862	Died at Fayetteville, Arkansas, March 18, 1863.

First regiment Arkansas cavalry volunteers. Mustered into service August 7, 1862, (three years;) mustered out August 23, 1865.

COMPANY M—Continued.

Names.	Rank.	Enlistment.	Muster.	Remarks.
Hooper, Benjamin	Private	Sept. 22, 1862	Oct. 1, 1862	Died at Van Buren, Arkansas, September 2, 1864.
James, Drury	Corporal	Sept. 8, 1862	Oct. 1, 1862	Died at Fayetteville, Arkansas, February 2, 1863.
Jones, Martin V	Private	July 27, 1863	Aug. 31, 1863	Died at Cassville, Missouri, October 16, 1863, of wounds received in action.
Locklier, Lorett	....do....	Mar. 20, 1863	Nov. 20, 1863	Died at Cassville, Missouri, May 1, 1863.
McCullough, Marion R	....do....	Sept. 20, 1862	Oct. 1, 1862	Died at Fayetteville, Arkansas, January 23, 1863.
Stiles, Robert R	Sergeant	Sept. 29, 1862	Oct. 2, 1862	Died at Springfield, Missouri, November 18, 1862.
Stiles, John	Private	Aug. 13, 1862	Oct. 1, 1862	Died at Springfield, Missouri, November 10, 1863.
West, Francis M	....do....	Aug. 13, 1862	Aug. 31, 1862	Died at Fayetteville, Arkansas, October 17, 1863.
Discharged.				
Bigger, John M	Private	Aug. 15, 1862	Oct. 1, 1862	Discharged to accept promotion, November 1, 1862.
Bays, Benton H	Corporal	Oct. 16, 1862	Oct. 20, 1862	Discharged for disability June 4, 1863.
Callen, Augustus D	Private	Sept. 2, 1862	Oct. 1, 1862	Discharged for promotion June 30, 1863.
....Hiram C	....do....	Aug. 27, 1862	Oct. 1, 1862	Discharged for disability March 20, 1863.
Hembree, Lewis	....do....	Aug. 29, 1862	Oct. 1, 1862	Discharged for disability July 2, 1863.
Joy, James R	Sergeant	Mar. 20, 1863	Aug. 31, 1863	Discharged for promotion April 14, 1864.
Johnson, William O	....do....	Sept. 10, 1862	Oct. 1, 1862	Discharged for disability caused by wounds received in action May 21, 1863.
Jones, Benjamin	Private	Aug. 6, 1863	Aug. 31, 1863	Discharged for disability December 14, 1863.
Kessee, John	....do....	July 27, 1863	Aug. 31, 1863	Discharged for disability from wounds March 30, 1865.
Luttrell, James	....do....	Oct. 16, 1862	Oct. 20, 1862	Discharged for disability March 30, 1863.
Martin, George A	....do....	Sept. 17, 1862	Oct. 1, 1862	Discharged for disability April 14, 1863.
Meek, Lewis	....do....	Mar. 20, 1863	Aug. 31, 1863	Discharged for disability December 8, 1863.
Morris, Doctor B	Sergeant	Aug. 26, 1862	Oct. 1, 1862	Discharged for disability February 1, 1865.
Rainey, Joseph P	....do....	July 22, 1862	Oct. 1, 1862	Discharged for promotion April 1, 1864.
Rowe, George W	....do....	Sept. 14, 1862	Oct. 1, 1862	Discharged for promotion March 2, 1864.
Todd, John P	....do....	Oct. 14, 1862	Aug. 31, 1863	Discharged for promotion June 4, 1865.
Vaughan, William R	Private	Aug. 26, 1862	Oct. 1, 1862	Discharged for disability March 9, 1863.
Woodbridge, William S	Sergeant	Sept. 13, 1862	Oct. 1, 1862	Discharged for promotion July 1, 1863.
Woolsey, Andrew C	Private	Aug. 29, 1862	Oct. 1, 1862	Discharged for disability March 20, 1863.
Walker, William T	....do....	Sept. 2, 1862	Oct. 1, 1862	Discharged for disability December 1, 1863.
Deserted.				
Bruman, James	Private	Jan. 16, 1864	Oct. 15, 1862	Deserted at Fayetteville, Arkansas, January 20, 1864.
Bays, Jerome	....do....	Oct. 12, 1862	Apr. 30, 1864	Deserted at Springfield, Missouri, August 9, 1863.
Caldwell, Thomas	....do....	Feb. 22, 1864	Oct. 1, 1862	Deserted at Van Buren, Arkansas, August 7, 1864.
Dunham, William	....do....	Aug. 28, 1862	Oct. 1, 1862	Deserted at Fayetteville, Arkansas, December 15, 1862.
Fine, William M	....do....	Aug. 28, 1862	Oct. 1, 1862	Deserted at Springfield, Missouri, August 30, 1863.
Gatewood, Andrew	....do....	Aug. 29, 1862	Oct. 1, 1862	Deserted at Fayetteville, Arkansas, September 29, 1864.
Hess, Hiram	....do....	Sept. 18, 1862	Oct. 1, 1862	Deserted at Fayetteville, Arkansas, December 26, 1863.
Johnson, Colbert	....do....	Nov. 29, 1862	Nov. 29, 1862	Deserted at battle of Prairie Grove, December 7, 1862.
Nichols, Leeper	....do....	Aug. 3, 1862	Aug. 7, 1862	Deserted at Springfield, Missouri, October 12, 1862.

REPORT OF THE ADJUTANT GENERAL OF ARKANSAS. 55

Oxford, John W	do	Feb. 2, 1864	Deserted at Fayetteville, Arkansas, February 7, 1864.
Ruff, David C	do	Aug. 29, 1862	Deserted at Springfield, Missouri, October —, 1862.
Scott, Jacob	do	Aug. 28, 1862	Deserted at Fayetteville, Arkansas, March 28, 1865.
Stratt, Joseph A	do	Aug. 26, 1862	Deserted at Fayetteville, Arkansas, April 11, 1863.
Stewart, James	do	Feb. 23, 1863	Deserted at Fayetteville, Arkansas, April 11, 1863.
Todd, Owen W	do	Sept. 10, 1862	Deserted at Fayetteville, Arkansas, April 11, 1863.
Todd, Elijah S	do	Sept. 10, 1862	Deserted March 10, 1864.
Thomason, Harmon	do	Sept. 12, 1862	Deserted at Fayetteville, Arkansas, April 11, 1863.
Wisdom, Joseph R	do	Mar. 16, 1863	Deserted at Fayetteville, Arkansas, June 28, 1864.
Walduss, Allen B	do	Aug. 31, 1862	Deserted at Fort Smith, Arkansas, October 5, 1863.
Wilson, John	Sergeant	Sept. 14, 1862	Deserted at Fayetteville, Arkansas, December 26, 1863.
Wilkinson, Thomas	do	Feb. 2, 1864	Deserted

FIRST ARKANSAS CAVALRY VOLUNTEERS.—HISTORICAL MEMORANDA.

On the 29th day of March, 1862, while the "Army of the Southwest" was lying at Cross Timbers, Missouri, M. La Rue Harrison, of the 36th Illinois infantry volunteers, applied for and received authority from General Curtis to recruit a company for the 6th Missouri cavalry volunteers, and proposed to enlist citizens of the State of Arkansas, many of whom had escaped conscription, and were then entering various regiments in the national army.

On the 12th of May, 1862, eleven men from Washington county, Arkansas, made their appearance at the post of Cassville, Missouri, and were sworn into the service of the United States; on the 18th of the same month about twenty more were added, and on the 1st of June the organization, numbering forty-five men, moved from Cassville to join a battalion of the 6th Missouri cavalry volunteers, then stationed at Forsyth, Missouri. On the march, Captain Harrison learned that many more men than men enough to complete one squadron were on their way from Arkansas to join him, and he telegraphed to Hon. John S. Phelps, tendering through him, to the President, would accept the regiment, provided it was completed within twenty days. Subsequent telegrams prolonged the time for an additional twenty days; and on the 3d day of July, 1862, the following letter was received:

ADJUTANT GENERAL'S OFFICE, *Washington, June 16, 1862.*

SIR: The Secretary of War hereby authorizes you to raise a regiment of cavalry from the loyal men of Arkansas, to be completed by the 20th of July, and to be mustered into service, subsisted, clothed, mounted, and armed at Springfield, Missouri, by the United States government.

The regiment will be mustered into the service for three years or the war, and will be organized as prescribed by act of Congress, approved July 29, 1861, entitled "An act to increase the present military establishment of the United States," as follows:

[The form of organization, being substantially like that of other cavalry commands, is omitted.]

Lieutenant Colonel Mills, of the 24th Missouri volunteers, commanding at Springfield, Missouri, or other officer who may be placed in command at that place, will act as mustering officer, and will make the necessary requisitions for arms, accoutrements, horses, subsistence, medical stores, clothing, camp and garrison equipage, and all other supplies that may be required for the regiment, on the proper staff officers at St. Louis, Missouri, or other convenient place in the department of the Mississippi.

I am, sir, very respectfully, your obedient servant,

L. THOMAS, *Adjutant General.*

M. LA RUE HARRISON, Esq., *Springfield, Missouri.*

Recruiting parties had already been sent into various parts of Arkansas, and squads of from six to thirty men were constantly arriving at Springfield and enlisting in the regiment. On the 20th of June a raid was made into Fayetteville, Arkansas, from Cassville, by a detachment of the 1st Missouri and 2d Wisconsin cavalry, under command of Major Hubbard, at which time 115 recruits were brought out, mostly from Washington county.

July 1, Captain Harrison, with about 200 recruits, left Cassville with the 37th Illinois infantry, and established his rendezvous at Springfield, Missouri. July 3, the authority for mustering having been received, four companies were mustered into the service, and on the 7th day of August Colonel Harrison was, by order of Brigadier General E. B. Brown, appointed chief engineer for the district of southwest Missouri. On the 11th day of August Colonel Harrison was, ordered to join the command of General Brown in the field, west of Mount Vernon, Missouri. It was engaged, September 15 and October 13, in the battles near Newtonia, Missouri, and during the campaign furnished most of the scouts, guides, and messengers for the army, besides being frequently engaged in skirmishes with the enemy's scouting and reconnoitring parties. On the 2d day of October, 1862, the regimental organization of twelve companies was completed.

On the 3d day of October, 1862, the Second battalion, having been mounted and armed, was sent to the southwest to join the Army of the Frontier, under General Schofield, and during that month it, with the 1st, constituted the advance of that army in its march through northwestern Arkansas. On the return of General Schofield, about the 20th of October, these battalions were stationed at Elkhorn Tavern and Cassville as outposts, and there remained until the next forward movement of that army. November 11, three companies of the 3d battalion, under command of Lieutenant Colonel Bishop, left Springfield and joined the regiment at Elkhorn Tavern, on Pea Ridge, which place was held by him as the extreme outpost south of the 2d and 3d divisions of the Army of the Frontier, until its second advance, which resulted in the battle of Prairie Grove.

On the 5th of December, in obedience to orders from General Herron, Colonel Harrison, who had been relieved from duty as chief engineer of the district of southwest Missouri, left Elkhorn with eight companies of the regiment and a train of twenty wagons, and moved forward to join General Blunt, then at Cane Hill, Arkansas. On the night of the 6th the detachment camped at Prairie Grove, ten miles southwest of Fayetteville. During the night orders were received from General Blunt for the detachment to move at daybreak and join General Solomon near Rhea's Mill. Messengers also brought information from General Blunt that the enemy were west of Cane Hill, and would probably attack him in the morning; that the road between himself and Colonel Harrison was clear.

At daylight on the morning of the 7th the detachment moved forward, but at sunrise was met by detachments of Missouri troops retreating, who had been attacked by Hindman's advance at their camp, two miles south of Illinois creek. A determined attack was made by the enemy at this point, and within half an hour a serious panic ensued, which resulted in the capture of the train of the 1st cavalry and the temporary demoralization of the regiment. Falling back to the Walnut Grove church, Colonel Harrison rallied his men upon the right of General Herron's army, which was met at that point, and advanced with it to Prairie Grove.

On the following day Colonel Harrison made a raid south to the Boston mountains, pursuing some of the routed detachments of Hindman's army, and capturing twenty-nine prisoners.

1863.—On the 8th of January a detachment, under command of Lieutenants Thompson and Vaughan, participated in the defeat of Marmaduke at Springfield, Missouri; Lieutenant Vaughan and Sergeant L. D. Jernigan were severely wounded during the engagement. About the 25th of January a detachment, commanded by Captain Galloway, participated in a raid into Van Buren, under command of Lieutenant Colonel Stuart, 10th Illinois cavalry, at which time a steamer and 315 prisoners were captured. On the 3d of February a detachment of eighty-three men, under Captain Galloway, routed 150 rebels near White Oak creek, in Franklin county, and on the following morning Captain R. E. Travis was mortally wounded in an attack upon a party of guerillas who had fortified themselves in a log-house near Thurlkill's ferry, on the Arkansas river.

On the 18th of April, at sunrise, the post of Fayetteville was attacked by the rebel General W. L. Cabell with a force of 1,200 men and two pieces of artillery. After four hour's severe fighting he was routed with serious loss. The defending force consisted of about 350 men of the 1st Arkansas cavalry and a portion of four companies of the 1st Arkansas infantry. The remainder of the 1st infantry and one company of the 1st cavalry were held in reserve. Neither artillery nor defensive works of any kind were used by the national troops. About this time, owing to the ordering of large numbers of troops from the department of Missouri to Vicksburg, most of the distant outposts were withdrawn, and, in obedience to orders from General Curtis, Fayetteville was abandoned on the 25th of April, and its garrison arrived in Springfield, Missouri, on the 4th of May. On the 9th of August Captain R. H. Wimpy, with two mountain howitzers and a detachment of the regiment, joined Colonel Catherwood, 6th cavalry, Missouri State militia, in a raid southwest across the Arkansas river, participating in the engagements at Pineville, Missouri, Backbone mountain, Arkansas, and in several skirmishes, marching over 500 miles.

In September Colonel Harrison attacked a detachment of rebels under Coffee, in the Seneca Nation, pursuing them down the Indian line to Round Prairie, Arkansas, and on the 22d of that month the 1st cavalry re-occupied Fayetteville. On the 4th of October a detachment of the regiment, 450 strong, with two sections of battery A, 1st Arkansas light artillery, and one section of mountain howitzers, under command of Colonel Harrison, left Fayetteville in pursuit of the rebel General Shelby, who at the time was moving north from Neosho, Missouri, with 2,000 men and two pieces of artillery. Marching through Pineville, Newtonia, Granby, Carthage, Lamar, and Greenfield towards Warsaw, countermanding orders turned the column towards Bowers's Mill, and thence by way of Mount Vernon and Cassville to Fayetteville to relieve the garrison at that place, which was being seriously threatened by a superior force under the rebel Colonel Brooks. At sunrise on the 15th of October a part of the detachment, while in camp at Cross Timbers, and having in charge a train of 25 wagons loaded with supplies for Fayetteville, was attacked by Brooks, but through the timely return of Colonel Harrison, who, having gone forward towards Fayetteville with a portion of his men, had heard the firing, the attack was repelled. On the 23d of October a portion of the regiment, with its howitzer battery, under command of Major Hunt, joined General McNeil at Huntsville, taking the advance in the pursuit of General Shelby across the Arkansas river.

On the 7th of November an expedition, 435 strong, under Colonel Harrison, left Fayetteville, moving eastward, and on the morning of the 9th routed a force of rebels near King's river; and again on the following day, at sunrise at Kingston, at noon on the Dry fork of King's river, and in the evening near Mulberry mountain. On the 11th and 12th Captain John I. Worthington drove the same irregular forces across the Arkansas river, carrying his howitzers by hand across the Frog Bayou mountain; and on the 23d and 25th engaged and routed bands of guerillas near Sugar Loaf mountain, in Marion county, and on Richland creek, in Searcy county—the last time with considerable loss. Lieutenant L. D. Jernigan was here severely wounded and taken prisoner.

1864.—During the months of January and February a detachment of the regiment, commanded by Captains Galloway and Boteführ, served in Carroll, Marion, and Searcy counties, under orders from Brigadier General C. B. Holland, from the district of southwest Missouri. They were engaged repeatedly with the enemy, and received high praise in General Holland's official report.

During this year detachments of the regiment were very frequently engaged with guerillas, who were still infesting northwestern Arkansas, and on the 28th of October a concerted attack upon Fayetteville was defeated. On the 3d of October the town was again attacked by a largely superior force, detached from General Price's army, then lying at Cane Hill, the whole under the command of Major General Fagan. The defending force consisted of about 800 of the 1st Arkansas cavalry and such home guards, citizens, and stragglers as could be brought together, the whole numbering 1,128 men. A fort and rifle-pits had been constructed, and the attack, though not pressed with all the vigor that would have been expected, was continued persistently through the day, several attempts to gain the fort and rifle-pits being gallantly repelled. On the following morning the army of General Curtis, then in pursuit of Price, arrived, and, re-enforced by the 1st cavalry, continued the pursuit to the Arkansas river. Here the great raid terminated, and with it active operations on this portion of the frontier.

All summer long the 1st cavalry had been actively employed against the enemy, who increased in strength until in the autumn they swarmed through the country; but Price's retreat and the approach of winter secured, for a time, comparative quiet.

1865.—During this year a relentless warfare was carried on against the small bands of guerillas who infested northwestern Arkansas, and many were killed. The news of the surrender of General E. Kirby Smith, then commanding the Trans-Mississippi department of the Confederate States, was not received in northwestern Arkansas until about the 1st of July, after which quiet was mainly restored; and on the 23d of August the 1st Arkansas cavalry was mustered out of the service. From May, 1863, until the disbanding of the regiment a cornet band was maintained at the private expense of the officers, and at the close of the war the instruments were presented to the city of Fayetteville.

REPORT OF THE ADJUTANT GENERAL OF ARKANSAS 57

Second regiment Arkansas cavalry volunteers. Mustered into service March 18, 1864, (three years;) mustered out August 20, 1865.

FIELD AND STAFF.

Names.	Rank.	Enlistment.	Date of rank.	Remarks.
John E. Phelps	Colonel	June 9, 1862	Mar. 18, 1864	Mustered out with regiment; appointed from 2d lieutenant 3d United States cavalry. Brevetted brigadier general for gallant and meritorious services during the war, with rank from March 13, 1865.
Hugh Cameron	Lieutenant colonel	Sept. 21, 1861	Feb. 20, 1864	Appointed 1st lieutenant 2d Kansas cavalry November 7, 1861; promoted captain 2d Kansas cavalry December 27, 1861. Brevetted colonel and brigadier general March 14, 1867, with rank from March 13, 1865; mustered out with regiment.
Jeremiah Hackett	Major	Dec. 25, 1863	Mar. 7, 1864	Promoted from captain company H; mustered out with regiment.
James A. Melton	do		Mar. 3, 1864	Resigned February 20, 1865.
Archibald B. Freeburn	do	Sept. 10, 1862	Feb. 25, 1864	Promoted from captain company B; resigned March 6, 1865.
Henry H. Maynard	Surgeon	Aug. 8, 1862	Mar. 17, 1864	Promoted from assistant surgeon 18th Iowa infantry; mustered out with regiment.
John D. Hocker	Assistant surgeon	Oct. 30, 1863	Nov. 2, 1863	Appointed from civil life; mustered out with regiment.
Alexander B. Turner	do	Sept. 3, 1864	Sept. 3, 1864	Do.
Louis Rémiatte	Adjutant	Dec. 1, 1861	Oct. 30, 1863	Appointed from sergeant major 2d Kansas cavalry; mustered out with regiment.
George Morley	Regimental quartermaster	July 7, 1862	Oct. 30, 1863	Appointed from sergeant company B; mustered out with regiment.
Pleasant G. Potter	Regimental com. subsistence.	Mar. 3, 1864	Mar. 3, 1864	Appointed from civil life; mustered out with regiment.

NON-COMMISSIONED STAFF.

Names.	Rank.	Enlistment.	Date of rank.	Remarks.
Miles Keener	Sergeant major	Nov. 10, 1863	July 12, 1865	Appointed from sergeant company I; mustered out with regiment.
James Massey	do	July 8, 1863	July 8, 1863	Appointed from private company B; reduced to the ranks and transferred to company B, July 23, 1864.
Joseph C. McClure	do	Sept. 10, 1863	July 26, 1864	Appointed from sergeant company H; promoted to 2d lieutenant company L, March 1, 1865.
Robert Hatfield	do	Nov. 14, 1863	Mar. 1, 1865	Appointed from company K; reduced to the ranks and transferred to company K, July 12, 1865.
Pleasant W. Hamblin	Quartermaster sergeant	Nov. 14, 1863	July 1, 1865	Appointed from company K; mustered out with regiment.
James T. Murphy	do	Aug. 10, 1862	April 14, 1864	Appointed from corporal company B; mustered out at Memphis, Tennessee.
James A. Claxton	Commissary sergeant	Nov. 17, 1862	April 20, 1863	Appointed from private company C; mustered out with regiment.
Edward H. Kilburn	Veterinary surgeon	Aug. 4, 1862	Sept. 21, 1864	Appointed from private company B; mustered out with regiment.
Charles White	Hospital steward	July 18, 1863	May 1, 1864	Appointed from private company F; mustered out with regiment.
Cyrus A. Raney	Chief trumpeter	July 5, 1863	Mar. 1, 1864	Appointed from private company C; mustered out with regiment.
John Tiner	Saddler sergeant	July 12, 1863	May 1, 1864	Appointed from saddler company E; mustered out with regiment.

Second regiment Arkansas cavalry volunteers. Mustered into service March 18, 1864, (three years;) mustered out August 20, 1865.

COMPANY A.

Names.	Rank.	Enlistment.	Date of rank.	Remarks.
Dennis W. Roberts	Captain	Nov. 3, 1863	Mar. 7, 1864	Appointed, from civil life, 1st lieutenant company A; mustered out with regiment.
Joseph P. Rainey	1st lieutenant	Mar. 7, 1864	Mar. 7, 1864	Discharged at Memphis, Tennessee, February 27, 1865.
Laban N. Garrett	2d lieutenant	Mar. 7, 1864	Mar. 7, 1864	Dismissed at Memphis, Tennessee, February 18, 1865.
William D. Moore	do	Mar. 1, 1864	Feb. 28, 1865	Appointed from 1st sergeant company M; mustered out with regiment.
Benjamin F. Hobbs	1st sergeant	Aug. 1, 1863	Mar. 2, 1864	Mustered out with regiment.
Thomas K. O'Kelley	Quartermaster sergeant	Mar. 23, 1864	Mar. 20, 1865	Do.
James G. Walker	Commissary sergeant	July 1, 1864	Mar. 20, 1865	Do.
Eli F. Holt	Sergeant	Aug. 25, 1863	Mar. 7, 1864	Do.
Eli J. Black	do	Oct. 1, 1863	Mar. 8, 1864	Do.
Josiah C. Watts	do	Oct. 1, 1863	Mar. 8, 1864	Do.
James N. Wheeler	do	Oct. 1, 1863	Mar. 8, 1864	Do.
Samuel Harris	do	Oct. 1, 1863	Mar. 20, 1865	Do.
Samuel Murphy	Corporal	Sept. 1, 1863	Mar. 8, 1864	Do.
William N. Edwards	do	July 12, 1863	Mar. 8, 1864	Do.
Mark B. Lewis	do	Sept. 25, 1863	Mar. 8, 1864	Do.
George W. Miller	do	July 1, 1864	Mar. 20, 1865	Do.
William J. Bulington	do	Jan. 19, 1864	Mar. 20, 1865	Do.
John R. Graham	do	Oct. 1, 1863	Mar. 20, 1865	Do.
Jesse Arnhart	do	Nov. 1, 1863		Do.
Francis M. Bottler	Trumpeter	July 19, 1863	Mar. 20, 1865	Do.
Asbury Tyler	Blacksmith	Oct. 1, 1863	Mar. 8, 1864	Do.
William M. Morris	Saddler	July 1, 1864	June 7, 1865	Do.
			Muster.	
Black, James N	Private	Oct. 1, 1863	Nov. 23, 1863	Do.
Brison, George A	do	Dec. 5, 1863	Dec. 12, 1863	Do.
Brewer, Jackson D	do	Aug. 1, 1863	Nov. 23, 1863	Do.
Causby, Charles	do	Oct. 1, 1863	Nov. 23, 1863	Do.
Chastine, Abner H	do	Oct. 1, 1863	Nov. 23, 1863	Do.
Dougherty, Hugh	do	Aug. 19, 1863	Nov. 1, 1863	Do.
Edlin, Robert P	do	Aug. 1, 1863	Nov. 1, 1863	Do.
Foster, Robert I	do	Aug. 1, 1863	Nov. 1, 1863	Do.
Fassett, John C	do	Aug. 1, 1863	Nov. 1, 1863	Do.
Green, Gasawa	do	Aug. 1, 1863	Nov. 1, 1863	Do.
Gillingham, Clemons	do	Oct. 1, 1863	Dec. 12, 1863	Do.
Goddard, Francis M	do	Jan. 1, 1864	Jan. 28, 1864	Do.
Gregory, William	do	Oct. 1, 1863	Nov. 23, 1863	Do.
Gregory, George L	do	Oct. 1, 1863	Nov. 23, 1863	Do.
Gustin, Lafayette W	do	Aug. 20, 1863	Nov. 1, 1863	Do.
Holt, Alfred P	do	Sept. 25, 1863	Nov. 23, 1863	Do.
Herrald, Paschal G	do	Oct. 1, 1863	Nov. 23, 1863	Do.
Harris, Milton	do	Oct. 1, 1863	Nov. 23, 1863	Do.

REPORT OF THE ADJUTANT GENERAL OF ARKANSAS. 59

Name	Rank	Enlisted	Discharged	Remarks
Hill, William T	do	Jan. 1, 1864	Mar. 15, 1864	Do.
Holman, James M	do	Jan. 1, 1864	Mar. 15, 1864	Do.
Killgore, John F	do	Aug. 1, 1863	Nov. 1, 1863	Do.
Killgore, Albert K	do	Aug. 1, 1863	Nov. 1, 1863	Do.
Lynch, Abraham	do	Sept. 25, 1863	Nov. 23, 1863	Do.
McElhany, William	do	Aug. 27, 1863	Nov. 1, 1863	Do.
Mills, John	do	Sept. 1, 1863	Nov. 1, 1863	Do.
Mills, James M	do	Nov. 30, 1863	Dec. 12, 1863	Do.
Morris, John	do	Aug. 8, 1863	Nov. 1, 1863	Do.
Mhoon, Wilson R	do	Sept. 25, 1863	Nov. 25, 1863	Do.
Mosley, James	do	Jan. 15, 1864	Jan. 28, 1864	Do.
Murray, Richard	do	Aug. 13, 1863	Nov. 1, 1863	Do.
Murray, James F	do	Nov. 1, 1863	Nov. 23, 1863	Do.
O'Kelley, William H	do	Mar. 23, 1864	Apr. 9, 1864	Do.
O'Kelley, James S	do	Mar. 23, 1864	Apr. 9, 1864	Do.
Patty, Isaac I	do	Jan. 17, 1864	Feb. 22, 1864	Do.
Pattis, John	do	Sept. 25, 1863	Nov. 23, 1863	Do.
Roller, George S	do	Dec. 5, 1863	Dec. 12, 1863	Do.
Roller, Archibald	do	Dec. 5, 1863	Dec. 12, 1863	Do.
Robinson, John T	do	July 25, 1863	Nov. 1, 1863	Do.
Roberts, Louis	do	Oct. 1, 1863	Nov. 23, 1863	Do.
Rainwater, John	do	Jan. 15, 1864	Jan. 28, 1864	Do.
Rainwater, Abraham	do	Jan. 15, 1864	Jan. 28, 1864	Do.
Rush, William H	do	May 15, 1864	June 20, 1864	Do.
Stowbough, Andrew	do	Aug. 14, 1863	Nov. 1, 1863	Do.
Smith, Paschal W	do	Aug. 1, 1863	Nov. 1, 1863	Transferred to Invalid Corps; no discharge furnished on muster out of regiment.
Slemmons, James M	do	Mar. 4, 1864	Apr. 9, 1864	Mustered out with regiment.
Sons, Enoch	do	Oct. 1, 1863	Nov. 27, 1863	Sick in general hospital Memphis, Tennessee; no discharge furnished on muster out of regiment.
Tyler, Caleb	do	June 9, 1864	June 20, 1864	Mustered out with regiment.
Wright, Bartlett	do	Nov. 30, 1863	Dec. 12, 1863	Do.
Watts, Martin J	do	Oct. 1, 1863	Nov. 23, 1863	Do.

Discharged.

Name	Rank	Enlisted	Discharged	Remarks
Butler, William	Trumpeter	July 19, 1863	Nov. 1, 1863	Discharged at Memphis, Tennessee, May 28, 1865.
Brotherton, Benjamin H	Private	Oct. 1, 1863	Nov. 23, 1863	Discharged at Memphis, Tennessee, May 28, 1865.
Beall, James M	do	Dec. 2, 1863	Dec. 12, 1863	Discharged at Memphis, Tennessee, May 31, 1865.
Barnes, John W	do	Sept. 25, 1863	Nov. 23, 1863	Discharged at Memphis, Tennessee, April 28, 1865.
Carpenter, Green B	do	Aug. 23, 1863	Nov. 1, 1863	Discharged for disability, at Springfield, Missouri, January 25, 1865.
Hobbs, Francis M	do	Aug. 1, 1863	Nov. 1, 1863	Discharged to accept appointment as 2d lieutenant company F, September 9, 1864.
Killgore, John	do	Aug. 1, 1863	Nov. 1, 1863	Discharged for disability, at Springfield, Missouri, December 13, 1864.
Killgore, James O	do	Aug. 11, 1863	Nov. 1, 1863	Discharged at Memphis, Tennessee, May 17, 1865.
Long, Edward	do	Sept. 25, 1863	Nov. 23, 1863	Discharged for disability, at Springfield, Missouri, May 6, 1865.
Lynch, William	do	Mar. 23, 1864	April 9, 1864	Discharged at Memphis, Tennessee, May 15, 1865.
Rainey, George W	do	Nov. 1, 1863	Dec. 12, 1863	Discharged at Memphis, Tennessee, May 31, 1865.
Sons, James	do	Sept. 1, 1863	Nov. 1, 1863	Discharged for disability, at Cassville, Missouri, September 29, 1864.
Seitzler, Henry	do	Sept. 1, 1863	Nov. 1, 1863	Discharged at Memphis, Tennessee, April 28, 1865.
Wheeler, Richard A	do	Oct. 1, 1863	Nov. 22, 1863	Discharged at Memphis, Tennessee, April 28, 1865.

Transferred.

Name	Rank	Enlisted	Discharged	Remarks
Felkins, Thomas	Private	July 19, 1863	Nov. 1, 1863	Transferred to company D April 1, 1864.
Williams, Cicero	do	Sept. 1, 1863	Nov. 1, 1863	Transferred to company M May 1, 1864.

60   REPORT OF THE ADJUTANT GENERAL OF ARKANSAS.

Second regiment Arkansas cavalry volunteers.   Mustered into service March 18, 1864, (three years;) mustered out August 20, 1865.

COMPANY A—Continued.

Names.	Rank.	Enlistment.	Muster.	Remarks.
Killed.				
Bowyer, Cornelius	Private	Jan. 17, 1864	Feb. 22, 1864	Killed in action in Carroll county, Arkansas, April 15, 1864.
Carroll, Christopher C	do	July 1, 1864	July 23, 1864	Killed in action at Memphis, Tennessee, February 9, 1865.
Dardanelle, Edward P	do	Dec. 10, 1863	Dec. 12, 1863	Killed in action in Newton county, Arkansas, April 12, 1864.
Hill, James B	do	Jan. 17, 1864	Feb. 22, 1864	Killed in action in Carroll county, Arkansas, April 11, 1864.
Roller, Enoch	do	Sept. 5, 1863	Nov. 27, 1863	Killed in action at Berryville, Arkansas, January 11, 1864.
Wright, Benjamin	do	Aug. 13, 1863	Nov. 1, 1863	Killed in action in Carroll county, Arkansas, April 16, 1864.
Died.				
Gibson, James M	Private	Feb. 19, 1864	Mar. 15, 1864	Died at Cassville, Missouri, August 27, 1864.
Gray, Price	do	Nov. 22, 1863	Nov. 28, 1863	Died at Alton, Illinois, December 14, 1864.
Hall, William H	do	Jan. 17, 1864	April 9, 1864	Died at Berryville, Arkansas, June 18, 1864.
Pointer, James S	do	Mar. 1, 1864	Mar. 15, 1864	Died at Memphis, Tennessee, July 1, 1865.
Raper, Beston A	do	Aug. 1, 1863	Nov. 1, 1863	Died at Memphis, Tennessee, May 19, 1865.
Smith, George W	do	Jan. 25, 1864	Jan. 28, 1864	Died at Memphis, Tennessee, February 14, 1865.
Smeadley, William H	do	Dec. 9, 1863	Dec. 12, 1863	Died at Cape Girardeau, Missouri, January 25, 1865.
Vaughan, Eli F	do	Oct. 1, 1863	Nov. 23, 1863	Died at Memphis, Tennessee, February 25, 1865.
Deserted.				
Atterbury, Matthew F	Private	July 1, 1864	July 23, 1864	Deserted at Cape Girardeau, Missouri, January 12, 1865.
Duningham, Levi J	do	Aug. 1, 1863	Nov. 1, 1863	Deserted at Cape Girardeau, Missouri, January 12, 1865.
Gray, James R	do	Nov. 7, 1863	Mar. 15, 1864	Deserted at Springfield, Missouri, December 16, 1864.
Gray, William A	do	Nov. 1, 1863	Mar. 15, 1864	Deserted at Springfield, Missouri, February 15, 1865.
Hadley, James H	do	July 1, 1864	July 23, 1864	Deserted at Cape Girardeau, Missouri, January 12, 1865.
Jones, John H	do	Jan. 17, 1863	Feb. 22, 1864	Deserted at Perryville, Arkansas, June 16, 1864.
Jones, Gideon A	do	Jan. 17, 1864	Feb. 22, 1864	Deserted at Perryville, Arkansas, June 16, 1864.
Keyes, John W	do		Jan. 20, 1864	Deserted at Springfield, Missouri, December 13, 1864.
Myers, Anthony	do	July 18, 1863	Mar. 1, 1863	Deserted at Cape Girardeau, Missouri, January 12, 1865.
Kelly, Joseph M	do	Mar. 27, 1864	April 9, 1864	Deserted at Springfield, Missouri, December 13, 1864.
Parker, James D	do	Mar. 7, 1864	Mar. 15, 1864	Deserted at Springfield, Missouri, December 16, 1864.
Ramsey, Joseph	do	July 19, 1863	Nov. 1, 1863	Deserted at Burroughville, Arkansas, April 1, 1864.
Ramsey, James	do	July 19, 1863	Nov. 1, 1863	Deserted at Burroughville, Arkansas, April 1, 1864.
Ramsey, John	do	July 19, 1863	Nov. 1, 1863	Deserted at Burroughville, Arkansas, April 1, 1864.
Rose, Kindred	do	Sept. 1, 1863	Nov. 1, 1863	Deserted at Cassville, Missouri, December 8, 1863.
Steel, William F	do	Nov. 1, 1863	Nov. 23, 1863	Deserted at Springfield, Missouri, December 16, 1864.
Tubbs, Erastus M	do	Sept. 1, 1863	Nov. 1, 1863	Deserted at Springfield, Missouri, December 16, 1864.

REPORT OF THE ADJUTANT GENERAL OF ARKANSAS. 61

Name	Rank		Date of rank.	Muster.	Remarks
Archibald B. Freeborn	Captain		Sept. 10, 1862	Sept. 10, 1862	Appointed from civil life; promoted to major February 25, 1864.
Albert A. Irvin	....do....		—, 1862	Feb. 25, 1864	Appointed 2d lieutenant from civil life on organization of company; mustered out with regiment.
Harley S. Wait	1st lieutenant		July 16, 1862	Aug. 10, 1862	Mustered out at St. Louis, Missouri, on consolidation of companies A and B.
Andrew J. Garner	....do....		April 9, 1863	Feb. 25, 1864	Mustered out with regiment.
James Hester	2d lieutenant		Oct. 1, 1862	Oct. 30, 1862	Appointed 2d lieutenant February 25, 1864; killed in action at Richland, Arkansas.
Henry H. Rogers	....do....		Aug. 17, 1862	Sept. 6, 1864	Appointed from private, 7th Minnesota infantry; mustered out with regiment.
Henry M. Young	Sergeant		Aug. 10, 1862	June 3, 1863	Mustered out with regiment.
Edward Brandt	Corporal		June 26, 1863	June 29, 1863	Do.
Prince Mark	....do....		Dec. 12, 1862	June 2, 1863	Do.
Jeremiah Norris	Blacksmith		Aug. 1, 1863	Aug. 2, 1863	Do.
John H. J. Hall	Farrier		June 27, 1863	June 29, 1863	Do.
John B. Cooksey	Saddler		June 13, 1863	June 13, 1863	Do.
James W. Davis	Teamster		July 2, 1863	July 23, 1863	Do.
William W. Davis	....do....		July 6, 1863	July 6, 1863	Do.
Begnette, Henry C	Private		Sept. 1, 1863	Feb. 17, 1864	Do.
Cranch, David	....do....		Dec. 12, 1862	June 3, 1863	Do.
Cooksey, James	....do....		May 15, 1863	June 3, 1863	In confinement at Alton, Illinois, by sentence of G. C. M.; no discharge furnished on muster out of company.
Doss, Thomas	....do....		Nov. 1, 1863	Nov. 6, 1863	Mustered out with regiment.
Epley, Josephus	....do....		Feb. 1, 1864	Feb. 20, 1864	Do.
Ford, Nathaniel	....do....		Nov. 29, 1862	June 3, 1863	Do.
Fisher, John A	....do....		June 14, 1863	June 23, 1863	Do.
Garrett, Lyechsey	....do....		June 23, 1863	June 25, 1863	Do.
Gohen, Anthony	....do....		June 29, 1863	June 29, 1863	Do.
Herrod, Joseph	....do....		Feb. 1, 1864	Feb. 20, 1864	Do.
Hooper, James	....do....		July 2, 1863	Sept. 12, 1863	Do.
Johnston, Francis H	....do....		July 1, 1863	July 2, 1863	Do.
Jones, Thomas	....do....		Feb. 1, 1864	Feb. 20, 1864	Do.
Jones, Martin	....do....		Feb. 1, 1864	Feb. 20, 1864	Do.
Jennings, Falton	....do....		Feb. 1, 1864	Feb. 20, 1864	Sick in general hospital, Springfield, Missouri, since December 14, 1864; no discharge furnished on muster out of company.
Lofler, Bradford	....do....		Mar. 18, 1864	Mar. 31, 1864	Mustered out with regiment.
Matthews, Horatio C	....do....		Dec. 13, 1862	June 3, 1863	Do.
Mussey, James	....do....		July 18, 1863	July 18, 1863	On recruiting service for 46th Missouri infantry since August 2, 1864; no discharge furnished on muster out of company.
Muir, William	....do....		Sept. 4, 1863	Feb. 17, 1864	Mustered out with regiment.
Quigley, John	....do....		June 2, 1863	June 3, 1863	Do.
Rieff, Lemuel T	....do....		Dec. 9, 1862	June 3, 1863	Do.
Robertson, Decatur	....do....		Feb. 10, 1864	Feb. 29, 1864	Do.
Randall, Carroll W	....do....		July 24, 1863	July 27, 1863	Do.
Snow, Benjamin	....do....		July 11, 1863	Sept. 13, 1863	Do.
Sullens, Reilly	....do....		Feb. 1, 1864	Mar. 19, 1864	Do.
Taylor, William H	....do....		Dec. 12, 1862	June 3, 1863	Do.

Second regiment Arkansas cavalry volunteers. Mustered into service March 18, 1864, (three years;) mustered out August 20, 1865.

COMPANY B—Continued.

Names.	Rank.	Enlistment.	Muster.	Remarks.
Van Voorhies, John	Private	Aug. 25, 1862	Sept. 10, 1862	Mustered out with regiment.
Rector, Willis	Colored cook	Mar. 18, 1864	Aug. 30, 1864	Do.
Discharged.				
Austin, William	Corporal	Aug. 10, 1862	June 3, 1863	Discharged at Memphis, Tennessee, July 10, 1865.
Armitage, John	Sergeant	Aug. 20, 1862	June 3, 1863	Discharged at Memphis, Tennessee, June 26, 1865.
Barlow, Lester	Private	Aug. 10, 1862	June 3, 1863	Discharged for disability at Helena, Arkansas.
Burgin, Lemuel T	do	Aug. 10, 1862	June 3, 1863	Discharged at Memphis, Tennessee, June 26, 1865.
Blennings, Samuel C	do	Aug. 10, 1862	June 3, 1863	Do.
Blalock, Joshua	do	Aug. 10, 1862	June 3, 1863	Do.
Casey, Daniel	Corporal	Sept. 5, 1862	Oct. 30, 1862	Discharged for disability at Helena, Arkansas, May 10, 1863.
Coan, Squire B	Private	Sept. 3, 1862	June 3, 1863	Discharged at Memphis, Tennessee, June 26, 1865.
Cristman, Morton B	do	July 22, 1862	June 3, 1863	Do.
Cumming, Daniel	do	Aug. 3, 1862	June 3, 1863	Do.
Delk, Thomas	do	Aug. 29, 1862	June 3, 1863	Do.
Doss, Samuel	do	Nov. 29, 1862	June 3, 1863	Do.
Escuzar, Mitchell	do	Aug. 2, 1862	June 3, 1863	Discharged at Memphis, Tennessee, July 10, 1865.
Fevins, Martin	Corporal	June 2, 1862	June 3, 1863	Discharged at Memphis, Tennessee, June 26, 1865.
Fowler, Benjamin	Private	Sept. 1, 1862	June 3, 1863	Do.
Grutch, John	Corporal	Oct. 3, 1862	June 3, 1863	Do.
Graham, Samuel	Private	Aug. 3, 1862	Sept. 8, 1862	Discharged for disability at St. Louis, Missouri, July 15, 1863.
Green, Madison	do	Sept. 20, 1862	June 3, 1863	Discharged at Memphis, Tennessee, June 26, 1865.
Gratiot, Ambrose	do	Aug. 2, 1862	June 3, 1863	Discharged at Springfield, Missouri.
Humbles, James	do	Aug. 18, 1862	June 3, 1863	Discharged at Memphis, Tennessee, July 9, 1865.
Hendricks, James L	Sergeant	Aug. 10, 1862	June 3, 1863	Discharged at Memphis, Tennessee, July 20, 1865.
Hendricks, James J	Private	Aug. 16, 1862	June 3, 1863	Discharged at Memphis, Tennessee, June 26, 1865.
Kirby, William	do	Aug. 23, 1862	Sept. 10, 1862	Discharged for disability at Helena, Arkansas, October 23, 1862.
Kennon, Benjamin	do	Sept. 2, 1862	June 3, 1863	Discharged at Memphis, Tennessee, June 26, 1865.
Long, Simeon	do	Aug. 2, 1862	June 3, 1863	Do.
Lewis, Hiram	Corporal	Aug. 10, 1862	June 3, 1863	Discharged at Memphis, Tennessee, July 12, 1865.
Ledford, John	Sergeant	Aug. 27, 1862	June 3, 1863	Discharged at Memphis, Tennessee, July 19, 1865.
Morley, George	1st sergeant	July 7, 1862	June 3, 1863	Discharged to accept promotion October 30, 1863.
Mills, Charles W	Private	Sept. 2, 1862	June 3, 1863	Discharged at Memphis, Tennessee, June 26, 1865.
Matthews, Marshall D	do	Oct. 3, 1862	June 3, 1863	Discharged at Memphis, Tennessee, July 15, 1865.
Mauigun, John H	do	June 23, 1863	June 24, 1863	Discharged at Memphis, Tennessee, June 15, 1865.
Mentone, John	do	Aug. 6, 1863	Aug. 6, 1863	Discharged at Memphis, Tennessee, July 13, 1865.
Moore, John	do	Aug. 18, 1862	June 3, 1863	Sentenced to ten years' imprisonment at Jefferson City.
Prisock, James	do	Aug. 17, 1862	June 3, 1863	Discharged at Memphis, Tennessee, June 26, 1865.
Prisock, Samuel	do	Aug. 17, 1862	June 3, 1863	Do.
Purse, Melvin	do	July 2, 1862	June 3, 1863	Do.
Randall, John F	1st sergeant	July 27, 1862	June 3, 1863	Do.
Randolph, Madison	Private	Aug. 8, 1862	June 3, 1863	Discharged at Memphis, Mennessee, June 10, 1865.

REPORT OF THE ADJUTANT GENERAL OF ARKANSAS. 63

Restle, Leger	Sergeant	Aug. 3, 1862	June 3, 1863	Discharged at Memphis, Tennessee June 26, 1865.
Sykes, Frederick	do	Aug. 10, 1862	June 3, 1863	Do.
Sharp, John	do	Aug. 2, 1862	June 3, 1863	Discharged at Memphis, Tennessee July 10, 1865.
Slephy, Daniel	Private	Aug. 6, 1862	June 3, 1863	Discharged at Memphis, Tennessee, July 7, 1865.
St. Clair, Charles	do	Aug. 27, 1862	June 3, 1863	Discharged at Memphis, Tennessee, June 26, 1865.
Stenson, James	do	Sept. 17, 1862	June 3, 1863	Do.
Turner, Joseph	do	Aug. 22, 1862	Sept. 10, 1862	Discharged for disability at Helena, Arkansas, May —, 1863.
Walsh, Edward	Corporal	Sept. 12, 1862	June 3, 1863	Discharged at Memphis, Tennessee, June 26, 1865.
Willson, Joseph	Private	Aug. 10, 1862	June 3, 1863	Do.
Waggoner, Matthias	do	Aug. 18, 1862	June 3, 1863	Discharged for disability at Springfield, Missouri, February 9, 1864.
Transferred.				
Cooper, Jeddison J	Private	Sept. 5, 1862	June 3, 1863	Transferred to Veteran Reserve Corps July 2, 1864.
Husson, Francis	do	Sept. 16, 1862	June 3, 1863	Transferred to Veteran Reserve Corps August 12, 1863.
Kilburn, Edward H	do	Aug. 4, 1862	June 3, 1863	Appointed regimental veterinary surgeon September 21, 1864.
Murphy, James T	Corporal	Aug. 10, 1862	June 3, 1863	Appointed regimental quartermaster sergeant April 14, 1864.
Thorn, William C	Private	July 31, 1862	June 3, 1863	Transferred to company G May 4, 1864.
Died.				
Avrick, William	Private	Aug. 11, 1862	Sept. 10, 1862	Died at Helena, Arkansas, September 28, 1862.
Alfeing, Richard	do	Aug. 26, 1862	Sept. 20, 1862	Died at Helena, Arkansas, October 17, 1862.
Brown, John	do	Aug. 10, 1862	Sept. 10, 1862	Died at Helena, Arkansas, October 15, 1862.

COMPANY C.

			Date of rank.	
William F. Orr	Captain	April 23, 1861	April 11, 1864	First enrolment as private in Lyon guards, Missouri; second enrolment September 21, 1861, as private in company L, 10th Illinois cavalry volunteers; appointed 2d lieutenant company C, 2d Arkansas cavalry, February 8, 1864; mustered out with regiment.
Hugh R. Creighton	1st lieutenant	Aug. 21, 1861	April 11, 1864	First enrolment company A, 3d Illinois cavalry volunteers; discharged December 13, 1863; appointed 1st lieutenant company C from civil life; mustered out with regiment.
Robert B. Patton	2d lieutenant	Sept. 29, 1863	Sept. 20, 1864	Appointed from sergeant company I; mustered out with regiment.
Benjamin F. Russell	1st sergeant	Jan. 31, 1863	April 20, 1863	Mustered out with regiment.
George M. Ray	Company sergeant	Jan. 31, 1863	April 20, 1863	Do.
Green B. Hill	Quartermaster sergeant	May 14, 1863	June 29, 1863	Do.
William W. Ferguson	Sergeant	Jan. 1, 1863	April 2, 1863	Do.
Robert Strickland	do	Jan. 1, 1863	April 1, 1864	Appointed from private for gallant conduct at Piney Mountain, Arkansas; mustered out with regiment.
Jonathan Cunningham	do	July 5, 1863	July 9, 1863	Mustered out with regiment.
Philip M. Shipton	do	Sept. 10, 1863	April 11, 1864	Do.
Lindsay R. Lee	Corporal	Jan. 1, 1863	April 20, 1863	Wounded in action at Dardanelle, Arkansas, November 23, 1863; mustered out with regiment.
James F. Ferguson	do	Jan. 1, 1863	April 20, 1863	Mustered out with regiment.
Lyman E. Meeker	do	Nov. 19, 1862	April 20, 1863	Do

Second regiment Arkansas cavalry volunteers. Mustered into service March 18, 1864, (three years,) mustered out August 20, 1865.

COMPANY C—Continued.

Names.	Rank.	Enlistment.	Date of rank.	Remarks.
Warren G. Ball	Corporal	July 18, 1864	July 18, 1864	Mustered out with regiment.
James E. Shannon	do	May 16, 1863	June 29, 1863	Do.
John W. Priscott	do	Jan. 1, 1863	April 20, 1863	Do.
Henry C. Bone	do	April 20, 1863	June 29, 1863	Do.
Samuel Earnhardt	Blacksmith	Nov. 8, 1862	April 20, 1863	Do.
Wiley Lockamay	Farrier	Sept. 1, 1863	April 11, 1864	Do.
Robert C. J. Matlock	Trumpeter	April 4, 1863	April 20, 1863	Do.
Walter D. Weaver	do	Jan. 1, 1864	Feb. 26, 1864	Wounded in breast and head at Richland, Arkansas, May 3, 1864; mustered out with regiment.
			Muster.	
Allen, John M	Private	Nov. 15, 1862	April 20, 1863	Mustered out with regiment.
Anderson, James	do	May 8, 1863	June 29, 1863	Do.
Anderson, Daniel T	do	May 31, 1863	June 29, 1863	Do.
Burge, John	do	Jan. 1, 1863	April 20, 1863	Do.
Burge, Seth G	do	Oct. 27, 1863	April 20, 1863	Do.
Bishop, Gustavus	do	Feb. 1, 1864	Feb. 23, 1864	Wounded with loss of right eye at Piney Mountain, Arkansas, April 6, 1864; mustered out with regiment.
Bailes, John R	do	Jan. 1, 1864	Feb. 26, 1864	Wounded accidentally March 8, 1864; mustered out with regiment.
Bailey, John C	do	Nov. 24, 1862	April 20, 1863	Mustered out with regiment.
Bishop, William A	do	June 21, 1864	June 21, 1864	Do.
Bishop, Joseph A	do	June 21, 1864	June 21, 1864	Accidentally wounded in line of duty October 16, 1864; mustered out with regiment.
Bell, William W	do	June 18, 1864	June 18, 1864	Mustered out with regiment.
Barnwell, George W	do	June 5, 1863	Feb. 26, 1864	Do.
Carter, Charles	do	Jan. 1, 1864	Feb. 26, 1864	Do.
Carter, William	do	May 20, 1863	June 29, 1863	Do.
Cox, Ammon B	do	Sept. 10, 1863	April 11, 1864	Do.
Cravins, John H	do	Sept. 1, 1864	Feb. 24, 1865	Do.
Danby, William A	do	Oct. 21, 1863	Feb. 26, 1864	Do.
Danby, George W	do	Oct. 31, 1863	Feb. 26, 1864	Do.
Danby, Martin	do	Feb. 24, 1864	Feb. 26, 1864	Do.
Dean, Charles A	do	Jan. 27, 1863	April 20, 1863	Do.
Ford, Benjamin F	do	Nov. 23, 1862	April 20, 1863	Do.
Forrester, Robert C	do	Jan. 1, 1864	Aug. 25, 1864	Do.
Forrster, Eli T	do	Jan. 12, 1865	Feb. 24, 1865	Do.
Ferguson, John D	do	Jan. 1, 1863	April 20, 1863	Do.
Ferguson, Daniel	do	Nov. 23, 1862	April 20, 1863	Absent in arrest at Cape Girardeau, Missouri; no discharge furnished on muster out of regiment.
Floyd, Henry	do	Feb. 1, 1863	June 29, 1863	Mustered out with regiment.
Ferguson, George W	do	Feb. 1, 1864	Feb. 26, 1864	Do.
Hammond, Henry	do	Jan. 31, 1863	April 20, 1863	Do.
Kelley, John M	do	Nov. 17, 1862	April 20, 1863	Absent in arrest; sentenced to ten years' confinement in Missouri State prison; no discharge furnished on muster out of regiment.

REPORT OF THE ADJUTANT GENERAL OF ARKANSAS. 65

Name	Rank	Enlisted	Mustered	Remarks
Lemonds, John R			June 18, 1864	Mustered out with regiment.
Lawson, Francis M	do	July 5, 1864	July 5, 1864	Do.
Meeker, Asa M	do	Nov. 19, 1862	April 20, 1863	Do.
Mass, James M	do	Jan. 18, 1863	April 20, 1863	Do.
Moser, Henry	do	Jan. 31, 1863	April 20, 1863	Do.
Mattock, John R	do	Oct. 27, 1862	April 20, 1863	Do.
Mobley, John R	do	Jan. 31, 1863	April 20, 1863	Do.
Masters, Henry F	do	Jan. 31, 1863	April 20, 1863	Do.
May, McDonald	do	April 9, 1864	June 11, 1864	Do.
Moser, Elkanah	do	Jan. 1, 1864	Aug. 25, 1864	Do.
Moser, George W	do	Jan. 1, 1864	Feb. 26, 1864	Do.
Meeks, Richard	do	June 18, 1864	June 18, 1864	Do.
Palmer, James A	do	July 5, 1863	July 9, 1863	Do.
Primm, George W	do	Jan. 31, 1863	April 20, 1863	Do.
Purvis, Wilson A	do	Jan. 1, 1863	April 20, 1863	Do.
Panter, Lorenzo D	do	Jan. 31, 1863	April 20, 1863	Do.
Palsten, John M	do	July 16, 1864	July 18, 1864	Do.
Qualls, Robert	do	April 9, 1864	June 11, 1864	Do.
Robinson, Lewis	do	Jan. 15, 1864	Aug. 25, 1864	Do.
Ray, John T	do	Jan. 1, 1864	Aug. 25, 1864	Do.
Russel, Christopher C	do	Jan. 1, 1864	Aug. 25, 1864	Do.
Russell, Daniel J	do	Jan. 31, 1863	April 20, 1863	Do.
Ross, William H	do	Jan. 31, 1863	April 20, 1863	Do.
Stoner, John M	do	July 5, 1863	July 9, 1863	Wounded in action June 7, 1864, Swan creek, Mo.; mustered out with regiment.
Shipton, William H	do	April 29, 1863	June 29, 1863	Absent, sick in hospital at Mound city, Illinois; no discharge furnished on muster out of regiment.
Storey, William S	do	Oct. 19, 1863	April 20, 1863	Mustered out with regiment.
Spreaks, George W	do	Sept. 10, 1863	April 11, 1864	Do.
Wolf, Isaiah M	do	Sept. 12, 1863	April 11, 1864	Do.
Willingham, James	do	Feb. 1, 1864	Feb. 23, 1864	Do.
Watson, Benjamin L	do	Jan. 1, 1864	Aug. 25, 1864	Do.
Crump, Robert	Cook	Mar. 1, 1864	Aug. 25, 1864	Do.
Drayton, Grover E	do	Mar. 1, 1864	Aug. 25, 1864	Do.

Discharged.

Name	Rank	Enlisted	Mustered	Remarks
Britton, John	Private	June 21, 1863	April 20, 1864	Discharged by sentence of general court-martial June 6, 1864.
Baker, Jasper N	do	June 1, 1863	April 20, 1864	Discharged for disability March 3, 1865.
Balls, John R	do	June 1, 1863	April 20, 1864	Discharged May 2, 1865.
Danvy, Alfred	do	Sept. 11, 1862	June 29, 1863	Discharged June 30, 1865.
Gore, Thomas M	do	Aug. 20, 1862	June 29, 1863	Discharged June 30, 1865.
Horton, James M	do	Aug. 20, 1862	June 29, 1863	Do.
Horton, Thomas J	Saddler	Jan. 1, 1863	April 28, 1863	Do.
Harrell, William	Private	Sept. 20, 1862	April 11, 1864	Discharged June 16, 1865.
Harris, William	Corporal	Sept. 20, 1862	June 29, 1863	Discharged June 30, 1865.
Jacobs, William P	Private	Sept. 20, 1862	June 29, 1863	Do.
Miller, James W	Sergeant	Jan. 1, 1863	April 20, 1863	Discharged for disability June 4, 1864.
Meeker, Hiram R	Private	Jan. 1, 1863	April 20, 1863	Discharged for disability May 22, 1863.
Marshall, Charles W	do	Jan. 5, 1863	April 20, 1863	Discharged for disability December 24, 1864.
Phillips, Josiah	do	Jan. 5, 1863	July 9, 1863	Discharged May 4, 1865.
Scott, Henry	do	Nov. 16, 1862	April 20, 1863	Discharged June 10, 1865.
Steward, Thomas H	Sergeant			

Second regiment Arkansas cavalry volunteers. Mustered into service March 18, 1864, (three years;) mustered out August 20, 1865.

COMPANY C—Continued.

Names.	Rank.	Enlistment.	Muster.	Remarks.
Smith, Eldridge	Corporal	Jan. 1, 1863	April 20, 1863	Discharged for disability October 31, 1864, contracted in line of duty on Shelby's raid in 1863.
Wilson, Andy J	Private	Nov. 2, 1862	April 20, 1863	Discharged; accidentally wounded June 2, 1865.
Oliver, Theodore	Sergeant	April 24, 1863	June 29, 1863	Discharged to accept promotion March 8, 1864.
Died.				
Burkett, George E	Private	June 12, 1863	June 29, 1863	Died at Cassville, Missouri, February 24, 1864, of consumption, and exposure in line of duty.
Butler, Wilson	do	Sept. 20, 1862	Oct. 4, 1862	Died at Springfield, Missouri, October 6, 1862; accidentally shot.
Ballard, William R	do	Jan. 1, 1863	April 20, 1863	Died at Cassville, Missouri, November 9, 1863, of typhoid fever.
Bayless, William A	do	Oct. 2, 1863	Feb. 26, 1864	Died at Springfield, Missouri, December 9, 1864, of chronic diarrhoea.
Brock, Francis M	do	Mar. 24, 1863	April 20, 1863	Killed in action at Richland, Arkansas, May 3, 1864.
Chandrin, Henry	do	Jan. 1, 1863	April 20, 1863	Died at Memphis, Tennessee, of remittent fever, March 13, 1865.
Goodrich, Charles	do	Sept. 10, 1863	April 11, 1864	Killed in action at Richland, Arkansas, May 3, 1864.
Harly, George	do	Oct. 27, 1862	April 20, 1863	Died at Memphis, Tennessee, of disease of the lungs, June 10, 1865.
Jones, Jesse	do	Jan. 1, 1863	April 20, 1863	Died at Cassville, Missouri, of pneumonia, January 17, 1864.
Low, Hervey	do	Jan. 1, 1863	Never	Died at Ironton, Missouri, of lung fever, April 7, 1863.
Luster, William A	do	July 5, 1863	July 9, 1863	Killed by guerillas at Swan creek, Missouri, May 22, 1864.
Lemars, Samuel	do	July 18, 1864	July 18, 1864	Died at St. Louis, Missouri, of pneumonia, August 3, 1864.
Larramo, William J	do	June 13, 1864	Aug. 25, 1864	Died at Memphis, Tennessee, of chronic diarrhoea, April 7, 1865.
Moss, Joseph L	do	Jan. 18, 1863	April 20, 1863	Died at Springfield, Missouri, of pneumonia, October 6, 1863.
McAdams, Robert P	do	Mar. 14, 1863	June 29, 1863	Died at Berryville, Arkansas, of pneumonia, January 25, 1864.
Mattock, John W	Corporal	Oct. 27, 1862	April 20, 1863	Killed in action at Richland, Arkansas, May 3, 1864.
Miller, John E	Private	Sept. 12, 1863	April 11, 1864	Do.
Montgomery, James	do	July 5, 1864	July 5, 1864	Died at Springfield, Missouri, of pneumonia, October 2, 1864.
Neighbors, Elijah	do	Sept. 20, 1862	Oct. 4, 1862	Died at Helena, Arkansas, of pneumonia, May 23, 1863.
Partin, Dildatha	do	Sept. 21, 1862	Oct. 4, 1862	Died at Schofield, Barracks, Missouri, of pneumonia, May 23, 1863.
Partin, Joshua	do	Sept. 21, 1862	Oct. 4, 1862	Died at Helena, Arkansas, of measles, December 31, 1862.
Porterfield, Robert	do	Sept. 21, 1862	Oct. 4, 1862	Died at Helena, Arkansas, of typhoid fever, March 23, 1863.
Powell, William L	do	Jan. 1, 1863	April 20, 1863	Died at Cape Girardeau, Missouri, of typhoid fever, August 12, 1863.
Queen, Reuben	do	Sept. 21, 1862	Oct. 4, 1862	Died at Jefferson barracks, Missouri, of erysipelas, February 22, 1865.
Queen, James	do	Sept. 21, 1862	Oct. 4, 1862	Died at Helena, Arkansas, of typhoid fever, April 8, 1863.
Rives, John H	do	Oct. 21, 1862	Never	Died at Ironton, Missouri, of lung fever, March 17, 1863.
Russell, Thomas C	do	Jan. 31, 1863	April 20, 1863	Killed in action on King's river, Arkansas, January 10, 1864.
Reynolds, Allen S	do	Aug. 20, 1862	June 29, 1863	Died at Springfield, Missouri, of small pox, December 19, 1864.
Stennett, Felix J	do	Sept. 21, 1862	Oct. 4, 1862	Died at Schofield barracks, Missouri, of typhoid fever, May 23, 1863.
Sewell, James H	do	Oct. 21, 1862	April 20, 1863	Died at Springfield, Missouri, of typhoid fever, October 12, 1863.
Smith, Thomas H	do	April 9, 1863	April 20, 1863	Killed in action at Richland, Arkansas, May 3, 1864.
Deserted.				
Butler, Martin L	Private	Sept. 20, 1862	Oct. 4, 1862	Deserted at Cape Girardeau, Missouri, September 10, 1863.

REPORT OF THE ADJUTANT GENERAL OF ARKANSAS. 67

Name	Rank			Remarks
Duncan, William A	do	Jan. 1, 1863	April 20, 1863	Deserted at Cape Girardeau, Missouri, January 13, 1865.
Duncan, John W	do	April 1, 1864	April 11, 1864	Do. do.
Green, James M	do	July 18, 1864	July 18, 1864	Deserted at Evening Shade, Arkansas, December 31, 1864.
Hodges, Stephen J	do	June 12, 1863	Never.....	Deserted at Arcadia, Missouri, June 24, 1863.
Rood, Jesse	do	Mar. 1, 1863	April 20, 1863	Deserted at Cape Girardeau, Missouri, August 21, 1863.
Tuggle, Lawson O	do	July 18, 1863	April 20, 1863	Deserted at Cape Girardeau, Missouri, January 13, 1865.
Wollard, John R	do	July 5, 1863	July 9, 1863	Do.
Van Embough, Jacob	do	July 5, 1863	July 9, 1863	Deserted at Batesville, Arkansas, June 30, 1864.

Transferred.

Name	Rank			Remarks
Baker, Joseph N	Private	April 1, 1864	April 11, 1864	Transferred to company D, June 2, 1864.
Claxton, James A	do	Nov. 17, 1862	April 20, 1863	Appointed commissary sergeant, non-commissioned staff March 1, 1864.
Porterfield, James T	do	Sept. 21, 1862	Oct. 4, 1862	Transferred to 9th legion invalid corps, September 8, 1863.
Raney, Cyrus A	do	July 5, 1863	July 9, 1863	Appointed chief trumpeter, non-commissioned staff, March 1, 1864.

COMPANY D.

Name	Rank		Date of rank.	Remarks
John C. Bailey	Captain	Nov. —, 1861	Mar. 16, 1864	Appointed from private company E, 2d Kansas cavalry, to 2d lieutenant company G, 2d Arkansas cavalry; discharged for disability at Springfield, Missouri, December 1, 1864.
Roland Hawkins	1st lieutenant	Aug. 29, 1862	Oct. 31, 1863	Appointed from private company I, 2d Kansas cavalry; mustered out with regiment.
Lemuel R. Jones	2d lieutenant	Jan. 15, 1864	Mar. 16, 1864	Discharged at Springfield, Missouri, December 1, 1864.
Samuel Cecil	1st sergeant	July 19, 1863	Jan. 1, 1865	Mustered out with regiment.
George H. T. Dodson	Quartermaster sergeant	July 19, 1863	June 1, 1865	Do.
Samuel H. Spears	Commissary sergeant	Feb. 10, 1864	June 1, 1865	Do.
John W. Keeton	Sergeant	Oct. 6, 1863	June 1, 1865	Do.
John D. Nixon	do	Feb. 19, 1864	June 1, 1865	Do.
Simon Barker	do	July 19, 1863	Nov. 1, 1863	Do.
Francis M. Chafin	Corporal	July 20, 1863	Nov. 1, 1865	Do.
Samuel S. Reynolds	do	Oct. 6, 1863	June 1, 1865	Do.
Frederick E. Shaddock	do	Oct. 6, 1863	June 1, 1865	Do.
Harman P. Chafin	do	Aug. 6, 1864	June 1, 1865	Do.
Robert Riggs	do	Mar. 1, 1864	June 1, 1865	Do.
John H. Estes	do	Feb. 10, 1864	Feb. 19, 1864	Do.
William R. Chafin	Trumpeter			Do.

Name	Rank		Muster.	Remarks
Bramlette, William	Private	Feb. 10, 1864	Feb. 19, 1864	Do.
Braswell, John	do	July 19, 1863	Feb. 19, 1864	Do.
Coyle, Charles A	do	July 19, 1863	Nov. 1, 1863	Do.
Cooper, James C	do	July 19, 1863	Nov. 1, 1863	Do.
Criner, Joseph	do	Oct. 15, 1863	Feb. 1, 1864	Do.
Chism, William	do	July 19, 1863	Nov. 1, 1863	Do.
Cummins, Claibourne	do	July 20, 1863	Mar. 10, 1864	Do.

Second regiment Arkansas cavalry volunteers. Mustered into service March 18, 1864, (three years;) mustered out August 20, 1865.

COMPANY D—Continued.

Names.	Rank.	Enlistment.	Muster.	Remarks.
Dickey, Hamilton C	Private	May 4, 1864	June 11, 1864	Mustered out with regiment.
Dickey, James M	do	Feb. 10, 1864	Feb. 19, 1864	Do.
Davis, Richard	do	July 18, 1863	Nov. 1, 1863	Do.
Davis, Ambrose L	do	Feb. 10, 1864	Feb. 19, 1864	Do.
Eoff, George	do	May 4, 1864	June 11, 1864	Do.
Eddings, James	do	May 4, 1864	June 11, 1864	Do.
Ford, Joseph	do	May 1, 1864	June 11, 1864	Do.
Freeman, Squire	do	July 18, 1863	Nov. 1, 1863	Do.
Freeman, James	do	May 4, 1864	June 11, 1864	Do.
Fowler, Nelson	do	Feb. 10, 1864	Feb. 19, 1864	Do.
Greenhan, Geo. W	do	July 18, 1863	Nov. 1, 1863	Do.
Gasevie, William	do	Feb. 10, 1864	Feb. 19, 1864	Do.
Gillmore, Kelsey	do	Dec. 1, 1863	Feb. 1, 1864	Do.
Harris, William G	do	Oct. 15, 1863	Feb. 1, 1864	Do.
Harris, James C	do	Oct. 15, 1863	Feb. 1, 1864	Do.
Hall, William C	do	May 4, 1864	June 11, 1864	Do.
Hill, Joseph	do	Feb. 10, 1864	Feb. 19, 1864	Do.
Hill, William M	do	Oct. 6, 1863	Dec. 15, 1863	Do.
Humphrey, Francis M	do	Mar. 1, 1864	Mar. 2, 1864	Do.
Jones, Thomas R	do	July 20, 1863	Nov. 1, 1863	Do.
Jones, Benjamin	do	Oct. 15, 1863	Feb. 1, 1864	Do.
Jones, Enoch	do	Oct. 15, 1863	Feb. 1, 1864	Do.
Key, Elisha C	do	Feb. 10, 1864	Feb. 19, 1864	Do.
Key, George W	do	Feb. 10, 1864	Feb. 19, 1864	Do.
Keeton, Alfred J	do	Feb. 10, 1864	Feb. 19, 1864	Do.
Keeton, Martin L	do	Feb. 10, 1864	Feb. 19, 1864	Do.
McCutchen, Andrew J	do	July 20, 1863	Nov. 1, 1863	Do.
McCutchen, Alexander C	do	Feb. 10, 1864	Feb. 19, 1864	Do.
Martin, Nathaniel	do	July 20, 1863	Nov. 1, 1863	Do.
McDougall, Archibald	do	July 19, 1863	Nov. 1, 1863	Do.
Myers, Henry	do	Feb. 10, 1864	Feb. 19, 1864	Do.
Myers, David	do	Feb. 10, 1864	Feb. 19, 1864	Do.
Mines, Larkin H	do	July 20, 1863	Nov. 1, 1863	Do.
Madduck, John M	do	Oct. 6, 1863	Dec. 15, 1863	Do.
Nixon, James	do	May 4, 1864	June 11, 1864	Do.
Powers, John	do	Feb. 10, 1864	Feb. 19, 1864	Do.
Payne, John W	do	July 20, 1863	Nov. 1, 1863	Do.
Pate, John	do	July 10, 1864	Feb. 1, 1864	Do.
Penn, John H	do	Oct. 6, 1863	Dec. 15, 1863	Do.
Rickman, John R. B	do	Aug. 28, 1863	Nov. 1, 1863	Do.
Riddle, David V	do	Feb. 10, 1864	Feb. 19, 1864	Do.
Robbman, James M	do	Feb. 10, 1864	Feb. 19, 1864	Do.
Riggs, James	do	July 20, 1863	Nov. 1, 1863	Do.

REPORT OF THE ADJUTANT GENERAL OF ARKANSAS. 69

Reynolds, John D	do	July 20, 1863	Nov. 1, 1863	Do.
Salmon, James W	do	May 4, 1864	June 11, 1864	Do.
Spears, Pleasant H	do	July 19, 1863	Nov. 1, 1863	Do.
Smith, John	do	July 19, 1863	Nov. 1, 1863	Do.
Smith, Martin	do	July 19, 1863	Nov. 1, 1863	Do.
Smith, Alfred	do	Feb. 10, 1864	Feb. 19, 1864	Do.
Sexton, Daniel	do	Feb. 10, 1864	Feb. 19, 1864	Do.
Shules, William A	do	May 4, 1864	June 11, 1864	Do.
Shules, Lucius W	do	Oct. 6, 1863	Dec. 15, 1863	Do.
Shadducks, Leon	do	Oct. 6, 1863	Dec. 15, 1863	Do.
Skaggs, Solomon	do	Oct. 6, 1863	Dec. 15, 1863	Do.
Smith, William F	do	Oct. 6, 1863	Dec. 15, 1863	Do.
Taylor, George W	do	May 4, 1864	June 11, 1864	Do.
Williams, Wiley	do	Oct. 15, 1863	Feb. 1, 1864	Do.
Wheeler, Isham	do	Mar. 9, 1864	Mar. 10, 1864	Do.
Young, James H	do	May 4, 1864	June 11, 1864	Do.
Young, John C	do	July 19, 1863	Nov. 1, 1863	Do.
Yates, Alexander	do	July 19, 1863	Nov. 1, 1863	Do.
Yates, Arwin	do	July 19, 1863	Nov. 1, 1863	Do.
Discharged.				
Brimage, Ezekiel	Private	July 19, 1863	Nov. 1, 1863	Discharged at Memphis, Tennessee, May 28, 1865.
Baker, Joseph N	do	Apr. 1, 1864	Apr. 11, 1864	Discharged at Memphis, Tennessee, May 18, 1865.
Kelley, Eli M	do	July 19, 1863	Nov. 1, 1863	Discharged for disability at Springfield, Missouri, February 20, 1865.
Jones, Lemuel R	do	July 19, 1863	Nov. 1, 1863	Discharged, to accept promotion, at Springfield, Missouri, March 16, 1865.
Snow, William	Corporal	July 19, 1863	Nov. 1, 1863	Discharged at Memphis, Tennessee, January 7, 1865.
Transferred.				
Hooper, James	Private	July 20, 1863	Nov. 1, 1863	Transferred to company B, November 1, 1863.
Robertson, Decatur A	do	Feb. 1, 1864	Feb. 19, 1864	Transferred to company B, June 1, 1864.
Snow, Benjamin	do	July 19, 1863	Nov. 1, 1863	Transferred to company B, November 1, 1863.
Died.				
Downey, Martin H	Private	Feb. 10, 1864	Feb. 19, 1864	Died in general hospital at Springfield, Missouri, of typhoid malaria fever, November 18, 1864.
Dearing, Abner H	do	Apr. 20, 1864	June 11, 1864	Died in general hospital at Memphis, Tennessee, April 27, 1865.
Felkins, Thomas	do	July 19, 1863	Nov. 1, 1863	Died in general hospital at Springfield, Missouri, October 17, 1864.
Higgs, Francis M	do	Feb. 10, 1864	Feb. 19, 1864	Killed in action near Jasper, Arkansas, May 31, 1864.
Hullums, James L	do	Oct. 1, 1863	Dec. 15, 1863	Died at Cassville, Missouri, January 15, 1864.
Howard, John W	do	July 19, 1863	Nov. 1, 1863	Killed in action near Jasper, Arkansas, May, 31, 1864.
Lyles, Absalom	Corporal	July 20, 1863	Nov. 1, 1863	Died in general hospital at Memphis, Tennessee, February 8, 1865.
Lane, Andrew E	Private	Feb. 10, 1864	Feb. 19, 1864	Died in general hospital at Memphis, Tennessee, August 2, 1865.
Miller, Jacob	Trumpeter	July 20, 1863	Nov. 1, 1863	Died in general hospital at Memphis, Tennessee, March 20, 1865.
Mancs, William	Private	Oct. 22, 1863	Feb. 29, 1864	Killed in action near Jasper, Arkansas, April 28, 1864.
McLenn, Robert O	do	July 20, 1863	Nov. 1, 1863	Died in general hospital at Cassville, Missouri, November 1, 1863.
Riddle, James A	do	Feb. 10, 1864	Feb. 19, 1864	Died in general hospital at Springfield, Missouri, March 13, 1864.
Wright, Benjamin	do	Feb. 10, 1864	Feb. 19, 1864	Died in general hospital at Springfield, Missouri, May 2, 1864.

70   REPORT OF THE ADJUTANT GENERAL OF ARKANSAS.

Second regiment Arkansas cavalry volunteers.   Mustered into service March 18, 1864, (three years;) mustered out August 20, 1865.

COMPANY D—Continued.

Names.	Rank.	Enlistment.	Muster.	Remarks.
Deserted.				
Boyred, Shirley	Private	July 19, 1863	Nov. 1, 1863	Deserted at ——, ——, ——.
Curnihan, Green S	do	Feb. 10, 1864	Feb. 19, 1864	Deserted at Forsyth, Missouri, June 14, 1864.
Crutchfield, Marion D	Blacksmith	Feb. 10, 1864	Feb. 19, 1864	Deserted at Springfield, Missouri, December 14, 1864.
Eoff, Robert M	Private	Feb. 10, 1864	Feb. 19, 1864	Deserted at Forsyth, Missouri, June 14, 1864.
Hampton, James	do	July 20, 1863	Nov. 1, 1863	Deserted at Ozark, Missouri, August 3, 1864.
Johnson, John J	do	Feb. 10, 1864	Feb. 19, 1864	Deserted at Forsyth, Missouri, June 14, 1864.
Johnson, Daniel	do	Oct. 1, 1863	Dec. 15, 1863	Deserted in Carroll county, Arkansas, January 24, 1864.
Kincaid, Preston	do	Oct. 15, 1863	Feb. 1, 1864	Deserted at Springfield, Missouri, December, 14, 1864.
Moore, Isaac	do	Feb. 10, 1864	Feb. 19, 1864	Deserted at Forsyth, Missouri, June 14, 1864.
Moon, Edward	do	Feb. 10, 1864	Feb. 19, 1864	Deserted at Springfield, Missouri, December 14, 1864.
Stewart, Henry	do	Oct. 6, 1863	Dec. 15, 1863	Deserted at Springfield, Missouri, October 8, 1864.
Tenney, Edward	do	July 19, 1863	Nov. 1, 1863	Deserted at Ozark, Missouri, August 3, 1864.
Thompson, William H	do	Feb. 10, 1864	Feb. 19, 1864	Deserted at Ozark, Missouri, August 4, 1864.
Voss, William J	do	Oct. 6, 1863	Dec. 15, 1863	Deserted in Stone county, Missouri, July 22, 1864.

COMPANY E.

Names.	Rank.	Enlistment.	Date of rank.	Remarks.
Jesse Millsaps	Captain	Dec. 21, 1863	Dec. 21, 1863	Appointed from civil life; discharged at Springfield, Missouri, December 6, 1864.
Henry C. Bell	do	Dec. 3, 1861	Mar. 1, 1865	Appointed from private 2d Kansas cavalry to 1st lieutenant company 1 2d Arkansas cavalry. Mustered out with regiment.
Joseph Brown	1st lieutenant	Dec. 21, 1863	Dec. 21, 1863	Appointed from civil life; discharged at Cassville, Missouri, September 27, 1864.
Henry C. Kelly	do	——, 1861	Oct. 17, 1863	Appointed from private company E 2d Kansas cavalry; died near Bellefonte, Arkansas, of wounds received in action, March 25, 1864.
Sanford H. Sweet	2d lieutenant	July 12, 1863	June 21, 1864	Appointed from private company —; mustered out with regiment.
Gasham A. McElroy	1st sergeant	July 12, 1863	July 1, 1865	Mustered out with regiment
Thomas E. Beverage	Quartermaster sergeant	July 12, 1863	Sept. 14, 1863	Do.
William E. Sutter	Commissary sergeant	July 12, 1863	July 1, 1865	Do.
Thomas Millsaps	Sergeant	July 12, 1863	Sept. 14, 1863	Do.
John F. Treadwell	do	Sept. 15, 1863	July 1, 1865	Do.
Nathan A. Sanders	do	July 12, 1863	Sept. 14, 1863	Do.
Henry Reed	do	July 12, 1863	July 1, 1865	Do.
Levi J. Hodges	Corporal	Sept. 15, 1863	Oct. 29, 1863	Do.
James A. Williams	do	July 12, 1863	July 1, 1865	Do.
James M. Colton	do	Oct. 12, 1863	July 1, 1865	Do.
James B. Church	do	July 12, 1863	July 1, 1865	Do.

REPORT OF THE ADJUTANT GENERAL OF ARKANSAS. 71

Name	Rank		Muster	
Martin L. Watts	do		Oct. 27, 1863	July 1, 1865	Do.
James P. McMinn	do		July 12, 1863	July 1, 1865	Do.
John W. Brown	Blacksmith		July 12, 1863	Sept. 14, 1863	Do.
Logan Millsaps	Saddler		July 12, 1863	Sept. 14, 1863	Do.
Aday, John W.	Private		July 12, 1863	Sept. 14, 1863	Do.
Brook, Osney	do		Aug. 1, 1863	Sept. 14, 1863	Do.
Baker, John E.	do		Sept. 1, 1863	Oct. 29, 1863	Do.
Baker, Caleb C.	do		Aug. 20, 1863	Sept. 14, 1863	Do.
Baker, Andrew	do		Sept. 1, 1863	Oct. 29, 1863	Do.
Baker, Willis	do		July 14, 1863	Sept. 14, 1863	Do.
Crouch, Solomon	do		July 12, 1863	Oct. 29, 1863	Do.
Campbell, William C.	do		July 12, 1863	Oct. 29, 1863	Do.
Colton, George T.	do		July 12, 1863	Oct. 29, 1863	Do.
Cypert, William P.	do		July 14, 1863	Sept. 14, 1863	Do.
Gwinn, Peyton	do		Sept. 14, 1863	Sept. 14, 1863	Do.
Gwinn, Samuel	do		July 14, 1863	Sept. 14, 1863	Do.
Haslip, Melvin	do		July 12, 1863	Oct. 29, 1863	Do.
Hargrove, Eldridge P.	do		Sept. 14, 1863	Sept. 14, 1863	Do.
Helms, John W.	do		July 12, 1863	Oct. 29, 1863	Do.
Horner, Anos H.	do		Sept. 15, 1863	Oct. 29, 1863	Do.
James, Redin W.	do		July 12, 1863	Oct. 29, 1863	Do.
McBride, James F.	do		June 4, 1864	July 2, 1864	Do.
McBlmurry, George	do		July 12, 1863	Sept. 14, 1863	Do.
Needsome, Levander	do		July 12, 1863	Oct. 29, 1863	Do.
Pitts, Lorenzo D	do		April 20, 1864	April 20, 1864	Do.
Reaves, James	do		Aug. 1, 1863	Sept. 14, 1863	Do.
Runyon, Abraham	do		July 14, 1863	Sept. 14, 1863	Do.
Runyon, George W.	do		May 8, 1864	July 2, 1864	Do.
Smalley, Josiah	do		Sept. 10, 1864	Nov. 19, 1864	Do.
Shoemake, James	do		July 14, 1863	Sept. 14, 1863	Do.
Shoemake, Thomas	do		July 12, 1863	Sept. 14, 1863	Do.
Seaton, Nicholas	do		May 15, 1864	July 2, 1864	Do.
Stroud, Jesse	do		July 12, 1863	Oct. 29, 1863	Do.
Siler, James N	do		July 12, 1863	Oct. 29, 1863	Do.
Sykes, Russell G.	do		July 12, 1863	Oct. 29, 1863	Do.
Sykes, William P.	do		July 12, 1863	Sept. 14, 1863	Do.
Thompson, William	do		July 12, 1863	Sept. 14, 1863	Do.
Treace, John	do		July 12, 1863	Sept. 14, 1863	Do.
Tripp, William	do		July 12, 1863	Sept. 14, 1863	Do.
Vaughan, James W	do		Aug. 1, 1863	Sept. 14, 1863	Do.
Woolridge, Lewis	do		July 12, 1863	Oct. 29, 1863	Do.
Watts, William A.	do		July 12, 1863	Oct. 29, 1863	Do.
Warner, Gideon	do		July 12, 1863	Oct. 29, 1863	Do.
Wallen, Jackson J.	do		Mar. 1, 1864	July 28, 1864	Do.

Second regiment Arkansas cavalry volunteers. Mustered into service March 18, 1864, (three years;) mustered out August 20, 1865.

COMPANY E—Continued.

Names.	Rank.	Enlistment.	Muster.	Remarks.
Transferred.				
Arnhart, Jesse	Private	Nov. 1, 1863	Nov. 23, 1863	Transferred to company A January 1, 1864.
Chastain, Amos H	do	Oct. 1, 1863	Nov. 23, 1863	Do.
Sous, Enoch	do	Oct. 1, 1863	Nov. 23, 1863	Do.
Tiner, John	Saddler	July 12, 1863	Oct. 29, 1863	Appointed saddler sergeant non-commissioned staff May 1, 1864.
Watts, Josiah	Private	Oct. 1, 1863	Nov. 23, 1863	Transferred to company A January 1, 1864.
Watts, Martin L	do	Oct. 1, 1863	Nov. 23, 1863	Do.
Discharged.				
William C. Thorn	1st sergeant	July 30, 1862	Aug. 9, 1862	Discharged at La Grange, Tennessee, June 21, 1865.
James B. Wamack	Sergeant	July 12, 1863	Sept. 14, 1863	Discharged at Memphis, Tennessee, May 28, 1865.
John R. Wallen	do	Aug. 12, 1863	Oct. 29, 1863	do.
Edward Stapleton	Trumpeter	Aug. 1, 1863	Sept. 14, 1863	Do.
Aday, Edmund	Private	July 17, 1863	Sept. 14, 1863	Discharged for disability at Memphis, Tennessee, April 22, 1865.
Curry, Benjamin F	do	Sept. 15, 1863	Oct. 29, 1863	Discharged at Springfield, Missouri, May 27, 1865.
Carter, Isaac	do	July 12, 1863	Oct. 29, 1863	Discharged for disability at Cassville, Missouri, August 20, 1864.
Cypert, William T	do	July 12, 1863	Oct. 29, 1863	Discharged at Memphis, Tennessee, May 28, 1865.
Easley, Edward F	do	July 14, 1863	Oct. 29, 1863	Do.
Eakins, Joseph	do	July 12, 1863	Sept. 14, 1863	Discharged for disability at Cassville, Missouri, August 20, 1864.
Green, David S	do	July 12, 1863	Oct. 29, 1863	Discharged at Memphis, Tennessee, May 28, 1865.
Hassell, Jordan	do	July 12, 1863	Sept. 14, 1863	Do.
Reed, Matthew W	do	July 12, 1863	Sept. 14, 1863	Do.
Seaton, John W	do	July 12, 1863	Sept. 14, 1863	do.
Shockley, Richard	do	July 14, 1863	Oct. 29, 1863	Discharged for disability at Cassville, Missouri, July 4, 1864.
Died.				
Francis M. Aday	Sergeant	July 12, 1863	Oct. 29, 1863	Died at Cassville, Missouri, January 5, 1864.
John Humphries	do	July 12, 1863	Sept. 14, 1863	Killed in action on King's river, Arkansas, April 16, 1864.
Arter, Nathan J	Private	July 12, 1863	Sept. 14, 1863	Died at Memphis, Tennessee, April 6, 1865.
Baker, Eldridge	do	Sept. 13, 1863	Oct. 29, 1863	Killed in action on King's river, Arkansas, April 16, 1864.
Currey, William H	do	July 14, 1863	Sept. 14, 1863	Died at Memphis, Tennessee, April 11, 1863.
Church, Larkin	do	July 12, 1863	Sept. 14, 1863	Died in Pope county, Arkansas, of wounds received in action, March 21, 1865.
Earley, Martin V	do	Oct. 25, 1863	Oct. 29, 1863	Died at Berryville, Arkansas, January 30, 1864.
Eakins, Joseph B	do	July 12, 1863	Sept. 14, 1863	Died at Cassville, Missouri, August 3, 1864.
Eakins, William A	do	July 12, 1863	Sept. 14, 1863	Died at Cape Girardeau, Missouri, January 14, 1865.
Hargrove, John	do	July 12, 1863	Oct. 29, 1863	Do.
Hawkins, Green T	do	April 23, 1864	July 2, 1864	Died at La Grange, Tennessee, July 29, 1865.
Kenyan, Holden W	do	May 18, 1864	July 2, 1864	Died near Powhattan, Arkansas, in the field, December 14, 1864.

REPORT OF THE ADJUTANT GENERAL OF ARKANSAS. 73

Queens, Theodore J	do	Oct. 27, 1863	Oct. 29, 1863	Killed in action on King's river, Arkansas, April 16, 1864.
Weeks, Gamblin	do	July 12, 1863	Sept. 14, 1863	Died at Cassville, Missouri, August 12, 1864.

Deserted.

Henderson, Henry	Private	July 12, 1863	Sept. 14, 1863	Deserted at Cassville, Missouri, October 14, 1864.

COMPANY F.

			Date of rank.	
James L. Powell	Captain	June 11, 1862	Nov. 23, 1863	Appointed from private company A, 1st Arkansas cavalry, to fill original vacancy; resigned May 18, 1865.
John A. Edwards	1st lieutenant		Jan. 31, 1864	Discharged May 25, 1864, on tender of resignation.
Whitefield C. Lefors	do	, 1863	Sept. 19, 1864	Appointed from sergeant same company; mustered out with regiment.
Francis M. Hobbs	2d lieutenant	Aug. 1, 1863	Sept. 9, 1864	Appointed from private company A; mustered out with regiment.
John N. Bingham	do		Jan. 31, 1864	Discharged August 20, 1864, on tender of resignation.
Andrew B. Anderson	1st sergeant	Aug. 10, 1863	Sept. 14, 1863	Mustered out with regiment.
Jesse Littrell	Quartermaster sergeant	Mar. 7, 1864	Mar. 15, 1864	Do.
Alexander A. Duckworth	Commissary sergeant	July 18, 1863	Sept. 14, 1863	Do.
Jennis H. Farrar	Sergeant	July 12, 1863	Sept. 14, 1863	Do.
James H. Gist	do	July 12, 1863	Sept. 14, 1863	Do.
John Sullivan	do	July 28, 1863	Sept. 14, 1863	Do.
Matthew Soater	do	Oct. 1, 1863	Nov. 19, 1863	Do.
John Adcock	Corporal	Oct. 1, 1863	Nov. 19, 1863	Do.
Enoch Meek	do	July 12, 1863	Sept. 14, 1863	Do.
Ambrose M. Ryan	do	Oct. 1, 1863	Nov. 19, 1863	Do.
John Hogan	do	Oct. 1, 1863	Nov. 19, 1863	Do.
Lemon C. Wright	do	Oct. 1, 1863	Nov. 19, 1863	Do.
Richard J. Maxwell	do	Dec. 7, 1863	Dec. 25, 1863	Do.
John R. Blevins	do	July 12, 1863	Sept. 14, 1863	Sick in hospital at Memphis, Tennessee, since March 24, 1865; no discharge furnished on muster out of regiment.
Jacob Meek	do	July 12, 1863	Sept. 14, 1863	Mustered out with regiment.
James Tallerson	Blacksmith	Oct. 1, 1863	Nov. 19, 1863	Do.
James Douthit	do	Oct. 1, 1863	Nov. 19, 1863	Do.
Nicholas Nail	Saddler	Dec. 10, 1863	Jan. 14, 1864	Do.
			Muster.	
Auvenshine, Elias	Private	July 12, 1863	Sept. 14, 1863	Do.
Anderson, Christopher C	do	July 18, 1863	Sept. 14, 1863	Do.
Aday, William	do	Oct. 1, 1863	Nov. 19, 1863	Do.
Ausborne, Jonathan	do	July 12, 1863	Sept. 14, 1863	Do.
Brown, William	do	Oct. 1, 1863	Nov. 19, 1863	Do.
Bell, Enoch	do	Oct. 1, 1863	Nov. 19, 1863	Do.
Blair, Constantine	do	Oct. 1, 1863	Nov. 19, 1863	Do.
Blevins, William	do	Oct. 18, 1863	Nov. 19, 1863	Do.
Blevins, Jesse	do	July 12, 1863	Sept. 14, 1863	Do.
Bridges, Allen W	do	July 18, 1863	Sept. 14, 1863	Do.
Barris, Henry A	do	Nov. 20, 1863	Nov. 20, 1863	Do.

Second regiment Arkansas cavalry volunteers. Mustered into service March 18, 1864, (three years;) mustered out August 20, 1865.

COMPANY F—Continued.

Names.	Rank.	Enlistment.	Muster.	Remarks.
Cleburne, John F. G.	Private	Aug. 14, 1863	Sept. 14, 1863	Mustered out with regiment.
Cannon, William L.	do	Mar. 1, 1864	June 28, 1864	Do.
Conan, Silas	do	Mar. 1, 1864	June 28, 1864	Do.
Dowthit, Woodey	do	Oct. 1, 1863	Nov. 19, 1863	Do.
Davis, James S.	do	Aug. 14, 1863	Sept. 14, 1863	Do.
Duckworth, Jonathan	do	July 29, 1863	Sept. 14, 1863	Do.
Davenport, John	do	Jan. 10, 1864	Feb. 1, 1864	Do.
Dickerson, Wiley	do	Mar. 7, 1864	Mar. 15, 1864	Do.
Dickerson, Britton	do	Mar. 7, 1864	Mar. 15, 1864	Do.
Dickerson, Nathaniel	do	Mar. 7, 1864	Mar. 15, 1864	Do.
Dickerson, Robert	do	Mar. 7, 1864	Mar. 15, 1864	Do.
Farrar, John H.	do	July 12, 1863	Sept. 14, 1863	Do.
Farrar, Nicholas G.	do	July 12, 1863	Sept. 14, 1863	Do.
Goodal, Robert	do	Mar. 1, 1864	June 28, 1864	Do.
Garrett, Thomas	do	Nov. 20, 1863	Nov. 20, 1863	Do.
Holcomb, Henderson	do	Oct. 1, 1863	Nov. 19, 1863	Do.
Hogan, Francis P.	do	Oct. 1, 1863	Nov. 19, 1863	Do.
Horn, Jacob	do	Aug. 8, 1863	Sept. 14, 1863	Sick at Springfield, Missouri, since December 14, 1864; no discharge furnished on muster out of regiment.
Herd, William	do	Oct. 1, 1863	Nov. 19, 1863	Mustered out with regiment.
Howard, Asaph	do	Mar. 7, 1864	Mar. 15, 1864	Do.
Jeffrey, John	do	July 12, 1863	Sept. 14, 1863	Do.
Lynch, John	do	Oct. 1, 1863	Nov. 19, 1863	Do.
Morgan, De Kalb	do	Oct. 1, 1863	Nov. 19, 1863	Do.
Morrison, James A.	do	Aug. 22, 1863	Sept. 14, 1863	Do.
Meek, John	do	July 12, 1863	Sept. 14, 1863	Do.
Matthews, James	do	Dec. 10, 1863	Jan. 4, 1864	Do.
McCullough, Robert	do	Aug. 12, 1863	Sept. 14, 1863	Do.
Mason, Joseph	do	Dec. 25, 1863	Jan. 4, 1864	Do.
Phillips, Preston	do	Oct. 1, 1863	Nov. 19, 1863	Do.
Rhea, Claiborne	do	Oct. 1, 1863	Nov. 19, 1863	Do.
Ross, John	do	Sept. 14, 1863	Sept. 14, 1863	Do.
Rutledge, William	do	Mar. 7, 1864	Mar. 15, 1864	Do.
Sisk, Abner	do	July 12, 1863	Sept. 14, 1863	Do.
Standridge, Richard	do	May 1, 1864	June 28, 1864	Do.
Teney, George	do	July 12, 1863	Sept. 14, 1863	On furlough; sick at Little Rock since April 23, 1865; no discharge furnished on muster out of regiment.
Wimpy, Thomas J.	do	July 18, 1863	Sept. 14, 1863	Mustered out with regiment.
Woodsome, James H.	do	Oct. 1, 1863	Nov. 19, 1863	Do.
Ward, Edward	do	Oct. 1, 1863	Nov. 19, 1863	Do.
Wilson, James	do	Dec. 10, 1863	Jan. 4, 1864	Do.
Wilson, John	do	Mar. 7, 1864	Mar. 15, 1864	Do.

REPORT OF THE ADJUTANT GENERAL OF ARKANSAS.

Name	Rank		Date	Remarks
Wilson, Lewis	do		Mar. 7, 1864	Do.
Wright, Allen	do		Oct. 1, 1863	Do.
Willard, Samuel	do		Mar. 1, 1864	Do.

Discharged.

Name	Rank		Date	Remarks
Dickerson, George A	Private	Mar. 7, 1864	Mar. 15, 1864	Discharged for disability at Springfield, Missouri, May 27, 1865.
Ellis, Alexander A	do	Dec. 25, 1863	Feb. 1, 1864	Discharged at Memphis, Tennessee, May 28, 1865.
Jettand, Robert	do	Dec. 1, 1864		Do.
Kessinger, Miles H	do	July 12, 1863	Sept. 14, 1863	Discharged for disability at Cassville, Missouri, August 20, 1864.
Kesterson, Darius P	do	July 29, 1863	Sept. 14, 1863	Discharged for disability at Cassville, Missouri, November 9, 1864.
Lenningham, Calvin	do	Oct. 18, 1863	Nov. 21, 1863	Discharged at Memphis, Tennessee, May 28, 1865.
Morris, William	do	Oct. 1, 1863	Nov. 19, 1863	Do.
Stapleton, Edward	do	Aug. 9, 1863	Sept. 14, 1863	Discharged for disability at Cassville, Missouri, November 1, 1864.
Tugus, Emanuel	do	Sept. 14, 1863	Sept. 14, 1863	Discharged at Memphis, Tennessee, June 5, 1865.
Miller, John	Trumpeter	July 24, 1863	Sept. 14, 1863	Discharged at Memphis, Tennessee, May 28, 1865.

Transferred.

Name	Rank		Date	Remarks
Black, Eli J	Private	Oct. 1, 1863	Nov. 19, 1863	Transferred to company A January 1, 1864.
Cansby, Charles	do	Oct. 1, 1863	Nov. 19, 1863	Do.
Graham, John	do	Oct. 1, 1863	Nov. 19, 1863	Do.
Gray, William A	do	Mar. 7, 1864	Mar. 15, 1864	Transferred to company A May 1, 1864.
Gray, James B	do	Mar. 7, 1864	Mar. 15, 1864	Do.
Goodman, James	do	Mar. 7, 1864	Mar. 15, 1864	Transferred to company G May 1, 1864.
Gregory, William	do	Oct. 1, 1863	Nov. 19, 1863	Transferred to company A January 1, 1864.
Harris, William	do	Oct. 1, 1863	Nov. 19, 1863	Do.
Lynch, William	do	Mar. 7, 1864	Mar. 15, 1864	Do.
Parker, James	do	Oct. 1, 1863	Nov. 19, 1863	Transferred to company A May 1, 1864.
Roberts, Lewis	do	Aug. 10, 1863	Sept. 14, 1863	Transferred to company A January 1, 1864.
Runnion, Abraham	do	Oct. 1, 1863	Nov. 19, 1863	Transferred to coupany E May 1, 1864.
Tyler, Asbury	do	Oct. 1, 1863	Nov. 19, 1863	Transferred to company A January 1, 1864.
Wheeler, James N	do	Oct. 1, 1863	Sept. 14, 1863	Do.
White, Charles	do			Appointed hospital steward, non-commissioned staff, May 1, 1864.

Died.

Name	Rank		Date	Remarks
Thomas C. Pollard	Corporal	Dec. 25, 1863	Feb. 1, 1864	Killed in action at Boonville, Missouri, October 11, 1864.
Thomas E. Smith	do	Oct. 1, 1863	Nov. 19, 1863	Died at Springfield, Missouri, May 29, 1864.
Gallant, William	Private	Oct. 1, 1863	Nov. 19, 1863	Died at Cassville, Missouri, January 17, 1864.
Gallant, Joab	do	Oct. 1, 1863	Nov. 19, 1863	Killed in action at Buffalo creek, Arkansas, May 3, 1864.
Hodges, William	do	Mar. 1, 1864		Died at Springfield, Missouri, November 18, 1864.
Harrold, Robert	do	Oct. 1, 1863	Nov. 19, 1863	Died at Cape Girardeau, Missouri, January 18, 1865.
Hogan, Lamartine	do	July 12, 1863	Sept. 14, 1863	Died at Springfield, Missouri, October 2, 1863.
Holcomb, Newton	do	Oct. 1, 1863	Nov. 19, 1863	Died at Memphis, Tennessee, March 9, 1865.
Laney, Ephraim	do	Aug. 14, 1863	Sept. 14, 1863	Died at Fayetteville, Arkansas, January 22, 1864.
Meek, Simeon	do	July 12, 1863	Sept. 14, 1863	Killed in action in Carroll county, Arkansas, April 5, 1864.
Murray, John	do	Nov. 20, 1863	Nov. 20, 1863	Killed in action on Richland creek, Arkansas, April 5, 1864.
Nooner, William	do	Oct. 1, 1863	Nov. 19, 1863	Died at Cassville, Missouri, January 12, 1864.
Rounceville, James	do	Oct. 1, 1863	Nov. 19, 1863	Killed in action on Richland creek, Arkansas, May 3, 1864.
Tygart, John	do	July 18, 1863	Sept. 14, 1863	Killed in action on Richland creek, Arkansas, May 3, 1864.
Williams, Spencer	do	Oct. 1, 1863	Nov. 19, 1863	Died at Cussville, Missouri, December 16, 1863.

Second regiment Arkansas cavalry volunteers. Mustered into service March 18, 1864, (three years;) mustered out August 20, 1865.

COMPANY F—Continued.

Names.	Rank.	Enlistment.	Muster.	Remarks.
White, William E.	Private	Oct. 1, 1863	Nov. 19, 1863	Killed in action in Carroll county, Arkansas, April 5, 1864.
Williamson, David	do	July 30, 1863	Sept. 14, 1863	Killed in action on Richland creek, Arkansas, May 3, 1864.
Wilbanks, Joshua	do	July 20, 1863	Sept. 14, 1863	Killed at Memphis, Tennessee, by an unknown hand, April 12, 1865.

Deserted.

Douthit, Richard P.	Private	Oct. 1, 1863	Nov. 19, 1863	Deserted from furlough in Yell county, Arkansas, May 17, 1864.
Dickerson, Joseph	do	Mar. 7, 1864	Mar. 15, 1864	Deserted at Berryville, Arkansas, April 1, 1864; afterwards killed by U. S. troops.
Faulkner, George A.	do	Mar. 7, 1864	Mar. 15, 1864	Deserted at Berryville, Arkansas, April 1, 1864.
Nail, Charles	do	Dec. 10, 1863	Jan. 4, 1864	Deserted at Cassville, Missouri, January 15, 1864; killed in Benton county, Arkansas, April, 1865.
Smith, Henry	do	Mar. 7, 1864	Mar. 15, 1864	Killed at Berryville, Arkansas, April 1, 1864.

COMPANY G.

Names.	Rank.	Enlistment.	Date of rank.	Remarks.
Martin E. O'Brien	Captain	June 3, 1862	Oct. 5, 1863	Appointed to fill original vacancy from 1st sergeant company C, 1st Arkansas cavalry; mustered out with regiment.
Rufus K. Milam	1st lieutenant	Sept. 9, 1863	Nov. 1, 1863	Dismissed.
John S. Chastain	2d lieutenant	Sept. 7, 1863	April 9, 1864	Appointed from 1st sergeant same company; resigned.
John C. Bailey	1st sergeant	Nov. —, 1861	Oct. 23, 1863	Discharged to accept promotion as captain of company D.
James F. Milam	1st sergeant	Sept. 20, 1863	Oct. 9, 1863	Mustered out with regiment.
John W. Smith	Quartermaster sergeant	Sept. 21, 1863	Oct. 9, 1863	Do.
Elisha B. Meadors	Commissary sergeant	Sept. 19, 1863	Oct. 9, 1863	Do.
Rowlin W. Moore	Sergeant	Sept. 21, 1863	Oct. 9, 1863	Do.
William Daily	do	Sept. 19, 1863	Oct. 9, 1863	Do.
Andrew H. Bannister	do	Sept. 17, 1863	Oct. 9, 1863	Do.
John C. Rogers	Corporal	Sept. 7, 1863	Oct. 9, 1863	Do.
Elisha B. Meadors	do	Sept. 19, 1863	Oct. 9, 1863	Do.
James C. C. Rogers	do	Nov. 3, 1863	Dec. 3, 1863	Do.
William Bell	do	July 5, 1864	July 18, 1864	Do.
Samuel Case	do	Sept. 22, 1863	Oct. 9, 1863	Do.
Mark Hatley	Bugler	Sept. 19, 1863	Oct. 9, 1863	Do.
William C. Sliger	Blacksmith	Sept. 20, 1863	Oct. 9, 1863	Do.
Pleasant Cheek	Farrier	Sept. 21, 1863	Oct. 9, 1863	Do.
			Muster.	
Arnold, Henry C.	Private	Sept. 7, 1863	Oct. 9, 1863	Do.

Name	Rank	Date	Date	Remarks
Biagg, James	do	Sept. 16, 1863	Oct. 9, 1863	Do.
Blevins, Squire	do	Sept. 10, 1863	Oct. 9, 1863	Do.
Bridges, Green B	do	Sept. 13, 1863	Oct. 9, 1863	Do.
Beckwith, Farris B	do	Sept. 1, 1864	Jan. 28, 1864	Do.
Brown, James B	do	Jan. 11, 1864	Jan. 28, 1864	Do.
Blackwell, Richard	do	Jan. 11, 1864	Jan. 28, 1864	Do.
Coyle, David	do	Sept. 7, 1863	Oct. 9, 1863	Do.
Chastain, Madison M. C.	do	Sept. 7, 1863	Oct. 3, 1863	Do.
Chastain, Joseph C	do	Sept. 7, 1863	Dec. 9, 1863	Do.
Cornelius, Garrett	do	Sept. 1, 1863	Oct. 9, 1863	Do.
Caruth, Jesse	do	Sept. 19, 1863	Oct. 9, 1863	Do.
Cotton, John C	do	Sept. 17, 1863	Oct. 9, 1863	Do.
Clary, John S.	do	Sept. 7, 1863	Oct. 9, 1863	Do.
Corey, Joel C	do	July 18, 1864	Sept. 15, 1863	Do.
Curry, Josephus	do	July 18, 1864	Dec. 8, 1864	Do.
Easley, John	do	Sept. 7, 1863	Oct. 9, 1863	Do.
Fillegan, Michael	do	Sept. 6, 1863	Oct. 9, 1863	Do.
Felters, James	do	Sept. 9, 1863	Oct. 9, 1863	Do.
Frazier, William B	do	Sept. 18, 1863	Oct. 9, 1863	Do.
Gunter, John L	do	Sept. 19, 1863	Oct. 9, 1863	Do.
Garrett, Robert	do	Sept. 21, 1863	Oct. 9, 1863	Do.
Greene, Isaac N	do	Dec. 24, 1863	Mar. 15, 1864	Do.
Goodman, James	do	Sept. 1, 1863	Oct. 9, 1863	Do.
Howard, Samuel	do	Sept. 10, 1863	Oct. 9, 1863	Do.
Holland, Thomas H	do	Sept. 18, 1863	Oct. 9, 1863	Do.
Hudson, Benjamin F	do	Sept. 8, 1863	Dec. 14, 1863	Do.
Jones, Jesse R	do	Nov. 23, 1864	Dec. 8, 1864	Do.
Meadors, William B	do	Sept. 14, 1863	Oct. 9, 1863	Do.
Moore, Francis M	do	Sept. 17, 1863	Oct. 9, 1863	Do.
Moore, McLewis	do	Sept. 14, 1863	Oct. 9, 1863	Do.
Niedeffer, John	do	Sept. 11, 1863	Oct. 9, 1863	Do.
Odin, Andrew J.	do	Sept. 20, 1863	Oct. 9, 1863	Do.
Overbay, Thomas	do	Sept. 17, 1863	Oct. 9, 1863	Do.
Overbay, Shed	do	Sept. 11, 1863	Oct. 9, 1863	Do.
Perkins, Joseph	do	Sept. 12, 1863	Oct. 9, 1863	Do.
Parker, Cheslie	do	Sept. 7, 1863	Oct. 9, 1863	Do.
Pate, Wesley W	do	Nov. 4, 1863	Dec. 9, 1863	Do.
Rogers, Greene N	do	Sept. 8, 1863	Dec. 3, 1863	Do.
Stephens, Gideon G	do	Sept. 19, 1863	Dec. 14, 1863	Do.
Smoot, John	do	Sept. 9, 1863	Oct. 9, 1863	Do.
Sherridan, Madison	do	Mar. 25, 1864	Oct. 9, 1863	Do.
Trammel, Harrison	do	Sept. 22, 1863	April 8, 1864	Do.
Turner, George A	do	Aug. 22, 1864	Oct. 9, 1863	Do.
Wilburne, Lemuel	do		Sept. 15, 1864	Do.
White, William	do			Do.
Discharged.				
Phillips, James P	Private	Sept. 10, 1863	Oct. 9, 1863	Discharged to accept promotion.
Bishop, Joshua	do	Sept. 8, 1863	Oct. 9, 1863	Discharged for disability February 15, 1865; wounded severely May 5, 1864, in the lungs.
Muntooth, John	do	Sept. 13, 1863	Oct. 9, 1863	Discharged for disability April 10, 1865.

Second regiment Arkansas cavalry volunteers. Mustered into service March 18, 1864, (three years ;) mustered out August 20, 1865.

Names.	Rank.	Enlistment.	Muster.	Remarks.
Bannister, William H	Private	Sept. 9, 1863	Oct. 9, 1863	Mustered out May 17, 1865.
Maness, John W	do	April 1, 1864	April 8, 1864	Discharged for disability July 7, 1865.
Transferred.				
Beaver, Samuel J	Private	July 22, 1863	Oct. 9, 1863	Transferred to company M March 4, 1864.
Parkes, John C	do	Sept. 8, 1863	Oct. 9, 1863	Transferred to company H March 4, 1864.
Moore, George W	do	Sept. 18, 1863	Oct. 9, 1863	Transferred to company M March 4, 1864.
Sage, Eli	do	Sept. 10, 1863	Oct. 9, 1863	Transferred to company H March 4, 1864.
Stanfield, James E	do	Sept. 1, 1863	Oct. 9, 1863	Transferred to company M March 4, 1864.
Stanfield, Samuel P	do	Sept. 1, 1863	Oct. 9, 1863	Do.
Southerland, William H	do	Aug. 26, 1863	Oct. 9, 1863	Do.
Died.				
Martin L. Moore	Sergeant	Sept. 19, 1863	Oct. 9, 1863	Died in general hospital at Springfield, Missouri, November 4, 1864.
John Felters	Corporal	Sept. 6, 1863	Oct. 9, 1863	Died of wounds received while on duty with guard October 29, 1863.
James L. Alford	Bugler	Sept. 19, 1863	Oct. 9, 1863	Died in general hospital at Memphis, Tennessee, April 30, 1865.
Blevins, Robert	Private	Sept. 14, 1863	Oct. 9, 1863	Died in general hospital at Springfield, Missouri, October 13, 1863.
Meadors, Gideon	do	Sept. 19, 1863	Oct. 9, 1863	Killed by rebels in Crawford county, Arkansas, November 12, 1863.
Moore, James	do	Sept. 7, 1863	Dec. 3, 1863	Died in post hospital at Cassville, Missouri, January 12, 1864.
Campbell, Levi C	do	July 23, 1863	Oct. 9, 1863	Died of wounds received in action January 21, 1864.
Laine, John W	do	Oct. 5, 1863	Oct. 9, 1863	Killed in action at Buffalo Creek, Arkansas, May 1, 1864.
Locklear, Stephen G	do	Sept. 7, 1863	Oct. 9, 1863	Killed in action at Richland, Arkansas, May 3, 1864.
Meadors, Joseph B	do	Nov. 4, 1863	Dec. 28, 1864	Do.
McDonald, John B	do	Jan. 22, 1864	Jan. 3, 1863	Do.
Sherman, Henry	do	Nov. 4, 1863	Dec. 3, 1863	Do.
Sherman, William J	do	Sept. 19, 1863	Oct. 9, 1863	Killed in action at Buffalo Creek, Arkansas, May 1, 1864.
Cagle, Leonard	do	Sept. 7, 1863	Oct. 9, 1863	do.
Ward, William	do	Sept. 22, 1863	Oct. 9, 1863	Died in general hospital at Fort Smith, Arkansas, February 10, 1865.
Mantooth, Jasper	do	Sept. 9, 1863	Oct. 9, 1863	Died in general hospital at Springfield, Missouri, January 20, 1865.
Maness, George F	do	Mar. 25, 1864	Mar. 31, 1864	Died in general hospital at Memphis, Tennessee, March 5, 1865.
				Died in general hospital at Memphis, Tennessee, April 3, 1865.
Deserted.				
Henry Hess	Sergeant	Sept. 20, 1863	Oct. 9, 1863	Deserted at La Grange, Tennessee, July 6, 1865.
John P. Nolan	Corporal	Sept. 11, 1863	Oct. 9, 1863	Do.
Peters, Elbert	Private	Nov. 16, 1863	Dec. 3, 1863	Deserted at Cassville, Missouri, March 10, 1864.
Norwick, Crocket	do	Mar. 18, 1864	Mar. 31, 1863	Deserted at Forsyth, Missouri, June 1, 1864.
Garrett, Thomas	do	Sept. 12, 1863	Oct. 9, 1863	Deserted at White River, Missouri, July 25, 1864.
Jones, Clemons C	do	Jan. 20, 1864	Jan. 28, 1864	do.
McCertney, George W	do	Sept. 11, 1863	Oct. 9, 1863	Deserted at White River, Missouri, July 10, 1864.
Haggard, Solomon J	do	July 20, 1864	Sept. 15, 1864	Deserted at Cassville, Missouri, October 10, 1864.
Morrison, Joel	do	July 30, 1864	Sept. 15, 1864	do.
Allen, John	do	Sept. 18, 1863	Oct. 9, 1863	Deserted at Springfield, Missouri, December 3, 1864.

REPORT OF THE ADJUTANT GENERAL OF ARKANSAS. 79

Name	Rank	Date	
Irvin, Rigdon J	do	Sept. 20, 1863	Oct. 9, 1863	Deserted at Springfield, Missouri, December 14, 1864.
Davis, Robert R	do	Sept. 7, 1863	Oct. 9, 1863	Deserted at La Grange, Tennessee, July 6, 1865.
Ward, Jerry	do	Sept. 12, 1863	Oct. 9, 1863	Do. do.
Trammel, Wharton	do	Sept. 8, 1863	Oct. 9, 1863	Deserted at La Grange, Tennessee, July 8, 1865.
Cantrell, John C	do	Sept. 18, 1863	Oct. 9, 1863	Do. do.
Ferguson, John W	do	Sept. 7, 1863	Oct. 9, 1863	Do. do.
Meadows, Jacob W	do	Nov. 4, 1863	Dec. 3, 1863	Do.

COMPANY H.

Name	Rank		Date of rank.	
Jeremiah Hackett	Captain	Dec. 25, 1863	Dec. 25, 1863	Appointed from civil life to fill original vacancy; discharged to accept promotion as major.
Orrin S. Fahnestock	do	Nov. 18, 1861	April 4, 1864	Appointed from sergeant 3d Kansas battery to 2d lieutenant January 30, 1864; mustered out with regiment.
James B. Stephens	1st lieutenant	Sept. 22, 1863	Oct. 7, 1863	Discharged ———.
William H. Bell	2d lieutenant	Aug. 13, 1863	Oct. 7, 1863	Appointed from 1st sergeant; discharged ———.
George S. Statham	1st sergeant	Sept. 9, 1863	Oct. 7, 1863	Mustered out with regiment.
James W. McKinney	Company Q. M. sergeant	Sept. 12, 1863	Oct. 7, 1863	Do.
Robert J. Hill	Sergeant	Sept. 17, 1863	Oct. 7, 1863	Do.
John McGregor	do	Oct. 1, 1863	Dec. 13, 1863	Do.
Berry B. Putnam	do	Sept. 16, 1863	June 1, 1865	Do.
William H. Blackman	do	Sept. 12, 1863	Oct. 7, 1863	Do.
James E. McBride	Corporal	Sept. 26, 1863	Oct. 7, 1863	Do.
Henry Ross	do	Sept. 9, 1863	Oct. 7, 1863	Do.
John B. Tucker	do	Dec. 3, 1863	Jan. 28, 1864	Do.
William H. Wilkins	do	Oct. 1, 1863	Dec. 15, 1863	Do.
Benjamin T. Henley	do	Sept. 9, 1863	June 1, 1865	Do.
Blomfield L. Durham	do	Sept. 6, 1863	June 1, 1865	Do.
William T. Box	do	Sept. 9, 1863	Oct. 7, 1863	Do.
Armstead T. Patterson	Farrier	Oct. 10, 1863	April 2, 1864	Do.
John W. McDavis	Saddler	Sept. 23, 1863	Oct. 7, 1863	Do.
Solomon Barnes	Bugler	Oct. 1, 1863	Dec. 15, 1863	Do.
William R. McKinney	do			Do.
Randolph Patterson			Muster.	
Alexander, Phillimon	Private	Sept. 6, 1863	Jan. 28, 1864	Do.
Adams, Allen	do	Sept. 17, 1864	Feb. 24, 1865	Do.
Barnes, Lewis	do	Sept. 13, 1863	Oct. 7, 1863	Do.
Barnes, Leonard	do	Sept. 9, 1863	Oct. 7, 1863	Do.
Barnes, James B	do	Oct. 1, 1863	Dec. 15, 1863	Do.
Barnes, Robert	do	Nov. 19, 1863	Dec. 22, 1863	Do.
Barnes, Robert B	do	Nov. 17, 1863	Jan. 28, 1864	Do.
Barnett, Hiram	do	Sept. 6, 1863	Dec. 15, 1863	Sick in general hospital, Springfield, Missouri, since December 14, 1864; no discharge furnished on muster out of company.

REPORT OF THE ADJUTANT GENERAL OF ARKANSAS.

Second regiment Arkansas cavalry volunteers. Mustered into service March 18, 1864, (three years;) mustered out August 20, 1865.

COMPANY H—Continued.

Names.	Rank.	Enlistment.	Muster.	Remarks.
Blackman, James K	Private	Oct. 1, 1863	Dec. 15, 1863	Mustered out with regiment.
Bridges, James M	do	Sept. 18, 1863	Oct. 7, 1863	Do.
Briggs, Archibald	do	Sept. 6, 1863	Oct. 7, 1863	Do.
Brownfield, Jasper P	do	Jan. 25, 1865	Feb. 2, 1865	Do.
Barrett, John A	do	Sept. 8, 1863	Oct. 7, 1863	Do.
Birch, Wesley	do	Dec. 4, 1863	Dec. 22, 1863	Do.
Chaplin, Alnous	do	Sept. 18, 1863	Oct. 7, 1863	Do.
Cleburne, Benjamin B	do	Oct. 1, 1863	Dec. 15, 1863	Wounded in the head at the battle of the Osage, October 25, 1864.
Coleman, Stephen T	do	Sept. 17, 1863	Oct. 7, 1863	Mustered out with regiment.
Courvay, Joseph	do	Sept. 9, 1863	Oct. 7, 1863	Do.
Corlew, Alphonso	do	Dec. 4, 1863	Dec. 22, 1863	Absent on furlough; sick, and supposed to be unable to travel. No discharge furnished on muster out of company.
Caruth, David	do	Sept. 6, 1863	Oct. 7, 1863	Mustered out with regiment.
Drake, John O	do	Sept. 8, 1863	Oct. 7, 1863	Do.
Duncan, Charles C	do	Sept. 17, 1863	Oct. 7, 1863	Do.
Elwood, William L	do	Nov. 17, 1863	Jan. 28, 1864	Do.
Evans, Winfield S	do	Sept. 17, 1863	Oct. 7, 1863	Do.
Eubanks, Yerby W	do	Nov. 2, 1863	Dec. 22, 1863	Do.
Good, Benjamin H	do	Sept. 23, 1863	Oct. 7, 1863	Do.
Haynes, William H	do	Sept. 12, 1863	Oct. 7, 1863	Do.
Hardwick, James L	do	Sept. 10, 1863	Oct. 7, 1863	Do.
Hughes, George P	do	Sept. 6, 1863	Dec. 15, 1863	Do.
Hulsey, Thomas	do	Oct. 1, 1863	Dec. 15, 1863	Do.
Henley, William	do	Dec. 7, 1863	Dec. 22, 1863	Do.
Johnson, Henry	do	Sept. 1, 1864	Sept. 4, 1864	Do.
Kepper, Thomas	do	Sept. 17, 1863	Oct. 7, 1863	Do.
Keller, John	do	Sept. 16, 1863	Oct. 7, 1863	Do.
McGlothlin, Warren M	do	Sept. 16, 1863	Oct. 7, 1863	Do.
McGlothlin, James W	do	Jan. 26, 1863	Feb. 2, 1865	Do.
Morrison, John	do	Sept. 6, 1863	April 2, 1864	Do.
Martin, William H	do	Oct. 1, 1863	Dec. 15, 1863	Do.
Mathis, Jesse B	do	Sept. 1, 1863	Oct. 7, 1863	Do.
Parker, William E	do	Dec. 5, 1863	Dec. 22, 1863	Do.
Person, John R	do	Sept. 7, 1863	Oct. 7, 1863	Do.
Rowe, William F	do	Sept. 27, 1863	Oct. 7, 1863	Do.
Sanderson, Frank	do			Sentenced to one year's imprisonment, and to forfeit $10 per month during confinement. No discharge furnished on muster out.
Sorrels, Joseph	do	Oct. 1, 1863	Dec. 15, 1863	Mustered out with regiment.
Smith, James W	do	Sept. 18, 1863	Oct. 7, 1863	Do.
Snodgrass, James M	do	Jan. 26, 1863	Feb. 2, 1865	Absent in confinement at St. Louis, Missouri, since January 26, 1865. No discharge furnished on muster out of company.
Tucker, William A	do	Jan. 26, 1863	Dec. 15, 1863	Mustered out with regiment.
Weaver, Andrew J	do	Oct. 1, 1863	Oct. 7, 1863	Do.

REPORT OF THE ADJUTANT GENERAL OF ARKANSAS. 81

Name	Rank	Enlisted	Mustered in	Remarks
Weaver, Crawford	do	Sept. 17, 1863	Oct. 7, 1863	Do.
Weatherford, Alexander L	do	Sept. 23, 1863	Oct. 7, 1863	Do.
Wibbing, Henry F	do	Sept. 7, 1863	Oct. 7, 1863	Do.
Wren, James B	do	Sept. 13, 1863	Oct. 7, 1863	Do.
Younger, Joshua	do	Sept. 10, 1863	Oct. 7, 1863	Do.
Discharged.				
William C. Brower	Sergeant	Sept. 9, 1863	Oct. 7, 1863	Discharged at Memphis, Tennessee, May 26, 1865.
Lucius L. Joyner	do	Sept. 7, 1863	Oct. 7, 1863	Discharged for disability, at Springfield, Missouri, December 13, 1864.
James A. Mickle	do	Sept. 6, 1863	Dec. 15, 1863	Discharged July 24, 1865.
Adams, Isaac	Private	Oct. 1, 1863	Dec. 15, 1863	Discharged at Memphis, Tennessee, May 28, 1865.
Barnes, Martin	do	Sept. 9, 1863	Oct. 7, 1863	Discharged at Memphis, Tennessee, May 18, 1865.
Bloodworth, Timothy W	do	Sept. 13, 1863	Oct. 7, 1863	Discharged for disability, at Springfield, Missouri, September 31, 1864.
Bloodworth, James M	do	Sept. 11, 1863	Oct. 7, 1863	Discharged at Memphis, Tennessee, May 31, 1865.
Hodges, William L	do	Sept. 7, 1863	Oct. 7, 1863	Discharged for disability, at Springfield, Missouri, December 13, 1864.
Sage, Eli	do	Sept. 7, 1863	Oct. 7, 1863	Discharged at Memphis, Tennessee, May 28, 1865.
Sambeth, Leonard	do	Sept. 10, 1863	Oct. 7, 1863	Discharged at Memphis, Tennessee, May 28, 1865.
Sarsols, William M	do	Sept. 1, 1863	Sept. 4, 1864	Discharged at Memphis, Tennessee, May 25, 1865.
Wolf, Josiah	do	Nov. 29, 1863	Dec. 22, 1863	Discharged for disability, at Springfield, Missouri, January 12, 1864.
Transferred.				
Joseph C. McClure	Sergeant	Sept. 10, 1863	Oct. 7, 1863	Transferred to non-commissioned staff as sergeant major July 26, 1864.
Blevins, William R	Private	Dec. 5, 1863	Dec. 15, 1863	Transferred to company F March 16, 1864.
Maxfield, Richard J	do	Dec. 5, 1863	Dec. 15, 1863	Do.
Died.				
John L. Haynes	Sergeant	Sept. 12, 1863	Oct. 7, 1863	Died at Cassville, Missouri, of disease, April 1, 1864.
Thomas J. Rasberry	Corporal	Sept. 20, 1863	Oct. 7, 1863	Died at Memphis, Tennessee, April 17, 1865.
Barnes, Morgan B	Private	Sept. 13, 1863	Oct. 7, 1863	Killed accidentally at Fort Smith, Arkansas, June 25, 1864.
Brewer, George W	do	Oct. 1, 1863	Dec. 15, 1863	Died at St. Louis, Missouri, January 30, 1865.
Ellis, Alexander L	do	Sept. 23, 1863	Oct. 7, 1863	Died at Fort Smith, Arkansas, November 26, 1863.
Fry, Andrew J	do	Sept. 6, 1863	Oct. 7, 1863	Died at Springfield, Missouri, February 21, 1865.
McGehee, Eli	do	Sept. 7, 1863	Oct. 7, 1863	Died at Springfield, Missouri, October 28, 1864.
Parris, Alfred	do	Oct. 1, 1863	Dec. 15, 1863	Died at Springfield, Missouri, August 25, 1864.
Perry, Joseph W	do	Sept. 6, 1863	Oct. 7, 1863	Died at Cassville, Missouri, October 24, 1863.
Deserted.				
Jackson Wilkinson	Corporal	Sept. 10, 1863	Oct. 7, 1863	Deserted, from furlough, August 26, 1864.
John T. Keffer	Saddler	Sept. 8, 1863	Oct. 7, 1863	Deserted at Springfield, Missouri, December 14, 1864.
Adams, Daniel	Private	Nov. 3, 1863	Dec. 22, 1863	Deserted at Cassville, Missouri, March 5, 1864.
Anderson, Jesse	do	Sept. 2, 1863	Oct. 7, 1863	Deserted at Springfield, Missouri, December 14, 1864.
Baykin, Samuel G	do	Sept. 7, 1863	Oct. 7, 1863	Do.
Barnett, Elijah	do	Sept. 6, 1863	Dec. 15, 1863	Do.
Jones, Wiley	do	Nov. 29, 1863	Dec. 22, 1863	Do.
Jones, John	do	Oct. 1, 1863	Dec. 22, 1863	Deserted at Lagrange, Tennessee, July 11, 1865.
Rupe, Joseph B	do	Sept. 18, 1863	Oct. 7, 1863	Deserted at Lagrange, Tennessee, May 16, 1865.

Mis. Doc. 53——6

82 REPORT OF THE ADJUTANT GENERAL OF ARKANSAS.

Second regiment Arkansas cavalry volunteers. Mustered into service March 18, 1864, (three years;) mustered out August 20, 1865.

COMPANY I.

Names.	Rank.	Enlistment.	Date of rank.	Remarks.
James Duff	Captain	Dec. 9, 1861	Dec. 3, 1863	Appointed from sergeant company C, 2d Kansas cavalry volunteers, to fill original vacancy; mustered out with regiment.
Henry C. Bell	1st lieutenant		Dec. 3, 1863	Appointed from private company C, 2d Kansas cavalry, to fill original vacancy; promoted captain company C, March 6, 1865; mustered out with regiment.
William G. Graves	2d lieutenant			Discharged ——— ———, ———.
John Williams	1st sergeant	Sept. 25, 1863	Dec. 3, 1863	Mustered out with regiment.
Samuel S. French	Company commissary serg't	Sept. 16, 1863	Dec. 3, 1863	Do.
Robert R. Harris	Sergeant	Sept. 16, 1863	Dec. 3, 1863	Do.
George McElroy	do	Oct. 27, 1863	Dec. 3, 1863	Do.
Robert T. Baines	do	Oct. 31, 1863	Dec. 3, 1863	Do.
John D. McClury	do	Oct. 1, 1863	Dec. 3, 1863	Do.
John Conoway	Corporal	Sept. 16, 1863	Dec. 3, 1863	Do.
Drowry Rowland	do	Sept. 16, 1863	Dec. 3, 1863	Do.
Alfred H. Muffett	do	Nov. 13, 1863	Dec. 3, 1863	Do.
William S. Patton	do	Sept. 29, 1863	Dec. 3, 1863	Do.
John H. Barrett	do	Feb. 2, 1864	Feb. 20, 1864	Do.
John H. Parish	do	Sept. 29, 1863	Dec. 3, 1863	Do.
Thomas J. Jimison	Bugler	Nov. 12, 1863	Dec. 3, 1863	Do.
Jesse G. Low	do	Sept. 12, 1863	Dec. 3, 1863	Do.
William G. Sparks	Farrier	Sept. 28, 1863	Dec. 3, 1863	Do.
James Mathis	Blacksmith	Feb. 2, 1864	Feb. 20, 1864	Do.
			Muster.	
Alexander, David R.	Private	Mar. 14, 1864	June 28, 1864	Do.
Alexander, Joseph R.	do	Mar. 14, 1864	June 28, 1864	Do.
Andrews, James R.	do	Apr. 17, 1864	June 28, 1864	Do.
Anderson, William	do	Sept. 30, 1863	Dec. 3, 1863	Do.
Breedlove, Irvin E.	do	May 14, 1864	June 28, 1864	Absent without leave since August 13, 1865.
Braswell, Mathias	do	May 14, 1864	June 28, 1864	Mustered out with regiment.
Buckner, John W.	do	Oct. 18, 1863	Dec. 3, 1863	Do.
Boydstone, David C	do	Nov. 14, 1863	Dec. 3, 1863	Do.
Baxter, Jasper	do	Sept. 28, 1863	Dec. 3, 1863	Do.
Castleberry, James D.	do	Oct. 19, 1863	Mar. 4, 1864	Do.
Cotner, John C.	do	Nov. 18, 1863	Dec. 3, 1863	Do.
Chanceller, Andrew J.	do	Nov. 13, 1863	Dec. 3, 1863	Do.
Church, Colonel B.	do	Sept. 29, 1863	Dec. 3, 1863	Absent, sick in general hospital, Fort Smith, Arkansas, since March 26, 1864; no discharge furnished on muster out of company.
Dammons, Wilson	do	Oct. 12, 1863	Dec. 3, 1863	Mustered out with the regiment.
Davis, James T.	do	Nov. 20, 1863	Dec. 3, 1863	Do.
Dunnigan, George	do	Feb. 2, 1864	Feb. 20, 1864	Do.
Eerles, Samuel	do	Sept. 29, 1862	Dec. 3, 1863	Do.

REPORT OF THE ADJUTANT GENERAL OF ARKANSAS. 83

Name	Rank	Date 1	Date 2	Remarks
Eubanks, Archibald	do	Oct. 31, 1863	Dec. 3, 1863	Do.
Eppler, John V	do	Oct. 18, 1863	Dec. 3, 1863	Do.
Farmer, Andrew J	do	Oct. 21, 1863	Dec. 3, 1863	Do.
Glisson, Burton	do	Oct. 19, 1863	Dec. 3, 1863	Do.
Gipson, Isaac	do	Sept. 28, 1863	Dec. 3, 1863	Do.
Hunt, Jesse A	do	Oct. 18, 1863	Dec. 3, 1863	Do.
Hughes, Isaac	do	Sept. 28, 1863	Dec. 3, 1863	Do.
Hendrix, James	do	Oct. 1, 1863	Dec. 3, 1863	Do.
Jones, John B	do	Nov. 16, 1863	Dec. 3, 1863	Do.
Keener, Gilbert	do	Nov. 10, 1863	Dec. 3, 1863	Do.
Kennedy, Isham	do	Nov. 7, 1863	Dec. 3, 1863	Do.
Lee, Benjamin F	do	Sept. 22, 1863	Dec. 3, 1863	Do.
Langley, Meredith C	do	Nov. 14, 1863	Dec. 3, 1863	Do.
Long, John B	do	Sept. 16, 1863	Dec. 3, 1863	Do.
Long, Milford	do	Sept. 16, 1863	Dec. 3, 1863	Do.
Lewis, James T	do	Nov. 11, 1863	Dec. 3, 1863	Do.
Metcalf, Isaac F	do	Oct. 29, 1863	Dec. 3, 1863	Do.
McClary, James	do	Oct. 1, 1863	Dec. 3, 1863	Do.
Mulhollen, James M	do	Sept. 21, 1863	Dec. 3, 1863	On detached service since April 20, 1864; no discharge furnished on muster out of regiment.
Parrish, George W	do	Sept. 29, 1863	Dec. 3, 1863	Mustered out with regiment.
Pace, Kinchen	do	Oct. 14, 1863	Dec. 3, 1863	Do.
Patty, Obed. W	do	Feb. 2, 1864	Feb. 20, 1864	Do.
Phillips, Daniel	do	May 14, 1864	June 28, 1864	Do.
Phillips, Miles H	do	May 14, 1864	June 28, 1864	Do.
Rowland, Elijah	do	Sept. 16, 1863	Dec. 3, 1863	Do.
Rowland, Alonzo J	do	Sept. 30, 1863	Dec. 3, 1863	Do.
Raines, William M	do	Sept. 30, 1863	Dec. 3, 1863	Sent to St. Louis, Missouri, to be transferred to Invalid Corps; no official notice received to what regiment or company; no discharge furnished on muster out of regiment.
Rewis, Benjamin F	do	Sept. 28, 1863	Dec. 3, 1863	Mustered out with regiment.
Riley, William D	do	Sept. 16, 1863	Dec. 3, 1863	Do.
Sturfitt, Allen	do	Nov. 7, 1863	Dec. 3, 1863	Do.
Styles, William	do	Oct. 29, 1863	Dec. 3, 1863	Do.
Styles, John	do	Oct. 30, 1863	Dec. 3, 1863	Do.
Styles, William M. D	do	Nov. 16, 1863	Dec. 3, 1863	Do.
Styles, Thomas	do	Oct. 30, 1863	Dec. 3, 1863	Do.
Smith, Thomas	do	Oct. 12, 1863	Dec. 3, 1863	Do.
Stone, John W	do	Oct. 21, 1863	Dec. 3, 1863	Do.
Still, Stephen J	do	Oct. 17, 1864	June 28, 1864	Do.
Spencer, Alfred A	do	Sept. 16, 1863	Dec. 3, 1863	Do.
Spencer, Absalom B	do	Sept. 16, 1863	Dec. 3, 1863	Do.
Tutt, James	do	Feb. 18, 1864	Mar. 4, 1864	Do.
Vernon, William	do	Nov. 4, 1863	Dec. 3, 1863	Do.
Vandergriff, James	do	Sept. 16, 1863	Dec. 3, 1863	Do.
Vincennon, Eli	do	Sept. 27, 1864	Nov. 4, 1864	Do.
Williams, Matthew A	do	Oct. 13, 1863	Dec. 3, 1863	Do.
Williams, George W	do	Nov. 11, 1863	Dec. 3, 1863	Do.

Discharged.

| Robert B. Patten | Sergeant | Sept. 29, 1863 | Dec. 3, 1863 | Discharged for appointment to 2d lieutenant company C, September 16, 1864. |

84   REPORT OF THE ADJUTANT GENERAL OF ARKANSAS.

Second regiment Arkansas cavalry volunteers. Mustered into service March 18, 1864, (three years;) mustered out August 20, 1865.

COMPANY I—Continued.

Names.	Rank.	Enlistment.	Muster.	Remarks.
Hale, Harvey	Private	Oct. 2, 1864	Nov. 26, 1864	Discharged May 17, 1865.
Place, John W	do	Nov. 8, 1863	Dec. 3, 1863	Discharged for disability, October 27, 1864.
Still, John M	do	Feb. 8, 1864	Mar. 14, 1864	Discharged July 10, 1865.
Transferred.				
Miles Keener	Sergeant	Nov. 10, 1863	Dec. 3, 1863	Transferred to non-commissioned staff as sergeant major, July 12, 1865.
Chastain, Joseph C	Private	Sept. 7, 1863	Dec. 3, 1863	Transferred to company G, January 4, 1864.
Moore, James	do	Sept. 7, 1863	Dec. 3, 1863	Do.
Menter, Jacob	do	Nov. 4, 1863	Dec. 3, 1863	Do.
Menter, Joseph	do	Nov. 16, 1863	Dec. 3, 1863	Do.
Peters, Elbert	do	Sept. 7, 1863	Dec. 3, 1863	Do.
Rogers, John	do	Nov. 12, 1863	Dec. 3, 1863	Do.
Rogers, James C. C	do	Nov. 3, 1863	Dec. 3, 1863	Do.
Sherman, Henry	do	Nov. 2, 1863	Dec. 3, 1863	Do.
Stephens, Gideon G	do			Do.
Died.				
John Hughes	Sergeant	Sept. 28, 1863	Dec. 3, 1863	Killed in action at Richland creek, Arkansas, May 3, 1864.
Robert D. Harris	Corporal	Sept. 16, 1863	Dec. 3, 1863	Killed in action at Richland creek, Arkansas, October 17, 1864.
Barnes, Balem B	Private	Mar. 23, 1864	Mar. 26, 1864	Died in general hospital, Memphis, Tennessee, of pneumonia, February 27, 1865.
Durnett, Francis M	do	Feb. 2, 1864	Feb. 20, 1864	Killed in action at Richland creek, Arkansas, May 3, 1864.
Bledsoe, William P	do	Nov. 14, 1863	Dec. 3, 1863	Do.
Dilda, Charles F	do	Nov. 11, 1863	Dec. 3, 1863	Died of wounds received in action, May 3, 1864.
Campbell, Thomas	do	Sept. 30, 1863	Dec. 3, 1863	Killed in action at Richland creek, Arkansas, May 3, 1864.
Evans, Frederick G	do	Mar. 3, 1863	June 28, 1864	Killed in general hospital, Memphis, Tennessee, of diarrhœa, February 18, 1865.
Harris, Alexander L	do	Sept. 16, 1863	Dec. 3, 1863	Killed in action in Barry county, Missouri, June 25, 1864.
Hale, John J	do	July 25, 1864	Nov. 26, 1864	Died in general hospital, Memphis, Tennessee, of measles, January 27, 1865.
Keys, John	do	April 18, 1864	Never	Killed in action at Richland, Arkansas, May 30, 1864.
Martin, Joha S	do	Sept. 16, 1863	Dec. 3, 1863	Died in general hospital, Cape Girardeau, Mo., of inflammation of lungs, Feb. 6, 1865.
Patton, Harvey C	do	Sept. 29, 1863	Dec. 3, 1863	Died in general hospital, Springfield, Missouri, of congestive fever, January 1, 1864.
Powell, Robert Y	do	Oct. 22, 1863	Dec. 3, 1863	Died in the field of typhoid fever, May 20, 1864.
Ralph, William H	do	Mar. 6, 1864	Mar. 26, 1864	Died in general hospital, Memphis, Tennessee, of inflammation of lungs, Mar. 25, 1865.
Winchester, John	do	Nov. 10, 1863	Dec. 3, 1863	Died at Berryville, Arkansas, of congestion, February 6, 1864.
Wilson, Thomas	do	Sept. 25, 1863	Dec. 3, 1863	Died in regimental hospital, of pneumonia, March 24, 1864.
Deserted.				
Hale, William	Private	Aug. 26, 1864	Nov. 26, 1864	Deserted at Springfield, Missouri, Dec. 13, 1864.
Townson, John W	do	Mar. 25, 1864	Mar. 26, 1864	Deserted at Forsyth, Missouri, May 27, 1864.
Bendlow, Irvin E	do	May 14, 1864	June 28, 1864	Deserted August 13, 1865.

REPORT OF THE ADJUTANT GENERAL OF ARKANSAS. 85

COMPANY K.

			Date of rank.	
Samuel P. Dickinson	Captain	Sept. 9, 1862	Dec. 2, 1863	Appointed from private 13th Kansas infantry; mustered out with regiment.
William P. Warner	1st lieutenant		Dec. 21, 1863	Discharged for disability, May 18, 1865.
James S. Bryen	2d lieutenant		Jan. 8, 1864	Discharged for disability, May 28, 1864.
James K. Dickinson	....do	Sept. 10, 1864	Mar. 1, 1865	Appointed from private same company; mustered out with regiment.
Hiram R. Summer	1st sergeant	Jan. 23, 1864	Jan. 25, 1864	Mustered out with regiment.
Charles W. Richmond	Commissary sergeant	Nov. 14, 1863	Dec. 18, 1863	Do.
George H. Springer	Quartermaster sergeant	Nov. 14, 1863	Dec. 18, 1863	Do.
Thomas J. Hardcastle	Sergeant	Nov. 14, 1863	Mar. 1, 1865	Do.
John C. Barnes	...do	Nov. 14, 1863	Dec. 18, 1863	Do.
William F. Hoyt	...do	Jan. 1, 1865	Mar. 1, 1865	Do.
Samuel McCowan	...do	Nov. 14, 1863	Dec. 18, 1863	Do.
John N. Stanley	Corporal	Nov. 14, 1863	Dec. 18, 1863	Do.
David C. Resterson	...do	Nov. 14, 1863	Dec. 18, 1863	Do.
Woodson D. Parker	...do	Nov. 14, 1863	Dec. 18, 1863	Do.
Uriah J. Nichols	...do	Nov. 14, 1863	Mar. 1, 1865	Do.
Houston Taylor	...do	Nov. 14, 1863	Dec. 18, 1863	Sick in general hospital at Rolla, Missouri, since May 30, 1865; no discharge furnished on muster out of regiment.
Peter Lewis	...do	Nov. 14, 1863	Dec. 18, 1863	Mustered out with regiment.
William A. Nye	Bugler	July 6, 1864	July 6, 1864	Do.
Albert W. Hampton	...do	Nov. 14, 1863	Dec. 18, 1863	Do.
Thomas F. Alstatt	Blacksmith	Nov. 14, 1863	Dec. 18, 1863	Do.
Charles J. Oliver	Farrier	Nov. 14, 1863	Oct. 31, 1864	Do.
John Cowan	Saddler	Nov. 14, 1863	Aug. 31, 1864	Do.
			Muster.	
Armstrong, Harrison	Private	Nov. 14, 1863	Dec. 18, 1863	Do.
Armstrong, John	...do	Nov. 14, 1863	Dec. 18, 1863	Do.
Alstatt, John W.	...do	Nov. 14, 1863	Dec. 18, 1863	Do.
Adams, William A.	...do	Nov. 14, 1863	Dec. 18, 1863	Do.
Adams, James	...do	Jan. 20, 1864	Feb. 16, 1864	Do.
Belt, William B.	...do	Nov. 14, 1863	Dec. 18, 1863	Do.
Belt, Robert	...do	Nov. 2, 1864	Nov. 3, 1864	Do.
Barnes, James	...do	Nov. 14, 1863	Dec. 18, 1863	Do.
Brashear, James M.	...do	Nov. 14, 1863	Dec. 18, 1863	Do.
Crinson, George W.	...do	Nov. 14, 1863	Dec. 18, 1863	Do.
Conatser, James B.	...do	Nov. 14, 1863	Feb. 16, 1864	Do.
Clevinger, John H.	...do	Nov. 14, 1863	Dec. 18, 1863	Do.
Deckard, David M.	...do	Jan. 1, 1865	Jan. 1, 1865	Sick in general hospital at Memphis, Tennessee, since March 9, 1865; no discharge furnished on muster out of regiment.
English, George W.	...do	Nov. 14, 1863	Dec. 18, 1863	Mustered out with regiment.
English, Charles	...do	Nov. 14, 1863	Dec. 18, 1863	Do.
Foster, Samuel	...do	Nov. 14, 1863	Dec. 18, 1863	Do.
Freeman, Thomas B.	...do	May 15, 1864	July 2, 1864	Do.
Gibson, Pleasant A.	...do	Nov. 14, 1863	Dec. 18, 1863	Do.
Gifford, William	...do	Nov. 14, 1863	Dec. 18, 1863	Do.
Gambel, William J.	...do	May 15, 1864	July 2, 1864	Do.

86 REPORT OF THE ADJUTANT GENERAL OF ARKANSAS.

Second regiment Arkansas cavalry volunteers. Mustered into service March 18, 1864, (three years;) mustered out August 20, 1865.

COMPANY K—Continued.

Names.	Rank.	Enlistment.	Muster.	Remarks.
Hardcastle, Benjamin	Private	Nov. 14, 1863	Dec. 18, 1863	Mustered out with regiment.
Holder, John	do	Nov. 14, 1863	Dec. 18, 1864	Do.
Hatfield, Robert	do	Nov. 14, 1863	Dec. 18, 1864	Do.
Harden, Thomas	do	Mar. 2, 1865	Mar. 2, 1865	Do.
Johnson, Richard L	do	Jan. 1, 1865	Jan. 1, 1865	Absent without leave since January 25, 1865.
Jackson, James	do	Nov. 20, 1863	Feb. 15, 1864	Mustered out with regiment.
Kirby, James	do	Nov. 14, 1863	Dec. 18, 1863	Do.
Knox, Lorenzo D	do	Nov. 14, 1863	Dec. 18, 1863	Do.
Kirk, Samuel	do	Nov. 14, 1863	Dec. 18, 1863	Do.
Lee, William R	do	Nov. 14, 1863	Dec. 18, 1863	Sick in general hospital at Springfield, Missouri, since March 16, 1864; no discharge furnished on muster out of regiment.
Lee, James	do	Nov. 2, 1864	Nov. 3, 1864	Mustered out with regiment.
McAllister, Joseph	do	Nov. 14, 1863	Dec. 18, 1864	Do.
McMurray, James C	do	Nov. 14, 1863	Dec. 18, 1864	Do.
McMurray, William	do	Jan. 20, 1864	Feb. 16, 1864	Do.
McCartney, George T	do	Nov. 14, 1863	Dec. 18, 1863	Do.
Morse, Samuel	do	Nov. 14, 1863	Dec. 18, 1863	Do.
Mercer, David H	do	Nov. 14, 1863	Dec. 18, 1863	Do.
McIntosh, Bluford	do	Nov. 14, 1863	Dec. 18, 1863	Do.
Maxfield, Macklin	do	Nov. 14, 1863	Dec. 18, 1863	Do.
Maxfield, Goodson A	do	Nov. 14, 1863	Dec. 15, 1813	Do.
Nichols, Alven A	do	Nov. 14, 1863	Dec. 18, 1863	Do.
Nichols, David	do	Nov. 14, 1863	Dec. 18, 1863	Do.
Nichols, James H	do	Nov. 14, 1863	Dec. 18, 1863	Do.
Nichols, John	do	Feb. 18, 1865	Feb. 18, 1865	Do.
Nichols, George W	do	Feb. 18, 1865	Feb. 18, 1865	Do.
Nichols, Russell R	do	Nov. 15, 1863	Dec. 18, 1863	Do.
Nichols, Larkin	do	Nov. 14, 1863	Dec. 18, 1863	Do.
Nichols, Martin	do	April 15, 1864	July 2, 1864	Do.
Nichols, John W	do	Sept. 10, 1864	Sept. 15, 1864	Do.
Nichols, Pleasant	do	Nov. 14, 1863	Dec. 18, 1863	Do.
Pierce, Samuel	do	July 9, 1864	July 18, 1864	Do.
Price, Alexander	do	Sept. 10, 1864	Sept. 15, 1864	Do.
Pipkins, Edward	do	Nov. 14, 1863	Dec. 18, 1863	Do.
Rodgers, Jesse	do	Nov. 14, 1863	Dec. 18, 1863	Do.
Smith, Thomas M	do	Nov. 14, 1863	Dec. 18, 1863	Do.
Smedley, Abner G	do	Nov. 14, 1863	Dec. 18, 1863	Do.
Sutherland, James M	do	Jan. 1, 1865	Jan. 1, 1863	Sick in general hospital at Memphis, Tennessee, since March 2, 1865; no discharge furnished on muster out of regiment.
Steward, Benjamin F	do			Mustered out with regiment.
Taylor, John	do	Nov. 14, 1863	Dec. 18, 1863	Do.
Tucker, Andrew J	do	Sept. 10, 1864	Sept. 15, 1864	Do.
Thompson, William	do	Nov. 14, 1863	Dec. 18, 1863	Do.

REPORT OF THE ADJUTANT GENERAL OF ARKANSAS. 87

Name	Rank			Remarks
Thompson, Moses A	do	Nov. 14, 1863	Dec. 18, 1863	Do.
Wilson, William	do	Nov. 14, 1863	Dec. 18, 1863	Sick in general hospital at Springfield, Missouri, since October 18, 1864; no discharge furnished out of regiment.
Wilsey, Daniel	do	Jan. 20, 1864	Feb. 16, 1864	Mustered out with regiment.
Wolf, Samuel D	do	Jan. 1, 1865	Jun. 1, 1865	Do.
Reed, Jacob	do	Feb. 24, 1865	Feb. 24, 1865	Do.
McCracken, William	do	Feb. 24, 1865	Feb. 24, 1865	Do.

Discharged.

Wiley B. Sartin	Sergeant	Nov. 14, 1863	Dec. 18, 1863	Discharged May 28, 1865.
James Cargile	Corporal	Nov. 14, 1863	Dec. 18, 1863	Discharged May 31, 1865.
John C. Nichols	do	Nov. 14, 1863	Dec. 18, 1863	Discharged July 17, 1865.
Bench, James	Private	Nov. 14, 1863	Dec. 18, 1863	Discharged for disability, December 13, 1864.
Williams, Thomas C	do	Nov. 14, 1863	Dec. 18, 1863	do.
Williams, Ira	do	Dec. 15, 1863	Feb. 16, 1864	Discharged.

Transferred.

| Hamblin, Pleasant W | Private | Nov. 14, 1863 | Dec. 18, 1863 | Appointed to non-commissioned staff as quartermaster sergeant July 1, 1865. |

Died.

Marcus A. Hogan	Sergeant	Nov. 14, 1863	Dec. 18, 1863	Killed in action at Richland, Arkansas, May 3, 1864.
Lewis, John	Private	Jan. 5, 1864	Jan. 5, 1864	Died in general hospital at Springfield, Missouri, of gunshot wounds, Feb. 10, 1864.
Estes, Alexander M	do	Nov. 14, 1863	Dec. 18, 1863	Killed in action at Richland, Arkansas, May 3, 1864.
Oliver, Robert A	do	Nov. 14, 1863	Dec. 18, 1863	Do.
Snoddy, Henry	do	Nov. 14, 1863	Dec. 18, 1863	do.
Thompson, Isaac	do	Jan. 20, 1864	Feb. 16, 1864	do.
Tilford, James S	do	July 9, 1864	July 9, 1864	Died in general hospital, Springfield, Missouri, August 15, 1864.
Rice, Bird C	do	Nov. 14, 1863	Dec. 18, 1863	Died in general hospital, Springfield, Missouri, October 5, 1864, of remittent fever.
Campbell, Jerry C	do	Dec. 24, 1863	Dec. 26, 1863	Died in general hospital, Memphis, Tennessee, March 27, 1865.
Balautine, Jesse	do	Nov. 14, 1863	Dec. 18, 1863	Killed by guerillas at Johnson, Arkansas, July 2, 1864.
Waller, John	do	Nov. 14, 1863	Dec. 18, 1863	Killed by guerillas on Boston mountain, while on furlough, July 1, 1864.

Deserted.

David A. Nichols	Sergeant	Nov. 14, 1863	Dec. 18, 1863	Deserted while on detached service at Franklin, Arkansas, July 8, 1864.
Jeremiah Blaylock	Bugler	Nov. 14, 1863	Dec. 18, 1863	Deserted at Clipper's mill, Arkansas, May 16, 1864.
Calvin C. Hasten	do	Jan. 20, 1864	Feb. 16, 1864	do.
James M. Hayes	Farrier	Nov. 14, 1863	Dec. 18, 1863	Deserted while on detached service at Franklin, Arkansas, July 8, 1864.
Wood, James F	Private	Nov. 14, 1863	Dec. 18, 1863	Deserted at Springfield, Missouri, February 18, 1864.
Pendergrass, John P	do	Nov. 14, 1863	Dec. 18, 1863	Deserted while on leave of absence at Franklin, Arkansas, joined the enemy, February 28, 1864.
McAllister, William C	do	Nov. 14, 1863	Dec. 18, 1863	Deserted near Cassville, Missouri, March 18, 1864.
Smith, John	do	Nov. 14, 1863	Dec. 18, 1863	Deserted from furlough, Franklin county, Arkansas, May 27, 1864.
Edgin, Thomas P	do	Nov. 14, 1863	Dec. 18, 1863	Deserted from escort duty near Fayetteville, Arkansas, May 30, 1864.
Hagley, James G	do	Nov. 14, 1863	Dec. 18, 1863	Do.
Nicks, George W	do	Nov. 14, 1863	Dec. 18, 1863	Deserted at Cassville, Missouri, June 12, 1864.
Patty, John C	do	Jan. 20, 1864	Feb. 16, 1864	Do.
Snoddy, James R	do	Nov. 14, 1863	Dec. 18, 1863	Do.
Campbell, James N. D	do	Nov. 14, 1863	Dec. 18, 1863	Deserted while on march near Cassville, Missouri, June 24, 1864.

Second regiment Arkansas cavalry volunteers. Mustered into service March 18, 1864, (three years;) mustered out August 20, 1865.

COMPANY K—Continued.

Names.	Rank.	Enlistment.	Muster.	Remarks.
McAllister, John	Private	Nov. 14, 1863	Dec. 18, 1863	Deserted while on march near Cassville, Missouri, June 24, 1864.
Hill, William R	do	Jan. 23, 1864	Jan. 26, 1864	Deserted from furlough, Franklin county, Arkansas, July 30, 1864.
Nichols, George W	do	Nov. 14, 1863	Dec. 18, 1863	Deserted at Springfield, Missouri, October 17, 1864.
Crain, John	do	Nov. 14, 1863	Dec. 18, 1863	Deserted at Springfield, Missouri, November 29, 1864.
Robinson, James H	do	Jan. 3, 1864	Jan. 5, 1864	Deserted at Rolla, Missouri, December 24, 1864.
Taylor, Eli M	do	Nov. 14, 1863	Dec. 18, 1864	Deserted at Cairo, Illinois, January 1, 1865.
Harris, Pleasant R. W	do	Nov. 14, 1863	Dec. 18, 1864	Deserted near Springfield, Missouri, December 16, 1864.

COMPANY L.

Names.	Rank.	Enlistment.	Date of rank.	Muster.	Remarks.
William Bowling	Captain		March 8, 1864		Appointed from civil life to fill original vacancy; resigned ——.
Theodore Oliver	do	April 25, 1863	March 1, 1865		Appointed 1st lieutenant from sergeant company C ——; mustered out with regiment.
Andrew W. Wyman	1st lieutenant	—, 1861	Jan. 30, 1864		Appointed from 1st Iowa cavalry to fill original vacancy; dismissed ——.
Alvis Smith	2d lieutenant		March 8, 1864		Resigned ——.
Joseph McClure	do	Sept. 10, 1863	March 1, 1865		Appointed from sergeant major; mustered out with regiment.
John A. Davis	1st sergeant	Oct. 10, 1863	Jan. 26, 1864		Mustered out with regiment.
John Q. West	Quartermaster sergeant	Oct. 10, 1863	Jan. 26, 1864		Do.
Benjamin Hargraves	Commissary sergeant	Oct. 10, 1863	Jan. 26, 1864		Do.
Charles Pense	Sergeant	Oct. 10, 1863	Jan. 26, 1864		Do.
William H. Busbong	do	Oct. 10, 1863	Jan. 26, 1864		Absent—sick in general hospital, Springfield, Missouri, December 13, 1864; no discharge furnished on muster out of regiment.
Lewis Simpson	do	Oct. 10, 1863	Jan. 26, 1864		Mustered out with regiment.
Andrew J. Peters	do	Oct. 10, 1863	Jan. 26, 1864		Do.
John F. Meadows	Corporal	Oct. 10, 1863	Jan. 26, 1864		Do.
Yonger Neal	do	Oct. 10, 1863	Jan. 26, 1864		Do.
James M. Ford	do	Oct. 10, 1863	Jan. 26, 1864		Do.
Enoch P. Davis	do	Oct. 10, 1863	Jan. 26, 1864		Do.
Henderson C. Rankins	do	Oct. 10, 1863	Jan. 26, 1854		Do.
Isaac G. Pollard	do	Oct. 10, 1863	Jan. 26, 1864		Do.
William Maynor	do	Oct. 10, 1863	Jan. 26, 1864		Do.
James Steel	Bugler	Oct. 10, 1863	Jan. 26, 1864		Do.
John Buck	Farrier	Oct. 10, 1863	Jan. 26, 1864		Do.
Thomas Gazaway	Blacksmith	Oct. 10, 1863	Jan. 26, 1864		Do.
John McIntyre	Farrier	Oct. 10, 1863	Jan. 26, 1864		Do.
Andrew Fugett	Saddler	Oct. 10, 1863	Jan. 26, 1864		Do.

REPORT OF THE ADJUTANT GENERAL OF ARKANSAS. 89

			Muster.	
Arrington, Lewis	Private	Oct. 10, 1863	Jan. 26, 1864	Do.
Arrington, Jose	do	Oct. 10, 1863	Jan. 26, 1864	Do.
Brewer, Melton	do	Oct. 10, 1863	Jan. 26, 1864	Do.
Boyd, Joseph	do	Oct. 10, 1863	Jan. 26, 1864	Do.
Barnes, John	do	Oct. 10, 1863	Jan. 26, 1864	Do.
Bryson, William D	do	Jan. 22, 1864	Jan. 26, 1864	Do.
Burton, James H	do	Mar. 29, 1864	Apr. 18, 1864	Do.
Briscoe, Martin	do	May 3, 1864	June 6, 1864	Do.
Craig, Zeblin P	do	Oct. 10, 1863	Jan. 26, 1864	Absent; sick in general hospital, Springfield, Missouri, since December 13, 1864; no discharge furnished on muster out of regiment.
Carney, William	do	Oct. 10, 1863	Jan. 26, 1864	Mustered out with regiment.
Covington, Richard	do	Oct. 10, 1863	Jan. 26, 1864	Do.
Dean, David H	do	Oct. 10, 1863	Jan. 26, 1864	Do.
Dean, John W	do	Oct. 10, 1863	Jan. 26, 1864	Do.
Duvall, William C	do	Oct. 10, 1863	Jan. 26, 1864	Do.
Dyer, George H	do	Oct. 10, 1863	Jan. 26, 1864	Do.
Good, Willey	do	Oct. 10, 1863	Jan. 26, 1864	Do.
Gregory, Hiram	do	Oct. 10, 1863	Jan. 26, 1864	Do.
Holman, Joseph	do	Oct. 10, 1863	Jan. 26, 1864	Do.
Howard, William	do	Oct. 10, 1863	Jan. 26, 1864	Do.
Howell, John W	do	Oct. 10, 1863	Jan. 26, 1864	Do.
Hendricks, Thomas S	do	Jan. 22, 1864	Jan. 26, 1864	Do.
Ivey, James A	do	Oct. 10, 1863	Jan. 26, 1864	Do.
Jackson, James K	do	Oct. 10, 1863	Jan. 26, 1864	Do.
Kuykendall, James	do	Oct. 10, 1863	Jan. 26, 1864	Do.
Killingworth, James	do	Oct. 10, 1863	Jan. 26, 1864	Do.
Maples, Joseph	do	Oct. 10, 1863	Jan. 26, 1864	Do.
Miller, John W., sr	do	Oct. 10, 1863	Jan. 26, 1864	Do.
Miller, Daniel M	do	Oct. 10, 1863	Jan. 26, 1864	Do.
McCurdy, James	do	Oct. 10, 1863	Jan. 26, 1864	Do.
Meadows, Archibald	do	Oct. 10, 1863	Jan. 26, 1864	Do.
Marshall, George	do	Oct. 10, 1863	Jan. 26, 1864	Do.
Moss, William	do	Oct. 10, 1863	Jan. 26, 1864	Do.
Pense, Joseph	do	Oct. 10, 1863	Jan. 26, 1864	Do.
Pope, David	do	Oct. 10, 1863	Jan. 26, 1864	Do.
Pope, John T	do	Oct. 10, 1863	Jan. 26, 1864	Do.
Pope, Martin V	do	Oct. 10, 1863	Jan. 26, 1864	Do.
Penter, George	do	Oct. 10, 1863	Jan. 26, 1864	Do.
Penter, William	do	Oct. 10, 1863	Jan. 26, 1864	Do.
Parker, Andrew	do	Oct. 10, 1863	Jan. 26, 1864	Do.
Stephenson, Samuel	do	Oct. 10, 1863	Jan. 26, 1864	Do.
Stephenson, John A	do	Oct. 10, 1863	Jan. 26, 1864	Absent; sick in general hospital, Memphis, Tennessee, since May 29, 1865, no discharge furnished on muster out of regiment.
Sigroves, Alvin	do	Oct. 10, 1864	Jan. 26, 1864	Absent; sick in general hospital, Springfield, Missouri, since December 13, 1864; no discharge furnished on muster out of regiment.
Sagely, John C	do	Oct. 10, 1863	Jan. 26, 1864	Mustered out with regiment.
Taylor, Walter F. M	do	May 30, 1864	June 6, 1864	Do.
Wilburn, William	do	Oct. 10, 1863	Jan. 26, 1864	Do.

Second regiment Arkansas cavalry volunteers. Mustered into service March 18, 1864, (three years;) mustered out August 20, 1865.

COMPANY I—Continued.

Names.	Rank.	Enlistment.	Muster.	Remarks.
Discharged.				
Dean, James T	Private	Oct. 10, 1863	Jan. 26, 1864	Discharged June 6, 1865.
Jackson, John J	do	Oct. 10, 1863	Jan. 26, 1864	Discharged May 16, 1865.
Kirkpatrick, William J	do	Oct. 10, 1863	June 6, 1864	Discharged May 28, 1865.
Miller, John W	do	Oct. 10, 1863	Jan. 30, 1864	Discharged July 1, 1865.
Rankin, Francis M	do	Oct. 10, 1863	Jan. 30, 1864	Discharged July 17, 1865.
Sheppard, Jesse P	do	Oct. 10, 1863	Jan. 30, 1864	Discharged June 5, 1865.
Taylor, Thomas J	do	Oct. 10, 1863	Jan. 30, 1864	Discharged May 16, 1865.
Wilburn, Curtis	do	Oct. 10, 1863	Jan. 30, 1864	Discharged May 28, 1865.
Died.				
Jasper N. Brown	Corporal	Oct. 10, 1863	Jan. 26, 1864	Died at Memphis, Tennessee, April 24, 1865.
Forbus, William P	Private	Oct. 10, 1863	Jan. 26, 1864	Died at Memphis, Tennessee, April 27, 1865.
Stephenson, Robert W	do	Oct. 10, 1863	Jan. 26, 1864	Died at Memphis, Tennessee, February 4, 1865.
Spoon, John	do	Oct. 10, 1863	Jan. 26, 1864	Died at Memphis, Tennessee, April 19, 1865.
Turner, Richard	do	Oct. 10, 1863	Jan. 26, 1864	Died at Memphis, Tennessee, May 13, 1865.
Tabor, William	do	Oct. 10, 1863	Jan. 26, 1864	Died at Memphis, Tennessee, May 31, 1865.
Deserted.				
John W. Weise	Sergeant	Oct. 10, 1863	Jan. 26, 1864	Deserted at Springfield, Missouri, December 12, 1864.
Wiley B. Wagner	Corporal	Oct. 10, 1863	Jan. 26, 1864	Deserted at Cassville, Missouri, June 27, 1864.
Andrew Couch	Bugler	Oct. 10, 1863	Jan. 26, 1864	Deserted at Clepper's Mills, Arkansas, April 16, 1864.
Bashan, Christopher	Private	Oct. 10, 1863	Jan. 26, 1864	Deserted at Cassville, Missouri, July 18, 1864.
Jones, Thomas	do	Oct. 10, 1863	Jan. 26, 1864	Deserted at Yellville, Arkansas, May 8, 1864.
Marlar, Thomas W	do	Oct. 10, 1863	Jan. 26, 1864	Deserted at Springfield, Missouri, March 13, 1864.
Melton, James M	do	Oct. 10, 1863	Jan. 26, 1864	Deserted at Springfield, Missouri, December 12, 1864.
Maynor, Wesley	do	Oct. 10, 1863	Jan. 26, 1864	Deserted at Springfield, Missouri, September 1, 1864.
Meltor, Samuel A	do	Oct. 10, 1863	Jan. 26, 1864	Deserted at Clepper's Mills, Arkansas, April 16, 1864.
Pearce, John C	do	Oct. 10, 1863	Jan. 26, 1864	Deserted at Memphis, Tennessee, May 9, 1865.
Thomas, Marchant	do	Oct. 10, 1863	Jan. 26, 1864	Deserted at Springfield, Missouri, December 12, 1864.

COMPANY M.

			Date of rank.	Muster.
George W. Moore	Captain	—, 1861	Mar. 14, 1864	Appointed from civil life to fill original vacancy; mustered out with regiment.
James Gipson	1st lieutenant	—, 1861	Mar. 14, 1864	Appointed from civil life to fill original vacancy; discharged for disability.
James P. Phillips	2d lieutenant	Sept. 10, 1863	Mar. 16, 1864	Appointed from private company G to fill original vacancy; mustered out with regiment.
Thomas H. Peel	1st sergeant	July 28, 1863	May 1, 1865	Mustered out with regiment.
Eastin Irby	Commissary sergeant	Nov. 1, 1863	Jan. 28, 1864	Do.
Shadrick Waller	Quartermaster sergeant	Sept. 2, 1863	Jan. 29, 1864	Do.
George W. Moore	Sergeant	Sept. 18, 1863	Oct. 9, 1863	Do.
William Caler	....do....	Jan. 28, 1864	Feb. 19, 1864	Do.
George R. Haggard	....do....	Sept. 25, 1863	May 1, 1865	Appointed from corporal; mustered out with regiment.
Samuel Stanfield	....do....	Sept. 1, 1863	May 1, 1865	do.
A. Y. Jones	Corporal	Dec. 3, 1863	Jan. 28, 1864	Mustered out with regiment.
Thomas J. Caler	....do....	Jan. 28, 1864	Feb. 19, 1864	Do.
Noble J. McBride	....do....	Jan. 28, 1864	Jan. 28, 1864	Do.
John F. Murphy	....do....	Jan. 28, 1864	Feb. 19, 1864	Do.
Benj. F. Coley	....do....	Jan. 28, 1864	Feb. 19, 1864	Do.
William Lay	....do....	Jan. 28, 1864	May 1, 1865	Do.
John A. Rambo	....do....	Jan. 28, 1864	May 1, 1864	Do.
James B. Reeves	....do....	jun. 28, 1864	May 1, 1865	Do.
Sylvester Bryant	Blacksmith	Sept. 10, 1863	Jan. 28, 1864	Do.
William C. Haggard	Farrier	Mar. 1, 1864	Mar. 9, 1864	Do.
Irvin Ash	Bugler	Feb. 10, 1864	Feb. 19, 1864	Do.
Johnson Beaver	....do....	July 22, 1863	Oct. 9, 1863	Do.
Andrew, James	Private	Jan. 28, 1864	Feb. 19, 1864	Do.
Aleredge, Ruphis	....do....	Mar. 1, 1864	Mar. 9, 1864	Do.
Brown, Jesse G.	....do....	Jan. 28, 1864	Feb. 19, 1864	Do.
Baker, John R.	....do....	Jan. 28, 1864	Feb. 19, 1864	Do.
Baker, Jesse M	....do....	Jan. 28, 1864	Feb. 19, 1864	Do.
Beaver, James	....do....	Feb. 20, 1864	Mar. 9, 1864	Do.
Barnes, Joseph	....do....	Jan. 28, 1864	Feb. 19, 1864	Do.
Cassel, Jackson	....do....	Jan. 28, 1864	Feb. 19, 1864	Do.
Coatney, James H.	....do....	Jan. 28, 1864	Jan. 28, 1864	In general hospital, Springfield, Missouri, since December 10, 1864; no discharge furnished on muster out of regiment.
Coatney, William	....do....	Jan. 12, 1864	Jan. 28, 1864	Mustered out with regiment.
Fairwell, Wilda	....do....	Jan. 22, 1864	Jan. 28, 1864	Do.
Farmer, John	....do....	Feb. 19, 1864	Feb. 20, 1864	Do.
George, Jesse B.	....do....	Dec. 3, 1863	Jan. 28, 1864	Do.
Harris, John A.	....do....	Jan. 28, 1864	Feb. 19, 1864	Do.
Horton, Ananias W	....do....	Jan. 28, 1864	Feb. 19, 1864	Do.
Hill, David C.	....do....	Dec. 3, 1863	Jan. 28, 1864	Do.
Houston, John G	....do....	Nov. 3, 1863	Jan. 28, 1864	Sick in general hospital, Cape Girardeau, Missouri; no discharge furnished on muster out of regiment.
Harrison, David L.	....do....	Mar. 7, 1864	Mar. 9, 1864	Mustered out with regiment.
Kester, Isaac W.	....do....	Jan. 28, 1864	Feb. 19, 1864	Do.

Second regiment Arkansas cavalry volunteers. Mustered into service March 18, 1864, (three years;) mustered out August 20, 1865.

COMPANY M—Continued.

Names.	Rank.	Enlistment.	Muster.	Remarks.
Kimball, Andrew W	Private	Jan. 28, 1864	Feb. 19, 1864	Mustered out with regiment.
Looney, Joseph S	do	Jan. 28, 1864	Jan. 28, 1864	Do.
Martin, Cornelius	do	Dec. 12, 1863	Jan. 28, 1864	Do.
Myers, Isaac W	do	Jan. 1, 1864	Jan. 28, 1864	Do.
Moore, William H	do	Jan. 28, 1864	Feb. 19, 1864	Do.
Mear, James L	do	Jan. 28, 1864	Feb. 19, 1864	Do.
McGuirk, William B	do	Jan. 28, 1864	Feb. 19, 1864	Do.
Price, Asa B	do	Dec. 3, 1863	Jan. 28, 1864	Do.
Price, John W	do	Nov. 20, 1863	Jan. 28, 1864	Do.
Proctor, James	do	Feb. 20, 1864	Feb. 20, 1864	Do.
Phillips, William C	do	Jan. 28, 1864	Jan. 28, 1864	Do.
Sarrels, William L	do	Jan. 28, 1864	Feb. 19, 1864	Do.
Standredge, James P	do	Dec. 9, 1863	Jan. 28, 1864	Do.
Scraggins, James A	do	Jan. 1, 1864	Jan. 28, 1864	Do.
Scraggins, Lafayette	do	Feb. 20, 1864	Mar. 9, 1864	Do.
Simpson, Jasper	do	Jan. 15, 1864	Mar. 9, 1864	Do.
Southerland, William	do	Aug. 26, 1863	Oct. 9, 1863	Sick in general hospital, Springfield, Missouri, since November 9, 1864; has descriptive roll; no discharge furnished.
Thompson, John C	do	Jan. 28, 1864	Feb. 19, 1864	Mustered out with regiment.
Thomas, Malachi	do	Jan. 28, 1864	Feb. 19, 1864	Do.
Trendwell, Joseph	do	Jan. 28, 1864	Feb. 19, 1864	Do.
Tucker, Joseph B	do	Jan. 28, 1864	Feb. 19, 1864	Do.
Woods, Samuel J	do	Jan. 28, 1864	Feb. 19, 1864	Do.
Woods, R. M	do	Jan. 28, 1864	Feb. 19, 1864	Do.
Watts, Albert	do	Jan. 28, 1864	Feb. 19, 1864	Do.
Willis, Cephas	do	Jan. 28, 1864	Feb. 19, 1864	Do.
Wilson, James A	do	Jan. 28, 1864	Feb. 19, 1864	Do.
Walker, John J	do	Dec. 5, 1863	Jan. 28, 1864	Do.
Wallen, Simpson	do	Sept. 2, 1863	Jan. 28, 1864	Do.
Williams, Cicero J	do	Sept. 1, 1863	Nov. 3, 1863	Do.
Stephens, Weathers	do	Mar. 2, 1864	April 13, 1864	Do.
Discharged.				
Will S. Moore	1st sergeant	Mar. 1, 1864	April 13, 1864	Discharged to receive promotion, February 28, 1865.
Allen Weathers	Sergeant	Jan. 12, 1864	Feb. 19, 1864	Discharged July 10, 1865.
Bohannon, Albert	Private	Jan. 15, 1864	Jan. 28, 1864	Discharged for disability, March 1, 1865.
George, Thomas O	do	Dec. 3, 1863	Jan. 28, 1864	Discharged June 7, 1865.
Stanfield, James	do	Sept. 1, 1863	Oct. 9, 1863	Discharged for disability, June 4, 1864.
Tucker, William N	do	Dec. 1, 1864	Jan. 28, 1864	Discharged for disability, December 6, 1864.
Woods, Osiah	do	Jan. 28, 1864	Feb. 19, 1864	Discharged for disability, March 30, 1865.

REPORT OF THE ADJUTANT GENERAL OF ARKANSAS. 93

Transferred.

Name	Rank	Date enrolled	Date mustered	Remarks
Alexander, Phillimon	Private	Sept. 6, 1863	Jan. 28, 1864	Transferred to company H, July 1, 1864.
Barnes, Robert B	do	Nov. 17, 1863	Jan. 28, 1864	Do.
Blackwell, Richard	do	Jan. 31, 1864	Feb. 19, 1864	Transferred to company G, March 1, 1864.
Doss, Thomas H	do	Nov. 25, 1863	Jan. 28, 1864	Transferred to company B, September 1, 1864.
Elwood, William L	do	Nov. 17, 1863	Jan. 28, 1864	Transferred to company H, July 1, 1864.
Godard, Francis M	do	Jan. 15, 1864	Jan. 28, 1864	Transferred to company A, July 1, 1864.
Henley, Benjamin F	do	Dec. 3, 1863	Jan. 28, 1864	Transferred to company H, July 1, 1864.
Jones, Clement C	do	Jan. 24, 1864	Jan. 28, 1864	Transferred to company G, March 1, 1864.
Mosby, James	do	Dec. 3, 1863	Jan. 28, 1864	Transferred to company A, July 1, 1864.
McDowell, John B	do	Jan. 18, 1864	Jan. 28, 1864	Transferred to company G, March 1, 1864.
Rainwaters, John	do	Jan. 13, 1864	Jan. 28, 1864	Transferred to company A, July 1, 1864.
Rainwaters, Abraham	do	Jan. 13, 1864	Jan. 28, 1864	Do.
Smith, George W	do	Jan. 13, 1864	Jan. 28, 1864	Do.

Died.

Name	Rank	Date enrolled	Date mustered	Remarks
Colley, James P	Private	Aug. 26, 1863	Jan. 28, 1864	Died in general hospital, Memphis, Tennessee, April 26, 1865.
Epperson, William J	do	Jan. 28, 1864	Feb. 19, 1864	Died in general hospital, Memphis, Tennessee, March 23, 1865.
McCarson, William C	do	Jan. 28, 1864	Feb. 19, 1864	Died in general hospital, Springfield, Missouri, April 3, 1865.
Truce, Henry	do	Jan. 28, 1864	Feb. 19, 1864	Killed May 22, 1864, on his way to join his company from escort duty, May 22, 1864.
Banks, Melvin	do	Jan. 15, 1864	Jan. 28, 1864	Was taken from his home while on furlough and killed by rebels, July 24, 1864.

Deserted.

Name	Rank	Date enrolled	Date mustered	Remarks
Adkins, John J	Corporal	Dec. 3, 1863	Feb. 1, 1864	Deserted on the march near Lindon, Missouri, December 13, 1864.
Banks, Jefferson	Private	Jan. 28, 1864	Feb. 19, 1864	Deserted at Talbot's barreus, Arkansas, December 20, 1864.
Beaver, Martin A	do	Feb. 20, 1864	Nov. 19, 1864	Do.
Brownen, Lewis L	do	Jan. 28, 1864	Feb. 19, 1864	Do.
Gilbert, Robert	do	Jan. 28, 1864	Feb. 19, 1864	Deserted near Yellville, Arkansas, May 14, 1864.
Hunter, Joseph B	do	Jan. 23, 1864	Jan. 28, 1864	Deserted near Forsyth, Missouri, July 24, 1864.
Jones, C. A	do	April 25, 1864	Never	Deserted near Ozark, Missouri, August 5, 1864.
Scraggins, Crittenden	do	Feb. 6, 1864	Mar. 9, 1864	Deserted from leave of absence, October 20, 1864.
Steward, Felix G	do	Dec. 3, 1863	Jan. 28, 1864	Deserted from a scout near Forsyth, Missouri, July 24, 1864.
Scott, Jacob	Sergeant	Dec. 13, 1863	Jan. 28, 1864	Deserted near Lindon, Missouri, December 15, 1864.

SECOND ARKANSAS CAVALRY VOLUNTEERS.—HISTORICAL MEMORANDA.

In July, 1862, authority was given to Colonel W. James Morgan, of Missouri, to raise a regiment, to be called the First Arkansas Mounted Rangers, and his headquarters and rendezvous were established at Helena. Nearly four hundred recruits were enrolled, and company A, Captain J. William Demby, and company B, Captain Archibald B. Freeburn, were organized and mustered into the service. Many circumstances had already unfortunately transpired to make the men displeased with their position. Their location was unhealthy; they were ignorant of the economy of a soldier's life; age had incapacitated many of them for duty; sickness was prevailing to an unusual extent; and, to add to their embarrassments, Colonel Morgan was dismissed the service. Company C at this time lacked but a few men of its minimum, and when Colonel Morgan's dismissal became known desertions were frequent, and the company was never mustered in. The designation of the regiment was now changed by Governor Phelps to the "Second Arkansas Cavalry volunteers." Recruiting still continued, but under many discouraging circumstances, and, at last, to the relief of all, the following order was issued:

Special Orders, No. 69.

HEADQUARTERS DISTRICT OF EAST ARKANSAS, *Helena, May 2, 1863.*

The commanding officer of 2d regiment Arkansas cavalry will turn over to the proper officers all government property in the possession of his regiment without delay, and will forthwith embark, with his entire command, on transports, and proceed to St. Louis, Missouri, and report to the commanding general of the department of the Missouri, that the regiment may be consolidated with some other Arkansas regiment. Quartermaster's department will furnish the necessary transportation.

By order of Major General PRENTISS:

JAMES O. PIERCE, *A. A. A. G.*

At this time company C had become entirely disintegrated, the few remaining men having been transferred to companies A and B, which themselves were but skeleton organizations when they set out for St. Louis. Shortly after their arrival the following order was issued:

HEADQUARTERS ST. LOUIS DISTRICT, *St. Louis, Missouri, May 31, 1863.*

Special Orders, No. 121.

II.—In accordance with orders received from headquarters department of the Missouri, by indorsement on letter of A. F. Eno, adjutant general and secretary of Arkansas, of May 28, 1863, companies A and B of 2d Arkansas cavalry will be consolidated immediately into one company, to be called company B, 2d Arkansas cavalry.

In compliance with orders, Captain A. B. Freeburn, of company B, First Lieutenant A. A. Irwin, of company A, and Second Lieutenant Andrew J. Garner, of company B, will be retained as the officers of the consolidated company.

Captain James W. Demby, of company A, and First Lieutenant Harley S. Wait, of company B, will be mustered out of service of the United States. Captain D. W. Cheek, A. C. M., St. Louis, Missouri district, will make the consolidation named in the order.

By order of Brigadier General DAVIDSON:

HENRY C. FILLEBROWN, *Captain and Assistant Adjutant General.*

On the 2d day of June this consolidation was made and the supernumerary officers were mustered out.

In August, 1863, John E. Phelps was appointed a commissioner to take charge of this new organization, and with it as a nucleus to raise a regiment still to be known as the 2d Arkansas cavalry. Rendezvousing at Springfield and Cassville, Missouri, his energy and success were such that on the 18th day of March, 1864, he was mustered in as colonel, twelve full companies having been raised. Prior to this event, Colonel Phelps and his energetic subordinate officers had penetrated time and again into Arkansas, always bringing out recruits, and never failing to inspire the loyal citizens of the State with increased faith in the ultimate triumph of their cause. With reference to some of the services rendered by this regiment, Lieutenant Colonel Hugh Cameron, who earlier in the rebellion was captain of company F, 2d Kansas cavalry volunteers, writes as follows:

"As captain of company F, 2d Kansas cavalry, while on duty in Arkansas, in 1862–'63, I never failed to find faithful scouts and reliable guides among the citizens. When, at Dardanelle, during the months of November and December, 1863, with eighty-five armed men, ('Mountain Feds,') surrounded by more than six hundred renegade Missouri rebels, I was sustained and re-enforced as often as necessary by the citizens of Pope and Yell counties, under the direction of Burk Johnson and the late William Stout, during which time over five hundred recruits were added to the federal army, and not a single case of treachery on the part of any citizen was discovered. Shortly after this, I became an officer in the 2d Arkansas cavalry, and served with the regiment to the close of the war. And in justice to Arkansas troops let me say, that for watchfulness, cheerful obedience, and courage, they had, in my judgment, no superiors. Under the command of judicious and brave officers, they were seldom defeated or surprised. The march from Dardanelle to Cassville, Missouri, in January, 1864, with a number of prisoners equal to one-third of the entire armed force, was as orderly and as well executed as any ever performed by old and well-disciplined troops.

"The encounter on Richland creek, Arkansas, May 4, 1864, in which Colonel Jackman and a force of over two hundred rebels were dislodged and put to flight by Colonel Phelps with one hundred of his regiment, was as desperate, perhaps, as any of the war.

"The pursuit of a detachment of eight hundred rebels from Buck prairie to Upshaw Farm, Missouri, on the 29th of October of the same year, resulted in the death of over sixty and the capture of thirty-seven of the detachment—a number equal to one-fourth of the entire federal command, composed principally of the 2d Arkansas cavalry and Missouri troops.

"A scout through Berryville, Rolling and Marshall prairies, Yellville, and Talbot's barrens, Arkansas, a distance of about four hundred miles, was performed in ten days, without loss of life or property, in the month of November, 1864, by one hundred and fifty men of the 2d Arkansas cavalry. In the region through which we passed several thousand rebels of General Price's command were scattered. On this occasion, rebel Major Mooney and twenty-six of his men were captured and conveyed to Springfield, Missouri, and several were killed and wounded, among whom were Major Lauderdale and Lieutenant Hastings. I have instanced the above to illustrate the character of the service in which Arkansas troops were constantly employed—a service dangerous to those engaged as well as important to the government, but of which scarcely anything yet is publicly known, and for which the actors have received comparatively no credit."

Upon this subject it is gratifying also to be permitted to publish the subjoined letter from Hon. J. P. C. Shanks, a member of the Fortieth Congress, from the State of Indiana: *

During the Shelby raid into Missouri in the fall of 1863, Colonel Phelps was frequently called upon for scouts and detachments of men, and in the following winter when northwestern Arkansas was alive with guerillas, performed essential service for the government. Between Fayetteville, Washington county, where the 1st Arkansas cavalry was then stationed, and Batesville, on White river, held by Colonel Livingston, of the 1st Nebraska infantry, then commanding the district of northeastern Arkansas, there was a wide belt of country north of the Arkansas river wholly unprotected by posts or stations, and in which were many Union men. These it was important to relieve, and into this section detachments of the 2d Arkansas cavalry were frequently sent, accomplishing much good in this respect, and breaking up and scattering the marauding bands with which the country was infested. Once only, on Richland creek, were they defeated.

Of an expedition undertaken in January, 1864, and which is characteristic of much of the warfare of the border, L. Rémiatte, late adjutant of the regiment, writes as follows: "I left Cassville, Missouri, January 17, and went with the expedition to Burrongliville, Searcy county. In several skirmishes the guerillas were defeated with loss—at Crooked creek, Tomahawk gap, and on Rolling prairie. I returned to Cassville about the 10th of February, having been left on the edge of Rolling prairie in charge of the whole force of the regiment and the train of refugees collected there under my protection. Upwards of one hundred and twenty wagons, with all sorts of trains, were depending upon me to escort them safely through to Missouri. I had to provide forage for all the stock or allow them to starve on the road, and yet, in order to protect the refugees, had to keep them together. By taking almost impassable roads I managed to avoid difficulty, and at last succeeded in bringing the train safely through. An attack made by guerillas on the Osage was repelled."

Connected with the raid of General Price into Missouri in the autumn following, the 2d Arkansas distinguished itself, moving from Springfield to Rolla, one hundred and ten miles, in fifty-six hours; in subsequent marches, skirmishes and battles, it was almost invariably in the advance; and at Jefferson city, Russelville, California, Boonville, Dover, Independence, Big Blue, the Osage and Newtonia, behaved most gallantly. After the battle at Newtonia, the chase was continued on to the Arkansas river, and throughout it all, the 2d cavalry were prompt and efficient in the pursuit.

Returning to Springfield, Missouri, November 15, 1864, they were ordered across the country to Memphis, Tennessee, which place they reached on the 25th day of January, 1865. Their journey through northeastern Arkansas, over mountains and through swamps, across bayous and swollen streams, was severe, and guerillas were a constant source of annoyance and delay.

In Mississippi and Tennessee the regiment was actively on duty, scouting and guerilla hunting, until it was mustered out August 20, 1865. It was stationed successively at Germantown, La Fayette and Lagrange, Tennessee, and Senatobia, Mississippi, capturing, at various times, over three hundred prisoners.

After the surrender of General Taylor a detachment of this regiment garrisoned Holly Springs, Mississippi, and on leaving the place, Lieutenant Colonel Cameron in command, received a flattering testimonial from the citizens, with reference to the manner in which he discharged the difficult and delicate duties devolved upon him while conscientiously and fully performing his obligations to the government. A merited tribute to the good order and discipline of the men of the regiment was likewise bestowed.

At a meeting of the regiment held at Lagrange, Tennessee, shortly before the muster out, the following resolutions were adopted:

Whereas the necessity for united martial action which called us together no longer exists, our work being done, and our cause gloriously triumphant, it becomes us before disbanding, to make some disposal of the proud old banner which has never trailed, and which we have borne triumphantly upon many a bloody field; and

Whereas it is desirable that a relic so dear to the hearts of those who have followed it should be preserved as a testimonial of what we have done: Therefore, be it resolved by the officers and men of the 2d regiment Arkansas volunteer cavalry:

1. That we have the names of the battles of "Independence," "Big Blue," and "Osage," ordered by the War Department to be put upon our banner embroidered thereon, and that it then be presented to the governor of the State of Arkansas to be preserved among the archives of the State.

2. That we claim that our flag is entitled to have upon it the additional battles of Richland, Limestone Valley, Pine Mountains, Jefferson City, Boonville, Dover, Newtonia, and Upshaw Farm, where our boys did service that our enemies will long remember.

[This flag was afterwards received by the governor and is now among the archives of the State.]

3. That we refer with pride to the promotions received by our commanding officer, Colonel John E. Phelps, who, while commanding the regiment, was breveted brigadier general of volunteers, and captain, major, and lieutenant colonel in the regular army.

4. That the regiment do hereby tender their thanks to Mrs. Mary Phelps, who presented it with this flag. They are happy in being able to say to her that she committed it into the keeping of true soldiers, who will long remember the noble hearted and charitable donor with thankful feelings; and we deem her worthy of the nation's gratitude and the gratitude of every officer and soldier in the regiment.

5. That we appoint Major H. H. Maynard, surgeon, Captain D. W. Roberts, company A, and Captain H. C. Bell, company E, as a committee to have the names of the battles embroidered on the flag, and have it forwarded to Little Rock to be disposed of as directed.

6. That the Memphis, Tennessee, St. Louis, Missouri, Springfield, Missouri, and Arkansas papers be requested to publish these resolutions, and that Mrs. Phelps and the governor of the State of Arkansas be furnished with a copy.

* "FORTIETH CONGRESS, UNITED STATES, *Washington, D. C., March 8, 1867.*

"GENERAL: I am informed that you are about publishing, through the kindness of the United States Senate, your official report, and that your State being in the hands of disloyal men, refuses to publish the services of those gallant men of Arkansas who served their country in the field in defence of the Union and Constitution.

"Permit me to tender this expression of my high regard for, and confidence in, the men who composed the 2d Arkansas cavalry, commanded by Colonel John E. Phelps, Lieutenant Colonel Hugh Cameron, and Major Jeremiah Hackett. This regiment was in my command for some time at and near Memphis, Tennessee, and in several long and severe marches, and I take pleasure in attesting the uniform good character of the troops, and the energy, integrity, and efficiency of the officers; and permit me to make especial reference to the field officers above named.

"I make this statement as a just tribute to those men who were loyal and true under every adversity.

"With highest regards, I am, sir, yours truly,

"J. P. C. SHANKS, *late Colonel 7th Indiana Cavalry and Brevet Brigadier General.*

"Brigadier General A. W. BISHOP, *Adjutant General of the State of Arkansas.*"

Third regiment Arkansas cavalry volunteers. Mustered into service February 10, 1864, (three years;) mustered out June 30, 1865.

FIELD AND STAFF.

Names.	Rank.	Enlistment.	Date of rank.	Remarks.
Abraham H. Ryan	Colonel	—, 1861	Feb. 10, 1864	Promoted from captain 17th Illinois infantry to fill original vacancy; mustered out with regiment.
Irving W. Fuller	Lieutenant colonel	—, 1861	Dec. 1, 1863	Promoted from captain 1st Missouri cavalry; resigned April 24, 1865.
Harry Van Houston	Major	Dec. 1, 1863	Dec. 1, 1863	Resigned September 28, 1864.
Thaddeus S. Clarkson	......do......	Dec. 14, 1863	Dec. 15, 1863	Resigned September 10, 1864.
George F. Lovejoy	......do......	Feb. 11, 1864	Feb. 17, 1864	Resigned August 13, 1864.
Daniel W. Mason	......do......		Dec. 18, 1864	Appointed from private 1st Iowa cavalry to 1st lieutenant and adjutant, to fill original vacancy; mustered out with regiment.
David Hamilton	......do......	—, 1863	Feb. 24, 1865	Appointed from civil life to 1st lieutenant; promoted to captain February 9, 1864; mustered out with regiment.
Abner D. Thomas	Surgeon		Dec. 26, 1863	Promoted from assistant surgeon of Merrill's Horse, to fill original vacancy; mustered out with regiment.
John W. Madison	Assistant surgeon		Jan. 10, 1864	Appointed from hospital steward, 8th Missouri cavalry, to fill original vacancy; mustered out with regiment.
Francis S. Peiro	......do......		Mar. 22, 1864	Appointed 2d assistant surgeon from private 126th Illinois infantry; mustered out with regiment.
Samuel O. Green	Adjutant		Mar. 30, 1865	Appointed from private 3d Michigan cavalry; mustered out with regiment.
Albert Harrell	Regimental quartermaster	Nov. 27, 1863	Dec. 1, 1863	Dismissed February 13, 1864.
David Russell	......do......		Feb. 14, 1864	Appointed from regimental quartermaster sergeant 36th Iowa infantry; mustered out with regiment.
Samuel B. Jellison	Regimental com. subsistence.	Dec. 2, 1863	Dec. 3, 1863	Resigned March 1, 1865.
David A. Thompson	......do......		Mar. 30, 1865	Appointed from private 29th Iowa infantry; mustered out with regiment.

NON-COMMISSIONED STAFF.

Names.	Rank.	Enlistment.	Date of rank.	Remarks.
Wilson G. Gray	Sergeant major	Sept. 13, 1863	May 10, 1864	Appointed from private of company K; reduced at his own request October 10, 1864.
Henry A. Gill	......do......	Nov. 16, 1863	Nov. 20, 1864	Appointed from sergeant company C; mustered out with regiment.
John A. Anderson	Quartermaster sergeant	Sept. 23, 1863	Mar. 18, 1864	Appointed from sergeant company B; mustered out with regiment.
Edward Snyder	Commissary sergeant	Oct. 30, 1863	Apr. 15, 1864	Appointed from private company D; mustered out with regiment.
William Weeks	Saddler sergeant	Feb. 6, 1864	June 15, 1864	Appointed from saddler of company E; reduced to the ranks for absence without leave December 22, 1864.
Anthis B. Gaylor	......do......	Feb. 4, 1864	Dec. 15, 1864	Appointed from private of company L; mustered out with regiment.
Peter F. Saylors	Hospital steward	Oct. 18, 1863	June 17, 1864	Appointed from private company A; mustered out with regiment.
James S. Gwinn	......do......	Oct. 14, 1863	July 1, 1864	Appointed from private company F; mustered out with regiment.
Thomas D. Hawkins	Chief trumpeter	Sept. 23, 1863	Aug. 1, 1864	Appointed from bugler of company B; mustered out with regiment.
Morgan Maybee	Veterinary surgeon		May 10, 1865	Appointed from private 3d Michigan volunteer cavalry; mustered out with regiment.

REPORT OF THE ADJUTANT GENERAL OF ARKANSAS.

COMPANY A.

Name	Rank		Date of rank.	Muster.	Remarks
Elisha W. Dodson	Captain	—, 1863	Nov. 29, 1863		Appointed from private to 1st lieutenant October 18, 1863; dismissed Feb. 13, 1864.
David Turner	...do...		Feb. 16, 1864		Promoted captain from 1st lieutenant 28th Wisconsin infantry volunteers; resigned October 28, 1864.
George H. Hand	1st lieutenant	Oct. 18, 1863	Nov. 29, 1863		Appointed from private 15th Illinois cavalry; resigned February 21, 1864.
John W. Pennington	...do...	Oct. 18, 1863	Mar. 5, 1864		Appointed from private to sergeant October 29, 1863; resigned May 17, 1864.
Lawson S. Mitchum	2d lieutenant		Oct. 29, 1863		Appointed from private; resigned March 5, 1864.
Richard C. Ludwick	...do...		Feb. 1, 1865		Appointed sergeant October 29, 1863; mustered out with regiment.
Lucelius W. Hale	1st sergeant	Nov. 12, 1863	Nov. 1, 1864		Appointed corporal December 8, 1863; commissary sergeant December 18, 1863.
William J. Berryman	Commissary sergeant	Nov. 8, 1863	Feb. 4, 1865		Appointed corporal November 20, 1864; mustered out with regiment.
Albert Coninger	Corporal	Oct. 18, 1863	Feb. 20, 1865		Mustered out with regiment.
John Furr	...do...	Nov. 8, 1863	Feb. 4, 1865		Do.
John Cooper	...do...	Oct. 18, 1863	Nov. 20, 1864		Do.
Peter T. Welch	...do...	Oct. 18, 1863	Nov. 20, 1864		Do.
John J. King	Farrier and blacksmith	Nov. 12, 1863	Dec. 1, 1863		Do.
Henry C. Smith	Bugler	Nov. 19, 1863	Jan. 1, 1865		Do.
Bradley, Samuel S	Private	Nov. 19, 1863		Dec. 1, 1863	Do.
Brewer, George H	...do...	Oct. 18, 1863		Oct. 29, 1863	Do.
Churchill, James J	...do...	Oct. 18, 1863		Oct. 29, 1863	Do.
Cloninger, Alfred L	...do...	Oct. 18, 1863		Oct. 29, 1863	Do.
Cloninger, John R	...do...	Oct. 18, 1863		Oct. 29, 1863	Do.
Cooper, Samuel H	...do...	Nov. 8, 1863		Nov. 21, 1863	Do.
Campbell, John M	...do...	Oct. 18, 1863		Oct. 29, 1863	Do.
Collier, Green A	...do...	Oct. 18, 1863		Oct. 29, 1863	Do.
Chronister, Douglas H	...do...	Oct. 18, 1863		Oct. 29, 1863	Do.
Cook, John J	...do...	Oct. 18, 1863		Oct. 29, 1863	Do.
Epps, Romelius S	...do...	Oct. 18, 1863		Oct. 29, 1863	Do.
Epps, Doctor C	...do...	Nov. 19, 1863		Nov. 21, 1863	Do.
Fulton, Levi T	...do...	Oct. 18, 1863		Oct. 29, 1863	Do.
Freeman, Richard	...do...	Nov. 8, 1863		Nov. 21, 1863	Do.
Guess, Calvin E	...do...	Oct. 18, 1863		Oct. 29, 1863	Do.
Harkey, John J	...do...	Nov. 8, 1863		Nov. 21, 1863	Do.
Hughey, John	...do...	Nov. 8, 1863		Nov. 21, 1863	Do.
Hart, William	...do...	Nov. 19, 1863		Dec. 1, 1863	Do.
Harvill, Philip J	...do...	Oct. 18, 1863		Oct. 29, 1863	Do.
Kindrick, Obadiah	...do...	Nov. 19, 1863		Dec. 1, 1863	Do.
Maddux, James H	...do...	Oct. 18, 1863		Oct. 29, 1863	Do.
May, Robert C	...do...	Oct. 18, 1863		Oct. 29, 1863	Do.
Moore, William N	...do...	Jan. 13, 1864		June 14, 1864	Do.
McCay, William	...do...	Oct. 18, 1863		Oct. 29, 1863	Do.
McAnulty, James C	...do...	Oct. 18, 1863		Oct. 29, 1863	Do.
Nichols, Zachariah	...do...	Oct. 18, 1863		Oct. 29, 1863	Do.
Parker, Lewis	...do...	Oct. 18, 1863		Oct. 29, 1863	Do.
Reed, William A	...do...	Nov. 8, 1863		Nov. 21, 1863	Do.
Reed, John F	...do...	Oct. 18, 1863		Oct. 29, 1863	Do.

Miss. Doc. 53——7

REPORT OF THE ADJUTANT GENERAL OF ARKANSAS.

Third regiment Arkansas cavalry volunteers. Mustered into service February 10, 1864, (three years;) mustered out June 30, 1865.

COMPANY A—Continued.

Names.	Rank.	Enlistment.	Muster.	Remarks.
Rackley, Robert P	Private	Oct. 18, 1863	Oct. 29, 1863	Mustered out with regiment.
Shul, Henry W	do	Oct. 18, 1863	Oct. 29, 1863	Do.
Shul, Rufus F	do	Oct. 18, 1863	Oct. 29, 1863	Do.
Shul, John W	do	Jan. 19, 1863	May 25, 1863	Do.
Scatterfield, Noah W	do	Oct. 18, 1863	Oct. 29, 1863	Do.
Sullivan, Daniel	do	Nov. 8, 1863	Nov. 21, 1863	Do.
Welch, Levi J	do	Oct. 18, 1863	Oct. 29, 1863	Do.
Welch, David C	do	Oct. 18, 1863	Oct. 29, 1863	Do.
Webb, George W	do	Oct. 18, 1863	Oct. 29, 1863	Do.
Western, John	do	Oct. 18, 1863	Oct. 29, 1863	Do.
Mustered out in accordance with special instructions from the War Department, dated Adjutant General's Office, April 5, 1865—discharges to take effect May 22, 1865.				
John W. Hess	Quartermaster sergeant	Nov. 19, 1863	Dec. 1, 1863	Appointed corporal December 10, 1863; sergeant July 1, 1864.
William W. Scoggins	Sergeant	Oct. 18, 1863	Oct. 29, 1863	Appointed corporal November 20, 1864; sergeant February 4, 1865.
La Fayette Brashears	Corporal	Nov. 8, 1863	Nov. 21, 1863	Appointed corporal June 1, 1864.
John M. Bradley	Saddler	Oct. 18, 1863	Oct. 29, 1863	Appointed sergeant October 29, 1863; saddler February 4, 1865.
Carpenter, William P	Private	Oct. 18, 1863	Oct. 29, 1863	
Curtis, James C	do	Oct. 18, 1863	Oct. 29, 1863	
Fronaberger, Laban L	do	Nov. 8, 1863	Oct. 29, 1863	
Findley, Lorenzo D	do	Nov. 19, 1893	Dec. 1, 1863	
Findley, John	do	Oct. 18, 1863	Oct. 29, 1863	
Hess, Samuel W	do	Oct. 18, 1863	Oct. 29, 1863	
Kirkpatrick, George D	do	Oct. 18, 1863	Oct. 29, 1863	
Kindrick, Thomas P	do	Nov. 19, 1863	Dec. 1, 1863	
Motley, John R	do	Nov. 8, 1863	Nov. 21, 1863	
Mason, William A	do	Nov. 8, 1863	Nov. 21, 1863	
Owens, Harvey C	do	Oct. 18, 1863	Oct. 29, 1863	
Russell, William H	do	Oct. 18, 1863	Oct. 29, 1863	
Staley, George G	do	Oct. 18, 1863	Oct. 29, 1863	
Shinn, Alphus M	do	Oct. 18, 1863	Dec. 1, 1863	
Wither, Jasper N	do	Oct. 18, 1863	Oct. 18, 1863	
Webb, Elisha F	do	Nov. 8, 1863	Nov. 21, 1863	

Died.

James M. Howell	Sergeant	Oct. 18, 1863	Oct. 29, 1863	Died of pneumonia in general hospital, Little Rock, Arkansas, April 15, 1864.
Anderson L. Rhoades	Corporal	Oct. 18, 1863	Oct. 29, 1863	Died of pneumonia in private hospital, Lewisburg, Arkansas, March 4, 1865.
Bishop, Marion P	Private	Oct. 18, 1863	Oct. 29, 1863	Died in regimental hospital, Lewisburg, Arkansas, July 31, 1864.
Burris, William J	do	Oct. 18, 1863	Oct. 29, 1863	Died of typhoid fever, Lewisburg, Arkansas, August 1, 1864.

REPORT OF THE ADJUTANT GENERAL OF ARKANSAS. 99

Harkey, William J	do	Nov. 8, 1863		Died of scurvy in military prison, Little Rock, Arkansas, July 7, 1864.
Long, William	do	Oct. 18, 1863		Died of pneumonia, Little Rock, Arkansas, March 13, 1864.
Maddux, John R	do	Oct. 18, 1863		Died of remittent fever, Lewisburg, Arkansas, July 16, 1864.
May, James F	do	Nov. 19, 1863		Died of wounds received accidentally, Lewisburg, Arkansas, July 10, 1864.
Neal, William P	do	Oct. 18, 1863		Died of small pox, Lewisburg, Arkansas, August 3, 1864.
Stancil, John D	do	Oct. 18, 1863		Died of pneumonia, Little Rock, Arkansas, March 10, 1864.
Shul, Nelson M	do	Oct. 18, 1863		Died of chronic diarrhœa while on furlough, June 1, 1864.
Staley, Ezekiel	do	Oct. 18, 1863		Died of chronic diarrhœa, Lewisburg, Arkansas, December 5, 1864.
Webb, George M, (2d)	do	Oct. 18, 1863		Died of pneumonia, Norristown, Arkansas, May 9, 1865.
Yaw, Nelson	do	Nov. 19, 1863		Died of remittent fever, Little Rock, Arkansas, October 7, 1864.
Discharged.				
Stancil, William C	Private	Oct. 18, 1863	Oct. 29, 1863	For disability, August 5, 1864.
Deserted.				
John C. Crawford	Sergeant	Oct. 18, 1863	Oct. 29, 1863	Appointed sergeant June 3, 1864; deserted at Lewisburg, Arkansas, July 1, 1864.
James C. Hickey	do	Nov. 8, 1863	Dec. 1, 1863	Appointed corporal December 1, 1864; sergeant February 1, 1865; deserted March 21, 1865.
Branch, William L	Private	Nov. 8, 1863	Dec. 1, 1863	Deserted at Lewisburg, Arkansas, June 17, 1864.
Branch, John	do	Nov. 10, 1863	Dec. 1, 1863	Deserted at Lewisburg, Arkansas, July 12, 1864.
Brown, Allen	do	Oct. 18, 1863	Oct. 29, 1863	Deserted at Lewisburg, Arkansas, April 20, 1865.
Carter, Rufus	do	Nov. 8, 1863	Nov. 21, 1863	Deserted at Lewisburg, Arkansas, July 12, 1864.
Garner, Coffee	do	Oct. 18, 1863	Oct. 29, 1863	Do.
Heflin, Alexander	do	Oct. 18, 1863	Oct. 29, 1863	Deserted at Little Rock, Arkansas, September 19, 1864.
Hess, George W	do	Nov. 19, 1863	Dec. 1, 1863	Deserted at Lewisburg, Arkansas, December 10, 1864.
King, Moses	do	Nov. 19, 1863	Dec. 1, 1863	Deserted at Lewisburg, Arkansas, September 19, 1864.
Richardson, Willis J	do	Oct. 18, 1863	Oct. 29, 1863	Deserted at Little Rock, Arkansas, September 19, 1864.
Richardson, John A	do	Nov. 8, 1863	Nov. 21, 1863	Deserted at Little Rock, Arkansas, September 8, 1864.
Scott, William M	do	Nov. 8, 1863	Nov. 21, 1863	Deserted at Little Rock, Arkansas, September 19, 1864.
Shul, William T	do	Oct. 18, 1863	Dec. 1, 1863	Deserted at Little Rock, Arkansas, June 17, 1864.
Worldley, John	do	Oct. 18, 1863	Oct. 29, 1863	Deserted at Little Rock, Arkansas, March 13, 1864.
Webb, William E	do	Oct. 18, 1863	Oct. 29, 1863	Deserted at Little Rock, Arkansas, September 19, 1864.
Walker, Joseph	do	Nov. 19, 1863	Dec. 1, 1863	Do.
Stinett, William L	do	Oct. 18, 1863	Oct. 28, 1863	Do.
Transferred.				
Saylors, Peter J	Private	Oct. 18, 1863	Oct. 29, 1863	Appointed corporal October 29, 1863; transferred to non-commissioned staff as hospital steward.

COMPANY B.

			Date of rank.	
John J. Gibbons	Captain		Nov. 29, 1865	Promoted captain from 1st lieutenant; mustered out with regiment.
Charles M. Greene	1st lieutenant	Nov. 29, 1863	Nov. 29, 1863	Appointed from civil life; mustered out with regiment.
Bluford Gordon	2d lieutenant	Sept. 23, 1863	Nov. 29, 1863	Died at officers' hospital, Little Rock, Arkansas, of consumption, October 26, 1864.

100   REPORT OF THE ADJUTANT GENERAL OF ARKANSAS.

Third regiment Arkansas cavalry volunteers. Mustered into service February 10, 1864, (three years;) mustered out June 30, 1865.

COMPANY B—Continued.

Names.	Rank.	Enlistment.	Date of rank.	Remarks.
Joseph W. Bond	2d lieutenant	Oct. 18, 1864	Nov. 18, 1864	Appointed from 1st sergeant company —; mustered out with regiment.
Louis Powell, sen	Sergeant	Sept. 23, 1863	Sept. 23, 1863	In confinement May 2, 1865; no discharge on muster out of regiment.
Abraham Eaton	do	Oct. 24, 1863	Mar. 29, 1864	Corporal to March 29, 1864; mustered out with regiment.
Joseph Aldridge	Corporal	Dec. 20, 1863	Dec. 22, 1864	Mustered out with regiment.
Basil Overton	do	Apr. 14, 1864	Feb. 10, 1865	Do.
Nathaniel E. Hawkins	do	June 10, 1864	Dec. 22, 1864	Do.
John T. Gooch	do	Sept. 18, 1864	Feb. 10, 1865	Do.
Jeremiah Duvall	do	Nov. 18, 1864	May 16, 1865	Do.
Jonathan Roane	do	Sept. 23, 1863	Oct. 29, 1863	Do.
William Seago	Bugler	Apr. 14, 1864	Sept. 23, 1864	Do.
			Muster.	
Brents, Wesley C	Private	Mar. 22, 1864	May 16, 1865	Do.
Brock, Wiley R	do	June 16, 1864	Sept. 29, 1864	Do.
Bannore, James	do	Jan. 2, 1865	May 20, 1865	Do.
Baker, Moses R	do	Sept. 23, 1863	May 29, 1863	Do.
Carr, George M	do	Oct. 24, 1863	Nov. 7, 1863	Do.
Childers, John A	do	Dec. 18, 1864	May 16, 1865	Do.
Childers, William P	do	Sept. 23, 1863	Oct. 29, 1865	Do.
Greer, William	do	Sept. 23, 1863	Oct. 29, 1865	Do.
Hale, John A	do	June 19, 1864	Sept. 23, 1864	Do.
Nulton, Henry	do	Sept. 23, 1863	Oct. 29, 1863	Do.
Parks, Joseph	do	July 29, 1864	May 16, 1865	Do.
Powell, Ambrose	do	Apr. 14, 1864	Nov. —,	Do.
Powell, Harden	do	Oct. 31, 1864	May 16, 1865	In confinement in military prison, Little Rock, Arkansas; no discharge on muster out of regiment.
Phillips, Joseph W	do	Sept. 23, 1863	Oct. 29, 1863	
Rainwaters, Jackson D	do	Oct. 29, 1864	May 16, 1865	Mustered out with regiment.
Whitesides, Lewis	do	Apr. 14, 1864	Sept. 23, 1864	Do.
Willis, William	do	Nov. 14, 1863	Nov. 25, 1863	Do.
Williams, Jacob A	do	Sept. 6, 1864	Sept. 23, 1864	Do.
Webb, William H	do	Sept. 19, 1864	Sept. 23, 1864	Do.
Wages, Morgan J	do	Nov. 25, 1863	Dec. 5, 1863	In confinement awaiting sentence; no discharge on muster out of regiment.
Mustered out in accordance with special instructions from the War Department, dated April 5, 1865—discharges to take effect May 22, 1865.				
Hiram Overton	1st sergeant	Oct. 24, 1863	Nov. 7, 1863	Corporal from organization; appointed sergeant March 29, 1864, reduced May 7, 1864; appointed sergeant November 18, 1864.
James M. Stout	Quartermaster sergeant	Sept. 23, 1863	Oct. 29, 1863	Appointed quartermaster sergeant from corporal, March 29, 1864.

REPORT OF THE ADJUTANT GENERAL OF ARKANSAS. 101

Name	Rank	Date	Date	Notes
William L. Bunts	Sergeant	Sept. 23, 1863	Oct. 29, 1863	Appointed from corporal March 29, 1864.
James H. Gordon	do	Sept. 23, 1863	Oct. 29, 1863	Appointed August 23, 1864.
David L. Jenkins	do	Sept. 23, 1863	Oct. 29, 1863	Appointed from corporal July 1, 1864.
Elias Malone	Corporal	Sept. 23, 1863	Nov. 3, 1863	Appointed corporal July 1, 1864.
Thomas Furguson	do	Sept. 23, 1863	Nov. 25, 1863	Appointed corporal August 23, 1864.
William G. Cobb	do	Nov. 14, 1863	Nov. 3, 1863	Appointed corporal March 29, 1864.
William C. Brown	Blacksmith	Nov. 1, 1863	Oct. 29, 1863	
Alexander Kerley	Saddler	Sept. 23, 1863	Oct. 29, 1863	
Henry Sledge	Teamster	Sept. 23, 1863	Nov. 25, 1863	
Allen, Squire	Private	Nov. 14, 1863	Dec. 5, 1863	
Aldridge, Peter	do	Nov. 25, 1863	Oct. 29, 1863	
Bateman, William H	do	Sept. 23, 1863	Nov. 7, 1863	
Bateman, Calvin E	do	Oct. 24, 1863	Oct. 29, 1863	
Broadway, Richard B	do	Sept. 23, 1863	Oct. 29, 1863	
Bennett, William R	do	Sept. 23, 1863	Oct. 29, 1863	
Brook, Richard	do	Sept. 23, 1863	Dec. 30, 1863	
Bond, John M	do	Dec. 20, 1863	Oct. 29, 1863	
Brim, John	do	Sept. 23, 1863	Oct. 29, 1863	
Burns, Wilburn	do	Sept. 23, 1863	Oct. 29, 1863	
Cough, Hugh	do	Sept. 23, 1863	Oct. 29, 1863	
Collins, George	do	Sept. 23, 1863	Nov. 29, 1863	
Cowan, Andrew J	do	Nov. 14, 1863	Nov. 25, 1863	
Castleberry, Sanford V	do	Nov. 14, 1863	Nov. 29, 1863	
Clifton, Alfred N	do	Sept. 23, 1863	Nov. 7, 1863	
Davis, Benjamin B	do	Oct. 24, 1863	Nov. 3, 1863	
Durham, William	do	Nov. 1, 1863	Oct. 29, 1863	
Durham, John	do	Sept. 23, 1863	Oct. 29, 1863	
Freeman, Jesse	do	Sept. 23, 1863	Oct. 29, 1863	
Garrison, George W	do	Sept. 23, 1863	Oct. 29, 1863	
Garrison, Allen W	do	Sept. 23, 1863	Oct. 29, 1863	
Garrison, James F	do	Sept. 23, 1863	Oct. 29, 1863	
Hasty, Matthew	do	Dec. 18, 1863	Dec. 22, 1863	
Hogue, William J	do	Sept. 23, 1863	Oct. 29, 1863	
Keen, William J	do	Sept. 23, 1863	Oct. 29, 1863	
Kendrick, William D	do	Sept. 23, 1863	Nov. 3, 1863	
Kendrick, John J	do	Sept. 23, 1863	Oct. 29, 1863	
Lewis, William C	do	Sept. 23, 1863	Oct. 29, 1863	
Mindard, William	do	Sept. 23, 1863	Oct. 29, 1863	
Mahun, Dempsey	do	Sept. 23, 1863	Oct. 29, 1863	
Meuse, John S	do	Sept. 23, 1862	Oct. 29, 1863	
Powell, Lewis J	do	Sept. 23, 1863	Oct. 29, 1863	
Ryan, Thomas	do	Sept. 23, 1863	Oct. 29, 1863	
Roberts, William H	do	Nov. 29, 1863	Dec. 5, 1863	
Rowell, John A	do	Sept. 23, 1863	Oct. 29, 1863	
Reid, William J	do	Nov. 14, 1863	Nov. 25, 1863	
Sledge, Thomas P	do	Sept. 23, 1863	Oct. 29, 1863	
Salter, Andrew J	do	Sept. 23, 1863	Oct. 29, 1863	
Stobaugh, James	do	Sept. 23, 1863	Oct. 29, 1863	
Stobaugh, John J	do	Sept. 23, 1863	Oct. 29, 1863	
Upchurch, Thomas A	do	Sept. 23, 1863	Oct. 29, 1863	
Upchurch, William A	do	Sept. 23, 1863	Oct. 29, 1863	
Whitson, John	do	Sept. 23, 1863	Oct. 29, 1863	

102 REPORT OF THE ADJUTANT GENERAL OF ARKANSAS.

Third regiment Arkansas cavalry volunteers. Mustered into service February 10, 1864, (three years;) mustered out June 30, 1865.

COMPANY B—Continued.

Names.	Rank.	Enlistment.	Muster.	Remarks.
Wages, William	Private	Sept. 23, 1863	Oct. 29, 1863	
Williams, William K	do	Dec. 18, 1863	Dec. 22, 1863	
Williams, John M	do	Dec. 18, 1863	Dec. 22, 1863	
Williams, Allen T	do	Nov. 14, 1863	Nov. 25, 1863	
Yates, William B	do	Nov. 14, 1863	Nov. 25, 1863	
Killed since action.				
Carpenter, Felix A	Private	Sept. 23, 1863	Oct. 29, 1863	Killed in action at White Oak Creek, Ark., September 29, 1864.
Missing in action.				
Atkinson, James	Private	Oct. 24, 1863	Nov. 7, 1863	Missing since action at Glassey Village, Ark., September 8, 1864.
Died.				
Jones, Ezra	Private	Sept. 23, 1863	Oct. 29, 1863	Died of pneumonia at Little Rock, Arkansas, November 10, 1863.
Roberts, John L	do	Sept. 23, 1863	Oct. 29, 1863	Died of pneumonia at Little Rock, Arkansas, November 14, 1863.
Adams, George	do	Dec. 18, 1863	Dec. 22, 1863	Died of pneumonia at Lewisburg, Arkansas, March 11, 1864.
Bateman, Eaton R	do	Oct. 24, 1863	Nov. 7, 1863	Died of measles at Lewisburg, Arkansas, March 27, 1864.
Ballard, William P	do	Nov. 14, 1863	Nov. 25, 1863	Died of fever at Lewisburg, Arkansas, May 1, 1864.
Allen, William B	do	Sept. 23, 1863	Oct. 29, 1863	Died of measles at Lewisburg, Arkansas, April 11, 1864.
Bridges, William R	do	Dec. 18, 1863	Dec. 22, 1863	Died of small-pox at Lewisburg, Arkansas, June 15, 1864.
Davis, John E	do	Sept. 23, 1863	Oct. 29, 1863	Died of small-pox at Lewisburg, Arkansas, May 11, 1864.
Campbell, William H	do	Nov. 28, 1864	Never	Died of pneumonia at Lewisburg, Arkansas, January 28, 1865.
Roberts, John W	do	Sept. 23, 1863	Oct. 29, 1863	Died of small-pox in Conway county, Arkansas, September 15, 1864.
Scott, William	do	Oct. 24, 1863	Nov. 7, 1863	Died of pneumonia in hospital December 27, 1864.
Verden, Leander	do	Dec. 4, 1863	Dec. 5, 1863	Died of measles in regimental hospital April 8, 1864.
Plunket, James	Sergeant	Sept. 23, 1863	Oct. 29, 1863	Died of small-pox at Lewisburg, Arkansas, April 18, 1864.
Teague, Nathaniel	Private	Sept. 23, 1863	Oct. 29, 1863	Died of pneumonia at Little Rock, Arkansas, December 11, 1863.
Discharged.				
Bond, Joseph W	1st sergeant	Sept. 23, 1863	Oct. 29, 1863	Discharged to accept promotion November 12, 1864.
Brocke, Sheppard S	Blacksmith	Sept. 23, 1863	Oct. 29, 1863	Discharged for disability February 11, 1865.
Hendricks, William J	Private	Oct. 24, 1863	Nov. 7, 1863	Discharged for disability January 30, 1865.
Heine, Preston B	do	June 29, 1864	Sept. 23, 1863	Discharged for disability April 5, 1865.
Kinkade, William	do	Nov. 1, 1863	Nov. 3, 1863	Discharged for disability April 23, 1865.
Miller, Wesley C	do	Nov. 14, 1863	Nov. 25, 1863	Do.
Roades, Samuel J	do	Dec. 18, 1863	Dec. 22, 1863	Discharged for disability January 15, 1865.
Stobough, Edmund S	do	Sept. 23, 1863	Oct. 29, 1863	Discharged for disability January 30, 1865.
Stockton, Jonathan D	do	Sept. 23, 1863	Oct. 29, 1863	Discharged by order April 4, 1865.
Treadway, John M	do	Sept. 23, 1863	Oct. 29, 1863	Discharged for disability December 14, 1864.

REPORT OF THE ADJUTANT GENERAL OF ARKANSAS. 103

Name	Rank	Date		Remarks
Treadway, Francis M	do	Nov.	14, 1863	Discharged for disability April 23, 1865.
Upchurch, David H	do	Sept.	23, 1863	Discharged for disability October 15, 1864.
Upchurch, George	do	Sept.	23, 1863	Do.
Whitson, Calvin	do	Oct.	24, 1863	Discharged on account of wounds received in action, October 15, 1864.

Deserted.

Name	Rank	Date		Remarks
Gooch, Thomas L	Private	Sept.	18, 1864	Deserted October 29, 1864.
Steward, Richard W	do	Mar.	23, 1864	Deserted at Lewisburg, Arkansas, June 9, 1864.
Vinson, Thomas	do	Sept.	23, 1863	Deserted at Lewisburg, Arkansas, September 17, 1864.
Davis, John M	do	Nov.	14, 1863	Deserted from confinement under charges of absence without leave May 20, 1865.

Transferred.

Name	Rank	Date		Remarks
Anderson, John A	Sergeant	Sept.	23, 1863	Transferred to non-commissioned staff of regiment March 18, 1864.
Hawkins, Thomas	Bugler	Sept.	23, 1863	Transferred to non-commissioned staff as chief bugler August 1, 1864.

COMPANY C.

Name	Rank	Date of rank		Remarks
John W. Gill	Captain	Oct.	25, 1863	Promoted from 1st lieutenant; resigned October 15, 1864.
Marion M. Gates	1st lieutenant	Dec.	21, 1863	Ordered to be mustered as captain from October 18, 1864; killed in action December 2, 1864, in Perry county, Arkansas.
John L. W. Matthews	2d lieutenant	Oct.	17, 1864	Promoted from 2d lieutenant; mustered out with regiment.
John H. Huggins	Sergeant	Oct.	17, 1864	Appointed from 1st sergeant October 18, 1864; mustered out with regiment.
Green Griffin	Sergeant	Mar.	22, 1864	Appointed from private August 12, 1864; mustered out with regiment.
James Griffin	Corporal	Mar.	22, 1864	Appointed from private; mustered out with regiment.

Name	Rank	Muster		Remarks
Bostick, Joshua	Private	Sept.	5, 1864	Mustered out with regiment.
Cushman, George	do	May	1, 1864	Do.
Evans, Leroy	do	Nov.	16, 1863	Do.
Evans, Alfred	do	July	8, 1864	Do.
Gee, John A	do	July	17, 1864	Do.
Gee, Miltus V	do	July	6, 1864	Do.
Gee, Charles H	do	July	6, 1864	Do.
Grinaway, Robert	do	June	11, 1864	Do.
Hale, John	do	Nov.	22, 1863	Do.
Hickman, James D	do	Oct.	25, 1863	Do.
Hunter, George W	do	Oct.	25, 1863	In confinement in military prison, Little Rock, Arkansas, since February 29, 1864.
Jennings, Thomas D	do	Oct.	25, 1863	Mustered out with regiment.
Morgan, John	do	Nov.	11, 1864	Do.
McConnel, James W	do	Aug.	16, 1864	Do.
Nicholson, John	do	Oct.	25, 1863	In confinement at Lewisburg, Arkansas, awaiting trial.
Parks, Levi	do	Nov.	1, 1864	Mustered out with regiment.
Patrick, Henry	do	Mar.	22, 1864	Do.
Robertson, Alexander	do	Aug.	16, 1864	Do.

Third regiment Arkansas cavalry volunteers. Mustered into service February 10, 1864, (three years;) mustered out June 30, 1865.

COMPANY C—Continued.

Names.	Rank.	Enlistment.	Muster.	Remarks.
Storey, James	Private	April 12, 1864	June 11, 1864	Mustered out with regiment.
Seabolt, William A	do	Oct. 25, 1863	Nov. 3, 1863	Do.
Stubblefield, John R	do	July 14, 1864	July 14, 1864	Do.
Watson, William	do	Jan. 11, 1865	May 25, 1865	Do.
Mustered out in accordance with special instructions from War Department, Adjutant General's Office, dated April 5, 1865; discharges to date May 22, 1865.				
William P. Hambright	1st sergeant	Oct. 25, 1863	Nov. 3, 1863	Sergeant from enlistment; 1st sergeant since December 26, 1864.
George F. Sloan	Quartermaster sergeant	Oct. 25, 1863	Nov. 3, 1863	Quartermaster sergeant from enlistment.
Joseph B. Wood	Commissary sergeant	Oct. 25, 1863	Nov. 3, 1863	Sergeant from enlistment; commissary sergeant since May 11, 1864.
James O. Higgins	Sergeant	Oct. 25, 1863	Nov. 3, 1863	Appointed from private April 16, 1864.
James Edwards	Corporal	Oct. 25, 1863	Nov. 3, 1863	Appointed April 16, 1864.
William Clemons	do	Oct. 25, 1863	Nov. 3, 1863	Do.
Newton Brown	Blacksmith	Oct. 25, 1863	Nov. 3, 1863	Appointed June 30, 1864.
Green Young	do	Oct. 25, 1863	Nov. 3, 1863	Blacksmith from enlistment.
Brazil, William	Private	Nov. 16, 1863	Dec. 1, 1863	
Brazil, Valentine	do	Oct. 25, 1863	Nov. 3, 1863	
Billings, Wilson	do	Oct. 25, 1863	Nov. 3, 1863	
Brandon, John R	do	Oct. 25, 1863	Nov. 3, 1863	
Baskins, William	do	Oct. 25, 1863	Nov. 3, 1863	
Baskins, Lafayette	do	Oct. 25, 1863	Nov. 3, 1863	
Dacus, William H	do	Nov. 16, 1863	Dec. 1, 1863	
Fitch, Ransom	do	Oct. 25, 1863	Nov. 3, 1863	
Gordon, Alfred	do	Nov. 16, 1863	Dec. 1, 1863	Prisoner of war from November 16, 1863, to November 1, 1864.
Grace, William	do	Oct. 25, 1863	Nov. 3, 1863	
Hunter, John P	do	Oct. 25, 1863	Nov. 3, 1863	
Hunter, Larkin	do	Oct. 25, 1863	Nov. 3, 1863	
Hasper, John W	do	Oct. 25, 1863	Nov. 3, 1863	
Hadlock, John	do	Oct. 25, 1863	Nov. 3, 1863	
Johnson, Alfred	do	Oct. 25, 1863	Nov. 3, 1863	
Johnston, Robert H	do	Oct. 25, 1863	Nov. 3, 1863	
Jones, Jesse	do	Nov. 16, 1863	Dec. 1, 1863	
Lewis, Dennis D	do	Oct. 25, 1863	Nov. 3, 1863	
Leak, James	do	Oct. 25, 1863	Nov. 3, 1863	
Leach, Alexander	do	Nov. 16, 1863	Dec. 1, 1863	
Leach, William	do	Nov. 16, 1863	Dec. 1, 1863	
Mathis, Thomas E	do	Oct. 25, 1863	Nov. 3, 1863	
Mathis, John W	do	Oct. 25, 1863	Nov. 3, 1863	
Morris, Francis	do	Oct. 25, 1863	Nov. 3, 1863	
McCabe, Marion	do	Oct. 25, 1863	Nov. 3, 1863	

REPORT OF THE ADJUTANT GENERAL OF ARKANSAS. 105

Name	Rank	Enlisted	Mustered out	Remarks
McCabe, John	do	Oct. 25, 1863	Nov. 3, 1863	
McDonald, Julius	do	Oct. 25, 1863	Nov. 3, 1863	
May, Joshua	do	Oct. 25, 1863	Nov. 3, 1863	
Nicholson, Lafayette	do	Oct. 25, 1863	Nov. 3, 1863	
Posey, William R	do	Oct. 25, 1863	Nov. 3, 1863	
Pryor, Green	do	Oct. 25, 1863	Nov. 3, 1863	
Pinson, David	do	Oct. 25, 1863	Nov. 3, 1863	
Pinson, George W	do	Oct. 25, 1863	Nov. 3, 1863	
Ragsdale, Jesse	do	Oct. 25, 1863	Nov. 3, 1863	
Roddy, James E	do	Oct. 25, 1863	Nov. 3, 1863	
Smith, John E	do	Oct. 25, 1863	Nov. 3, 1863	
Watson, Josiah	do	Oct. 25, 1863	Nov. 3, 1863	
Waller, George W	do	Nov. 16, 1863	Dec. 1, 1863	

Killed in action.

Name	Rank	Enlisted	Mustered out	Remarks
McGehee, William	Private	Oct. 25, 1863	Nov. 3, 1863	Killed in action in Perry county, Arkansas, December 6, 1864.
Pasten, Dixon	do	Oct. 25, 1863	Nov. 3, 1863	Do.

Died.

Name	Rank	Enlisted	Mustered out	Remarks
George A. Cunningham	Commissary sergeant	Oct. 25, 1863	Nov. 3, 1863	Died in regimental hospital, Lewisburg, Arkansas, August 11, 1864.
William Crouch	Corporal	Oct. 25, 1863	Nov. 3, 1863	Died at Lewisburg, Arkansas, September 4, 1864.
Joseph Heaton	do	Oct. 25, 1863	Nov. 3, 1863	Died at Lewisburg, Arkansas, July 16, 1864.
Wesley H. Johnson	do	Oct. 25, 1863	Nov. 3, 1863	Died at Lewisburg, Arkansas, January 21, 1864.
Edmond Wade	Blacksmith	Oct. 25, 1863	Nov. 3, 1863	Died in hospital, Little Rock, Arkansas, June 3, 1864.
John Graves	Private	Oct. 25, 1863	Nov. 3, 1863	Died in military prison, Little Rock, Arkansas, September 30, 1864.
Alvis, William	do	Mar. 22, 1864	Never	Died in hospital, Lewisburg, Arkansas, August 12, 1864.
Griffin, Young F	do	Mar. 22, 1864	Never	Died in hospital, Lewisburg, Arkansas, April 20, 1864.
Hoffman, Francis	do	Oct. 25, 1863	Nov. 3, 1863	Died in hospital, Lewisburg, Arkansas, July 1, 1864.
Howell, John	do	Oct. 25, 1863	Nov. 3, 1863	Died in Perry county, Arkansas, February 24, 1863.
Higgins, Michael	do	Oct. 25, 1863	Nov. 3, 1863	Died in hospital, Lewisburg, Arkansas, March 8, 1865.
Irvin, Alexander	do	Oct. 25, 1863	Nov. 3, 1863	Died at Lewisburg, Arkansas, November 24, 1863.
Lewis, John	do	Oct. 25, 1863	Nov. 3, 1863	Died in hospital, Little Rock, Arkansas, October 20, 1864.
McGehee, Robert	do	Oct. 25, 1863	Nov. 3, 1863	Died in hospital, Lewisburg, Arkansas, June 4, 1864.
Morris, William	do	Oct. 25, 1863	Nov. 3, 1863	Died in hospital, Lewisburg, Arkansas, August 10, 1864.
Newton, Isaac	do	Oct. 25, 1863	Nov. 3, 1863	Died in hospital, Lewisburg, Arkansas, June 15, 1864.
Pruit, William S	do	Oct. 25, 1863	Nov. 3, 1863	Died in hospital, Lewisburg, Arkansas, June 17, 1864.
Pinson, Reuben	do	Oct. 25, 1863	Nov. 3, 1863	Died in military prison, Little Rock, Arkansas, October 10, 1864.
Robertson, Elisha M	do	Oct. 25, 1863	Nov. 3, 1863	Died in hospital, Little Rock, Arkansas, October 20, 1864.
Robertson, Elisha	do	Oct. 25, 1863	Nov. 3, 1863	Died in military prison, Little Rock, Arkansas, June 16, 1864.
Reed, Joseph	do	Oct. 25, 1863	Nov. 3, 1863	Died in hospital, Lewisburg, Arkansas, July 6, 1864.
Reed, Henry	do	Oct. 25, 1863	Nov. 3, 1867	Died in hospital, Lewisburg, Arkansas, December 1, 1864.
Reed, William H	do			

Discharged.

Name	Rank	Enlisted	Mustered out	Remarks
Morris, Chessley	Private	Nov. 16, 1863	Dec. 1, 1863	For disability, March 31, 1864, having contracted small-pox while in the discharge of his duty, which rendered him totally blind.

Deserted.

Name	Rank	Enlisted	Mustered out	Remarks
Brazil, John	Private	Jan. 6, 1865	Never	Deserted April 2, 1865.

Third regiment Arkansas cavalry volunteers. Mustered into service February 10, 1864, (three years;) mustered out June 30, 1865.

COMPANY C—Continued.

Names.	Rank.	Enlistment.	Muster.	Remarks.
Brazil, Thomas	Private	Jan. 19, 1865	Never	Deserted April 28, 1865.
Brazil, Andrew J	do	Jan. 5, 1865	Never	Deserted May 21, 1865.
Graves, William	do	Oct. 25, 1863	Nov. 3, 1863	Deserted March 2, 1865.
Joslin, George	do	Sept. 5, 1864	Never	Deserted October 26, 1864.
Hopper, Gilam	do	Oct. 25, 1863	Nov. 3, 1863	Deserted April 2, 1865.
Mhoon, John	do	Oct. 25, 1863	Nov. 3, 1863	Deserted March 1, 1865.
Perrine, Austin T	do	Oct. 25, 1863	Nov. 3, 1863	Deserted September 7, 1864.
Robertson, John	Corporal	Oct. 25, 1863	Nov. 3, 1863	Deserted April 2, 1865.
Welburn, William	Private	Oct. 25, 1863	Nov. 3, 1863	Deserted September 7, 1864.
Wade, John	do	Oct. 25, 1863	Nov. 3, 1863	Escaped from confinement at Lewisburg, Arkansas, June 5, 1865.

Transferred.

Names.	Rank.	Enlistment.	Muster.	Remarks.
Gill, Murray A	Sergeant	Nov. 16, 1863	Dec. 1, 1863	Transferred to non-commissioned staff November 20, 1864.

COMPANY D.

Names.	Rank.	Date of rank.	Muster.	Remarks.
James F. Clear	Captain	Dec. 4, 1863	Dec. 4, 1863	Appointed from civil life; dismissed October 15, 1864.
Robert W. Wylie	do	Feb. 1, 1865	Feb. 1, 1865	Appointed from sergeant 3d Missouri cavalry to 1st lieutenant of company D, December 3, 1863; mustered out with regiment.
John Macklencate	1st lieutenant	Feb. 1, 1865	Feb. 1, 1865	Appointed from sergeant company A, 3d Michigan cavalry; mustered out with regiment.
Jacob Graves	2d lieutenant	Dec. 11, 1863	Dec. 11, 1863	Appointed from civil life; resigned August 8, 1864.
William J. McDonald	do	Feb. 1, 1865	Feb. 1, 1865	Appointed sergeant December 2, 1864; 1st sergeant February 1, 1865; mustered out with regiment.
Thomas Grery	1st sergeant	Oct. 30, 1863	Feb. 1, 1865	Appointed corporal December 2, 1863; sergeant July 18, 1864; mustered out with regiment.
Solomon Childers	Quartermaster sergeant	Nov. 15, 1863	July 18, 1864	Appointed from private; mustered out with regiment.
Christopher C. Price	Commissary sergeant	Oct. 30, 1863	Dec. 2, 1863	Appointed from private December 2, 1863; mustered out with regiment.
William Blackburn	Sergeant	Nov. 15, 1863	Oct. 30, 1864	Appointed corporal July 25, 1864; mustered out with regiment.
Ransom Shinn	do	Oct. 7, 1863	May 1, 1865	Appointed from corporal; mustered out with regiment.
Thomas Graves	Corporal	Oct. 30, 1863	Dec. 2, 1863	Mustered out with regiment.
James M. Graves	do	Nov. 15, 1863	July 25, 1864	Do.
Martin V. Harchfield	do	Oct. 30, 1863	Oct. 30, 1864	Do.
William W. Garrison	do	Oct. 30, 1863	Oct. 30, 1864	Do.
James G. Underwood	do	Nov. 15, 1863	May 1, 1865	Do.
John E. Hagler	Bugler	Nov. 15, 1863	Nov. 15, 1864	Do.
Jesse S. Lunsford	do	Nov. 15, 1863	Nov. 15, 1864	Do.
William Erwood	Wagoner	Nov. 15, 1863	Dec. 2, 1863	Do.

REPORT OF THE ADJUTANT GENERAL OF ARKANSAS. 107

Name	Rank		Muster	
Amburn, Reuben	Private	Jan. 10, 1865	May 25, 1865	Do.
Brown, Montgomery	do	Oct. 30, 1863	Nov. 7, 1863	Do.
Brown, Benton L	do	Oct. 30, 1863	Nov. 7, 1863	Do.
Brock, Russell	do	Nov. 15, 1863	Dec. 2, 1863	Do.
Brewer, William	do	Nov. 15, 1863	Dec. 2, 1863	Do.
Burton, John W	do	Nov. 15, 1863	Dec. 2, 1863	Do.
Counts, Henry C	do	Oct. 30, 1863	Nov. 7, 1863	Do.
Compton, Oliver P	do	Oct. 30, 1863	Nov. 7, 1863	Do.
Cobb, William D	do	Dec. 2, 1864	Dec. 2, 1864	Do.
Drake, Allen	do	Oct. 30, 1863	Nov. 7, 1863	Do.
Edwards, John L	do	Oct. 30, 1863	Nov. 7, 1863	Do.
Foley, Allen	do	Nov. 15, 1863	Dec. 2, 1863	Do.
Frazier, George	do	Nov. 15, 1863	Dec. 2, 1863	Do.
Gray, John W	do	Oct. 30, 1863	Nov. 7, 1863	Do.
Gray, Charles P	do	Dec. 23, 1864	Dec. 23, 1864	Do.
Hensley, George W	do	Nov. 15, 1863	Dec. 2, 1863	Do.
Huffstidler, James N	do	Nov. 15, 1863	Nov. 2, 1863	Do.
Honeycutt, Laban M	do	Oct. 30, 1863	Nov. 7, 1863	Do.
Haurir, Levi	do	Sept. 5, 1864	Sept. 5, 1864	Do.
Kirkpatrick, James	do	Jan. 11, 1865	May 25, 1865	Do.
Lime, John	do	Nov. 15, 1863	Dec. 2, 1863	Do.
Lunsford, William	do	Nov. 15, 1863	Dec. 2, 1863	Do.
Lunsford, Monroe	do	Nov. 15, 1863	Dec. 2, 1863	Do.
Parliam, John	do	Oct. 30, 1863	Nov. 7, 1863	Do.
Parrish, James M	do	Nov. 15, 1863	Dec. 2, 1863	Do.
Powell, Robert B	do	Nov. 15, 1863	Dec. 2, 1863	Do.
Peatray, John	do	Nov. 15, 1863	Dec. 2, 1863	Do.
Price, James F	do	Oct. 30, 1863	Nov. 7, 1863	Do.
Price, Robert	do	Nov. 12, 1864	Nov. 12, 1864	Do.
Sterling, Milton	do	Oct. 30, 1863	Nov. 7, 1863	Do.
Snider, George	do	Nov. 15, 1863	Dec. 2, 1863	Do.
Smith, James W	do	Nov. 15, 1863	Dec. 2, 1863	Do.
Smith, John	do	Nov. 15, 1863	Dec. 2, 1863	Do.
Smith, Henry A	do	Nov. 2, 1864	Nov. 2, 1864	Do.
Stiven, James W	do	Oct. 18, 1864	Nov. 18, 1864	Do.
Thompson, Stephen	do	Oct. 30, 1863	Nov. 7, 1863	Do.
Taylor, Thomas	do	Nov. 15, 1863	Dec. 2, 1863	Do.
Thomas, Adam	do	Nov. 15, 1863	Nov. 2, 1863	Do.
Underwood, Reuben	do	Oct. 30, 1863	Nov. 7, 1863	Do.
Underwood, Malachi	do	Nov. 15, 1863	Dec. 2, 1863	Do.
Vassar, Charles	do	Nov. 15, 1863	Dec. 2, 1863	Do.
Wilt, John	do	Nov. 15, 1863	Dec. 2, 1863	Do.
Waterson, Robert A	do	Nov. 15, 1863	Dec. 2, 1863	Do.
Wroper, George	do	Oct. 30, 1863	Nov. 7, 1863	Do.
Wyatt, John D	do	Dec. 12, 1864	Dec. 12, 1864	Do.

108 REPORT OF THE ADJUTANT GENERAL OF ARKANSAS.

Third regiment Arkansas cavalry volunteers. Mustered into service February 10, 1864, (three years;) mustered out June 30, 1865

COMPANY D—Continued.

Names.	Rank.	Enlistment.	Muster.	Remarks.
Mustered out in accordance with special instructions from the War Department, Adjutant General's Office, dated April 5, 1865—discharges to take effect May 22, 1865.				
Isaac Griffin	Sergeant	Nov. 15, 1863	Dec. 2, 1863	Appointed corporal December 2, 1863; sergeant July 25, 1864.
John Robinson	do	Oct. 30, 1863	Nov. 7, 1863	Appointed corporal December 2, 1863; sergeant August 31, 1864.
Henry C. Parrish	do	Oct. 30, 1863	Nov. 7, 1863	Appointed corporal December 2, 1863; sergeant October 30, 1864.
Zebulon J. Garrison	Corporal	Oct. 30, 1863	Nov. 7, 1863	Appointed corporal July 25, 1864.
David Parish	do	Nov. 15, 1863	Dec. 2, 1863	Do.
William R. Shopton	Farrier and blacksmith	Oct. 30, 1863	Nov. 7, 1863	Appointed blacksmith and farrier December 2, 1863.
Brewer, Joseph D	Private	Oct. 30, 1863	Nov. 7, 1863	
Burnham, Isaac B	do	Oct. 30, 1863	Nov. 7, 1863	
Belkhead, John	do	Nov. 15, 1863	Dec. 2, 1863	
Cox, James S. F	do	Oct. 30, 1863	Nov. 7, 1863	
Faman, John	do	Oct. 30, 1863	Nov. 7, 1863	
Griffin, Benjamin F	do	Nov. 15, 1863	Dec. 2, 1863	
Garrison, Elias A	do	Oct. 30, 1863	Nov. 7, 1863	
Garrison, Moses J	do	Oct. 30, 1863	Nov. 7, 1863	
Guthrie, Edward	do	Oct. 30, 1863	Nov. 7, 1863	
Haddox, Isaac	do	Oct. 30, 1863	Nov. 7, 1863	
Hames, Milton A	do	Nov. 15, 1863	Dec. 2, 1863	
Shopton, Alpheus T	do	Oct. 30, 1863	Nov. 7, 1863	
Smith, William J	do	Oct. 30, 1863	Nov. 7, 1863	
Tillman, John	do	Oct. 30, 1863	Nov. 7, 1863	
Willett, Edward H	do	Oct. 30, 1863	Nov. 7, 1863	
Willeutt, Barney Y	do	Oct. 30, 1863	Nov. 7, 1863	
Killed in action.				
Tillman, James	Private	Oct. 30, 1863	Nov. 7, 1863	Killed in action at Dardanelle, Arkansas, May 12, 1864.
Died.				
Coleman, Harrison G	Private	Oct. 30, 1863	Nov. 7, 1863	Died of smallpox at Lewisburg, Arkansas, August 16, 1864.
Hodges, William F	do	Oct. 30, 1863	Nov. 7, 1863	Died at Lewisburg, Arkansas, April 1, 1863.
Honeycutt, James A	do	Oct. 30, 1863	Nov. 7, 1863	Died of congestive chills, at Russellville, Arkansas, March 19, 1865.
Tillman, William	Sergeant	Nov. 15, 1863	Dec. 2, 1863	Died at Lewisburg, Arkansas, August 3, 1864.
Underwood, Robert F	Private	Oct. 30, 1863	Nov. 7, 1863	Died at Little Rock, Arkansas, January 1, 1864.
Fielden, James	do	Nov. 15, 1863	Dec. 2, 1863	Died at Little Rock, Arkansas, March 1, 1864.

REPORT OF THE ADJUTANT GENERAL OF ARKANSAS. 109

Discharged.

Baker, William A	Private	Oct. 30, 1863	Nov. 7, 1863	Discharged for disability, at Lewisburg, Arkansas, April 18, 1865.
Jones, Bradford L	do	Oct. 30, 1863	Nov. 7, 1863	Do.

Deserted.

Harrison Gilbert	Corporal	Nov. 15, 1863	Dec. 2, 1863	Appointed corporal Nov. 30, 1864; deserted at Lewisburg, Arkansas, Feb. 18, 1865.
Samuel Poe	Bugler	Nov. 15, 1863	Dec. 2, 1863	Bugler from enlistment, deserted at Lewisburg, Arkansas, September 1, 1864.
Arnold, William L	Private	Nov. 15, 1863	Dec. 2, 1863	Deserted at Lewisburg, Arkansas, August 12, 1864.
Branden, Jasper N	do	Nov. 15, 1863	Dec. 2, 1863	Deserted at Dardanelle, Arkansas, May 15, 1864.
Bailey, Rufus A	do	Nov. 15, 1863	Dec 2, 1863	Deserted at Lewisburg, Arkansas, August 6, 1864.
Barnum, William J	do	Oct. 30, 1863	Nov. 7, 1863	Deserted at Dardanelle, Arkansas, May 15, 1864.
Huckaby, Alfred	do	Oct. 30, 1863	Nov. 7, 1863	Deserted at Lewisburg, Arkansas, August 17, 1864.
Hanley, Marvin	do	Nov. 15, 1863	Dec. 2, 1863	Deserted at Lewisburg, Arkansas, February 1, 1865.
Kirvin, John W	do	Oct. 20, 1863	Nov. 7, 1863	Deserted at Dardanelle, Arkansas, May 15, 1864.
Lauderdale, James A	do	Nov. 15, 1863	Dec. 2, 1863	Do.
Phasir, Meigs D	do	Nov. 15, 1863	Nov. 7, 1863	Do.
Smith, Gilman	do	Oct. 30, 1863	Nov. 7, 1863	Deserted at Lewisburg, Arkansas, January 12, 1865.
Spicer, Stephen D	do	Oct. 30, 1863	Dec. 2, 1863	Deserted at Dardanelle, Arkansas, May 15, 1864.
Thompson, Newman	do	Nov. 15, 1863	Nov. 7, 1863	Do.
Utley, John C	do	Oct. 30, 1863	Dec. 2, 1863	Do.
Utley, Ralph	do	Nov. 15, 1863	Dec. 2, 1863	Deserted at Lewisburg, Arkansas, September 1, 1864.
Webb, Wesley	do	Oct. 30, 1863	Nov. 7, 1863	Deserted at Dardanelle, Arkansas, May 15, 1864.
Young, David	do	Nov. 15, 1863	Dec. 2, 1863	Do.

Transferred.

Snyder, Edward	Private	Oct. 30, 1863	Nov. 7, 1863	Transferred to regimental non-commissioned staff as com'sary sergeant Mar. 4, 1864.

COMPANY E.

			Date of rank.	
Thomas Boles	Captain	Feb. 5, 1864	Feb. 5, 1864	Appointed from civil life; mustered out ——, 1864.
Robert W. Wishard	do		Oct. 18, 1864	Appointed from 1st sergeant of company I 1st Missouri cavalry to 1st lieutenant February 5, 1864; mustered out with regiment.
Patrick B. King	1st lieutenant	Oct. 15, 1863	Oct. 18, 1864	Promoted from 2d lieutenant October 18, 1864; mustered out with regiment.
William M. Boler	2d lieutenant	Dec. 23, 1863	June 20, 1864	Appointed from sergeant October 18, 1864; mustered out with regiment.
James M. Tatum	1st sergeant	Dec. 23, 1863	June 20, 1864	Appointed from private; mustered out with regiment.
David C. Wood	Quartermaster sergeant	Dec. 23, 1863	Oct. 1, 1864	Do.
John L. Worsham	Sergeant	Oct. 15, 1863	Nov. 19, 1863	Do.
Andrew J. Chance	Corporal	Dec. 23, 1863	Nov. 19, 1863	Mustered out with regiment.
John Herrin	do	Oct. 15, 1863	Dec. 30, 1863	Do.
William A. Cornelius	do	Oct. 15, 1863	Nov. 19, 1863	Do.
James T. Maxwell	do	Feb. 1, 1864	Sept. 4, 1864	Do.
John M. Priest	do	Feb. 6, 1864	Nov. 1, 1864	Do.
John P. Newbern	Farrier	Oct. 15, 1863	Nov. 19, 1863	Do.
Carr Allen	Bugler	Oct. 15, 1863	Nov. 19, 1863	Do.
John B. Morgan	do	Oct. 15, 1863	Nov. 19, 1863	Do.

Third regiment Arkansas cavalry volunteers. Mustered into service February 10, 1864, (three years;) mustered out June 30, 1865.

COMPANY E—Continued.

Names.	Rank.	Enlistment.	Muster.	Remarks.
Bean, Peter K	Private	Dec. 23, 1863	Dec. 30, 1863	In confinement under charges; no discharge furnished on muster out of regiment.
Box, Lewis	do	Oct. 15, 1863	Nov. 19, 1863	Mustered out with regiment.
Boggur, William	do	Feb. 1, 1864	Feb. 4, 1864	Do.
Brown, William	do	Mar. 25, 1865	May 23, 1865	Do.
Brown, Thomas	do	Mar. 25, 1865	May 23, 1865	Do.
Cooper, Oliver	do	Feb. 6, 1864	Feb. 8, 1864	Do.
Carpenter, Abraham	do	Nov. 21, 1864	April 29, 1865	Do.
Castelbury, David	do	Oct. 15, 1863	Nov. 19, 1863	Do.
Dean, Nathaniel	do	Feb. 1, 1864	Feb. 4, 1864	Do.
Ezell, William	do	Feb. 10, 1864	Mar. 4, 1864	Do.
Fry, Quinn J	do	Oct. 15, 1863	Nov. 19, 1863	Do.
Grigsby, James	do	Oct. 15, 1863	Nov. 19, 1863	Do.
Gaskins, Henderson	do	Oct. 15, 1863	Nov. 19, 1863	Do.
Gilbreath, Lorenzo D	do	Dec. 23, 1863	Dec. 30, 1863	Do.
Gross, Alfred	do	Aug. 29, 1864	Sept. 23, 1864	Do.
Greenwood, Lewis T	do	Jan. 14, 1864	Sept. 23, 1864	Do.
Hinley, Lafayette	do	Feb. 1, 1864	Feb. 4, 1864	Do.
Hawkins, John W	do	Feb. 1, 1864	Feb. 4, 1864	Do.
Hunt, Peter	do	Mar. 22, 1864	May 17, 1864	Do.
Harper, James W	do	Oct. 15, 1863	Nov. 19, 1863	Do.
Hutchinson, Harry C	do	Oct. 15, 1863	Nov. 19, 1863	Do.
King, Joseph S	do	Oct. 15, 1863	Nov. 19, 1863	Do.
King, Linza	do	June 12, 1864	Sept. 23, 1864	Do.
Lambert, James R. P	do	Feb. 1, 1864	Feb. 4, 1864	Do.
Ladd, Richard	do	Feb. 1, 1864	Feb. 4, 1864	Do.
McClenden, Lewis	do	Oct. 15, 1863	Nov. 19, 1863	Do.
McClenden, Mason G	do	Oct. 15, 1863	Nov. 19, 1863	Do.
Miller, David	do	Oct. 15, 1863	Nov. 19, 1863	Do.
Miller, Rufus	do	Dec. 23, 1863	Dec. 23, 1863	Do.
McCann, George W	do	Dec. 23, 1863	Dec. 23, 1863	Do.
Meeks, William P	do	Feb. 6, 1864	Feb. 8, 1864	Do.
Norman, William P	do	Feb. 1, 1864	Feb. 4, 1864	Do.
Parker, Ralph	do	Oct. 13, 1863	Nov. 19, 1863	Do.
Pugh, Henry M	do	Feb. 1, 1864	Feb. 4, 1864	Do.
Qualls, David	do	Feb. 10, 1864	Mar. 4, 1864	Do.
Qualls, Isaac	do	Dec. 13, 1864	April 29, 1865	Do.
Sherrill, Eli P	do	June 12, 1864	April 29, 1865	Do.
Sherrill, Leeman R	do	June 12, 1864	April 29, 1865	Do.
Taylor, William M	do	Dec. 7, 1864	April 29, 1865	Do.
Whaley, Jesse A	do	Dec. 6, 1864	April 29, 1865	Do.
Miles, William N	do	Oct. 15, 1863	Nov. 19, 1863	Do.

REPORT OF THE ADJUTANT GENERAL OF ARKANSAS. 111

Mustered out in accordance with special instructions from the War Department, dated Adjutant General's Office, April 5, 1865—discharges to take effect May 22, 1865.

Name	Rank	Enlisted	Mustered	Remarks
George W. Lemour	Sergeant	Oct. 15, 1863	Nov. 19, 1863	
James H. Lemour	do	Oct. 15, 1863	Nov. 19, 1863	
Francis M. Gilbreath	do	Dec. 23, 1863	Dec. 30, 1863	
George A. Morgan	do	Oct. 15, 1863	Nov. 19, 1863	
Blagg, Benjamin F	Private	Oct. 15, 1863	Nov. 19, 1863	
Blagg, Michael B	do	Oct. 15, 1863	Nov. 19, 1863	
Brown, Robert J	do	Feb. 1, 1864	Feb. 4, 1864	
Cole, Francis M	do	Oct. 15, 1863	Nov. 19, 1864	
Garner, William	do	Oct. 15, 1863	Nov. 19, 1864	
Horrin, Jonathan	do	Oct. 15, 1863	Feb. 4, 1864	
Furguson, Robert V	do	Oct. 15, 1863	Nov. 19, 1863	
Fowler, Thomas J	do	Oct. 15, 1863	Nov. 19, 1863	
Forgy, John	do	Feb. 1, 1864	Feb. 4, 1864	
Jones, William H	do	Dec. 23, 1863	Dec. 30, 1863	
Jones, Leonard	do	Oct. 15, 1863	Nov. 19, 1863	
Kirker, William H	do	Dec. 23, 1863	Dec. 30, 1863	
Morgan, William T	do	Dec. 23, 1863	Dec. 30, 1863	
McClain, John	do	Dec. 23, 1863	Dec. 30, 1863	
McClenden, Laban H	do	Oct. 15, 1863	Nov. 19, 1863	
Parker, John	do	Dec. 23, 1863	Dec. 30, 1863	
Turner, Samuel	do	Oct. 15, 1863	Nov. 19, 1863	
Taylor, Joseph D	do	Oct. 15, 1863	Nov. 19, 1863	
Griffith, John	Blacksmith	Oct. 15, 1863	Nov. 19, 1863	

Died.

Name	Rank	Enlisted	Mustered	Remarks
Luther G. Floyd	Sergeant	Oct. 15, 1863	Nov. 19, 1863	Died at Lewisburg, Arkansas, August 19, 1864.
Wade W. Morgan	Corporal	Oct. 15, 1863	Nov. 19, 1863	Do.
Bailey Oller	do	Oct. 15, 1863	Nov. 19, 1863	Died at Lewisburg, Arkansas, February 23, 1865.
James M. Ryan	do	Oct. 15, 1863	Nov. 19, 1863	Died at Lewisburg, Arkansas, February 4, 1864.
Michael E. Aikman	Private	Oct. 15, 1863	Nov. 19, 1863	Died at Little Rock, Arkansas, July 1, 1864.
Banister, Joseph S	do	Oct. 15, 1863	Nov. 19, 1863	Died at Little Rock, Arkansas, January 18, 1864.
Carter, James T	do	Oct. 15, 1863	Nov. 19, 1863	Died at Little Rock, Arkansas, January 17, 1864.
Cook, Daniel C	do	Oct. 15, 1863	Nov. 19, 1863	Died at Little Rock, Arkansas, June 19, 1864.
Fry, James F	do	Oct. 15, 1863	Nov. 19, 1863	Died at Little Rock, Arkansas, April 28, 1864.
Morgan, John C	do	Oct. 15, 1863	Nov. 19, 1863	Died at Little Rock, Arkansas, December 8, 1863.
Stone, Thomas J	do	Feb. 1, 1864	Feb. 4, 1864	Died at Little Rock, Arkansas, October 25, 1864.

Deserted.

Name	Rank	Enlisted	Mustered	Remarks
Hugh A. Morgan	Sergeant	Oct. 15, 1863	Nov. 19, 1863	Deserted at Lewisburg, Arkansas, November 8, 1864.
Thomas B. Clifton	do	Aug. 29, 1864	Sept. 23, 1864	do.
Chandler, Alpheus	Private	Aug. 29, 1864		Deserted at Lewisburg, Arkansas, September 5, 1864.
Douthit, Sanford C	do	Oct. 15, 1863	Nov. 19, 1863	Deserted at Lewisburg, Arkansas, November 8, 1864.
Fetridge, William	do	July 1, 1864		Deserted at Lewisburg, Arkansas, January 10, 1864.

112   REPORT OF THE ADJUTANT GENERAL OF ARKANSAS.

Third regiment Arkansas cavalry volunteers. Mustered into service February 10, 1864, (three years;) mustered out June 30, 1865.

COMPANY E—Continued.

Names.	Rank.	Enlistment.	Muster.	Remarks.
Garner, William, sr	Private	Oct. 15, 1863	Nov. 19, 1863	Deserted at Lewisburg, Arkansas, January 1, 1864.
Garrett, John	do	Oct. 15, 1863	Nov. 19, 1863	Deserted at Lewisburg, Arkansas, November 8, 1864.
Hutchinson, Robert	do	Oct. 15, 1863	Nov. 19, 1863	Deserted at Lewisburg, Arkansas, November 16, 1864.
Kress, Franklin P	do	Feb. 6, 1864	Feb. 8, 1864	Deserted at Lewisburg, Arkansas, November 8, 1864.
Millsap, George W	do	Oct. 15, 1863	Nov. 19, 1863	Do.
Miller, John H	do	Oct. 15, 1863	Nov. 19, 1863	Deserted at Lewisburg, Arkansas, January 1, 1864.
Newsom, Richard B	do	Dec. 23, 1863	Dec. 30, 1863	Deserted at Mount Ida, Arkansas, April 5, 1864.
Ramsey, John	do	Jan. 1, 1864		Deserted at Little Rock, Arkansas, January 10, 1864.
Wilson, John	do	Oct. 15, 1863	Nov. 19, 1863	Deserted at Lewisburg, Arkansas, November 8, 1864.
Discharged.				
Kilburn, John	Private	Dec. 23, 1863	Dec. 30, 1863	Discharged for disability at Little Rock, Arkansas, November 7, 1864.
Morgan, John	do	Oct. 15, 1863	Nov. 19, 1863	Discharged for disability at Little Rock, Arkansas, March 13, 1865.
Welch, Andrew	do	Dec. 23, 1863	Dec. 30, 1863	Discharged for disability at Little Rock, Arkansas, April 17, 1864.
Welch, Joseph	do	Dec. 23, 1863	Dec. 30, 1863	Discharged for disability at Little Rock, Arkansas, November 7, 1864.

COMPANY F.

Names.	Rank.	Enlistment.	Date of rank.	Remarks.
Bright W. Henning	Captain	Oct. 14, 1863	Feb. 5, 1864	Appointed 1st lieutenant November 19, 1863; dismissed October 16, 1864.
John M. ——	1st lieutenant		Feb. 28, 1865	Appointed from sergeant company I, 1st Missouri cavalry; mustered out with regiment.

			Muster.	
Hiram Dacus	2d lieutenant	Dec. 15, 1863	Feb. 28, 1865	Appointed from civil life; mustered out with regiment.
William H. Lyon	Sergeant	Oct. 14, 1863	Oct. 30, 1864	Mustered out with regiment.
Marcus L. Sattenfield	Corporal	Oct. 14, 1863	Oct. 30, 1864	Do.
William Dacus	Bugler	Oct. 14, 1863	Oct. 1, 1864	Do.
Daniel Frobaugh	Blacksmith	Jan. 20, 1864	Oct. 1, 1864	Do.
Lewis Miller	Saddler	Oct. 14, 1863	Dec. 1, 1864	Do.
Bouregamer, Thomas D	Private	Dec. 15, 1863	Dec. 30, 1863	Do.
Clemton, William	do	Oct. 14, 1863	Nov. 19, 1863	Do.
Campbell, Thomas J	do	Dec. 15, 1863	Dec. 30, 1863	Do.
George, Harding W	do	Oct. 14, 1863	Nov. 19, 1863	Do.
Hill, William A	do	Oct. 14, 1863	Nov. 19, 1863	Do.
Hunt, Joel	do	Dec. 1, 1864	May 5, 1865	Do.

REPORT OF THE ADJUTANT GENERAL OF ARKANSAS. 113

Name	Rank			Remarks
Hunt, John C	do	Jan. 9, 1865	May 5, 1865	Do.
Harney, Clemons E	do	Oct. 14, 1863	Nov. 19, 1863	Do.
Inman, Hezekiah J	do	Jan. 20, 1864	Jan. 20, 1864	Do.
Ledel, Milton	do	Oct. 14, 1863	Nov. 19, 1863	Do.
Muse, John A	do	Oct. 14, 1863	Nov. 19, 1863	Do.
McMillins, Jesse	do	Oct. 14, 1863	Nov. 19, 1863	Do.
Manney, Samuel	do	Oct. 14, 1863	Nov. 19, 1853	Do.
Nix, Isom	do	June 18, 1864	May 5, 1865	Do.
Preiwtt, William	do	Oct. 14, 1863	Nov. 19, 1863	Do.
Pledge, Simeon	do	Oct. 14, 1863	Nov. 19, 1863	Do.
Sloan, ————	do	Oct. 14, 1863	Nov. 19, 1863	Do.
Sloan, Thomas A	do	Oct. 14, 1863	Nov. 19, 1863	Do.
Satterfield, Peter L	do	Dec. 13, 1863	Dec. 30, 1863	Do.
Taylor, Thomas J	do	Dec. 13, 1863	Nov. 17, 1863	Do.
Williams, Lewis	do	June 20, 1864	June 21, 1864	Do.

Mustered out in accordance with special instructions from War Department, dated Adjutant General's Office, April 5, 1865; discharges to take effect May 22, 1865.

John F. Briggs	Sergeant	Oct. 14, 1863	Nov. 19, 1863	
Ripley J	do	Oct. 14, 1863	Nov. 19, 1863	
Elisha P. Johnson	do	Oct. 14, 1863	Nov. 19, 1863	
Malcomb McClumey	do	Oct. 14, 1863	Nov. 19, 1863	
James M. Cook	Corporal	Oct. 14, 1863	Nov. 19, 1863	
John R. Page	do	Oct. 14, 1863	Nov. 19, 1863	
James M. Bennett	do	Dec. 15, 1863	Dec. 30, 1863	
Bennett, Hugh M	Private	Jan. 20, 1864	Jan. 20, 1864	
Cheat, Thomas J	do	Oct. 14, 1863	Nov. 19, 1863	
Fastin, Erastus	do	Oct. 14, 1863	Nov. 19, 1863	
George, Pubert	do	Jan. 20, 1864	Jan. 20, 1864	
Gwinn, Joseph C	do	Oct. 14, 1863	Nov. 19, 1863	
Huckaby, Ferdinand F	do	Dec. 15, 1863	Dec. 30, 1863	
Hames, ————	do	Dec. 15, 1863	Dec. 30, 1863	
Hunter, William P	do	Oct. 14, 1863	Nov. 19, 1863	
Johnson, Ben	do	Oct. 14, 1863	Nov. 19, 1863	
————, Joseph	do	Oct. 14, 1864	Nov. 19, 1863	
————, Henry	do	Oct. 14, 1863	Nov. 19, 1863	
Morse, James A	do	Oct. 14, 1863	Nov. 19, 1863	
Morris, William A	do	Oct. 14, 1863	Nov. 19, 1863	
Stinnett, Joseph	do	Oct. 14, 1863	Nov. 19, 1863	
Smith, William B	do	Oct. 14, 1863	Nov. 19, 1863	
Tate, James M	do	Oct. 14, 1863	Nov. 19, 1863	

Killed in action.

Taylor, Hampton	do	Oct. 14, 1863	Nov. 19, 1863	Killed by the enemy November 30, 1864.
Fox, Norton	do	Nov. 19, 1863	Never	Killed in action December 18, 1864.
Fickens, Samuel	do	June 1, 1864	June 20, 1864	Killed by the enemy June 18, 1865.

Mis. Doc. 53——8

114 REPORT OF THE ADJUTANT GENERAL OF ARKANSAS.

Third regiment Arkansas cavalry volunteers. Mustered into service February 10, 1864, (three years;) mustered out June 30, 1865.

COMPANY F—Continued.

Names.	Rank.	Enlistment.	Muster.	Remarks.
Missing since action.				
Lees, Griffin	Private	Oct. 14, 1863	Nov. 19, 1863	Missing on Camden expedition; died since in hospital, Memphis, Tennessee.
Jones, Thomas M	Sergeant	June 1, 1864	June 20, 1864	Appointed sergeant July 1, 1864; missing since action on Point Remove creek, Ark.
Died.				
Joseph Crabtree	Sergeant	Dec. 15, 1863	Dec. 30, 1863	Died from wounds received in the line of duty, April 7, 1865.
Samuel Huckaby	do	Dec. 15, 1863	Dec. 30, 1863	Died at Lewisburg, Arkansas, March 1, 1865.
Daniel D. Crownove	Corporal	Oct. 14, 1863	Nov. 19, 1863	Died in hospital, Little Rock, Arkansas.
Cannon, John	Private	June 20, 1864	Never	Died in hospital, Little Rock, Arkansas, February 22, 1864.
Cannon, George W	do	Oct. 14, 1863	Nov. 19, 1863	Died in hospital, Little Rock, Arkansas, February 5, 1864.
Gantt, Joseph C	do	Oct. 14, 1863	Nov. 19, 1863	Died in hospital, Little Rock, Arkansas, May 18, 1864.
Giger, John	do	Oct. 14, 1863	Nov. 19, 1863	Died in hospital, Little Rock, Arkansas, April 18, 1864.
Page, Nathaniel	do	Dec. 15, 1863	Dec. 30, 1863	Died in hospital, Lewisburg, Arkansas, April 1, 1865.
Scaggs, John C	do	Oct. 14, 1863	Nov. 19, 1863	Died in hospital, Little Rock, Arkansas, June 18, 1864.
Taylor, Benjamin F	do	Oct. 14, 1863	Nov. 10, 1863	Died in hospital, Camden, Arkansas, April 18, 1864.
Wysinger, James E	do	Oct. 14, 1863	Nov. 19, 1863	Died in hospital, Little Rock, Arkansas, June 20, 1864.
Walker, William	do	Oct. 14, 1863	Nov. 19, 1863	Died in hospital, Little Rock, Arkansas, February 3, 1864.
Deserted.				
B——, William	Private	Oct. 14, 1863	Nov. 19, 1863	Deserted July 12, 1864.
Buchanan, John A	do	Oct. 14, 1863	Nov. 19, 1863	Deserted September 7, 1864.
Brenen, Joseph	do	Dec. 13, 1863	Dec. 30, 1863	Do.
Crownove, James J	do	Oct. 14, 1863	Nov. 19, 1863	Do.
Crownove, William	do	Oct. 14, 1863	Nov. 19, 1863	Do.
Crownove, John	do	Oct. 14, 1863	Nov. 19, 1863	Do.
Dees, Alexander	do	Oct. 14, 1863	Nov. 19, 1863	Do.
Donald, Noah	do	Oct. 14, 1863	Nov. 19, 1863	Do.
Griger, George S	do	Oct. 14, 1863	Nov. 19, 1863	Do.
George, James G	do	Feb. 10, 1864	Feb. 20, 1864	Do.
Gray, William	do	Oct. 14, 1863	Oct. 19, 1863	Do.
Haney, Thaddeus L	do	Oct. 14, 1863	Oct. 19, 1863	Do.
Haney, William	do	Feb. 10, 1864	Feb. 20, 1864	Do.
Haney, John	do	Feb. 10, 1864	Feb. 20, 1864	Do.
Ivey, John	do	Oct. 14, 1863	Nov. 19, 1863	Do.
Mills, Charles B	do	Oct. 14, 1863	Nov. 19, 1863	Do.
Mills, John A	do	Oct. 14, 1863	Nov. 19, 1863	Do.
Mullinax, Isaac G	do	Dec. 15, 1863	Dec. 30, 1863	Do.
Munally, James S	do	Oct. 14, 1863	Nov. 19, 1863	Do.
Powers, Lewis	do	Oct. 14, 1863	Nov. 19, 1863	Do.
Pinney, Francis	do	Oct. 14, 1863	Nov. 19, 1863	Do.

REPORT OF THE ADJUTANT GENERAL OF ARKANSAS. 115

Thomas, James K	do	Oct. 14, 1863	Nov. 19, 1863	Do.
White, Francis M	do	Oct. 14, 1863	Nov. 19, 1863	Do.

Discharged.

Mitchell, William	Private	Dec. 15, 1863	Dec. 30, 1863	Discharged by order, December 15, 1864.

Transferred.

Gwinn, James S	Sergeant	Oct. 14, 1863	Nov. 19, 1863	Appointed sergeant November 19, 1863; transferred to non-commissioned staff June 1, 1864.

COMPANY G.

		Date of rank.	
Leander S. Driscomb	Captain		1st lieutenant from organization; honorably discharged June 10, 1865.
George P. Carr	do	Dec. 22, 1863	1st lieutenant from December 22, 1863; mustered out with regiment.
Orville Gillett, Jr	1st lieutenant	Oct. 18, 1864	Appointed from sergeant 3d Michigan cavalry; mustered out with regiment.
James H. Reynolds	2d lieutenant	Oct. 18, 1864	Appointed from civil life; dismissed October 16, 1864.
Elijah L. Allen	do	Dec. 22, 1863	Appointed from 1st sergeant; mustered out with regiment.
Andrew B. Henry	1st sergeant	Oct. 18, 1864	Appointed from private; mustered out with regiment.
Daniel B. Norwood	Quartermaster sergeant	Jan. 3, 1865	
Francis M. Mallett	Sergeant	Nov. 21, 1863	Do.
Charles Simmons	do	July 4, 1864	Do.
Frederick H. Donnell	do	July 4, 1864	Appointed from corporal; mustered out with regiment.
Jasper N. Reese	do	July 4, 1864	do.
Mack C. Hensley	Corporal	Jan. 3, 1865	Mustered out with regiment.
William Davis	do	July 4, 1864	Do.
George W. Dalton	do	Oct. 28, 1863	Do.
Pleasant W. Reynolds	do	Dec. 13, 1863	Do.
Joseph Watson	do	Oct. 28, 1863	Do.
Rufus B. Edwards	Blacksmith	June 9, 1864	Do.
		Dec. 1, 1863	

Muster.

Atkinson, Newton	Private	Dec. 13, 1863	Dec. 20, 1863	Sick at Little Rock, Arkansas, since October, 1864; no discharge furnished on muster out of regiment.
Burtrain, Alexander	do	Oct. 28, 1863	Nov. 21, 1863	Mustered out with regiment.
Baskins, William J	do	Nov. 9, 1864	Nov. 9, 1864	Do.
Burkett, John	do	Dec. 13, 1863	Dec. 20, 1863	Do.
Bradley, Isaac T	do	June 21, 1864	Sept. 23, 1864	Do.
Burress, James B	do	Oct. 28, 1863	Nov. 21, 1863	Do.
Baskins, Isaac W	do	Nov. 22, 1864	Nov. 22, 1864	Do.
Brown, Richard M	do	Oct. 28, 1863	Nov. 21, 1863	Do.
Brown, George C	do	Oct. 28, 1863	Nov. 21, 1863	Do.
Brady, James W	do	Jan. 10, 1865	Jan. 10, 1865	Do.

116 REPORT OF THE ADJUTANT GENERAL OF ARKANSAS.

Third regiment Arkansas cavalry volunteers. Mustered into service February 10, 1864, (three years;) mustered out June 30, 1865.

COMPANY G—Continued.

Names.	Rank.	Enlistment.	Muster.	Remarks.
Bizzell, John E	Private	Jan. 23, 1865	Jan. 23, 1865	Mustered out with regiment.
Brewer, Edward S	do	Jan. 23, 1865	Jan. 23, 1865	Do.
Dedwilder, John W	do	Aug. 27, 1864	Sept. 23, 1864	Do.
Evans, Leroy	do	Nov. 14, 1863	Nov. 25, 1864	In hospital; no discharge given on muster out of regiment.
Estep, Samuel W	do	Dec. 7, 1864	Dec. 7, 1864	Mustered out with regiment.
Fowler, David	do	Oct. 28, 1863	Nov. 21, 1863	Do.
Glenn, Andrew P	do	Dec. 1, 1863	Dec. 8, 1863	Do.
Goodnight, William J	do	Dec. 1, 1863	Dec. 8, 1863	Do.
Haley, Thomas	do	Oct. 28, 1863	Nov. 2, 1863	Do.
Henderson, Thomas F	do	Dec. 13, 1863	Dec. 20, 1863	Do.
Henderson, William P	do	Dec. 13, 1863	Dec. 20, 1863	Do.
Harness, Thomas	do	Oct. 28, 1863	Nov. 2, 1863	Do.
Heffington, Henry	do	Oct. 28, 1863	Nov. 2, 1863	Do.
Harwood, Austin F	do	Oct. 28, 1863	Nov. 2, 1863	Do.
Hogue, Gideon C	do	Nov. 14, 1863	Nov. 25, 1864	Do.
Harkrider, William	do	Dec. 7, 1863	Dec. 7, 1864	Do.
Jones, Alpha B	do	Dec. 1, 1863	Dec. 8, 1863	Permanently disabled by a gunshot wound received in the line of duty at —— Mills, Arkansas; mustered out with regiment.
Jennings, James R	do	Nov. 14, 1863	Nov. 25, 1863	Sick in general hospital, Little Rock, Arkansas; discharged from hospital; no discharge furnished on muster out of regiment.
Johnson, Thomas J	do	Dec. 20, 1863	Dec. 30, 1863	Mustered out with regiment.
Martin, Noah	do	Oct. 28, 1863	Nov. 21, 1863	Do.
McGinty, Robert N	do	June 21, 1864	Sept. 22, 1864	Do.
Mathews, John W	do	Oct. 28, 1863	Nov. 21, 1863	Do.
Maxwell, Thomas J	do	Jan. 1, 1865	Jan. 1, 1865	Do.
O'Neal, David	do	Dec. 1, 1863	Dec. 8, 1863	Do.
Pruitt, John	do	Oct. 28, 1863	Nov. 21, 1863	Do.
Powell, James E	do	Dec. 23, 1864	Dec. 23, 1864	In guard-house at Lewisburg, Arkansas, since February 17, 1865.
Reynolds, Jesse A	do	Dec. 1, 1863	Dec. 8, 1863	Mustered out with regiment.
Reynolds, George M	do	Nov. 28, 1864	Nov. 28, 1864	Do.
Sanders, Hiram	do	Oct. 28, 1863	Nov. 21, 1863	Do.
Thorn, William B	do	Dec. 13, 1863	Dec. 20, 1863	Do.
Starr, Andrew J	do	Oct. 28, 1863	Nov. 21, 1863	Do.
Tapp, James	do	Oct. 28, 1863	Nov. 21, 1863	Do.
McGlone, Theodore P	do	Oct. 28, 1863	Nov. 21, 1863	Do.
Adams, Hiram G	do	April 2, 1865	April 2, 1865	Do.
Russell, John M	do	Dec. 8, 1863	Dec. 8, 1863	Do.
Reynolds, Jesse M	do	Oct. 28, 1863	Nov. 21, 1863	Do.
Mafford, Lewis J	do	Oct. 28, 1863	Nov. 21, 1863	Do.
Lancaster, Andrew J	do	Oct. 28, 1863	Nov. 21, 1863	Do.
Middleton, John C	do	Oct. 29, 1863	Nov. 21, 1863	Do.

REPORT OF THE ADJUTANT GENERAL OF ARKANSAS. 117

Mustered out in accordance with special instructions from the War Department, dated Adjutant General's Office, April 5, 1865; discharges to take effect May 22, 1865.

Name	Rank	Date	Date	Remarks
James H. Blair	Sergeant	Dec. 1, 1863	Dec. 8, 1863	Appointed from corporal April 6, 1865.
Alvin G. Woodworth	Corporal	Oct. 28, 1863	Nov. 21, 1863	Appointed corporal January 3, 1865.
Aaron Crouch	do	Dec. 1, 1863	Dec. 8, 1863	
Joseph Matthews	Bugler	Dec. 13, 1863	Dec. 20, 1863	
John N. Curtis	Saddler	Dec. 13, 1863	Dec. 20, 1863	
John W. Blair	do	Dec. 1, 1863	Dec. 8, 1863	Appointed saddler January 1, 1865.
Belcher, George R.	Private	Oct. 28, 1863	Nov. 21, 1863	
Cashrago, Lewis	do	Dec. 1, 1863	Dec. 8, 1863	
Flatford, William N.	do	Oct. 28, 1863	Nov. 21, 1863	
Griggs, Cheesley	do	Oct. 28, 1863	Nov. 21, 1863	
Hankins, James W.	do	Dec. 1, 1863	Dec. 8, 1863	
Mallett, George W.	do	Dec. 1, 1863	Dec. 8, 1863	
Mathews, Jesse R. W.	do	Dec. 13, 1863	Dec. 20, 1863	
Mobbs, John A.	do	Dec. 13, 1863	Dec. 20, 1863	
Qualls, John B.	do	Dec. 1, 1863	Dec. 8, 1863	
Qualls, William M.	do	Dec. 1, 1863	Dec. 8, 1863	
Reeder, James K.	do	Dec. 1, 1863	Dec. 8, 1863	
Satterfield, Isaac S.	do	Dec. 1, 1863	Dec. 8, 1863	
Smith, James	do	Dec. 1, 1863	Dec. 8, 1863	
Shoemake, Jesse	do	Oct. 28, 1863	Nov. 21, 1863	
Townsend, Robert M.	do	Oct. 28, 1863	Nov. 21, 1863	
Reynolds, Presley G.	do	Dec. 13, 1863	Dec. 20, 1863	
McGinty, Thomas	do	Oct. 28, 1863	Nov. 21, 1863	
Brown, William M.	do	Dec. 1, 1863	Dec. 8, 1863	

Missing in action.

Spence, James	Private	Oct. 28, 1863	Nov. 21, 1863	Captured at Camp Texas, Arkansas, March 22, 1864.
Reynolds, William A.	do	Oct. 28, 1863	Nov. 21, 1863	Do.
Patty, Obed	do			Captured September 8, 1864.

Died.

Chance, Purnell	Private	Dec. 1, 1863	Dec. 8, 1863	Died of chronic diarrhœa at Little Rock, Arkansas, June 23, 1864.
Clarkson, Charles W.	do	Dec. 1, 1863	Dec. 8, 1863	Died of remittent fever at Little Rock, Arkansas, April 16, 1864.
Denton, William A.	do	Oct. 28, 1863	Dec. 8, 1863	Died near Little Rock, Arkansas, January 19, 1864.
Justice, William	do	Dec. 1, 1863	Nov. 2, 1864	Died near Lewisburg, Arkansas, December 8, 1864.
Moore, John A.	do	Oct. 28, 1863	Dec. 8, 1863	Died of pneumonia at Little Rock, Arkansas, October 1, 1863.
Parish, Thomas	do	Dec. 1, 1863	Nov. 21, 1863	Died at Lewisburg, Arkansas, April 3, 1865.
Reynolds, Henry	do	July 4, 1864	Dec. 8, 1864	Died of chronic diarrhœa at Little Rock, Arkansas, December 10, 1864.

Discharged.

| Smith, John L. | Private | Feb. 16, 1864 | Never | Discharged by order. |
| Elijah L. Allen | 1st sergeant | Dec. 13, 1863 | Dec. 20, 1863 | Discharged for promotion to 2d lieutenant. |

Third regiment Arkansas cavalry volunteers. Mustered into service February 10, 1864, (three years;) mustered out June 30, 1865.

COMPANY G—Continued.

Names.	Rank.	Enlistment.	Muster.	Remarks.
Zadock Wooker	Corporal	Oct. 28, 1863	Nov. 21, 1863	Discharged at Lewisburg, Arkansas, May 17, 1865.
Justice, John G	Private	Dec. 1, 1863	Dec. 8, 1863	Discharged by order April 23, 1865.
Presley, Wyley	do	Aug. 10, 1864	Never	
Lovell C. Obar	Commissary sergeant	Oct. 28, 1863	Nov. 21, 1863	Discharged to accept civil office.
Reynolds, John R	Private	Oct. 28, 1863	Nov. 21, 1863	Discharged March 17, 1865.
Deserted.				
David Goodnight	Sergeant	Dec. 1, 1863	Dec. 8, 1863	Deserted at Lewisburg, Arkansas, September 8, 1864.
William M. Midleton	Corporal	Oct. 28, 1863	Nov. 21, 1863	Deserted at Little Rock, Arkansas, October 21, 1864.
Brown, Reuben F	Private	Dec. 1, 1863	Dec. 8, 1863	Deserted from guard-house, May 24, 1865.
Baskins, Aaron Thomas	do	Jan. 4, 1865	Never	Deserted May 22, 1865.
Davis, Wait C	do	Oct. 28, 1863	Nov. 21, 1863	Deserted October 21, 1864.
Davidson, John	do	Oct. 28, 1863	Nov. 21, 1863	Deserted from hospital at Little Rock, Arkansas, December 10, 1864.
Graham, William A	do	Oct. 28, 1863	Nov. 21, 1863	Deserted from guard-house, April 3, 1865.
Hall, John A. W	do	Dec. 13, 1863	Dec. 20, 1863	Deserted at Little Rock, Arkansas, October 21, 1864.
Heffington, William F	do	Oct. 28, 1863	Dec. 20, 1863	Do.
Heffington, Elisha J	do	Dec. 13, 1863	Dec. 20, 1863	Do.
Lamar, Stephen E	do	Oct. 28, 1863	Nov. 21, 1863	Deserted at Little Rock, Arkansas, May 6, 1864.
Lincleoln, George W	do	Dec. 13, 1863	Dec. 20, 1863	Deserted at Little Rock, Arkansas, May 18, 1864.
Morris, William J	do	Oct. 28, 1863	Oct. 21, 1863	Deserted at Little Rock, Arkansas, October 21, 1864.
Patrick, Henry F	do	Oct. 28, 1863	Nov. 21, 1863	Deserted at Lewisburg, Arkansas, February 23, 1865.
Pope, William Andrew	do	Feb. 7, 1865	Never	Deserted at Little Rock, Arkansas, October 21, 1864.
Thompson, James W	do	Dec. 13, 1863	Dec. 20, 1863	Do.
Turpens, Thomas C	do	Oct. 23, 1863	Nov. 2, 1863	Deserted, (date unknown,) 1864.
Hall, Isum R	do	Dec. 1, 1863	Dec. 8, 1863	Deserted from guard-house at Lewisburg, Arkansas, May 24, 1865.
Wilson, Charles	do	Oct. 28, 1863	Nov. 21, 1863	Deserted at Little Rock, Arkansas, October 21, 1864.
Wilson, Richard J	do	Oct. 28, 1863	Nov. 21, 1863	Deserted from guard-house, May 24, 1864.
Williams, James R. P	do	Feb. 10, 1865	Never	Deserted at Lewisburg, Arkansas, May 22, 1865.

COMPANY H.

Names.	Rank.	Enlistment.	Date of rank.	Remarks.
David F. Edington	Captain	Nov. 22, 1863	Feb. 23, 1864	Promoted from 1st lieutenant; shot in the thigh and drowned in attempting to swim the Arkansas river during an engagement with General Shelby's command, May 16, 1864.
Frank Peale	1st lieutenant	Feb. 23, 1864	Feb. 23, 1864	Mustered out with regiment.
John M. Harkey	2d lieutenant	Feb. 23, 1864	Feb. 23, 1864	Do.
John D. Gilchrist	Commissary sergeant	Feb. 13, 1864	Apr. 1, 1865	Do.

REPORT OF THE ADJUTANT GENERAL OF ARKANSAS.   119

Name	Rank		Muster		
William H. Moore	Corporal	Dec. 23, 1863	May 5, 1864	Do.
James H. Walkup	Bugler	Oct. 28, 1863	Dec. 9, 1863	Do.
Robert C. Yonnes	do	Jan. 8, 1864	Apr. 1, 1865	Do.
William Akins	Saddler	Jan. 20, 1864	Feb. 25, 1864	Do.
Apple, George	Private	Oct. 28, 1863	Nov. 28, 1863	Do.
Bridgeman, William F	do	Feb. 13, 1864	Feb. 13, 1864	Do.
Clifton, William	do	Jan. 11, 1864	Jan. 13, 1864	Do.
Crane, Erasmus	do	Sept. 3, 1864	Sept. 23, 1864	Do.
Ferguson, William H	do	Oct. 28, 1863	Nov. 22, 1863	Do.
Gardner, Thaddius	do	Oct. 28, 1863	Nov. 22, 1863	Do.
Gunter, William M	do	Oct. 28, 1863	Nov. 22, 1863	Do.
Gray, Martin V	do	Oct. 28, 1863	Nov. 22, 1863	Do.
Gower, Jackson	do	Feb. 13, 1864	Feb. 13, 1864	Do.
Harkey, Jacob S	do	Oct. 28, 1863	Nov. 22, 1863	Do.
Hubble, James	do	Oct. 28, 1863	Nov. 22, 1863	Do.
Jones, John T	do	Dec. 28, 1863	Dec. 22, 1863	Do.
James, Columbus J	do	Oct. 28, 1863	Nov. 22, 1863	Do.
Lynch, Caleb B	do	Feb. 9, 1864	Feb. 9, 1864	Do.
Martin, Samuel M	do	Oct. 28, 1863	Nov. 22, 1863	Do.
Martin, Isaac N	do	Oct. 28, 1863	Nov. 22, 1863	Do.
McCarroll, Hugh B	do	Oct. 28, 1863	Nov. 22, 1863	Do.
Neal, John	do	Nov. 21, 1863	May 25, 1864	Do.
Ott, William	do	Feb. 12, 1864	Feb. 12, 1864	Do.
Parker, Meredith	do	Dec. 8, 1863	Dec. 8, 1864	Do.
Rowland, Hiram E	do	Feb. 12, 1864	Feb. 12, 1864	Do.
Smith, James E	do	Oct. 28, 1863	Nov. 2, 1863	Do.
Smith, Joseph	do	Mar. 3, 1864	Mar. 23, 1864	Do.
Sloan, Winfield S	do	Sept. 3, 1864	Sept. 23, 1863	Do.
Thompson, Thomas	do	Oct. 28, 1863	Nov. 22, 1863	Do.
Tucker, Solomon	do	Dec. 23, 1863	Dec. 30, 1863	Do.
Treat, John W	do	Feb. 2, 1864	Feb. 12, 1864	Do.
Witt, George W	do	Oct. 28, 1863	Nov. 22, 1863	Do.
Westmoreland, Moses B	do	Dec. 8, 1863	Dec. 8, 1863	Do.
Walker, John A	do	Dec. 31, 1863	Jan. 13, 1864	Do.
Killed in action.				
John W. Lane	Private	Oct. 28, 1863	Nov. 22, 1863	Captured in an engagement with guerillas, and hung near Dardanelle, Arkansas, May 24, 1864.
Died.				
Joseph W. Ferguson	Sergeant	Oct. 28, 1863	Nov. 22, 1863	Died in post-house near Dardanelle, Arkansas, May 4, 1864.
William W. Saddler	Corporal	Oct. 28, 1863	Nov. 22, 1863	Died in hospital, Lewisburg, Arkansas, April 8, 1864.
Barley, Cason	Private	Oct. 28, 1863	Nov. 22, 1863	do.
Bone, Hugh C	do	Dec. 23, 1863	Dec. 20, 1863	Died in hospital, Lewisburg, Arkansas, April 1, 1864.
Cooper, Nelson	do	Oct. 28, 1863	Nov. 22, 1863	Died in hospital, Lewisburg, Arkansas, March 11, 1864.
Cooper, John	do	Jan. 11, 1864	Jan. 13, 1864	Died in hospital, Little Rock, Arkansas, October 24, 1864.
Harkey, Martin M	do	Oct. 22, 1863	Nov. 22, 1863	Died in hospital, Little Rock, Arkansas, March 17, 1864.
Harkey, Eli	do	Oct. 28, 1863	Nov. 22, 1863	Died in hospital, Little Rock, Arkansas, November 4, 1864.

Third regiment Arkansas cavalry volunteers. Mustered into service February 10, 1864, (three years;) mustered out June 30, 1865.

COMPANY H—Continued.

Names.	Rank.	Enlistment.	Muster.	Remarks.
James, William H	Private	Oct. 28, 1863	Nov. 22, 1863	Died in hospital, Lewisburg, Arkansas, April 27, 1864.
James, John J	do	Oct. 28, 1863	Nov. 22, 1863	Died in hospital, Lewisburg, Arkansas, April 9, 1865.
Kennerly, Doctor G	do	Dec. 8, 1863	Dec. 8, 1863	Died in pest-house near Dardanelle, Arkansas, May 17, 1864.
McBride, Andrew J	do	Jan. 21, 1864	Jan. 27, 1864	Died in hospital, Lewisburg, Arkansas, May 10, 1864.
McCarley, Isaac C	do	Oct. 23, 1863	Nov. 22, 1863	Died in hospital, Lewisburg, Arkansas, January 8, 1865.
Onsley, William	do	Nov. 8, 1863	Dec. 8, 1863	Died in hospital, Little Rock, Arkansas, October 18, 1864.
Parham, Jesse R	do	Dec. 23, 1863	Dec. 30, 1863	Died in hospital, Lewisburg, Arkansas, March 31, 1864.
Rivers, Robert D	do	Oct. 28, 1863	Nov. 22, 1863	Died at his residence in Yell county, Arkansas, December 20, 1863.
Vandeyrer, James C	do	Oct. 28, 1863	Nov. 22, 1863	Died in hospital, Little Rock, Arkansas, January 30, 1864.
Wilson, John M	do	Oct. 28, 1863	Nov. 22, 1863	Died at his residence in Yell county, Arkansas, January 3, 1864.
Deserted.				
James M. Moore	Quartermaster sergeant	Oct. 28, 1863	Dec. 30, 1863	Deserted near Lewisburg, Arkansas, August 28, 1864.
John T. Turner	Sergeant	Oct. 28, 1863	Nov. 22, 1863	Deserted at Lewisburg, Arkansas, May 19, 1864.
Reuben Vandyre	Corporal	Oct. 28, 1863	Nov. 22, 1863	Do.
George W. Lewis	Farrier	Oct. 28, 1863	Dec. 30, 1863	Do.
Brown, Lorenzo K	Private	Oct. 28, 1863	Dec. 30, 1863	Do.
Dell, Seborn E	do	Oct. 28, 1863	Dec. 1, 1863	Deserted at Lewisburg, Arkansas, August 18, 1864.
Fuller, John W	do	Dec. 23, 1863	Dec. 30, 1863	Deserted at Lewisburg, Arkansas, May 19, 1864.
Feiro, Williamson	do	Oct. 28, 1863	Oct. 22, 1863	Deserted at Lewisburg, Arkansas, October 31, 1864.
Hodges, George W	do	Nov. 22, 1863	Jan. 20, 1864	Deserted near Dardanelle, Arkansas, August 12, 1864.
Hubbell, James	do	Oct. 28, 1863	Nov. 22, 1863	Deserted at Lewisburg, Arkansas, August 28, 1864.
James, William	do	Oct. 28, 1863	Nov. 22, 1863	Deserted at Lewisburg, Arkansas, October 31, 1864.
Lowery, Isaac P	do	Feb. 13, 1864	Nov. 22, 1863	Deserted at Lewisburg, Arkansas, May 19, 1864.
Lippe, Isaac	do	Oct. 28, 1863	Dec. 30, 1863	Deserted at Lewisburg, Arkansas, September 8, 1864.
Lippe, John W	do	Oct. 28, 1863	Nov. 22, 1863	Deserted at Lewisburg, Arkansas, November 17, 1864.
Lynch, Lewis	do	Feb. 10, 1864	Feb. 10, 1864	Deserted between Little Rock and Lewisburg, Arkansas, December 15, 1864.
Miller, Robert R	do	Oct. 29, 1863	Nov. 22, 1863	Deserted between Little Rock and Lewisburg, Arkansas, May 20, 1864.
McCarley, Thomas B	do	Oct. 28, 1863	Oct. 28, 1863	Deserted at Lewisburg, Arkansas, August 28, 1864.
McClung, John	do	Oct. 28, 1863	Nov. 22, 1863	Deserted near Lewisburg, Arkansas, September 9, 1864.
Patterson, James R	do	Oct. 28, 1863	Nov. 22, 1863	Deserted at Lewisburg, Arkansas, August 28, 1864.
Patterson, William A	do	Oct. 28, 1863	Nov. 22, 1863	Do.
Reay, James G	do	Dec. 23, 1863	Dec. 30, 1863	Deserted near Lewisburg, Arkansas, October 31, 1864.
Stanfield, Aaron	do	Feb. 13, 1864	Feb. 13, 1864	Deserted at Lewisburg, Arkansas, May 19, 1864.
Sexton, Harrison	do	Nov. 22, 1863	Dec. 23, 1863	Deserted near Lewisburg, Arkansas, July 30, 1864.
Smith, Obadiah	do	Oct. 23, 1863	Nov. 22, 1863	Deserted at Lewisburg, Arkansas, August 28, 1864.
Scott, William	do	Dec. 23, 1863	Dec. 30, 1863	Deserted at Lewisburg, Arkansas, September 9, 1864.
Smith, William	do	Oct. 28, 1863	Nov. 22, 1863	Deserted near Lewisburg, Arkansas, October 31, 1864.
Simon, James A	do	Jan. 13, 1864	Feb. 13, 1864	Deserted at Lewisburg, Arkansas, February 5, 1865.
Underwood, John F	do	Dec. 23, 1863	Jan. 27, 1864	Deserted at Lewisburg, Arkansas, May 19, 1864.
Wiggins, David	do	Oct. 28, 1863	Nov. 22, 1863	Deserted at Lewisburg, Arkansas, September 29, 1864.
Welch, Green B	do	Oct. 28, 1863	Nov. 22, 1863	Deserted near Lewisburg, Arkansas, October 31, 1864.

REPORT OF THE ADJUTANT GENERAL OF ARKANSAS. 121

Discharged.

Thomas H. Walker	Farrier	Dec. 23, 1863	Discharged for disability December 17, 1864.
Davis, George W	Private	Aug. 8, 1864	Discharged by sentence of G. C. M. May 9, 1865.

Transferred.

Henry A. Messengill	Corporal	Dec. 23, 1863	Transferred to 1st Arkansas infantry May 5, 1864.
James, James B	Private	Dec. 31, 1863	Do.
Johnson, Eli	do	Dec. 23, 1863	Do.
Jones, William N	do	Dec. 23, 1863	Do.
McBride, James	do	Jan. 20, 1864	Do.

COMPANY I.

			Date of rank.	
Archibald D. Napier	Captain	Nov. 21, 1863	Feb. 14, 1864	1st lieutenant from organization; dismissed October 15, 1864.
William M. Williams	1st lieutenant	Nov. 21, 1863	Feb. 1, 1865	Appointed from private to 2d lieutenant; mustered out with regiment.
William H. Ritter	1st lieutenant		Feb. 14, 1864	Killed in action at Cypress Bridge May 13, 1864.
Wallace H. Hickox	do	Nov. 21, 1863	Feb. 1, 1865	Mustered out with regiment.
William L. Conely	2d lieutenant	Nov. 21, 1863	Feb. 1, 1865	Appointed from sergeant February 1, 1865; mustered out with regiment.
Ebenezer B. Jamison	1st sergeant	Nov. 21, 1863	Feb. 1, 1865	Sergeant from enlistment; mustered out with regiment.
John H. McElroy	Quartermaster sergeant	Dec. 17, 1863	Nov. 10, 1864	Do.
Thomas G. McElroy	Commissary sergeant	Nov. 21, 1863	Feb. 1, 1865	Do.
James Bratton	Sergeant	Dec. 17, 1863	Dec. 17, 1863	Mustered out with regiment.
Reuben P. Vaughan	do	Nov. 21, 1863	Nov. 1, 1863	Do.
James H. Ellis	do	Jan. 20, 1864	Nov. 10, 1864	Appointed from corporal; mustered out with regiment.
John S. Stephenson	do	Feb. 1, 1864	Feb. 1, 1865	Do.
Francis Kykendall	do	Dec. 17, 1863	May 20, 1864	Do.
James J. Harrington	Corporal	Jan. 11, 1864	May 20, 1864	Mustered out with regiment.
Charles Pemberton	do	Dec. 17, 1863	May 20, 1864	Do.
John Bratton	do	Feb. 1, 1864	May 20, 1864	Do.
William J. Kelly	do	Feb. 1, 1864	Nov. 10, 1864	Do.
David Boyd	do	Nov. 21, 1863	Feb. 1, 1865	Do.
Commodore Pleasonton	do	July 15, 1864	Feb. 1, 1865	Do.
Abram C. Henry	Bugler	Dec. 29, 1864	Dec. 29, 1864	Do.
John H. Williams	do	June 15, 1864	Feb. 10, 1865	Do.
William Mathews	Artificer	Feb. 1, 1864	Feb. 1, 1865	Do.
Hiram M. Barnes	Blacksmith	Nov. 21, 1863	Nov. 21, 1863	Do.
Gambrel Bartelett				

		Muster.		
Ashur, William H	Private	Dec. 17, 1863	Dec. 30, 1864	Mustered out with regiment.
Atwell, George S	do	June 15, 1864	Sept. 27, 1864	Do.
Brimage, William P	do	Nov. 21, 1863	Dec. 1, 1863	Do.
Brenkey, Bumphus B	do	Dec. 17, 1863	Dec. 30, 1863	Do.
Brenkey, William	do	Jan. 19, 1865		

Third regiment Arkansas cavalry volunteers. Mustered into service February 10, 1864, (three years;) mustered out June 30, 1865.

COMPANY I—Continued.

Names.	Rank.	Enlistment.	Muster.	Remarks.
Barnes, Joshua R	Private	Nov. 21, 1863	Dec. 1, 1863	Mustered out with regiment.
Barnes, Green A	do	Nov. 21, 1863	Dec. 1, 1863	Do.
Barnes, Washington	do	Dec. 17, 1863	Dec. 30, 1863	Do.
Bratton, Francis M	do	Dec. 17, 1863	Dec. 30, 1863	Do.
Bratton, John B	do	Feb. 17, 1864	Mar. 2, 1864	Do.
Bratton, Benjamin	do	Aug. 25, 1864	Sept. 30, 1864	Do.
Bartlett, William P	do	Feb. 1, 1864	Feb. 13, 1864	Do.
Branham, James F	do	Aug. 20, 1864	Sept. 27, 1864	Do.
Branshaw, James F	do	Aug. 20, 1864	Sept. 27, 1864	Do.
Conley, Epaphroditus	do	Jan. 13, 1864	Sept. 30, 1864	Do.
Curtis, Hillery	do	Jan. 15, 1864	Sept. 27, 1864	Do.
Curtis, William B	do	Sept. 12, 1864	April 29, 1865	Do.
Curtiss, James T	do	June 15, 1864	Sept. 27, 1864	Do.
Caughman, Franklin	do	June 15, 1864	April 29, 1865	Do.
Cooper, William	do	Dec. 30, 1864	Sept. 27, 1864	Do.
Deavers, George W	do	Dec. 17, 1863	Dec. 30, 1863	Do.
Duncan, William	do	Nov. 21, 1863	Dec. 1, 1863	Do.
Eoff, John	do	Mar. 1, 1864	Mar. 2, 1864	Do.
Emos, Moses	do	Aug. 1, 1864	Sept. 27, 1864	Do.
Finley, John H	do	July 1, 1864	Sept. 27, 1864	Do.
Gray, John W	do	July 1, 1864	Sept. 27, 1864	Do.
Hollabough, John M	do	Feb. 1, 1864	Feb. 13, 1864	Do.
Henry, Nathaniel M	do	July 6, 1864	Sept. 30, 1864	Do.
Henly, Joshua L	do	Jan. 12, 1865	May 1, 1865	Do.
Henly, David	do	Dec. 30, 1864	April 29, 1865	Do.
Harris, Joseph	do	Dec. 17, 1863	Dec. 30, 1863	Do.
Hale, George W	do	Nov. 21, 1863	Dec. 1, 1863	Do.
Kimbrell, William F	do	Dec. 17, 1863	Dec. 30, 1863	Do.
Lay, John W	do	Nov. 21, 1863	Dec. 1, 1863	Do.
Luna, Peter M	do	Mar. 1, 1864	Mar. 2, 1864	Do.
McDaniel, William	do	Nov. 21, 1863	Mar. 30, 1864	Do.
McDaniel, Robert	do	Feb. 1, 1864	Feb. 13, 1864	Do.
Morrison, Lewis C	do	Aug. 25, 1864	Sept. 27, 1864	Do.
Morrison, James L	do	Dec. 17, 1863	Dec. 30, 1863	Do.
Molley, Samuel J	do	Dec. 30, 1863	April 29, 1865	Do.
Owens, Charles	do	Nov. 21, 1863	Dec. 14, 1863	Do.
Peyton, Alexander A	do	Nov. 21, 1863	Dec. 14, 1863	Do.
Peyton, John H	do	Jan. 19, 1865	May 1, 1865	Do.
Petty, William G	do	Nov. 21, 1863	Dec. 1, 1863	Do.
Prigg, Isaac J	do	Nov. 21, 1863	Dec. 1, 1865	Do.
Patterson, Elisha	do	July 25, 1863	Sept. 30, 1864	Do.
Russell, William J	do	Nov. 21, 1863	Dec. 14, 1863	Do.
Ring, John	do			

REPORT OF THE ADJUTANT GENERAL OF ARKANSAS. 123

Name	Rank	Enlisted	Mustered	Remarks
Ragland, Robert	do		Aug. 2, 1864	Do.
Riley, James W	do		Jan. 9, 1865	Do.
Riley, Samuel	do		Mar. 17, 1865	Do.
Sutterfield, Nathaniel	do		Jan. 26, 1864	Do.
Steward, William C	do		Nov. 21, 1863	Do.
Seaton, Christopher M	do		Nov. 21, 1863	Do.
Taylor, David B	do		Dec. 1, 1863	Do.
Taylor, Henry A	do		Jan. 19, 1865	Do.
Wallace, Lafayette	do		Nov. 21, 1863	Do.

Died.

Name	Rank	Enlisted	Mustered	Remarks
George W. Arnhart	Sergeant	Feb. 1, 1864	Feb. 13, 1864	Sergeant from organization; died in hospital at Lewisburg, Arkansas, February 25, 1865.
James R. Bartlett	Blacksmith	Nov. 21, 1863	Dec. 1, 1863	Died of measles at Carroll Farm, Arkansas, April 7, 1864.
Ballmeyer, John	Private	July 12, 1864	Sept. 27, 1864	Died of measles at Lewisburg, Arkansas, May 5, 1865.
Davis, Joshua S	do	Dec. 17, 1863	Feb. 2, 1864	Died of small-pox at Lewisburg, Arkansas, May 13, 1864.
Dapriese, Isaac M	do	Nov. 21, 1863	Dec. 1, 1863	Died of small-pox at Lewisburg, Arkansas, July 6, 1864.
Foster, Eizy B	do	Dec. 17, 1863	Dec. 30, 1863	Died in hospital at Little Rock, Arkansas, December 10, 1864.
Henderson, Ransom	do	Nov. 21, 1863	Dec. 1, 1863	Died of chronic diarrhoea in Van Buren county, Arkansas, October 22, 1864.
McDaniel, Henry M	do	Nov. 21, 1863	Dec. 1, 1863	Died of measles at Carroll Farm, Arkansas, March 15, 1864.
McElroy, William	do	July 1, 1864	Sept. 27, 1864	Died of measles at Lewisburg, Arkansas, April 26, 1865.
Mathews, Lewis	do	June 15, 1864	Sept. 30, 1864	Died in hospital at Lewisburg, Arkansas, March 9, 1865.
Nichols, Isaac C	do	Nov. 21, 1863	Dec. 1, 1863	Died at Lewisburg, Arkansas, March 25, 1865.
Pyton, Elias J	do	Nov. 21, 1863	Dec. 1, 1863	Died in hospital at Little Rock, Arkansas, March 2, 1864.
Parker, Elijah	do	Nov. 21, 1863	Dec. 1, 1863	Died in hospital at Little Rock, Arkansas, April 1, 1864.
Sweeden, Robert	do	Nov. 21, 1863	Dec. 1, 1863	Died of small-pox at Lewisburg, Arkansas, June 25, 1864.
Sweeden, James J	do	Nov. 21, 1863	Dec. 1, 1863	Died at Little Rock, Arkansas, January 19, 1864.
Sanders, John L	do	Jan. 4, 1864	Jan. 19, 1864	Died in Van Buren county, Arkansas, February 2, 1864.
Whitmore, Henry W	do	Nov. 21, 1863	Dec. 1, 1863	Died at Lewisburg, Arkansas, March 5, 1864.

Deserted.

Name	Rank	Enlisted	Mustered	Remarks
Thomas P. Nichols	Sergeant	Nov. 21, 1863	Dec. 1, 1863	Deserted at Lewisburg, Arkansas, April 24, 1864.
William Robertson	Corporal	Nov. 21, 1863	Dec. 1, 1863	Deserted at Lewisburg, Arkansas, May 13, 1864.
William D. Holmes	do	Feb. 1, 1864	Feb. 13, 1864	do.
Robert M. Emerson	do	Dec. 17, 1863	Dec. 30, 1863	Corporal from organization; deserted at Lewisburg, Arkansas, May 17, 1864.
James L. Sanders	do	Nov. 21, 1863	Dec. 1, 1863	Deserted at Lewisburg, Arkansas, April 24, 1864.
Brown, John	Private	Jan. 10, 1865	Never	Deserted at Lewisburg, Arkansas, April 24, 1864.
Clark, Benjamin	do	Nov. 21, 1863	Dec. 1, 1863	Deserted at Lewisburg, Arkansas, March 25, 1865.
Causey, Frederick	do	Nov. 21, 1863	Dec. 1, 1863	Deserted in Polk county, Arkansas, January 25, 1865.
Dean, Amos	do	Dec. 17, 1863	Dec. 30, 1863	Deserted at Armstrong Farm, Arkansas, April 24, 1864.
Ellet, Andrew J	do	Dec. 17, 1863	Dec. 30, 1863	Deserted at Armstrong Farm, Arkansas, April 4, 1864.
Gross, James	do	Nov. 21, 1863	Dec. 1, 1863	Deserted at Lewisburg, Ark., April 24, 1864; was killed for robbing July 10, 1864.
Hendricks, George W	do	Jan. 19, 1865	Never	Deserted at Lewisburg, Arkansas, September 6, 1864.
Hill, Jesse C	do	Dec. 17, 1863	Dec. 30, 1863	Deserted at Lewisburg, Arkansas, March 24, 1865.
Hale, William	do	Dec. 17, 1863	Dec. 30, 1863	Deserted at Lewisburg, Arkansas, May 13, 1864.
Howard, Jarda	do	Jan. 23, 1865	Never	Deserted on a scout February 8, 1864.
Meek, Lewis	do	Dec. 17, 1863	Dec. 30, 1863	Deserted at Lewisburg, Arkansas, March 30, 1865.
Meek, John	do	Dec. 17, 1863	Dec. 30, 1863	Deserted on a scout in Pope county, Arkansas, December 26, 1863.
Maleray, William H	do	Feb. 17, 1864	Feb. 13, 1864	Deserted at Armstrong Farm, Arkansas, April 4, 1864.
Martin, Nathaniel M	do	Feb. 1, 1864	Feb. 13, 1864	Deserted at Lewisburg, Arkansas, May 17, 1864.
				Do.

Third regiment Arkansas cavalry volunteers. Mustered into service February 10, 1864, (three years;) mustered out June 30, 1865.

COMPANY I—Continued.

Names.	Rank.	Enlistment.	Muster.	Remarks.
Newman, Ayres	Private	Nov. 21, 1863	Dec. 1, 1863	Deserted at Little Rock, Arkansas, October 8, 1864.
Nichols, Thomas I.	do	Feb. 1, 1864	Mar. 2, 1864	Deserted at Lewisburg, Arkansas, May 26, 1864.
O'Neal, Beakburn	do	May 17, 1864	Sept. 27, 1864	Deserted at Lewisburg, Arkansas, February 20, 1865.
Parks, Theophilus	do	Nov. 21, 1863	Dec. 1, 1863	Deserted on a scout December 8, 1863.
Parks, John C	do	Nov. 21, 1863	Dec. 1, 1863	Do.
Sweeden, sr., James	do	Feb. 1, 1864	Feb. 13, 1864	Deserted at Lewisburg, Arkansas, March 4, 1865.
Sweeden, Pearson	do	Nov. 21, 1863	Dec. 1, 1863	Deserted on a scout September 16, 1864.
Standridge, John	do	Dec. 17, 1863	Dec. 30, 1863	Deserted on a scout in Pope county, Arkansas, December 8, 1863.
Standridge, Richard	do	Nov. 21, 1863	Dec. 1, 1863	do
Vickery, William	do	Nov. 21, 1863	Dec. 1, 1863	Deserted at Lewisburg, Arkansas, April 24, 1864.
Discharged.				
Henry J. Gibson	Sergeant	Dec. 17, 1863	Dec. 30, 1863	Discharged for disability.
Barnes, James J	Corporal	Jan. 26, 1864	Feb. 2, 1864	Discharged for disability May 29, 1865.
Kimbree, Eli M.	Private	Nov. 21, 1863	Dec. 1, 1863	Discharged for disability.
Page, Samuel	do	Nov. 21, 1863	Dec. 1, 1863	Do.
Womble, Allen	do	June 15, 1864	Sept. 27, 1864	Do.

COMPANY K.

Names.	Rank.	Date of rank.	Muster.	Remarks.
David Hamilton	Captain	Dec. 1, 1863	Feb. 9, 1864	Promoted to major February 1, 1865; mustered out with regiment.
John W. Jay	1st lieutenant	Feb. 9, 1864	Feb. 9, 1864	Resigned May 10, 1864.
J. L. Koonce	do		Feb. 1, 1865	Appointed 2d lieutenant from sergeant third Illinois cavalry February 9, 1864; mustered out with regiment.
Thomas M. Alexander	2d lieutenant	Feb. 1, 1864	Feb. 1, 1865	Promoted from 1st sergeant; mustered out with regiment.
Abraham E. Davis	Corporal	Dec. 14, 1863	June 9, 1864	Mustered out with regiment.
George M. Brown	do	Feb. 1, 1864	June 9, 1864	Do.
Benjamin F. Gray	do	May 11, 1864	Mar. 27, 1865	Do.
			Muster.	
Andrew J., Amesworthy	Private	Dec. 30, 1863	Jan. 8, 1864	Do.
Arnold, William	do	Jan. 13, 1864	Feb. 8, 1864	Do.
Baxley, Asa P.	do	Nov. 8, 1863	Nov. 16, 1863	Do.
Barnes, William	do	Dec. 14, 1863	Dec. 20, 1863	Do.
Barron, James	do	Nov. 15, 1863	Dec. 4, 1863	Do.
Bowden, William J	do	Feb. 1, 1864	Feb. 8, 1864	Do.
Cunningham, Andrew	do	Sept. 13, 1864	Sept. 23, 1864	Do.

REPORT OF THE ADJUTANT GENERAL OF ARKANSAS. 125

Name	Rank	Enlisted	Mustered out	Remarks
Cornwell, John R		Nov. 27, 1864	April 29, 1865	Do.
Davis, Richard	do	Feb. 1, 1864	Feb. 8, 1864	Do.
Gray, Wilson G	do	Sept. 13, 1864	Feb. 8, 1865	Do.
Gray, Thomas J	do	May 11, 1864	Sept. 23, 1864	Do.
Gray, Aaron P	do	Feb. 1, 1864	Feb. 8, 1864	Do.
Gray, William	do	Feb. 1, 1864	Feb. 8, 1864	Do.
Harrington, Andrew J	do	Jan. 2, 1865	Jan. 2, 1865	Do.
Jones, Francis M	do	Nov. 22, 1863	Dec. 1, 1863	Do.
McGhee, Ransom	do	Aug. 5, 1864	Sept. 23, 1864	Do.
Morris, Mathew M	do	Feb. 1, 1864	Feb. 8, 1864	Do.
Owens, Thomas	do	Feb. 1, 1864	Feb. 8, 1864	Do.
Pain, Andrew H	do	Nov. 7, 1864	Apr. 29, 1865	Do.
Pollard, James H	do	Mar. 7, 1865	Mar. 7, 1865	Do.
Parks, Samuel W	do	Mar. 11, 1864	Sept. 23, 1864	Do.
Ryan, Patrick	do	Nov. 8, 1863	Nov. 16, 1863	Do.
Ramsey, Harrison	do	July 28, 1864	Sept. 23, 1864	Do.
Ramsey, Marion	do	Sept. 5, 1864	Sept. 23, 1864	Do.
Renford, James	do	Jan. 1, 1864	Jan. 5, 1864	Do.
Sutterfield, James W	do	Feb. 1, 1864	Feb. 8, 1864	Do.
Filly, John	do	July 12, 1864	Sept. 23, 1864	Do.
Wiley, Jasper N	do	Dec. 14, 1863	Dec. 20, 1863	Do.
Webb, James E	do	Aug. 21, 1864	Sept. 23, 1864	Do.
Webb, William A	do	Aug. 21, 1864	Sept. 23, 1864	Do.
Wills, Joseph B	do	Nov. 8, 1863	Nov. 16, 1863	Do.

Mustered out in accordance with special instructions from the War Department, dated Adjutant General's Office, April 5, 1865—discharges to take effect May 22, 1865.

Name	Rank	Enlisted	Mustered out	Remarks
Lorenzo D. Jones	1st sergeant	Nov. 22, 1863	Dec. 1, 1863	Promoted commissary sergeant February 8, 1864, to 1st sergeant March 27, 1865.
Reuben D. Etheridge	Sergeant	Nov. 22, 1863	Dec. 1, 1863	Promoted sergeant February 8, 1864.
William L. Baker	do	Feb. 1, 1864	Feb. 8, 1864	Do.
William H. Huffins	do	Feb. 1, 1864	Feb. 8, 1864	Do.
Ransom M. Simpson	do	Nov. 22, 1863	Dec. 1, 1863	Promoted corporal February 8, 1864, to sergeant June 9, 1864.
Samuel A. Lisk	do	Feb. 1, 1864	Feb. 8, 1864	Promoted corporal June 9, 1864, to sergeant August 23, 1864.
James J. Spann	do	Nov. 22, 1863	Nov. 26, 1863	Promoted corporal February 8, 1864, to sergeant March 27, 1865
John W. Plunkett	do	Feb. 1, 1864	Dec. 1, 1863	Do.
Francis M. Duvall	Corporal	Nov. 8, 1863	Dec. 1, 1863	Promoted corporal February 8, 1864.
William D. Prescott	do	Nov. 22, 1863	Dec. 20, 1863	Promoted corporal June 9, 1864.
Emanuel F. Hollabough	do	Nov. 22, 1863	Dec. 1, 1863	Do.
Charles Johnson	do	Dec. 14, 1863	Jan. 8, 1864	Promoted corporal October 29, 1864.
Peter H. T. Horton	do	Feb. 1, 1864	Feb. 8, 1864	Promoted corporal March 27, 1865.
David A. Morrison	Blacksmith	Dec. 21, 1863	Feb. 8, 1864	Blacksmith from organization of company.
Francis Murphy	Bugler	Feb. 1, 1864	Dec. 1, 1864	
Davis, William	Private	Feb. 1, 1864	Feb. 8, 1864	
Harrington, James	do	Dec. 14, 1863	Dec. 20, 1863	
Horton, James A	do	Feb. 1, 1864	Feb. 8, 1864	
House, Marion	do	Feb. 1, 1864	Feb. 8, 1864	
Hensley, William M	do	Feb. 1, 1864	Feb. 8, 1864	
Hensley, Alfred M	do	Feb. 1, 1864	Feb. 8, 1864	

Third regiment Arkansas cavalry volunteers. Mustered into service February 10, 1864, (three years;) mustered out June 30, 1865.

COMPANY K—Continued.

Names.	Rank.	Enlistment.	Muster.	Remarks.
Jones, William A	Private	Dec. 14, 1863	Dec. 20, 1863	
Jackson, Andrew J	do	Feb. 1, 1864	Feb. 8, 1864	
McBain, James T	do	Feb. 1, 1864	Feb. 8, 1864	
Middleton, Richard T	do	Feb. 1, 1864	Feb. 8, 1864	
Mattall, Levi E	do	Nov. 22, 1863	Dec. 1, 1863	
Nix, Burton	do	Nov. 8, 1863	Nov. 16, 1863	
Pipkins, James	do	Dec. 14, 1863	Dec. 20, 1863	
Parks, Zachariah	do	Feb. 1, 1864	Feb. 8, 1864	
Parks, John M	do	Feb. 1, 1864	Feb. 8, 1864	
Roan, William H	do	Feb. 1, 1864	Feb. 8, 1864	
Rorie, Absalom J	do	Feb. 1, 1864	Feb. 8, 1864	
Ross, William J	do	Nov. 22, 1863	Dec. 1, 1863	
Sisk, Arthur R	do	Feb. 1, 1864	Feb. 8, 1864	
Sutterfield, William J	do	Feb. 1, 1864	Feb. 8, 1864	
Shipman, Jacob	do	Feb. 1, 1864	Feb. 8, 1864	
Tilly, James W	do	Feb. 1, 1864	Feb. 8, 1864	
Tilly, Henry	do	Feb. 1, 1864	Feb. 8, 1864	
Died.				
John W. Horton	Sergeant	Feb. 1, 1864	Feb. 8, 1864	Died in hospital at Little Rock, Arkansas.
Oliver, Richmond	do	Nov. 15, 1863	Dec. 4, 1863	Died at Little Rock, Arkansas.
Chandler, Daniel F	Private	Nov. 22, 1863	Dec. 1, 1863	Died at Little Rock, Arkansas, August 7, 1864.
Carter, Wiley W	do	Feb. 11, 1864	Feb. 11, 1864	Died in hospital at Little Rock, Arkansas, February 18, 1864.
Dunkin, Stephen B	do	Aug. 10, 1864	Sept. 23, 1864	Died in hospital at Little Rock, Arkansas, October 21, 1864.
Goodman, Pleasant R	do	Feb. 1, 1864	Feb. 8, 1864	Died in hospital at Lewisburg, Arkansas, July 24, 1864.
Horton, Isaac E	do	Feb. 1, 1864	Feb. 8, 1864	Died in hospital at Lewisburg, Arkansas, April 15, 1864.
Jones, John H	do	Nov. 18, 1863	Dec. 20, 1863	Died in hospital at Lewisburg, Arkansas, June 6, 1864.
Murphy, John	do	Nov. 22, 1863	Dec. 1, 1863	Died in hospital at Lewisburg, Arkansas, August 16, 1864.
Marimon, Andrew G	do	Feb. 5, 1865	Never.	Died in hospital at Lewisburg, Arkansas, May 13, 1865.
McGhee, Thomas	do	Feb. 9, 1864	Feb. 11, 1864	Died in hospital at Little Rock, Arkansas, December 9, 1864.
Price, John	do	Nov. 8, 1863	Nov. 16, 1863	Died in hospital at Little Rock, Arkansas, May 3, 1864.
Polk, James K	do	Feb. 1, 1864	Feb. 8, 1864	Died in hospital at Little Rock, Arkansas, March 8, 1864.
Rorie, Andrew J	do	Aug. 10, 1864	Never.	Died in hospital at Lewisburg, Arkansas, January 3, 1865.
Roberts, John A	do	Nov. 8, 1863	Nov. 16, 1863	Died in hospital at Little Rock, Arkansas, March 6, 1864.
Shipman, Ervin A	do	Feb. 1, 1864	Feb. 8, 1864	Died in hospital at Lewisburg, Arkansas, June 18, 1864.
Webb, Joseph H	do	Dec. 14, 1863	Dec. 20, 1863	Died in hospital at Little Rock, Arkansas, April 6, 1864.
Williams, Peter W	do	Nov. 8, 1863	Nov. 14, 1863	Died in hospital at Little Rock, Arkansas, March 23, 1864.
Discharged.				
Davis, George L	Private	Feb. 1, 1864	Feb. 8, 1864	Discharged for disability ——, ——.
Tilly, William	do	Feb. 1, 1864	Feb. 8, 1864	Do.

Deserted.

Name	Rank			Remarks
Baker, James M.	Corporal	Feb. 1, 1864	Feb. 8, 1864	Deserted from a scout May 26, 1864.
Campbell, James H.	Private	Dec. 18, 1863	Dec. 18, 1863	Deserted at Lewisburg, Arkansas, September 3, 1864.
Campbell, William L.	do	Dec. 18, 1863	Dec. 20, 1863	Do.
Collins, William H.	do	Nov. 22, 1863	Dec. 20, 1863	Deserted at Lewisburg, Arkansas, May 18, 1864.
Eaves, John T.	do	July 1, 1864	Never	Deserted at Lewisburg, Arkansas, September 17, 1864.
Jones, David J.	do	Dec. 18, 1863	Dec. 20, 1863	Deserted at Lewisburg, Arkansas, October 20, 1864.
Kelly, James W.	do	Dec. 21, 1863	Dec. 22, 1863	Deserted at Lewisburg, Arkansas, September 13, 1864.
Mills, Alonzo	do	Nov. 22, 1863	Dec. 4, 1863	Deserted at Lewisburg, Arkansas, May 18, 1864.
Morris, Henry	do	Feb. 1, 1864	Feb. 4, 1864	Deserted at Lewisburg, Arkansas, May 7, 1864.
Patterson, Rufus R.	do	Dec. 31, 1863	Jan. 8, 1864	Deserted at Lewisburg, Arkansas, October 20, 1864.
Patterson, William H. H.	do	Dec. 31, 1863	Jan. 8, 1864	Do.
Shipman, James E.	do	Feb. 1, 1864	Feb. 8, 1864	Deserted from a scout July 4, 1864.
Shipman, William L.	do	Feb. 1, 1864	Feb. 8, 1864	Deserted from a scout August 16, 1864.
Thompson, Benjamin	Sergeant	Dec. 14, 1863	Dec. 20, 1863	Deserted at Lewisburg, Arkansas, May 18, 1864.
Triplith, Lafayette	Corporal	Dec. 14, 1863	Dec. 20, 1863	Do.
Vyars, William	Private	Dec. 14, 1863	Dec. 20, 1863	Deserted at Lewisburg, Arkansas, September 3, 1864.
Vyars, John	do	Mar. 5, 1864	Never	Deserted at Little Rock, Arkansas, May 26, 1864.
Vilt, Andrew J.	Bugler	Feb. 15, 1865		Deserted at Lewisburg, Arkansas, April 23, 1865.

COMPANY L.

Name	Rank		Date of rank.	Remarks
Anthony Hinkle	Captain		Feb. 14, 1864	Appointed lieutenant January 8, 1864; dismissed October 8, 1864.
Frederick A. Williams	do		Nov. 12, 1864	Appointed 1st lieutenant February 14, 1864; mustered out with regiment.
William A. Lenox	1st lieutenant		Nov. 12, 1864	Promoted from sergeant 3d Michigan cavalry; resigned.
Pleasant H. Simmons	2d lieutenant		Feb. 13, 1864	Appointed from private; discharged for disability.
Madison E. Moore	do	Oct. 18, 1864	Oct. 17, 1864	Appointed from private to 1st sergeant March 8, 1864; mustered out with regiment.
William Carter	1st sergeant	Dec. 27, 1864	Oct. 20, 1864	Sergeant from enrolment; mustered out with regiment.
John J. Dickens	Commissary sergeant	July 17, 1864	Jan. 1, 1865	Promoted from private; mustered out with regiment.
George W. Carter	Sergeant	Jan. 17, 1864	Jan. 17, 1864	Sergeant from enrolment; mustered out with regiment.
Abraham Oliver	do	Jan. 8, 1864	Jan. 1, 1865	Appointed from corporal; mustered out with regiment.
Charles P. Williams	do	Feb. 5, 1864	Jan. 8, 1865	Appointed corporal April 5, 1864; mustered out with regiment.
Reuben M. Norwood	do	Jan. 14, 1864	April 1, 1865	Appointed from corporal; mustered out with regiment.
Philip Howell	Corporal	Jan. 15, 1864	Jan. 15, 1864	Mustered out with regiment.
James F. Standlee	do	Jan. 8, 1864	May 3, 1864	Do.
Francis E. Henry	do	Jan. 20, 1864	Dec. 20, 1864	Do.
Richard P. Bryant	do	Dec. 29, 1864	Jan. 1, 1865	Do.
Daniel E. Burnett	do	Feb. 5, 1864	Jan. 1, 1865	Do.
John M. Baringame	do	July 25, 1864	Jan. 1, 1865	Do.
John Adams	do	Jan. 4, 1864	Jan. 1, 1865	Do.
John W. Buckner	do	Feb. 4, 1864	Jan. 1, 1865	Do.
Monroe Gilchrist	Farrier	Feb. 4, 1864	Feb. 4, 1864	Do.

Muster.

Name	Rank			
Allen, Hiram S.	Private	Jan. 4, 1864	Feb. 2, 1864	Do.
Atkins, Benjamin D.	do	Jan. 25, 1864	Feb. 2, 1864	Do.
Atkinson, John M.	do	Sept. 21, 1864	Sept. 29, 1864	Do.

128   REPORT OF THE ADJUTANT GENERAL OF ARKANSAS.

Third regiment Arkansas cavalry volunteers. Mustered into service February 10, 1864, (three years;) mustered out June 30, 1865.

COMPANY L—Continued.

Names.	Rank.	Enlistment.	Muster.	Remarks.
Boykin, Benjamin	Private	Feb. 4, 1864	Feb. 8, 1864	Mustered out with regiment.
Blythe, George W	do	Jan. 12, 1864	Feb. 8, 1864	Do.
Brady, William	do	Feb. 29, 1864	Mar. 2, 1864	Do.
Brinley, John	do	April 22, 1864	Sept. 27, 1864	Do.
Banks, Peter W	do	Aug. 2, 1864	Sept. 30, 1864	Do.
Carr, James E	do	Dec. 28, 1863	Feb. 8, 1864	Do.
Dickens, Thomas M	do	Dec. 28, 1863	Jan. 8, 1864	Do.
Dickens, Francis M	do	Dec. 28, 1863	Jan. 8, 1864	Do.
Dickens, Andrew J	do	Aug. 19, 1864	Sept. 27, 1864	Do.
Doyle, Michael C	do	Aug. 4, 1864	Sept. 27, 1864	Do.
Dowdy, Isaac	do	July 27, 1864	Sept. 27, 1864	Do.
Davis, James P	do	Sept. 1, 1864	Sept. 27, 1864	Do.
Dyarnatt, Walter F	do	Sept. 2, 1864	Sept. 27, 1864	Do.
Edwards, William B	do	Jan. 16, 1864	Feb. 2, 1864	Do.
Ferguson, John A	do	Jan. 18, 1864	Feb. 8, 1864	Do.
Feugna, John F	do	Feb. 5, 1864	Feb. 8, 1864	Do.
Freeland, Joseph J	do	Feb. 28, 1864	Mar. 2, 1864	Do.
Fryer, Francis L	do	July 4, 1864	Sept. 27, 1864	Do.
Glenn, Robert	do	Jan. 29, 1864	Feb. 2, 1864	Do.
Griffith, Benjamin F	do	Feb. 7, 1864	Feb. 8, 1864	Do.
Gross, William	do	Feb. 8, 1864	Feb. 8, 1864	Do.
Henry, James M	do	Jan. 20, 1864	Feb. 2, 1862	Do.
Heine, James M	do	June 20, 1864	Sept. 27, 1864	Do.
Heine, Jesse A	do	Feb. 6, 1864	Feb. 8, 1864	Do.
Henderson, James M	do	Jan. 25, 1864	Feb. 2, 1864	Do.
Hooper, William H. H	do	July 21, 1864	Sept. 27, 1864	Do.
Hensley, James J	do	Sept. 4, 1864	Sept. 27, 1864	Do.
Howard, Edward	do	Sept. 4, 1864	Sept. 27, 1864	Do.
Lyons, Marairean J	do	Apr. 22, 1864	Sept. 27, 1864	Do.
Lackey, James R	do	Jan. 18, 1864	Feb. 2, 1864	Do.
Lackey, George W	do	Jan. 18, 1864	Feb. 2, 1864	Do.
Lewellen, James F	do	July 23, 1864	Sept. 27, 1864	Do.
Lovell, William	do	Dec. 4, 1864		Do.
Lilly, William H	do	Feb. 29, 1864	Mar. 2, 1864	Do.
Miller, William F	do	Aug. 3, 1864	Sept. 27, 1864	Do.
McGhee, John	do	Jan. 11, 1864	Jan. 13, 1864	Do.
Martin, William F	do	Jan. 4, 1864		Do.
Mathews, Thomas J	do	Jan. 14, 1864	Feb. 2, 1864	Do.
McDaniel, Francis A	do	Jan. 8, 1864	Feb. 8, 1864	Do.
Nichols, Harvey B	do	July 27, 1864	Sept. 27, 1864	Do.
Newberry, Robert M	do	Sept. 2, 1864	Sept. 27, 1864	Do.
Oliver, Henry	do	Jan. 8, 1864		Do.
O'Neal, James K	do	Jan. 29, 1864	Feb. 2, 1864	Do.

REPORT OF THE ADJUTANT GENERAL OF ARKANSAS.   129

Name	Rank	Enrolled	Mustered in	Remarks
O'Neal, Charles	do	Sept. 2, 1864	Sept. 27, 1864	Do.
Parrott, Larkin B	do	July 23, 1864	Sept. 27, 1864	Do.
Rhodes, Sylvester	do	Nov. 22, 1864		Do.
Shillings, James M	do	Jan. 1, 1864	Jan. 8, 1864	Do.
Sherman, John H	do	Feb. 6, 1864	Feb. 8, 1864	Do.
Simmons, William B	do	Jan. 1, 1864	Jan. 8, 1864	Do.
Shewmake, Jesse	do	July 30, 1864	Sept. 27, 1864	Do.
Stone, John D	do	Jan. 18, 1865		Do.
Sullivan, William P	do	Jan. 8, 1864	Feb. 2, 1864	Do.
Tindall, Howell	do	Jan. 28, 1864	Feb. 2, 1864	Do.
Tarkington, Howell	do	Jan. 14, 1864	Feb. 2, 1864	Do.
Usey, William S	do	Jan. 16, 1864	Feb. 2, 1864	Do.
Willis, John R	do	Jan. 18, 1864	Feb. 2, 1864	Do.
Warden, Joseph	do	July 18, 1864	Sept. 27, 1864	Do.
Williams, George R	do	Jan. 1, 1864	Jan. 8, 1864	Do.
White, David N	do	Jan. 20, 1864		Do.
Wilson, Robert C	do	Jan. 1, 1862	Jan. 8, 1864	Do.

Killed in action.

Butler, William B	Private	Jan. 29, 1864	Feb. 2, 1864	Killed in a skirmish near Quitman, Arkansas, March 26, 1864.
Harden, James A	do	Feb. 29, 1864	Mar. 2, 1864	Do.
Lilly, Anthony W	Corporal	Jan. 24, 1864	Feb. 29, 1864	Do.
Oliver, William	Private	Jan. 4, 1864	Feb. 8, 1864	Do.
Wann, William A	do	Jan. 27, 1864	Feb. 2, 1864	Do.

Missing in action.

| Collingsworth, Bartley M | Private | Jan. 18, 1864 | Feb. 2, 1864 | Missing in action May 19, 1864. |
| Printon, James | Corporal | Jan. 18, 1864 | Jan. 6, 1865 | Do. |

Died.

Allen, Solomon M	Private	Feb. 24, 1863	Feb. 2, 1864	Died in hospital at Little Rock, Arkansas, March 17, 1864.
Atkins, Leonidas F	do	Jan. 13, 1864	Feb. 2, 1864	Died of measles at Little Rock, Arkansas, March 18, 1864.
Dickens, William L	do	Jan. 12, 1864	Feb. 29, 1864	Died of measles at Little Rock, Arkansas, March 12, 1864.
Dowdy, William S	do	Feb. 2, 1864	Never	Died at Lewisburg, Arkansas, September 4, 1864.
Griffith, William S	do	Jan. 8, 1864	Feb. 2, 1864	Died of measles at Little Rock, Arkansas, March 9, 1864.
Gross Edward	do	Feb. 2, 1864	Feb. 2, 1864	Died of pneumonia at Lewisburg, Arkansas, April 9, 1864.
Garrett, Franklin E	do	Aug. 3, 1864	Never	Died of pneumonia at Lewisburg, Arkansas, October 30, 1864.
Killingsworth, Charles	do	Feb. 1, 1864	Feb. 8, 1864	Died of pneumonia at Lewisburg, Arkansas, September 23, 1864.
McMillen, John H	do	Jan. 20, 1864	Feb. 2, 1864	Died of pneumonia at Little Rock, Arkansas, March 14, 1864.
Mabry, Fleming A	do	Jan. 25, 1864	Feb. 2, 1864	Died of pneumonia at Lewisburg, Arkansas, July 9, 1864.
Newberry, John C	do	Jan. 8, 1864	Feb. 2, 1864	Died of consumption at Little Rock, Arkansas, February —, 1864.
Pruit, John J	do	Jan. 18, 1864	Feb. 8, 1864	Died of small-pox at Lewisburg, Arkansas, June 1, 1864.
Perrons, Joseph J	do	July 18, 1864	Never	Died in hospital at Lewisburg, Arkansas, August 23, 1864.
Shillings, Lewis J	do	Jan. 23, 1864	Feb. 2, 1864	Died of measles at Little Rock, Arkansas, March 13, 1864.
Wilson, William F	do	Jan. 1, 1864	Jan. 8, 1864	Died of typhoid fever at Lewisburg, Arkansas, April 29, 1864.
Woodworth, Henry P	do	Jan. 20, 1864	Feb. 8, 1864	Died of typhoid fever at Little Rock, Arkansas, April 23, 1864.
Waley, William R	do	Jan. 18, 1864	Feb. 8, 1864	Died of typhoid fever at Little Rock, Arkansas, March 2, 1864.
Witt, James S	do	Jan. 2, 1864	Feb. 2, 1864	Died of small-pox at Lewisburg, Arkansas, June 13, 1863.
Waley, David W	do	Jan. 18, 1864	Feb. 2, 1864	Died at Lewisburg, Arkansas, in hospital, August 28, 1864.

Mis. Doc. 53——9

Third regiment Arkansas cavalry volunteers. Mustered into service February 10, 1864, (three years;) mustered out June 30, 1865.

COMPANY L—Continued.

Names.	Rank.	Enlistment.	Muster.	Remarks.
Bodwin, William P.	Private	Jan. 14, 1864	Feb. 2, 1864	Died at Little Rock, Arkansas, September 16, 1864.
Lumpkins, George H.	...do...	Jan. 5, 1864	Feb. 2, 1864	Died in hospital at Lewisburg, Arkansas, September 16, 1864.
Letbetter, Lenah S.	...do...	Feb. 11, 1864	Feb. 19, 1864	Died in hospital at Little Rock, Arkansas, April 29, 1864.
Morton, William B.	...do...	June 21, 1864	Never	Died in penitentiary at Little Rock, Arkansas, January 30, 1865.
Deserted.				
Bryant, Henry J.	...do...	Jan. 8, 1864	Never	Deserted, May 19, 1865.
Batty, Franklin E.	...do...	Aug. 27, 1864	Jan. 8, 1865	Deserted, November 1, 1864.
Bowind, William	...do...	July 19, 1864	Never	Deserted, May 19, 1865.
Clifton, William L.	...do...	July 28, 1864	Sept. 27, 1864	Deserted, October 19, 1864.
Dyson, Thomas M.	...do...	Jan. 8, 1864	Never	Deserted, August 30, 1864.
Edmondson, Manley B.	...do...	Jan. 8, 1864	July 25, 1864	Deserted, October 13, 1864.
Gullett, Hine A.	...do...	Aug. 14, 1864	Never	Deserted, September 11, 1864.
Joslin, Samuel J.	...do...	Jan. 23, 1864	Sept. 27, 1864	Deserted, October 13, 1864.
Lacefield, William J.	...do...	Feb. 2, 1864	Feb. 29, 1864	Do.
Martin, Newton	...do...	Feb. 29, 1864	Mar. 2, 1864	Deserted, May 28, 1864.
Middleton, Alexander F.	...do...	Mar. 2, 1864	Aug. 3, 1864	Deserted, May 18, 1864.
Murray, Wesley J.	...do...	Feb. 29, 1864	Never	Deserted, August 30, 1864.
Mabry, James E.	...do...	Mar. 2, 1864	Mar. 8, 1864	Deserted, November 5, 1864.
Tindall, James A.	...do...	Jan. 16, 1864	Never	Deserted, May 19, 1864.
Tarkington, Thomas	...do...			Deserted, July 28, 1864.
Discharged.				
Brinley, Jasper	...do...	Aug. 4, 1864	Never	Discharged, September 27, 1864.
Carrington, Leonidas	Sergeant	Jan. 29, 1864	Feb. 2, 1864	Discharged, June 19, 1864; sergeant from enrolment.
Hinkle, William K.	Private	Jan. 1, 1864	Feb. 19, 1864	Discharged, June 19, 1864.
Moore, Nathaniel W.	...do...	Jan. 8, 1864	Feb. 2, 1864	Do.
Moore, James S.	...do...	Jan. 1, 1864	Jan. 8, 1864	Do.
Nichols, James A.	...do...	July 28, 1864	Never	Discharged, September 27, 1864.
Phillipps, Bethel	...do...	July 23, 1864	Never	Do.
Turner, William	...do...	Jan. 21, 1864	Feb. 2, 1864	Discharged, October 7, 1864.

COMPANY M.

		Date of rank.	Muster.	
Benjamin F. Taylor	Captain	Feb. 10, 1864	Feb. 10, 1864	Captain from organization of company; mustered out with regiment.
William H. Lee	1st lieutenant	Feb. 10, 1864	Feb. 10, 1864	Resigned, February 6, 1865.
Darwin E. Hand	do		May 1, 1865	Promoted from private 3d Michigan cavalry; mustered out with regiment.
George A. Winslow	2d lieutenant	Feb. 10, 1864	Feb. 10, 1864	Dismissed, May 9, 1865.
Mastin Hensley	1st sergeant	Jan. 1, 1864	Feb. 10, 1864	1st sergeant from organization of company; mustered out with regiment.
James Young	Commissary sergeant	Jan. 28, 1864	Feb. 10, 1864	Commissary sergeant from organization of company; mustered out with regiment.
Uriah J. Sutterfield	Sergeant	Jan. 28, 1864	Feb. 10, 1864	Sergeant from organization of company; mustered out with regiment.
Samuel R. Sutterfield	Corporal	Feb. 5, 1864	Oct. 17, 1864	Corporal from organization of company; mustered out with regiment.
William J. Young	do	Jan. 28, 1864	Feb. 10, 1864	Corporal from organization of company; mustered out with regiment.
Harry Kitchens	do	Jan. 28, 1864	Mar. 1, 1864	Mustered out with regiment.
James Gaddy	Bugler	Jan. 28, 1864	June 4, 1864	Mustered out with regiment.
Thomas E. Brown	Saddler	Jan. 28, 1864	Feb. 10, 1864	Do.
John G. Rosie	Blacksmith	Jan. 28, 1864	Feb. 10, 1864	Blacksmith from organization of company; mustered out with regiment.
Davis Casey	Teamster	Jan. 1, 1864	Oct. 18, 1864	Mustered out with regiment.
Allseed, Samuel	Private	Jan. 28, 1864	Feb. 2, 1864	Do.
Bonds, Richard W	do	July 27, 1864	Sept. 23, 1864	Do.
Bone, William F	do	July 15, 1864	Sept. 23, 1864	Do.
Bonds, Andrew J	do	Nov. 14, 1864	Nov. 14, 1864	Do.
Clark, Jeremiah	do	Jan. 28, 1864	Feb. 2, 1864	Do.
Cooper, Newton	do	Jan. 1, 1864	Feb. 2, 1864	Do.
Danon, John	do	Jan. 28, 1864	Feb. 2, 1864	Do.
Davis, Wesley	do	July 1, 1864	Sept. 23, 1864	Do.
Fox, Richard	do	Jan. 28, 1864	Feb. 2, 1864	Do.
Goodnight, John	do	April 6, 1864	Sept. 23, 1864	Do.
Hughast, Samuel M	do	July 30, 1864	Sept. 23, 1864	Do.
Hopson, William S	do	Aug. 20, 1864	Feb. 2, 1865	Do.
Highley, Martin	do	Jan. 1, 1864	Dec. 23, 1864	Do.
Hensley, Benjamin	do	Dec. 8, 1864	Dec. 8, 1864	Do.
Hensley, Nathaniel	do	Dec. 12, 1864	Dec. 12, 1864	Do.
Jackson, John	do	Aug. 20, 1864	Aug. 20, 1864	Do.
Jackson, Richard	do	Jan. 28, 1864	Feb. 4, 1864	Do.
Kaistle, Moses	do	Nov. 28, 1864	Nov. 28, 1864	Do.
Lafferty, Dallas	do	Nov. 28, 1864	Nov. 29, 1864	Do.
Lafferty, Alfred	do	Jan. 28, 1864	Feb. 2, 1864	Do.
Massey, Thomas G	do	Jan. 28, 1864	Feb. 2, 1864	Do.
Mastin, Peter	do	April 6, 1864	Sept. 23, 1864	Do.
Mastin, James J	do	Jan. 28, 1864	Feb. 2, 1864	Do.
Martin, James H	do	Dec. 30, 1864	Dec. 30, 1864	Do.
Martin, William M	do	July 10, 1864	Sept. 23, 1864	Do.
Mannel, John F	do	Sept. 9, 1864	Sept. 9, 1864	Do.
Owens, Zachariah	do	Aug. 3, 1864	Sept. 23, 1864	Do.
Pierce, James T	do	Dec. 30, 1864	Dec. 30, 1864	Do.
Potter, Andrew A	do	Jan. 1, 1864	Feb. 12, 1864	Do.
Renfro, Joseph	do			Do.

132   REPORT OF THE ADJUTANT GENERAL OF ARKANSAS.

Third regiment Arkansas cavalry volunteers. Mustered into service February 10, 1864, (three years;) mustered out June 30, 1865.

COMPANY M—Continued.

Names.	Rank.	Enlistment.	Muster.	Remarks.
Talley, Robertson	Private	Jan. 28, 1864	Feb. 2, 1864	Mustered out with regiment.
Watkins, Carmine	do	July 27, 1864	July 27, 1864	Do.
Mustered out in accordance with special instructions from the War Department, dated Adjutant General's Office, April 5, 1865—discharges to take effect May 22, 1865.				
Asa C. Hanna	Quartermaster sergeant	Jan. 1, 1864	Feb. 2, 1864	Corporal from organization; appointed quartermaster sergeant October 17, 1864.
Ebenezer D. Arnold	Sergeant	Jan. 1, 1864	Feb. 2, 1864	Appointed from private October 17, 1864.
John W. Metcalf	do	Feb. 5, 1864	Feb. 13, 1864	Sergeant from organization of company.
William S. Boyd	do	Feb. 5, 1864	Feb. 13, 1864	Do.
John W. Harness	do	Jan. 28, 1864	Feb. 2, 1864	Do.
Joseph M. Kesner	Corporal	Jan. 28, 1864	Feb. 2, 1864	Appointed corporal October 17, 1864.
Alex. C. Stephenson	do	Jan. 28, 1864	Feb. 2, 1864	Appointed corporal April 1, 1864.
Jefferson Lane	do	Jan. 28, 1864	Feb. 2, 1864	Corporal from organization of company.
George W. Early	do	Feb. 5, 1864	Feb. 13, 1864	Do.
Alexander Bohannon	do	Feb. 5, 1864	Feb. 13, 1864	Do.
James H. Kelly	Blacksmith	Jan. 28, 1864	Feb. 2, 1864	
Arnold, John	Private	Jan. 1, 1864	Feb. 2, 1864	
Arnold, William	do	Jan. 1, 1864	Feb. 2, 1864	
Ashley, John F.	do	Feb. 5, 1864	Feb. 13, 1864	
Barnett, David	do	Jan. 1, 1864	Feb. 2, 1864	
Copeland, Alexander	do	Jan. 28, 1864	Feb. 2, 1864	
Dawson, Eli	do	Feb. 5, 1864	Feb. 13, 1864	
Early, Adam K.	do	Feb. 5, 1864	Feb. 13, 1864	
Ellis, William	do	Feb. 5, 1864	Feb. 13, 1864	
Hanna, James A.	do	Jan. 1, 1864	Feb. 2, 1864	
Hynchey, William W.	do	Jan. 1, 1864	Feb. 2, 1864	
Hartman, Jonathan	do	Jan. 28, 1864	Feb. 2, 1864	
Harris, John	do	Jan. 28, 1864	Feb. 2, 1864	
Harness, Roan	do	Jan. 28, 1864	Feb. 2, 1864	
Kelly, Jabez H.	do	Jan. 28, 1864	Feb. 2, 1864	
Kelly, John H.	do	Feb. 5, 1864	Feb. 13, 1864	
McDaniel, Samuel	do	Jan. 1, 1864	Feb. 2, 1864	
Maler, John H.	do	Jan. 1, 1864	Feb. 2, 1864	
Mathis, John W.	do	Feb. 13, 1864	Mar. 6, 1864	
Pierce, William	do	Jan. 1, 1864	Feb. 2, 1864	
Ragland, Jesse B.	do	Jan. 28, 1864	Feb. 2, 1864	
Reid, John E.	do	Jan. 28, 1864	Feb. 2, 1864	
Sutterfield, Peter M.	do	Jan. 28, 1864	Feb. 2, 1864	

Sutterfield, Henry P	do	Jan. 28, 1864	Feb. 2, 1864
Stephenson, James W	do	Feb. 2, 1864	Feb. 2, 1864
Wastman, Franklin	do	Jan. 1, 1864	Feb. 2, 1864
Watts, Benjamin G	do	Jan. 28, 1864	Feb. 2, 1864

Discharged.

Harris, Wm. B	Private	Jan. 28, 1864	Feb. 2, 1864	Discharged for disability January 3, 1865.

Missing in action.

Whitmuse, William	Private	Aug. 1, 1864	Never	Missing since September 8, 1864.

Died.

Arnold, Jacob	Private	Jan. 1, 1864	Feb. 2, 1864	Died of inflammation of lungs, Lewisburg, Arkansas, February 1, 1865.
Begley, Hiram	do	Jan. 28, 1864	Feb. 2, 1864	Died in Searcy county, Arkansas, February 25, 1864.
Cash, Levi	do	Jan. 1, 1864	Feb. 2, 1864	Died at Lewisburg, Arkansas, January 17, 1865.
Garrison, Samuel	do	Jan. 28, 1864	Feb. 2, 1864	Died of chronic diarrhœa, Little Rock, Arkansas, August 14, 1864.
Jackson, Andrew	do	Jan. 28, 1864	Feb. 2, 1864	Died of general debility, Little Rock, Arkansas, October 1, 1864.
Jackson, William	do	Jan. 5, 1864	Feb. 13, 1864	Died of typhoid fever, Lewisburg, Arkansas, January 24, 1865.
Sutterfield, Armanius	do	Jan. 28, 1864	Feb. 2, 1864	Died at Lewisburg, Arkansas, September 2, 1864.
Young, jr., William J	do	Jan. 28, 1864	Feb. 2, 1864	Died at Little Rock, Arkansas, March 18, 1864.

Deserted.

Allseed, William J	Private	Jan. 28, 1864	Feb. 2, 1864	Deserted at Springfield, Arkansas, May 25, 1864.
Boyd, James	do	Feb. 5, 1864	Feb. 13, 1864	Deserted at Lewisburg, Arkansas, May 11, 1864.
Begley, Thomas	do	Feb. 5, 1864	Feb. 13, 1864	Deserted at Lewisburg, Arkansas, May 25, 1865.
Colley, Francis M	do	Feb. 5, 1864	Feb. 13, 1864	Deserted at Lewisburg, Arkansas, June 2, 1864.
Husley, Joseph	do	Jan. 28, 1864	Feb. 2, 1864	Deserted at Lewisburg, Arkansas, September 6, 1864.
Hastings, John D	do	Feb. 5, 1864	Feb. 13, 1864	Deserted at Lewisburg, Arkansas, May 18, 1864.
Jones, Stephen	do	Jan. 28, 1864	Feb. 2, 1864	Deserted at Little Rock, Arkansas, October 10, 1864.
Potter, William	do	Jan. 28, 1864	Feb. 2, 1864	Deserted at Lewisburg, Arkansas, May 25, 1865.
Potter, Melekiah B	do	Feb. 5, 1864	Feb. 13, 1864	Do.
Roberts, James E	do	Jan. 28, 1864	Feb. 2, 1864	Deserted at Lewisburg, Arkansas, September 6, 1864.
Watts, Yell	do	Feb. 5, 1864	Feb. 13, 1864	Deserted at Little Rock, Arkansas, October 10, 1864.

THIRD ARKANSAS CAVALRY VOLUNTEERS.—HISTORICAL MEMORANDA.

After the occupation of Little Rock by General Steele in September, 1863, it was soon found that there also many citizens of Arkansas were loyal, and would fight for the flag, and the following authority for raising the 3d regiment of Arkansas cavalry volunteers was accordingly given:

HEADQUARTERS ARMY OF ARKANSAS. *Little Rock, Arkansas, October 26, 1863.*

Special Orders, No. 64.

[Extract.]

IV.—Captain A. H. Ryan, 17th Illinois infantry, is hereby authorized to raise a regiment of cavalry, to be designated the 3d Arkansas cavalry; the regiment to be recruited and mustered into service as the War Department may determine; the regiment to be rendezvoused at Little Rock. The officers of the regiment will be designated by Captain Ryan, and approved by the commanding general of troops in central Arkansas, and submitted to the War Department for approval and orders. Private Harry F. Van Houten, company A, 13th Illinois volunteer infantry, will aid Captain Ryan in the organization of the regiment.

By order of Major General F. STEELE:

GEORGE O. SOKALSKI, *First Lieutenant 2d Cavalry and A. A. A. G.*

The authority thus given by General Steele was shortly afterwards confirmed by the commanding general of the department of the Missouri, and the raising of the regiment was vigorously proceeded with. At this time the exigencies of the service were such in the department of Arkansas that it was necessary that all troops raised should be put at once upon active field duty. It was therefore a desideratum, kept constantly in view, to make the 3d Arkansas cavalry efficient in the shortest time practicable, and men of ability and experience were selected as field and staff officers. For officers in the line one lieutenant was chosen for each company from regiments that had seen service, and the remaining officers were Arkansians, who had been actively engaged in recruiting for the regiment. The regiment was mustered into the service on the 10th day of February, 1864, and was immediately ordered into the field.

In a report made to this office February 4, 1865, by First Lieutenant Frank Pease, of company H, the following succinct statement of the operations of the regiment to that time appears: "On the organization of the regiment, two battalions were sent up the Arkansas river to hold a large scope of territory infested by numerous guerilla bands, who were robbing and murdering Union families in the most barbarous manner that human depravity could invent. Territory held by these marauders was soon wrested from their hands by the 3d cavalry, and comparative quiet restored. One battalion remained in camp at Little Rock until an expedition was sent out to the Ouachita river under General Steele; that battalion accompanied the expedition, and participated in all the engagements of the entire campaign.

"The regiment, since its organization, has been engaged in clearing the country of the numerous predatory bands which have cursed this district with their infamous operations since the inception of the rebellion, and by it a large number of them have been killed and wounded. Being stationed remotely from supplies, and constituting an extreme outpost to Little Rock, the regiment has necessarily performed a large amount of labor, sometimes subsisting on half or quarter rations. The extent of territory protected and occupied was large, and, at the same time, to avoid being cut off from our base of supplies by greatly superior forces, we were taught vigilance and the imperative necessity of giving the enemy a wholesome dread of the regiment."

For some months prior to the date of this communication the regiment was stationed at Lewisburg, on the Arkansas river, where it was of great service to General Steele. Detachments were constantly on the alert, scouring the country, breaking up the lesser haunts of the enemy; and it is to be regretted that more minute details of their achievements cannot be given.

The regiment was mustered out of the service at Lewisburg on the 30th day of June, 1865.

REPORT OF THE ADJUTANT GENERAL OF ARKANSAS. 135

Fourth regiment Arkansas cavalry volunteers. Mustered into service December 29, 1864, (three years;) mustered out June 30, 1865.

FIELD AND STAFF.

Names.	Rank.	Enlistment.	Date of rank.	Remarks.
La Fayette Gregg	Colonel	Dec. 29, 1864	Dec. 29, 1864	Appointed from civil life to fill original vacancy; mustered out with regiment.
Horace L. Moore	Lieutenant colonel	—, 1861	Mar. 29, 1864	Promoted from 1st lieutenant company D, 2d Kansas cavalry, to fill original vacancy; mustered out with regiment.
Lyman G. Bennett	Major		Dec. 8, 1863	Appointed from private to adjutant; promoted from adjutant to major, resigned August 26, 1864.
Willis Jones	....do	Jan. 19, 1864	Jan. 20, 1864	Appointed from civil life to fill original vacancy; discharged October 3, 1864.
Horace S. Greeno	....do	—, 1861	Oct. 16, 1864	Promoted from captain 6th Kansas cavalry, *vice* Lyman G. Bennett, resigned; mustered out with regiment.
Albert O. Vincent	....do		May 24, 1864	Promoted major 1st Arkansas cavalry, April 23, 1864, from 1st lieutenant 2d U. S. artillery; transferred to 4th Arkansas cavalry, May 24, 1864, to fill vacancy, *vice* Major Willis Jones, mustered out; muster out suspended.
M. Hazen White	....do		Oct. 16, 1864	Promoted from 1st lieutenant 22d Ohio infantry; mustered out with regiment.
Franklin M. Warford	Surgeon		Jan. 27, 1864	Promoted from assistant surgeon 3d Iowa cavalry to fill original vacancy; mustered out with regiment.
A. B. Fryrear	Assistant surgeon	Feb. 5, 1864	Feb. 5, 1864	Appointed from civil life; resigned July 27, 1864.
Porter J. Andrews	Adjutant		April 7, 1864	Appointed from corporal 30th Iowa infantry; transferred to company D as 1st lieutenant.
Nathaniel W. Welliver	....do		Oct. 16, 1864	Appointed from private 1st Iowa cavalry to fill vacancy caused by transfer of Lieutenant Porter J. Andrews; promoted to captain of company D, *vice* Norton, mustered out.
Charles T. Jordan	Regimental quartermaster	Dec. 5, 1863	Dec. 5, 1863	Appointed from civil life; resigned January 27, 1864.
John C. Parrish	....do	Jan. 31, 1864	Jan. 31, 1864	Appointed from civil life; resigned August 5, 1864.
Henry L. Bosquet	....do		Dec. 30, 1864	Appointed from private 33d Iowa infantry to fill vacancy caused by resignation of John C. Parrish; mustered out with regiment.
John C. Curtis	Regimental com. subsistence.	Feb. 5, 1864	Feb. 5, 1864	Appointed from civil life; resigned August 22, 1864.
Samuel B. Evans	....do		Oct. 16, 1864	Appointed from commissary sergeant 33d Iowa infantry to fill vacancy caused by resignation of John C. Curtis; mustered out with regiment.

NON-COMMISSIONED STAFF.

Robert W. Bodell	Veterinary surgeon		Dec. 15, 1864	Appointed from private company B 1st Iowa cavalry; mustered out with regiment.
John Jeffers	Hospital steward	Feb. 28, 1864	Mar. 8, 1865	Appointed from 1st sergeant company M; mustered out with regiment.
Michael Dodd	....do	Feb. 16, 1864	June 1, 1865	Appointed from private company E.

136 REPORT OF THE ADJUTANT GENERAL OF ARKANSAS.

Fourth regiment Arkansas cavalry volunteers. Mustered into service December 29, 1864, (three years;) mustered out June 30, 1865.

NON-COMMISSIONED STAFF—Continued.

Names.	Rank.	Enlistment.	Date of rank.	Remarks.
Thomas J. Ross	Sergeant major	Feb. 13, 1864	Feb. 28, 1864	Appointed from sergeant company E; mustered out June 6, 1865.
Albert Harrell	do	—, 1861	June 7, 1865	Appointed from 29th Illinois infantry; mustered out with regiment.
Pleasant Hixon	Quartermaster sergeant	Sept. 21, 1864	Dec. 10, 1864	Appointed from 1st sergeant company A.
Thomas H. Ritter	Commissary sergeant	Jan. 14, 1864	Feb. 17, 1864	Appointed from commissary sergeant company D; mustered out with regiment.
Noah J. Baumgartner	Saddler sergeant	Mar. 23, 1864	April 23, 1864	Appointed from private company G; mustered out with regiment.
Charles Raber	Chief bugler	Jan. 13, 1864	June 3, 1864	Appointed from bugler company I; mustered out with regiment.

COMPANY A.

Names.	Rank.	Enlistment.	Date of rank.	Remarks.
Joel Brown	Captain		Dec. 10, 1863	Appointed 1st lieutenant November 18, 1863; died of typhoid fever at Little Rock, Arkansas, July 20, 1864.
Henry R. Newcomb	do	Dec. 10, 1863	Oct. 16, 1864	Mustered out with regiment.
David W. Babb	1st lieutenant		Jan. 1, 1864	Appointed from private 1st Arkansas infantry, Jan. 1, 1864; deserted June 15, 1864.
Hiram Selsor	do		Nov. 3, 1864	Appointed from sergeant 3d Missouri cavalry; mustered out with regiment.
George A. White	2d lieutenant	—, 1862	Dec. 12, 1863	Appointed from private company E, 1st Arkansas cavalry; discharged July 3, 1864.
James H. Law	do		July 22, 1864	Appointed from commissary sergeant company —; mustered out.
Isaac W. Ray	1st sergeant	May 20, 1864	Nov. 1, 1864	Appointed corporal July 23, 1864; mustered out with regiment.
Thomas Harris	Quartermaster sergeant	Sept. 20, 1863	May 1, 1865	Appointed from corporal; mustered out with regiment.
Francis M. Lancaster	Commissary sergeant	Sept. 20, 1863	July 23, 1864	Appointed from private; mustered out with regiment.
Francis M. Neal	Sergeant	Sept. 20, 1863	Dec. 10, 1863	Mustered out with regiment.
William Brown	do	Sept. 20, 1863	Dec. 10, 1863	Do.
John N. Neal	do	May 30, 1864	Nov. 1, 1864	Do.
Francis M. Davis	do	Sept. 20, 1863	Nov. 1, 1864	Appointed from private; mustered out with regiment.
Ephraim Hixon	Corporal	Sept. 20, 1863	Dec. 10, 1863	Do.
Henry Horn	do	Sept. 20, 1863	Dec. 10, 1863	Mustered out with regiment.
James A. Friar	do	Sept. 20, 1863	Dec. 10, 1863	Do.
Michael Reed	do	Sept. 20, 1863	Mar. 20, 1865	Do.
James R. Sevley	do	Sept. 20, 1863	Mar. 20, 1865	Do.
James Farmer	do	Sept. 20, 1863	Mar. 20, 1865	Do.
Thomas Anderson	do	Nov. 21, 1863	Mar. 20, 1865	Do.
Joseph Reed	Trumpeter	Sept. 20, 1863	Mar. 1, 1865	Do.
William Reed	do	Sept. 20, 1863	Mar. 1, 1865	Do.
Joseph Friar	Farrier	Dec. 6, 1863	Mar. 1, 1865	Do.
James J. McBride	do	Sept. 20, 1863	Mar. 1, 1865	Do.
William R. Sivley	Saddler	Sept. 20, 1863	Mar. 1, 1865	Do.
			Muster.	
Arnold, John T.	Private	Feb. 18, 1864	Feb. 29, 1864	Do.

REPORT OF THE ADJUTANT GENERAL OF ARKANSAS. 137

Name	Rank		Date		Remarks
Brown, Pleasant H		do	Dec. 1, 1863	Dec. 10, 1863	Do.
Brady, Oliver M		do	Sept. 20, 1863	Dec. 10, 1863	Do.
Cummings, Leroy		do	Sept. 20, 1863	Dec. 10, 1863	Do.
Carter, Peter		do	Apr. 6, 1864	Aug. 31, 1864	Do.
Doyle, John		do	Sept. 20, 1863	Dec. 12, 1863	Do.
Ewing, Francis M		do	Sept. 20, 1863	Dec. 10, 1863	Do.
Ewing, Benjamin F		do	Nov. 18, 1863	Dec. 10, 1863	Do.
Farmer, John		do	Nov. 26, 1863	Dec. 10, 1863	Do.
Farmer, Josiah A		do	Sept. 20, 1863	Dec. 10, 1863	Do.
Graves, Jacob		do	Sept. 20, 1863	Dec. 10, 1863	Do.
Genin, James P		do	Dec. 1, 1863	Dec. 10, 1863	Do.
Homer, John C		do	Sept. 20, 1863	Dec. 10, 1863	Do.
Homer, James M		do	Sept. 20, 1863	Dec. 10, 1863	Do.
Homer, Shelby C		do	Sept. 20, 1863	Dec. 10, 1863	Do.
Humphrey, Hustes		do	Sept. 20, 1863	Dec. 10, 1863	Do.
Hartley, J'el L		do	Sept. 20, 1863	Dec. 10, 1863	Do.
Hamilton, Thomas J		do	Sept. 20, 1863	Dec. 10, 1863	Do.
Horn, Joseph		do	Sept. 20, 1863	Dec. 10, 1863	Do.
Houser, Samuel		do	Oct. 18, 1863	Dec. 12, 1863	Do.
Hicks, George C		do	Sept. 20, 1863	Oct. 31, 1863	Do.
Lasater, William M		do	Sept. 20, 1863	Dec. 10, 1863	Do.
Lasater, Burrell		do	Sept. 20, 1863	Dec. 12, 1863	Do.
Maples, Daniel J		do	Sept. 20, 1863	Dec. 12, 1863	Do.
Moore, John A		do	Dec. 1, 1863	Dec. 12, 1863	Do.
Peeler, Andrew		do	Sept. 20, 1863	Dec. 12, 1863	Do.
Partin, William E		do	Sept. 20, 1863	Dec. 10, 1863	Do.
Reed, Shipman		do	Sept. 20, 1863	Dec. 10, 1863	Do.
Robertson, James F		do	Sept. 20, 1863	Dec. 10, 1863	Do.
Sorey, John		do	Sept. 20, 1863	Dec. 10, 1863	Do.
Sively, James M		do	Sept. 20, 1863	Feb. 29, 1864	Do.
Simpson, Richard F		do	Nov. 18, 1863	Dec. 10, 1863	Do.
Wheeler, Francis C		do	Dec. 1, 1863	Dec. 10, 1863	Do.
Webster, Francis M		do	Sept. 20, 1863	Dec. 10, 1863	Do.
Williams, William H		do	Jan. 4, 1864	Feb. 29, 1864	Do.
Killed in action.					
Andrew N. George	Private		Sept. 20, 1863	Dec. 10, 1863	Killed in a skirmish on Saline river February 15, 1864.
Missing in action.					
Alexander, James M	Private		Sept. 20, 1863	Dec. 10, 1863	Missing in action at Dardanelle, Arkansas, on the night of May 16, 1864.
Land, James M		do	Nov. 24, 1863	Dec. 10, 1863	Do.
Kilgore, Charles		do	Sept. 20, 1863	Dec. 10, 1863	Do.
Died.					
Belshey, Joseph	Private		Mar. 10, 1864	Aug. 31, 1864	Died of pneumonia at cavalry depot, Arkansas, February 23, 1864.
Boyd, William T		do	Nov. 25, 1863	Dec. 12, 1863	Died of chronic diarrhœa at Devall's Bluff, Arkansas, February 5, 1865.
Carter, James		do	Sept. 20, 1863	Dec. 10, 1863	Died of typhoid fever at Little Rock, Arkansas, July 19, 1864.
Geurin, Robert M		do	Dec. 1, 1863	Dec. 10, 1863	Died of typhoid fever, at St. Louis, Missouri, September 22, 1864.

138   REPORT OF THE ADJUTANT GENERAL OF ARKANSAS.

Fourth regiment Arkansas cavalry volunteers. Mustered into service December 29, 1864, (three years;) mustered out June 30, 1865.

COMPANY A—Continued.

Names.	Rank.	Enlistment.	Muster.	Remarks.
Jasper, Homer	Private	Sept. 20, 1863	Dec. 10, 1863	Died of chronic diarrhœa at Duvall's Bluff, Arkansas, May 2, 1865.
Keed, John	do	Sept. 20, 1863	Dec. 10, 1863	Died of chronic diarrhœa at Duvall's Bluff, Arkansas, March 12, 1865.
Lester, Edward	do	Sept. 20, 1863	Dec. 10, 1863	Died of typhoid fever, at Little Rock, Arkansas, July 12, 1864.
Long, Isaac	do	Oct. 29, 1863	Dec. 12, 1863	Died of dropsy at Duvall's Bluff, Arkansas, November 30, 1864.
Lasater, James L	do	Sept. 20, 1863	Dec. 12, 1863	Died of chronic diarrhœa at Duvall's Bluff, Arkansas, March 4, 1865.
Lewellen, John	do	June 1, 1864	Sept. 28, 1864	Died of chronic diarrhœa at Duvall's Bluff, Arkansas, March 10, 1865.
McCabe, Matthew	do	Sept. 20, 1863	Dec. 12, 1863	Died of pneumonia at Duvall's Bluff, Arkansas, April 15, 1865.
Neatherton, Henry H	do	Sept. 20, 1863	Dec. 12, 1863	Died of typhoid fever at Little Rock, Arkansas, July 25, 1864.
Neal, James P	do	Nov. 28, 1863	Dec. 12, 1863	Died of chronic diarrhœa at Duvall's Bluff, Arkansas, April 21, 1865.
Sear, Albert R	do	Sept. 20, 1863	Dec. 10, 1863	Died of chronic diarrhœa at Little Rock, Arkansas, November 3, 1864.
Selvadge, James J. A	do	Sept. 20, 1863	Dec. 12, 1863	Died of pneumonia at Duvall's Bluff, Arkansas, April 25, 1865.
Turner, James L	do	Sept. 20, 1863	Dec. 10, 1863	Died of chronic diarrhœa at Little Rock, Arkansas, December 5, 1864.
Wright, Elijah	do	Sept. 20, 1863	Dec. 10, 1863	Died of chronic diarrhœa at Little Rock, Arkansas, July 20, 1864.
Waldron, James B	do	Sept. 20, 1863	Dec. 10, 1863	Died of measles at Little Rock, Arkansas, June 25, 1864.
Weathen, John	do	Sept. 20, 1863	Dec. 10, 1863	Died of congestive fever in hospital March 22, 1864.
Discharged.				
Craven, Joseph	Private	Sept. 20, 1863	Dec. 12, 1863	Mustered out per telegram dated Washington, D. C., May 3, 1865, to take effect May 22, 1865.
Carter, William	do	Sept. 20, 1863	Dec. 10, 1863	Discharged by sentence of general court martial.
Ewing, George W	do	Sept. 20, 1863	Dec. 10, 1863	Mustered out per telegram dated Washington, D. C., May 3, 1865, to take effect May 22, 1865.
McClyen,	do	Sept. 20, 1863	Dec. 10, 1863	Mustered out nnder telegram dated Washington, D. C., May 3, 1865, to take effect May 22, 1865.
Polland, Jasper M	do	Sept. 20, 1863	Dec. 10, 1863	Discharged for disability at Duvall's Bluff, Arkansas, March 25, 1865.
Tyner, Jesse L	do	Sept. 20, 1863	Dec. 12, 1863	Mustered out per telegram from Washington, D. C., May 3, 1865, to take effect May 22, 1865.
Webster, Joseph G	do	Sept. 20, 1863	Dec. 10, 1863	Mustered out per telegram from Washington, D. C., May 3, 1865, to take effect May 22, 1865.
Deserted.				
Bring, William	Private	Dec. 1, 1863	Dec. 10, 1863	Deserted at Dardanelle, Arkansas, May 16, 1864.
Cames, John	do	Dec. 6, 1863	Dec. 10, 1863	Deserted from military prison Little Rock, Arkansas, ——.
Davis, John	do	Nov. 5, 1863	Dec. 10, 1863	Deserted at Dardanelle, Arkansas, May 17, 1864.
Row, William	do	Sept. 20, 1863	Dec. 10, 1863	Deserted at Little Rock, Arkansas, June 30, 1864.
Smith, Joseph H	do	Nov. 18, 1863	Dec. 10, 1863	Deserted at Dardanelle, Arkansas, May 16, 1864.
Smith, Julian	do	Sept. 20, 1863	Dec. 10, 1863	Deserted at Dardanelle, Arkansas, May 17, 1864.
Stuart, Pleasant	do	Dec. 8, 1863	Dec. 10, 1863	Detailed as scout, August 17, 1864; deserted ——.
Transferred.				
Hixon, Pleasant	Private	Sept. 20, 1863	Dec. 10, 1863	Appointed regimental quartermaster sergeant January 1, 1865.

REPORT OF THE ADJUTANT GENERAL OF ARKANSAS. 139

COMPANY B.

			Date of rank.	Muster.
James R. Laferty	Captain	Dec. 10, 1863	Jan. 9, 1864	Appointed 1st lieutenant December 10, 1863, to fill original vacancy; promoted captain to fill original vacancy; mustered out with regiment.
Henry White	1st lieutenant			Resigned at Little Rock, Arkansas, October 5, 1864.
John J. Storm	do		April 30, 1865	Appointed from private of company H, 2d Colorado infantry volunteers, to fill vacancy caused by resignation of Henry White; mustered out with regiment.
Porter J. Andrew	2d lieutenant		Jan. 9, 1864	Promoted to regimental adjutant April 7, 1864.
Wallace H. Hickox	do		April 11, 1864	Appointed from quartermaster sergeant of 15th Illinois cavalry, vice Lieut. Andrews promoted; mustered out at Little Rock, Arkansas, October 5, 1864.
Frederick J. Moore	do	Dec. 18, 1863	Oct. 18, 1864	Appointed from private of company B; mustered out with regiment.
William Armstrong	1st sergeant	Nov. 23, 1863	Mar. 23, 1864	Appointed from private; mustered out with regiment.
John R. Plunket	Quartermaster sergeant	Oct. 10, 1863	Jan. 9, 1864	Do.
James A. Chitwood	Commissary sergeant	Oct. 10, 1863	Jan. 9, 1864	Do.
Francis M. Marlem	Sergeant	Nov. 14, 1863	Jan. 9, 1864	Do.
James W. Hart	do	Nov. 23, 1863	Jan. 9, 1864	Do.
Allen W. Plunket	do	Oct. 10, 1863	Jan. 9, 1864	Do.
Nathan M. Howard	do	Oct. 10, 1863	Jan. 9, 1864	Do.
Aaron Chitwood	Corporal	Oct. 10, 1863	Jan. 9, 1864	Mustered out with regiment.
Edmund P. Chitwood	do	Oct. 10, 1863	Jan. 9, 1864	Do.
James C. Plunket	do	Nov. 23, 1863	Jan. 9, 1864	Do.
Thomas J. Gollahise	do	Nov. 30, 1863	Jan. 9, 1864	Do.
Alvin J. Moore	do	Jan. 1, 1864	Jan. 9, 1864	Do.
James R. Brune	Bugler	Nov. 20, 1863	Dec. 10, 1863	Do.
James M. Hampton	do	Jan. 9, 1864	Jan. 9, 1864	Do.
Benn, Samuel	Private	June 16, 1864	Aug. 26, 1864	Mustered out with regiment.
Bennett, James L	do	Oct. 10, 1863	Dec. 10, 1863	Do.
Bust, Joseph F	do	Dec. 18, 1863	Jan. 1, 1864	Do.
Chitwood, Aurelian H	do	Oct. 10, 1863	Dec. 10, 1863	Do.
Chitwood, Andrew R	do	Oct. 10, 1863	Dec. 10, 1863	Do.
Chitwood, Drury L	do	Nov. 16, 1863	Dec. 10, 1863	Do.
Davis, William R	do	Dec. 18, 1863	Jan. 1, 1864	Do.
Draper, John	do	Dec. 18, 1863	Dec. 10, 1863	Do.
Foster, Samuel J	do	Nov. 14, 1863	Dec. 10, 1863	Do.
Foster, John W	do	Oct. 10, 1863	Dec. 10, 1863	Do.
Graham, William T	do	Nov. 14, 1863	Dec. 10, 1863	Do.
Hawser, Joseph N	do	Oct. 10, 1863	Dec. 10, 1863	In military prison, Little Rock, Ark.; no discharge furnished on muster out of reg'nt.
Hampton, Benjamin A	do	Nov. 10, 1863	Dec. 10, 1863	Mustered out with regiment.
Lasley, Francis M	do	Jan. 1, 1864	Jan. 1, 1864	Do.
Murray, Jeremy	do	Oct. 10, 1863	Dec. 10, 1863	Do.
McAllister, Underwood	do	Nov. 29, 1863	Dec. 10, 1863	Do.
Pruitt, William H	do	Jan. 9, 1864	Jan. 9, 1864	Do.
Prine, Lloyd W	do	Dec. 18, 1863	Jan. 9, 1864	Do.
Rose, Samuel B	do	Oct. 10, 1863	Dec. 10, 1863	Do.
Rogers, William R	do	Nov. 21, 1863	Dec. 10, 1863	Do.
Rice, John Q	do	Nov. 14, 1863	Dec. 10, 1863	Do.

140   REPORT OF THE ADJUTANT GENERAL OF ARKANSAS.

Fourth regiment Arkansas cavalry volunteers. Mustered into service December 29, 1864, (three years;) mustered out June 30, 1865.

COMPANY B—Continued.

Names.	Rank.	Enlistment.	Muster.	Remarks.
Stillwell, Green D	Private	Dec. 18, 1863	Jan. 1, 1864	Mustered out with regiment.
Sykes, Levander	do	Dec. 18, 1863	Jan. 1, 1864	Do.
Trinity, Hume B	do	Nov. 14, 1863	Dec. 10, 1863	Do.
Taylor, Sanford V	do	Dec. 18, 1863	Jan. 1, 1864	Do.
Tharp, John	do	Dec. 18, 1863	Dec. 10, 1863	Do.
Ward, David	do	Nov. 14, 1863	Dec. 10, 1863	
Wimberly, William	do	Nov. 21, 1863	Dec. 10, 1863	In military prison, Little Rock, Ark.; no discharge furnished on muster out of reg'nt.
McElhany, Thomas	Colored cook	Jan. 18, 1864	Feb. 28, 1864	Mustered out with regiment.

Discharged.

Randell, S. Green	Sergeant	Oct. 10, 1863	Dec. 10, 1863	Mustered out per telegram from the War Department dated May 3, 1865; was promoted sergeant January 9, 1864.
Newton J. Hibbs	Corporal	Oct. 10, 1863	Dec. 10, 1863	Mustered out from hospital at Duvall's Bluff, Arkansas, per telegram dated War Department, May 3, 1865; appointed from private January 9.1864.
Johnson, Philip P	Private	Oct. 10, 1863	Dec. 10, 1863	Discharged for disability.
Abernethy, John	do	Oct. 10, 1863	Dec. 10, 1863	Discharged at hospital, Little Rock, Arkansas, June 12, 1865.
Bennett, Joseph	do	Nov. 18, 1863	Dec. 10, 1863	Discharged for promotion to captain of company K July —, 1864.
Collin, Henry C	do	Nov. 21, 1863	Dec. 10, 1863	Discharged from hospital at Little Rock, Arkansas, per order dated May 3, 1865.
Draper, Joseph	do	Dec. 8, 1863	Dec. 10, 1863	Discharged by order for informal enlistment.
Green, James M	do	Oct. 10, 1863	Dec. 10, 1863	Discharged from hospital at Little Rock, Arkansas, May 3, 1865.
Moore, Frederick J	do	Nov. 14, 1863	Dec. 10, 1863	Discharged for promotion to 2d lieutenant of company B.
Smith, David	do	Jan. 19, 1864	Dec. 10, 1863	Discharged from hospital at Duvall's Bluff, Arkansas, May 3, 1865.
Douglass, Jonathan L	do	Nov. 28, 1863	Dec. 10, 1863	Discharged from hospital at Little Rock, Arkansas; June 16, 1865.

Died.

John D. McElhanon	Sergeant	Dec. 17, 1863	Jan. 1, 1864	Killed by guerillas near Dardanelle, Arkansas, April 6, 1864.
Thomas Green	Corporal	Nov. 14, 1863	Dec. 10, 1863	Do.
John A. Ryan	do	Nov. 20, 1863	Dec. 10, 1863	Died of chronic diarrhœa at Duvall's Bluff, Arkansas, April 6, 1865.
Adams, John	Private	Oct. 10, 1863	Dec. 10, 1863	Died in hospital at Dardanelle, Arkansas, May 4, 1864.
Chitwood, Ezekiel	do	Dec. 7, 1863	Dec. 10, 1863	Died in hospital at Little Rock, Arkansas, November 1, 1864.
Chitwood, Richard	do	Nov. 24, 1863	Jan. 1, 1864	Died in hospital at Little Rock, Arkansas, February 2, 1865.
Hart, William F	do	Dec. 18, 1863	Jan. 1, 1864	Died at Norristown, Arkansas, May 20, 1864.
Kelly, Michael H	do	Nov. 14, 1863	Dec. 10, 1863	Died of chronic diarrhœa at Little Rock, Arkansas, March 11, 1865.
Luster, David	do	Jan. 18, 1864	Feb. 29, 1864	Died in hospital at Duvall's Bluff, Arkansas, April 11, 1865.
Murray, John	do	Oct. 10, 1863	Dec. 10, 1863	Died in hospital at Duvall's Bluff, Arkansas, November 14, 1864.
Murray, Howlett	do	Oct. 10, 1863	Dec. 10, 1863	Died in hospital at Little Rock, Arkansas, January 18, 1865.
Moore, James M	do	Nov. 14, 1863	Dec. 10, 1863	Died of typhoid fever at Little Rock, Arkansas, October 5, 1864.
Moore, Walter R	do	Oct. 10, 1863	Dec. 10, 1863	Died in hospital at Duvall's Bluff, Arkansas, December 11, 1861.
McElhanon, James	do	Nov. 14, 1863	Dec. 10, 1863	Killed by guerillas August 16, 1864.
Rogers, John W	do	Nov. 21, 1863	Dec. 10, 1863	Died of chronic diarrhœa at Jefferson Barracks December 6, 1864.
Riggs, William C	do	Dec. 18, 1863	Jan. 1, 1864	Died in hospital at Little Rock, Arkansas, August 16, 1864.

REPORT OF THE ADJUTANT GENERAL OF ARKANSAS. 141

Name	Rank	Date of enlistment	Date of rank	Remarks
Smith, James	do	Nov. 20, 1863	Dec. 10, 1863	Killed at Dardanelle, Ark., in an affray with a private of same company, April 1, 1864.
Sinclair, Robert W	do	Jan. 9, 1864	Jan. 9, 1864	Died in hospital at Little Rock, Arkansas, February 3, 1865.
Kemp, George	do	Sept. 9, 1864	Never	Died of chronic diarrhoea at Duvall's Bluff, Arkansas, February 5, 1865.

Deserted.

Name	Rank	Date of enlistment	Date of rank	Remarks
Collier, Abraham	Private	Dec. 18, 1863	Jan. 1, 1864	Deserted at Dardanelle, Arkansas, May 10, 1864.
Frazier, William J	do	Nov. 19, 1863	Dec. 10, 1863	Deserted at Dardanelle, Arkansas, May 20, 1864.
Chandler, Ralton B	do	Aug. 26, 1864	Aug. 26, 1864	Deserted at Little Rock, Arkansas, August 30, 1864.
Kinney, Andrew J	do	Oct. 10, 1863	Dec. 10, 1863	Deserted at Little Rock, Arkansas, August 16, 1864.
Moore, George W	do	Jan. 9, 1864	Jan. 9, 1864	Deserted at Dardanelle, Arkansas, March 6, 1864.
McPherson, George R	do	Nov. 18, 1863	Dec. 10, 1863	Deserted at Dardanelle, Arkansas, May 20, 1864.
Mooney, Israel	do	Dec. 18, 1863	Jan. 1, 1864	Do.
McLain, Joseph	do	Dec. 18, 1863	Jan. 1, 1864	Do.
Needham, Robert A	do	Dec. 18, 1863	Jan. 1, 1864	Do.
Needham, Richard C	do	May 3, 1864	Never	Deserted at Little Rock, Arkansas, December 31, 1864.
Johnson, John E	do	Jan. 9, 1864	Jan. 9, 1864	do.
Ogden, William R	do	Aug. 26, 1864	Aug. 26, 1864	Deserted at Dardanelle, Arkansas, ——, ——.
Ross, Franklin	do	Jan. 5, 1864	Jan. 9, 1864	Deserted at Little Rock, Arkansas, August 30, 1864.
Rogers, James T	do	Jan. 5, 1864	Jan. 9, 1864	Deserted at Dardanelle, Arkansas, May 20, 1864.
Witcher, William J	do	Jan. 5, 1864	Jan. 1, 1864	Deserted at Dardanelle, Arkansas, ——, ——.
White, John	do	Dec. 18, 1863	Jan. 1, 1864	Deserted at Dardanelle, Arkansas, do.
Vernon, William M	do	Jan. 9, 1864	Jan. 9, 1864	Do.

COMPANY C.

Name	Rank	Date of enlistment	Date of rank	Remarks
Henry Wood	Captain		Jan. 29, 1864	Appointed from private 2d Kansas cavalry to 1st lieutenant December 10, 1863; resigned May 26, 1865.
Duncan Holliday	1st lieutenant		April 7, 1864	Appointed from private 2d Kansas cavalry; resigned August 26, 1864.
William A. Sullivan	do		Oct. 18, 1864	Appointed from sergeant major 9th Iowa cavalry; mustered out with regiment.
Hugh Quinn	2d lieutenant		Jan. 30, 1864	Appointed from private 2d Kansas cavalry; promoted to captain company D June 23, 1864.
John W. Ayres	do	Nov. 24, 1863	Sept. 19, 1864	Appointed from private 3d Missouri cavalry; resigned May 12, 1865.
John W. Stout	1st sergeant	Dec. 28, 1863	Mar. 4, 1864	Appointed from private March 4, 1864; mustered out with regiment.
Alfred C. Stout	Quartermaster sergeant	Dec. 28, 1863	Dec. 21, 1864	Appointed from private December 21, 1864; mustered out with regiment.
William J. Johnson	Commissary sergeant	Dec. 28, 1863	Mar. 4, 1864	Appointed from private March 4, 1864; mustered out with regiment.
William C. Chambers	Sergeant	Oct. 19, 1863	Mar. 4, 1864	do.
William N. Stout	do	Nov. 28, 1863	Mar. 4, 1864	do.
Stephen R. Ashmore	do	Dec. 28, 1863	Mar. 4, 1864	do.
John N. Mathews	do	Dec. 21, 1863	Mar. 4, 1864	do.
John B. Furguson	Corporal	Dec. 27, 1863	Mar. 4, 1864	Mustered out with regiment.
Thomas Herolson	do	Dec. 28, 1863	Mar. 4, 1864	Do.
Andrew J. Vampelt	do	Dec. 6, 1863	Mar. 4, 1864	Do.
Martin E. Hearkey	do	Dec. 29, 1863	Mar. 4, 1864	Do.
Zachariah Sinclair	do	Jan. 28, 1864	Nov. 7, 1864	Do.
Edmund Schofeld	Bugler	Nov. 3, 1863	Dec. 15, 1864	Do.
Joseph Vick	do	Mar. 17, 1864	Dec. 15, 1864	Do.

142   REPORT OF THE ADJUTANT GENERAL OF ARKANSAS.

Fourth regiment Arkansas cavalry volunteers.   Mustered into service December 29, 1864, (three years;) mustered out June 30, 1865.

COMPANY C—Continued.

Names.	Rank.	Enlistment.	Date of rank.	Muster.	Remarks.
William J. Brigham	Saddler	Dec. 27, 1863	Mar. 16, 1865		Mustered out with regiment.
John N. Stewart	Farrier	Dec. 19, 1863	April 14, 1865		Do.
William Linsay	do	Nov. 25, 1863	April 14, 1865		Do.
Ashmore, Robert D	Private	Dec. 28, 1863	Jan. 28, 1864		Do.
Ballard, John	do	Sept. 20, 1863	Jan. 28, 1864		In arrest since June 3, 1865, at Little Rock, Arkansas; no discharge furnished on muster out of regiment.
Bernard, John	do	Oct. 20, 1863	Dec. 10, 1863		Mustered out with regiment.
Bernard, Isaac D	do	Oct. 20, 1863	Dec. 10, 1863		Do.
Brown, Jesse M	do	Nov. 3, 1863	Dec. 10, 1863		Do.
Brown, James A	do	Jan. 20, 1864	Jan. 28, 1864		Do.
Brown, David	do	Nov. 2, 1863	Dec. 10, 1863		Do.
Bryant, Lorenzo D	do	Dec. 27, 1863	Jan. 28, 1864		Do.
Chambers, Green B	do	Oct. 23, 1863	Dec. 10, 1863		Do.
Carline, John N	do	Nov. 17, 1863	Dec. 10, 1863		Do.
Caruthers, Samuel	do	Oct. 29, 1863	Dec. 10, 1863		Do.
Colbert, John	do	Oct. 19, 1863	Dec. 10, 1863		Do.
Crawford, William C	do	Oct. 24, 1863	Dec. 10, 1863		Do.
Davis, Casper A	do	Dec. 19, 1863	Jan. 28, 1864		Do.
Fruman, James R	do	Jan. 29, 1864	Feb. 29, 1864		Do.
Hanna, Andrew J	do	Oct. 28, 1863	Dec. 10, 1863		Do.
Harlon, Robert	do	Oct. 28, 1863	Dec. 10, 1863		Do.
Holmesley, Francis M	do	Sept. 20, 1863	Dec. 10, 1863		Do.
Hudson, George N	do	Oct. 19, 1863	Dec. 10, 1863		Do.
Lay, James	do	Sept. 20, 1863	Jan. 28, 1864		Do.
Melican, Williams	do	Jan. 22, 1864	Jan. 28, 1864		Do.
McCulley, John A	do	Mar. 2, 1864	April 25, 1864		Do.
Mullins, James M	do	Dec. 30, 1863	Jan. 28, 1864		Do.
Mullins, Pinkney M	do	Dec. 29, 1863	Jan. 28, 1864		Do.
Mustain, Holland C	do	Oct. 10, 1863	Dec. 10, 1863		Do.
Parker, John C	do	Dec. 20, 1863	Jan. 28, 1864		Do.
Rainey, Robert B	do	Nov. 23, 1863	Dec. 10, 1863		Do.
Stout, James A	do	Dec. 28, 1863	Jan. 28, 1864		Do.
Strickland, Zachariah	do	Dec. 28, 1863	Jan. 28, 1864		Do.
Steward, George N	do	Nov. 30, 1863	Dec. 10, 1863		Do.
Swader, William	do	Nov. 4, 1863	Dec. 10, 1863		Do.
Todd, William	do	April 29, 1864	April 29, 1864		Do.
Todd, James	do	April 29, 1864	April 29, 1864		Do.
Todd, Alexander	do	April 29, 1864	April 29, 1864		Do.
Tate, Joseph D	do	Dec. 1, 1863	Dec. 10, 1863		Do.
Voss, Daniel	do	Dec. 29, 1863	Jan. 28, 1864		Do.

REPORT OF THE ADJUTANT GENERAL OF ARKANSAS. 143

Name	Rank			
Webb, Hampton M	do	Dec. 28, 1863	Jan. 28, 1864	Do.
Missing in action.				
Howard, Isaac B	do	Jan. 20, 1864	Jan. 28, 1864	Supposed to have been killed May 18, 1865.
Died.				
Melchisedec C. Reynolds	Corporal	Nov. 13, 1863	Dec. 10, 1863	Died of measles, Little Rock, Arkansas, July 7, 1864.
Bartin, Hezekiah A	Private	Oct. 19, 1863	Dec. 10, 1863	Died August 1, 1864.
Brown, Lorenzo D	do	Jan. 20, 1864	Feb. 29, 1864	Died of chronic diarrhœa at Devall's Bluff, Arkansas, April 15, 1865.
Bookout, John	do	Nov. 27, 1864	Dec. 10, 1864	Died of chronic diarrhœa at Devall's Bluff, Arkansas, April 30, 1865.
Brown, Obadiah W	do	Feb. 6, 1864	Feb. 29, 1864	Died at Fort Smith, Arkansas, July 8, 1864.
Colbert, Moses C	do	Oct. 20, 1863	Dec. 10, 1863	Died at Fort Smith, Arkansas, July 8, 1864.
Johnson, William S	do	Dec. 1, 1863	Jan. 28, 1864	Died of measles at Little Rock, Arkansas, July 11, 1864.
Jones, James R	do	Dec. 12, 1863	Jan. 28, 1864	Died of erysipelas, Duvall's Bluff, Arkansas, February 21, 1865.
Montgomery, Samuel H	do	Jan. 9, 1864	Jan. 9, 1864	Died of wounds received at Clarksville, Arkansas, March 16, 1864.
Nichols, William P	do	Nov. 25, 1863	Dec. 10, 1863	Died of measles at Little Rock, Arkansas, July 7, 1864.
Nichols, Moses C	do	Oct. 19, 1863	Dec. 10, 1863	Died of wounds received from one of his comrades, January 20, 1864.
Nichols, Wilson L	do	Oct. 19, 1863	Dec. 10, 1863	Died of wounds received from guerillas, January 21, 1864.
Nichols, William	do	Jan. 9, 1864	Jan. 9, 1864	Died of chronic diarrhœa, Little Rock, Arkansas, December 20, 1864.
Pitts, David L	do	Dec. 21, 1863	Jan. 28, 1864	Died in hospital, Duvall's Bluff, Arkansas, February 7, 1865.
Stout, Peter	do	Oct. 22, 1863	Dec. 10, 1863	Died of chronic diarrhœa, Duvall's Bluff, Arkansas, December 1, 1864.
Strickland, James M	do	Dec. 29, 1863	Jan. 28, 1864	Fell dead in company street, January 22, 1865.
Thompson, Joseph M	do	Sept. 20, 1863	Jan. 28, 1864	Died of chronic diarrhœa, Dardanelle, Arkansas, April 12, 1864.
Deserted.				
Bradshaw, Samuel K	Private	Jan. 9, 1864	Jan. 9, 1864	Deserted at Dardanelle, Arkansas, May 5, 1864.
Chronister, James M	do	Jan. 9, 1864	Jan. 9, 1864	Deserted at Dardanelle, Arkansas, May 17, 1864.
Clark, Levi C	do	Nov. 5, 1863	Dec. 10, 1863	Deserted at Little Rock, Arkansas, September 26, 1864.
Emmert, Jacob S	do	Jan. 9, 1864	Jan. 9, 1864	Deserted at Galley Rock, Arkansas, May 20, 1864.
Hill, Alston	do	Nov. 27, 1863	Dec. 10, 1863	Deserted at Dardanelle, Arkansas, May 18, 1864.
Howard, William C	do	Jan. 20, 1864	Jan. 28, 1864	Deserted at Dardanelle, Arkansas, May 17, 1864; returned from desertion January 15, 1865; sentenced to confinement and hard labor for three years in military prison.
Jones, John	do	Jan. 9, 1864	Jan. 9, 1864	Deserted at Dardanelle, Arkansas, May 17, 1864.
Jacket, Jesse	do	Jan. 30, 1864	Feb. 29, 1864	do.
Jacket, Lewis	do	Jan. 19, 1864	Jan. 28, 1864	Deserted at Lewisburg, Arkansas, January 5, 1865.
Lambert, John E	do	Jan. 9, 1864	Jan. 9, 1864	Deserted at Little Rock, Arkansas, September 26, 1864.
Macon, George N	do	Dec. 2, 1863	Jan. 28, 1864	Deserted at Dardanelle, Arkansas, January 9, 1864.
Nelson, William M	do	Nov. 13, 1863	Dec. 10, 1863	Deserted at Dardanelle, Arkansas, May 17, 1864.
Posey, Pinkney C	do	Jan. 9, 1864	Jan. 9, 1864	Deserted at Dardanelle, Arkansas, May 5, 1864.
Ward, Thomas A	do	Jan. 16, 1864	Jan. 28, 1864	Deserted at Dardanelle, Arkansas, May 17, 1864.
Webb, James W	do	Oct. 3, 1863	Dec. 10, 1863	Deserted at Little Rock, Arkansas, September 27, 1864.
Discharged.				
John Penn	Corporal	Dec. 28, 1863	Jan. 28, 1864	Discharged for disability June 10, 1865.
Crenshaw, David	Private	Nov. 24, 1863	Dec. 10, 1863	Discharged for disability at Little Rock, Arkansas, September 25, 1864.
Chambers, Bennett	do	Oct. 24, 1863	Dec. 10, 1863	Discharged for disability at Duvall's Bluff, Arkansas, March 2, 1865.
Reynolds, William H	do	Nov. 28, 1863	Dec. 10, 1863	Discharged for disability at Duvall's Bluff, Arkansas, February 22, 1865.
Stout, James	do	Oct. 10, 1863	Dec. 10, 1863	Discharged for disability at Little Rock, Arkansas, April 21, 1865.

Fourth regiment Arkansas cavalry volunteers. Mustered into service December 29, 1864, (three years;) mustered out June 30, 1865.

COMPANY D.

Names.	Rank.	Enlistment.	Date of rank.	Remarks.
George H. Hand	Captain		Mar. 9, 1864	Appointed from private company H, 15th Illinois cavalry, to fill original vacancy; resigned June 22, 1864.
Hugh Quinn	do		Jan. 23, 1864	Appointed from sergeant company A, 2d Kansas cavalry, to 2d lieutenant, January 28, 1864, to fill original vacancy; mortally wounded in action July 13, 1864; died July 16, 1864.
Julius H. Norton	do		Sept. 19, 1864	Appointed from private company H, 5th Illinois cavalry, vice Quinn, killed; honorably mustered out May 15, 1865.
Nathaniel W. Welliver	do		June 20, 1865	Appointed regimental adjutant March 20, 1865, from private 1st Iowa cavalry; promoted captain, vice Norton, mustered out; mustered out with regiment.
Jonas B. Spiva	1st lieutenant	Feb. 19, 1864	Feb. 16, 1864	Appointed from civil life to fill original vacancy; resigned August 16, 1864.
Porter J. Andrews	do		Apr. 7, 1864	Appointed from corporal company D, 36th Iowa infantry, to 2d lieutenant company B; promoted to adjutant April 7, 1864; transferred to company D, vice Welliver, transferred to adjutant; mustered out with regiment.
William B. Bostick	2d lieutenant		Mar. 13, 1864	Appointed from private 1st Arkansas infantry to fill original vacancy; mustered out October 15, 1864.
Nelson J. Baker	do		June 21, 1864	Appointed from sergeant 25th Ohio battery, vice Bostick, mustered out; promoted to 1st lieutenant company I, vice Downs, promoted captain; mustered out with regiment.
William Sutton	1st sergeant	Jan. 16, 1864	Mar. 7, 1864	Appointed from private; mustered out with regiment.
John J. Willis	Quartermaster sergeant	Aug. 24, 1864	Sept. 1, 1861	Do.
Charles R. Kymes	Commissary sergeant	Mar. 10, 1864	Oct. 1, 1861	do.
Turner Goldin	Sergeant	Mar. 30, 1864	Aug. 24, 1864	do.
John Neston	do	Feb. 20, 1864	Aug. 17, 1864	do.
Handy C. Tomelson	do	Feb. 6, 1864	Mar. 23, 1864	do.
Terrill M. Mimens	do	Jan. 14, 1864	Nov. 1, 1864	do.
Eli R. Burrow	do	Jan. 14, 1864	Nov. 1, 1864	do.
James H. Biddle	Corporal	Jan. 17, 1864	Mar. 8, 1864	Mustered out with the regiment.
James Earnest	do	Jan. 29, 1864	Mar. 7, 1864	Do.
George W. Barentine	do	Jan. 14, 1864	Mar. 7, 1864	Do.
George R. Chapman	do	Jan. 14, 1864	Sept. 7, 1864	Do.
George W. Carpenter	do	Mar. 10, 1864	Jan. 31, 1865	Do.
William Irons	do	Dec. 8, 1863	Jan. 31, 1865	Do.
Michael W. Blocket	do	Jan. 14, 1864	May 20, 1865	Do.
Jep. Miller	do	Feb. 5, 1864	Feb. 17, 1864	Do.
John M. Kinney	Bugler			Do.
			Muster.	
Ambler, William P	Private	Feb. 1, 1864	Feb. 17, 1864	Undergoing sentence of general court-martial at Little Rock, Arkansas; no discharge furnished on muster out of regiment.
Abbott, Stephen	do	Mar. 10, 1864	Mar. 20, 1864	Mustered out with regiment.
Burnett, William T	do	Jan. 16, 1864	Feb. 17, 1864	Do.
Burnett, Isaac F	do	Jan. 8, 1864	Feb. 17, 1864	Do.

REPORT OF THE ADJUTANT GENERAL OF ARKANSAS 145

Name	Rank	Date 1	Date 2	Remarks
Bates, James H		Jan. 16, 1864	Feb. 17, 1864	Do.
Bates, Christopher C	do	Jan. 16, 1864	Feb. 17, 1864	Do.
Barentine, Alexander	do	Jan. 14, 1864	Feb. 17, 1864	Do.
Barentine, Elijah	do	Jan. 14, 1864	Feb. 17, 1864	Do.
Blocker, James W	do	Dec. 22, 1863	April 21, 1864	Do.
Blakely, James H	do	Mar. 8, 1864	Feb. 12, 1864	Do.
Brady, Ripley P	do	Jan. 14, 1864	Feb. 13, 1864	Do.
Campbell, Jarrett M	do	Mar. 10, 1864	Mar. 21, 1864	Do.
Crawford, Wesley J	do	Feb. 5, 1864	Mar. 5, 1864	Do.
Denny, John P	do	Feb. 1, 1864	Mar. 12, 1864	Do.
Dowdy, Green	do	Jan. 14, 1864	Mar. 12, 1864	Do.
Fisher, Josiah	do	Jan. 14, 1864	Mar. 12, 1864	Do.
Graves, Gillian	do	Jan. 14, 1864	Feb. 17, 1864	Do.
Graves, Allison	do	Nov. 21, 1863	April 21, 1864	Do.
Golden, William	do	Jan. 14, 1864	Feb. 17, 1864	Do.
Hankins, Wright	do	Jan. 14, 1864	Feb. 17, 1864	Do.
Hankins, James	do	Jan. 14, 1864	Feb. 17, 1864	Do.
Herron, Jonathan	do	Jan. 14, 1864	Mar. 12, 1864	Do.
Hulsey, Benjamin F	do	Feb. 22, 1864	Feb. 17, 1864	Do.
Hybarger, Andrew J	do	Feb. 11, 1864	Feb. 17, 1864	Do.
Irons, Jonathan	do	Feb. 2, 1864	Feb. 17, 1864	Do.
Jackson, Thomas	do	Oct. 16, 1863	Feb. 17, 1864	Do.
Kinsey, Benjamin F	do	Jan. 14, 1864	Feb. 17, 1864	Do.
Kessiah, James H	do	Jan. 14, 1864	Feb. 17, 1864	Do.
Kelly, Henry	do	Nov. 21, 1863	April 21, 1864	Do.
Lamb, Frank A	do	Feb. 22, 1864	Mar. 12, 1864	Do.
Lamb, Columbus	do	Feb. 11, 1864	Mar. 12, 1864	Do.
Martin, Thomas L	do	Jan. 14, 1864	Feb. 17, 1864	Do.
Mannis, Jasper	do	Jan. 14, 1864	Feb. 17, 1864	Do.
McCay, Thomas	do	Jun. 18, 1864	June 16, 1864	Do.
Phillips, John F	do	Mar. 10, 1864	Mar. 2, 1864	Do.
Priddy, John D	do	Jan. 14, 1864	Feb. 17, 1864	Do.
Ritter, Malcolm S	do	Jan. 14, 1864	Feb. 17, 1864	Do.
Ralls, Thomas	do	Jan. 14, 1864	Feb. 17, 1864	Do.
Robbins, David	do	Jan. 14, 1864	Feb. 17, 1864	Do.
Spears, Nathan M	do	Jan. 15, 1864	April 21, 1864	Do.
Spears, John	do	Mar. 10, 1864	Mar. 21, 1864	Do.
Sherley, James W	do	Mar. 10, 1864	Feb. 17, 1864	Do.
Smith, Thomas	do	Jan. 14, 1864	Mar. 21, 1864	Do.
Smith, James A	do	Jan. 14, 1864	Feb. 17, 1864	Do.
Tucker, Joseph	do	Mar. 10, 1864	Mar. 21, 1864	Do.
Vansickles, Miles	do	Jan. 14, 1864	Feb. 17, 1864	Do.
Wallace, jr., Drew A	do	Feb. 5, 1863	Feb. 17, 1864	Do.
Wages, William T	do	Oct. 5, 1863	Feb. 17, 1864	Do.
Williams, John	do	Jan. 5, 1864	Feb. 17, 1864	Do.
Wilson, James D	do			Do.
Wright, John D	do			Do.

Killed in action.

Name	Rank	Date 1	Date 2	Remarks
Edge, John	Private	Jan. 14, 1864	Feb. 17, 1864	Killed in action near Cedar Glades, Arkansas, March 1, 1864.
Golden, Clayburn	do	Feb. 2, 1864	Feb. 17, 1864	Killed in action near Cedar Glades, Arkansas, May 17, 1864.

Mis. Doc. 53——10

Fourth regiment Arkansas cavalry volunteers. Mustered into service December 29, 1864, (three years;) mustered out June 30, 1865.

COMPANY D—Continued.

Names.	Rank.	Enlistment.	Muster.	Remarks.
Martin, Nathaniel	Private	Jan. 14, 1864	April 21, 1864	Killed in action near Benton, Arkansas, July 6, 1864.
Ritter, John D	do	Jan. 14, 1864	Feb. 17, 1864	Killed in action near Cedar Glades, Arkansas, March 1, 1864.
Died.				
Zachariah Phillips	Corporal	Jan. 14, 1864	Feb. 17, 1864	Appointed corporal March 7, 1864; died of diarrhœa ——.
Nicholas Fisher	do	Jan. 16, 1864	Feb. 17, 1864	Appointed corporal March 7, 1864; died August 24, 1864.
James Ralph	do	Oct. 16, 1863	Feb. 17, 1864	Appointed corporal March 7, 1864; died September 1, 1864.
Bentley, Francis M	Private	Feb. 3, 1864	Feb. 17, 1864	Died of fever at Little Rock, Arkansas, March 22, 1864.
Bradley, William R	do	Feb. 7, 1864	Feb. 17, 1864	Died of pneumonia April 29, 1864.
Brown, William	do	Jan. 7, 1864	Feb. 17, 1864	Died of typhoid fever July 3, 1864.
Bostick, Francis A	do	Jan. 15, 1864	Feb. 17, 1864	Died of pneumonia at Little Rock, Arkansas, January 7, 1865.
Brashears, Mathew	do	Jan. 14, 1864	Feb. 17, 1864	Died of diarrhœa at Little Rock, Arkansas, March 2, 1865.
Blakely, John J	do	Mar. 8, 1864	Mar. 12, 1864	Died of diarrhœa May 11, 1865.
Curley, Jesse	do	June 24, 1864	June 24, 1864	Died of diarrhœa, in hospital, December 28, 1865.
Carpenter, John	do	Aug. 1, 1864	Aug. 1, 1864	Died of diarrhœa February 20, 1864.
Eldridge, Daniel T	do	Oct. 16, 1863	Feb. 17, 1864	Died of pneumonia April 22, 1864.
Fulton, Winford	do	Jan. 6, 1864	Feb. 17, 1864	Died in hospital, of fever, September 14, 1864.
Glidewell, Robert R	do	Jan. 14, 1864	Feb. 17, 1864	Died of diarrhœa July 12, 1864.
Godwin, Joseph	do	Jan. 14, 1864	Feb. 17, 1864	Died in hospital, of diarrhœa, September 14, 1864.
Herron, Carter	do	Jan. 14, 1864	Feb. 17, 1864	Died in hospital, of diarrhœa, August 11, 1864.
Hall, Jasper	do	Jan. 14, 1864	Feb. 17, 1864	Died of congestive chills January 11, 1865.
Huddleston, David	do	Nov. 23, 1863	Mar. 21, 1864	Died of pneumonia March 2, 1865.
Haskins, William H	do	Jan. 14, 1864	Feb. 17, 1864	Died of diarrhœa April 30, 1865.
Kendrick, James A	do	Jan. 14, 1864	Feb. 17, 1864	Died at home, of pneumonia, February 17, 1865.
Lewis, Barnett	do	Jan. 14, 1864	Feb. 17, 1864	Died of typhoid fever August 7, 1864.
Mathews, William	do	Jan. 14, 1864	Jan. 17, 1864	Died of inflammation of lungs August 11, 1864.
Tidwell, John	do	Jan. 14, 1864	Jan. 17, 1864	Died June 24, 1864.
Sproud, John J	do	Jan. 14, 1864	Jan. 17, 1864	Died May 27, 1864.
Deserted.				
Buyton, William M	Private	Feb. 3, 1864	Feb. 17, 1864	Deserted at Little Rock, Arkansas, May 12, 1864; killed by guerillas.
Sanders, Jesse	do	Feb. 5, 1864	Feb. 17, 1864	Deserted at Little Rock, Arkansas, October 8, 1864.
Drew, sr., Wallace A	do	Mar. 10, 1864	Mar. 21, 1864	Deserted with horse, arms, and equipments, July 15, 1864.
Discharged.				
Jacob Vanderslice	Sergeant	Jan. 14, 1864	Feb. 17, 1864	Appointed sergeant August 11, 1864; discharged May 27, 1865.
Fisher, Elisha	Private	Jan. 16, 1864	Mar. 12, 1864	Discharged May 29, 1865.
Fulton, Daniel	do	Feb. 5, 1864	Feb. 17, 1864	Do.
Hall, Joshua C	do	Nov. 21, 1863	Apr. 21, 1864	Discharged for disability, December 25, 1864.
Lamb, Reuben	do			

REPORT OF THE ADJUTANT GENERAL OF ARKANSAS. 147

Name	Rank	Muster		Remarks
Pettijohn, George W	do	Jan. 14, 1864	Feb. 17, 1864	Discharged for promotion April 27, 1864.
Turner, Robert L	do	Dec. 2, 1863	Apr. 21, 1864	Discharged May 19, 1865.
White, Jefferson C	do	Jan. 8, 1864	Feb. 17, 1864	Discharged March 2, 1865.
Wolsey, William J	do	Jan. 14, 1864	Feb. 17, 1864	Discharged May 23, 1865.

Transferred.

Name	Rank	Muster		Remarks
Harrell, Albert	Private	Mar. 28, 1864	May 4, 1864	Transferred to non-commissioned staff as quartermaster sergeant.
Ritter, Thomas H	do	Jan. 14, 1864	Feb. 7, 1864	Transferred to non-commissioned staff as sergeant major.

COMPANY E.

Name	Rank	Date of rank.	Remarks
George W. Smith	Captain	Mar. 29, 1864	Appointed from 1st sergeant company D, 11th Kansas cavalry, to 1st lieutenant, to fill original vacancy; promoted captain of company E, to fill original vacancy; mustered out with regiment.
Howard Schuyler	do	June 3, 1865	Appointed from private company I, 11th Kansas cavalry, to 1st lieutenant company E; mustered out with regiment.
James L. Garner	1st lieutenant	Apr. 18, 1864	Appointed from civil life to fill original vacancy; mustered out October 5, 1864.
Robert Sutherland	2d lieutenant	May 1, 1864	Appointed from sergeant 2d Missouri cavalry, May 1, 1864, to fill original vacancy; mustered out with regiment.

Name	Rank	Date of rank.	Remarks
James B. Sutton	1st sergeant	June 21, 1863	Appointed from private; mustered out with regiment.
John A. Conley	Quartermaster sergeant	Nov. 12, 1863	Do.
Alexander H. Armstrong	Commissary sergeant	Feb. 25, 1864	Do.
Rufus Turner	Sergeant	Dec. 19, 1863	Do.
Henry J. Wadden	do	Oct. 1, 1863	Do.
John Parks	do	Oct. 1, 1863	Do.
Columbus C. Coffee	Corporal	Oct. 1, 1863	Appointed from private; mustered out with regiment.
Benjamin H. Garey	do	Jun. 9, 1864	Do.
John V. Frost	do	Oct. 1, 1863	Do.
John H. Wiseman	do	Jan. 19, 1864	Do.
William A. Lewis	Bugler	Mar. 18, 1864	Do.
Edward Parks	Farrier	Oct. 13, 1863	Do.

Name	Rank	Muster		Remarks
Adcock, Shelby B	Private	Jan. 19, 1864	Jan. 28, 1864	Mustered out with regiment.
Aiken, Jesse B	do	Feb. 27, 1864	Feb. 28, 1864	Do.
Blevins, Edward	do	Feb. 27, 1864	Feb. 28, 1864	Do.
Corley, William Y	do	Apr. 22, 1864	Apr. 28, 1864	Do.
Carter, James S	do	Oct. 1, 1863	Dec. 10, 1863	Do.
Carter, Michael B	do	Oct. 1, 1863	Dec. 10, 1863	Do.
English, James	do	Feb. 16, 1864	Feb. 28, 1864	Do.
Ezell, Clayborne	do	Oct. 1, 1863	Jan. 13, 1864	Sick in general hospital, Duvall's Bluff, Arkansas, since April, 1865; no discharge furnished on muster out of regiment.
Gilley, William R	do	Feb. 19, 1864	Feb. 28, 1864	Mustered out with regiment.
Hooker, John A	do	Feb. 20, 1864	Feb. 28, 1864	Do.

Fourth regiment Arkansas cavalry volunteers. Mustered into service December 29, 1864, (three years;) mustered out June 30, 1865.

COMPANY E—Continued.

Names.	Rank.	Enlistment.	Muster.	Remarks.
Harkey, Jacob T	Private	Feb. 27, 1864	Feb. 28, 1864	Mustered out with regiment.
Kirkwood, James H	do	Dec. 16, 1863	Jan. 13, 1864	Do.
Key, William G	do	Dec. 20, 1863	Jan. 13, 1864	Do.
Martin, Daniel W	do	Jan. 20, 1864	Jan. 28, 1864	Do.
McDaniel, Granville W	do	Jan. 30, 1864	Feb. 28, 1864	Do.
McLane, William S	do	Jan. 20, 1864	Jan. 28, 1864	Do.
McMinn, John M	do	Feb. 12, 1864	Feb. 12, 1864	Do.
Nichols, Andrew J	do	Dec. 12, 1863	Jan. 13, 1864	Do.
Pitts, John H	do	Feb. 14, 1864	Feb. 28, 1864	Do.
Poindexter, John H	do	Oct. 13, 1863	Dec. 10, 1863	Do.
Robbins, John M	do	Nov. 13, 1863	Dec. 10, 1863	Do.
Reed, Alfred D	do	Oct. 1, 1863	Jan. 13, 1864	Do.
Smith, Bradford	do	Oct. 1, 1863	Dec. 10, 1863	Do.
Thompson, Carlin	do	Oct. 1, 1863	Jan. 13, 1864	Do.
Wilbanks, Louis	do	Aug. 27, 1864	Aug. 27, 1864	Do.
Killed in action.				
Harris, Frederick	Private	Nov. 7, 1863	Dec. 10, 1863	Shot by guerillas in Johnson county, Arkansas, May 27, 1864.
Key, James G	do	Dec. 30, 1863	Jan. 13, 1864	Shot by guerillas in Johnson county, Arkansas, March 10, 1864.
Madden, Nelson	do	Nov. 15, 1863	Dec. 10, 1863	Killed in a skirmish near Little Rock, Arkansas, July 18, 1864.
Smith, William A	do	Dec. 16, 1863	Jan. 13, 1864	Shot by guerillas near Dardanelle, Arkansas, May 18, 1864.
Died.				
Baker, Zachariah	Farrier	Oct. 14, 1863	Dec. 10, 1863	Died of jaundice at Little Rock, Arkansas, September 12, 1864.
Beck, William F	Private	Nov. 10, 1863	Dec. 10, 1863	Died of scurvy at Little Rock, Arkansas, August 28, 1864.
Bird, William	do	Jan. 22, 1864	Jan. 28, 1864	Died of fever at Little Rock, Arkansas, November 12, 1864.
Churchman, William H	do	Oct. 1, 1863	Dec. 10, 1863	Died of inflammation of brain at Dardanelle, Arkansas, March 6, 1864.
Churchman, Stephen	do	Oct. 1, 1863	Dec. 10, 1863	Died of congestion of the brain at Dardanelle, Arkansas, April 3, 1864.
Churchman, John	do	Oct. 1, 1863	Dec. 10, 1863	Died of dysentery at Duvall's Bluff, Arkansas, April 3, 1865.
Carrol, John A	do	Nov. 12, 1863	Dec. 10, 1863	Died of small-pox at Duvall's Bluff, Arkansas, April 22, 1865.
Coats, Thomas J	do	Jan. 18, 1864	Jan. 28, 1864	Died of diarrhoea at Little Rock, Arkansas, July 17, 1864.
Forehand, David	do	Nov. 12, 1863	Dec. 10, 1863	Died of pneumonia at Little Rock, Arkansas, June 13, 1864.
Foster, John C	do	Feb. 24, 1864	Feb. 29, 1864	Died of fever at Little Rock, Arkansas, August 30, 1864.
Hicks, John S	do	Feb. 12, 1864		Died of flux at Little Rock, Arkansas, September 16, 1864.
Morris, Nathan M	do	Feb. 27, 1864	Feb. 28, 1864	Died of chronic rhrumatism at Little Rock, Arkansas, November 9, 1864.
Poindexter, James F	do	Oct. 1, 1863	Dec. 10, 1863	Died of chronic diarrhoea at Duvall's Bluff, Arkansas, December 8, 1864.
Romines, John	do	Oct. 1, 1863		Died of small-pox at Duvall's Bluff, Arkansas, May 3, 1865.
Sugg, Joseph C	do	Feb. 14, 1864	Feb. 29, 1864	Died of chronic diarrhoea at Duvall's Bluff, Arkansas, March 29, 1865.
				Died of chronic diarrhoea at Duvall's Bluff, Arkansas, May 12, 1865.

REPORT OF THE ADJUTANT GENERAL OF ARKANSAS. 149

Discharged.

Name	Rank	Date	Remarks
Gilley, Jasper	Corporal	Feb. 20, 1864	Discharged from hospital May 22, 1865.
Coose, Nicholas W	Private	Dec. 30, 1863	Do.
De Hart, Milton	do	Dec. 25, 1863	Discharged for disability December 17, 1864.
Ezell, David	do	Oct. 1, 1863	Discharged May 3, 1865.
Long, Thomas P	do	Oct. 15, 1863	Do.
Witson, Robert D	do	Jan. 23, 1864	Discharged for disability February 3, 1865.

Deserted.

Name	Rank	Date	Remarks
Truett, James E	1st sergeant	Feb. 5, 1864	Deserted at Dardanelle, Arkansas, May 16, 1864.
Bruce, David L	Private	April 5, 1864	Deserted at Dardanelle, Arkansas, April 22, 1864.
Carroll, William R	do	Oct. 22, 1863	Deserted at Dardanelle, Arkansas, March 30, 1865.
Condely, William H	do	Dec. 2, 1863	Deserted at Dardanelle, Arkansas, December 25, 1863.
Davis, Wallace P	do	Feb. 3, 1864	Deserted at Dardanelle, Arkansas, May 16, 1864.
Davis, John J	do	Feb. 3, 1864	Do.
Daugherty, Hugh	do	Jan. 21, 1864	Do.
Donaldson, Otto B	do	Dec. 28, 1863	Do.
Hatchet, G. T	do	Feb. 16, 1864	Deserted at Dardanelle, Arkansas, May 11, 1864.
Hudson, Franklin P	do	Feb. 18, 1864	Deserted at Dardanelle, Arkansas, May 16, 1864.
Jones, Alexander S. M	do	Feb. 9, 1864	Do.
Kirkpatrick, Mason C	do	Feb. 20, 1864	Do.
N——, Henry M	do	Dec. 25, 1863	Do.
N——, William M	do	Feb. 12, 1864	Do.
Peters, William H	do	Jan. 13, 1864	Do.
Rhoades, Arthur	do	Dec. 1, 1863	Deserted at Duvall's Bluff, Arkansas, October 14, 1864.
Russell, Perry	do	April 5, 1864	Deserted at Dardanelle, Arkansas, April 22, 1864.
Sugg, William	do	Oct. 22, 1863	Deserted at Little Rock, Arkansas, August 28, 1864.
Wiley, William C	do	Dec. 28, 1863	Deserted March 4, 1864.
Wiley, John B	do	Dec. 28, 1863	Do.

Transferred.

Name	Rank	Date	Remarks
Ross, Thomas J	Sergeant	Feb. 13, 1864	Appointed corporal March 3, 1864; sergeant October 28, 1864; transferred for promotion January 1, 1865.
Dodd, Michael	Private	Feb. 16, 1864	Appointed hospital steward June 1, 1865.

COMPANY F.

Name	Rank	Date of rank.	Remarks
William H. Warner	Captain		Appointed from private in company H, 15th Illinois cavalry, to fill original vacancy; mustered out with regiment.
Thomas Whitten	1st lieutenant	April 7, 1864	Appointed from civil life to fill original vacancy; mustered out October 5, 1864.
William H. McKinley	do	Oct. 18, 1864	Appointed from corporal in company E, 2d Missouri cavalry, vice Whitten mustered out; mustered out with regiment.
John N. Jones	2d lieutenant	April 7, 1864	Appointed from private in company F to fill original vacancy; mustered out with regiment.
Nori N. Chaffin	1st sergeant	Nov. 19, 1863	Appointed from private; mustered out with regiment.

Fourth regiment Arkansas cavalry volunteers. Mustered into service December 29, 1864, (three years;) mustered out June 30, 1865.

COMPANY F—Continued.

Names.	Rank.	Enlistment.	Date of rank.	Remarks.
William A. Green	Commissary sergeant	Nov. 19, 1863	April 7, 1864	Appointed from private; mustered out with regiment.
William J. Neighbors	Sergeant	Nov. 20, 1863	April 7, 1864	Do.
Robert M. Gibbons	do	Jan. 2, 1864	Dec. 14, 1864	Appointed corporal October 14, 1864; mustered out with regiment.
Richard A. Wright	Corporal	Nov. 17, 1863	April 7, 1864	Mustered out with regiment.
Joseph Skates	do	Mar. 24, 1864	April 7, 1864	Do.
David Trofford	do	Nov. 4, 1863	April 7, 1864	Do.
William R. Massengale	do	Mar. 28, 1864	May 10, 1864	Do.
George W. Clingan	do	Mar. 24, 1864	July 20, 1864	Do.
Morgan Ussery	do	Nov. 19, 1863	July 25, 1864	Do.
William M. Maybie	do	Mar. 28, 1864	Dec. 20, 1864	Do.
Richard J. Whitten	Bugler	Nov. 20, 1863	April 6, 1864	Do.
Rice Harris	do	Nov. 19, 1863	April 6, 1864	Do.
William A. Hughes	Blacksmith	Dec. 22, 1863	April 6, 1864	Do.
			Muster.	
Anthony, Salvador	Private	Nov. 17, 1863	April 6, 1864	Do.
Blankinship, Elisha	do	Nov. 19, 1863	April 6, 1864	Do.
Bell, Isaac	do	Mar. 24, 1864	April 6, 1864	Do.
Blodsoe, Benjamin F	do	Nov. 20, 1863	April 6, 1864	Do.
Crow, Isaac	do	Nov. 17, 1863	April 6, 1864	Do.
Crow, James	do	Dec. 21, 1864	Feb. 24, 1865	Do.
Davis, Barney P	do	Nov. 19, 1863	April 6, 1864	Do.
Denham, William	do	Nov. 19, 1863	April 6, 1864	Do.
Denham, James	do	Nov. 19, 1863	April 6, 1864	Do.
Duggan, Arnett S	do	Nov. 19, 1863	April 6, 1864	Do.
Duggan, Samuel	do	Dec. 21, 1863	Feb. 24, 1864	Do.
Elmore, John	do	May 14, 1864	June 10, 1864	In confinement at Little Rock since June 5, 1865; no discharge furnished on muster out of regiment.
Fora, Sterling B	do	Jan. 2, 1864	June 10, 1864	Mustered out with regiment.
Flynn, Patrick	do	Mar. 1, 1864	April 6, 1864	Do.
Garner, William	do	Nov. 20, 1863	April 6, 1864	Do.
Garner, John H	do	Nov. 20, 1863	April 6, 1864	Do.
Griffin, John J	do	June 2, 1864	June 10, 1864	Do.
Hurd, James P	do	Jan. 27, 1864	April 29, 1864	Do.
Hardin, William F. D	do	Nov. 19, 1863	April 6, 1864	Do.
Hughes, General M	do	Mar. 28, 1864	April 6, 1864	Do.
Hill, Pleasant B	do	Feb. 20, 1864	April 6, 1864	Do.
Hight, Thomas C	do	Nov. 19, 1863	April 6, 1864	Do.
Helms, Lemuel	do	Nov. 19, 1863	April 6, 1864	Do.
Johnson, John F, 1st	do	Nov. 25, 1863	April 6, 1864	Do.
Johnson, John F, 2d	do	Nov. 17, 1863	April 6, 1864	Do.
Lamb, Lewis	do	Mar. 24, 1864	April 6, 1864	Do.

REPORT OF THE ADJUTANT GENERAL OF ARKANSAS. 151

Name	Rank	Date	Date	Remarks
Locket, Enoch S		Mar. 25, 1864	April 29, 1864	Do.
Lowery, Nathan	do	Nov. 19, 1863	April 6, 1864	Do.
Lamb, Thomas	do	Mar. 24, 1864	April 6, 1864	Do.
Moore, Enoch	do	Dec. 5, 1863	April 6, 1864	Do.
Osborne, Jesse J	do	Nov. 19, 1863	April 6, 1864	Do.
Parker, Alexander W	do	Nov. 19, 1863	April 6, 1864	Do.
Plemens, John M	do	Nov. 19, 1863	April 6, 1864	Do.
Perry, Clayborne	do	Nov. 20, 1863	April 6, 1864	Do.
Richards, George W	do	Jan. 18, 1864	April 6, 1864	Do.
Sutton, Martin	do	Jan. 18, 1864	April 6, 1864	Do.
Sutton, Carroll	do	Nov. 19, 1863	April 6, 1864	Do.
Sterling, William	do	Nov. 19, 1863	April 6, 1864	Do.
Slaight, James	do	Nov. 19, 1863	April 6, 1864	Do.
Taylor, John F	do	Nov. 19, 1863	April 6, 1864	Do.
Ussery, Albert C	do	Nov. 19, 1863	April 6, 1864	Do.
Walker, William J	do	Nov. 19, 1863	April 6, 1864	Do.
Worley, Neal	do	Nov. 19, 1863	April 6, 1864	Do.
Whitton, Samuel A	do	Nov. 20, 1863	April 6, 1864	Do.
Watkins, John	do	Mar. 30, 1864	April 6, 1864	Do.

Died.

Name	Rank	Date	Date	Remarks
George W. Sevier	Quartermaster sergeant	Nov. 19, 1863	April 6, 1864	Died of chronic diarrhoea at Little Rock, Arkansas, May 13, 1865.
Thomas P. Gilbert	Sergeant	Nov. 19, 1863	April 6, 1864	Died of chronic diarrhoea at Duvall's Bluff, Arkansas, December 15, 1864.
William Galligor	Corporal	Mar. 24, 1864	April 6, 1864	Died of chronic diarrhoea at Little Rock, Arkansas, May 5, 1864.
Alfred M. King	do	Mar. 30, 1864	April 6, 1864	Wounded in action at Hot Springs, Arkansas, April 19, 1864; killed by guerillas July 30, 1864.
Thomas N. Montgomery	do	Nov. 19, 1863	April 6, 1864	Died of congestive chills at Little Rock, Arkansas, July 30, 1864.
Mathew Norman	do	Nov. 20, 1863	April 6, 1864	Died of chronic diarrhoea at Little Rock, Arkansas, May 9, 1864.
Berry, Nathan A	Private	Nov. 19, 1863	April 6, 1864	Died of pneumonia at Duvall's Bluff, Arkansas, January 3, 1865.
Biddy, Daniel	do	Nov. 19, 1863	April 6, 1864	Died of chronic diarrhoea at Little Rock, Arkansas, May 27, 1864.
Burrill, Abner G	do	Nov. 19, 1863	April 6, 1864	Died of chronic diarrucea at Little Rock, Arkansas, July 28, 1864.
Benton, William	do	Jan. 7, 1864	April 6, 1864	Died of chronic diarrhoea at Little Rock, Arkansas, July 25, 1864.
Bankston, William H	do	Nov. 19, 1863	April 6, 1864	Died of whooping-cough at Duvall's Bluff, Arkansas, November 15, 1864.
Chaffin, John C	do	Nov. 19, 1863	April 12, 1864	Died of fever at Little Rock, Arkansas, August 26, 1864.
Daniels, Ephraim	do	Dec. 10, 1863	April 6, 1864	Died of fever at Little Rock, Arkansas, November 13, 1864.
Ferfer, Eli	do	Nov. 22, 1863	April 6, 1864	Died of chronic diarrhoea at Little Rock, Arkansas, February 26, 1865.
Gibbons, John D	do	Jan. 2, 1864	April 29, 1864	Died of pneumonia at Little Rock, Arkansas, June 16, 1864.
Gilley, Warren	do	Nov. 19, 1863	April 6, 1864	Died of chronic diarrhoea at Little Rock, Arkansas, December 30, 1864.
Hurd, Jeremiah	do	Jan. 27, 1864	April 6, 1864	Died of pneumonia at Duvall's Bluff, Arkansas, January 18, 1865.
Hardin, William P	do	Nov. 19, 1863	April 6, 1864	Died of chronic diarrhoea at Duvall's Bluff, Arkansas, April 15, 1865.
Johnson, Robert	do	Mar. 21, 1864	Feb. 24, 1864	Died of chronic diarrhoea at Duvall's Bluff, Arkansas, March 16, 1865.
Lamb, Drury	do	June 2, 1864	June 10, 1864	Died of chronic diarrhoea at Little Rock, Arkansas, September 13, 1864.
McGuire, Isaac	do	Mar. 28, 1864	April 6, 1864	Died of fever at Little Rock, Arkansas, July 12, 1864.
Moore, Thomas	do	Mar. 28, 1864	April 12, 1864	Died of chronic diarrhoea at Little Rock, Arkansas, July 20, 1864.
Skates, Thomas	do	Mar. 24, 1864	April 6, 1864	Died of chronic diarrhoea at Little Rock, Arkansas, May 5, 1864.
Suit, Ralph	do	Nov. 19, 1863	April 6, 1864	Died of chronic diarrhoea at Duvall's Bluff, Arkansas, March 11, 1865.
Spencer, Jacob C	do	Nov. 19, 1863	April 6, 1864	Died of pneumonia at Duvall's Bluff, Arkansas, December 23, 1864.
Trout, James R	do	Mar. 24, 1864	April 6, 1864	Died in hospital at Little Rock, Arkansas, July 30, 1864.
Till, George W	do	Nov. 19, 1863	April 6, 1864	Died of chronic diarrhoea at Little Rock, Arkansas, April 6, 1865.
Watkins, William	do	Mar. 30, 1864	April 6, 1864	Died of fever at Little Rock, Arkansas, August 10, 1864.
Webb, James A	do	Nov. 19, 1863	April 6, 1864	Died of chronic diarrhoea at Little Rock, Arkansas, May 9, 1865.

Fourth regiment Arkansas cavalry volunteers. Mustered into service December 29, 1864, (three years;) mustered out June 30, 1865.

COMPANY F—Continued.

Names.	Rank.	Enlistment.	Muster.	Remarks.
Discharged.				
Edmund Richards	Sergeant	Nov. 20, 1863	April 6, 1864	Discharged for disability.
James C. Parker	do	Nov. 17, 1863	April 6, 1864	Discharged June 6, 1865.
Brown, Floyd O	Private	Mar. 30, 1864	April 29, 1864	Discharged for disability December 13, 1864.
Brown, John A	do	Mar. 24, 1864	April 6, 1864	Discharged June 6, 1865.
Brown, John C	do	Mar. 24, 1864	April 6, 1864	Do.
Baggs, Elbert	do	Nov. 19, 1863	April 6, 1864	Discharged May 22, 1865.
Carson, John H	do	Nov. 20, 1863	April 6, 1864	Discharged February 14, 1865.
Cox, John Q	do	Nov. 19, 1863	April 6, 1864	Discharged June 6, 1865.
Gillham, Elisha G	do	Mar. 30, 1864	April 6, 1864	Discharged May 22, 1865.
Jones, John	do	Nov. 19, 1863	April 6, 1864	Discharged for promotion April 7, 1864.
Musgrove, Francis M	do	Nov. 19, 1863	April 6, 1864	Discharged for disability March 15, 1865.
Neighbors, Levi S	do	Mar. 28, 1864	April 12, 1864	Discharged for disability February 21, 1865.
Pate, Allen P	do	Nov. 19, 1863	April 6, 1864	Discharged for disability February 1, 1865.
Parker, Rufus	do	Nov. 17, 1863	April 6, 1864	Discharged to accept promotion April 28, 1864.
Reaves, Lewis	do	Mar. 24, 1864	April 6, 1864	Discharged for disability February 1, 1865.
Deserted.				
Frank, Virgil L	Private	Jan. 22, 1864	April 29, 1864	Deserted at Benton, Arkansas, August 29, 1864.
Gunn, William H	do	Nov. 19, 1863	April 6, 1864	Do.
McDonald, Daniel	do	Nov. 23, 1864	April 6, 1864	Deserted at Little Rock, Arkansas, August 31, 1864.
Pippins, Ebenezer	do	Nov. 17, 1863	April 6, 1864	Deserted at Little Rock, Arkansas, October 22, 1864.
Reynolds, Abel S	do	Dec. 14, 1863	April 6, 1864	Deserted at Little Rock, Arkansas, August 31, 1864.

COMPANY G.

Names.	Rank.	Date of rank.	Remarks.
William J. Green	Captain	April 29, 1864	Appointed from corporal 15th Illinois cavalry volunteers to fill original vacancy; resigned July 31, 1864.
Edson S. Bastin	do	Oct. 16, 1864	Appointed from private company G 28th Wisconsin infantry volunteers, vice Green, resigned; mustered out with regiment.
Josiah H. Danby	1st lieutenant	Mar. 8, 1864	Appointed from civil life to fill original vacancy; mustered out with regiment.
George W. Pettijohn	2d lieutenant	April 29, 1864	Do.
William C. Wallace	1st sergeant	Feb. 6, 1864	Mustered out with regiment.
Andrew J. Tate	Quartermaster sergeant	Feb. 25, 1864	Do.
Andrew H. Murchison	Commissary sergeant	Feb. 6, 1864	Do.
John L. Webb	Sergeant	Feb. 6, 1864	Do.

REPORT OF THE ADJUTANT GENERAL OF ARKANSAS.   153

Name	Rank	Enlisted	Muster	Remarks
Dempsey T. Barnes	do	Feb. 6, 1864	April 29, 1864	Do.
Joel Cummings	do	Feb. 6, 1864	July 24, 1864	Corporal from organization of company; mustered out with regiment.
Cicero Tiner	Corporal	Feb. 6, 1864	April 29, 1864	Mustered out with regiment.
Elbott L. Majors	do	Feb. 6, 1864	April 29, 1864	Do.
Green Johnson	do	Mar. 24, 1864	July 24, 1864	Do.
John R. Ruskin	do	Feb. 28, 1864	Mar. 15, 1865	Do.
Alfred Pare	Bugler	Aug. 10, 1864	Nov. 30, 1864	Do.
Andrews, Tarleton	Private	Feb. 23, 1864	Feb. 25, 1864	Do.
Allen, James L	do	Mar. 23, 1864	Apr 1 23, 1864	Do.
Allen, Pinkney	do	Mar. 23, 1864	April 23, 1864	Do.
Bierman, Charles	do	Feb. 6, 1864	Feb. 25, 1864	Do.
Browning, Mitchell	do	Feb. 25, 1864	Feb. 27, 1864	Do.
Carter, William	do	Feb. 2, 1864	April 23, 1864	Do.
Clark, William A. N	do	June 21, 1864	Aug. 25, 1864	Do.
Davis, Nicholas J	do	Aug. 27, 1864	Sept. 28, 1864	Do.
Estrus, Jasper	do	Mar. 23, 1864	April 23, 1864	Do.
Favor, Joseph	do	Feb. 6, 1864	Feb. 23, 1864	Do.
Ga dy, Charles W	do	Aug. 10, 1864	Aug. 25, 1861	Do.
Gibbs, George W	do	Feb. 2, 1964	April 29, 1864	Do.
Grayson, Enoch B	do	Aug. 10, 1864	Aug. 25, 1864	Do.
Hawkins, Franklin	do	Mar. 6, 1864	April 8, 1864	Do.
Johnson, James R	do	Mar. 24, 1864	April 8, 1864	Do.
King, Thomas	do	Oct. 29, 1864	Oct. 31, 1864	Do.
Kinsey, Jesse L	do	Mar. 21, 1864	April 23, 1864	Do.
Kindrick, Young M	do	Mar. 21, 1864	April 23, 1864	Do.
Lavender, John T	do	Feb. 6, 1864	Feb. 25, 1864	Do.
Lawry, James T	do	Mar. 25, 1864	April 8, 1864	Do.
Marlin, Henry	do	Feb. 6, 1864	Feb. 25, 1864	Do.
McMahoney, Augustus	do	Mar. 23, 1864	Aug. 25, 1864	Do.
Morning, George W	do	Aug. 10, 1864	Aug. 25, 1864	Do.
Nutt, Sampson	do	Feb. 6, 1864	Feb. 25, 1864	Do.
Owen, William K	do	Aug. 24, 1864	Sept. 28, 1864	Do.
Parker, Joel R	do	Mar. 21, 1864	April 23, 1864	Do.
Polk, William	do	Aug. 26, 1864	Oct. 31, 1864	Do.
Price, William R	do	Mar. 16, 1864	April 23, 1864	Do.
Rawls, John F	do	Feb. 2, 1864	April 23, 1861	Do.
Sammons, William	do	Mar. 24, 1864	April 23, 1864	Do.
Scarberry, William	do	Mar. 21, 1864	April 23, 1864	Do.
Simpson, Lewis D	do	Feb. 6, 1864	Feb. 25, 1864	Do.
Smith, Doctor T	do	Mar. 23, 1864	April 23, 1864	Do.
Stearns, David	do	Feb. 27, 1864	Mar. 8, 1864	Do.
Stringfellow, William T	do	Feb. 6, 1864	Feb. 25, 1864	Do.
Turner, John J	do	Feb. 6, 1864	Feb. 25, 1864	Do.
Vaughan, Charles W	do	Feb. 6, 1864	Feb. 25, 1864	Do.
Watts, Alexander	do	Feb. 6, 1864	Feb. 25, 1864	Do.
Wilson, Eli G	do	Feb. 6, 1864	Feb. 25, 1864	Do.
Woodrum, William S	do	Feb. 25, 1864	Feb. 27, 1864	Do.
Bugg, William D	do	Feb. 6, 1864	Feb. 25, 1864	Do.
Carter, James M	do	Feb. 21, 1864	Feb. 25, 1864	Do.

154 REPORT OF THE ADJUTANT GENERAL OF ARKANSAS.

Fourth regiment Arkansas cavalry volunteers. Mustered into service December 29, 1864, (three years;) mustered out June 30, 1865.

COMPANY G—Continued.

Names.	Rank.	Enlistment.	Muster.	Remarks.
Owens, Henry	Private	Feb. 6, 1864	Feb. 25, 1864	Mustered out with regiment.
Missing in action.				
Carter, James B	...do...	Feb. 2, 1864	April 23, 1864	Missing since skirmish at Caddo Gap July 12, 1864.
Discharged.				
Isaac Newcome	Sergeant	Feb. 6, 1864	Mar. 8, 1864	Discharged for disability January 27, 1865, caused by wounds received in action at Duvall's Bluff, Arkansas.
Charles Hoover	Corporal	Feb. 6, 1864	Feb. 25, 1864	Discharged May 22, 1865.
Davis, Benjamin F	Private	Mar. 4, 1864	April 8, 1864	Dishonorably discharged January 23, 1865.
Hoover, Joseph	...do...	Feb. 6, 1864	Feb. 25, 1864	Discharged May 22, 1865.
Jennings, James P	...do...	Mar. 23, 1864	April 23, 1864	Discharged June 9, 1865.
Echols, James	...do...	Mar. 21, 1864	April 23, 1864	Discharged June 12, 1865.
Mathews, Stephen R	...do...	Feb. 6, 1864	Feb. 25, 1864	Discharged June 9, 1865.
Snyder, Charles F	...do...	Feb. 6, 1864	Feb. 23, 1864	Discharged May 22, 1865.
Transferred.				
Noah J. Bumgarner	Corporal	Mar. 23, 1864	April 23, 1864	Transferred to non-commissioned staff as saddler sergeant, January 1, 1865.
Died.				
William Mitchell	Sergeant	Feb. 6, 1864	Feb. 25, 1864	Died of chronic diarrhœa at Little Rock, Arkansas, August 21, 1864; sergeant from organization of company.
Stephen H. Snyder	...do...	Feb. 6, 1864	Feb. 25, 1864	Died of chronic diarrhœa at Duvall's Bluff, Arkansas, January 17, 1865; corporal from organization of company; appointed sergeant August 29, 1864.
James H. Jennings	Corporal	Mar. 23, 1864	April 23, 1864	Died of chronic diarrhœa at Little Rock, Arkansas, July 26, 1864; corporal from organization of company.
John O. Ross	...do...	Feb. 6, 1864	Feb. 25, 1864	Died of inflammation of the brain at Little Rock, Arkansas, June 27, 1864; corporal from organization of company.
George F. Ross	...do...	Feb. 6, 1864	Feb. 25, 1864	Died of inflammation of the lungs at Duvall's Bluff, Arkansas, April 20, 1865; corporal from organization of company.
Bankston, John R	Private	Feb. 6, 1864	Feb. 25, 1864	Died of measles at Little Rock, Arkansas, May 5, 1864.
Black, George F	...do...	Mar. 21, 1864	April 23, 1864	Died of poison at Little Rock, Arkansas, (accidentally,) July 30, 1864.
Bowlin, William	...do...	Feb. 6, 1864	Feb. 25, 1864	Died of pneumonia at Pine Bluff, Arkansas, March 14, 1864.
Bugg, Morgan	...do...	Mar. 22, 1864	April 8, 1864	Accidentally shot at Duvall's Bluff, Arkansas, January 2, 1865.
Burnett, Mason	...do...	Mar. 23, 1864	April 23, 1864	Died of chronic diarrhœa at Little Rock, Arkansas, July 3, 1864.
Carley, Edmund	...do...	Mar. 25, 1864	April 29, 1864	Died of pneumonia at Little Rock, Arkansas, May 10, 1864.
Davis, Edward	...do...	Feb. 6, 1864	Feb. 25, 1864	Died of chronic diarrhœa at Duvall's Bluff, Arkansas, March 15, 1865.
Dulin, James S	...do...	Aug. 27, 1864	Sept. 28, 1864	Died of complex variola at Duvall's Bluff, Arkansas, April 29, 1865.
Eno, Jefferson	...do...	Feb. 25, 1864	Feb. 27, 1864	Died of measles at Little Rock, Arkansas, May 16, 1864.

Name	Rank	Date	Remarks
Gathin, James	do	Feb. 25, 1864	Died of variola at Duvall's Bluff, Arkansas, April 21, 1865.
Gilbert, Jilson	do	Feb. 6, 1864	Died of chronic diarrhœa at Little Rock, Arkansas, July 27, 1864.
Hamlin, George W	do	Feb. 6, 1864	Died of chronic diarrhœa at Duvall's Bluff, Arkansas, February 20, 1865.
Harris, Henry	do	Feb. 6, 1864	Died of chronic diarrhœa at Brownsville, Arkansas, February 4, 1865.
Henry, Albert H	do	Feb. 27, 1864	Died of chronic diarrhœa at Duvall's Bluff, Arkansas, March 30, 1865.
Purnell, James M	do	Mar. 24, 1864	Died of pneumonia at Little Rock, Arkansas, April 26, 1864.
Raines, James W	do	Feb. 6, 1864	Died of pneumonia at Pine Bluff, Arkansas, March 14, 1864.
Rawls, Joseph C	do	Feb. 25, 1864	Died of chronic diarrhœa at Duvall's Bluff, Arkansas, November 24, 1864.
Secrest, James H	do	Mar. 21, 1864	Died of erysipelas at Little Rock, Arkansas, June 25, 1864.
Taber, Elisha R	do	April 23, 1864	Died of chronic diarrhœa at Duvall's Bluff, Arkansas, April 15, 1864.
Treadway, James A	do	April 8, 1864	Died of chronic diarrhœa at Little Rock, Arkansas, May 2, 1864.
Wilson, Allen K	do	Feb. 25, 1864	Died at Little Rock, Arkansas, September 24, 1864.
Wright, Eli J	do	Mar. 21, 1864	Killed accidentally with the blow of a fist while boxing at Little Rock, Arkansas, August 1, 1864.

Deserted.

Name	Rank	Date	Remarks
Elisha Flora	Corporal	Mar. 12, 1864	Deserted at Little Rock, Arkansas, June 9, 1864.
John V. Mathews	Bugler	Mar. 23, 1864	Deserted at Little Rock, Arkansas, June 11, 1864.
Bowles, John M	Private	Mar. 23, 1864	Deserted at Little Rock, Arkansas, June 5, 1864.
Patten, William	do	Feb. 22, 1864	Deserted at Little Rock, Arkansas, March 15, 1864.
Smith, Henry	do	Mar. 28, 1864	Deserted at Little Rock, Arkansas, July 20, 1864.
Wright, Isaac W	do	Mar. 24, 1864	Deserted at Little Rock, Arkansas, August 29, 1864.
Young, Isaiah	do	Aug. 10, 1864	Deserted at Little Rock, Arkansas, September 17, 1864.

COMPANY H.

Name	Rank	Date of rank.	Muster.	Remarks
John F. Landers	Captain	May 9, 1864		Appointed from private to fill original vacancy; mustered out with regiment.
Rufus Parker	1st lieutenant	April 30, 1864		Appointed from private of company F to fill original vacancy; mustered out with regiment.
John W. Plumlee	2d lieutenant	May 11, 1864	Jan. 20, 1863	Appointed from sergeant, company E, 1st Arkansas cavalry, to fill original vacancy; mustered out with regiment.
John N. McCallum	1st sergeant	June 1, 1864	Dec. 27, 1863	Appointed from private; mustered out with regiment.
Thomas W. Bean	Quartermaster sergeant	April 21, 1864	May 2, 1864	Do.
Samuel Parker	Commissary sergeant	April 21, 1864	Nov. 17, 1863	Do.
Thomas J. Strown	Sergeant	June 30, 1864	May 2, 1864	Do.
John M. Stapp	do	June —, 1864	Jan. 25, 1864	Do.
John Hawkins	Corporal	April 21, 1864	Nov. 17, 1863	
William A. Dye	do	Oct. 15, 1864	April 20, 1864	Mustered out with regiment.
John C. Harper	do	Nov. 12, 1864	June 5, 1864	Do.
Robert B. Turner	Blacksmith	April 1, 1864	Mar. 28, 1864	Do.
Ambrose H. White	Bugler	Nov. 30, 1864	Nov. 10, 1864	Do.
Bennett, John J	Private	April 21, 1864	Mar. 30, 1864	Do.
Blanchard, Larisco F	do	May 5, 1864	Mar. 31, 1864	Do.
Brown, William	do	May 5, 1864	Mar. 31, 1864	Do.

156 REPORT OF THE ADJUTANT GENERAL OF ARKANSAS

Fourth regiment Arkansas cavalry volunteers. Mustered into service December 29, 1864, (three years;) mustered out June 30, 1865.

COMPANY H—Continued.

Names.	Rank.	Enlistment.	Muster.	Remarks.
Brown, James G	Private	Mar. 31, 1864	May 5, 1864	Mustered out with regiment.
Beshes, Henry	do	Feb. 23, 1864	May 5, 1864	Do.
Chastain, Benjamin	do	Mar. 21, 1864	April 21, 1864	Do.
Curr, John J	do	Nov. 17, 1863	April 21, 1864	Do.
Cox, Dennis B	do	Nov. 17, 1863	April 21, 1864	Do.
Chastain, William F	do	Feb. 14, 1864	April 21, 1864	Do.
Dyer, Andrew J	do	Nov. 6, 1863	April 21, 1864	Do.
Dyer, John	do	Mar. 25, 1864	May 5, 1864	Do.
Fulton, Conrad	do	Sept. 8, 1864	Sept. 28, 1864	Do.
Goodwin, William R	do	Feb. 28, 1864	May 5, 1864	Do.
Haynes, William R	do	April 20, 1864	April 21, 1864	Do.
Harper, John M	do	June 5, 1864	June 9, 1864	Do.
McIntosh, James T	do	Jan. 10, 1864	April 25, 1864	Do.
Muse, Stephen	do	Feb. 28, 1864	May 5, 1864	Do.
Muse, Mallory B	do	Feb. 28, 1864	May 5, 1864	Do.
Nutt, Adolphus T	do	Nov. 17, 1863	April 21, 1864	Do.
Peaceyhouse, James H	do	April 20, 1864	May 5, 1864	Do.
Paint, James H	do	April 14, 1864	April 21, 1864	Do.
Perry, James	do	Mar. 31, 1864	May 5, 1864	Do.
Parker, Thomas C	do	Dec. 27, 1863	Sept. 28, 1864	Do.
Tollerson, Christopher	do	Dec. 27, 1863	Sept. 28, 1864	Do.
Tollerson, James A	do	Aug. 18, 1864	Sept. 28, 1864	Do.
Tollerson, Shelby U	do	Dec. 27, 1863	Sept. 28, 1864	Do.
White, James F	do	Nov. 10, 1864	Nov. 10, 1864	Do.
Died.				
Littleton, Arnold	Corporal	July 25, 1864	Sept. 28, 1864	Died at Duvall's Bluff, Arkansas, January 26, 1865; promoted corporal November 2, 1864.
Beshers, Larkin R	Private	Feb. 28, 1864	May 5, 1864	Died at Little Rock, Arkansas, August 13, 1864.
Bussell, Rodman	do	Jan. 25, 1864	June 9, 1864	Died at Duvall's Bluff, Arkansas, September 26, 1864.
Chambers, Ely E	do	Feb. 15, 1864	April 21, 1864	Died at Little Rock, Arkansas, June 7, 1864.
Chastain, John W	do	May 33, 1864	April 21, 1864	Died at Little Rock, Arkansas, July 6, 1864.
Collens, Francis M	do	April 28, 1864	May 5, 1864	Died at Little Rock, Arkansas, June 6, 1864.
Fowler, John	do	April 15, 1864	April 21, 1864	Died at Little Rock, Arkansas, September 4, 1864.
Goodwin, John W	do	Feb. 28, 1864	May 5, 1864	Died at Little Rock, Arkansas, October 5, 1864.
Hawkins, John S	do	Mar. 31, 1864	May 5, 1864	Died at Little Rock, Arkansas, July 4, 1864.
Hall, William W	do	April 27, 1864	June 9, 1864	Died at Little Rock, Arkansas, December 14, 1864.
Nutt, Haller D	do	Nov. 17, 1864	April 21, 1864	Died at Little Rock, Arkansas, August 27, 1864.
Osborne, James D	do	Nov. 17, 1864	April 21, 1864	Died at Little Rock, Arkansas, July 21, 1864.
Parker, William	do	Dec. 27, 1863	Sept. 28, 1864	Died at Duvall's Bluff, Arkansas, November 8, 1864.
Stricklin, Christopher C	do	Feb. 14, 1864	April 21, 1864	Died at Little Rock, Arkansas, May 20, 1864.
Taylor, James M	do	April 22, 1864	April 25, 1864	Died at Little Rock, Arkansas, January 8, 1865.

Name	Rank	Enlisted	Mustered	Remarks
Walton, David A	do	Nov. 17, 1863	April 21, 1864	Died at Little Rock, Arkansas, September 2, 1864.
Wallace, Thomas	do	April 20, 1864	April 21, 1864	Died at Duvall's Bluff, Arkansas, September 2, 1864.
Discharged.				
Beshears, William R	do	Feb. 15, 1864	April 25, 1864	Discharged for disability, December 29, 1864.
Cobler, Joseph F	do	Mar. 26, 1864	April 21, 1864	Discharged for disability, January 26, 1865.
Compton, James	do	April 20, 1864	April 21, 1864	Do.
Harper, William H	do	April 20, 1864	April 21, 1864	Discharged for being a minor, June 5, 1864.
Lanning, John M	do	Feb. 28, 1864	April 25, 1864	Discharged June 6, 1865.
Powers, Holloway	do	Nov. 17, 1863	April 21, 1864	Discharged February 18, 1865.
White, John L	do	June 25, 1864	Never	Discharged by sentence of G. C. M.
Transferred to 2d Missouri artillery, May 30, 1864, per General Order No. 112, department of Arkansas.				
George W. Sutton	1st sergeant	Feb. 1, 1864	April 21, 1864	Appointed sergeant April 21, 1864.
Moses D. Brownman	Commissary sergeant	Mar. 19, 1864	April 21, 1864	Appointed from private April 21, 1864.
William L. Richey	Sergeant	Feb. 14, 1864	April 21, 1864	Do.
Murrell D. Fletcher	do	Feb. 25, 1864	April 21, 1864	Do.
Amos E. Gentry	do	Feb. 14, 1864	April 21, 1864	Do.
Alfred D. Stephens	do	Feb. 14, 1864	April 21, 1864	Do.
Thomas R. Beshers	Corporal	Jan. 25, 1864	April 21, 1864	Appointed corporal April 21, 1864.
Isaac Janway	do	Feb. 8, 1864	April 21, 1864	Do.
William H. James	do	Feb. 14, 1864	April 21, 1864	Do.
General C. Litlow	do	Feb. 14, 1864	April 21, 1864	Do.
Herman F. Swinford	do	Feb. 28, 1864	April 21, 1864	Do.
Balden, Thomas J	Private	Feb. 14, 1864	April 21, 1864	
Brashears, William	do	Feb. 16, 1864	April 21, 1864	
Brazil, William R	do	Feb. 14, 1864	April 21, 1864	
Brazil, George W	do	Feb. 15, 1864	April 21, 1864	
Beshers, George W	do	Feb. 28, 1864	April 21, 1864	
Chambers, William C	do	Feb. 16, 1864	April 21, 1864	
Ewing, Alexander	do	Feb. 8, 1864	April 21, 1864	
Ewing, Jerry	do	Feb. 8, 1864	April 21, 1864	
Echols, Augustus	do	Dec. 25, 1863	April 25, 1864	
Graves, Giles R	do	Mar. 11, 1864	April 21, 1864	
Goodwin, John F	do	Dec. 25, 1863	April 25, 1864	
Hutchinson, Wm. C	do	Feb. 25, 1864	April 21, 1864	
Long, William B	do	Feb. 14, 1864	April 21, 1864	
Meredith, John	do	Nov. 17, 1863	April 21, 1864	
Meredith, David L	do	Feb. 14, 1864	April 21, 1864	
Mehuse, William A	do	Feb. 14, 1864	April 21, 1864	
Mehuse, Robert H	do	Feb. 14, 1864	April 21, 1864	
Pepper, David F	do	Feb. 14, 1864	April 21, 1864	
Stainer, Michael D	do	Dec. 28, 1863	April 21, 1864	
Stricklin, William	do	Feb. 14, 1864	April 21, 1864	
Tuck, Robert M	do	Mar. 19, 1864	April 21, 1864	
Deserted.				
Richard M. Bennett	1st sergeant	May 6, 1864	June 9, 1864	Deserted at Little Rock, Arkansas, September 14, 1864.

158 REPORT OF THE ADJUTANT GENERAL OF ARKANSAS.

Fourth regiment Arkansas cavalry volunteers. Mustered into service December 29, 1864, (three years;) mustered out June 30, 1865.

COMPANY H—Continued.

Names.	Rank.	Enlistment.	Muster.	Remarks.
Bledsoe, William	Private	Nov. 25, 1863	April 21, 1864	Deserted at Little Rock, Arkansas, July 4, 1864.
Benton, Colbert	do	April 15, 1864	May 5, 1864	Do.
Burnett, Nath'niel W	do	May 7, 1864	June 9, 1864	Deserted at Little Rock, Arkansas, May 11, 1864.
Burnett, Charles L	do	May 10, 1864	June 9, 1864	Deserted at Little Rock, Arkansas, September 14, 1864.
Bussell, Thomas P	do	June 21, 1864	Never	Deserted at Little Rock, Arkansas, August 29, 1864.
Bussell, James	do	June 21, 1864	Never	Do.
Clingman, Francis M	do	Dec. 26, 1863	June 9, 1864	Deserted at Little Rock, Arkansas, August 10, 1864.
Dyer, D. M	do	Mar. 28, 1864	April 25, 1864	Deserted at Little Rock, Arkansas, May 11, 1864.
D-nham, Nathaniel P	do	April 25, 1864	April 25, 1864	Deserted at Little Rock, Arkansas, August 20, 1864.
Davis, John	do	Mar. 9, 1864	May 5, 1864	Deserted at Littl- Rock, Arkansas, August 29, 1864.
Fryer, John M	do	June 3, 1864	June 9, 1864	Deserted at Little Rock, Arkansas, May 12, 1864.
G—, John	do	Mar. 28, 1864	April 25, 1864	Deserted at Little Rock, Arkansas, October 1, 1864.
James, George	do	May 25, 1864	May 5, 1864	Deserted at Little Rock, Arkansas, September 19, 1864.
McCarley, Hiram H	do	Mar. 9, 1864	May 5, 1864	Deserted at Little Rock, Arkansas, August 29, 1864.
Snodgrass, Elijah F	do	Mar. 25, 1864	April 25, 1864	Deserted at Little Rock, Arkansas, October 1, 1864.
Willhight, David P	do	April 23, 1864	April 25, 1864	Deserted at Little Rock, Arkansas, May 11, 1864.
Walker, Houston C	do	Jan. 6, 1864	June 9, 1864	Deserted at Little Rock, Arkansas, August 19, 1864.

COMPANY I.

Names.	Rank.	Enlistment.	Date of rank.	Muster.	Remarks.
Emory E. Knowlton	Captain		Oct. 16, 1864		Appointed from sergeant 25th Ohio battery; resigned May 14, 1865.
Dioclesian L. Downs	do		June 20, 1865		Appointed from private company I to 2d lieutenant June 3, 1864; promoted 1st lieutenant July 27, 1864; promoted captain, vice Knowlton, resigned; mustered out with regiment.
Henry Stocks	1st lieutenant		June 3, 1864		Appointed from sergeant company E, 15th Illinois cavalry, to fill original vacancy; resigned July 25, 1864.
Nelson P. Baker	do	June 20, 1865	June 20, 1865		Appointed from sergeant 25th Ohio battery to 2d lieutenant October 19, 1864; mustered out with regiment.
Henry Gregory	2d lieutenant	Feb. 25, 1864	Nov. 10, 1864		Appointed from private 1st Iowa cavalry; resigned March 13, 1865.
Andrew J. Crawford	1st sergeant	Dec. 11, 1863	Oct. 16, 1864		Mustered out with regiment.
James W. Crisp	Quartermaster sergeant	Dec. 27, 1863	Oct. 16, 1864		Do.
Virgil C. Bingham	Commissary sergeant	Dec. 27, 1863	Oct. 16, 1864		Do.
Wesley T. Breeding	Sergeant	Apr. 2, 1864	May 14, 1865		Do.
Clark Smith	do	Nov. 26, 1864	May 13, 1865		Do.
Eliand Hill	do	Dec. 11, 1863	Oct. 16, 1864		Do.
Joseph W. Langston	Corporal	Mar. 14, 1864	Nov. 1, 1864		Do.
Crawford Nichols	do				Do.

REPORT OF THE ADJUTANT GENERAL OF ARKANSAS. 159

				Muster.		
Robert H. Dieson	do		Apr. 15, 1864		Jan. 28, 1865	Do.
Alfred N. Evans	do		Jan. 18, 1864		Jan. 28, 1865	Do.
Bevel, Fletcher C		Private	May 17, 1864	June 3, 1864		Do.
Burton, William		do	Mar. 27, 1864	June 3, 1864		Do.
Council, Allen		do	Dec. 26, 1863	June 3, 1864		Do.
Cruig, Andrew J		do	Jan. 6, 1864	June 3, 1864		Do.
Crocket, Elias M		do	Apr. 15, 1864	June 3, 1864		Do.
Cyrus, John		do	May 18, 1864	June 3, 1864		Do.
Edwards, Cornelius		do	Jan. 19, 1864	June 3, 1864		Do.
Farmer, Jonathan		do	Feb. 12, 1864	June 30, 1864		Do.
Gardenhier, Thomas		do	Apr. 20, 1864	Apr. 20, 1864		Do.
Gnuter, Lewis		do	Apr. 1, 1864	Apr. 1, 1864		Do.
Hunt, James		do	Mar. 19, 1864	June 3, 1864		Do.
Hunt, Taylor O		do	Mar. 19, 1864	June 3, 1864		Do.
Havens, Jesse L		do	Apr. 19, 1864	June 3, 1864		Do.
Henry, Gabriel C		do	Apr. 22, 1864	Apr. 22, 1864		Do.
Hofner, Samuel		do	Apr. 22, 1864	Apr. 22, 1864		Do.
Hearn, Thomas		do	Jan. 14, 1864	Jan. 14, 1864		In military prison under sentence of general court-martial; no discharge given on muster out of regiment.
Harper, William		do	Dec. 27, 1863	June 3, 1864		Mustered out with regiment.
Howard, Thomas		do	Apr. 20, 1864	Apr. 20, 1864		Do.
Latton, Thomas		do	Jan. 15, 1864	June 3, 1864		Do.
Lensk, William		do	Apr. 3, 1864	Apr. 3, 1864		Do.
Marshall, William		do	Jan. 19, 1864	June 3, 1864		Do.
Marsh, Thomas L		do	Jan. 19, 1864	June 3, 1864		Do.
McCniars, John W		do	Mar. 16, 1864	June 3, 1864		Do.
Myrick, William B		do	Apr. 12, 1864	June 3, 1864		Do.
Province, Sampson P		do	Mar. 12, 1864	June 3, 1864		Do.
Parnell, Thomas E		do	Mar. 3, 1864	Mar. 3, 1864		Do.
Sanford, Clayton		do	Jan. 6, 1864	June 3, 1864		Do.
Sumner, Monroe L		do	July 12, 1864	July 12, 1864		Do.
Smith, Edward		do	Jan. 25, 1864	June 3, 1864		Do.
Truesdail, John F		do	Jan. 17, 1864	June 3, 1864		Do.
Vanderpool, Thomas		do	Apr. 3, 1864	Apr. 3, 1864		Do.
Wood, Richard		do	Nov. 26, 1864	Dec. 14, 1864		Do.
Welliver, Jacob		do	Apr. 18, 1864	Apr. 18, 1864		Do.
Walker, John T		do	Dec. 13, 1863	July 1, 1864		Do.
Winsberry, Drury M		do	Feb. 29, 1864	June 3, 1864		Do.
Discharged.						
Andrews, John W		Private	Dec. 12, 1863	June 31, 1864		Discharged May 22, 1865.
Boatwright, John A		do	May 3, 1864	May 3, 1864		Discharged May 3, 1865.
Gwin, Alexander		do	Apr. 11, 1864	Apr. 11, 1864		Discharged at Duvall's Bluff, Arkansas, November 21, 1864.
Henderson, Andrew		do	Jun. 19, 1864	June 3, 1864		Discharged, per sentence of general court-martial, February 10, 1865.
Hansewright, John		do	Apr. 20, 1864	Apr. 20, 1864		Discharged for disability February 14, 1865.
Mathis, Isaac		do	Mar. 15, 1864	Mar. 16, 1864		Do.
Rober, Alexander		do	Jan. 15, 1864	June 31, 1864		Discharged for promotion.
Stewart, Robert E		do	Dec. 29, 1863	Jan. 31, 1864		Discharged, per sentence of general court-martial, February 5, 1865.

160 REPORT OF THE ADJUTANT GENERAL OF ARKANSAS.

Fourth regiment Arkansas cavalry volunteers. Mustered into service December 29, 1864, (three years;) mustered out June 30, 1865.

COMPANY I—Continued.

Names.	Rank.	Enlistment.	Muster.	Remarks.
Tillery, William	Private	Apr. 25, 1864	June 31, 1864	Discharged, per sentence of general court-martial, February 16, 1865.
Died.				
Bates, Samuel	Corporal	Mar. 12, 1864	June 3, 1864	Died at Little Rock, Arkansas, in hospital, November 5, 1865; appointed corporal October 16, 1864.
Castile, Eben A	Private	Apr. 11, 1864	June 3, 1864	Died in hospital, Duvall's Bluff, Arkansas, December 23, 1864.
Crisp, Ansel	....do	Feb. 16, 1864	June 3, 1864	Died at Little Rock, Arkansas, September 28, 1864.
Edwards, Jesse L	....do	Jan. 19, 1864	June 3, 1864	Died in hospital, Duvall's Bluff, Arkansas, December 25, 1864.
Gwin, William	....do	Apr. 11, 1864	Apr. 11, 1864	Died in hospital, Duvall's Bluff, Arkansas, November 21, 1864.
Lewis, James	Bugler	Jan. 15, 1864	June 3, 1864	Died in hospital, Duvall's Bluff, Arkansas, September 5, 1865.
Miller, Calvin L	Private	July 12, 1864	July 12, 1864	Died in hospital, Duvall's Bluff, Arkansas, December 4, 1864.
Mitchelly, William U	....do	Dec. 27, 1863	June 3, 1864	Died in hospital, Duvall's Bluff, Arkansas, March 11, 1865.
Murray, John A	....do	Apr. 9, 1864	Apr. 9, 1864	Died at Duvall's Bluff, Arkansas, January 22, 1865.
Owens, George W	....do	Mar. 12, 1864	June 3, 1864	Died in hospital at Duvall's Bluff, Arkansas, February 23, 1865.
Philpot, Franz M	....do	Apr. 8, 1864	June 3, 1864	Died in hospital at Duvall's Bluff, Arkansas, November 15, 1864.
Roper, David	Sergeant	Feb. 12, 1864	June 3, 1864	Died in hospital at Duvall's Bluff, Arkansas, February 14, 1865.
Ropp, William	....do	Dec. 14, 1863	June 3, 1864	Died in hospital at Duvall's Bluff, Arkansas, January 1, 1865.
Smith, William M	Private	Dec. 12, 1863	June 3, 1864	Died in hospital at Duvall's Bluff, Arkansas, August 10, 1864.
Stroud, William	....do	Apr. 15, 1864	Apr. 15, 1864	Died in hospital at Duvall's Bluff, Arkansas, November 3, 1864.
Wilmot, William	....do	Apr. 5, 1864	Apr. 6, 1864	Died in hospital at Helena, Arkansas, April 27, 1865.
Williford, Oliver P	Sergeant	Apr. 8, 1864	June 8, 1864	Died in hospital at Duvall's Bluff, Arkansas, March 8, 1865.
Deserted.				
Bugley, Joseph	Private	Dec. 11, 1863	June 3, 1864	Deserted at Duvall's Bluff, Arkansas, November 1, 1864.
Benton, George L	....do	Apr. 9, 1864	June 3, 1864	Deserted at Helena, Arkansas, January 6, 1864.
Cypert, Robert B	....do	June 13, 1864	June 10, 1864	Deserted at Little Rock, Arkansas, August 1, 1864.
Davis, Benjamin	....do	Mar. 14, 1864	June 3, 1864	Deserted at Little Rock, Arkansas, September 10, 1864.
Helms, Jo.1	....do	Mar. 14, 1864	June 3, 1864	Do.
Jones, Philip	....do	Dec. 28, 1863	June 3, 1864	Deserted at Little Rock, Arkansas, August 1, 1864.
Johnson, Lawrence	....do	Mar. 22, 1864	June 3, 1864	Deserted at Caddo Gap, Arkansas, July 14, 1864.
Reetan, James M	....do	Mar. 22, 1864	June 3, 1864	Do.
Martin, Edward	....do	Feb. 18, 1864	June 3, 1864	Do.
Murray, John W	....do	July 12, 1864	July 12, 1864	Deserted at Little Rock, Arkansas, August 1, 1864.
Williams, Moses	....do	Dec. 16, 1863	June 3, 1864	Deserted at Little Rock, Arkansas, September 10, 1864.
Wintenberry, John T. O	....do	Mar. 8, 1864	June 3, 1864	Do.

REPORT OF THE ADJUTANT GENERAL OF ARKANSAS. 161

COMPANY K.

Name	Rank	Muster	Date of rank	Remarks
Joseph Bennett	Captain		June 18, 1864	Appointed from private company B; mustered out October 5, 1864.
William J. Patton	do	May 18, 1862	April 1, 1865	Promoted from 1st lieutenant company A, 1st Arkansas cavalry, vice Bennett, mustered out; mustered out with regiment.
James W. Stephenson	1st lieutenant	Mar. 28, 1864	Mar. 28, 1864	Appointed from civil life to fill original vacancy; died November 17, 1864.
Henry D. Sevier	2d lieutenant	June 18, 1864	June 18, 1864	Appointed from civil life to fill original vacancy; mustered out October 5, 1864.
Herman Hesse	do		Oct. 24, 1864	Appointed 2d lieutenant, vice Sevier, mustered out; mustered out with regiment.
William B. Wallingsford	1st sergeant	May 11, 1864	June 30, 1864	Appointed from private; mustered out with regiment.
Lovett S. Hibbs	Commissary sergeant	Jan. 25, 1864	May 1, 1864	Do.
Romulus L. Allen	Quartermaster sergeant	Feb. 20, 1864	Jan. 1, 1865	Do.
John M. Mustain	Sergeant	Feb. 3, 1864	May 1, 1864	Do.
Andrew J. Ogden	Corporal	Nov. 19, 1863	May 1, 1864	Mustered out with regiment.
Elbert Greene	do	Feb. 9, 1864	May 1, 1864	Do.
John Doile	Bugler	May 28, 1864	June 30, 1864	Do.
			Muster.	
Arnell, John	Private	Dec. 8, 1863	April 13, 1864	In prison under sentence of G. C. M. since April 26, 1865; no discharge furnished on muster out of regiment.
Barnes, James B	do	Aug. 25, 1864	Feb. 27, 1865	Mustered out with regiment.
Barton, Isaac W	do	Jan. 25, 1864	Feb. 29, 1864	Do.
Barton, Daniel H	do	Dec. 26, 1863	Feb. 29, 1864	Do.
Brinson, Richard C	do	Sept. 1, 1864	Sept. 1, 1864	Do.
Barringer, William A	do	Aug. 26, 1864	Aug. 26, 1864	Do.
Carpenter, John W	do	Dec. 17, 1863	April 13, 1864	Do.
Carlisle, Henry	do	Dec. 3, 1863	April 13, 1864	Do.
Davis, William R	do	May 11, 1864	May 11, 1864	Do.
Ford, C. S	do	Dec. 5, 1863	April 13, 1864	Do.
Gray, James N	do	Jan. 17, 1864	Feb. 29, 1864	Do.
Gestwhite, James	do	May 28, 1864	May 28, 1864	Do.
Hanley, John	do	Feb. 4, 1864	Feb. 29, 1864	Do.
Huddleston, George W	do	May 11, 1864	May 11, 1864	In confinement under sentence of G. C. M. since April 29, 1865; no discharge furnished on muster out of regiment.
Jones, Samuel M	do	Feb. 24, 1864	Feb. 29, 1864	Mustered out with regiment.
Lofton, Samuel	do	Feb. 15, 1864	April 13, 1864	Do.
Morrow, Isaac J	do	Feb. 15, 1864	Feb. 29, 1864	Do.
Mathews, Jasper M	do	Jan. 20, 1864	Feb. 29, 1864	Do.
Miller, James H	do	Mar. 1, 1864	April 13, 1864	Do.
Miller, Andrew P	do	Mar. 1, 1864	April 13, 1864	Do.
McGee, James	do	Mar. 8, 1864	April 15, 1864	Do.
Mustain, Shadrack	do	Mar. 1, 1864	April 13, 1864	Do.
Pruitt, William C	do	Jan. 11, 1864	April 13, 1864	Do.
Redden, Mathew	do	April 9, 1864	April 13, 1864	Do.
Scott, John B	do	Dec. 8, 1863	Feb. 29, 1864	Do.
Smith, John A	do	Mar. 10, 1864	April 13, 1864	Do.
Shelby, James L	do	April 24, 1864	April 13, 1864	Do.
Vaughan, Elisha	do	Feb. 19, 1864	Feb. 29, 1864	Do.
Witt, David	do	Jan. 3, 1864	Feb. 29, 1864	Do.

Mis. Doc. 53——11

162 REPORT OF THE ADJUTANT GENERAL OF ARKANSAS

Fourth regiment Arkansas cavalry volunteers. Mustered into service December 29, 1864, (three years;) mustered out June 30, 1865.

COMPANY K—Continued.

Names.	Rank.	Enlistment.	Muster.	Remarks.
Wolcott, William H	Private	Jan. 9, 1864	Feb. 29, 1864	Mustered out with regiment.
Williamson, Thomas E	do	Feb. 25, 1864	Feb. 29, 1864	Do.
Ware, David L	do	May 11, 1864	May 11, 1864	Do.
Walker, Robert W	do	Nov. 17, 1863	April 13, 1864	Do.
Ware, Phillips	do	April 12, 1864	April 13, 1864	Do.
Missing in action.				
Allen, John	Private	May 11, 1864	May 11, 1864	Missing in action in Montgomery county, Arkansas, July 11, 1864.
Barnett, Newton	do	Feb. 11, 1864	Feb. 29, 1864	Missing in action at Darr Arkansas, May 16, 1864.
Barnett, Silas L	do	Feb. 11, 1864	Feb. 29, 1864	do.
Cravins, Robert B	do	Feb. 11, 1864	Feb. 29, 1864	Do.
Dorris, Celcus J	do	Jan. 27, 1864	Feb. 29, 1864	Do.
McGuire, James P	do	Feb. 11, 1864	Feb. 29, 1864	Do.
Robinson, John H	do	Jan. 27, 1864	Feb. 29, 1864	Do.
Saunders, Isaac	do	Mar. 17, 1864	April 13, 1864	Do.
Williams, Zachariah	do	Mar. 17, 1864	April 13, 1864	Do.
Wathan, William M	do	Jan. 9, 1864	Feb. 29, 1864	Do.
Died.				
Jacob Greene	Corporal	Feb. 9, 1864	Feb. 29, 1864	Died of chronic diarrhœa at Duvall's Bluff, Arkansas, April 28, 1865.
Cline, John W. L	Private	June 9, 1864	June 9, 1864	Died of chronic diarrhœa at Duvall's Bluff, Arkansas, March 19, 1865.
Davis, Jesse	do	May 11, 1864	May 11, 1864	Died of pneumonia at Duvall's Bluff, Arkansas, November 21, 1864.
Martin, John D. H	do	Nov. 19, 1863	Feb. 29, 1864	Died of dysentery at Little Rock, Arkansas, October 1, 1864.
McGuire, Thomas	do	Jan. 16, 1864	April 13, 1864	Died of fever at Little Rock, Arkansas, August 29, 1864.
McCaskill, Alexander	do	May 11, 1864	May 11, 1864	Died of pneumonia at Little Rock, Arkansas, May 14, 1865.
Pitts, Isaac	do	Dec. 5, 1863	April 13, 1864	Died of chronic diarrhœa at Little Rock, Arkansas, November 5, 1864.
Tingle, Shadrack	do	Dec. 8, 1863	Feb. 29, 1864	Died of measles at Little Rock, Arkansas, June 1, 1864.
Deserted.				
John A. Rains	Sergeant	Nov. 10, 1863	Feb. 29, 1864	Deserted near Little Rock, Arkansas, October 7, 1864.
James M. Tyson	do	Jan. 10, 1864	Feb. 29, 1864	Deserted at Duvall's Bluff, Arkansas, January 14, 1864.
James M. Kelly	do	Feb. 25, 1864	Feb. 29, 1864	Deserted at Dardanelle, Arkansas, May 16, 1864.
James Perrymore	Corporal	Feb. 15, 1864	Feb. 29, 1864	do.
Archibald Rowlan	do	Feb. 18, 1864	Feb. 29, 1864	do.
George Gilbert	do	May 11, 1864	May 11, 1864	Deserted near Little Rock, Arkansas, September 28, 1864.
Brown, John H	Private	Dec. 8, 1863	Feb. 29, 1864	Deserted near Little Rock, Arkansas, June 1, 1864.
Byrd, Samuel J	do	Feb. 24, 1864	Feb. 29, 1864	Deserted at Dardanelle, Arkansas, May 16, 1864.
Carter, Morgan	do	Feb. 24, 1864	Feb. 29, 1864	Do.
Cowger, James B	do	Feb. 10, 1864	Feb. 29, 1864	Do.
Collins, William D	do	Feb. 3, 1864	Feb. 29, 1864	Do.

Name	Rank	Muster		Remarks
Cantrell, Alfred	do	Feb.	28, 1864	Feb. 29, 1864	Do.
Dugan, Newton	do	Feb.	15, 1864	Feb. 29, 1864	Do.
Frazier, Thomas H	do	Feb.	5, 1864	Feb. 29, 1864	Do.
Hill, Albert C	do	Jan.	10, 1864	Feb. 29, 1864	Do.
Montgomery, William C	do	Feb.	3, 1864	Feb. 29, 1864	Do.
Moss, James W	do	Mar.	29, 1864	April 13, 1864	Do.
Newton, Isaac H	do	Jan.	30, 1864	Feb. 29, 1864	Do.
Roush, Jonathan H	do	Dec.	11, 1863	Feb. 29, 1864	Deserted at Duvall's Bluff, Arkansas, February 9, 1865.
Smith, Francis R	do	Feb.	19, 1864	Feb. 29, 1864	Deserted at Dardanelle, Arkansas, May 16, 1864.
Smith, Henry W	do	April	7, 1864	April 13, 1864	do.
Sanders, Isaac B	do	May	11, 1864	May 11, 1864	Deserted near Little Rock, Arkansas, September 18, 1864.

Discharged.

Name	Rank	Muster		Remarks
James C. Keys	Sergeant	Dec.	8, 1863	April 13, 1864	Discharged May 18, 1865.
Gallant, James	Private	Mar.	10, 1864	April 13, 1864	Discharged for disability December 15, 1864.
Graham, John W	do	Dec.	11, 1863	Feb. 29, 1864	do.
Grigsby, James M	do	Jan.	15, 1864	Feb. 29, 1864	Discharged for disability March 2, 1865.
Helms, Franklin	do	May	23, 1864	May 28, 1864	Discharged for disability February 11, 1865.
Stow, Robert W	do	Feb.	25, 1864	Feb. 29, 1864	Discharged for disability March 13, 1865.

COMPANY L.

Name	Rank	Muster		Remarks
James S. Clark	Captain		July 25, 1864	Appointed from private company H, 10th Illinois cavalry, to fill original vacancy. Resigned March 9, 1865.
Alexander D. Ross	do		June 2, 1865	Appointed from sergeant company D, 1st Missouri cavalry, October 25, 1864, to 1st lieutenant company L; mustered out with regiment.
Alonzo B. Clymer	1st lieutenant	May 20, 1864	May 20, 1864	Appointed to fill original vacancy; mustered out October 5, 1864.
Benjamin T. Powell	2d lieutenant		Oct. 20, 1864	Appointed from private company D, 5th Illinois cavalry, to fill original vacancy. Resigned May 8, 1865.
William T. Blankenship	1st sergeant	Mar. 24, 1864	Aug. 1, 1864	Mustered out with regiment.
William E. Osborn	Quartermaster sergeant	June 25, 1864	Aug. 1, 1864	Do.
Joseph Burleson	Commissary sergeant	Apr. 18, 1864	Aug. 1, 1864	Absent, sick, Duvall's Bluff, Ark.; no discharge given on muster out of regiment.
Benjamin L. Bridges	Sergeant	June 21, 1864	Aug. 1, 1864	Mustered out with regiment.
John S. Fincher	do	May 2, 1864	Oct. 25, 1864	Do.
William J. Reed	do	June 25, 1864	Oct. 25, 1864	Do.
William F. M. Carpenter	Corporal	June 25, 1864	Oct. 25, 1864	Do.
William J. Blue	do	Sept. 12, 1864	Oct. 25, 1864	Do.
Robert Suit	do	Apr. 8, 1864	Oct. 25, 1864	Do.
James A. Campbell	do	June 21, 1864	Oct. 25, 1864	Do.
Montgomery P. Campbell	do	June 25, 1864	Oct. 25, 1864	Do.
John W. Howard	do	June 21, 1864	Oct. 25, 1864	Do.
Charles Stallcup	Farrier	June 1, 1864	Feb. 10, 1865	Do.
Jesse E. Sanders	Bugler	June 21, 1864	Sept. 1, 1864	Do.

Muster.

Atkinson, William A	Private	June 5, 1864	June 5, 1864	Do.
Brown, Josiah	do	Mar. 24, 1864	May 12, 1864	Do.
Beck, Samuel	do	June 21, 1864	June 21, 1864	Do.

164 REPORT OF THE ADJUTANT GENERAL OF ARKANSAS.

Fourth regiment Arkansas cavalry volunteers. Mustered into service December 29, 1864, (three years;) mustered out June 30, 1865.

COMPANY L—Continued.

Names.	Rank.	Enlistment.	Muster.	Remarks.
Bradbury, William C	Private	May 24, 1864	May 24, 1864	Mustered out with regiment.
Carpenter, Stephen H	do	June 21, 1864	June 21, 1864	Do.
Carpenter, Green	do	June 21, 1864	June 21, 1864	Do.
Cooker, Ethelbert S	do	May 10, 1864	May 12, 1864	Do.
Carter, Joseph C	do	July 13, 1864	July 13, 1864	Do.
Crow, Amos A	do	June 25, 1864	June 25, 1864	Do.
Dorasongh, John T	do	Mar. 24, 1864	May 12, 1864	Do.
Hendrix, Nathan	do	Mar. 24, 1864	May 12, 1864	On detached service in ambulance corps, Little Rock, Arkansas; no discharge given on muster out of regiment.
Henson, James S	do	Mar. 24, 1864	May 12, 1864	Mustered out with regiment.
Hawkins, Albert L	do	June 21, 1864	June 21, 1864	Do.
Horner, Philip	do	June 21, 1864	June 21, 1864	Do.
Hubble, Thomas J	do	Apr. 3, 1864	Apr. 3, 1864	Do.
Horn, James B	do	June 25, 1864	June 25, 1864	Do.
Keen, Joel	do	June 25, 1864	June 25, 1864	Do.
Mordin, Francis M	do	Apr. 30, 1864	May 12, 1864	Absent, sick in general hospital; no discharge given on muster out of regiment.
Miteham, Hezekiah	do	May 31, 1864	May 31, 1864	Mustered out with regiment.
Morgan, Thomas M	do	June 25, 1864	June 25, 1864	Absent, sick in general hospital; no discharge given on muster out of regiment.
Nichols, Louis	do	Apr. 24, 1864	May 12, 1864	Mustered out with regiment.
Nichols, Samuel	do	June 4, 1864	June 4, 1864	Do.
Parker, Thomas F	do	Apr. 28, 1864	May 12, 1864	Do.
Rodgers, Alfred	do	Jan. 20, 1864	May 12, 1864	Do.
Ross, John B	do	May 5, 1864	May 12, 1864	Do.
Richardson, Stephen W	do	May 20, 1864	May 20, 1864	Do.
Rowe, Riley	do	June 21, 1864	June 21, 1864	Do.
Smith, Thomas E	do	Mar. 24, 1864	May 12, 1864	Do.
Suit, Andrew J	do	Apr. 8, 1864	May 12, 1864	Do.
Suggs, Arrick	do	June 2, 1864	June 2, 1864	Absent on detached service in ambulance corps; no discharge given on muster out of regiment.
Small, Joseph W	do	June 2, 1864	June 21, 1864	Mustered out with regiment.
Taylor, Green W	do	Jan. 20, 1864	May 12, 1864	Do.
White, John J	do	Apr. 20, 1864	May 12, 1864	Do.
Wright, Henry L	do	June 21, 1864	June 21, 1864	Do.
Watson, William N	do	June 25, 1864	June 25, 1864	Do.
Widener, John J	do	June 25, 1864	June 25, 1864	Do.
Young, Henry H	do	June 4, 1864	June 4, 1864	Do.
Young, Andrew J	do	June 4, 1864	June 4, 1864	Do.
Yerkey, Henry C	do	June 4, 1864	June 4, 1864	Do.
Watson, Henry	do	June 25, 1864	June 25, 1864	Do.

REPORT OF THE ADJUTANT GENERAL OF ARKANSAS. 165

Died.

Buell, Henry	Private	May 16, 1864	Died in hospital June 25, 1864.
Buell, Samuel	do	May 16, 1864	Died in hospital July 22, 1864.
Bankston, James M	do	May 16, 1864	Died in hospital, of chronic diarrhœa, September 14, 1864.
Diggs, John A	do	June 25, 1864	Died of chronic diarrhœa at Little Rock, Arkansas, September 30, 1864.
Emmons, William	do	May 24, 1864	Died of dysentery September 15, 1864.
Emmons, Jonathan	do	May 24, 1864	Died of intermittent fever at Little Rock, Arkansas, September 1, 1864.
McCain, Andrew J	do	June 1, 1864	Died of chronic diarrhœa at Little Rock, Arkansas, August 18, 1864.
Rodgers, John A	do	Mar. 24, 1864	Died of phthisis pulmonalis at Little Rock, Arkansas, August 13, 1864.
Radden, James A	do	Apr. 18, 1864	Died of chronic diarrhœa at Little Rock, Arkansas, July 22, 1864.
Scott, William	do	May 28, 1864	Died in hospital May 31, 1864.
Walls, John D	do	May 16, 1864	Died of chronic diarrhœa July 16, 1864.
Sterling, Wiley	do	June 21, 1864	Died at Duvall's Bluff, Arkansas, November 22, 1864.
Maybee, James	do	July 15, 1864	Died of chronic diarrhœa December 14, 1864.
Stinnett, David	do	Dec. 27, 1864	Died of phthisic at Little Rock, Arkansas.
Lautrip, Meredith M	do	Mar. 17, 1864	Died of chronic diarrhœa August 15, 1864.
Matlock, George B	do	Jan. 21, 1864	Died of chronic diarrhœa February 22, 1864.
Tweedle, John	do	June 1, 1864	Died of chronic diarrhœa May 18, 1865.
Williams, John	do	Mar. 24, 1864	Died of chronic diarrhœa August 15, 1864.
Hawthorn, Noah	do	June 1, 1864	Died of chronic diarrhœa June 3, 1865.

Discharged.

Brown, Willis	Private	Mar. 24, 1864	Discharged for disability February 12, 1865.
Holcomb, John	do	June 25, 1864	Discharged May 22, 1865.
Lilly, Sampson H	do	July 13, 1864	Discharged June 10, 1865.
Ottwell, William J	do	Apr. 18, 1864	Do.

Deserted.

Amos, Charles L	Private	June 26, 1864	Deserted at Camp Fishback, Arkansas, July 9, 1864.
Ballard, Andrew J	do	Apr. 18, 1864	Deserted at Camp Fishback, Arkansas, August 2, 1864.
D———, Benjamin F	do	May 12, 1864	do.
Maffott, Calvin V	do	Apr. 20, 1864	Deserted at Camp Fishback, Arkansas, August 20, 1864.
S———, James M	do	May 10, 1864	Deserted at Camp Fishback, Arkansas, August 2, 1864.
Sexton, Martin V	do	Apr. 30, 1864	Escaped from guard-house December 10, 1864.

Transferred to 2d Missouri artillery May 29, 1864, per General Order No. 112, headquarters department of Arkansas.

Brown, William D	Private	Feb. 2, 1864	May 12, 1864
Brown, George	do	Feb. 26, 1864	May 12, 1864
Brown, William B	do	Mar. 14, 1864	May 12, 1864
Billingsley, Samuel A	do	Feb. 14, 1864	May 12, 1864
Chambers, Thomas W	do	Mar. 24, 1864	May 12, 1864
Crow, John P	do	Jan. 5, 1864	May 12, 1864
Gullet, Benjamin T	do	Feb. 2, 1864	May 12, 1864
Hawkins, James M	do	Mar. 24, 1864	May 12, 1864
Jack, John A	do	Feb. 20, 1864	May 12, 1864
Parker, John W	do	Jan. 20, 1864	May 12, 1864

Fourth regiment Arkansas cavalry volunteers. Mustered into service December 10, 1864, (three years;) mustered out June 30, 1865.

COMPANY M.

Names.	Rank.	Enlistment.	Date of rank.	Remarks.
Frederick F. Burlock	Captain		Dec. 31, 1864	Promoted from adjutant 33d Iowa infantry; resigned April 11, 1865.
William J. Hunter	do		Jan. 25, 1865	Appointed from sergeant company I, 6th Kansas cavalry, to fill original vacancy of 1st lieutenant company M, 4th Arkansas cavalry; promoted captain June 20, 1865; mustered out with regiment.
John Tennant	2d lieutenant	Oct. 7, 1861	Oct. 18, 1864	Appointed from sergeant co. F, 6th Kansas cavalry; mustered out with regiment.
Thaddeus Blakely	1st sergeant	Nov. 3, 1864	Jan. 3, 1865	Appointed from private; mustered out with regiment.
Wm. S. Meadows	Commissary sergeant	Aug. 1, 1864	Jan. 3, 1865	Do.
Zephaniah Roberts	Quartermaster sergeant	Mar. 17, 1864	Jan. 3, 1865	Do.
John P. Chappell	Sergeant	April 1, 1864	Jan. 3, 1865	Do.
Samuel Hardesty	do	Feb. 20, 1864	Jan. 3, 1865	Do.
John C. Gaynor	do	Mar. 28, 1864	Jan. 3, 1865	Do.
Stephen Wilson	Corporal	Feb. 25, 1864	Jan. 3, 1865	Do.
Thornsberry Davis	do	Feb. 22, 1864	Jan. 3, 1865	Do.
Joseph Smith	do	April 1, 1864	Jan. 3, 1865	Do.
Calvin C. Morris	do	Nov. 1, 1864	Jan. 3, 1865	Do.
John C. Gillham	do	Feb. 19, 1864	Jan. 3, 1865	Do.
William Davis	do	Feb. 28, 1864	Jan. 3, 1865	Do.
William Tyra	Bugler	July 25, 1864	July 25, 1864	Do.
			Muster.	
Boyd, William	Private	Mar. 7, 1864	Mar. 7, 1864	Mustered out with regiment.
Byrum, Jasper P	do	May 23, 1864	May 23, 1864	Do.
Brewer, Henry H	do	Sept. 7, 1864	Sept. 7, 1864	Do.
Brisco, William R	do	Feb. 20, 1864	Feb. 20, 1864	Do.
Balyen, Jacob	do	May 30, 1864	May 30, 1864	Do.
Caffield, David W	do	Mar. 5, 1864	Mar. 5, 1864	Do.
Emerson, James	do	Feb. 23, 1864	Feb. 23, 1864	Do.
Echols, Augustus	do	Dec. 25, 1863	Dec. 25, 1863	Do.
Goodwin, John F	do	Dec. 25, 1863	Dec. 25, 1863	Do.
Griffin, Lewis L	do	Nov. 12, 1864	Nov. 12, 1864	Do.
Grangeene, Oliver	do	May 13, 1864	May 13, 1864	Do.
Goff, William R	do	Mar. 16, 1864	Mar. 16, 1864	Do.
Graham, Philip	do	April 1, 1864	April 1, 1864	Do.
Jack, Daniel	do	April 13, 1864	April 13, 1864	Do.
Kelly, Marion	do	July 31, 1864	July 31, 1864	Do.
Looper, Isaac D	do	April 1, 1864	April 1, 1864	Do.
Matlock, James P	do	Mar. 25, 1864	Mar. 25, 1864	Do.
Mahaney, Paul	do	Mar. 2, 1864	Mar. 2, 1864	Do.
Morris, John W. B	do	June 25, 1864	June 25, 1864	Do.
Moss, Francis M	do	June 10, 1864	June 10, 1864	Do.
Nobles, William	do	Nov. 2, 1864	Nov. 2, 1864	Do.
Pawley, Daniel B	do	Sept. 26, 1864	Sept. 26, 1864	Do.
Pawley, William L	do	Sept. 18, 1861	Sept. 18, 1864	Do.

REPORT OF THE ADJUTANT GENERAL OF ARKANSAS. 167

Payne, William P	do		April 14, 1864	Do.
Richardson, Balsam	do		Mar. 7, 1864	In confinement under sentence of G. C. M., from June 9, 1865; no discharge given on muster out of regiment.
Southworth, Peter H	do		Sept. 23, 1864	Mustered out with regiment.
Trout, William G. W	do		Aug. 1, 1864	Do.
Tweedle, William A	do		Sept. 12, 1864	Do.
Winchester, James	do		July 26, 1864	Do.
Waddle, Mark	do		Mar. 29, 1864	Do.
Waddle, Abraham	do		Feb. 5, 1864	Do.
Whisenhunt, Mathews	do		Sept. 26, 1864	Do.
Williams, Leatris	do		July 26, 1864	Do.
Waggoner, Andrew J	do		Dec. 9, 1864	Do.
Died.				
Alexander, Jeremiah	Private		Jan. 25, 1864	Died at Little Rock, Arkansas, August 6, 1864.
Blair, James C	do		Sept. 1, 1864	Died at Duvall's Bluff, Arkansas, January 28, 1865.
Cellars, John W	do		Feb. 20, 1864	Died at Little Rock, Arkansas, June 7, 1865.
Hartley, Jesse H	do		Mar. 8, 1864	Died at Little Rock, Arkansas, August 26, 1864.
Housewright, Wesley	do		April 6, 1864	Died at Duvall's Bluff, Arkansas, March 26, 1865.
Harmon, Lafayette	do		Sept. 20, 1864	Died at Duvall's Bluff, Arkansas, March 11, 1865.
Harris, Columbus L	do		Oct. 3, 1864	Died at Duvall's Bluff, Arkansas, August 26, 1865.
Kirkham, Hiram L	do		Nov. 12, 1864	Died at Duvall's Bluff, Arkansas, May 1, 1865.
Martin, Jonathan J	do		April 1, 1864	Died at Duvall's Bluff, Arkansas, December 12, 1864.
McElroy, Gilmore K. D	Sergeant		Aug. 1, 1864	Died at Little Rock, Arkansas, May 20, 1865.
Phillips, Thomas	Private		April 1, 1864	Died at Little Rock, Arkansas, December 23, 1864.
Smith, John	do		Mar. 4, 1864	Died at Little Rock, Arkansas, October 29, 1864.
Simpson, Austin	do		Aug. 1, 1864	Died at Duvall's Bluff, Arkansas, April 18, 1865.
Winchester, David	do		July 26, 1864	Died at Duvall's Bluff, Arkansas, November 13, 1864.
Discharged.				
Bevans, Jason W	Private		April 1, 1864	Discharged May 22, 1865.
Breeding, Peter C	do		Sept. 1, 1864	Discharged for disability March 2, 1865.
Call, Jacob	do		Mar. 16, 1864	Discharged May 22, 1865.
Emerson, Green	do		Feb. 23, 1864	Discharged May 27, 1865.
Emerson, Henry	do		Feb. 23, 1864	Discharged for disability March 2, 1865.
Lovell, Daniel	do		April 22, 1864	Do.
Partin, Holaway	do		Feb. 21, 1864	Discharged for disability February 3, 1865.
Smith, John	do		Mar. 29, 1864	Discharged May 22, 1865.
Whitlock, John D	do		April 1, 1864	
Deserted.				
Grimes, James P	Private		April 1, 1864	Deserted at Little Rock, Arkansas, August 28, 1864.
Howard, Allen W	do		Aug. 1, 1864	Deserted at Little Rock, Arkansas, October 25, 1864.
Kirkham, James F	do		Aug. 1, 1864	Do.
Reed, Andrew J	do		Aug. 1, 1864	Do.
Sisemore, Harmon	do		Feb. 28, 1864	Deserted at Little Rock, Arkansas, August 28, 1864.
Smith, Jesse	do		June 16, 1864	Deserted at Little Rock, Arkansas, May 17, 1865.
White, Leonard H	do		Mar. 28, 1864	Deserted at Little Rock, Arkansas, August 28, 1864.
Williams, John N	do		Feb. 19, 1864	Do.
Transferred.				
Jeffers, John	1st sergeant		Feb. 28, 1864	Transferred to non-commissioned staff, as hospital steward, March 8, 1865.

FOURTH ARKANSAS CAVALRY VOLUNTEERS.—HISTORICAL MEMORANDA.

The raising of the 4th regiment Arkansas cavalry volunteers was begun in November, 1863, and completed on the muster in of Lafayette Gregg as colonel, December 29, 1864. Meantime companies of the regiment, as rapidly as organized, were placed on active duty and experienced the usual vicissitudes of the service.

The following communication, received shortly before the muster out of the regiment, (June 30, 1865,) gives an account of its organization and services:

HEADQUARTERS FOURTH REGIMENT ARKANSAS CAVALRY,
Little Rock, Arkansas, June 8, 1865.

SIR: In reply to your communication of to-day requesting a history of this regiment I have the honor to state: The organization of the regiment was commenced under the direction of William M. Fishback in the month of November, 1863. The first battalion was mustered in for one year or during the war, but the muster was declared invalid by the Adjutant General of the army, and in the month of December that battalion was disbanded, and the regiment commenced reorganizing as a three years' organization. The regiment filled up quite rapidly until the disastrous expedition of General Steele in the month of March, 1864, which discouraged enlistments, and the organization of the regiment was not completed till December 29, 1864.

The following is a statement of the completion of the organization of each company: "A" company was organized by Captain Joel Brown on the 12th day of December, 1863, at Little Rock, Arkansas; "B" company by Captain James R. Lafferry on the 9th day of January, 1864, at Little Rock, Arkansas; "C" company by Captain Henry Wood on the 28th day of January, 1864, at Little Rock, Arkansas; "D" company by Captain George H. Hand, on the 5th day of March, 1864, at Little Rock, Arkansas; "E" company by Captain George W. Smith, on the 29th day of March, 1864, at Little Rock, Arkansas; "F" company by Captain William H. Warner, on the 7th day of April, 1864, at Little Rock, Arkansas; "G" company by Captain William J. Green, on the 29th day of April, 1864, at Little Rock, Arkansas; "H" company by Captain John F. Sanders, on the 7th day of May, 1864, at Little Rock, Arkansas; "I" company by Captain Emory E. Knowlton, on the 16th day of October, 1864, at Little Rock, Arkansas; "K" company by Captain Joseph Bennett, on the 18th day of June, 1864, at Little Rock, Arkansas; "L" company by Captain James S. Clark, on the 15th day of July, 1864, at Little Rock, Arkansas; "M" company by Captain Frederick F. Burlock, on the 31st day of December, 1864, at Little Rock, Arkansas.

Although the regiment, as such, has never been in any general engagements, detachments of it have been in several skirmishes and fights. A portion of company G was in a fight at Mount Elba, Arkansas, on the 30th day of March, 1864. Companies A, B, C, E, and K were in a fight at Dardanelle, Arkansas, when that place was attacked by the rebel General Shelby's command, on the 16th day of May, 1864. The regiment also had a severe skirmish with the enemy on Saline river, Arkansas, on the 16th day of July, 1864, in which the brave Captain Hugh Quin was killed.

Portions of the regiment have also been in several other skirmishes at different times, and a large number of bushwhackers have at various times been captured by it.

I am, very respectfully, your obedient servant,

HORACE L. MOORE,
Lieutenant Colonel Commanding Regiment.

A. W. BISHOP, *Adjutant General, State of Arkansas.*

The regiment was mustered out at Little Rock, Arkansas, on the 30th day of June, 1865.

REPORT OF THE ADJUTANT GENERAL OF ARKANSAS.

First regiment Arkansas infantry volunteers. Mustered into service March 25, 1863, (three years;) mustered out August 10, 1865.

FIELD AND STAFF.

Names.	Rank.	Enlistment.	Date of rank.	Remarks.
James M. Johnson	Colonel	Mar. 25, 1863	Mar. 25, 1863	Entered service of the United States as volunteer aide to General Curtis, April 15, 1862; mustered out with regiment.
Elhanon J. Searle	Lieutenant colonel	—, 1861	Feb. 27, 1863	Promoted from captain company M, 10th Illinois cavalry; mustered out with regiment.
Elijah D. Ham	Major	Mar. 10, 1863	Mar. 10, 1863	Entered the United States service as a volunteer aide to General Curtis, March —, 1862; resigned March 22, 1864.
Francis M. Johnson	do	Feb. 9, 1863	June 9, 1864	Entered the United States service as a scout, April 15, 1862; promoted from 1st lieutenant company B; mustered out with regiment.
William B. Waterman	Surgeon	May 12, 1863	Dec. 9, 1863	Appointed from civil life; mustered out with regiment.
Thomas B. Drake	Assistant surgeon	Mar. 25, 1863	Mar. 25, 1863	Appointed from 1st Iowa cavalry; discharged May 18, 1863.
Harvey H. Bolinger	do	Feb. 1, 1863	Mar. 25, 1863	Appointed from civil life; resigned April 10, 1864.
Robert B. Campfield	do	June 10, 1864	June 10, 1864	Appointed from private company I, 18th Iowa infantry; mustered out with regiment.
Francis Springer	Chaplain	—, 1861	April 11, 1863	Appointed from civil life; entered service as chaplain 10th Illinois cavalry; discharged to accept post chaplaincy at Fort Smith, Arkansas.
John M. Leard	do	May 24, 1864	June 10, 1864	Appointed from private company F, 12th Kansas infantry; mustered out with regiment.
Francis M. Sams	Adjutant	Mar. 10, 1863	Mar. 25, 1863	Appointed from civil life; resigned March 19, 1864.
William Patterson	do		April 20, 1864	Appointed from private company F, 2d Colorado cavalry; mustered out with regiment.
Crittenden C. Wells	Regimental quartermaster	June 23, 1862	Mar. 25, 1863	Promoted from 2d lieutenant company B, 1st Arkansas cavalry; dismissed July 31, 1863.
Jonathan H. Hewes	do	Aug. 1, 1863	Aug. 1, 1863	Appointed from civil life; mustered out with regiment.

NON-COMMISSIONED STAFF.

Names.	Rank.	Enlistment.	Date of rank.	Remarks.
Josiah S. Turney	Sergeant major	Mar. 20, 1863	Mar. 1, 1864	Appointed from sergeant company K; mustered out with regiment.
William Banksum	do	Feb. 18, 1863	Mar. 25, 1863	Was sergeant major from organization; reduced July 1, 1863; transferred to company D.
Maxwell C. McBroom	do	Jan. 29, 1863	Feb. 23, 1863	Appointed sergeant major July 1, 1863; reduced to the ranks and assigned to duty in company B, June 30, 1864; killed in Madison county, Arkansas, August 15, 1864.
Patrick H. Oliver	Commissary sergeant	June 20, 1863	Aug. 1, 1864	Appointed from private company K; mustered out with regiment.
Thomas Goad	do	Jan. 31, 1863	Feb. 23, 1863	Commissary sergeant from organization; reduced and transferred to company B, July 31, 1864.
Joseph A. Brown	Quartermaster sergeant	May 20, 1863	Aug. 1, 1864	Appointed from private company K; mustered out with regiment.

First regiment Arkansas infantry volunteers. Mustered into service March 25, 1863, (three years;) mustered out August 10, 1865.

NON-COMMISSIONED STAFF—Continued.

Names.	Rank.	Enlistment.	Date of rank.	Remarks.
Henry Sears	Quartermaster sergeant		Aug. 1, 1863	Appointed from sergeant company F; reduced and assigned to duty as private in company F, July 31, 1864.
Daniel V. Dow	Hospital steward	Mar. 1, 1863	July 1, 1863	Appointed from private company E; mustered out with regiment.
Leroy M. Kindrick	Principal musician	Feb. 14, 1863	Aug. 1, 1864	Appointed from corporal company A; mustered out with regiment.
Henry F. Edmondson	......do......	Mar. 1, 1863	May 1, 1865	Appointed from 1st sergeant company E; transferred for promotion to company F, October 31, 1863.
Thomas Bates	......do......	Feb. 14, 1863	Nov. 1, 1863	Appointed from private company A; reduced and assigned to duty as private in company A, July 31, 1864.
James Ledbetter	Fife major	Feb. 15, 1863	July 1, 1863	Appointed from private company G; mustered out with regiment.

COMPANY A.

Names.	Rank.	Enlistment.	Date of rank.	Remarks.
Randall Smith	Captain	......, 1861	Feb. 14, 1863	Appointed from 37th Illinois infantry; dismissed March 10, 1865.
Daniel E. Sutcliffe	......do......	Feb. ......, 1863	June 23, 1865	Promoted from 1st lieutenant of company E, vice Smith, dismissed; mustered out with regiment.
Samuel Bard	1st lieutenant	Feb. 14, 1863	Feb. 14, 1863	Appointed from civil life to fill original vacancy; promoted to captain of company I August 22, 1864.
Winphrey W. Robinson	......do......	Feb. 15, 1863	June 22, 1865	Appointed from sergeant of company G, vice Bard, promoted; mustered out with regiment.
Clarence R. Smith	2d lieutenant	Feb. 14, 1863	Feb. 14, 1863	2d lieutenant from organization; dismissed January 1, 1865.
John M. Robinson	......do......	April 20, 1863	June 23, 1865	Appointed from 1st sergeant of company C, vice Smith, dismissed; mustered out with regiment.
George T. Waldron	1st sergeant	Sept. 1, 1863	June 1, 1864	Appointed from corporal to sergeant October 7, 1862; mustered out with regiment.
William C. Reeves	Sergeant	Feb. 14, 1863	Mar. 20, 1863	Appointed from corporal; mustered out with regiment.
Gilson N. Stephens	......do......	Feb. 14, 1863	April 30, 1863	Do.
George W. Gillcoat	......do......	Feb. 14, 1863	June 24, 1863	do.
John J. Hutchinson	Corporal	Feb. 14, 1863	Sept. 1, 1863	Mustered out with regiment.
William H. Mayo	......do......	Feb. 14, 1863	July 1, 1863	Do.
Shepherd H. Blackburn	......do......	Feb. 14, 1863	Sept. 1, 1863	Do.
James Vaught	......do......	Sept. 1, 1863	Sept. 1, 1863	Do.
Thomas Burgoon	......do......	Feb. 14, 1863	June 1, 1864	Do.
Andrew J. Williams	......do......	Sept. 1, 1863	June 24, 1865	Do.
			Muster.	
Ashworth, Andrew	Private	Feb. 14, 1863	Feb. 14, 1863	Do.
Anderson, Thomas	......do......	Sept. 1, 1863	Feb. 26, 1864	Do.
Burgoon, John	......do......	Feb. 14, 1863	Feb. 14, 1863	Do.
Boren, Robert C	......do......	Feb. 14, 1863	Feb. 14, 1863	Do.

REPORT OF THE ADJUTANT GENERAL OF ARKANSAS. 171

Name		Date enlisted	Date mustered	
Bledsoe, Hezekiah		Feb. 14, 1863	Feb. 14, 1863	Do.
Bledsoe, George W	do	Feb. 14, 1863	Feb. 14, 1863	Do.
Burkett, William	do	Feb. 14, 1863	Feb. 14, 1863	Do.
Blankenship, Jacob	do	Feb. 14, 1863	Feb. 14, 1863	Do.
Bates, Thomas J	do	Feb. 14, 1863	Feb. 14, 1863	Do.
Bates, John C	do	Feb. 14, 1863	Feb. 14, 1863	Do.
Bates, Robert E	do	Sept. 1, 1863	Sept. 1, 1864	Do.
Bailey, William C	do	Feb. 24, 1864	Feb. 26, 1864	Do.
Bynum, Luke C	do	Sept. 1, 1863	Feb. 26, 1864	Do.
Bowen, Darwin H	do	Sept. 1, 1863	Feb. 26, 1864	Do.
Capps, William	do	Feb. 14, 1863	Feb. 14, 1863	Do.
Collins, James	do	Feb. 14, 1863	Feb. 14, 1863	Do.
Coburn, James L	do	Sept. 1, 1863	Feb. 26, 1864	Do.
Campbell, Thomas J	do	Sept. 1, 1863	Feb. 26, 1864	Do.
Campbell, George M	do	Sept. 1, 1863	Feb. 26, 1864	Do.
Cornelius, William	do	Sept. 1, 1863	Feb. 26, 1864	Do.
Cartwright, Joseph	do	Feb. 14, 1863	Feb. 14, 1863	Do.
Carroll, John	do	Feb. 14, 1863	Feb. 14, 1863	Do.
Chapman, Daniel	do	Feb. 14, 1863	Feb. 14, 1863	Do.
Evans, Joseph	do	Feb. 14, 1863	Feb. 14, 1863	Do.
Gibson, David	do	Feb. 14, 1863	Feb. 14, 1863	Do.
Graham, Wilson	do	Feb. 14, 1863	Feb. 14, 1863	Do.
Graham, Peter	do	July 1, 1863	Aug. 12, 1863	Do.
Goddard, Jesse	do	Feb. 14, 1863	Feb. 14, 1863	Do.
Gregg, Benson W	do	Feb. 14, 1863	Feb. 14, 1863	Do.
Hill, John W	do	Feb. 14, 1863	Feb. 14, 1863	Do.
Hill, Richard H	do	Feb. 14, 1863	July 16, 1863	Do.
Hill, Wiley H	do	Feb. 14, 1863	Feb. 14, 1863	Do.
Happy, James H	do	Feb. 14, 1863	Feb. 14, 1863	Do.
Hopper, William J	do	Feb. 14, 1863	Feb. 14, 1863	Do.
Haddox, John J	do	Sept. 1, 1863	Feb. 26, 1864	Do.
Killingsworth, Archibald	do	Aug. 1, 1863	Mar. 1, 1865	Do.
Lewellen, Jacob	do	Feb. 14, 1863	Feb. 14, 1863	Do.
Lallis, Richard	do	Sept. 1, 1863	Feb. 26, 1864	Do.
Luper, Gilbert C	do	Feb. 14, 1863	Feb. 14, 1863	Do.
McGuirk, Lewis	do	Sept. 1, 1863	Feb. 26, 1864	Do.
McCoy, George	do	Sept. 1, 1863	Feb. 26, 1864	Do.
Martin, Henry	do	Feb. 14, 1863	Feb. 14, 1863	Do.
Martin, Caleb	do	Feb. 14, 1863	Feb. 14, 1863	Do.
Mayo, John W	do	Feb. 14, 1863	Feb. 14, 1863	Do.
Monds, Lorenzo	do	Feb. 14, 1863	Feb. 14, 1863	Do.
Neal, Elias	do	Dec. 1, 1863	Feb. 26, 1864	Do.
Phelan, William	do	Feb. 14, 1863	Feb. 14, 1863	Do.
Queen, Thomas	do	Feb. 24, 1863	Feb. 26, 1864	Do.
Russell, William	do	Feb. 14, 1863	Feb. 14, 1863	Do.
Russell, John	do	Feb. 14, 1863	Feb. 14, 1863	Do.
Ritter, Daniel	do	Feb. 14, 1863	Feb. 14, 1863	Do.
Reed, William J	do	Sept. 1, 1863	Mar. 1, 1865	Do.
Smith, Bluford A	do	Feb. 14, 1863	Feb. 14, 1863	Do.
Slater, Milo	do	Feb. 14, 1863	Feb. 14, 1863	Do.
Sensebough, Christian	do	Feb. 14, 1863	Feb. 14, 1863	Do.
Simmons, William	do	Feb. 14, 1863	Feb. 14, 1863	Do.

172   REPORT OF THE ADJUTANT GENERAL OF ARKANSAS

First regiment Arkansas infantry volunteers. Mustered into service March 25, 1863, (three years;) mustered out August 10, 1865.

COMPANY A—Continued.

Names.	Rank.	Enlistment.	Muster.	Remarks.
Sawyers, Archibald	Private	Dec. 7, 1863	Feb. 26, 1864	Mustered out with regiment.
Shrader, James	do	Sept. 1, 1863	Feb. 26, 1864	Do.
Taylor, William	do	Feb. 24, 1864	Feb. 26, 1864	Do.
Taylor, Francis M	do	Feb. 24, 1864	Feb. 26, 1864	Do.
Terry, Ansel D	do	Feb. 14, 1863	Feb. 14, 1863	Do.
Wells, Washington A	do	Feb. 14, 1863	Feb. 14, 1863	Do.
Wilsie, Micher	do	Feb. 14, 1863	Feb. 14, 1863	Do.
Wilsie, Jasper	do	Feb. 14, 1863	Feb. 14, 1863	Do.
Wolf, William	do	Feb. 14, 1863	Feb. 14, 1863	Do.
Young, John	do	Feb. 14, 1863	Feb. 14, 1863	Do.
Young, Anderson	do	Feb. 14, 1863	Feb. 14, 1863	Do.
Killed.				
Stow, George, (negro)	Cook	Jan. 1, 1864	Feb. 26, 1864	Killed.
Discharged.				
Bledsoe, William	Private	Feb. 14, 1863	Feb. 14, 1863	Discharged June 25, 1865.
Gillcoat, John	Corporal	Feb. 14, 1863	Feb. 14, 1863	Discharged for disability March 1, 1865.
Marrs, Samuel P	Private	Feb. 14, 1863	Feb. 14, 1863	Discharged June 24, 1865.
Musgraves, Andrew	do	Feb. 14, 1863	Feb. 14, 1863	Discharged to accept civil office (member of legislature) July 1, 1865.
Miller, Oliver P	do	Feb. 14, 1863	Feb. 14, 1863	Discharged June 16, 1865.
Neil, Thomas	do	Feb. 14, 1863	Feb. 14, 1863	Discharged from hospital March 1, 1865.
Phelan, Josiah R	do	Feb. 14, 1863	Feb. 14, 1863	do.
Petty, John	do	Feb. 14, 1863	Feb. 14, 1863	Discharged June 16, 1865.
Richardson, Joseph	do	Feb. 14, 1863	Feb. 14, 1863	Discharged from hospital February 22, 1864.
Sawyers, Henry A	Sergeant	Feb. 14, 1863	Feb. 14, 1863	Discharged for disability July 10, 1865.
Transferred.				
Le Roy M. Kendrick	Private	Feb. 14, 1863	Feb. 14, 1863	Appointed from corporal to principal musician August 1, 1864.
Died.				
Boren, John	Private	Feb. 14, 1863	Feb. 14, 1863	Died of pneumonia at Waldron, Arkansas, February 8, 1864.
Cox, Albert	do	Feb. 14, 1863	Feb. 14, 1863	Died of fever near Fayetteville, Arkansas, April 26, 1863.
Cockrell, Shadrack	do	Feb. 14, 1863	Feb. 14, 1863	Died of wounds received in battle, at Fayetteville, Arkansas, April 18, 1863.
Copeland, Martin	do	Feb. 26, 1863	Feb. 26, 1863	Died of fever at Fort Smith, Arkansas, September 2, 1864.
Counts, William	do	Feb. 14, 1863	Feb. 14, 1863	Died of pneumonia at Fayetteville, Arkansas, March 7, 1863.
England, William C	do	Feb. 14, 1863	Feb. 14, 1863	Died of wounds received from enemy, June 1, 1863.
Graham, Elihu	do	Dec. 1, 1863	Feb. 26, 1864	Died in hands of enemy at Camden, Arkansas, July 9, 1864.
Gibson, Joseph D	1st sergeant	Feb. 14, 1863	Feb. 14, 1863	Died of pneumonia at Fort Smith, Arkansas, June 4, 1865.

REPORT OF THE ADJUTANT GENERAL OF ARKANSAS.   173

Name	Rank	Date of enlistment	Remarks
Gregg, Wesley F	Private	April 1, 1864	Died of pneumonia at Fort Smith, Arkansas, May 14, 1865.
Lavin, William	do	Feb. 14, 1863	Died of fever at Springfield, Missouri, June 30, 1863.
Moore, Evan	do	Feb. 14, 1863	Died of fever at Fayetteville, Arkansas, April 2, 1863.
Rogers, John	Sergeant	Feb. 14, 1863	Died of fever at Fort Smith, Arkansas, September 11, 1863.
Russell, William H	do	Feb. 14, 1863	Died of fever at Fayetteville, Arkansas, April 16, 1863.
Snowden, Joseph	Private	July 16, 1863	Died of fever at Waldron, Arkansas, December 6, 1863.
Sawyers, Jeptha	do	Aug. 12, 1863	Died of wounds received from enemy, August 1, 1864.
Tackley, James	do	Feb. 14, 1863	Died of wounds received in battle, April 21, 1863.
White, Thomas M	do	Feb. 14, 1863	Died of fever at Springfield, Missouri, June 20, 1863.
Woods, Charles	1st sergeant	Feb. 14, 1863	Died of fever at Fayetteville, Arkansas, March 15, 1863.

Deserted.

Name	Rank	Date of enlistment	Remarks
Cummings, William	Private	Feb. 24, 1864	Deserted at Jenny Lind, Arkansas, July 30, 1864.
Cannon, Francis M	do	Feb. 14, 1863	Deserted at Fayetteville, Arkansas, April 4, 1863.
Graham, Alexander	do	Feb. 14, 1863	Deserted at Fayetteville, Arkansas, April 17, 1863.
Howell, James H	do	Feb. 14, 1863	Deserted at Fayetteville, Arkansas, April 5, 1863.
Henrett, Francis E	do	Feb. 14, 1863	Deserted at Fayetteville, Arkansas, April 1, 1863.
Miles, Levi	do	Feb. 14, 1863	Deserted at Fayetteville, Arkansas, April 17, 1863.
Perdue, John	do	Sept. 19, 1863	Deserted at Fort Smith, Arkansas, June 30, 1864.
Savin, William H	do	Feb. 14, 1863	Deserted at Fayetteville, Arkansas, April 20, 1863.
Sumner, Mathew M	Sergeant	Feb. 14, 1863	Deserted at Fayetteville, Arkansas, April 10, 1863.
Stewart, Albert	Private	Sept. 1, 1863	Deserted at Van Buren, Arkansas, July 11, 1864.

COMPANY B.

Name	Rank	Date of rank	Remarks
Elitle Haynes	Captain	Feb. 23, 1863	Appointed from civil life; resigned December 15, 1863.
Thomas H. Scott	do	July 24, 1862	Appointed from commissary sergeant 1st Arkansas cavalry; 2d lieutenant, February 23, 1863; mustered out with regiment.
Francis M. Johnson	1st lieutenant	Feb. 9, 1863	1st lieutenant from organization of company; promoted major June 9, 1864, vice E. D. Ham, resigned.
Felix G. Eubanks	do	Mar. —, 1863	1st sergeant from organization of company; appointed 1st lieutenant, vice Johnson, promoted; mustered out with regiment.
Albert K. Berry	2d lieutenant	June 22, 1865	Appointed from private, vice Scott, promoted; mustered out with regiment.
John Upton	1st sergeant	June 4, 1863	Appointed from sergeant; mustered out with regiment.
Samuel M. Haynes	Sergeant	Jan. 29, 1863	Sergeant from organization of company; mustered out with regiment.
Nathan H. Cox	do	Feb. 23, 1863	Do.
William J. Seaman	do	Feb. 21, 1863	Do.
Robert B. Carter	do	Jan. 29, 1863	Do.
Michael Hoppers	Corporal	Feb. 23, 1863	Appointed from corporal; mustered out with regiment.
Isaiah T. Upton	do	Feb. 4, 1863	Mustered out with regiment.
Sinclair Cox	do	Feb. 23, 1863	Do.
John W. Brown	do	Nov. 20, 1863	Do.
William R. King	do	Sept. 1, 1863	Do.
Harlin Keeling	do	Feb. 23, 1863	Do.
John W. Banks	do	Feb. 4, 1863	Do.
Burrell Ledbetter	do	Feb. 2, 1863	Do.

First regiment Arkansas infantry volunteers. Mustered into service March 25, 1863, (three years;) mustered out August 10, 1865.

COMPANY B—Continued.

Names.	Rank.	Enlistment.	Muster.	Remarks.
Bolinger, Jasper	Private	Jan. 28, 1863	Feb. 23, 1863	Mustered out with regiment.
Beasley, James	do	Feb. 18, 1863	Feb. 23, 1863	Do.
Beasley, Thomas	do	Feb. 18, 1863	Feb. 23, 1863	Do.
Beasley, Josiah	do	Sept. 1, 1863	Feb. 26, 1864	Do.
Brien, George W	do	Feb. 21, 1863	Feb. 23, 1863	Do.
Boyd, John	do	Feb. 21, 1863	Feb. 23, 1863	Do.
Boyd sr., Robert	do	Feb. 21, 1863	Feb. 23, 1863	Do.
Boyd, jr., Robert	do	Oct. 1, 1863	Feb. 26, 1864	Do.
Bolinger, Isaac N	do	Feb. 23, 1863	Feb. 28, 1863	Do.
Brunk, Thomas J	do	Sept. 1, 1863	Feb. 26, 1864	Do.
Bradley, William	do	Sept. 1, 1863	Feb. 26, 1864	Do.
Burgess, Perry A	do	Dec. 1, 1863	Feb. 26, 1864	Do.
Bearkley, Right	do	Sept. 1, 1864		Do.
Casey, Henson	do	Jan. 29, 1863	Feb. 23, 1863	Do.
Cox, Joshua	do	Feb. 23, 1863	Feb. 23, 1863	Do.
Coleman, Enos	do	Feb. 23, 1863	Feb. 23, 1863	Do.
Clark, Hiram	do	Mar. 31, 1865	April 30, 1865	Do.
Dotson, Samuel F	do	Feb. 2, 1863	Feb. 28, 1863	Do.
Dotson, Noah B	do	Mar. 1, 1863	Aug. 12, 1863	Do.
Dotson, William S	do	Mar. 1, 1863	Aug. 12, 1863	Do.
Dansey, Alexander	do	Feb. 21, 1863	Feb. 23, 1863	Do.
Downey, John D	do	Feb. 1, 1864	Feb. 28, 1864	Do.
Dennis, George W	do	Oct. 1, 1864	Feb. 28, 1865	Do.
Dennis, Mathew	do	Mar. 1, 1863	Mar. 10, 1863	Do.
Forrester, William B	do	Jan. 29, 1863	Feb. 23, 1863	Do.
Forester, James	do	Feb. 4, 1863	Feb. 23, 1863	Do.
Goad, Thomas	do	Jan. 26, 1863	Feb. 23, 1863	Do.
Horton, Rundy	do	Feb. 2, 1863	Feb. 23, 1863	Do.
Horton, William D	do	April 1, 1863	Aug. 12, 1863	Do.
Herrimon, Joseph	do	Feb. 25, 1863	Feb. 25, 1863	Do.
Herrimon, Miles	do	Feb. 1, 1865	Feb. 12, 1863	Do.
Hague, Louis	do	Mar. 1, 1863	Aug. 12, 1863	Do.
Hague, William	do	Feb. 2, 1863	Feb. 23, 1863	Do.
Hopper, Samuel J	do	Feb. 23, 1863	Feb. 23, 1863	Do.
Herrimon, Samuel	do	Feb. 1, 1865	April 15, 1865	Do.
Ingram, Thomas	do	Feb. 1, 1865	April 15, 1865	Do.
Joyce, William	do	Jan. 31, 1863	Feb. 23, 1863	Do.
Johnson, Pleasant	do	Feb. 23, 1863	Feb. 27, 1863	Do.
Johnson, James C	do	Jan. 1, 1865	Feb. 20, 1865	Do.
Johnson, Calvin	do	Feb. 1, 1865	Feb. 28, 1865	Do.
Jones, William H	do	Feb. 27, 1865	Feb. 28, 1864	Do.
Lovett, Alfred	do	Sept. 1, 1863	Feb. 26, 1864	Do.
Lee, Robert	do	Feb. 1, 1865	April 15, 1865	Do.

REPORT OF THE ADJUTANT GENERAL OF ARKANSAS 175

Name	Rank	Date	Date	Remarks
Leadbetter, George		Feb. 1, 1865	April 15, 1865	Do.
Mabry, Jacob	do	Jan. 29, 1863	Feb. 23, 1863	Do.
McCoy, James	do	Feb. 21, 1863	Feb. 23, 1863	Do.
McCoy, Jasper	do	Feb. 24, 1864	Feb. 23, 1863	Do.
McElhaney, Henry J	do	Feb. 4, 1863	Feb. 23, 1863	Do.
McGarroch, Mathew	do	Feb. 4, 1863	Feb. 23, 1863	Do.
Mitchell, Shadrack J	do	Mar. 1, 1865	April 15, 1865	Do.
Nevels, John	do	Sept. 1, 1863	Feb. 26, 1864	Do.
Phillips, Reuben	do	Feb. 21, 1863	Feb. 25, 1863	Do.
Phillips, John	do	Mar. 1, 1863	Aug. 12, 1863	Do.
Powell, James	do	Oct. 1, 1863	Feb. 26, 1864	Do.
Reeves, Morgan G	do	Jan. 29, 1863	Feb. 23, 1863	Do.
Reeves, Francis M	do	Jan. 29, 1863	Feb. 23, 1863	Do.
Ray, John W	do	Feb. 12, 1863	Feb. 23, 1863	Do.
Robinson, John H	do	Oct. 1, 1863	Feb. 26, 1864	Do.
Robinson, George W	do	Feb. 1, 1865	Feb. 23, 1865	Do.
Seamans, McHenry	do	Feb. 22, 1863	Feb. 23, 1863	Do.
Seamans, Calvin B	do	Oct. 1, 1863	Feb. 26, 1864	Do.
Smith, Elihu	do	Oct. 1, 1863	Feb. 26, 1864	Do.
Stroop, Michael S	do	Oct. 1, 1863	Feb. 26, 1864	Do.
Smith, Warren	do	Feb. 12, 1863	Feb. 23, 1863	Do.
Scott, Henry C	do	Oct. 1, 1863	Feb. 26, 1864	Do.
Scott, Green B	do	Feb. 24, 1864	Feb. 26, 1864	Do.
Stone, James W	do	Feb. 1, 1864	Feb. 26, 1864	Do.
Smith, Jonathan	do	Jan. 31, 1863	Feb. 23, 1863	Do.
Sivley, John D	do	Feb. 12, 1863	Feb. 23, 1863	Do.
Slover, James	do	Feb. 12, 1863	Feb. 23, 1863	Do.
Thomas, Joseph	do	Feb. 1, 1863	Feb. 23, 1863	Do.
Teague, John C	do	Jan. 1, 1864	Feb. 26, 1864	Do.
Upton, John W	do	Oct. 1, 1863	Feb. 26, 1864	Do.
Upton, Josephus	do	Sept. 1, 1863	Jan. 20, 1865	Do.
Westmoreland, William	do	Jan. 29, 1863	Feb. 23, 1863	Do.
Williams, Isaac	do	Feb. 23, 1863	Feb. 23, 1863	Do.
Worthington, Wayne C	do	Feb. 12, 1863	Feb. 23, 1863	Do.
Wagnon, Beverly	do	Mar. 15, 1863	Mar. 15, 1863	Do.
Wagnon, John	do	Feb. 24, 1864	Feb. 24, 1864	Do.

Killed.

Horton, James	Private	Feb. 1, 1863	Feb. 23, 1863	Killed by the enemy in Madison county, Arkansas, May 30, 1864.
McBroom, Maxwell C	do	Jan. 29, 1863	Feb. 23, 1863	Killed by the enemy in Madison county, Arkansas, August 15, 1864.
Mitchell, John	do	Feb. 22, 1863	Feb. 23, 1863	Killed by the enemy in Madison county, Arkansas, September 9, 1864.
McChristian, Monroe	do	Jan. 29, 1863	Feb. 23, 1863	Killed by the enemy in Madison county, Arkansas, February 27, 1863.
Williams, David A	do	Feb. 23, 1863	Feb. 23, 1863	Killed by the enemy at Fort Smith, Arkansas, February 7, 1865.

Died.

Boyd, David	Private	Feb. 3, 1863	Feb. 23, 1863	Died of small-pox in Madison county, Arkansas, April 6, 1863.
Clark, Henderson	do	Jan. 29, 1863	Feb. 23, 1863	Died of pneumonia at Little Rock, Arkansas, January 27, 1865.
Lane, Isaiah T	do	Jan. 29, 1863	Feb. 23, 1863	Died of pneumonia at Waldron, Arkansas, January 17, 1864.
Laferry, John	do	Mar. 11, 1863	Mar. 11, 1863	Died of pneumonia at Springfield, Missouri, January 27, 1864.
Myers, William	do	Jan. 26, 1863	Feb. 23, 1863	Died at Fayetteville, Arkansas, February 25, 1863.

First regiment Arkansas infantry volunteers. Mustered into service March 25, 1863, (three years;) mustered out August 10, 1865.

COMPANY B—Continued.

Names.	Rank.	Enlistment.	Muster	Remarks.
Johnson, John	Private	Jan. 29, 1863	Feb. 23, 1863	Died of chronic diarrhœa at Fort Smith, Arkansas, April 8, 1864.
Rankins, William A	do	Sept. 1, 1863	Feb. 23, 1863	Died of chronic diarrhœa at Fort Smith, Arkansas, March 6, 1864.
Roskelly, William	do	Feb. 4, 1863	Feb. 23, 1863	Died of convulsions at Cassville, Missouri, September 1, 1863.
McElhaney, Joseph	do	Feb. 12, 1863	Feb. 23, 1863	Died of pneumonia at Fayetteville, Arkansas, March 12, 1863.
Tucker, John J	do	Feb. 23, 1863	Feb. 23, 1863	Died of chronic diarrhœa at Fort Smith, Arkansas, January 15, 1864.
Deserted.				
Boatright, Thomas J	Private	Feb. 23, 1863	Feb. 23, 1863	Deserted at Fort Smith, Arkansas, October 2, 1864.
Crow, Robert	do	Feb. 14, 1863	Feb. 23, 1863	Deserted at Fayetteville, Arkansas, February 25, 1863.
Downum, George W	do	Feb. 14, 1863	Feb. 23, 1863	Deserted at Fayetteville, Arkansas, March 25, 1863.
Gibbs, Benjamin F	do	Feb. 13, 1863	Feb. 23, 1863	do.
Garrett, Thomas E	do	Feb. 12, 1863	Feb. 23, 1863	Deserted at Fayetteville, Arkansas, April 26, 1863.
Mahon, Hezekiah	do	Feb. 10, 1863	Feb. 23, 1863	Deserted at Fayetteville, Arkansas, March 25, 1863.
Oxford, William B	do	Feb. 1, 1863	Feb. 23, 1863	Deserted at Fayetteville, Arkansas, April 25, 1863.
Oxford, John A	do	Feb. 1, 1863	Feb. 23, 1863	Do.
Perry, John L	do	Feb. 6, 1863	Feb. 23, 1863	Deserted at Fayetteville, Arkansas, February 27, 1863.
Sims, David W	do	Feb. 23, 1863	Feb. 23, 1863	Deserted at Fayetteville, Arkansas, April 26, 1863.
Smith, Eli	do	Feb. 1, 1863	Feb. 23, 1863	do.
Vernon, Vernon	do	Feb. 10, 1863	Feb. 23, 1863	do.
Discharged.				
Abbett, Larkin	Private	Sept. 1, 1863	Feb. 26, 1864	Discharged for disability, March 1, 1865.
Johnson, William C	do	Mar. 1, 1863	Mar. 1, 1863	Do.
McGlathlin, Martin	do	May 1, 1864	June 6, 1864	Do.
McGlathlin, John	do	May 1, 1864	June 6, 1864	Do.
McBroom, Alexander D	do	Feb. 23, 1863	Feb. 23, 1863	Shot to death by sentence of G. C. M, at Fort Smith, Arkansas, for desertion, April 21, 1865.

COMPANY C.

Names.	Rank.	Date of rank.	Remarks.
James R. Vanderpool	Captain	June 21, 1862	Promoted from private company B. 1st Arkansas cavalry, to fill original vacancy; mustered out with regiment.
Burrett A. Rogers	1st lieutenant	Feb. 12, 1863	1st lieutenant from organization; resigned August 1, 1863.
Leroy Cardner	do	Oct. 25, 1863	Appointed from civil life, vice Rogers, resigned. Mustered out with regiment.
William Cross	2d lieutenant	June 21, 1862	Appointed from private company B, 1st Arkansas cavalry, to fill original vacancy; mustered out with regiment.

REPORT OF THE ADJUTANT GENERAL OF ARKANSAS. 177

Name	Rank	Enlistment	Muster	Remarks
Vincent W. Murphy	1st sergeant	Feb. 27, 1863	Nov. 1, 1863	Appointed from private; mustered out with regiment.
Albert J. Reeves	Sergeant	Feb. 27, 1863	Mar. 1, 1864	Do.
James M. Henson	do	Feb. 12, 1863	Nov. 1, 1863	Appointed from corporal; mustered out with regiment.
Hiram Boyd	do	Feb. 12, 1863	Nov. 1, 1863	do.
Thomas B. Parker	Corporal	Feb. 12, 1863	Nov. 1, 1863	Mustered out with regiment.
John L-mar	do	Feb. 12, 1863	Nov. 1, 1863	Do.
Archibald W. Reynolds	do	Feb. 12, 1863	June 1, 1865	Do.
William Houston	do	Feb. 12, 1863	Jan. 1, 1864	Do.
Pleasant O. Chism	do	Feb. 12, 1863	June 1, 1864	Do.
David N. Roobell	do	Feb. 12, 1863	Dec. 1, 1863	Do.
Thomas C. Bethel	do	Feb. 12, 1863	June 1, 1865	Do.
George W. Keith	do	Feb. 12, 1863		
			Muster.	
Adams, William	Private	Feb. 25, 1863	Feb. 27, 1863	Mustered out with regiment.
Adams, Mathews	do	Feb. 12, 1863	Feb. 27, 1863	Do.
Brassfield, Sedrick P.	do	Feb. 12, 1863	Feb. 27, 1863	Do.
Cayburn, James N.	do	Feb. 12, 1863	Feb. 27, 1863	Do.
Cass, Jackson	do	Feb. 12, 1863	Feb. 27, 1863	Do.
Cooper, George W.	do	Feb. 12, 1863	Feb. 27, 1863	Do.
Carrolton, Lowery C.	do	Feb. 12, 1863	Feb. 27, 1863	Do.
Carrolton, John	do	Feb. 12, 1863	Feb. 27, 1863	Do.
Duncan, William K.	do	Mar. 1, 1863	Apr. 10, 1863	Do.
Faught, Thomas J	do	Feb. 12, 1863	Feb. 27, 1863	Do.
Hendricks, James	do	Feb. 12, 1863	Feb. 27, 1863	Do.
Hicks Isaac C	do	Feb. 12, 1863	Feb. 27, 1863	Do.
Houston, William H.	do	Feb. 12, 1863	Feb. 27, 1863	Do.
Henderson, Isam J.	do	Feb. 12, 1863	Feb. 27, 1863	Do.
Henley, Franklin	do	Feb. 12, 1863	Feb. 27, 1863	Do.
Houston, Harvey	do	Feb. 12, 1863	Feb. 27, 1863	Do.
Hodges, Anderson	do	Feb. 12, 1863	Feb. 27, 1863	Do.
Jones, James	do	Feb. 12, 1863	Feb. 27, 1863	Do.
Knight, Silas T.	do	Feb. 12, 1863	Feb. 27, 1863	Do.
Lawson, William	do	Feb. 12, 1863	Feb. 27, 1863	Do.
Matlock, John S.	do	Feb. 12, 1863	Feb. 27, 1863	Do.
Morgan, Joel	do	Feb. 12, 1863	Feb. 27, 1863	Do.
McCord, John	do	Mar. 1, 1865	Apr. 10, 1865	Do.
Nichols, Joseph A.	do	Mar. 1, 1865	Apr. 10, 1865	Do.
Nichols, John B	do	Feb. 12, 1863	Feb. 27, 1863	Do.
Owen, William	do	Feb. 12, 1863	Feb. 27, 1863	Do.
Owen, Aaron	do	Feb. 25, 1864	Feb. 26, 1864	Do.
Pitman, Francis	do	Oct. 1, 1864	Apr. 10, 1865	Do.
Pitman, George W.	do	Feb. 12, 1863	Feb. 27, 1863	Do.
Peace, Elbert M.	do	Feb. 12, 1863	Feb. 27, 1863	Do.
Powell, William L.	do	Feb. 12, 1863	Feb. 27, 1863	Do.
Reynolds, John H.	do	Feb. 12, 1863	Feb. 27, 1863	Do.
Reynolds, Edmond	do	Feb. 12, 1863	Feb. 27, 1863	Do.
Reynolds, Thomas O.	do	Nov. 5, 1864	Feb. 26, 1864	Do.
Reeves, David W.	do	Feb. 12, 1863	Feb. 27, 1863	Do.
Ross, Alexander	do	Feb. 12, 1863	Feb. 27, 1863	Do.
Ross, Martin	do			Do.

Mis. Doc. 53——12

178 REPORT OF THE ADJUTANT GENERAL OF ARKANSAS.

First regiment Arkansas infantry volunteers. Mustered into service March 25, 1863, (three years;) mustered out August 10, 1865.

COMPANY C—Continued.

Names.	Rank.	Enlistment.	Muster.	Remarks.
Sexton, Daniel	Private	Feb. 12, 1863	Feb. 27, 1863	Mustered out with regiment.
Shipman, Isaac N	do	Feb. 12, 1863	Feb. 27, 1863	Do.
Sumpter, James H	do	Feb. 12, 1863	Feb. 27, 1863	Do.
Sparks, Thomas	do	July 1, 1863	Feb. 26, 1864	Do.
Sparks, George W	do	Feb. 12, 1863	Feb. 27, 1863	Do.
Sparks, B. E	do	Feb. 12, 1863	Feb. 27, 1863	Do.
Sparks, Jesse	do	Feb. 12, 1863	Feb. 27, 1863	Do.
Standridge, Martin, Jr	do	Feb. 12, 1863	Feb. 27, 1863	Do.
Standridge, Jerry	do	Feb. 12, 1863	Feb. 27, 1863	Do.
Standridge, Samuel	do	Feb. 12, 1863	Feb. 27, 1863	Do.
Smith, Martin	do	Feb. 12, 1863	Feb. 27, 1863	Do.
Smith, Elisha	do	Aug. 1, 1863	Feb. 26, 1864	Do.
Tuna, Edmond	do	Feb. 12, 1863	Feb. 27, 1863	Do.
Villians, Abraham	do	Feb. 12, 1863	Feb. 27, 1863	Do.
Villians, Hezekiah	do	Mar. 1, 1865	Apr. 10, 1865	Do.
Vineyard, Jonathan	do	Feb. 12, 1863	Feb. 27, 1863	Do.
Waldrip, Henry J	do	Nov. 1, 1863	June 6, 1864	Do.
Ward, James H	do	Sept. 1, 1863	Feb. 26, 1864	Do.
Killed in action.				
Brisco, William	Corporal	Feb. 12, 1863	Feb. 27, 1863	Killed in action in Carroll county, Arkansas, May 10, 1863.
Conly, Virgil	Private	Feb. 12, 1863	Feb. 27, 1863	Killed in action in Pope county, Arkansas, May 28, 1863.
Chaffin, Henson C	do	Feb. 12, 1863	Feb. 27, 1863	Killed in action in Washington county, Arkansas, November 15, 1864.
Cecil, James M	do	Feb. 12, 1863	Feb. 27, 1863	Killed in action in Newton county, Arkansas, September 15, 1864.
Harp, Marion	do	Feb. 12, 1863	Feb. 27, 1863	do.
Meek, Francis M	do	Feb. 12, 1863	Feb. 27, 1863	Taken prisoner and killed in Carroll county, Arkansas, March 15, 1863.
Mulholland, John	do	Feb. 12, 1863	Feb. 27, 1863	Killed in action at Moscow, Arkansas, April 12, 1864.
Owen, John	do	Feb. 12, 1863	Feb. 27, 1863	Killed in action in Washington county, Arkansas, November 15, 1864.
Patterson, Duncan	do	Feb. 12, 1863	Feb. 27, 1863	Killed in action at Moscow, Arkansas, April 12, 1864.
Riggs, Benjamin	do	Feb. 12, 1863	Feb. 27, 1863	Killed in action in Newton county, Arkansas, September 15, 1864.
Died of disease.				
Bell, Joseph C	Private	Feb. 12, 1863	Feb. 27, 1863	Died of pneumonia at Waldron, Arkansas, January 17, 1864.
Corbell, William G	do	Feb. 12, 1863	Feb. 27, 1863	Died of fever at Cassville, Missouri, April 28, 1863.
Geyson, Cornelius	do	Sept. 1, 1863		Died in hospital at Fort Smith, Arkansas, February 29, 1864.
Henson, Joseph C	do	Feb. 12, 1863	Feb. 27, 1863	Died in Newton county, Arkansas, July 30, 1863.
Meek, William	do	Feb. 12, 1863	Feb. 27, 1863	Died of poison at Fayetteville, Arkansas, March 22, 1863.
Murphy, Isaac N	do	Feb. 12, 1863	Feb. 27, 1863	Died on furlough in Johnson county, Arkansas, March 20, 1864.
Owen, James	do	Feb. 12, 1863	Feb. 27, 1863	Died of fever at Fayetteville, Arkansas, March 1, 1863.
Peacock, Benjamin	do	Feb. 12, 1863	Feb. 27, 1863	Died of typhoid fever in Newton county, Arkansas, March 18, 1863.

REPORT OF THE ADJUTANT GENERAL OF ARKANSAS. 179

Name	Rank	Date 1	Date 2	Remarks
Standridge, Martin W	do	Feb. 12, 1863	Feb. 27, 1863	do.
Ward, Samuel	1st sergeant	Feb. 12, 1863	Feb. 27, 1863	Died of fever at Fayetteville, Arkansas, March 28, 1863.

Deserted.

Name	Rank	Date 1	Date 2	Remarks
Adams, Mathew	Private	Feb. 12, 1863	Feb. 27, 1863	Deserted at Fort Smith, Arkansas, November 15, 1864.
Brassfield, John L	do	Feb. 12, 1863	Feb. 27, 1863	Deserted at Fort Smith, Arkansas, September 1, 1864.
Chaffin, William R	do	Feb. 12, 1863	Feb. 27, 1863	Deserted at Waldron, Arkansas, January 20, 1864.
Carrolton, Lowry C	do	Feb. 12, 1863	Feb. 27, 1863	Deserted at Clarksville, Arkansas, May 16, 1864.
Carrolton, John	do	Feb. 12, 1863	Feb. 27, 1863	Deserted at Waldron, Arkansas, January 28, 1864.
Clayburn, John W	do	Feb. 12, 1863	Feb. 26, 1864	Deserted at Fort Smith, Arkansas, January 10, 1865.
Cooper, James	do	Feb. 12, 1863	Feb. 27, 1863	Deserted at Fort Smith, Arkansas, September 1, 1865.
Coppenger, Samuel	do	Feb. 12, 1863	Feb. 27, 1863	Deserted at Waldron, Arkansas, January 28, 1864.
Doolin, John	do	Feb. 12, 1863	Feb. 27, 1863	Deserted from prison, March 3, 1864.
Ford, Joseph	do	Feb. 12, 1863	Feb. 27, 1863	Deserted at Waldron, Arkansas, January 28, 1864.
Hodges, Anderson	do	Feb. 12, 1863	Feb. 27, 1863	Deserted at Fort Smith, Arkansas, January 1, 1865.
Houston, William H	do	Feb. 12, 1863	Feb. 27, 1863	Deserted at Fort Smith, Arkansas, January 10, 1865.
Hicks, Isaac C	do	Feb. 12, 1863	Feb. 27, 1863	Deserted at Waldron, Arkansas, February 21, 1864.
Jones, Lewis	do	Feb. 12, 1863	Feb. 27, 1863	Deserted at Fort Smith, Arkansas, April 1, 1864.
King, David	do	Feb. 12, 1863	Feb. 27, 1863	Deserted at Fort Smith, Arkansas, October 20, 1863.
Millsaps, Marion	do	Feb. 12, 1863	Feb. 27, 1863	Deserted at Fort Smith, Arkansas, January 10, 1865.
Patterson, James	do	Feb. 12, 1863	Feb. 27, 1863	Deserted at Waldron, Arkansas, January 28, 1864.
Patterson, John	do	Feb. 12, 1863	Feb. 27, 1863	Do.
Pease, Elbert M	do	Feb. 12, 1863	Feb. 27, 1863	Deserted at Fort Smith, Arkansas, January 10, 1865.
Powell, William L	do	Feb. 12, 1863	Feb. 27, 1863	Deserted at Waldron, Arkansas, January 28, 1864.
Standridge, Martin	do	Feb. 12, 1863	Feb. 27, 1863	Deserted at Fort Smith, Arkansas, March 1, 1861.
Standridge, Samuel	do	Feb. 12, 1863	Feb. 27, 1863	Deserted at Waldron, Arkansas, January 28, 1864.
Standridge, John	do	Feb. 12, 1863	Feb. 27, 1863	Deserted at Fort Smith, Arkansas, January 10, 1865.
Standridge, Jerry	do	Feb. 12, 1863	Feb. 27, 1863	Deserted at Fort Smith, Arkansas, March 1, 1865.
Smith, Elisha	do	Aug. 1, 1863	Feb. 26, 1864	Deserted at Fort Smith, Arkansas, January 10, 1865.
Snow, George W	do	Feb. 12, 1863	Feb. 27, 1863	Deserted at Fort Smith, Arkansas, September 1, 1865.
Smith, Martin	do	Feb. 12, 1863	Feb. 27, 1863	Do.
Wright, Nelson	do	Feb. 12, 1863	Feb. 27, 1863	Deserted at Waldron, Arkansas, January 28, 1864.
Williams, James	do	Feb. 12, 1863	Feb. 27, 1863	Deserted at Fort Smith, Arkansas, January 10, 1865.

Discharged.

Name	Rank	Date 1	Date 2	Remarks
Clark, Henry M	Private	Feb. 12, 1863	Feb. 27, 1863	Discharged for disability October 30, 1864.
Villans, William	do	Feb. 12, 1863	Feb. 27, 1863	Discharged for disability May 30, 1865.

Transferred.

Name	Rank	Date 1	Date 2	Remarks
Robinson, John M	1st sergeant	April 20, 1863	June 6, 1863	Appointed from private September 1, 1863; promoted to 2d lieutenant and transferred to company A.

180 REPORT OF THE ADJUTANT GENERAL OF ARKANSAS.

First regiment Arkansas infantry volunteers. Mustered into service March 25, 1863, (three years,) mustered out August 10, 1865.

COMPANY D.

Names.	Rank.	Enlistment.	Date of rank.	Remarks.
Ransom P. Rhodes	Captain	June 18, 1862	Feb. 27, 1863	Appointed from sergeant, company E, 1st Arkansas cavalry, to fill original vacancy; died at Fayetteville, Arkansas, of brain fever, March 13, 1863.
William H. Newman	do	July 26, 1861	Mar. 14, 1863	Appointed from sergeant, company D, 1st Iowa cavalry; mustered out with regiment.
Nathan H. Burns	1st lieutenant	—, 1861	Feb. 27, 1863	Appointed from sergeant, 10th Illinois cavalry; resigned, January 13, 1865.
George W. Gurley	do	Feb. 9, 1863	June 2, 1865	Appointed 2d lieutenant from 1st sergeant; promoted to 1st lieutenant vice Burns, resigned; mustered out with regiment.
John Arrington	2d lieutenant	Feb. 20, 1863	Feb. 27, 1863	2d lieutenant from organization of company; resigned, May 18, 1863.
James W. Burney	1st sergeant	Feb. 9, 1863	Nov. 9, 1863	Appointed from sergeant; mustered out with regiment.
William Stotts	Sergeant	Feb. 26, 1863	Feb. 27, 1863	Sergeant from organization of company; mustered out with regiment.
John F. Burney	do	Feb. 9, 1863	Aug. 25, 1863	Appointed from corporal; mustered out with regiment.
Silas Gordon	do	Feb. 9, 1863	May 18, 1863	Do.
Samuel D. Minks	do	Feb. 9, 1863	Nov. 9, 1863	Do.
Pleasant M. Gurley	Corporal	Feb. 9, 1863	Feb. 27, 1863	Date of appointment unknown. All company records destroyed on Camden expedition, in April, 1864; mustered out with regiment.
Edward Lee	do	Feb. 11, 1863	Feb. 27, 1863	Do.
James M. Clark	do	Feb. 20, 1863	Feb. 27, 1863	Do.
James A. Raney	do	Sept. 1, 1863	Fb. 26, 1864	Do.
John Albread	do	April 1, 1863	Aug. 12, 1863	Do.
Brantley B. Cluck	do	Feb. 23, 1863	Feb. 27, 1863	Do.
John S. Williams	do	Sept. 1, 1863	Feb. 26, 1864	Do.
William S. Grayson	do	Sept. 1, 1863	Feb. 26, 1864	Do.
			Muster.	
Albread, Thomas	Private	April 1, 1863	Aug. 12, 1863	Mustered out with regiment.
Albread, Solomon A	do	April 1, 1863	Aug. 12, 1863	Do.
Bates, Benjamin F	do	Feb. 9, 1863	Feb. 27, 1863	Do.
Brotherton, William	do	Feb. 9, 1863	Feb. 27, 1863	Do.
Brashears, Alonzo	do	Feb. 25, 1863	Feb. 27, 1863	Do.
Burris, Andrew	do	Feb. 22, 1863	Feb. 27, 1863	Do.
Burris, Isaac	do	Feb. 6, 1863	Feb. 27, 1863	Do.
Bowen, William	do	April 1, 1865	April 10, 1865	Do.
Burney, Thomas J	do	April 1, 1865	April 17, 1865	Do.
Bell, James F	do	Feb. 8, 1863	Feb. 27, 1863	Do.
Copeland, William	do	Feb. 8, 1863	Feb. 27, 1863	Do.
Copeland, John W	do	April 1, 1863	Aug. 12, 1863	Do.
Chapel, Lafton	do	Sept. 1, 1863	Feb. 26, 1864	Do.
Coffery, John	do	Sept. 1, 1863	June 6, 1864	Do.
Compton, Thomas	do	Feb. 10, 1863	Feb. 27, 1863	Do.
Cole, Lewis F	do	Sept. 1, 1863	Feb. 26, 1864	Do.
Davis, James K. Polk	do			
Dill, Wesley	do			

REPORT OF THE ADJUTANT GENERAL OF ARKANSAS. 181

Name	Rank	Date		Remarks
Dill, William	do	Sept. 1, 1863	Feb. 26, 1864	Do.
Ednes, Austin	do	July 1, 1863	Aug. 12, 1863	Do.
Ellis, James F	do	Sept. 1, 1863	Feb. 26, 1864	Do.
Edmonds, James	do	Sept. 1, 1863	Feb. 26, 1864	Do.
Edwards, James W	do	April 1, 1863	Aug. 12, 1863	Do.
Gwiley, Newton	do	Oct. 1, 1863	Feb. 26, 1864	Do.
Gallion, Benjamin T	do	Mar. 1, 1863	June 6, 1864	Do.
Gunter, William B	do	July 1, 1863	Aug. 12, 1863	Do.
Garner, James W	do	Feb. 11, 1863	Feb. 27, 1863	Do.
Hunter, James J	do	Feb. 11, 1863	Feb. 27, 1863	Do.
Hunter, Francis M	do	Sept. 1, 1863	June 6, 1864	Do.
Hunter, William	do	Sept. 1, 1863	Feb. 26, 1864	Do.
Kelsey, Francis C. J	do	Feb. 9, 1863	Feb. 27, 1863	Do.
Leadbetter, Lewis C. J	do	Feb. 26, 1863	Feb. 27, 1863	Do.
Leadbetter, George W	do	Feb. 8, 1863	Feb. 27, 1863	Do.
Lasater, Henderson	do	Feb. 4, 1863	Feb. 27, 1863	Do.
Laker, Willis	do	Feb. 25, 1863	Feb. 27, 1863	Do.
McElhaney, Wiley	do	Feb. 20, 1863	Feb. 27, 1863	Do.
Millsaps, Isaac	do	Feb. 12, 1863	Feb. 26, 1864	Do.
Morse, John	do	Sept. 1, 1863	Feb. 26, 1864	Do.
Mathews, Andrew J	do	Sept. 1, 1863	June 6, 1864	Do.
Mathews, James	do	Sept. 1, 1863	Feb. 26, 1864	Do.
Mathews, Leford	do	Oct. 1, 1863	Feb. 26, 1864	Do.
Macca, John W	do	Sept. 1, 1863	Feb. 26, 1864	Do.
Powell, William	do	Sept. 1, 1863	Feb. 27, 1863	Do.
Powell, John	do	Feb. 20, 1863	Feb. 27, 1863	Do.
Riggs, John	do	Feb. 20, 1863	Feb. 27, 1863	Do.
Steele, George W	do	Sept. 1, 1863	Feb. 26, 1864	Do.
Stansell, William L	do	Sept. 1, 1863	Feb. 26, 1864	Do.
Strickland, sr., William	do	Feb. 28, 1865	Feb. 28, 1865	Do.
Strickland, jr., William	do	Feb. 21, 1863	Feb. 27, 1863	Do.
Tate, Joseph H	do	Sept. 1, 1863	Feb. 26, 1864	Do.
Underwood, Bedford	do	Nov. 1, 1863	Feb. 26, 1864	Do.
Walker, James	do	Sept. 1, 1863	Feb. 26, 1864	Do.
Williams, John	do	Sept. 1, 1863	Feb. 26, 1864	Do.
Woodward, Abraham	do	July 3, 1863	Feb. 18, 1864	Do.
Wood, William	do			Do.
Woodly, Allen N	do			Do.

Killed.

Carnahan, Robert D	Private	Sept. 1, 1863	Feb. 26, 1864	Killed in Sebastian county, Arkansas, March 26, 1865.
Moore, Henry C	do	Feb. 14, 1863	Feb. 27, 1863	Killed near Fayetteville, Arkansas, April 26, 1863.
Mathews, James H	do	Feb. 18, 1863	Feb. 27, 1863	Killed at Linden, Missouri, May 9, 1863.
Walker, David	do	Feb. 9, 1863	Feb. 27, 1863	Killed in Washington county, Arkansas, August 12, 1864.

Died.

Joel Arrington	Corporal	Feb. 20, 1863	Feb. 27, 1863	Died of pneumonia at Cassville, Missouri, April 29, 1863.
Roger Fox	do	Feb. 7, 1863	Feb. 27, 1863	Died at Fort Smith, Arkansas, July 9, 1864.
Benjamin F. Clark	do	Feb. 20, 1863	Feb. 27, 1863	Died of wounds received in action, June 14, 1863.
Arrington, Alfred	Private	Feb. 20, 1863	Feb. 27, 1863	Died at Fayetteville, Arkansas, March 25, 1863.

182 REPORT OF THE ADJUTANT GENERAL OF ARKANSAS.

First regiment Arkansas infantry volunteers. Mustered into service March 25, 1863, (three years;) mustered out August 10, 1865.

COMPANY D—Continued.

Names.	Rank.	Enlistment.	Muster.	Remarks.
Cassel, Dillon	Private	Feb. 20, 1863	Feb. 27, 1863	Died of brain fever August 30, 1863.
Garrison, Daniel	do	Feb. 21, 1863	Feb. 27, 1863	Died at Fayetteville, Arkansas, March 1, 1863.
Glassup, Levi	do	Feb. 20, 1863	Feb. 27, 1863	Died at Fort Smith, Arkansas, January 18, 1864.
Johnston, John	do	July 1, 1863	Aug. 12, 1863	Died of smallpox in Polk county, Arkansas, July 23, 1864.
Land, William H	do	Sept. 1, 1863	Feb. 26, 1864	Died at Fort Smith, Arkansas, April 30, 1864.
Moore, Evan B	do	Feb. 14, 1863	Feb. 27, 1863	Died at Fayetteville, Arkansas, March 2, 1863.
Martin, Minor B	do	Sept. 1, 1863	Never	Died at Waldron, Arkansas, December 22, 1863.
Trent, Wesley	do	Sept. 1, 1863	Feb. 26, 1864	Died at Fort Smith, Arkansas, July 4, 1864.
Williams, Joseph	do	Sept. 1, 1863	Never	Died at Waldron, Arkansas, December 17, 1863.
——, Josiah	do	Feb. 16, 1863	Feb. 27, 1863	Died near Fayetteville, Arkansas, March 5, 1863.
Deserted.				
Grovemill, Griffith	Corporal	Feb. 12, 1863	Feb. 27, 1863	Deserted at Fayetteville, Arkansas, March 30, 1863.
Auerson, Lafayette	Private	Feb. 21, 1863	Feb. 27, 1863	Deserted at Springfield, Missouri, May 1, 1863.
Bell, John Presley	do	Feb. 13, 1863	Feb. 27, 1863	Deserted at Fayetteville, Arkansas, March 15, 1863.
Bingham, Thomas	do	Feb. 21, 1863	Feb. 27, 1863	Deserted at Cassville, Missouri, July 15, 1863.
Banksom, William	do	Feb. 18, 1863	Feb. 27, 1863	Deserted at Fort Smith, Arkansas, September 6, 1863.
Carroll, John	do	Feb. 14, 1863	Feb. 27, 1863	Deserted at Fayetteville, Arkansas, April 1, 1863.
Collins, William	do	Feb. 12, 1863	Feb. 27, 1863	Deserted at Fayetteville, Arkansas, March 25, 1863.
Clay, Alexander	do	Aug. 1, 1863	Never	Deserted at Waldron, Arkansas, November 30, 1863.
Doggin, John	do	Feb. 12, 1863	Feb. 27, 1863	Deserted at Fort Smith, Arkansas, March 25, 1863.
Fisher, William	do	Sept. 1, 1863	Never	Deserted at Fort Smith, Arkansas, August 9, 1864.
Housewright, Thomas	do	Feb. 21, 1863	Feb. 27, 1863	Deserted at Cassville, Missouri, August 1, 1863.
McClendon, John	do	Feb. 21, 1863	Feb. 27, 1863	Deserted at Fayetteville, Arkansas, April 1, 1863.
Mason, Lafayette	do	Feb. 14, 1863	Feb. 27, 1863	Deserted at Cassville, Missouri, August 13, 1863.
McKinney, George	do	Feb. 20, 1863	Feb. 27, 1863	Deserted at Fayetteville, Arkansas, February 28, 1863.
Mackey, Hugh	do	Sept. 1, 1863	Never	Deserted at Jenny Lind, Arkansas, February 25, 1864.
Officer, Robert H	do	Feb. 26, 1863	Feb. 27, 1863	Deserted at Fayetteville, Arkansas, March 30, 1863.
Oxford, Daniel	do	Feb. 14, 1863	Feb. 26, 1864	Deserted at Fayetteville, Arkansas, April 16, 1863.
Reynolds, Mark	do	Nov. 1, 1863	Feb. 27, 1863	Deserted at Fort Smith, Arkansas, September 16, 1864.
Smith, Rufus	do	Feb. 21, 1863	Feb. 27, 1863	Deserted at Springfield, Missouri, May 1, 1863.
Smith, Eli	do	Feb. 24, 1863	Feb. 27, 1863	Deserted at Fayetteville, Arkansas, April 1, 1863.
Thomas, Robert	do	Feb. 11, 1863	Feb. 27, 1863	Deserted at Fayetteville, Arkansas, April 3, 1863.
Taylor, Isaac	do	Feb. 15, 1863	Feb. 27, 1863	Deserted at Fayetteville, Arkansas, March 15, 1863.
Taylor, William	do	Sept. 1, 1863	Never	Deserted at Fort Smith, Arkansas, February 4, 1865.
Waddle, Abraham	do	Sept. 1, 1863	Never	Deserted at Jenny Lind, Arkansas, February 25, 1864.
Discharged.				
Jesse H. Stansell	1st sergeant	Feb. 9, 1863	Feb. 27, 1863	Discharged for promotion to 2d lieutenant of company C, 2d Arkansas infantry.
Jesse H. Millsaps	Corporal	Feb. 20, 1863	Feb. 27, 1863	Discharged for promotion to captain 2d Arkansas cavalry.
William Burney	do	April 1, 1863	Aug. 12, 1863	Discharged for disability March 1, 1865.

REPORT OF THE ADJUTANT GENERAL OF ARKANSAS. 183

Name	Rank	Date of muster	Remarks
Alwread, Marion E	Private	April 1, 1863	Discharged for insanity April 1, 1864.
Barnheart, Harfin	do	Oct. 1, 1863	Discharged for disability January 4, 1865.
Bokamon, William H	do	Feb. 9, 1863	Discharged for disability March 2, 1865.
Brashears, Harden	do	Feb. 20, 1863	Discharged June 23, 1865.
Cotton, Joseph	do	Oct. 1, 1863	Discharged for disability March 1, 1865.
Dill, John	do	Sept. 1, 1863	Do.
Kelsey, Levi	do	Sept. 1, 1863	Discharged June 28, 1865.
Leadbetter, Willey	do	Feb. 9, 1863	Discharged for disability March 1, 1865.
Shelton, James	do	Feb. 20, 1863	Discharged for disability March 2, 1865.
Snodgrass, James	do	Feb. 20, 1863	Discharged for disability March 1, 1865.

COMPANY E.

Name	Rank	Date of rank	Muster	Remarks
James M. Hutchings	Captain	Mar. 10, 1863	—, 1861	Appointed from company G, 2d Wisconsin cavalry, to fill original vacancy; resigned August 18, 1864.
John W. Spralding	do	Nov. 16, 1864	—, 1862	Appointed 1st lieutenant from private of company F, 1st Arkansas cavalry, to fill original vacancy; promoted captain, vice Hutchings, resigned; mustered out with regiment.
Daniel E. Sutcliffe	1st lieutenant	Nov. 16, 1864	Feb. —, 1863	2d lieutenant from organization of company; promoted captain of company A June 23, 1865.
Archibald T. Strand	1st sergeant	April 20, 1865	Mar. 1, 1863	Appointed from private to sergeant May 1, 1863; mustered out with regiment.
John C. Yaden	Sergeant	Sept. 1, 1863	Mar. 1, 1863	Appointed from private; mustered out with regiment.
Lewis Palmer	do	Feb. 1, 1864	Sept. 1, 1863	Do.
William R. Allen	do	May 1, 1863	Mar. 1, 1863	Do.
Frederick Hill	do	Feb. 1, 1865	Mar. 1, 1863	Do.
John T. English	Corporal	Mar. 10, 1863	Mar. 1, 1863	Corporal from organization of company; mustered out with regiment.
James Nass	do	May 1, 1863	Mar. 1, 1863	Mustered out with regiment.
Martin Stedzel	do	Mar. 10, 1863	Mar. 1, 1863	Corporal from organization of company; mustered out with regiment.
James N. Clevenger	do	Aug. 1, 1864	Mar. 1, 1863	Do.
James S. Ridge	do	May 1, 1863	Mar. 1, 1863	Do.
William H. H. Nass	do	Nov. 15, 1864	Mar. 1, 1863	Mustered out with regiment.
Anderson, Lafayette	Private		Mar. 1, 1863	Do.
Bell, Lorenzo D	do		Mar. 1, 1863	Do.
Blankinship, James	do		Mar. 1, 1863	Do.
Byrum, John M	do		Sept. 1, 1863	Do.
Byrum, William	do		Feb. 26, 1864	Do.
Byrum, George	do		Sept. 1, 1863	Do.
Brown, George W	do		Sept. 1, 1863	Do.
Brown, John W	do		Mar. 1, 1863	Do.
Crawford, William W	do		April 2, 1865	Do.
Cloer, John B	do		Feb. 15, 1863	Do.
Cloer, James H	do		Feb. 12, 1863	Do.
Crawford, James C	do		Mar. 1, 1863	Do.
Crosby, Samuel	do		Mar. 1, 1863	Do.

First regiment Arkansas infantry volunteers. Mustered into service March 25, 1863, (three years;) mustered out August 10, 1865.

COMPANY E—Continued.

Names.	Rank.	Enlistment.	Muster.	Remarks.
Corden, Alfred C	Private	Mar. 1, 1863	Mar. 10, 1863	Mustered out with regiment.
Coffee, Albert W	do	Sept. 1, 1863	Feb. 20, 1864	Do.
Douglass, Samuel M	do	Mar. 1, 1863	Mar. 10, 1863	Do.
Edwards, William	do	July 1, 1864	July 1, 1864	Do.
Franklin, William W	do	Mar. 1, 1863	Mar. 10, 1863	Do.
Gann, Daniel	do	Mar. 1, 1863	Mar. 10, 1863	Do.
Gaff, John H	do	Sept. 1, 1863	Feb. 26, 1864	Do.
Harris, General L	do	Mar. 1, 1863	Mar. 10, 1863	Do.
Harper, Thomas B	do	Mar. 1, 1863	Mar. 10, 1863	Do.
Huley, Howard	do	Nov. 9, 1863	Feb. 26, 1864	Do.
Johnson, Samuel H	do	Feb. 15, 1863	Mar. 10, 1863	Do.
Jones, William S	do	Mar. 1, 1863	Mar. 10, 1863	Do.
Kennedy, James J	do	Sept. 1, 1863	Feb. 26, 1864	Do.
Little, James	do	Mar. 1, 1863	Mar. 10, 1863	Do.
Michaels, Daniel	do	Mar. 1, 1863	April 10, 1865	Do.
McCaslin, Webster	do	Sept. 1, 1863	Feb. 26, 1864	Do.
Morrow, Jesse T	do	July 14, 1863	Aug. 12, 1863	Do.
Mitchell, Jesse H	do	April 12, 1863	April 12, 1863	Do.
Mitchell, Daniel C	do	April 12, 1863	April 12, 1863	Do.
Murphy, John	do	Mar. 10, 1863	Mar. 10, 1863	Do.
Norton, David	do	Mar. 1, 1863	Mar. 10, 1863	Do.
Norton, Marion	do	Sept. 1, 1863	Feb. 26, 1864	Do.
Obar, John	do	Sept. 1, 1863	Feb. 26, 1864	Do.
Ridge, Jacob	do	Mar. 1, 1863	May 10, 1863	Do.
Rigge, Presley B	do	Sept. 1, 1863	Feb. 26, 1863	Do.
Rupe, Ransom P	do	Mar. 1, 1863	Mar. 10, 1863	Do.
Rupe, Lewis	do	Mar. 1, 1863	Mar. 10, 1863	Do.
Rupe, Daniel	do	Mar. 1, 1863	Mar. 10, 1863	Do.
Rupe, David P	do	Mar. 1, 1863	Mar. 10, 1863	Do.
Rice, Alexander	do	Mar. 1, 1863	Mar. 10, 1863	Do.
Rutherford, Calvin R	do	Mar. 1, 1863	Mar. 10, 1863	Do.
Shaver, Vincent	do	Mar. 1, 1863	Mar. 10, 1863	Do.
Shelby, Eli	do	Mar. 1, 1863	Mar. 10, 1863	Do.
Stewart, Francis M	do	April 12, 1863	Feb. 26, 1864	Do.
Smith, John W	do	Sept. 1, 1863	Feb. 26, 1864	Do.
Smith, McHenry	do	Sept. 1, 1863	Feb. 26, 1864	Do.
Talkington, Joel D	do	Sept. 1, 1863	Feb. 26, 1864	Do.
Tharr, John W	do	Mar. 1, 1863	Mar. 10, 1863	Do.
Tharr, Joseph N	do	Mar. 1, 1863	Mar. 10, 1863	Do.
Underwood, Lewis C	do	Mar. 1, 1863	Mar. 10, 1863	Do.
Underwood, Jackson	do	Mar. 1, 1863	Mar. 10, 1863	Do.
Winn, David D	do	Mar. 1, 1863	Mar. 10, 1863	Do.
Walden, William	do	Mar. 1, 1863	Mar. 10, 1863	Do.

REPORT OF THE ADJUTANT GENERAL OF ARKANSAS. 185

Name	Rank	Enlisted	Discharged	Remarks
Williams, Thomas A	do	Mar. 1, 1865	April 10, 1865	Do.
Yaden, Thomas H	do	Sept. 1, 1863	Feb. 26, 1864	Do.

Killed.

| Jasper N. Keisey | Corporal | Mar. 1, 1863 | Mar. 10, 1863 | Killed at Greenwood, Arkansas, in spring of 1863. |
| Bull, Edward J | Private | Mar. 1, 1863 | Mar. 10, 1863 | By accidental discharge of a gun at Waldron, Arkansas, January 28, 1864. |

Missing in action.

| John Huckaby | Corporal | Feb. 15, 1863 | Mar. 10, 1863 | Missing in action at Jack's Ferry, Arkansas, April 30, 1864. |

Died.

Cloer, James	Private	Feb. 15, 1863	Mar. 10, 1863	Died near Fayetteville, Arkansas, March 16, 1863.
Corbell, Levran S	do	Mar. 1, 1863	Mar. 10, 1863	Died at Cassville, Missouri, April 30, 1863.
Brewer, John O	do	Mar. 1, 1863	Mar. 10, 1863	Died at Fayetteville, Arkansas, May 15, 1863.
Deatin, George W	do	Feb. 13, 1863	Mar. 10, 1863	Died at Fort Smith, Arkansas, June 3, 1865.
Huckaby, Thomas	do	Feb. 15, 1863	Mar. 10, 1863	Died at Fayetteville, Arkansas, March 20, 1863.
Looper, John	do	Feb. 15, 1863	Mar. 10, 1863	Do.
Looper, Irvin	do	Feb. 15, 1863	Mar. 10, 1863	Died at Fayetteville, Arkansas, April 1, 1863.
Mathew, George W	do	Mar. 1, 1863	Mar. 10, 1863	Died in hands of enemy, cause unknown, May 1, 1863.
See, Francis M	do	Sept. 1, 1863	Feb. 26, 1864	Died at Greenwood, Arkansas, March 15, 1864.
Shelby, Thomas	do	Mar. 1, 1863	Mar. 10, 1863	Died at Little Rock, Arkansas, August 2, 1864.
Ramsey, William J	do	Sept. 1, 1863	Feb. 26, 1864	Died at Fort Smith, Arkansas, February 29, 1865.
Swift, John D	do	Mar. 1, 1863	Mar. 10, 1863	Died at Springfield, Missouri, June 30, 1863.

Deserted.

Bingham, Thomas	Corporal	Mar. 1, 1863	Mar. 10, 1863	Deserted at Fayetteville, Arkansas, April 18, 1863.
Brassfield, Shadrack	Private	Mar. 1, 1863	Mar. 10, 1863	Deserted at Fayetteville, Arkansas, April 1, 1863.
Barbee, Edward	do	Sept. 1, 1863	Never	Deserted at Fayetteville, Arkansas, March 20, 1864.
Dawson, Joseph N	do	Sept. 1, 1863	Feb. 26, 1864	Deserted at Fort Smith, Arkansas, January 12, 1865.
Chipman, Issac	do	Mar. 1, 1863	Mar. 10, 1863	Deserted at Fort Smith, Arkansas, October 3, 1863.
Care, John D	do	Mar. 1, 1863	Mar. 10, 1863	Deserted at Fayetteville, Arkansas, October 31, 1863.
Collins, Joshua	do	Feb. 3, 1863	Mar. 10, 1863	Deserted at Fayetteville, Arkansas, April 2, 1863.
Glenn, George W	do	Mar. 1, 1863	Mar. 10, 1863	Deserted at Fort Smith, Arkansas, August 29, 1864.
Murphy, Isaac	do	Mar. 10, 1863	Mar. 10, 1863	Deserted at Fort Smith, Arkansas, October 3, 1863.
Murphy, Vincent	do	Mar. 10, 1863	Mar. 10, 1863	Do.
Nowlan, Thomas	do	Mar. 1, 1863	Mar. 10, 1863	Deserted at Fayetteville, Arkansas, April 30, 1863.
Reaves, Albert	do	Mar. 10, 1863	Mar. 10, 1863	Deserted at Fort Smith, Arkansas, October 3, 1863.
Rash, Preston	do	Mar. 1, 1863	Mar. 10, 1863	Deserted at Fayetteville, Arkansas, April 1, 1863.
Rash, Joseph	do	Mar. 1, 1863	Mar. 10, 1863	do.
Kotteridge, Roderick D	do	Sept. 1, 1863	Never	Deserted at Fort Smith, Arkansas, April 1, 1865.
Valins, William	do	Mar. 1, 1863	Mar. 10, 1863	Deserted at Fort Smith, Arkansas, October 3, 1861.
Williams, David, jr	do	Feb. 15, 1863	Mar. 10, 1863	Deserted at Elm Springs, Arkansas, April 29, 1863.

Discharged.

William Syerson	1st sergeant	Sept. 1, 1863	Feb. 26, 1864	Discharged for promotion to United States hospital steward, January 1, 1864.
James B. Stephens	Sergeant	Mar. 1, 1863	Mar. 10, 1863	Discharged for promotion to 1st lieutenant 2d Arkansas cavalry, December 18, 1863.
John Welch	Corporal	Mar. 1, 1863	Mar. 10, 1863	Discharged May 3, 1865.

First regiment Arkansas infantry volunteers. Mustered into service March 25, 1863, (three years;) mustered out August 10, 1865.

COMPANY E—Continued.

Names.	Rank.	Enlistment.	Muster.	Remarks.
Ake, William	Private	Sept. 1, 1863	Never	Discharged for disability February 26, 1864.
Bams, Joachim	do	Feb. 14, 1863	Mar. 10, 1863	Discharged for disability October 19, 1864.
Brooks, Jesse	do	Sept. 1, 1863	Never	Discharged for disability February 26, 1864.
Comstock, William	do	Sept. 1, 1863	Never	Discharged for disability January 13, 1864.
Casey, Washington W	do	Sept. 1, 1863	Never	Discharged for disability February 26, 1864.
Looman, Gilbert	do	Sept. 1, 1863	Never	Do. do.
Munley, William	do	Sept. 1, 1863	Feb. 26, 1864	Discharged May 3, 1865.
Spradling, George N	do	July 14, 1863	Aug. 12, 1863	Discharged for promotion to 2d lieutenant 2d Arkansas infantry, June 7, 1865.
Sling, Alexander	do	Sept. 1, 1863	Never	Discharged for disability January 15, 1864.
Ridge, John	do	Sept. 1, 1863	Never	Discharged for disability February 26, 1864.
Wilson, James T	do	Sept. 1, 1863	Never	Do. do.
Wilson, Charles H	do	Sept. 1, 1863	Never	Do. do.
Transferred.				
Henry F. Edmundson	1st sergeant	Mar. 1, 1863	Mar. 10, 1863	Appointed principal musician, non-commissioned staff, May 1, 1863.
Daw, David V	Private	Mar. 1, 1863	Mar. 10, 1863	Appointed to non-commissioned staff as hospital steward, July 1, 1863.
Dishonorably discharged.				
Stroud, Isaac L	Private	Mar. 1, 1863	Mar. 10, 1863	Per sentence of general court martial.
Vaughan, Elijah	do	Mar. 1, 1863	Mar. 10, 1863	Do. do.

COMPANY F.

Names.	Rank.	Enlistment.	Date of rank.	Remarks.
John McCoy	Captain	Mar. 10, 1863	Mar. 10, 1863	Appointed from civil life; resigned August 5, 1864.
George W. Raymond	do	—, 1861	Nov. 16, 1864	Appointed 2d lieutenant from private company D, 36th Illinois infantry, April 29, 1863; promoted to 1st lieutenant January 5, 1864; mustered out with regiment.
John F. Fesperman	1st lieutenant	June 21, 1862	Mar. 10, 1863	Appointed from private company K, 1st Arkansas cavalry, to fill original vacancy; killed in action near Jasper, Arkansas.
Henry F. Edmondson	do	Mar. 1, 1863	Jan. 1, 1865	Appointed from 1st sergeant of company E, 1st Arkansas infantry, May 1, 1863, to principal musician; to 2d lieutenant Jan. 5, 1864; mustered out with regiment.
John H. McClure	1st sergeant	Sept. 10, 1863	Feb. 25, 1864	Appointed from corporal; mustered out with regiment.
William Slusher	Sergeant	Mar. 1, 1863	Mar. 10, 1863	Sergeant from organization of company; mustered out with regiment.
Henry Sears	do	Mar. 1, 1863	Feb. 1, 1865	Appointed from corporal; mustered out with regiment.
Francis M. Blaylock	do	Sept. 10, 1863	May 2, 1865	Do. do.
Isaac Henderson	Corporal	Mar. 1, 1863	May 15, 1863	Mustered out with regiment.
William Long	do	Sept. 10, 1863	Sept. 15, 1863	Do.

REPORT OF THE ADJUTANT GENERAL OF ARKANSAS. 187

				Muster.
Zaddock P. Logan			Sept. 10, 1863	April 11, 1864	Do.
John T. Hathcock			Sept. 10, 1863	June 1, 1864	Do.
John L. Gilliam			Jan. 10, 1864	June 1, 1864	Do.
Calvan D. Weatherman			Sept. 10, 1863	May 18, 1865	Do.
Martin V. Rust			Sept. 10, 1863	May 18, 1865	Do.
Asher, James W	Private		Mar. 1, 1863	Mar. 10, 1863	Mustered out with regiment.
Baltimore, Wm	do		Sept. 10, 1863	Feb. 26, 1864	Do.
Brown, William	do		Sept. 10, 1863	Feb. 26, 1864	Do.
Brannon, James R	do		Sept. 10, 1863	Feb. 26, 1864	Do.
Cavin, William R	do		Mar. 1, 1863	Mar. 10, 1863	Do.
Crossen, Stephen L	do		Sept. 10, 1863	Feb. 26, 1864	Do.
Coker, Thomas	do		Sept. 10, 1863	Feb. 26, 1864	Do.
Casey, Lewis	do		Mar. 1, 1863	Mar. 10, 1863	Do.
Dullard, Lewis	do		Mar. 1, 1863	Mar. 10, 1863	Do.
Doshier, Richard	do		Sept. 10, 1863	Feb. 26, 1864	Do.
Doshier, Harrison	do		Sept. 10, 1863	Feb. 26, 1864	Do.
Ford, James R	do		Jan. 10, 1864	Feb. 26, 1864	Do.
Hamby, Isaac M	do		Mar. 1, 1863	Mar. 10, 1863	Do.
Hamilton, Thomas	do		Mar. 1, 1863	Mar. 10, 1863	Do.
Holt, Charles K	do		Mar. 1, 1863	Mar. 10, 1863	Do.
Henderson, William	do		Mar. 1, 1863	Mar. 10, 1863	Do.
Hodges, Calsway	do		Sept. 10, 1863	Feb. 26, 1864	Do.
Henderson, Thomas P	do		Sept. 10, 1863	Feb. 26, 1864	Do.
Hannah, Thomas J	do		Jan. 10, 1864	Feb. 22, 1865	Do.
Harp, William A	do		Mar. 6, 1863	Mar. 10, 1863	Do.
Jackson, Preston	do		Mar. 1, 1863	Mar. 10, 1863	Do.
Jones, Robert	do		Mar. 1, 1863	Mar. 10, 1863	Do.
Jones, Thomas R	do		Mar. 1, 1863	Mar. 10, 1863	Do.
Logan, Jasper N	do		Mar. 10, 1863	Feb. 26, 1864	Do.
McGuffee, James	do		Sept. 10, 1863	Mar. 10, 1863	Do.
Nichols, William	do		Mar. 1, 1863	Mar. 10, 1863	Do.
Owen, John	do		Mar. 1, 1863	Mar. 10, 1863	Do.
Oxford, John Y	do		Mar. 1, 1863	Mar. 10, 1863	Do.
Payne, Daniel M	do		Mar. 1, 1863	Mar. 10, 1863	Do.
Poppels, Nathan	do		Mar. 1, 1863	Mar. 10, 1863	Do.
Poppels, Smith	do		Mar. 1, 1863	Mar. 10, 1863	Do.
Prine, John B	do		Sept. 10, 1863	Feb. 25, 1864	Do.
Powell, Stanton	do		Mar. 1, 1863	Mar. 10, 1864	Do.
Poppels, John	do		Mar. 1, 1863	Mar. 10, 1864	Do.
Rowland, John	do		Mar. 1, 1863	Mar. 10, 1864	Do.
Ratterree, Wiley B	do		Sept. 10, 1863	Feb. 26, 1864	Do.
Redding, John	do		Sept. 10, 1863	Feb. 26, 1864	Do.
Redding, Isaac R	do		Sept. 10, 1863	Feb. 26, 1864	Do.
Rackley, William C	do		Mar. 1, 1863	Mar. 10, 1863	Do.
Robinson, Asaph	do		Sept. 10, 1863	Feb. 26, 1864	Do.
Snow, Ericus	do		Mar. 1, 1863	Mar. 10, 1863	Do.
Snow, Abijah	do		Mar. 1, 1863	Mar. 10, 1863	Do.
Siebold, Wm. R	do		June 10, 1863	Aug. 12, 1863	Do.
Thomas, Vincent	do		Mar. 1, 1863	Mar. 10, 1862	Do.

188   REPORT OF THE ADJUTANT GENERAL OF ARKANSAS.

First regiment Arkansas infantry volunteers. Mustered into service March 25, 1863, (three years;) mustered out August 10, 1865.

COMPANY F—Continued.

Names.	Rank.	Enlistment.	Muster.	Remarks.
Tidwell, Wesley	Private	Sept. 10, 1863	Feb. 26, 1864	Mustered out with regiment.
Wright, Seaburn	do	Mar. 1, 1863	Mar. 10, 1863	Do.
White, Wm. J.	do	Mar. 5, 1863	April 30, 1865	Do.
Wood, Christopher C	do	May 26, 1863	Aug. 12, 1863	Do.
Walker, George W	do	Sept. 10, 1863	Feb. 26, 1864	Do.
Young, Alvin	do	Mar. 1, 1863	Mar. 10, 1863	Do.
Young, Marion	do	Mar. 1, 1863	Mar. 10, 1863	Do.

Killed in action.

McPherson, Daniel	Corporal	Sept. 10, 1863	Feb. 26, 1864	Killed near Fort Smith, Arkansas, September 4, 1864.
Lasater, John H	Sergeant	Sept. 10, 1863	Feb. 26, 1864	Killed near Fort Smith, Arkansas, May 1, 1865.
Lasater, James H	Private	Jan. 10, 1864	Feb. 26, 1864	Killed near Fort Smith, Arkansas, September 4, 1864.
Parker, Thomas B	do	Mar. 1, 1863	Mar. 10, 1863	Killed by guerillas near Fayetteville, Arkansas, September 15, 1863.
Spurlock, Hiram	do	Mar. 1, 1863	Mar. 10, 1863	Killed in Newton county, Arkansas, November 16, 1864.
Williams, William	do	Mar. 1, 1863	Mar. 10, 1863	Do.
Young, Martin	do	Jan. 10, 1864	Feb. 26, 1864	Killed near Macon creek, Arkansas, April 13, 1864.

Died.

Cecil, James	Private	Mar. 1, 1863	Mar. 10, 1863	Died at Springfield, Missouri, May 29, 1863.
Criner, John	do	Mar. 10, 1863	Mar. 10, 1863	Died of wounds in Newton county, Arkansas, June 15, 1863.
Frazier, Joshua R	do	Sept. 10, 1863	Feb. 26, 1864	Died of erysipelas, at Springfield, Missouri, December 4, 1864.
Flood, David	do	Mar. 1, 1863	Mar. 10, 1863	Died of wounds in Newton county, Arkansas, June 8, 1863.
Holt, Williamson	do	Mar. 10, 1863	Mar. 10, 1863	Died of pneumonia at Fayetteville, Arkansas, May 29, 1863.
Harp, James C	Corporal	Mar. 1, 1863	Mar. 10, 1863	Died of poison at Fayetteville, Arkansas, March 10, 1863.
Hendrix, Green L	Private	Mar. 10, 1863	Mar. 10, 1863	Died of apoplexy at Fayetteville, Arkansas, May 21, 1863.
Hallum, Rufus A. J	do	Mar. 1, 1863	Mar. 10, 1863	Died of dropsy at Fort Smith, Arkansas, March 24, 1863.
Mayberry, William A	Corporal	Mar. 1, 1863	Mar. 10, 1863	Died of consumption at Fort Smith, Arkansas, April 10, 1864.
McClure, Robert A	Sergeant	Mar. 1, 1863	Mar. 10, 1863	Died of brain fever at Fort Smith, Arkansas, February 25, 1864.
Nixon, Joshua	Private	Sept. 10, 1863	Never	Died of measles at Fort Smith, Arkansas, December 24, 1863.
Redding, Marion D	do	Sept. 10, 1863	Feb. 26, 1864	Died of brain fever at Waldron, Arkansas, April 28, 1865.
Smith, James	do	Mar. 10, 1863	Mar. 10, 1863	Died of wounds in Newton county, Arkansas, February 17, 1864.
Slusher, George	do	Mar. 10, 1863	Mar. 10, 1863	Died of intermittent fever at Little Rock, Arkansas, May 29, 1863.
Tennison, Daniel	do	Mar. 10, 1863	Mar. 10, 1863	Died of wounds in Newton county, Arkansas, July 10, 1863.
Cassidy, John	do	Sept. 10, 1863	Feb. 26, 1864	Died of acute diarrhœa at Fort Smith, Arkansas, December 4, 1864.

Deserted.

Brasswell, John	Private	Mar. 10, 1863	Mar. 10, 1863	Deserted at Fayetteville, Arkansas, August 29, 1863.
Brasswell, Mathias	do	Mar. 10, 1863	Mar. 10, 1863	Do.
Cooper, James	Corporal	Mar. 10, 1863	Mar. 10, 1863	Do.

REPORT OF THE ADJUTANT GENERAL OF ARKANSAS. 189

Name	Rank	Date of enlistment	Date of muster	Remarks
Criner, Joseph	Private	Mar. 10, 1863	Mar. 10, 1863	Do.
Casey, Uriah	do	Mar. 10, 1863	Mar. 10, 1863	Do.
Casey, Miles P	do	Mar. 10, 1863	Mar. 10, 1863	Do.
Carlton, William C	do	Mar. 10, 1863	Mar. 10, 1863	Do.
Cheatam, Trauty F	do	Mar. 10, 1863	Mar. 10, 1863	Deserted at Jenny Lind, Arkansas, November 7, 1863.
Coltner, William D	do	Sept. 10, 1863	Feb. 26, 1864	Deserted at Fort Smith, Arkansas, January 11, 1865.
Davis, Richard	do	Mar. 10, 1863	Mar. 10, 1863	Deserted at Fayetteville, Arkansas, August 22, 1863.
Davis, Ambrose L	do	Mar. 10, 1863	Mar. 10, 1863	Deserted at Jenny Lind, Arkansas, November 7, 1863.
Ford, John A	do	Sept. 10, 1863	Feb. 26, 1864	Deserted at Fayetteville, Arkansas, August 22, 1863.
Gaswick, William	do	Mar. 10, 1863	Mar. 10, 1863	Deserted at Jenny Lind, Arkansas, November 7, 1863.
Gillmore, Kelsey	do	Mar. 1, 1863	Mar. 1, 1863	Do.
Hefley, Daniel	do	Mar. 10, 1863	Mar. 10, 1863	Deserted at Fayetteville, Arkansas, August 22, 1863.
Hefley, John B	do	Mar. 10, 1863	Mar. 10, 1863	Deserted at Jenny Lind, Arkansas, November 7, 1863.
Henderson, James	do	Mar. 10, 1863	Mar. 10, 1863	Deserted at Fayetteville, Arkansas, August 22, 1863.
Henderson, Allen	do	Mar. 10, 1863	Mar. 10, 1863	do.
Hallum, James L	Corporal	Mar. 1, 1863	Mar. 10, 1863	Deserted at Jenny Lind, Arkansas, November 7, 1863.
Harp, Samuel R	Private	Mar. 1, 1863	Mar. 10, 1863	Deserted at Fort Smith, Arkansas, March 25, 1864.
Jones, Lemuel R	do	Mar. 10, 1863	Mar. 10, 1863	Deserted at Fayetteville, Arkansas, August 22, 1863.
Jones, Benjamin	do	Mar. 10, 1863	Mar. 10, 1863	Do.
Liles, Absalom	do	Mar. 10, 1863	Mar. 10, 1863	Do.
McPherson, William L	do	Sept. 10, 1863	Feb. 26, 1864	Deserted at Fort Smith, Arkansas, July 1, 1864.
McElroy, Abraham	do	Mar. 10, 1863	Mar. 10, 1863	Deserted at Fayetteville, Arkansas, August 22, 1863.
Nichol, William B	do	Mar. 10, 1863	Mar. 10, 1863	Do.
Raab, Preston	do	Mar. 10, 1863	Mar. 10, 1863	Do.
Ra-n, Joseph	do	Mar. 10, 1863	Mar. 10, 1863	Do.
Riddle, Vinson	do	Mar. 10, 1863	Mar. 10, 1863	Do.
Smith, Gilbert	do	Mar. 10, 1863	Mar. 10, 1863	Do.
Smith, Alfred	do	Mar. 10, 1863	Mar. 10, 1863	Do.
Smith, John	do	Mar. 10, 1863	Mar. 10, 1863	Deserted at Jenny Lind, Arkansas, November 7, 1863.
Skaggs, Solomon	do	Mar. 10, 1863	Mar. 10, 1863	Deserted at Fayetteville, Arkansas, August 22, 1863.
Sexton, Timothy	do	Mar. 1, 1863	Mar. 1, 1863	Deserted at Jenny Lind, Arkansas, November 7, 1863.
Sexton, Daniel	do	Mar. 10, 1863	Mar. 10, 1863	Deserted at Fayetteville, Arkansas, August 22, 1863.
Sexton, Riley	do	Mar. 10, 1863	Mar. 10, 1863	Do.
Tennison, Thomas J	do	Mar. 10, 1863	Mar. 10, 1863	Do.
Minton, John R	do	Mar. 10, 1863	Mar. 10, 1863	Do.

Discharged.

Name	Rank	Date of enlistment	Date of muster	Remarks
Ford, John D	Private	Sept. 10, 1863	Feb. 26, 1864	Discharged for disability January 10, 1865.
Phillips, Absalom C	1st sergeant	Mar. 1, 1863	Mar. 10, 1864	Discharged for promotion to 2d lieutenant 2d Arkansas infantry February 25, 1864.
Powell, Martin	Private	Sept. 10, 1863	Feb. 26, 1864	Discharged for disability January 10, 1864.
Radford, Alfred H	do	Sept. 10, 1863	Feb. 26, 1864	Discharged for disability March 1, 1865.

COMPANY G.

Name	Rank	Date of rank	Date of muster	Remarks
George W. R. Smith	Captain	Mar. 15, 1863	Mar. 15, 1863	Appointed from civil life to fill original vacancy; mustered out with regiment.
John Johnson	1st lieutenant	Mar. 15, 1863	Mar. 15, 1863	Do.

190 REPORT OF THE ADJUTANT GENERAL OF ARKANSAS.

First regiment Arkansas infantry volunteers. Mustered into service March 25, 1863, (three years;) mustered out August 10, 1865.

COMPANY G—Continued.

Names.	Rank.	Enlistment.	Date of rank.	Remarks.
Simon P. Smith	2d lieutenant	Nov. —, 1862	Mar. 15, 1863	Appointed from private company A, 1st Arkansas cavalry, to fill original vacancy; mustered out with regiment.
Calaway Wash	1st sergeant	Feb. 15, 1863	Mar. 15, 1863	Appointed from private; mustered out with regiment.
Miles A. Rogers	Sergeant	Feb. 15, 1863	Mar. 15, 1863	do.
William Anderson	do	Mar. 15, 1863	Mar. 15, 1863	Do.
Alfred Johnson	do	Mar. 15, 1863	Mar. 15, 1863	Do.
William Tweedy	Corporal	Mar. 15, 1863	Mar. 15, 1863	Mustered out with regiment.
James Thomas	do	Aug. 10, 1863	Mar. 2, 1864	Do.
Andrew J. Sinnett	do	Mar. 15, 1863	Mar. 15, 1863	Do.
Joshua P. Drake	do	Feb. 21, 1863	Mar. 2, 1864	Do.
Joshua S. Jeffers	do	Feb. 15, 1863	Mar. 15, 1863	Do.
Madison Dunnaway	do	Feb. 15, 1863	Mar. 15, 1863	Do.
William Blackwell	do	Feb. 15, 1863	Mar. 15, 1863	Do.
James Wagers	do	Feb. 15, 1863	Mar. 15, 1863	Do.
			Muster.	
Austin, William	Private	June 15, 1863	Aug. 13, 1863	Do.
Aldridge, James M	do	Sept. 15, 1863	Feb. 26, 1864	Do.
Bohamnon, James	do	Mar. 15, 1863	Mar. 15, 1863	Do.
Bolinger, Frederick	do	Mar. 15, 1863	Mar. 15, 1863	Do.
Bolinger, William H	do	Mar. 15, 1863	Mar. 15, 1863	Do.
Bolinger, Wilson	do	Mar. 31, 1863	April 10, 1865	Do.
Brooks, Nathaniel	do	Feb. 15, 1863	Feb. 15, 1863	Do.
Bollard, Marges	do	Sept. 15, 1863	Feb. 26, 1864	Do.
Brewer, Elijah	do	Sept. 15, 1863	Feb. 26, 1863	Do.
Brown, James	do	Sept. 15, 1863	Feb. 26, 1864	Do.
Cassida, William	do	Mar. 15, 1863	Mar. 15, 1863	Do.
Casse'man, James	do	Feb. 15, 1862	Feb. 15, 1863	Do.
Cagle, Thomas	do	Sept. 15, 1863	Feb. 26, 1864	Do.
Cace, John	do	Sept. 15, 1863	Feb. 26, 1864	Do.
Drimnon, David	do	Mar. 15, 1863	Mar. 15, 1863	Do.
Drake, Pleasant	do	Feb. 15, 1863	Feb. 26, 1864	Do.
Drake, Elijah	do	Aug. 10, 1863	Feb. 26, 1863	Do.
Drake, Wilson	do	Aug. 10, 1863	Feb. 26, 1864	Do.
Drake, Benjamin	do	Feb. 21, 1863	Feb. 23, 1864	Do.
Driver, James	do	Mar. 31, 1865	April 10, 1865	Do.
Evans, Samuel	do	Feb. 15, 1863	Feb. 15, 1863	Do.
Gage, William	do	Mar. 15, 1863	Mar. 15, 1863	Do.
Gest, Alfred	do	Mar. 15, 1863	Mar. 15, 1863	Do.
Goad, Pinkney	do	Mar. 15, 1863	Mar. 18, 1863	Do.
Goad, Madison	do	Mar. 15, 1863	Mar. 15, 1863	De.
Gipson, Linsey	do	Feb. 15, 1863	Feb. 15, 1863	Do.

REPORT OF THE ADJUTANT GENERAL OF ARKANSAS 191

Name	Rank	Enlisted	Mustered in	Remarks
Hallis, Jacob		Feb. 15, 1863	Feb. 15, 1863	Do.
Hankins, William	do	Feb. 15, 1863	Feb. 15, 1863	Do.
Hale, George W	do	Feb. 15, 1863	Feb. 15, 1863	Do.
Huckaley, John R	do	Feb. 15, 1863	Feb. 15, 1863	Do.
Hopper, Frederick T	do	Feb. 15, 1863	Feb. 15, 1863	Do.
Hooper, William D	do	Mar. 15, 1863	Mar. 15, 1863	Do.
Johnson, John	do	Feb. 15, 1863	Feb. 15, 1863	Do.
Johnson, Martin	do	Feb. 10, 1863	Feb. 25, 1863	Do.
Keck, Christopher	do	Feb. 15, 1863	Feb. 15, 1863	Do.
Keck, John A	do	Feb. 15, 1863	Feb. 15, 1863	Do.
Keck, Isaac	do	Feb. 1, 1863	June 6, 1864	Do.
Logue, David	do	Mar. 15, 1863	Mar. 15, 1863	Do.
Mado, Louis	do	Feb. 15, 1863	Feb. 15, 1863	Do.
McMasters, William J	do	Mar. 15, 1863	Mar. 15, 1863	Do.
McKedy, Hezekiah	do	Feb. 15, 1863	Aug. 13, 1863	Do.
Neal, Arthur L	do	June 15, 1863	Feb. 23, 1863	Do.
Neal, James	do	Feb. 21, 1863	Feb. 25, 1865	Do.
Russell, James	do	Feb. 10, 1865	Feb. 15, 1865	Do.
Russell, Bennett	do	Feb. 15, 1863	Mar. 15, 1863	Do.
Russell, Steven	do	Feb. 10, 1865	Feb. 25, 1865	Do.
Rogers, James	do	Feb. 15, 1863	Feb. 15, 1863	Do.
Rogers, Jacob	do	Feb. 21, 1863	Feb. 23, 1863	Do.
Stover, William	do	Mar. 15, 1863	Aug. 13, 1863	Do.
Starnes, Nichols	do	Mar. 15, 1863	Aug. 13, 1863	Do.
Seals, John	do	Feb. 15, 1863	Feb. 15, 1863	Do.
Seals, Pleasant	do	Feb. 15, 1863	Feb. 15, 1863	Do.
Spencer, George W	do	Mar. 15, 1863	Mar. 15, 1863	Do.
Sisemore, Andrew J	do	Feb. 15, 1863	Feb. 15, 1863	Do.
Sisemore, Russell	do	June 1, 1864	June 7, 1864	Do.
Seals, Calaway	do	Mar. 31, 1865	April 10, 1865	Do.
Wagers, Wilson	do	Feb. 15, 1863	Feb. 15, 1863	Do.
Wagers, Ashley	do	Feb. 15, 1863	Feb. 15, 1863	Do.
Williams, Andrew J	do	Feb. 15, 1863	Feb. 15, 1863	Do.
Williams, Franklin	do	Feb. 15, 1863	Feb. 15, 1863	Do.
Williams, George W	do	Feb. 15, 1863	Feb. 15, 1863	Do.
Wagnon, Thomas	do	Feb. 15, 1863	Feb. 15, 1863	Do.
Wilson, James C	do	Sept. 15, 1863	Feb. 26, 1864	Do.
Young, William M	do	Aug. 10, 1863	Feb. 26, 1864	Do.

Killed in action.

Name	Rank	Enlisted	Mustered in	Remarks
Matlock, Samuel	Private	Feb. 15, 1863	Feb. 15, 1863	Killed in action in Missouri March 10, 1864.
McCoy, Newton	do	Mar. 15, 1863	Mar. 15, 1863	Killed in action in Madison county, Arkansas, September 17, 1863.
Spencer, Samuel	do	Mar. 15, 1863	Mar. 15, 1863	Killed in action near Waldron, Arkansas, January 16, 1864.
Tweedy, Robert R	do	Mar. 15, 1863	Mar. 15, 1863	Killed in action near Waldron, Arkansas, January 22, 1864.
Wootin, Jarvis I	do	Feb. 15, 1863	Feb. 15, 1863	Do.

Died.

Name	Rank	Enlisted	Mustered in	Remarks
Bandy, George W	Private	Sept. 15, 1863	Feb. 15, 1863	Died of fever at Waldron, Arkansas, December 15, 1863.
Drinnon, William S	do	Feb. 15, 1863	Feb. 15, 1863	Died of pneumonia at Flat Creek, Missouri, May 3, 1863.
Hillis, William	do	Feb. 15, 1863	Feb. 15, 1863	Died of fever at Fort Smith, Arkansas, October 10, 1864.

First regiment Arkansas infantry volunteers. Mustered into service March 25, 1863, (three years;) mustered out August 10, 1865.

COMPANY G—Continued.

Names.	Rank.	Enlistment.	Muster.	Remarks.
Lewis, Bennett	Private	Feb. 15, 1863	Feb. 15, 1863	Died of fever at Waldron, Arkansas, January 15, 1864.
McArver, Andrew J	do	Feb. 15, 1863	Feb. 15, 1863	Died of pneumonia at Fayetteville, Arkansas, April 11, 1863.
Staats, Moses	do	Feb. 15, 1863	Feb. 15, 1863	Died of inflammation of bowels at Fort Smith, Arkansas, October 4, 1863.
White, Thomas	do	Feb. 15, 1863	Feb. 15, 1863	Died of fever at Springfield, Arkansas, May 23, 1862.
Deserted.				
Benton, Mark	Private	Sept. 15, 1863		Deserted at Fort Smith, Arkansas, November 20, 1863.
Blackwell, Richard	do	Sept. 15, 1863		Do.
Cason, William G	do	Jan. 10, 1865	Feb. 25, 1865	Deserted at Fort Smith, Arkansas, April 15, 1865.
Jones, Wilson	do	Feb. 15, 1863		Deserted at Fayetteville, Arkansas, March 20, 1863.
Lemington, James	do	Feb. 15, 1863		Deserted at Fayetteville, Arkansas, March 16, 1863.
Mooney, William R	do	Sept. 15, 1863		Deserted at Springfield, Missouri, March 1, 1863.
Nelson, John	do	Mar. 15, 1863	Mar. 15, 1863	Deserted in Missouri May 23, 1863.
Perry, John	do	Feb. 15, 1863	Feb. 15, 1863	Deserted at Fayetteville, Arkansas, March 22, 1863.
Sharp, James	do	Feb. 15, 1863	Feb. 15, 1863	Deserted at Fayetteville, Arkansas, March 20, 1862.
Discharged.				
Winphrey W. Robinson	Sergeant	Feb. 15, 1863	Feb. 15, 1863	Discharged to accept appointment as 1st lieutenant company A.
Drennon, Hiram	Private	Feb. 15, 1863	Feb. 15, 1863	Discharged for disability November 29, 1864.
Leatherwood, James R	do	Feb. 15, 1863	Feb. 15, 1863	Discharged for disability November 25, 1864.
Rickey, Isom	do	Feb. 15, 1863	Feb. 15, 1863	Discharged May 3, 1865.
Thomas, Joseph	do	Feb. 15, 1863	Feb. 15, 1863	Discharged for disability November 25, 1864.
Wagers, Marvin	do	Feb. 15, 1863	Feb. 15, 1863	Discharged May 3, 1865.
Transferred.				
Leadbetter, James	Private	Feb. 15, 1863	Feb. 15, 1863	Transferred to non-commissioned staff as fife major June 15, 1863.

COMPANY H.

		Date of rank.	
William C. Parker	Captain	July 3, 1862	Appointed from private company E, 1st Arkansas cavalry, to fill original vacancy; mustered out with regiment.
John C. Miles	1st lieutenant	Sept. 25, 1862	Appointed from farrier company E, 1st Arkansas cavalry, to fill original vacancy; died at Waldron, Arkansas, of fever, December 1, 1863.

REPORT OF THE ADJUTANT GENERAL OF ARKANSAS. 193

Name	Rank	Enlisted	Muster	Remarks
Jonathan L. Jones	......do......	Mar. 10, 1863	June 6, 1864	Appointed 2d lieutenant from 1st Arkansas cavalry; promoted 1st lieutenant, vice Miles, deceased; mustered out with regiment.
James W. Searle	2d lieutenant	Dec. 20, 1863	Aug. 22, 1864	Appointed from commissary sergeant 17th Illinois cavalry; mustered out with regiment.
Samuel J. Shelton	1st sergeant	Mar. 10, 1863	Jan. 12, 1865	Appointed from sergeant; mustered out with regiment.
Samuel Barnhill	Sergeant	Mar. 10, 1863	Mar. 25, 1863	Appointed sergeant on organization of company; mustered out with regiment.
John W. Moore	......do......	Mar. 10, 1863	Jan. —, 1864	Appointed from corporal, January —, 1864; mustered out with regiment.
Richard L. Autry	......do......	Mar. 10, 1863	Sept. —, 1864	Appointed from corporal; mustered out with regiment.
James H. Robinson	......do......	Mar. 10, 1863	Jan. 1, 1865	Appointed from private; mustered out with regiment.
James D. Corley	Corporal	Mar. 10, 1863	Mar. 25, 1863	Wounded in action on Mulberry creek, October 18, 1864; no discharge given on muster out of regiment.
Joseph C. Adkins	......do......	Nov. 15, 1863	Aug. 18, 1864	Mustered out with regiment.
John J. Waggoner	......do......	Mar. 10, 1863	Dec. —, 1863	Do.
Caleb Thurman	......do......	Mar. 10, 1863	Dec. —, 1863	Do.
James K. Lee	......do......	Mar. 10, 1863	July —, 1864	Do.
Jesse A. Corley	......do......	Mar. 10, 1863	Jan. —, 1865	Do.
John L. Little	......do......	Sept. 1, 1863	Jan. —, 1865	Do.
John Moore	......do......	Sept. 1, 1863	Jan. 1, 1865	Do.
Allen W. Sams	Musician	Aug. 13, 1863	Feb. 26, 1864	Do.
Atchley, Claborne A	Private	Mar. 10, 1863	Mar. 25, 1863	Mustered out with regiment.
Bridges, John A	......do......	Mar. 1, 1865	April 1, 1865	Do.
Barnhill, Alexander	......do......	Mar. 10, 1863	Mar. 25, 1863	Do.
Barnard, Thomas	......do......	Sept. 23, 1863	Sept. 23, 1864	Do.
Barnes, John R	......do......	Mar. 10, 1863	Mar. 25, 1863	Do.
Beatty, William B	......do......	Mar. 10, 1863	Mar. 25, 1863	Do.
Butler, Edmund F	......do......	Mar. 10, 1863	Mar. 25, 1863	Do.
Butler, Thomas H	......do......	Mar. 10, 1863	Mar. 25, 1863	Do.
Brown, Isaac	......do......	Oct. 2, 1863	Feb. 26, 1864	Do.
Brown, James	......do......	Oct. 2, 1863	Feb. 26, 1864	Do.
Bowers, William	......do......	Mar. 1, 1863	June 6, 1864	Do.
Corley, Solomon O	......do......	Mar. 10, 1863	Mar. 25, 1863	Do.
Corley, Legrand H	......do......	April 1, 1865	April 1, 1865	Do.
Corley, John J	......do......	April 1, 1865	April 1, 1865	Do.
Clark, Hiram	......do......	Mar. 10, 1864	June 6, 1864	Do.
Doak, David	......do......	Mar. 10, 1863	Mar. 25, 1863	Do.
Doak, John	......do......	Mar. 10, 1863	Mar. 25, 1863	Do.
Dotson, John T	......do......	Mar. 10, 1863	Mar. 25, 1863	Do.
Davis, George	......do......	Mar. 10, 1863	Feb. 26, 1864	Do.
Eulaw, Michael A	......do......	Feb. 27, 1865	April 1, 1865	Do.
Frost, Jesse A	......do......	Mar. 10, 1863	Mar. 25, 1863	Do.
Freeman, Albert A	......do......	Oct. 2, 1863	Feb. 26, 1864	Do.
Hooper, Joseph F	......do......	Mar. 10, 1863	Mar. 25, 1863	Do.
Heavener, John	......do......	Oct. 2, 1863	Feb. 26, 1864	Do.
Heavener, Floyd	......do......	Oct. 2, 1863	Feb. 26, 1864	Do.
Houser, Henry	......do......	Mar. 10, 1863	Mar. 25, 1863	Do.
Houser, David	......do......	Mar. 10, 1863	Mar. 25, 1863	Do.
Harp, William J	......do......	Mar. 10, 1863	Mar. 25, 1863	Do.
Hayes, Cooper	......do......	Nov. 1, 1863	Feb. 26, 1864	Do.
Hendrix, William H	......do......	Mar. 1, 1865	April 1, 1865	Do.

Mis. Doc. 53——13

First regiment Arkansas infantry volunteers. Mustered into service March 25, 1863, (three years;) mustered out August 10, 1865.

COMPANY H—Continued.

Names.	Rank.	Enlistment.	Muster.	Remarks.
Johnson, Reuben J	Private	Mar. 10, 1863	Mar. 25, 1863	Mustered out with regiment.
Killian, Jesse	do	Nov. 1, 1863	Feb. 26, 1864	Do.
Larimore, Obadiah	do	Mar. 10, 1863	Mar. 25, 1863	Do.
Larimore, John F	do	Nov. 1, 1863	Feb. 26, 1864	Do.
Looman, H-nry W	do	Sept. 1, 1863	Feb. 26, 1864	Do.
Looman, Joel N	do	Sept. 1, 1863	Feb. 26, 1864	Do.
Lee, Samuel H	do	Mar. 10, 1863	Mar. 25, 1863	Do.
Lee, John C	do	Sept. 1, 1863	Feb. 26, 1864	Do.
Lee, Britton	do	Oct. 2, 1863	Feb. 26, 1864	Do.
Little, James	do	Sept. 1, 1863	June 6, 1864	Do.
Long, Robert H	do	Mar. 10, 1863	Mar. 25, 1863	Do.
McReynolds, James A	do	Mar. 10, 1863	Feb. 26, 1864	Do.
Mathews, Augustus	do	Feb. 1, 1864	Mar. 25, 1863	Do.
Mathews, Jeremiah	do	Mar. 10, 1863	Mar. 25, 1863	Do.
Mathews, Alfred	do	Mar. 10, 1863	Mar. 25, 1863	Do.
Mathews, William	do	Mar. 10, 1863	Mar. 25, 1863	Do.
Moore, William H	do	Mar. 10, 1863	Mar. 25, 1863	Do.
Mullenix, William F	do	Mar. 10, 1863	Mar. 25, 1863	Do.
Nobles, Lewis	do	Mar. 10, 1863	Mar. 25, 1863	Do.
Newlin, Nathaniel	do	Mar. 10, 1863	Mar. 25, 1863	Do.
Oliver, William J	do	Oct. 1, 1864	Oct. 1, 1864	Do.
Plumley, William	do	Mar. 10, 1863	Mar. 25, 1863	Do.
Philps, James W	do	Mar. 10, 1863	Mar. 25, 1863	Do.
Parker, Sergeant M	do	Mar. 10, 1863	Mar. 25, 1863	Do.
Parker, Micajah S	do	Sept. 1, 1863	Feb. 26, 1864	Do.
Parks, William J	do	Mar. 10, 1863	Mar. 25, 1863	Do.
Pinnell, Peter	do	Nov. 1, 1863	Feb. 26, 1864	Do.
Penick, Joseph	do	Dec. 1, 1863	Feb. 26, 1864	Do.
Ragon, Joseph E	do	Mar. 10, 1863	Mar. 25, 1863	Do.
Reed, Oliver	do	Mar. 10, 1863	Mar. 25, 1863	Do.
Reed, Mathew	do	Sept. 1, 1863	Feb. 26, 1864	Do.
Robinson, John W	do	Sept. 1, 1863	Feb. 26, 1864	Do.
Randolph, John T	do	Sept. 1, 1863	Feb. 26, 1864	Do.
Shaver, George W	do	Sept. 23, 1864	Sept. 25, 1864	Do.
Shipley, William	do	Mar. 10, 1863	Mar. 25, 1863	Do.
Shipley, James	do	Mar. 10, 1863	Mar. 25, 1863	Do.
Teague, George W	do	Mar. 10, 1863	Mar. 25, 1863	Do.
Truitt, Scott	do	Oct. 2, 1863	Feb. 26, 1864	Do.
Talbott, Davis	do	Nov. 1, 1863	Feb. 26, 1864	Do.
Trash, Edmund F	do	Mar. 10, 1863	Mar. 25, 1863	Do.
Turner, Judith D	do	Jan. 1, 1865	Jan. 1, 1865	Do.
Womack, Josiah C	do	Mar. 10, 1865	Mar. 25, 1863	Do.
Wells, George	do	Mar. 10, 1865	Mar. 25, 1863	Do.

REPORT OF THE ADJUTANT GENERAL OF ARKANSAS. 195

Name	Rank			Remarks
Wallace, Alfred	do	Sept. 1, 1863	Feb. 26, 1864	Do.
Worthington, James P	do	Apr. 5, 1863	Aug. 12, 1863	Do.
Watkins, Samuel	do	May 4, 1863	Aug. 12, 1863	Do.

Killed in action.

Name	Rank			Remarks
Larimore, Samuel	Private	Oct. 2, 1863	Feb. 26, 1864	Killed at Fort Smith, Arkansas, April 4, 1865.
Lee, Lovett	do	Mar. 10, 1863	Mar. 25, 1863	Killed by guerillas in Franklin county, Arkansas, May 14, 1864.
Lee, Thomas	do	May 1, 1863	Aug. 12, 1863	Killed by guerillas in Franklin county, Arkansas, November 15, 1864.
McKissick, John C	do	Nov. 1, 1863	Feb. 26, 1864	Killed at Camden, Arkansas, April 18, 1864.
Shackley, John	do	Mar. 10, 1863	Mar. 25, 1863	Killed at Fayetteville, Arkansas, April 18, 1864.
Wilkins, Benjamin F	do	Mar. 10, 1863	Mar. 25, 1863	Killed at Haguewood Prairie, September 27, 1863.

Died.

Name	Rank			Remarks
Anderson, Richard M	Sergeant	Mar. 10, 1863	Mar. 25, 1863	Died of brain fever, Fayetteville, Arkansas, April 29, 1863.
Bell, Richard	Private	Mar. 10, 1863	Mar. 25, 1863	Died in Franklin county, Arkansas, October 15, 1863.
Bryant, John	do	Mar. 10, 1863	Mar. 25, 1863	Died of congestion of the brain, Springfield, Missouri, May 6, 1863.
Brown, Thomas	do	Mar. 10, 1863	Mar. 25, 1863	Died of congestion of the brain, Springfield, Missouri, May 4, 1863.
Corley, Leroy F	do	Mar. 10, 1863	Mar. 25, 1863	Died of congestion of the brain, Fayetteville, Arkansas, April 19, 1861.
Corley, James	do	Sept. 23, 1863	Never	Died at Fort Smith, Arkansas, September 30, 1863.
Carter, Joseph	do	Mar. 10, 1863	Mar. 25, 1863	Died at Springfield, Missouri, May 2, 1863.
Hartley, John	do	Mar. 10, 1863	Mar. 25, 1863	Died at Fayetteville, Arkansas, April 2, 1863.
Hixon, John	do	Sept. 1, 1863	Feb. 26, 1864	Died at Fort Smith, Arkansas, February —, 1864.
Moore, James L	do	Mar. 10, 1863	Mar. 25, 1863	Died at Springfield, Missouri, May —, 1863.
McKinney, Jonathan	do	Oct. 1, 1863	Never	Died in Johnson county, Arkansas, May 1, 1864.
Nixon, Licurgus	do	Sept. 1, 1863	Never	Died at Waldron, Arkansas, February 1, 1864.
Glover, John P	do	Sept. 1, 1863	Never	Died at Fort Smith, Arkansas, December 1, 1863.
Lock, William	do	Mar. 10, 1863	Mar. 25, 1863	Died at Fort Smith, Arkansas, March 31, 1865.
Pitts, Isaac D	do	Sept. 1, 1863	Never	Died at Waldron, Arkansas, December 1, 1863.
Welliver, John W	do	Mar. 10, 1863	Mar. 25, 1863	Died at Fort Smith, Arkansas, September 15, 1863.
Welliver, Alexander	do	Mar. 10, 1863	Mar. 25, 1863	Died at Springfield, Missouri, April 30, 1863.
Welliver, Lawyer H	do	Mar. 10, 1863	Mar. 25, 1863	Died of measles at Cassville, Missouri, May 4, 1863.
Wadsworth, David	do	Mar. 10, 1863	Mar. 25, 1863	Died of fever, Springfield, Missouri, May —, 1863.

Deserted.

Name	Rank			Remarks
Wilson, John W	Private	Mar. 10, 1863	Mar. 25, 1863	Deserted at Fayetteville, Arkansas, April 18, 1863.
Thompson, Lewis	do	Mar. 10, 1863	Mar. 25, 1863	Do.
Banks, William	do	Aug. 12, 1863	Aug. 12, 1863	Deserted between Cassville and Fort Smith, Arkansas, August 14, 1863.
Cornelius, Isham	do	Aug. 12, 1863	Aug. 12, 1863	Do.
Ritchie, Daniel	do	Nov. 1, 1863	Feb. 26, 1864	Deserted at Fort Smith, Arkansas, August 25, 1864.
Hamilton, John L	do	Aug. 12, 1863	Aug. 12, 1863	Do.
Dobbs, Reuben	do	Mar. 12, 1864	Mar. 25, 1863	Deserted at Fayetteville, Arkansas, April 18, 1863.
Moore, George	do	Apr. 5, 1864	Never	Deserted at Fort Smith, Arkansas, January 20, 1865.

Discharged.

Name	Rank			Remarks
Brasswell, Charles L	Private	Mar. 10, 1863	Mar. 25, 1863	Discharged for disability March 1, 1865.
Brown, Joel	do	Mar. 10, 1863	Mar. 25, 1863	Discharged for promotion to captain 4th Arkansas cavalry.
Garner, James L	do	Mar. 10, 1863	Mar. 25, 1863	Discharged for promotion to lieutenant 4th Arkansas cavalry.
Laffery, James R	do	Mar. 10, 1863	Mar. 25, 1863	Discharged for promotion to captain 4th Arkansas cavalry.

First regiment Arkansas infantry volunteers. Mustered into service March 25, 1863, (three years;) mustered out August 10, 1865.

COMPANY H—Continued.

Names.	Rank.	Enlistment.	Muster.	Remarks.
Plumby, Isaac	Private	Mar. 10, 1863	Mar. 25, 1863	Discharged for wounds received in action at Haguewood Prairie, Sept. 27, 1863.
Pruitt, Samuel	do	Mar. 10, 1863	Mar. 25, 1863	Discharged for disability March 1, 1865.
Ragan, Jonathan C	do	Mar. 10, 1863	Mar. 25, 1863	Do.

COMPANY I.

Names.	Rank.	Enlistment.	Date of rank.	Remarks.
William J. Heffington	Captain	Mar. 20, 1863	Mar. 20, 1863	Captain from organization; killed by the enemy in Western Arkansas, August 15, 1863.
John Whiteford	do	Sept. 1, 1863	Never	Assigned to duty as captain September 1, 1863 ; acting from that date to May 16, 1864, then dropped from the rolls by order of Brigadier General Thayer, commanding district of frontier.
Samuel Bard	do	Feb. 14, 1863	Aug. 22, 1864	Promoted from 1st lieutenant, company A, vice Heffington, deceased; mustered out with regiment.
Aaron C. Terry	1st lieutenant	July 21, 1862	Mar. 20, 1863	Appointed 1st lieutenant from commissary sergeant company C, 1st Arkansas cavalry, to fill original vacancy ; resigned March 12, 1864.
Aaron L. Thompson	do	Mar. —, 1863	Nov. 16, 1864	Appointed from 1st sergeant, vice Terry, resigned ; mustered out with regiment.
Robert Morrison	2d lieutenant	Mar. 20, 1863	Mar. 20, 1863	Appointed from civil life; dropped from the rolls May 31, 1864.
Martin Deadwiley	1st sergeant	Mar. 20, 1863	Mar. 1, 1865	Appointed from sergeant; mustered out with regiment.
Andrew J. Fry	Sergeant	Mar. 1, 1863	Feb. 27, 1864	Appointed from private; mustered out with regiment.
John Shelton	do	Mar. 1, 1863	Feb. 27, 1864	Appointed from corporal; mustered out with regiment.
George H. Morgan	do	Mar. 17, 1863	May 31, 1865	Do.
John Spencer	do	Feb. 1, 1863	May 31, 1865	do.
John A. Rogers	Corporal	Mar. 20, 1863	Mar. 20, 1863	do.
John Angel	do	Oct. 1, 1863	Nov. 1, 1863	Mustered out with regiment.
John H. Swilling	do	Mar. 17, 1863	Feb. 27, 1864	Do.
William A. Carter	do	Mar. 17, 1863	Feb. 27, 1864	Do.
William N. Jones	do	Mar. 17, 1863	Sept. 1, 1864	Do.
Pleasant Blevin	do	May 28, 1864	Sept. 1, 1864	Do.
William Mitchell	do	Feb. 18, 1863	May 31, 1865	Do.
Harry Hall	do	Mar. 15, 1863	May 31, 1865	Do.

Names.	Rank.	Enlistment.	Muster.	Remarks.
Adams, George W	Private	Mar. 17, 1863	Mar. 20, 1863	Mustered out with regiment.
Aday, Boze J	do	Mar. 1, 1863	Apr. 30, 1865	Do.
Bernay, John W	do	Oct. 1, 1863	Feb. 26, 1864	Do

REPORT OF THE ADJUTANT GENERAL OF ARKANSAS. 197

Bridges, Freeling H	do	Mar. 1, 1863	Mar. 20, 1863	Do.
Britt, James B	do	Mar. 17, 1863	Mar. 20, 1863	Do.
Black, Marcus	do	Mar. 20, 1863	Mar. 20, 1863	Do.
Capps, James	do	Feb. 4, 1863	Mar. 20, 1863	Do.
Cooper, George W	do	Mar. 17, 1863	Mar. 20, 1863	Do.
Clay, Dibrell T	do	July 20, 1864	Apr. 20, 1865	Do.
Cayle, Charles T	do	Mar. 1, 1863	Mar. 20, 1863	Do.
Carter, John G	do	Mar. 17, 1863	Mar. 20, 1863	Do.
Calvert, William J	do	Mar. 1, 1863	Mar. 20, 1863	Do.
Calvert, Isaac W	do	Mar. 20, 1863	Mar. 20, 1863	Do.
East, Martin	do	Mar. 1, 1863	Mar. 20, 1863	Do.
Findely, Christopher C	do	Mar. 20, 1863	Mar. 20, 1863	Do.
Fry, Calvin M	do	Mar. 1, 1863	Mar. 20, 1863	Do.
Fink, Levi	do	July 1, 1863	Aug. 13, 1863	Do.
Fussell, John O	do	July 1, 1863	Mar. 20, 1863	Do.
Gann, Vinyard	do	Mar. 1, 1863	Mar. 20, 1863	Do.
Graves, Alonzo N	do	Mar. 20, 1863	Mar. 20, 1863	Do.
Hodges, John T	do	Feb. 1, 1865	Apr. 30, 1865	Do.
Harris, Samuel J	do	Mar. 20, 1863	Mar. 20, 1863	Do.
Hall, George W	do	Feb. 18, 1863	Mar. 20, 1863	Do.
Hall, James C	do	Apr. 2, 1865	Apr. 2, 1865	Do.
Hurley, Jacob	do	Mar. 15, 1863	Mar. 20, 1863	Do.
Jackson, Silas M	do	Mar. 17, 1863	Mar. 20, 1863	Do.
Kersey, George R	do	Sept. 1, 1863	Feb. 26, 1864	Do.
Kersey, Thomas	do	Sept. 1, 1863	Feb. 26, 1864	Do.
Kibbler, John B	do	Mar. 17, 1863	Mar. 20, 1863	Do.
Kirkwood, John H	do	Mar. 17, 1863	Mar. 20, 1863	Do.
Kerr, John	do	Apr. 2, 1865	Apr. 2, 1865	Do.
Keeland, William R	do	Apr. 2, 1865	Apr. 2, 1865	Do.
Keeland, John H	do	Feb. 18, 1863	Mar. 20, 1863	Do.
Lightfoot, Rufus	do	Feb. 18, 1863	Mar. 20, 1863	Do.
Lightfoot, John	do	Oct. 1, 1863	Feb. 26, 1864	Do.
Little, Wiley B	do	Nov. 5, 1864	June 2, 1865	Do.
Lofson, George A	do	Mar. 20, 1863	Mar. 20, 1863	Do.
Massengill, Henry A	do	Oct. 1, 1863	Oct. 1, 1863	Do.
Peters, William H	do	Oct. 1, 1863	Feb. 26, 1864	Do.
Peters, Hiram	do	Feb. 25, 1863	Mar. 20, 1863	Do.
Poole, Augustus C	do	Mar. 15, 1863	Aug. 13, 1863	Do.
Page, Calvin	do	July 1, 1863	Mar. 20, 1863	Do.
Priddy, John G	do	Mar. 15, 1863	Mar. 20, 1863	Do.
Ranson, William	do	Mar. 17, 1863	Mar. 20, 1863	Do.
Robinson, Isaac	do	Mar. 20, 1863	Mar. 20, 1863	Do.
Robinson, Darling G	do	Mar. 17, 1863	Mar. 20, 1863	Do.
Robinson, John R	do	Dec. 12, 1863	Feb. 26, 1864	Do.
Robinson, Jacob H	do	Mar. 17, 1863	Mar. 20, 1863	Do.
Rogers, Eddy J	do	Mar. 17, 1863	Mar. 20, 1863	Do.
Rogers, Joseph G	do	Mar. 1, 1863	Mar. 20, 1863	Do.
Ross, Perry	do	Feb. 1, 1863	Mar. 20, 1863	Do.
Scott, William	do	Dec. 1, 1863	Feb. 26, 1864	Do.
Shoemaker, Frederick	do	Mar. 1, 1863	Mar. 20, 1863	Do.
Spencer, James	do	Mar. 1, 1863	Mar. 20, 1863	Do.
Stephens, Sherod A	do	Mar. 1, 1863	Mar. 20, 1863	Do.

First regiment Arkansas infantry volunteers. Mustered into service March 25, 1863, (three years;) mustered out August 10, 1865.

COMPANY I—Continued.

Names.	Rank.	Enlistment.	Muster.	Remarks.
Swilling, George W	Private	Mar. 17, 1863	Mar. 20, 1863	Mustered out with regiment.
Sharp, John A	do	Mar. 17, 1863	Mar. 20, 1863	Do.
Straitt, Powhatan	do	Mar. 1, 1863	Mar. 20, 1863	Do.
Sisk, George W	do	Feb. 1, 1865	April 30, 1865	Do.
Wynn, Josiah	do	May 28, 1864	June 6, 1864	Do.
Wells, William	do	June 10, 1864	June 10, 1864	Do.
White, Berry	do	April 1, 1865	April 1, 1865	Do.
White, Thomas R	do	July 1, 1863	Feb. 26, 1864	Do.
White, Wilson C	do	Sept. 5, 1863	Feb. 26, 1864	Do.
Willis, William	do	Feb. 11, 1864	Feb. 26, 1864	Do.
Young, James	do	Mar. 20, 1863	Mar. 20, 1863	Do.

Killed in action.

Gann, Robert	Private	Mar. 1, 1863	Mar. 20, 1863	Killed in Sebastian county, Arkansas, November 14, 1863.
Hawkins, William	do	Mar. 15, 1863	Mar. 20, 1863	Killed at Haguewood Prairie, Arkansas, September 27, 1863.
Kersey, George W	do	Sept. 1, 1863	Feb. 26, 1864	Killed by a citizen in Fort Smith, Arkansas, January 9, 1865.
Morgan, John F	do	Mar. 17, 1863	Mar. 20, 1863	Accidentally shot by his own gun, August 1, 1862.
Shrewder, William L	do	Mar. 20, 1863	Mar. 20, 1863	Killed in Johnson county, Arkansas, May 15, 1865.

Died.

Bennett, William	Private	Mar. 17, 1863	Mar. 20, 1863	Died of bronchitis at Springfield, Missouri, May 15, 1863.
Colvert, Benjamin	do	Mar. 20, 1863	Mar. 20, 1863	Died of chronic diarrhœa at Springfield, Missouri, May 17, 1863.
Colvert, Joseph G	do	Mar. 20, 1863	Mar. 20, 1863	Died of chronic diarrhœa at Fort Smith, Arkansas, September 20, 1863.
McClendon, James	do	Feb. 6, 1863	Mar. 20, 1863	Died of typhoid fever at Cassville, Missouri, April 30, 1863.
McClendon, Leonard	do	Mar. 1, 1863	Mar. 20, 1863	Died of chronic diarrhœa at Springfield, Missouri, May 13, 1863.
McClendon, John F	do	Feb. 1, 1863	Mar. 20, 1863	Died of congestive chills at Waldron, Arkansas, November 17, 1863.
Oley, William P	do	July 1, 1863	Aug. 13, 1863	do.
Poole, Clayborne A	Corporal	Feb. 25, 1863	Mar. 20, 1863	Died of congestion of the lungs at Fort Gibson, Arkansas, September 6, 1863.
Rogers, Henry	Private	Mar. 17, 1863	Mar. 20, 1863	Died of chronic diarrhœa at Springfield, Missouri, August 25, 1863.
Snyder, George W	do	Mar. 1, 1863	Mar. 20, 1863	Died of typhoid fever at Yell county, Arkansas, November 10, 1863.
Spingston, Fenton	Sergeant	Mar. 20, 1863	Mar. 20, 1863	Died of erysipelas at Fort Smith, Arkansas, February 28, 1864.
Stephens, Pleasant P	Private	Mar. 2, 1863	Mar. 20, 1863	Died of typhoid fever at Fort Smith, Arkansas, October 29, 1864.
Truitt, John W	do	Mar. 15, 1863	Mar. 20, 1863	Died of typhoid fever at Fort Smith, Arkansas, September 4, 1864.

Deserted.

Angel, James	Private	Sept 1, 1863	Never	Deserted November 6, 1863.
Bell, E. G	do	Oct. 1, 1863	Never	Do.
Baker, Samuel W	do	Oct. 1, 1863	Feb. 26, 1864	Deserted October 30, 1864.
Fink, George	do	July 1, 1863	Aug. 3, 1863	Deserted September 27, 1863.
Fowler, William	do	Sept. 1, 1863	Never	Deserted February 16, 1864.

REPORT OF THE ADJUTANT GENERAL OF ARKANSAS. 199

Name	Rank	Date	Remarks
Gazaway, Thomas	do	Oct. 1, 1863	Deserted November 6, 1863.
Griffin, William P	do	Feb. 20, 1864	Deserted September 24, 1864.
Howard, William	do	Oct. 1, 1863	Deserted November 6, 1863.
Hanson, David W	do	Mar. 17, 1863	Do.
Hutchinson, Robert W	do	Mar. 17, 1863	Deserted February 16, 1864.
Johnson, John	do	Mar. 1, 1863	Deserted January 11, 1865.
Johnson, Eli	do	Mar. 20, 1863	Deserted November 1, 1864.
Mathews, Archibald	do	Mar. 1, 1863	Deserted March 20, 1863.
Morgan, William T	do	Mar. 20, 1863	Deserted February 16, 1864.
Morgan, John B	do	Mar. 17, 1863	Do.
Mitchell, William, (2)	do	Sept. 1, 1863	Do.
McBride, James	do	Mar. 17, 1863	Deserted September 24, 1864.
Oehler, Paul C	do	Feb. 5, 1863	Deserted January 10, 1865.
Peters, Andrew J	do	Oct. 1, 1863	Deserted November 6, 1863.
Peters, Michael	do	Oct. 1, 1863	Do.
Steel, Francis M	do	Oct. 1, 1863	Do.
Whitley, Henry	do	Sept. 1, 1863	Deserted February 16, 1864.
Wiggens, Isaac	do	Mar. 17, 1863	Deserted January 11, 1865.

Transferred.

Name	Rank	Date	Remarks
Webb, David W	Private	Mar. 15, 1863	Appointed 1st lieutenant 4th Arkansas cavalry.
Spiva, Jonas B	do	Feb. 18, 1863	Do.
White, Burrell T	do	Dec. 10, 1864	Dishonorably discharged June 19, 1865.

COMPANY K.

Name	Rank	Date of rank.	Remarks
Abial Stevens	Captain	—, 1861	Mar. 25, 1863	Appointed from quartermaster sergeant company F, 10th Illinois cavalry, to fill original vacancy; mustered out with regiment.
Lorenzo D. Jameson	1st lieutenant	Aug. 5, 1862	Mar. 18, 1863	Appointed from sergeant company H, 1st Arkansas cavalry, to fill original vacancy; discharged May 18, 1863.
Joseph D Rambo	do	—, 1862	May 18, 1863	Appointed from sergeant company B, 19th Iowa infantry, vice Jameson, discharged; mustered out with regiment.
Augustus T. Cullen	2d lieutenant	1862	Mar. 25, 1863	Appointed from sergeant 1st Arkansas cavalry; resigned November 16, 1864.
John F. Davis	1st sergeant	Feb. 18, 1863	Mar. 1, 1864	Appointed from private; mustered out with regiment.
Calvin E. Hurt	Sergeant	Mar. 15, 1863	Mar. 25, 1863	Do.
William A. Ayres	do	Mar. 20, 1863	May 1, 1863	Do.
George F. Palmer	do	Feb. 7, 1863	Mar. 1, 1864	Do.
George Francisco	do	Feb. 7, 1863	Mar. 1, 1864	Do.
Cornelius Emberton	Corporal	Mar. 15, 1863	June 1, 1865	Mustered out with regiment.
Riley M. Moore	do	Nov. 1, 1863	Oct. 1, 1864	Do.
Joseph Looper	do	Feb. 24, 1863	May 1, 1863	Do.
Jared Ball	do	Feb. 13, 1863	Mar. 1, 1864	Do.
John Wigthon	do	Feb. 15, 1863	Mar. 1, 1864	Do.
Clavis Depee	do	Mar. 20, 1863	June 1, 1865	Do.
Leven S. Corbell	do	Feb. 25, 1863	Mar. 1, 1864	Do.
John W. Garrison	do			Do.

First regiment Arkansas infantry volunteers. Mustered into service March 25, 1863, (three years;) mustered out August 10, 1865.

COMPANY K—Continued.

Names.	Rank.	Enlistment.	Muster.	Remarks.
Ayres, Leroy G.	Private	July 1, 1863	Aug. 12, 1863	Mustered out with regiment.
Benbrooks, James	do	Mar. 15, 1863	Mar. 25, 1863	Do.
Brown, Samuel D.	do	Mar. 20, 1863	Mar. 25, 1863	Do.
Brown, William J.	do	Mar. 20, 1863	Mar. 25, 1863	Do.
Brown, Jesse	do	Mar. 20, 1863	Mar. 25, 1863	Do.
Ball, William W.	do	Mar. 20, 1863	Mar. 25, 1863	Do.
Butler, Joshua A.	do	May 20, 1863	Aug. 12, 1863	Do.
Bane, John A.	do	Feb. 15, 1863	Mar. 25, 1863	Do.
Copeland, Josiah	do	Mar. 20, 1863	Mar. 25, 1863	Do.
Conger, Thomas	do	Mar. 20, 1863	Mar. 25, 1863	Do.
Craddock, William	do	Mar. 20, 1863	Mar. 25, 1863	Do.
Davis, Jacob L.	do	June 1, 1863	Aug. 12, 1863	Do.
Daniel, Erby	do	Mar. 15, 1863	Mar. 25, 1863	Do.
Daniels, Lewis	do	Mar. 15, 1863	April 25, 1863	Do.
Daniels, Thomas J.	do	Mar. 23, 1863	April 30, 1865	Do.
Dunlap, Benjamin F.	do	Feb. 15, 1863	Mar. 25, 1863	Do.
Ellis, David	do	Mar. 5, 1863	Mar. 25, 1863	Do.
Echols, Winfield S.	do	Mar. 1, 1863	Mar. 25, 1863	Do.
Francisco, Rufus	do	Feb. 28, 1863	Mar. 25, 1863	Do.
Gilliam, Lemuel J.	do	Mar. 20, 1863	Mar. 25, 1863	Do.
Gaddy, Jasper A.	do	Mar. 20, 1863	Aug. 12, 1863	Do.
Gafford, Jesse	do	Sept. 1, 1863	Feb. 26, 1864	Do.
Hurst, Fielding L.	do	Mar. 20, 1863	Mar. 25, 1863	Do.
Hewley, Alford W.	do	Mar. 20, 1863	Mar. 25, 1863	Do.
Hagan, Edward C.	do	Mar. 15, 1863	Mar. 25, 1863	Do.
Hait, John W.	do	Feb. 10, 1863	Feb. 27, 1863	Do.
Jones, Alexander W.	do	June 1, 1863	Aug. 12, 1863	Do.
Kerr, Spencer G.	do	June 1, 1863	Aug. 12, 1863	Do.
Kerr, Isaac R.	do	June 10, 1863	Aug. 12, 1863	Do.
Kerr, Robert B.	do	June 1, 1863	Aug. 12, 1863	Do.
Kuykendall, John	do	Mar. 20, 1863	Mar. 25, 1863	Do.
Lewellen, James	do	Mar. 15, 1863	Mar. 25, 1863	Do.
Lewis, Richard	do	Mar. 20, 1863	Mar. 25, 1863	Do.
Morris, Byron S.	do	Mar. 15, 1863	Mar. 25, 1863	Do.
McKinney, Jones B.	do	Feb. 4, 1863	Feb. 29, 1863	Do.
McCrary, Charles	do	Feb. 25, 1863	Feb. 29, 1863	Do.
Miller, Jacob L.	do	Feb. 4, 1863	Feb. 26, 1863	Do.
Mahoney, Crawford	do	Sept. 1, 1863	Feb. 26, 1864	Do.
Meddors, George W.	do	May 1, 1864	June 26, 1864	Do.
Meddors, Andrew J.	do	Mar. 15, 1863	Mar. 25, 1863	Do.
Oxford, Lafayette D.	do	Mar. 20, 1863	Mar. 25, 1863	Do.
Pertiler, Winfield S.	do			Do.

REPORT OF THE ADJUTANT GENERAL OF ARKANSAS. 201

Name	Rank	Enlisted	Date	Remarks
Poole, Thomas	do	Nov. 1, 1863	Feb. 26, 1864	Do.
Pope, Henry H	do	Jan. 1, 1864	Feb. 26, 1864	Do.
Pinkaman, Samuel	do	Feb. 15, 1863	Feb. 29, 1863	Do.
Pinkaman, James	do	Feb. 21, 1863	Feb. 29, 1863	Do.
Qualls, Joseph C	do	Mar. 20, 1863	Mar. 25, 1863	Do.
Ramsey, John W	do	Mar. 20, 1863	Mar. 25, 1864	Do.
Richardson, John	do	Nov. 1, 1863	June 20, 1865	Do.
Roberts, William C	do	Sept. 1, 1864	Feb. 20, 1865	Do.
Robertson, George W	do	Mar. 15, 1863	Mar. 25, 1863	Do.
Rose, Lemuel J	do	Mar. 20, 1863	Mar. 25, 1863	Do.
Self, William	do	Mar. 20, 1863	April 30, 1865	Do.
Self, Nathan	do	Mar. 23, 1865	Mar. 25, 1865	Do.
Sinclair, William	do	Feb. 24, 1865	Mar. 26, 1865	Do.
Shoptaw, Mathew T	do	Sept. 1, 1863	Feb. 26, 1864	Do.
Stone, William J	do	Feb. 4, 1864	Mar. 25, 1863	Do.
Strodes, William J	do	Mar. 20, 1863	Mar. 25, 1863	Do.
Tipton, Calvin	do	Mar. 20, 1863	Mar. 25, 1863	Do.
Weese, James	do	Feb. 27, 1863	Mar. 25, 1863	Sentenced by general court-martial to serve term of enlistment at hard labor, with loss of all pay and allowances; no discharge given on muster out of regiment.
Yancey, John	do			

Killed.

Name	Rank	Enlisted	Date	Remarks
Harp, Elijah	Private	May 1, 1863	Aug. 12, 1863	Killed by guerillas in Newton county, Arkansas, September 15, 1864.
Maybee, Morley	do	Nov. 1, 1863	Feb. 26, 1864	Killed by guerillas in Scott county, Arkansas, March 17, 1864.
Stout, Lemuel J	do	Sept. 1, 1863	Feb. 26, 1864	Do. do.
Tull, Franklin	do	Nov. 1, 1863	Feb. 20, 1864	Do. do.
Tull, George W	do	Nov. 1, 1863	Feb. 26, 1864	Do. do.

Died.

Name	Rank	Enlisted	Date	Remarks
Anderson, Enoch	Private	Mar. 15, 1863	Mar. 15, 1863	Died of brain fever at Fort Smith, Arkansas, June 13, 1864.
Benn, Joshua	do	Mar. 15, 1863	Mar. 15, 1863	Died of brain fever at Fort Blunt, in Cherokee Nation, November 15, 1863.
Carpenter, Benjamin	do	Mar. 15, 1863	Mar. 15, 1863	Died of brain fever at Springfield, Missouri, May 26, 1863.
Casey, Robert	do	Mar. 15, 1863	Mar. 15, 1863	Died of measles at Cassville, Missouri, May 1, 1863.
Casey, Miles P	do	Mar. 15, 1864	Mar. 15, 1864	Died of inflammation of the brain at Fort Smith, Arkansas, September 19, 1863.
Cooper, William	do	Mar. 15, 1863	Mar. 20, 1863	Died of measles at Flint Creek, Missouri, May 1, 1863.
Garner, John	do	July 1, 1863	Aug. 12, 1863	Died of congestive chills at Fort Smith, Arkansas, November 10, 1863.
Hawkins, James	do	Mar. 15, 1863	Mar. 15, 1863	Died of pneumonia at Springfield, Missouri, June 9, 1863.
Harkness, Joseph C	do	Mar. 20, 1863	Mar. 21, 1863	Died at Springfield, Missouri, September 21, 1863.
Harkness, James Y	do	Mar. 20, 1863	Mar. 20, 1863	Died of brain fever at Waldron, Arkansas, January 10, 1861.
Laferry, John W	do	Mar. 15, 1863	Mar. 15, 1863	Died of brain fever at Springfield, Missouri, June 29, 1863.
Lamb, Larkin F	do	Mar. 20, 1863	Mar. 20, 1863	Died of smallpox at Fort Smith, Arkansas, September 15, 1864.
Stevens, John W. C	do	Mar. 20, 1863	Mar. 20, 1863	Died of fever at Fort Smith, Arkansas, September 3, 1863.
Smith, Anthony	do	Mar. 20, 1863	Mar. 20, 1863	Died of congestive fever at Fort Smith, Arkansas, September 21, 1864.
Turney, Isom	do	Mar. 1, 1863	Mar. 1, 1863	Died of congestive fever at Fort Smith, Arkansas, September 14, 1864.

Deserted.

Name	Rank	Enlisted	Date	Remarks
Allison, William	Corporal	Mar. 15, 1863	Mar. 15, 1863	Deserted in Benton county, Arkansas, April 5, 1863.
Allison, Lorenzo	Private	Mar. 15, 1863	Mar. 15, 1863	Do.
Ayers, William	do	Mar. 15, 1863	Mar. 15, 1863	Deserted at Cassville, Missouri, April 5, 1863.
Brimage, Ezekiel	Corporal	Mar. 15, 1863	Mar. 15, 1863	Deserted in Newton county, Arkansas, April 17, 1863.

First regiment Arkansas infantry volunteers. Mustered into service March 25, 1863, (three years;) mustered out August 10, 1865.

COMPANY K—Continued.

Names.	Rank.	Enlistment.	Muster.	Remarks.
Blakemore, Fielding	Private	Mar. 15, 1863	Mar. 15, 1863	Deserted at Fayetteville, Arkansas, April 1, 1863.
Bara, William	do	Mar. 15, 1863	Mar. 20, 1863	Do. do.
Blankenship, Elisha	do	Sept. 1, 1863	Mar. 15, 1863	Deserted near Waldron, Arkansas, November 11, 1863.
Bird, Richard M	do	Mar. 15, 1863	Mar. 15, 1863	Deserted in Newton county, Arkansas, October 11, 1863.
Brimage, William C	do	Mar. 15, 1863	Mar. 15, 1863	Do.
Casey, William F	Corporal	Mar. 15, 1863	Mar. 15, 1863	Deserted in Newton county, Arkansas, January 5, 1863.
Dunham, George	Private	Mar. 15, 1863	Mar. 20, 1863	Deserted at Cassville, Missouri, May 1, 1863.
Goodman, James	do	Sept. 1, 1863		Deserted at Waldron, Arkansas, December 15, 1863.
Lewis, William	do	Mar. 20, 1863	Mar. 20, 1863	Deserted at Fayetteville, Arkansas, April 1, 1863.
Lewis, Charles T	do	Mar. 15, 1863	Mar. 20, 1863	Do.
McDaniel, Marmaduke	do	Mar. 15, 1863	Mar. 20, 1863	do.
Nobbet, John	do	Mar. 15, 1863	Mar. 15, 1863	do.
Oxford, John	Sergeant	Mar. 15, 1863	Mar. 15, 1863	Deserted at Fayetteville, Arkansas, April 25, 1863.
Oxford, Wilson	Corporal	Mar. 15, 1863	Mar. 20, 1863	Deserted at Waldron, Arkansas, December 15, 1863.
Preston, Benjamin M	Private	Mar. 20, 1863	Mar. 20, 1863	Deserted at Fayetteville, Arkansas, March 26, 1863.
Shockley, John	do	Mar. 20, 1863	Mar. 20, 1863	Deserted at Van Buren, Arkansas, October 31, 1863.
Sykes, Joseph	do	Mar. 20, 1863	Mar. 20, 1863	Deserted at Fayetteville, Arkansas, April 10, 1863.
Smith, Samuel	do	Mar. 20, 1863	Mar. 20, 1863	Do.
Smith, Benjamin F	do	Mar. 20, 1863	Mar. 20, 1863	do.
Tiney, Edward	do	Mar. 20, 1863	Mar. 20, 1863	Deserted at Waldron, Arkansas, January 5, 1862.
Webster, William A	Corporal	Mar. 15, 1863	Mar. 15, 1863	Deserted at Fayetteville, Arkansas, April 25, 1863.
Wilson, Waite	Private	Mar. 15, 1863	Mar. 15, 1863	Deserted at Fayetteville, Arkansas, April 1, 1863.
Discharged.				
Corbell, Josiah	Private	Mar. 20, 1863	Mar. 20, 1863	Discharged for disability March 1, 1865.
Gaddy, Samuel	do	May 10, 1863	Aug. 10, 1863	Do.
Kerr, Rolley C	do	June 1, 1863	Aug. 10, 1863	Discharged for disability November 24, 1864.
Ruff, David C	do	Feb. 27, 1863	Feb. 27, 1863	Discharged for promotion to captain 46th regiment Missouri enrolled militia, November 18, 1864.
Taylor, Benjamin F	Sergeant	Feb. 27, 1863	Feb. 27, 1863	Discharged for promotion to captain 3d Arkansas cavalry, February 14, 1864.
Thorn, Thomas	Private	Mar. 20, 1863	Mar. 25, 1863	Discharged May 3, 1865.
Transferred.				
Brown, Joseph A	Private	Mar. 20, 1863	Mar. 25, 1863	Transferred to non-commissioned staff as quartermaster sergeant August 1, 1864.
Oliver, Patrick H	do	June 20, 1863	Aug. 11, 1863	Transferred to non-commissioned staff as regimental commissary sergeant August 1, 1864.
Turney, Josiah S	Sergeant	Mar. 20, 1863	Mar. 25, 1863	Transferred to non-commissioned staff as sergeant major March 1, 1864.

HISTORICAL MEMORANDA.—FIRST ARKANSAS INFANTRY VOLUNTEERS.

In November, 1862, authority was given by Major General Schofield, then commanding the "Army of the Frontier," to Dr. James M. Johnson, of Huntsville, Madison county, Arkansas, to raise infantry troops from the State. This authority was general, one regiment to be completed, however, before another was undertaken; and such a course was to be pursued until a different policy should be determined upon.

Early in the war Dr. Johnson's Union sentiments were avowed, and in April, 1862, being able no longer to remain at home in safety, he left Huntsville with Isaac Murphy, now governor of the State, and his brother, F. M. Johnson, afterwards major 1st Arkansas infantry. Arriving at an outpost of the old "Army of the Southwest," at Keitsville, Missouri, he promptly reported to General Curtis, then in command of this army, and was placed upon his staff as a volunteer aid. Subsequently he rendered valuable services to Generals Schofield, Totten, and Herron, and accompanied the "Army of the Frontier," on its first march into northwestern Arkansas, in October, 1862, under the command of General Schofield. Returning with this army to Elkhorn Tavern, he received the authority alluded to, marched with the army in the campaign that terminated in the battle of Prairie Grove, and on the 25th day of March, 1863, the regiment was raised, and Dr. Johnson was mustered into the service as its colonel. The following communication from Major F. M. Johnson, then in command, gives some account of the subsequent services of the regiment:

"HEADQUARTERS FIRST ARKANSAS INFANTRY, *Fort Smith, Arkansas, June* 26, 1865.

"GENERAL: I have the honor to submit the following report:

"At the time of the muster in of J. M. Johnson as colonel of this regiment it numbered thirty-six commissioned officers and eight hundred and ten enlisted men, recruited in the previous sixty days in Madison, Washington, Newton, Benton, Searcy, and Crawford counties. It participated in the battle of Fayetteville, under the immediate command of Lieutenant Colonel E. J. Searle and Major E. D. Ham, on the 18th day of April, 1863, and marched for Springfield, Missouri, on the 25th day of that month. On the 6th day of July it was ordered to Cassville, Missouri, where it shortly afterwards arrived, and on the 17th day of August joined the Army of the Frontier, under command of Major General Blunt, at Fort Gibson, Cherokee Nation, pursued the rebels under Cooper and Stanwatie to Perryville, in the Choctaw Nation, and, returning to Fort Smith, was the first regiment to enter the garrison, on the first day of September, 1863. Shortly afterwards, by order of Brigadier General McNeil, the regiment proceeded to Waldron, and remained there until February, 1864, when it was again ordered to report at Fort Smith, to take part in the movement southward, under Brigadier General Thayer; left Fort Smith with the frontier division on the 24th day of March, 1864, forming part of the first brigade, under Colonel John Edwards; participated in the battle of Moscow, losing three men killed and several wounded; entered Camden on the 16th day of April, 1864, and was engaged in a reconnoissance of the enemy after the battle of Poisoned Springs; left Camden on the 26th of April, and, as part of the right wing of the Union army, was engaged with the enemy at the battle of Saline river, where it repulsed a strong flanking party with considerable loss to the enemy, and losing no men itself. On the first day of May, 1864, the regiment arrived at Little Rock, and proceeded thence to Fort Smith, where it arrived on the 17th day of the same month; since which time it has been engaged in escort and guard duty on the frontier. The greatest aggregate was in November, 1863—nine hundred and seventy-nine (979) officers and men; the lowest in March, 1865, seven hundred and seventy-four, (774;) present aggregate, seven hundred and eighty-eight, (788,) thirty-one (31) commissioned officers and seven hundred and fifty-seven (757) enlisted men.

"Very respectfully, your obedient servant,
"F. M. JOHNSON, *Major, Commanding Regiment.*

"A. W. BISHOP, *Adjutant General, Arkansas.*"

Aside from the operations of the regiment embraced in this brief *resumé*, detachments were frequently sent out to succor Union men—a duty which, from their familiarity with the country, they were particularly well qualified to discharge. In September, 1863, it became known at Fort Smith that several hundred men of this class had gathered together from the surrounding country, upon and near the Magazine mountain, whither they had been compelled to flee for security, and though generally having arms of their own, were much in need of ammunition. To relieve them, Captain William C. Parker, of the 1st Arkansas infantry, was directed to proceed, with sixty men, to their rendezvous; which he did, accomplishing the object for which he was sent. On his return, while crossing Hagnewood prairie, in Franklin county, he was suddenly confronted by the rebel General Shelby's command, then moving northward on his well-known raiding expedition into Missouri. A stubborn fight ensued, Captain Parker slowly falling back until he reached the timber, where the unequal contest was still carried on, until, finding himself nearly surrounded, he directed his men to escape as best they could. In this encounter he lost twenty-two men killed and taken prisoners, but killing and wounding nearly the same number of the enemy. Captain Parker himself succeeded with the rest of his men in arriving safely at Fort Smith, when instant measures being taken by Colonel Johnson to advise Colonel Harrison, then commanding at Fayetteville, of Shelby's march northward, the intelligence was quickly circulated through southwestern Missouri, and Shelby's movement was in a great measure frustrated.

As early as the summer of 1862 bands of Union men similar to that relieved by Captain Parker had, in various portions of western Arkansas, consorted together, and, though compelled by oppression and violence to leave their homes, were accustomed to take refuge among the hills and in the woods, and no extent of persecution succeeded in driving them from the State. Commonly known as "Mountain Feds," they were true to the Union to the last, and from time to time gave valuable assistance to the organized forces operating in various portions of the State. To those in command at Fayetteville, Fort Smith, Van Buren, Clarksville, and Dardanelle, they were especially serviceable, and though it would be difficult, if not impossible, now to recount their exploits, they will long be remembered in Arkansas as men whose loyalty was put to the severest tests, shining out conspicuously when the federal arm was not outstretched for their relief. Many of them entered various Arkansas regiments, the 1st infantry among the number, as the Union army advanced; but not until the rebellion was suppressed did some of them cease their irregular though necessary warfare. From Newton county they were never entirely driven, and through their resistance, which was specially organized and directed by James R. Vanderpool, of that county, captain of company C, 1st Arkansas infantry, rebel conscription therein was in a great measure defeated.

In Yell county William J. Heffington, well known in western Arkansas as "Wild Bill," maintained himself with a band of these men for months, when the surrounding country was held by the enemy, and repeated efforts were made for his capture. Afterwards reporting to Colonel Johnson with a number of his men, who were organized into a company, with himself as captain, he again moved southward of the Boston mountains, and crossing the Arkansas river, was preparing to conduct other citizens to the federal lines, when he heard of the abandonment of northwestern Arkansas by the Union forces, (April, 1863,) and determined to remain in the State. This he did until the August following, when he was killed by guerillas, near the Arkansas river, while going northward to procure relief for a large number of the Union men of his section of the State, who banded together in the vicinity of the Magazine, Short, and Petit Jean mountains, were successfully resisting all attempts at their capture. After the death of Heffington these men still held together, and on the occupation of Fort Smith and Little Rock by the Union forces, in the September following, the most of them enlisted in various Arkansas regiments, the 1st infantry among the number.

In November, 1863, while this regiment was stationed at Fort Smith, about three hundred of its men were vaccinated with spurious vaccine matter, a large number of whom were permanently disabled, and many others, whose disability unfitted them for duty, it became necessary to discharge.

On the 30th of October, 1863, while this regiment was on duty at Fort Smith, a mass meeting of Union men was held at that place, for the purpose of inaugurating measures that should lead to the restoration of civil government in the State, at which Colonel Johnson was unanimously nominated to represent the people of western Arkansas in the Congress of the United States. In November he was elected, and again in October, 1865, for the third congressional district. Though thus a member elect of the 38th and 39th Congresses, and necessarily called away from his regiment in his efforts to secure the recognition of the State government by Congress, he served with the regiment when not thus occupied, and with it was mustered out, at Fort Smith, on the 10th day of August, 1865.

Second regiment Arkansas infantry volunteers. Mustered into service July 6, 1864, (three years;) mustered out August 8, 1865.

FIELD AND STAFF.

Names.	Rank.	Enlistment.	Date of rank.	Remarks.
Marshall L. Stephenson	Colonel	—, 1861	July 6, 1864	Promoted from major 10th Illinois cavalry; mustered out with regiment.
Gideon M. Waugh	Lieutenant colonel	—, 1861	Jan. 24, 1864	Promoted from 2d lieutenant company G, 2d Kansas cavalry; resigned June 27, 1865.
Charles Braeunlich	Major	—, 1862	May 20, 1864	Promoted from 1st lieutenant and adjutant, 18th Iowa infantry volunteers; mustered out with regiment.
James W. Donnelley	Adjutant	Aug. 19, 1861	Feb. 15, 1864	Appointed from private company B, 37th Illinois infantry; mustered out with regiment.
Hosea L. Beardsley	Regimental quartermaster		Jan. 28, 1864	Appointed from 18th Iowa infantry volunteers; resigned October 19, 1864.
Robert S. Crampton	do		May 22, 1865	Honorably discharged as regimental quartermaster, 4th Arkansas infantry volunteers, October 2, 1864; appointed from civil life; mustered out with regiment.
Nicholas B. Hocker	Surgeon	Feb. 25, 1864	Feb. 25, 1864	Honorably discharged as surgeon 24th Missouri infantry volunteers, November 7, 1862; appointed from civil life; mustered out with regiment.
Albert R. Ayres	Assistant surgeon		July 11, 1864	Appointed from private company A, 3d Missouri cavalry volunteers, to hospital steward, April 25, 1863; mustered out with regiment.
William P. Bowers	do	July 12, 1864	July 12, 1864	Dismissed September 22, 1864.
Zachariah Keeton	Chaplain	Sept. 10, 1863	Aug. 2, 1864	Appointed from sergeant company D; mustered out with regiment.

NON-COMMISSIONED STAFF.

Names.	Rank.	Enlistment.	Date of rank.	Remarks.
Samuel Dial	Sergeant major	Sept. 10, 1863	June 30, 1864	Appointed from sergeant company D; mustered out with regiment.
John M. Williams	Hospital steward	Oct. 1, 1863	May 2, 1865	Appointed from private company C; mustered out with regiment.
Isaac D. Lay	Quartermaster sergeant	Sept. 10, 1863	July 6, 1864	Appointed from private company B; mustered out with regiment.
Samuel Vanniwegin	Color sergeant	Oct. 1, 1863	Dec. 9, 1863	Died of disease at Lewisburg, Arkansas.
Levi M. Satterfield	do	Oct. 15, 1863	Dec. 31, 1864	Appointed from 1st sergeant company K; mustered out with regiment.

COMPANY A.

Names.	Rank.	Enlistment.	Date of rank.	Remarks.
Christopher C. Casey	Captain	Dec. 7, 1863	Dec. 7, 1863	Appointed from civil life; resigned September 30, 1864.
James W. Pelts	1st lieutenant	Jan. 28, 1864	Jan. 28, 1864	Appointed from civil life; mustered out with regiment.
Moses Pearson	2d lieutenant	Jan. 28, 1864	Jan. 28, 1864	Appointed from civil life; discharged for physical disability June 28, 1864.
James M. Laster	do		July 9, 1864	Appointed from 1st sergeant; mustered out with regiment.
George G. Dunn	1st sergeant	Sept. 2, 1863	July 9, 1864	Appointed sergeant April 9, 1864; mustered out with regiment.
Thomas F. Acroggain	Sergeant	Sept. 2, 1863	Dec. 7, 1863	Appointed from private; mustered out with regiment.
Lorenzo D. Feague	do	Sept. 2, 1863	Dec. 7, 1863	Do.

Second regiment Arkansas infantry volunteers. Mustered into service July 6, 1864, (three years;) mustered out August 8, 1865.

COMPANY A—Continued.

Names.	Rank.	Enlistment.	Date of rank.	Remarks.
John Storms	Sergeant	Sept. 2, 1863	Dec. 7, 1863	Appointed from private; mustered out with regiment.
Thomas M. Smith	do	Sept. 2, 1863	Jan. 1, 1865	Do.
Elias M. Moore	Corporal	Sept. 2, 1863	Apr. 21, 1864	Mustered out with regiment.
James M Shields	do	Sept. 2, 1863	Dec. 7, 1863	Do.
James W. Melson	do	Sept. 2, 1863	Dec. 7, 1863	Do.
Hugh Warren	do	Sept. 2, 1863	Dec. 7, 1863	Do.
John Martin	do	Sept. 2, 1863	Jan. 10, 1865	Do.
Elijah M. Garner	do	Sept. 2, 1863	Jan. 10, 1865	Do.
Walter B. Sanders	do	Sept. 2, 1863	Dec. 7, 1863	Do.
			Muster.	
Allen, William	Private	Sept. 2, 1863	Dec. 7, 1863	Mustered out with regiment.
Bean, Michael M	do	Sept. 2, 1863	Dec. 7, 1863	Do.
Burman, John J	do	Sept. 2, 1863	Dec. 7, 1863	Do.
Beans, Thomas J	do	Sept. 2, 1863	Dec. 7, 1863	Do.
Bennett, James	do	Sept. 2, 1863	Dec. 7, 1863	Do.
Beasley, Quinton D	do	Sept. 2, 1863	Dec. 7, 1863	Do.
Childers, Joel	do	Sept. 2, 1863	Dec. 7, 1863	Do.
Cordell, George W	do	Sept. 2, 1863	Dec. 7, 1863	Do.
Cheek, James	do	Sept. 2, 1863	Dec. 7, 1863	Do.
Cowan, Stephen	do	Sept. 2, 1863	Dec. 7, 1863	Do.
Cooper, Thomas	do	Sept. 2, 1863	Dec. 7, 1863	Do.
Crumley, Terrell	do	Sept. 2, 1863	Dec. 7, 1863	Do.
Cooper, Nathan	do	Sept. 2, 1863	Dec. 7, 1863	Do.
Couch, Samuel H	do	Sept. 1, 1863	Dec. 7, 1863	Do.
Cordell, Andrew J	do	Mar. 1, 1864	June 28, 1864	Do.
Ely, Joseph	do	Sept. 2, 1863	Dec. 7, 1863	Do.
Hunt, John	do	Sept. 2, 1863	June 28, 1864	Do.
Hall, John F	do	Sept. 2, 1863	Dec. 7, 1863	Do.
Hill, George T	do	Sept. 2, 1863	Dec. 7, 1863	Do.
Jacobs, Henderson	do	Sept. 2, 1863	Dec. 7, 1863	Do.
Jacobs, Stockley	do	Sept. 2, 1863	Dec. 7, 1863	Do.
Jacobs, Howard J	do	Sept. 2, 1863	Dec. 7, 1863	Do.
Johnson, Hugh	do	Sept. 2, 1863	Dec. 7, 1863	Do.
Kirby, Jesse E	do	Sept. 2, 1863	Dec. 7, 1863	Do.
Long, Allen	do	Sept. 2, 1863	Dec. 7, 1863	Do.
Lasater, John	do	Sept. 2, 1863	Dec. 7, 1863	Do.
Melson, Francis M	do	Sept. 2, 1863	Dec. 7, 1863	Do.
Moore, Henry	do	Sept. 2, 1863	Dec. 7, 1863	Do.
Maxwell, Silas	do	Sept. 2, 1863	Jan. 16, 1864	Do.
Mathews, Enoch A	do	Sept. 2, 1863	Dec. 7, 1863	Do.
Mathews, Daniel J	do	Sept. 2, 1863	Dec. 7, 1863	Do.

REPORT OF THE ADJUTANT GENERAL OF ARKANSAS. 207

Name	Rank	Enlisted	Remarks
Pelts, Benjamin		Sept. 2, 1863	Dec. 7, 1863 Do.
Ragsdale, William	do	Sept. 2, 1863	Dec. 7, 1863 Do.
Reed, William	do	Sept. 2, 1863	Dec. 7, 1863 Do.
Reeves, Elisha H	do	Sept. 2, 1863	Dec. 7, 1863 Do.
Reeves, Jonathan H	do	Sept. 2, 1863	Dec. 7, 1863 Do.
Robbins, James F	do	Sept. 2, 1863	Dec. 7, 1863 Do.
Shelton, Stephen	do	Sept. 2, 1863	Dec. 7, 1863 Do.
Skaggs, Willis G	do	Sept. 2, 1863	Dec. 7, 1863 Do.
Sanders, Thomas	do	Sept. 2, 1863	Dec. 7, 1863 Do.
Vaught, Isaac J	do	Sept. 2, 1863	Dec. 7, 1863 Do.
Wood, William C	do	Sept. 2, 1863	Dec. 7, 1863 Do.
Warren, sr., Michael	do	Sept. 2, 1863	Dec. 7, 1863 Do.
Warren, jr., Michael	do	Sept. 2, 1863	Dec. 7, 1863 Do.
Warren, John	do	Sept. 2, 1863	Dec. 7, 1863 Do.
Warren, William	do	Sept. 2, 1863	Dec. 7, 1863 Do.
William, William H	do	Sept. 2, 1863	Dec. 7, 1863 Do.
Wilson, William J	do	Sept. 2, 1863	Dec. 7, 1863 Do.
White, James	do	May 1, 1864	June 28, 1864 Do.

Killed in action.

Name	Rank	Enlisted	Remarks
Sanders, Francis M	Sergeant	Sept. 2, 1863	Dec. 7, 1863	Killed by guerillas near Clarksville, Arkansas, December 31, 1864.
Chronister, George W	Private	Sept. 2, 1863	Dec. 7, 1863	Killed by guerillas near Clarksville, Arkansas, December 16, 1863.
Martin, James E	do	Sept. 2, 1863	Dec. 7, 1863	Killed by a sentinel while on picket at Cadron Mills, Arkansas.

Missing in action.

Name	Rank	Enlisted	Remarks
Ross, William F	Private	Jan. 1, 1864	Feb. 25, 1864	Missing in action at Jenkins's Ferry, Arkansas, April 30, 1864.

Died.

Name	Rank	Enlisted	Remarks
Bensley, Alexander W	Corporal	Sept. 2, 1863	Dec. 7, 1863	Died at Dardanelle, Arkansas, April 3, 1865.
Trotter, John W	do	Sept. 2, 1863	Dec. 7, 1863	Died of consumption at Lewisburg, Arkansas, July 26, 1865.
Skaggs, William	Private	Sept. 2, 1863	Dec. 7, 1863	Died of pneumonia at Clarksville, Arkansas, February 7, 1865.
Jacobs, Wesley M	do	Sept. 2, 1863	Dec. 7, 1863	Died at Huntersville, Arkansas, June 9, 1865.
McDaniel, John W	do	Sept. 2, 1863	Dec. 7, 1863	Died of breast complaint at Huntersville, Arkansas, July 8, 1865.
Oglesvie, William	do	Sept. 2, 1863	Dec. 7, 1863	Died at Lewisburg, Arkansas, August 16, 1865.
Ragsdale, Moses	do	Sept. 2, 1863	Dec. 7, 1863	Died of chronic diarrhœa at Lewisburg, Arkansas, August 29, 1864.
Owen, Walter B	do	Sept. 2, 1863	Dec. 7, 1863	Died of erysipelas at Clarksville, Arkansas, May 2, 1865.
Mathews, Lewis W	Corporal	Sept. 2, 1863	Dec. 7, 1863	Died on Mulberry mountain, Arkansas, March 7, 1864.
Chronister, James	Private	Sept. 2, 1863	Dec. 7, 1863	Died of fever at Clarksville, Arkansas, May 10, 1865.
Owen, James F	do	Sept. 2, 1863	Dec. 7, 1863	

Deserted.

Name	Rank	Enlisted	Remarks
Pinkney, David	Corporal	Sept. 2, 1863	Dec. 7, 1863	Deserted at Lewisburg, Arkansas, September 27, 1864.
Smith, John N	do	Sept. 2, 1863	Dec. 7, 1863	Do.
Arbough, Albert	Private	Sept. 2, 1863	Dec. 7, 1863	Do.
Cribbens, Thomas H	do	Sept. 2, 1863	Dec. 7, 1863	Deserted at Little Rock, Arkansas, September 27, 1864.
Edwards, Stoughton H	do	Sept. 2, 1863	Dec. 7, 1863	Deserted at Lewisburg, Arkansas, September 27, 1864.
Garner, John Q	do	Sept. 2, 1863	Dec. 7, 1863	Deserted at Clarksville, Arkansas, September 25, 1864.
Laster, Stephen	do	Sept. 2, 1863	Dec. 7, 1863	Deserted at Clarksville, Arkansas, June 13, 1864.

Second regiment Arkansas infantry volunteers. Mustered into service July 6, 1864, (three years;) mustered out August 8, 1865.

COMPANY A—Continued.

Names.	Rank.	Enlistment.	Muster.	Remarks.
Pelts, Pleasant J	Private	Sept. 2, 1863	Dec. 7, 1863	Deserted at Little Rock, Arkansas, September 25, 1864.
Reeves, Isaac N	do	Sept. 2, 1863	Dec. 7, 1863	Deserted at Lewisburg, Arkansas, July 21, 1864.
Swift, Marcellus	do	Sept. 2, 1863	Dec. 7, 1863	Do.
Swift, James T	do	Sept. 2, 1863	Dec. 7, 1863	Deserted at Lewisburg, Arkansas, July 23, 1864.
Swift, William	do	Sept. 2, 1863	Dec. 7, 1863	Deserted at Little Rock, Arkansas, September 25, 1864.
Thomasson, William	do	Sept. 2, 1863	Dec. 7, 1863	Deserted at Lewisburg, Arkansas, July 21, 1864.
Johnson, Henry W	do	Sept. 2, 1863	Dec. 7, 1863	Deserted at Clarksville, Arkansas, May 2, 1865.
Moulder, Alfred	do	Sept. 2, 1863	Dec. 7, 1863	Do.
Warren, James	do	Sept. 2, 1863	Dec. 7, 1863	Deserted at Fort Smith, Arkansas, July 4, 1865.

Discharged.

| Melson, Absalom B | Private | Sept. 2, 1863 | Dec. 7, 1863 | Discharged at Little Rock, Arkansas, for disability, November 3, 1864. |

COMPANY B.

Names.	Rank.	Enlistment.	Date of rank.	Remarks.
George C. Alden	Captain	—, 1862	Jan. 28, 1864	Appointed from sergeant of company B, 18th Iowa infantry; mustered out with regiment.
Charles P. Anderson	1st lieutenant	Feb. 16, 1864	Feb. 16, 1864	Appointed from civil life; discharged September 25, 1864.
James M. Oliver	do		May 22, 1865	Appointed from civil life to 2d lieutenant; promoted to 1st lieutenant, vice Anderson, discharged; mustered out with regiment.
Thomas H. Durham	1st sergeant	Sept. 10, 1863	Dec. 8, 1863	Appointed from private December 8, 1863; mustered out with regiment.
Thomas Cauthorn	Sergeant	Sept. 10, 1863	Dec. 8, 1863	do.
Wade H. Calvard	do	Oct. 1, 1863	Dec. 8, 1863	Do.
Thomas M. Hickerson	do	Nov. 22, 1863	Dec. 8, 1863	Do.
Henson S. Brown	do	Nov. 22, 1863	June 27, 1864	Appointed from corporal June 27, 1864; mustered out with regiment.
John C. Darks	Corporal	Sept. 10, 1863	Dec. 8, 1863	Mustered out with regiment.
John J. Gipson	do	Sept. 10, 1863	Dec. 8, 1863	Do.
James R. Walker	do	Sept. 10, 1863	Dec. 8, 1863	Do.
Thomas N. Ellington	do	Sept. 10, 1863	Jan. 24, 1864	Do.
James R. Morrison	do	Sept. 10, 1863	Jan. 26, 1864	Do.
Lewis P. Ellington	do	Sept. 10, 1863	Jan. 26, 1864	Do.
Russel C. Foster	do	Nov. 26, 1863	Sept. 16, 1864	Do.
Albert Marshall	do	Mar. 22, 1864	Sept. 16, 1864	Do.

REPORT OF THE ADJUTANT GENERAL OF ARKANSAS. 209

Name	Rank		Muster.	Mustered out with regiment.
Boydston, Asa	Private	Sept. 10, 1863	Dec. 8, 1863	Mustered out with regiment.
Brewer, William T	do	Sept. 10, 1863	Dec. 8, 1863	Do.
Barnard, James S	do	Dec. 16, 1863	Jan. 16, 1864	Do.
Brown, Margens D	do	Nov. 22, 1863	Dec. 8, 1863	Do.
Choate, Squire G	do	Nov. 12, 1863	Dec. 8, 1863	Do.
Choate, James P	do	Dec. 1, 1863	Dec. 8, 1863	Do.
Choate, Anthony L	do	April 2, 1865	April 2, 1865	Do.
Crawford, John	do	Sept. 10, 1863	Dec. 8, 1863	Do.
Clark, Franklin	do	Sept. 5, 1863	Jan. 16, 1864	Do.
Corio, Jared P	do	Jan. 16, 1864	Feb. 18, 1864	Do.
Evans, Calvin	do	Sept. 10, 1863	Dec. 8, 1863	Do.
Grist, Isaac F	do	Sept. 10, 1863	Dec. 8, 1863	Do.
Glenn, John	do	Sept. 10, 1863	Dec. 8, 1863	Do.
Green, Robert	do	Sept. 10, 1863	Jan. 16, 1864	Do.
Harper, James H	do	Sept. 10, 1863	Dec. 8, 1863	Do.
Harper, Lorenzo D	do	Sept. 10, 1862	Dec. 8, 1863	Do.
Harp, Joseph	do	Sept. 10, 1863	Dec. 8, 1863	Do.
Harp, Leonard	do	Sept. 10, 1863	Dec. 8, 1863	Do.
Harris, Wesley	do	Sept. 10, 1863	Dec. 8, 1863	Do.
Harris, Fenton M	do	April 1, 1865	April 1, 1865	Do.
Hooper, Peter W	do	Sept. 10, 1863	Dec. 8, 1863	Do.
Hooper, Miles B	do	Sept. 10, 1863	Dec. 8, 1863	Do.
Hardin, Neely L	do	Sept. 10, 1863	Dec. 8, 1863	Do.
Hamlin, Jasper L	do	Nov. 12, 1863	Dec. 8, 1863	Do.
Hyatt, Adams	do	Sept. 10, 1863	Jan. 15, 1864	Do.
Jones, Joseph A	do	Sept. 10, 1863	Dec. 8, 1863	Do.
James, Henry V	do	Sept. 10, 1863	Dec. 8, 1863	Do[?]
James, John	do	Sept. 10, 1863	Dec. 8, 1863	Do.
Jackson, John W	do	Jan. 1, 1864	Jan. 16, 1864	Do.
Johnson, Josiah	do	Sept. 10, 1863	Jan. 16, 1864	Do.
Job, James R	do	Sept. 10, 1863	Dec. 8, 1863	Do.
Lloyd, James A	do	Sept. 10, 1863	Dec. 8, 1863	Do.
Lloyd, George G	do	Sept. 10, 1863	Dec. 8, 1863	Do.
Lewellen, Jordan	do	Jan. 1, 1864	Jan. 16, 1864	Do.
Landers, John	do	Sept. 10, 1863	Dec. 8, 1863	Do.
Marshall, David	do	Oct. 25, 1863	Jan. 16, 1864	Do.
Martin, James	do	Sept. 10, 1863	Dec. 8, 1863	Do.
Oliver, Willoughby	do	Dec. 8, 1863	Dec. 8, 1863	Do.
Person, Andrew J	do	Nov. 13, 1863	Dec. 8, 1863	Do.
Skaggs, Chester A	do	Sept. 10, 1863	Dec. 8, 1863	Do.
Skaggs, Hudson F	do	Sept. 10, 1863	Dec. 8, 1863	Do.
Sexton, Jacob	do	Jan. 16, 1864	Feb. 18, 1864	Do.
Sexton, James	do	Jan. 16, 1864	Feb. 18, 1864	Do.
Sexton, William N	do	Jan. 20, 1864	May 17, 1864	Do.
Sutherland, Alexander	do	Nov. 28, 1863	Dec. 8, 1863	Do.
Smith, Robert J	do	Dec. 12, 1863	Jan. 16, 1864	Do.
Salsman, Charles	do	Sept. 10, 1863	Dec. 8, 1863	Do.
Venable, Joseph E	do	Nov. 12, 1863	Dec. 8, 1863	Do.
Wood, Elijah	do	Nov. 12, 1863	Dec. 8, 1863	Do.

Second regiment Arkansas infantry volunteers. Mustered into service July 6, 1864, (three years;) mustered out August 8, 1865.

COMPANY B—Continued.

Names.	Rank.	Enlistment.	Muster.	Remarks.
Killed in action.				
Chronister, James D	Private	Jan. 1, 1864	Jan. 16, 1864	Killed by guerillas at Clarksville, Arkansas, May 21, 1863.
Harris, Gillmore	...do...	Sept. 10, 1863	Dec. 8, 1863	Killed between Fort Smith and Clarksville, Arkansas, February 4, 1865.
Kelley, William J	...do...	Sept. 10, 1863	Dec. 8, 1863	Killed by guerillas in Franklin county, Arkansas, December 24, 1863.
Kyles, William	...do...	Nov. 12, 1863	Dec. 8, 1863	Killed in Yell county, Arkansas, April 13, 1865.
Kyle, Thomas	...do...	Sept. 10, 1863	Dec. 8, 1863	Killed between Fort Smith and Clarksville, Arkansas, February 4, 1865.
Died.				
Cook, James B	Corporal	Sept. 10, 1863	Dec. 8, 1863	Died at Lewisburg, Arkansas, August 14, 1864.
Bryanes, Edward	Private	Sept. 10, 1863	Dec. 8, 1863	Died of chronic diarrhœa, Jefferson Barracks, Missouri, November 9, 1864.
Hudson, Robert B	...do...	Nov. 22, 1863	Dec. 8, 1863	Died at Lewisburg, Arkansas, July 28, 1864.
Hooper, James A	...do...	Sept. 10, 1863	Jan. 16, 1864	Died at Huntersville, Arkansas, June 29, 1864.
Lamb, Alfred R	...do...	Sept. 10, 1863	Dec. 8, 1863	Died at Little Rock, Arkansas, November 12, 1864.
Lamb, Christopher C	...do...	Nov. 12, 1863	Dec. 8, 1863	Died at Fort Smith, Arkansas, April 21, 1865.
Metcalf, Martin H	...do...	Dec. 8, 1863	Dec. 8, 1863	Died at Lewisburg, Arkansas, August 1, 1864.
Nobles, William	...do...	Sept. 10, 1863	Dec. 8, 1863	Died at Fort Smith, Arkansas, April 9, 1865.
Nobles, James S	...do...	Sept. 10, 1863	Dec. 8, 1863	Died at Huntersville, Arkansas, June 11, 1864.
Pierson, James	...do...	Sept. 10, 1863	Dec. 8, 1863	Died at Lewisburg, Arkansas, August 24, 1864.
Tomlinson, John H	...do...	Sept. 10, 1863	Dec. 8, 1863	Died at Little Rock, Arkansas, October 6, 1864.
Uselton, Wiley L	...do...	Nov. 12, 1863	Dec. 8, 1863	Died at Fort Smith, Arkansas, December 16, 1863.
Waters, John H	...do...	Sept. 10, 1863	Dec. 8, 1863	Died of chronic diarrhœa, Little Rock, Arkansas, June 28, 1864.
Deserted.				
Donathan, Jeremiah	Sergeant	Sept. 10, 1863	Dec. 8, 1863	Deserted at Dardanelle, Arkansas, May 13, 1864.
Tricket, Albert	Corporal	Sept. 10, 1863	Dec. 8, 1863	Deserted at Little Rock, Arkansas, May 9, 1864.
Ford, William	Private	Nov. 12, 1863	Dec. 8, 1863	Deserted at Dardanelle, Arkansas, May 27, 1864.
Fellows, Francis M	...do...	Nov. 26, 1863	Dec. 8, 1863	Deserted at Huntersville, Arkansas, July 6, 1864.
Lewellen, Charles M	...do...	Sept. 10, 1863	Dec. 8, 1863	Deserted at Huntersville, Arkansas, September 26, 1864.
Lawson, Joel	...do...	Jan. 1, 1864	Jan. 16, 1864	Deserted at Clarksville, Arkansas, May 20, 1864.
Prator, Loyd	...do...	Nov. 12, 1863	Dec. 8, 1863	Deserted at Huntersville, Arkansas, September 26, 1864.
Transferred.				
Lay, Isaac D	Private	Sept. 10, 1863	Dec. 8, 1863	Transferred to non-commissioned staff as quartermaster sergeant, July 6, 1864.

REPORT OF THE ADJUTANT GENERAL OF ARKANSAS. 211

COMPANY C.

Name	Rank	Muster	Date of rank	Remarks
Nichols T. B. Schuyler	Captain		Jan. 28, 1864	Appointed from quartermaster sergeant company H, 2d Kansas cavalry, to fill original vacancy; mustered out with regiment.
Jesse H. Stansell	1st lieutenant		Jan. 28, 1864	Appointed from 1st sergeant company D, 1st Arkansas infantry, to fill original vacancy, mustered out with regiment.
George N. Spradling	2d lieutenant		Jan. 17, 1864	Appointed from private company E, 1st Arkansas infantry, to fill original vacancy; mustered out with regiment.
Barnett, John W	Sergeant	Oct. 1, 1863	Jan. 28, 1864	Appointed from private January 28, 1864; wounded and captured by the enemy at Jenkins's Ferry, April 30, 1864; exchanged March 25, 1865; was confined in stockade at Tyler, Texas; mustered out with regiment.
McNeely, Wm. H	do	Nov. 15, 1863	Feb. 28, 1864	Appointed from private; mustered out with regiment.
Barnes, James M	do	Nov. 1, 1863	July 1, 1864	Do.
Barnes, George W	do	Nov. 1, 1863	July 1, 1864	Do.
Comer, Timothy	do	Nov. 28, 1863	Jan. 28, 1864	do.
Leftwich, Wm. A	Corporal	Oct. 1, 1863	Jan. 28, 1864	do.
Owen, Wm. B	do	Oct. 1, 1863	Jan. 28, 1864	Mustered out with regiment.
Brown, William	do	Oct. 1, 1863	Nov. 1, 1864	Do.
Allen, William	Private	Oct. 1, 1863	Dec. 9, 1863	Do.
Allen, Richard	do	Sept. 1, 1864	Sept. 1, 1864	Do.
Barnard, Marcus M	do	Oct. 1, 1863	Dec. 9, 1863	Do.
Byrum, Alfred	do	Oct. 1, 1863	Dec. 22, 1863	Do.
Comer, John	do	Nov. 1, 1863	Dec. 9, 1863	Do.
Comer, Thomas	do	Nov. 15, 1863	Dec. 9, 1863	Do.
Chastine, Madison C	do	Nov. 1, 1863	Dec. 9, 1863	Do.
Davis, David	do	Oct. 1, 1863	Dec. 22, 1863	Do.
Foster, Jackson	do	Oct. 1, 1863	Dec. 22, 1863	Do.
Glass, Lucius M	do	Oct. 1, 1863	Dec. 9, 1863	Do.
Glass, Daniel B	do	Oct. 1, 1863	Dec. 9, 1863	Do.
Garner, Dixon	do	Dec. 1, 1863	Dec. 9, 1863	Do.
Garrison, Pleasant J	do	May 1, 1864	June 29, 1864	Do.
Houst, Jarrett	do	Nov. 1, 1863	Dec. 9, 1863	Do.
Hope, William P	do	Oct. 1, 1863	Dec. 9, 1863	Do.
Herron, Joshua	do	Nov. 1, 1863	Dec. 9, 1863	Do.
Hasket, George	do	Oct. 1, 1863	Dec. 9, 1863	Do.
Hasket, Joseph	do	Oct. 1, 1863	Oct. 30, 1863	Do.
Hickey, James	do	Sept. 15, 1863	Jan. 16, 1864	Do.
Hill, James M	do	Jan. 13, 1864	Dec. 21, 1864	Do.
Leftwich, Francis M	do	Oct. 1, 1863	Dec. 9, 1863	Do.
Leftwich, William J	do	Oct. 1, 1863	Dec. 9, 1863	Do.
Liston, Andrew J	do	Oct. 1, 1863	Dec. 9, 1863	Do.
Miller, Robert	do	Nov. 28, 1863	Dec. 9, 1863	Do.
McGeehee, John	do	Dec. 1, 1863	Dec. 9, 1863	Do.
McInturf, James M	do	Nov. 20, 1863	Dec. 9, 1863	Do.
Moulder, Thomas B	do	Nov. 24, 1863	Dec. 22, 1863	Do.
Purtain, Gabriel G	do	Nov. 1, 1863	Dec. 9, 1863	Do.

212 REPORT OF THE ADJUTANT GENERAL OF ARKANSAS.

Second regiment Arkansas infantry volunteers. Mustered into service July 6, 1864, (three years;) mustered out August 8, 1865.

COMPANY C—Continued.

Names.	Rank.	Enlistment.	Date of rank.	Remarks.
Smith, Benjamin F	Private	Oct. 1, 1863	Dec. 22, 1863	Mustered out with regiment.
Shanks, John	do	Dec. 12, 1863	Jan. 16, 1864	Do.
Spaniard, John	do	Sept. 1, 1863	Dec. 22, 1863	Do.
Stafford, Allen B	do	Dec. 1, 1863	Dec. 9, 1863	Do.
Willis, George W	do	Oct. 1, 1863	Dec. 9, 1863	Do.
Wadkins, William A	do	Jan. 1, 1864	Jan. 16, 1864	Do.

Killed in action.

Names.	Rank.	Enlistment.	Date of rank.	Remarks.
Butler, Robert	Private	Oct. 1, 1863	Dec. 9, 1863	Killed in Johnson county, Arkansas, January 14, 1865.
Bennett, Hugh	do	Jan. 1, 1864	Jan. 16, 1864	Killed in Johnson county, Arkansas, December 15, 1864.
Paschal, William R	do	Oct. 1, 1863	Dec. 22, 1863	Killed in Johnson county, Arkansas, January 7, 1865.
Smathers, Dewitt C	do	Oct. 1, 1863	Dec. 9, 1863	Killed in Marion county, Arkansas, March 14, 1864.

Died.

Names.	Rank.	Enlistment.	Date of rank.	Remarks.
Aidlatt, Thomas J	Private	Oct. 1, 1863	Dec. 9, 1863	Died at Little Rock, Arkansas, August 7, 1864.
Chastine, William T. T	do	Nov. 1, 1863	Dec. 9, 1863	Died at Lewisburg, Arkansas, August 1, 1864.
Domeron, Yancy	do	Oct. 5, 1863	Dec. 22, 1863	Died at Little Rock, Arkansas, January 7, 1865.
Glass, John J	Sergeant	Oct. 1, 1863	Dec. 9, 1863	Died at Huntersville, Arkansas, October 2, 1864.
Holland, William	Private	Nov. 1, 1863	Dec. 9, 1863	Died at Little Rock, Arkansas, June 8, 1864.
McHamill, Isaac	do	Nov. 27, 1863	Dec. 21, 1863	Died at Fort Smith, Arkansas, June 2, 1864.
McIntyre, Samuel	do	Oct. 5, 1863	Dec. 21, 1863	Died at Huntersville, Arkansas, June 13, 1864.
McIntyre, William	do	Oct. 1, 1863	Dec. 21, 1863	Died at Clarksville, Arkansas, March 15, 1864.
Miller, Andrew	do	Dec. 1, 1863	Dec. 21, 1863	Died at Huntersville, Arkansas, June 14, 1864.
Mayo, Daniel A. S	do	Oct. 1, 1863	Dec. 9, 1863	Died at Little Rock, Arkansas, June 9, 1864.
Ruyle, William M	do	Oct. 2, 1863	Jan. 16, 1864	Died at Little Rock, Arkansas, July 10, 1864.
Redding, Thomas	do	Jan. 1, 1864	Jan. 16, 1864	Died at Little Rock, Arkansas, May 7, 1864.
Stiles, Fernan	do	Nov. 1, 1863	Dec. 9, 1863	Died at Lewisburg, Arkansas, July 29, 1864.
Seff, George W	do	Oct. 1, 1863	Dec. 9, 1863	Died at Fort Smith, Arkansas, May 15, 1865.
Winn, John	do	Dec. 1, 1863	Dec. 21, 1863	Died at _____

Deserted.

Names.	Rank.	Enlistment.	Date of rank.	Remarks.
Acres, Isaac C	Private	Nov. 1, 1863	Dec. 9, 1863	Deserted at Lewisburg, Arkansas, August 7, 1864.
Bryant, William J	do	Nov. 1, 1863	Dec. 9, 1863	Do.
Collins, Miles S	do	Oct. 1, 1863	Dec. 9, 1863	Deserted at Clarksville, Arkansas, January 1, 1865.
Chaplain, Daniel	do	Oct. 1, 1863	Dec. 9, 1863	Deserted at Clarksville, Arkansas, March 18, 1864.
Cole, Eldrige J	do	Oct. 1, 1863	Dec. 9, 1865	Deserted at Fort Smith, Arkansas, November 18, 1864.
Finley, John	do	Nov. 1, 1863	Dec. 29, 1863	Deserted at Clarksville, Arkansas, March 26, 1864.
Finley, William M	do	May 1, 1864	June 29, 1864	Deserted at Little Rock, Arkansas, August 15, 1864.
Gleason, James	do	Jan. 1, 1864	June 29, 1864	Deserted at Fort Smith Arkansas, November 18, 1864.
Griffin, John P	do	Nov. 1, 1863	Dec. 9, 1863	Deserted at Lewisburg, Arkansas, May 15, 1864.

Name	Rank	Date of enlistment	Date of rank	Remarks
Jackson, Robert A	do	Jan. 1, 1864	Jan. 16, 1864	Deserted at Clarksville, Arkansas, March 25, 1864.
Liston, Samuel H	do	Oct. 1, 1863	Dec. 9, 1863	Deserted at Lewisburg, Arkansas, August 27, 1864.
Mayers, William	Corporal	Oct. 1, 1863	Dec. 9, 1863	Deserted at Fort Smith, Arkansas, January 1, 1865.
Maffett, James L	do	Dec. 1, 1863	Dec. 21, 1863	Deserted at Lewisburg, Arkansas, August 18, 1864.
Partain, Ezekiel	do	Jan. 1, 1864	Jan. 16, 1864	Deserted at Camden, Arkansas, March 30, 1864.
Shook, James	do	Oct. 1, 1863	Dec. 9, 1863	Deserted at Fort Smith, Arkansas, January 1, 1865.
Smathers, Elisha A	do	Oct. 1, 1863	Dec. 21, 1863	Deserted while on detached service August 1, 1864.
Sanders, William R	do	Dec. 1, 1863	Dec. 21, 1863	Deserted at Lewisburg, Arkansas, August 7, 1864.
Turrentine, Abram A	do	Jan. 1, 1864	Jan. 16, 1864	Deserted at Clarksville, Arkansas, March 25, 1864.
Turrentine, James M	do	Jan. 1, 1864	Jan. 16, 1864	Do.
Wood, Joshua	do	Nov. 28, 1863	Dec. 9, 1863	Deserted while on a scout December 12, 1863.
Discharged.				
Goodall, Isaac G	Corporal	Oct. 1, 1863	Dec. 9, 1863	Discharged May 31, 1865.
Smith, Thomas B	Private	Dec. 20, 1863	Jan. 16, 1864	Discharged May 18, 1865.
Transferred.				
Vaninwegin, Samuel Y	Private	Oct. 1, 1863	Dec. 9, 1863	Transferred to non-commissioned staff as regimental com'ry sergeant, July 6, 1864.
Williams, John M	do	Oct. 1, 1863	Dec. 21, 1863	Transferred to non-commissioned staff as hospital steward May 20, 1865.

COMPANY D.

Name	Rank	Date of enlistment	Date of rank	Remarks
Edward P. Taylor	Captain	Oct. 10, 1863	Jan. 28, 1864	Appointed from private; mustered out with regiment.
Benjamin J. Lang	1st lieutenant	—, 1862	Jan. 28, 1864	Appointed from 1st sergeant company H, 8th Missouri cavalry volunteers; resigned June 5, 1865.
George W. White	2d lieutenant	Sept. 10, 1863	Jan. 28, 1864	Appointed from private; mustered out with regiment.
Edward Dearmore	1st sergeant	Sept. 10, 1863	Dec. 12, 1863	Do.
John H. Martin	Sergeant	Sept. 10, 1863	Dec. 12, 1863	Do.
William J. Keeton	do	Sept. 10, 1863	Dec. 12, 1863	Do.
William J. Hunt	do	Sept. 10, 1863	Oct. 30, 1864	Do.
Gustavus G. Pitts	do	Sept. 10, 1863	Oct. 30, 1864	Do.
Beverly D. Hunt	Corporal	Sept. 10, 1863	July 24, 1864	Do.
Samuel S. Scott	do	Sept. 10, 1863	July 20, 1864	Do.
William H. Dearmore	do	Sept. 10, 1863	July 20, 1864	Do.
John Burress	do	Sept. 10, 1863	July 20, 1864	Do.
		Muster.		
Austin, Phillips W	Private	Sept. 10, 1863	Dec. 10, 1863	Mustered out with regiment.
Anthony, Isaac R	do	Sept. 14, 1863	Sept. 20, 1864	Do.
Bowen, William T	do	Sept. 10, 1863	Dec. 10, 1863	Do.
Brown, James	do	Sept. 10, 1863	Dec. 10, 1863	Do.
Brigance, Lafayette M	do	Sept. 10, 1863	Dec. 10, 1863	Absent sick in Yell county; no discharge given on muster out of regiment.
Brown, William	do	Sept. 10, 1863	Dec. 10, 1863	Mustered out with regiment.
Burnett, Perry J	do	Sept. 10, 1863	Dec. 10, 1863	

Second regiment Arkansas infantry volunteers.   Mustered into service July 6, 1864, (three years;) mustered out August 8, 1865.

COMPANY D—Continued.

Names.	Rank.	Enlistment.	Muster.	Remarks.
Bynum, William	Private	Mar. 10, 1864	June 18, 1864	Mustered out with regiment.
Burress, William G	do	Sept. 14, 1864	Sept. 20, 1864	Do.
Clark, William	do	Sept. 10, 1863	Dec. 10, 1863	Do.
Crockett, William	do	Sept. 10, 1863	Dec. 10, 1863	Do.
Dodridge, Ira	do	Sept. 10, 1863	Dec. 10, 1863	Do.
Daily, John H	do	Sept. 10, 1863	Dec. 10, 1863	Do.
Firman, Joseph	do	Sept. 10, 1863	Dec. 10, 1863	Do.
Gladen, William L	do	Sept. 10, 1863	Dec. 10, 1863	Do.
Gavett, William	do	Sept. 10, 1863	Dec. 10, 1863	Do.
Herring, James R	do	Sept. 10, 1863	Dec. 10, 1863	Do.
Harkey, William R	do	Sept. 10, 1863	Dec. 10, 1863	Do.
Hogan, John M	do	Sept. 10, 1863	Dec. 10, 1863	Do.
Humphries, Reuben	do	Sept. 10, 1863	Dec. 10, 1863	Do.
Hunt, John W	do	Sept. 10, 1863	Dec. 10, 1863	Do.
Jones, Andrew, jr	do	Sept. 10, 1863	Dec. 10, 1863	Do.
Jones, Jesse	do	Sept. 10, 1863	Dec. 10, 1863	Do.
Jackson, Newton J	do	Sept. 10, 1863	Dec. 10, 1863	Do.
Jackson, William	do	Sept. 10, 1863	Dec. 10, 1863	Do.
Jackson, James J	do	Sept. 10, 1863	Dec. 10, 1863	Do.
Keeton, George W	do	Sept. 10, 1863	Dec. 10, 1863	Do.
Kindrick, John	do	Nov. 19, 1864	May 5, 1865	Do.
Lasiter, Jesse B	do	Sept. 10, 1863	Dec. 10, 1863	Do.
Logan, William	do	Sept. 10, 1863	Dec. 10, 1863	Do.
Moore, William S	do	Sept. 10, 1863	Dec. 10, 1863	Do.
Martin, William A	do	Sept. 10, 1863	Dec. 10, 1863	Do.
McClain, James W	do	Sept. 10, 1863	Dec. 10, 1863	Do.
Myers, William	do	Sept. 10, 1863	Dec. 10, 1863	Do.
Porter, John	do	Sept. 10, 1863	Dec. 10, 1863	Do.
Powell, Elisha	do	Sept. 10, 1863	Dec. 10, 1863	Do.
Stokes, James M	do	Sept. 10, 1863	Dec. 10, 1863	Do.
Steward, Pleasant	do	Sept. 10, 1863	Dec. 10, 1863	Do.
Stone, Reynolds W	do	Sept. 10, 1863	Dec. 10, 1863	Do.
Scott, William T	do	Sept. 10, 1863	Dec. 10, 1863	Do.
Scott, Abraham	do	Sept. 10, 1863	Dec. 10, 1863	Do.
Scott, James A	do	Sept. 10, 1863	Dec. 10, 1863	Do.
Scott, James I	do	Sept. 10, 1863	Dec. 10, 1863	Do.
Walden, James A	do	Sept. 10, 1863	Dec. 10, 1863	Do.
Killed in action.				
Batson, Robert	Private	Sept. 12, 1863	Sept. 28, 1863	Killed by guerillas near Clarksville, Arkansas, March 20, 1865.

REPORT OF THE ADJUTANT GENERAL OF ARKANSAS. 215

Died.

Name	Rank			
Cotman, L. M.	Corporal	Sept. 10, 1863	Dec. 10, 1863	Died of dropsy at Clarksville, Arkansas, April 4, 1864.
Rhoades, Charles W.	do	Sept. 10, 1863	Dec. 10, 1863	Died of wounds received in action May 13, 1864.
Simmons, Thomas W.	Private	Sept. 10, 1863	Dec. 10, 1863	Died of measles at Lewisburg, Arkansas, July 4, 1864.
Bata, Asa	do	Sept. 10, 1863	Dec. 10, 1863	Died of consumption at Little Rock, Arkansas, July 4, 1864.
Bradley, Melvin R.	do	Sept. 10, 1863	Dec. 10, 1863	Died at Lewisburg, Arkansas, September 12, 1864.
Brown, Frederick	do	Mar. 25, 1864	June 28, 1864	Died of chronic diarrhœa at Little Rock, Arkansas, January 12, 1865.
Brown, James W.	do	Sept. 10, 1863	Dec. 10, 1863	Died of fever at Clarksville, Arkansas, May 3, 1865.
Coats, James	do	Sept. 10, 1863	Dec. 10, 1863	Died of fever at Lewisburg, Arkansas, September 6, 1864.
Caldwell, Daniel	do	Sept. 10, 1863	Dec. 10, 1863	Died at Fort Smith, Arkansas, May 19, 1864.
Faulkner, Ransom J.	do	Sept. 10, 1863	Dec. 10, 1863	Died of fever at Huntersville, Arkansas, September 26, 1864.
Gipson, Samuel	do	Sept. 10, 1863	Dec. 10, 1863	Died at Clarksville, Arkansas, March 17, 1864.
Hunt, Richard H.	do	Sept. 10, 1863	Dec. 10, 1863	Died at Little Rock, Arkansas, September 17, 1864.
Hunt, James M.	do	Sept. 10, 1863	Dec. 10, 1863	Died at Huntersville, Arkansas, September 20, 1864.
Jackson, Andrew J.	do	Mar. 12, 1864	June 28, 1864	Died of measles at Little Rock, Arkansas, November 6, 1864.
Marshall, William H.	do	Sept. 10, 1863	Dec. 10, 1863	Died at Fort Smith, Arkansas, June 2, 1864.
McLane, Calvin G.	do	Sept. 10, 1863	Dec. 10, 1863	Died of bilious fever at Huntersville, Arkansas, October 9, 1864.
Page, Posey	do	Feb. 9, 1864	Mar. 16, 1864	Died at Little Rock, Arkansas, December 13, 1864.
Sherman, Asa J.	do	Sept. 10, 1863	Dec. 10, 1863	Died of measles at Little Rock, Arkansas, July 18, 1864.
Scott, James R.	do	Sept. 10, 1863	Dec. 10, 1863	Died of measles at Little Rock, Arkansas, December 30, 1864.
Womack, William	do	Sept. 10, 1863	Dec. 10, 1863	Died of bilious fever at Lewisburg, Arkansas, July 25, 1864.
Yates, Daniel R.	do	Sept. 10, 1863	Dec. 10, 1863	Died of bilious fever at Clarksville, Arkansas, February 3, 1864.
Brewer, Neriah	do	Sept. 10, 1863	Jan. 16, 1864	Died of wounds received in action February 12, 1864.
Morgan, William K.	do	Sept. 10, 1863	Dec. 10, 1863	Died at Fort Smith, Arkansas, February 10, 1865.

Deserted.

Name	Rank			
Lorance, James S.	Corporal	Sept. 10, 1863	Dec. 10, 1863	Deserted at Lewisburg, Arkansas, September 28, 1864.
Colwell, Sherrod	Private	Sept. 10, 1863	Dec. 10, 1863	Do.
Colwell, Shelton	do	Sept. 10, 1863	Dec. 10, 1863	Do.
Curtis, William	do	Sept. 10, 1863	Dec. 10, 1863	Deserted at Little Rock, Arkansas, October 2, 1864.
Curtis, Wesley	do	Sept. 10, 1863	Dec. 10, 1863	Do.
Bevel, John P.	do	Sept. 10, 1863	Dec. 10, 1863	Deserted at Lewisburg, Arkansas, September 28, 1864.
Hogan, Edward L.	do	Sept. 10, 1863	Dec. 10, 1863	Deserted at Little Rock, Arkansas, October 2, 1864.
Harden, Moses G.	do	Sept. 10, 1864	June 28, 1864	Deserted at Strayhome's Landing, Arkansas, November 25, 1864.
Linn, W. G. M.	do	Sept. 10, 1863	Dec. 10, 1863	Deserted at Ives' Ford, Arkansas, January 31, 1865.
Scott, William	do	Sept. 10, 1863	Dec. 10, 1863	Deserted at Lewisburg, Arkansas, October 30, 1864.
Lewis, Abraham	do	Sept. 10, 1863	Dec. 10, 1863	Deserted; furloughed for fifteen days from April 27, 1865, absent without leave; supposed to have been killed by guerillas.

Discharged.

Name	Rank			
Deputy, William J.	Corporal	Sept. 10, 1863	Dec. 10, 1863	Discharged for disability at Little Rock, Arkansas, February 18, 1865.
Tater, Peter	Private	Sept. 10, 1863	Dec. 10, 1863	Discharged for disability at Little Rock, Arkansas, October 15, 1864.
Burton, Pleasant	do	Sept. 10, 1863	Dec. 10, 1863	Discharged for disability at Fort Smith, Arkansas, July 26, 1865.
Clark, Nelson S.	do	Sept. 10, 1863	Dec. 10, 1863	do.

Transferred.

Name	Rank			
Dial, Samuel	Sergeant	Sept. 10, 1863	Dec. 10, 1863	Transferred to non-commissioned staff as sergeant major, June 12, 1864.
Keeton, Zachariah	do	Sept. 10, 1863	Dec. 10, 1863	Transferred to field and staff as chaplain, August 3, 1864.

Second regiment Arkansas infantry volunteers. Mustered into service July 6, 1864, (three years;) mustered out August 8, 1865.

COMPANY E.

Names.	Rank.	Enlistment.	Date of rank.	Remarks.
Ambrose R. McPherson	Captain	June 16, 1864	June 16, 1864	Appointed from civil life; mustered out with regiment.
James E. Markell	1st lieutenant		Feb. 25, 1864	Appointed from sergeant of 3d Wisconsin cavalry; honorably discharged September 29, 1864.
Absalom P. Phillips	do		May 22, 1865	Appointed from 1st sergeant of company F, 1st Arkansas infantry, to 2d lieutenant, February 25, 1864; mustered out with regiment.
Wallis, George W	1st sergeant	Jan. 1, 1864	May 21, 1864	Appointed from private; mustered out with regiment.
McPherson, William L	Sergeant	Sept. 2, 1863	Jan. 1, 1864	Do.
Lovell, Robert L	do	Sept. 2, 1863	July 1, 1864	Do.
Black, Samuel J	do	Sept. 2, 1863	Feb. 1, 1865	Do.
Essex, Warren	do	Sept. 2, 1863	Feb. 1, 1865	Do.
Owen, William	Corporal	Jan. 1, 1864	July 1, 1864	Mustered out with regiment.
Wannick, John	do	Sept. 2, 1863	July 1, 1864	Do.
Campbell, Cyrus A	do	Sept. 2, 1863	Feb. 25, 1864	Do.
Burrews, David T	do	Feb. 15, 1864	Sept. 23, 1864	Do.
Curtis, Amos F	do	Sept. 2, 1863	April 1, 1865	Do.
Taff, Morgan D	do	Feb. 15, 1864	April 25, 1865	Do.
			Muster.	
Alexander, John J	Private	Sept. 2, 1863	Dec. 24, 1863	Do.
Bristow, William J	do	Sept. 2, 1863	Dec. 24, 1863	Do.
Bristow, John W	do	Sept. 2, 1863	Dec. 24, 1863	Do.
Byrd, James	do	Sept. 2, 1863	Dec. 24, 1863	Do.
Bowen, Hiram	do	Sept. 2, 1863	Dec. 24, 1863	Do.
Cowan, Stephen	do	Sept. 2, 1863	Dec. 24, 1863	Do.
Cowan, Robert	do	Sept. 2, 1863	Dec. 24, 1863	Do.
Cowan, Isaac	do	Sept. 2, 1863	Dec. 24, 1863	Do.
Cowan, Zachariah	do	Sept. 2, 1863	Dec. 24, 1863	Do.
Carlton, William C	do	Sept. 2, 1863	Dec. 24, 1863	Do.
Carlton, Marion	do	Sept. 2, 1863	Dec. 24, 1863	Do.
Couch, William	do	Oct. 28, 1863	Dec. 24, 1863	Do.
Couch, Isaac	do	Oct. 28, 1863	Dec. 24, 1863	Do.
Conch, James N	do	Sept. 2, 1863	Dec. 24, 1863	Do.
Casey, Anthony	do	Sept. 2, 1863	Dec. 24, 1863	Do.
Casey, Ambler	do	Feb. 15, 1864	Mar. 8, 1864	Do.
Coleman, Alexander	do	Jan. 1, 1864	Feb. 25, 1864	Do.
Causey, James A	do	Jan. 1, 1864	Feb. 25, 1864	Do.
Dodson, William S	do	Sept. 2, 1863	May 21, 1864	Do.
Douthit, Levi	do	Jan. 1, 1864	May 21, 1864	Do.
Ellington, William W	do	Jan. 1, 1864	Feb. 25, 1864	Do.
Farmer, James K	do	Sept. 2, 1863	Dec. 22, 1863	Do.
Gassett, William	do	Jan. 1, 1864	Feb. 25, 1864	Do.
Henderson, John	do			Do.

REPORT OF THE ADJUTANT GENERAL OF ARKANSAS. 217

Name	Rank	Enlisted	Expiration of service	Remarks
Harris, Charles	do	Sept. 2, 1863	Feb. 25, 1864	Do.
Hensley, John A	do	Feb. 15, 1864	Mar. 8, 1864	Do.
Kunkels, William	do	Sept. 2, 1863	Dec. 24, 1863	Do.
King, William P	do	Feb. 15, 1864	Mar. 8, 1864	Do.
Lawson, Reuben	do	Jan. 1, 1864	June 1, 1865	Do.
Lewis, John S	do	Sept. 2, 1863	Dec. 24, 1863	Do.
Mooney, William R	do	Sept. 2, 1863	Dec. 24, 1863	Do.
Mooney, John	do	Sept. 2, 1863	Dec. 24, 1863	Do.
Marshall, Thomas D	do	Sept. 2, 1863	Dec. 24, 1863	Do.
Pannel, John	do	Sept. 2, 1863	Dec. 24, 1863	Do.
Prewitt, William O	do	Sept. 2, 1863	Feb. 25, 1864	Do.
Prewitt, John	do	Sept. 2, 1863	Dec. 24, 1863	Do.
Potts, William H	do	Sept. 2, 1863	Dec. 24, 1863	Do.
Rash, Silas P	do	Sept. 2, 1863	Dec. 24, 1863	Do.
Reeves, James	do	Sept. 2, 1863	Dec. 24, 1863	Do.
Rainwaters, Hiram	do	Jan. 1, 1864	June 1, 1865	Do.
Saylors, William J	do	Feb. 15, 1864	Mar. 8, 1864	Do.
Self, Levi	do	Sept. 2, 1863	Dec. 24, 1863	Do.
Self, Allen	do	Sept. 2, 1863	Dec. 24, 1863	Do.
Thomas, Perry	do	Feb. 15, 1864	Mar. 8, 1864	Do.
Woodward, Willis	do	Sept. 2, 1863	Feb. 25, 1864	Do.
Woods, William	do	Sept. 2, 1863	Dec. 24, 1863	Do.
Watkins, Thomas J	do	Jan. 1, 1864	Feb. 25, 1864	Do.
Walls, George L	do	Feb. 15, 1864	Dec. 24, 1864	Do.
Wade, Asa	do	Sept. 2, 1863	Dec. 24, 1864	Do.
Middleton, Joseph	do	Sept. 2, 1863	Dec. 24, 1864	Do.

Killed in action.

Name	Rank	Enlisted	Expiration of service	Remarks
Brogden, Marion	Private	Jan. 1, 1864	Feb. 25, 1864	Killed at Jasper, Arkansas, March 13, 1864.
Hudson, Reuben A	do	Jan. 1, 1864	Feb. 25, 1864	Killed at Prairie D'Anne, Arkansas, April 13, 1864.
Daniel, John	do	Sept. 2, 1863	Dec. 24, 1863	Killed at Jasper, Arkansas, April 25, 1865.
Cooksey, Joseph	do	Jan. 1, 1864	Never	Killed at Jasper, Arkansas, March 13, 1864.

Died.

Name	Rank	Enlisted	Expiration of service	Remarks
Bow, Stephen A	Private	Sept. 2, 1863	Dec. 24, 1863	Died at Little Rock, Arkansas, May 22, 1864.
Cowen, William R	do	Sept. 2, 1863	Dec. 24, 1863	Died at Clarksville, Arkansas, May 28, 1865.
Harris, Nalbert A	do	Jan. 1, 1864	Feb. 25, 1864	Died at Lewisburg, Arkansas, August 28, 1864.
Johnson, William M	do	Feb. 15, 1864	Mar. 8, 1864	Died at Clarksville, Arkansas, February 17, 1865.
Mays, James	do	Jan. 1, 1864	May 21, 1864	Died at Little Rock, Arkansas, June 22, 1864.
Stagle, Frederick	do	Feb. 15, 1864	Mar. 8, 1864	
Leadford, John	do	Feb. 15, 1864	Mar. 8, 1864	Died at Little Rock, Arkansas, October 18, 1864.
Warren, William A. J	do	Sept. 2, 1863	Dec. 24, 1863	Died at Camden, Arkansas, June 24, 1865.
McCoy, William	do	Sept. 2, 1863	Dec. 24, 1863	Died at Clarksville, Arkansas, July 10, 1865.
Self, Isaac	do	Jan. ?, 1864	Never	Died at Fort Smith, Arkansas, March 3, 1864.

Deserted.

Name	Rank	Enlisted	Expiration of service	Remarks
Allen, Nathaniel G	Private	Feb. 15, 1864	Mar. 8, 1864	Deserted at Lewisburg, Arkansas, September 23, 1864.
Allen, Christopher C	do	Feb. 15, 1864	Mar. 8, 1864	Do.
Baysinger, William A	do	Jan. 1, 1864	Feb. 25, 1864	Deserted at Lewisburg, Arkansas, July 29, 1864.

Second regiment Arkansas infantry volunteers. Mustered into service July 6, 1864, (three years;) mustered out August 8, 1865.

COMPANY E—Continued.

Names.	Rank.	Enlistment.	Muster.	Remarks.
Casey, West A	Private	Jan. 1, 1864	Feb. 25, 1864	Deserted at Clarksville, Arkansas, April 1, 1864.
Cooper, John N	do	Sept. 2, 1863	Dec. 24, 1863	Do.
Cooper, Greenberry	do	Sept. 2, 1863	Dec. 24, 1863	Do.
Chapman, Thomas E	do	Sept. 2, 1863	Dec. 24, 1863	Deserted at Clarksville, Arkansas, May 10, 1865.
Farmer, William P	do	Sept. 2, 1863	Dec. 24, 1863	Deserted at Little Rock, Arkansas, June 8, 1864.
Frazier, Patrick T	do	Feb. 15, 1864	Mar. 8, 1864	Deserted at Lewisburg, Arkansas, September 23, 1864.
Hurst, John	do	Feb. 15, 1864	Mar. 8, 1864	Do.
Jackson, Thomas	do	Feb. 15, 1864	Mar. 8, 1864	Do.
Lawson, John	do	Jan. 1, 1864	Feb. 25, 1864	Deserted at Lewisburg, Arkansas, September 20, 1864.
Ply, Joseph	do	Feb. 15, 1864	Mar. 8, 1864	Deserted at Lewisburg, Arkansas, September 23, 1864.
Patten, William C	do	Feb. 15, 1864	Mar. 8, 1864	Do.
Patten, Mathew	do	Feb. 15, 1864	Mar. 8, 1864	Do.
Riggs, James R	do	Feb. 15, 1864	Mar. 8, 1864	Do.
Sullins, David C	do	Sept. 2, 1863	Dec. 24, 1863	Deserted at Little Rock, Arkansas, May 9, 1864.
Taylor, Elisha	do	Feb. 15, 1864	Mar. 8, 1864	Deserted at Lewisburg, Arkansas, September 23, 1864.
Young, Allen	do	Feb. 15, 1864	Mar. 8, 1864	Do.

Discharged.

McPherson, William F	Private	Sept. 2, 1863	Dec. 24, 1863	Mustered out at Fort Smith, Arkansas, June 21, 1865.

COMPANY F.

Names.	Rank.	Enlistment.	Date of rank.	Remarks.
John T. Loudon	Captain		June 15, 1864	Appointed 1st lieutenant from civil life; promoted captain June 15, 1864; mustered out with regiment.
Joseph P. Basham	1st lieutenant	Oct. 8, 1863	July 6, 1864	Appointed from 1st sergeant to 2d lieutenant May 14, 1864; to 1st lieutenant July 6, 1864; mustered out with regiment.
Charles H. Oliver	1st sergeant	Oct. 28, 1863	May 28, 1864	Appointed from sergeant.
Gilbert M. Shelby	Sergeant	Nov. 30, 1863	Feb. 20, 1864	Mustered out with regiment.
Raleigh B. L. Spinks	do	Oct. 19, 1863	Mar. 24, 1864	Do.
Peter Durnling	do	Oct. 17, 1863	Dec. 26, 1863	Do.
James R. Mangrum	Corporal	Oct. 19, 1863	Dec. 16, 1863	Do.
Benjamin F. Been	do	Oct. 8, 1863	Dec. 26, 1863	Do.
Geennett L. Oliver	do	Oct. 29, 1863	Mar. 1, 1864	Do.
Thomas W. Thurston	do	Jan. 20, 1864	June 16, 1865	Do.
William C. M. Caslin	do	Oct. 29, 1863	Mar. 24, 1864	Do.
William Overman	do	Oct. 19, 1863	Mar. 24, 1864	Do.

REPORT OF THE ADJUTANT GENERAL OF ARKANSAS. 219

Name	Rank		Muster	Remarks
James Basham		Jan. 21, 1864	Aug. 1, 1864	Mustered out with regiment.
Joseph W. Harper		Nov. 5, 1863	Aug. 1, 1864	Do.
Arter, Robert	Private	Oct. 10, 1863	Dec. 25, 1863	Do.
Anthony, Lorenzo	do	Oct. 10, 1863	Jan. 11, 1864	Do.
Been, Rufus L.	do	Oct. 1, 1863	Dec. 25, 1863	Do.
Bradshaw, William D.	do	Nov. 1, 1863	Dec. 25, 1863	Do.
Bradshaw, Samuel H.	do	Nov. 1, 1863	Dec. 25, 1863	Do.
Bradshaw, George W.	do	Nov. 1, 1863	Dec. 25, 1863	Do.
Bowen, William B.	do	Nov. 1, 1863	Dec. 25, 1863	Do.
Bowlin, Richard	do	Nov. 30, 1863	Jan. 11, 1864	Do.
Bowlin, John	do	Nov. 30, 1863	Dec. 25, 1863	Do.
Bowlin, Christopher	do	Nov. 30, 1863	Dec. 25, 1863	Do.
Barnard, James	do	Dec. 10, 1863	Dec. 25, 1863	Do.
Caton, Jeremiah	do	Dec. 22, 1863	Jan. 11, 1864	Do.
Caton, William	do	Oct. 19, 1863	Dec. 25, 1863	Do.
Crosby, William M.	do	Nov. 20, 1863	Dec. 25, 1863	Do.
Clamite, James H.	do	Dec. 1, 1863	Dec. 25, 1863	Do.
Comstock, Cumberland	do	Nov. 30, 1863	Jan. 10, 1864	Do.
Casey, John	do	Jan. 5, 1864	Jan. 11, 1864	Do.
Edwards, John A.	do	Oct. 24, 1863	Dec. 25, 1863	Do.
Gillstrap, John	do	Jan. 2, 1864	Jan. 11, 1864	Do.
Gore, Thomas	do	Nov. 10, 1863	Jan. 11, 1864	Do.
Johnson, James	do	Oct. 29, 1863	Dec. 25, 1863	Do.
Johnson, Elbert	do	Oct. 29, 1863	Dec. 25, 1863	Do.
Lewis, Redman R.	do	Oct. 28, 1863	Dec. 25, 1863	Do.
Lambert, Moses	do	Feb. 10, 1864	May 12, 1864	Do.
McCaslin, Henry M.	do	Oct. 29, 1863	Jan. 11, 1864	Do.
Manas, Wilson	do	Oct. 28, 1863	Dec. 25, 1863	Do.
Morris, John W.	do	Feb. 15, 1864	May 12, 1864	Do.
O'Niel, Marmaduke	do	Nov. 27, 1863	Dec. 25, 1863	Do.
Oliver, Edward T.	do	Dec. 5, 1863	Dec. 25, 1863	Do.
Oliver, William F.	do	Nov. 25, 1863	Dec. 25, 1863	Do.
Oliver, John W.	do	Feb. 12, 1864	May 12, 1864	Do.
Oliver, Richmond L.	do	May 12, 1864	May 12, 1864	Do.
Price, Martin	do	Oct. 28, 1863	Dec. 25, 1863	Do.
Pyles, Andrew J.	do	Oct. 20, 1863	Dec. 25, 1863	Do.
Pennington, Oliver	do	Dec. 19, 1863	Jan. 11, 1864	Do.
Peters, George W.	do			Missing after battle of Jenkins's Ferry, Arkansas, and dropped; escaped from enemy, and returned to his company January 14, 1865; mustered out with regiment.
Ross, Elijah	do	Oct. 19, 1863	Jan. 11, 1864	Mustered out with regiment.
Rhoades, William	do	Dec. 1, 1863	Dec. 25, 1863	Do.
Shelby, George J.	do	Nov. 30, 1863	Jan. 11, 1864	Do.
Sibley, John	do	Dec. 12, 1864	May 5, 1865	Do.
Turner, Andrew J.	do	Feb. 15, 1864	May 12, 1864	Do.
Tedford, John	do	Nov. 15, 1863	Dec. 28, 1863	Do.
Thurston, Hezekiah	do	Oct. 10, 1863	Jan. 11, 1864	Do.
Vaughan, Lilburn H.	do	Dec. 5, 1863	Dec. 25, 1863	Do.
Williams, Adolphus	do	Dec. 16, 1863	Jan. 11, 1864	Do.
Wells, Anthony D.	do	Dec. 1, 1863	Dec. 25, 1863	Do.

Second regiment Arkansas infantry volunteers. Mustered into service July 6, 1864, (three years;) mustered out August 8, 1865.

COMPANY F—Continued.

Names.	Rank.	Enlistment.	Muster.	Remarks.
Yandle, John F	Private	Feb. 1, 1864	May 12, 1864	Mustered out with regiment.
Killed in action.				
Ross, George W	Private	Oct. 18, 1863	Dec. 25, 1863	Killed at Jenkins's Ferry, Arkansas, April 30, 1864.
Missing in action.				
Brown, William A	Private	Dec. 19, 1863	Jan. 11, 1864	Missing at Jenkin's Ferry, Arkansas, April 30. 1864.
Died.				
Davis, John	Private	Jan. 11, 1864	Jan. 15, 1864	Died at Clarksville, Arkansas, February 25, 1864.
Cook, Josiah H	do	Nov. 9, 1863	Dec. 25, 1863	Died at Huntersville, Arkansas, June 19, 1864.
Aldridge, John	do	Nov. 29, 1863	Dec. 25, 1863	Died at Lewisburg, Arkansas, July 21, 1864.
Shaw, Thomas	do	Dec. 22, 1863	Jan. 11, 1864	Died at Lewisburg, Arkansas, July 23, 1864.
Allison, Samuel	do	Nov. 21, 1863	Dec. 25, 1863	Died at Lewisburg, Arkansas, July 30, 1864.
Carpenter, Samuel W	do	Jan. 12, 1864	May 12, 1864	Died at Lewisburg, Arkansas, August 3, 1864.
Carr, James	do	Nov. 30, 1863	Dec. 25, 1864	Died at Little Rock, Arkansas, July 24, 1864.
Morris, Adrian	do	Nov. 24, 1863	Dec. 25, 1864	Died at Lewisburg, Arkansas, December 18, 1864.
Gentry, Jackson A	do	Nov. 14, 1863	Dec. 25, 1864	Died at Fort Smith, Arkansas, of wounds, August 2, 1864.
Price, Thomas J	do	Dec. 21, 1863	Dec. 25, 1864	Died at Clarksville, Arkansas, of wounds, May 14, 1864.
Lynn, Elam P	do	Nov. 30, 1863	Dec. 25, 1864	Do.
Deserted.				
Bush, John A	Private	Dec. 2, 1863	Dec. 25, 1863	Deserted at Little Rock, Arkansas, June 30, 1864.
Lewis, George W	do	Jan. 6, 1864	Jan. 11, 1864	Deserted at Fort Smith, Arkansas, January 20, 1864.
Martin, James	do	Oct. 21, 1863	Dec. 28, 1863	Deserted at Fort Smith, Arkansas, December 26, 1863.
Needham, Henry	do	Jan. 26, 1864	May 12, 1864	Deserted at Lewisburg, Arkansas, August 15, 1864.
Phillips, Henry	do	Dec. 1, 1863	Dec. 25, 1863	Deserted at Fort Smith, Arkansas, December 26, 1863.
Corbitt, William J	do	Dec. 1, 1863	Dec. 25, 1863	Deserted at Fort Smith, Arkansas, February 1, 1865.
Ratcliffe, Aaron	do	Oct. 10, 1863	Jan. 11, 1864	Do.
Wright, John H	do	Dec. 19, 1863	Dec. 25, 1863	Do.
Discharged.				
Stephens, James	Private	Feb. 5, 1864	May 12, 1864	Discharged for disability at Little Rock, Arkansas, October 18, 1864.
Transferred.				
Campbell, Thomas	Corporal	Nov. 10, 1863	Dec. 25, 1863	Transferred to Invalid Corps at St. Louis, Missouri, October 18, 1864.

COMPANY G.

		Date of rank.	Muster.	
William P. Henderson	Captain	May 29, 1865		Appointed from sergeant of company H, 18th Iowa infantry; mustered out with regiment.
George D. Thayer	1st lieutenant		Nov. 25, 1863	Detached at headquarters Dist. of the Frontier until June 30, 1865, when resigned.
Moses M. Norris	1st sergeant		Nov. 25, 1863	Appointed from private; mustered out with regiment.
John W. Morris	Sergeant	Jan. 6, 1864	Nov. 25, 1863	Do.
Henry C. Ridling	do	Jan. 6, 1864	Nov. 25, 1863	Do.
William C. Lowry	do	Jan. 8, 1864	Feb. 25, 1863	Do.
Asbury Norris	do	Mar. 6, 1864	Nov. 25, 1863	Do.
David R. Dixon	Corporal	Jan. 6, 1864	Nov. 25, 1863	Mustered out with regiment.
John S. Laftis	do	Jan. 6, 1864	Dec. 26, 1863	Do.
George W. Harbison	do	Dec. 12, 1864	July 11, 1864	Do.
David Mayberry	do	Dec. 12, 1864	Nov. 25, 1863	Do.
Lemuel A. Loftis	do	Dec. 12, 1864	Nov. 25, 1863	Do.
John R. Blackwell	do	Jan. 6, 1864	Nov. 25, 1863	Do.
Adams, Henry	Private		Nov. 25, 1863	Do.
Barber, Sidney M	do		Jan. 10, 1864	Do.
Barrington, Joel W	do		July 11, 1864	Do.
Brown, Robert G	do		Nov. 25, 1864	Do.
Brown, Benjamin F	do		Nov. 25, 1864	Do.
Carter, McLim	do		Dec. 26, 1863	Do.
Chambers, George W	do		Nov. 25, 1863	Do.
Chambers, William	do		Mar. 30, 1864	Do.
Cox, John	do		Jan. 18, 1864	Do.
Clark, Thomas J	do		July 11, 1864	Do.
Dill, Solomon	do		Nov. 25, 1863	Do.
Denny, Jacob	do		Jan. 15, 1864	Do.
Denny, William	do		Feb. 1, 1864	Do.
Fry, James W	do		Dec. 26, 1863	Do.
Filpot, Jackson	do		Nov. 25, 1863	Do.
Filpot, William	do		Nov. 25, 1863	Do.
Filpot, John	do		Nov. 25, 1863	Do.
Frederick, Jesse	do		Feb. 16, 1864	Do.
Griffith, George	do		Feb. 25, 1864	Do.
Gibbs, William C	do		Dec. 26, 1864	Do.
Helton, Peter	do		Jan. 15, 1864	Do.
Holbrook, James	do		July 11, 1864	Do.
Ham, Davis	do		July 11, 1864	Do.
Howard, William	do		Sept. 19, 1864	Do.
Kirby, Benjamin F	do		Nov. 25, 1863	Do.
Lamsford, Abraham	do		July 11, 1864	Do.
McIntire, John T	do		Nov. 25, 1864	Do.
Pruitt, John D	do		Jan. 6, 1864	Do.
Pollock, James H	do		July 11, 1864	Do.
Posey, Jesse W	do		Feb. 15, 1865	Do.

Second regiment Arkansas infantry volunteers. Mustered into service July 6, 1864, (three years;) mustered out August 8, 1865.

COMPANY G—Continued.

Names.	Rank.	Enlistment.	Muster.	Remarks.
Posey, Devard	Private	Feb. 15, 1865	Feb. 15, 1865	Mustered out with regiment.
Robbins, Jacob M	do	Nov. 25, 1863	Jan. 6, 1864	Do.
Risenhoover, Robert P	do	Nov. 25, 1863	Jan. 6, 1864	Do.
Risenhoover, Joseph	do	Nov. 25, 1863	Jan. 6, 1864	Do.
Riggs, Cyrus	do	Mar. 10, 1864	June 30, 1864	Do.
Southern, William J	do	Jan. 10, 1864	June 30, 1864	Do.
Shed, John	do	Nov. 25, 1863	Jan. 6, 1864	Do.
Shed, Lorenzo D	do	Nov. 25, 1863	Jan. 6, 1864	Do.
Statam, Albert H	do	Sept. 1, 1864	Sept. 19, 1864	Do.
Southern, John	do	Dec. 3, 1864	Dec. 3, 1864	Do.
Parish, Walter M	do	Sept. 1, 1864	Sept. 19, 1864	Do.
Wimberly, Marion	do	Sept. 1, 1864	Sept. 1, 1864	Do.

Killed in action.

| Johnson, William | Private | Nov. 25, 1863 | Jan. 6, 1864 | Killed in action near Clarksville, Arkansas, May 18, 1864. |
| Murray, Hickerson | do | Mar. 5, 1864 | Sept. 19, 1864 | Killed in action near Clarksville, Arkansas, May 26, 1865. |

Died.

Crawford, Newton	Private	Dec. 26, 1863	Jan. 6, 1864	Died at Lewisburg, Arkansas, July 19, 1864.
Counts, Peter L	do	Nov. 25, 1863	Jan. 6, 1864	Do.
Cox, Elijah	do	Jan. 10, 1864	Jan. 30, 1864	Died at Little Rock, Arkansas, July 3, 1864.
Ford, Robert	do	Jan. 10, 1864	Jan. 30, 1864	Died at Lewisburg, Arkansas, August 4, 1864.
Gibbs, Jonathan C	do	Dec. 26, 1863	Jan. 6, 1864	Died at Little Rock, Arkansas, July 28, 1864.
McLendon, Abraham	do	Nov. 25, 1863	Jan. 6, 1864	Died at Lewisburg, Arkansas, August 7, 1864.
Parrish, Thomas J	do	Dec. 23, 1863	Jan. 6, 1864	Died at Lewisburg, Arkansas, July 23, 1864.
Posey, John	do	Jan. 10, 1864	Jan. 30, 1864	Died at Lewisburg, Arkansas, August 1, 1864.
Peavyhouse, William	do	Nov. 25, 1863	Jan. 6, 1864	Died at Clarksville, Arkansas, May 5, 1864.
Ridling, George W	do	Nov. 25, 1863	Jan. 6, 1864	Died at Clarksville, Arkansas, April 23, 1864.
Read, Matthew G	do	Nov. 25, 1863	Jan. 6, 1864	Died at Clarksville, Arkansas, March 18, 1864.
Risenhoover, Jacob W	do	Nov. 25, 1863	Jan. 6, 1864	Died at Clarksville, Arkansas, April 17, 1864.
Shedd, John B	do	Nov. 25, 1863	Jan. 6, 1864	Died at Lewisburg, Arkansas, July 28, 1864.
Wimberly, John	do	Nov. 25, 1863	Jan. 6, 1864	Died at Lewisburg, Arkansas, July 30, 1864.
Owens, George B	do	Nov. 25, 1863	Jan. 6, 1864	Died at Clarksville, Arkansas, November 19, 1865.

Discharged.

| Carter, James H | Private | Dec. 23, 1863 | Jan. 30, 1864 | Discharged July 2, 1865. |
| Griffith, Thomas | do | Dec. 26, 1863 | Jan. 6, 1864 | Discharged for disability July 26, 1865. |

Deserted.

Name	Rank	Date	Remarks
Cabler, Thomas H	Private	Nov. 25, 1863	Deserted at Clarksville, Arkansas, April 29, 1864.
Flinn, Francis M	do	Jan. 10, 1864	Do.
Gwinn, James F	do	Nov. 25, 1863	Do.
Guess, Peori	do	Dec. 26, 1863	Do.
Adam, Robert	do	Apr. 19, 1864	Deserted at Lewisburg, Arkansas, August 25, 1864.
Shedd, James	do	Nov. 25, 1863	Deserted at Clarksville, Arkansas, April 29, 1864.
Shockley, David	do	Dec. 26, 1863	Do.
Wimberly, Maj. H	do	Nov. 25, 1863	Do.
Wasson, William H	do	Jan. 10, 1864	Do.
Weare, John	Corporal	Nov. 25, 1863	Deserted at Little Rock, Arkansas, September 14, 1864.
Cargie, William	Private	Nov. 25, 1863	Deserted at Waldron, Arkansas, January 20, 1864.
Johnson, Thomas B	do	Nov. 25, 1863	Deserted at Dallas, Arkansas, January 18, 1864.
White, James	do	Nov. 25, 1863	Do.
Wimberly, General J	do	Dec. 26, 1863	Deserted at Fort Smith, Arkansas, December 31, 1864.

COMPANY H.

Name	Rank	Date of rank.	Muster.	Remarks
Charles E. Berry	Captain	Feb. 25, 1864		Appointed from private company E, 2d Kansas cavalry; mustered out with regiment.
Oliver H. Herrington	1st lieutenant	May 14, 1864		Appointed from corporal company F, 2d Kansas cavalry, May 14, 1864; resigned June 11, 1865.
Amos D. Amerson	1st sergeant	Dec. 31, 1864	Feb. 1, 1864	Appointed sergeant January 1, 1864; mustered out with regiment.
George W. Hancock	Sergeant	Jan. 1, 1864		Appointed from private; mustered out with regiment.
Joel Parsons	Corporal	Jan. 1, 1864	Dec. 11, 1863	Mustered out with regiment.
Cyrus W. Buchanan	do	Jan. 1, 1864	Dec. 8, 1863	Do.
Allen, Harmon	Private	Feb. 10, 1864	Jan. 11, 1864	Absent, sick at Lewisburg, Arkansas, since October 16, 1864; no discharge furnished at muster out of company.
Allison, William	do	Feb. 10, 1864	Jan. 9, 1864	Wounded at Jenkins's Ferry, April 30, 1864; carried to Pine Bluff, Arkansas; never heard of since; no discharge furnished on muster out of regiment.
Allen, Davis M	do	Feb. 18, 1864	Jan. 26, 1864	Mustered out with the regiment.
Baker, James A	do	Feb. 10, 1864	Jan. 1, 1864	Do.
Clifton, Thomas W	do	Feb. 10, 1864	Dec. 8, 1863	Do.
Chitwood, Joseph	do	Feb. 10, 1864	Jan. 1, 1864	Do.
Curtis, Benjamin	do	Feb. 10, 1864	Jan. 12, 1864	Do.
Ervin, John	do	Feb. 18, 1864	Jan. 27, 1864	Do.
Farmer, Abner H	do	Feb. 10, 1864	Dec. 5, 1863	Do.
Freeman, Lazarus	do	Feb. 10, 1864	Feb. 5, 1864	Do.
Looper, Henry M	do	Feb. 18, 1864	Feb. 1, 1863	Do.
Looper, Joseph R	do	Feb. 10, 1864	Dec. 1, 1863	Do.
McVey, James	do	Feb. 10, 1864	Feb. 15, 1864	Do.
Marsher, John R	do	Feb. 18, 1864	Feb. 12, 1864	Do.

Second regiment Arkansas infantry volunteers. Mustered into service July 6, 1864, (three years;) mustered out August 8, 1865.

COMPANY H—Continued.

Names.	Rank.	Enlistment.	Muster.	Remarks.
Marsher, John S.	Private	Jan. 26, 1864	Feb. 18, 1864	Mustered out with regiment.
Olar, Andrew J.	do	Dec. 1, 1863	Feb. 10, 1864	Do.
Post, Richard T.	do	Dec. 1, 1863	Feb. 10, 1864	Do.
Pitts, Hiram K.	do	Jan. 13, 1864	Feb. 18, 1864	Do.
Ross, William F.	do	Dec. 15, 1863	Feb. 18, 1864	Do.
Robothum, John	do	Jan. 1, 1864	Feb. 18, 1864	Do.
Singleton, Thomas	do	Jan. 18, 1864	Feb. 10, 1864	Do.
Shirley, Joseph	do	Jan. 1, 1864	Feb. 18, 1864	Do.
Woodard, Willis	do	Feb. 2, 1864	Feb. 18, 1864	Do.
Ward, Jasper N	do	Feb. 6, 1864	Feb. 18, 1864	Do.
Wright, Silas O.	do	Feb. 9, 1864	Feb. 18, 1864	Do.
Warren, Thomas.	do	Jan. 10, 1864	Mar. 8, 1864	Do.
Wood, Martin J.	do	Feb. 15, 1864	Mar. 8, 1864	Do.
Wood, John H.	do	Feb. 15, 1864	Mar. 8, 1864	Do.
Wood, George W.	do	Jan. 6, 1864	Feb. 10, 1864	Do.
Willhite, George A.	do	Jan. 8, 1864	Feb. 10, 1864	Do.
Willhite, John H.	do	Dec. 2, 1863	Feb. 10, 1864	Do.
Whinner, William D	do			

Died.

Ard, Eli	Private	Dec. 11, 1863	Feb. 18, 1864	Died at Lewisburg, Arkansas, August 15, 1864.
Baker, Thomas	do	Dec. 1, 1863	Feb. 10, 1864	Died at Little Rock, Arkansas, March 19, 1864.
Baxter, James	do	Dec. 1, 1863	Feb. 10, 1864	Died at Little Rock, Arkansas, May 24, 1864.
Chitwood, Joel	do	Dec. 13, 1863	Feb. 18, 1864	Died at Little Rock, Arkansas, June 23, 1864.
Chambers, John W.	do	Dec. 25, 1863	Feb. 18, 1864	Killed by guerillas near Clarksville, Arkansas, March 27, 1864.
Fiddler, William C	do	Jan. 9, 1864	Feb. 10, 1864	Died at Little Rock, Arkansas, October 21, 1864.
Gaston, William	do	Dec. 6, 1863	Feb. 10, 1864	Died at Fort Smith, Arkansas, February 14, 1864.
Hicks, John	do	Feb. 18, 1864	Feb. 18, 1864	Died at Lewisburg, Arkansas, November 3, 1864.
McCurley, Micajah	do	Feb. 8, 1864	Feb. 10, 1864	Died at Huntersville, Arkansas, July 10, 1864.
Magley, Riley William	do	Feb. 15, 1864	Mar. 8, 1864	Died at Huntersville, Arkansas, July 3, 1864.
Osborn, Jeremiah	do	Jan. 13, 1864	Feb. 18, 1864	Died at Lewisburg, Arkansas, July 28, 1864.
Pitts, Levi	do	Jan. 13, 1864	Feb. 18, 1864	Died at Huntersville, Arkansas, September 20, 1864.
Pitts, Elijah D.	do	Jan. 1, 1864	Feb. 10, 1864	Died at Huntersville, Arkansas, October 8, 1864.
Smith, Jasper	do	Jan. 1, 1864	Feb. 10, 1864	Died at Lewisburg, Arkansas, July 19, 1864.
Stout, General A. J.	do	Feb. 13, 1864	Feb. 18, 1864	Died at Little Rock, Arkansas, May 12, 1864.
Wood, John G.	do	Jan. 11, 1864	Feb. 10, 1864	Died at Lewisburg, Arkansas, November 15, 1864.

Deserted.

Bailey, William	Private	Jan. 1, 1864	Feb. 25, 1864	Deserted at Clarksville, Arkansas, March 4, 1864.
Boyd, Rolland	do	Jan. 1, 1864	Feb. 25, 1864	do.

REPORT OF THE ADJUTANT GENERAL OF ARKANSAS. 225

Name	Rank	Date	Remarks
Brown, Isaac B	do	Feb. 2, 1864	Deserted at Little Rock, Arkansas, May 4, 1864.
Curtis, Solomon	do	Jan. 12, 1864	Deserted at Little Rock, Arkansas, May 12, 1864.
Callahan, Mark R	do	Sept. 8, 1863	Do.
Casey, Jesse C	do	Sept. 8, 1863	Do.
Fryor, Thomas	do	Jan. 8, 1864	Deserted at Little Rock, Arkansas, March 24, 1864.
Fryor, James S	do	Jan. 7, 1864	Deserted at Clarksville, Arkansas, March 20, 1864.
Hickey, George C	do	Jan. 16, 1864	Deserted at Clarksville, Arkansas, March 1, 1864.
Henson, David C	do	Jan. 1, 1864	Do.
Hart, Silas C	do	Dec. 2, 1863	Deserted at Little Rock, Arkansas, September 11, 1864.
Jones, Alonzo J. W	do	Feb. 15, 1864	Deserted at Little Rock, Arkansas, May 12, 1864.
Lovehdy, John	do	Jan. 12, 1864	Deserted at Clarksville, Arkansas, March 1, 1864.
Lane, William	do	Dec. 3, 1863	Deserted at Ozark, Arkansas, September 15, 1864.
Lowrey, George M	do	Feb. 15, 1864	Deserted at Clarksville, Arkansas, March 1, 1864.
McElhaney, William	do	Feb. 15, 1864	Deserted at Little Rock, Arkansas, May 12, 1864.
McConnell, Miller	do	Jan. 11, 1864	Deserted at Clarksville, Arkansas, March 24, 1864.
Morton, James	do	Dec. 8, 1863	Deserted at Little Rock, Arkansas, May 12, 1864.
McKinney, Samuel J	do	Dec. 8, 1863	Do.
Mears, James	do	Feb. 15, 1864	Do.
McJones, Willey	do	Jan. 8, 1864	Deserted at Cadron, Arkansas, August 5, 1864.
Mitchell, Robert F	do	Feb. 15, 1864	Deserted at Little Rock, Arkansas, May 12, 1864.
Perkins, Andrew J	do	Dec. 1, 1863	Deserted at Reviler, Arkansas, March 28, 1864.
Penrod, Lewis	do	Dec. 1, 1863	Deserted at Clarksville, Arkansas, May 20, 1864.
Pearson, Lewis	do	Dec. 12, 1863	Deserted at Little Rock, Arkansas, May 12, 1864.
Robinson, Thomas	do	Dec. 11, 1863	Deserted at Cadron, Arkansas, August 14, 1864.
Tabor, Elijah	do	Feb. 15, 1864	Deserted at Little Rock, Arkansas, May 12, 1864.
White, Zachariah M	do	Feb. 8, 1864	Deserted at Little Rock, Arkansas, March 24, 1864.

Discharged.

Name	Rank	Date	Remarks
Wilkenson, Isaiah	Private	Feb. 15, 1864	Discharged by reason of wounds received in action at Yellville, Ark., April 6, 1864.

NOTE.—Joseph Taylor was borne on the rolls of this company as a recruit, and did good service as a soldier. He was killed at the battle of Jenkins's Ferry. Never mustered, for want of opportunity.

M. L. STEPHENSON, *Colonel, Commanding Regiment.*

COMPANY I.

Name	Rank	Date of rank	Remarks
Ira D. Bronson	Captain	May 14, 1862	Enlisted as private in company F 2d Kansas cavalry May 14, 1862; appointed 2d lieutenant 4th Arkansas infantry January 15, 1864; promoted to captain company A 4th Arkansas infantry May 10, 1864; transferred to company I 2d Arkansas infantry October 25, 1864; mustered out with regiment.
Samuel W. Brees	1st lieutenant	July 12, 1862	Enlisted as private company F 18th Iowa infantry July 12, 1862; mustered out with regiment.
William W. Tibbs	2d lieutenant	Oct. 25, 1864	Appointed from private company F 14th Kansas cavalry volunteers to 2d lieutenant company A 4th Arkansas infantry May 10, 1864; transferred to company I 2d Arkansas infantry October 25, 1864; mustered out with regiment.

Mis. Doc. 53——15

226 REPORT OF THE ADJUTANT GENERAL OF ARKANSAS.

Second regiment Arkansas infantry volunteers. Mustered into service July 6, 1864, (three years;) mustered out August 8, 1865.

COMPANY I—Continued.

Names.	Rank.	Enlistment.	Date of rank.	Remarks.
John W. Willis	1st sergeant	Jan. 11, 1864	May 3, 1864	Appointed from private.
Ezekiel Kindell	Sergeant	Jan. 25, 1864	Feb. 6, 1864	Mustered out with regiment.
William Shelton	do	Feb. 10, 1864	June 5, 1864	Do.
John W. Watson	do	Mar. 25, 1864	July 5, 1864	Do.
Thomas W. Redding	do	Feb. 6, 1864	Nov. 1, 1864	Do.
Jacob Queener	Corporal	Jan. 16, 1864	June 5, 1864	Do.
Jeremiah J. Tate	do	Dec. 6, 1863	Sept. 1, 1864	Do.
Isaac H. Grider	do	Jan. 25, 1864	Oct. 1, 1864	Do.
John Rogers	do	Mar. 28, 1864	Oct. 1, 1864	Do.
William F. Hodges	do	Jan. 18, 1864	Dec. 12, 1864	Do.
William W. Colton	do	Mar. 10, 1864	June 29, 1865	Do.
Elias Hays	do	Jan. 20, 1864	June 29, 1865	Do.
			Muster.	
Adams, William	Private	Apr. 12, 1864	July 25, 1864	Mustered out with regiment.
Allcock, William J	do	Feb. 25, 1864	May 18, 1864	On detached service at Springfield, Missouri; no discharge furnished on muster out of regiment.
Bynum, Kincher R	do	Jan. 17, 1864	Feb. 6, 1864	Mustered out with regiment.
Barrett, James D	do	Jan. 24, 1864	Feb. 6, 1864	Do.
Bledsoe, Abraham	do	Oct. 16, 1863	May 18, 1864	Do.
Boydston, Ezekiel B	do	Apr. 20, 1864	July 25, 1864	Do.
Baird, Benjamin W	do	Apr. 28, 1864	July 25, 1864	Absent, sick in hospital at Little Rock, Arkansas; no discharge furnished on muster out of regiment.
Bean, John T	do	Mar. 10, 1864	July 25, 1864	Mustered out with regiment.
Brazil, Richard I	do	Sept. 8, 1864	Sept. 21, 1864	Do.
Cooper, William J	do	Dec. 24, 1863	Feb. 25, 1864	Do.
Cooper, Winter E	do	Feb. 6, 1864	Feb. 25, 1864	Do.
Chambers, Hardy W	do	Jan. 25, 1864	Feb. 25, 1864	Absent, sick in hospital at Fort Leavenworth, Kansas; no discharge furnished on muster out of regiment.
Carlisle, Michael	do	Apr. 15, 1864	July 25, 1864	Mustered out with regiment.
Chapman, Joseph	do	Apr. 4, 1864	July 25, 1864	Do.
Clem, James N	do	Apr. 22, 1864	July 25, 1864	Do.
Dugan, Andrew J	do	Dec. 26, 1863	Feb. 25, 1864	Do.
Dinsmore, Nathaniel B	do	Mar. 24, 1864	July 25, 1864	Do.
Daniel, Robert	do	Mar. 28, 1864	July 25, 1864	Do.
Dunn, Hiram	do	Jan. 17, 1864	Feb. 6, 1864	Absent, on detached service in Newton county, Arkansas; no discharge furnished on muster out of regiment.
English, Benjamin	do	April 8, 1864	July 25, 1864	Absent, sick at Little Rock, Arkansas; no discharge furnished on muster out of regiment.
Fort, Lorenzo Q	do	Dec. 20, 1863	Feb. 25, 1864	do.
Ferguson, William T	do	Jan. 30, 1864	Feb. 6, 1864	Absent, sick at Roseville, Ark.; no discharge furnished on muster out of regiment. Mustered out with regiment.

Name		Enlisted	Mustered out	Remarks
Goulds, Isaiah J		April 20, 1864	July 25, 1864	Do.
Garner, John K	do	Jan. 20, 1864	Feb. 6, 1864	Do.
Hinton, James R	do	Dec. 26, 1863	July 25, 1864	Do.
Hudson, Zachariah	do	June 4, 1864	July 25, 1864	Do.
Hardcastle, Lumford	do	April 3, 1864	July 25, 1864	Do.
Hunt, George W	do	Dec. 12, 1863	July 25, 1864	Do.
Hunt, William	do	April 23, 1864	July 25, 1864	Do.
Hunt, John W	do	Dec. 6, 1863	July 25, 1864	Do.
Hunt, James	do	Dec. 6, 1863	Dec. 29, 1864	Do.
Hobles, George W	do	Feb. 25, 1864	Feb. 29, 1864	Do.
Hobles, John W	do	Jan. 23, 1864	Feb. 29, 1864	Do.
Hickey, Lewis H	do	Jan. 31, 1864	Feb. 6, 1864	Do.
Leming, Adolphus G	do	Mar. 4, 1864	July 25, 1864	Do.
Leming, Elijah	do	Mar. 4, 1864	July 25, 1864	Do.
Laster, Samuel H	do	Mar. 28, 1864	Aug. 20, 1864	Do.
Lewis, Thomas	do	April 21, 1864	July 25, 1864	Absent, sick in hospital at Fort Smith, Arkansas; no discharge furnished on muster out of regiment.
Ledgerwood, Samuel	do	Sept. 16, 1863	May 18, 1864	Mustered out with regiment.
Ledgerwood, George	do	Sept. 15, 1863	May 18, 1864	Do.
Lovell, Edmond	do	Jan. 4, 1864	May 18, 1864	Do.
Marshall, Richard J	do	Dec. 21, 1863	Feb. 29, 1864	Do.
Maynard, John W	do	Jan. 23, 1864	Feb. 29, 1864	Do.
McCord, Jack S	do	Mar. 11, 1864	July 25, 1864	Do.
Martin, Edmond T	do	April 21, 1864	Feb. 29, 1864	Do.
Murray, John L	do	Jan. 12, 1864	Feb. 6, 1864	Do.
Nash, Elijah	do	Mar. 11, 1864	July 25, 1864	Do.
Paine, Christopher C	do	Sept. 15, 1864	Sept. 21, 1864	Do.
Potts, John W	do	Feb. 8, 1864	Feb. 29, 1864	Do.
Porter, Henry	do	Dec. 23, 1863	Feb. 29, 1864	Do.
Price, John	do	Dec. 28, 1863	Feb. 29, 1864	Do.
Price, William	do	Feb. 16, 1864	Feb. 25, 1864	Do.
Pippin, Amos	do	April 20, 1864	July 25, 1864	Do.
Pearson, John B	do	April 20, 1864	Feb. 25, 1864	Do.
Palmer, Thomas	do	Jan. 6, 1864	Feb. 6, 1864	Do.
Reynolds, Edward	do	Jan. 20, 1864	Feb. 6, 1864	Do.
Ross, William C	do	Jan. 17, 1864	Feb. 6, 1864	Do.
Rodgers, George W	do	Jan. 1, 1864	May 28, 1864	Do.
Rodgers, William W	do	Jan. 17, 1864	Feb. 6, 1864	Do.
St. Clair, George W	do	Jan. 23, 1864	Feb. 29, 1864	Do.
Stokes, General S	do	Jan. 5, 1864	May 18, 1864	Do.
Smith, James C	do	Aug. 30, 1864	Sept. 21, 1864	Do.
Smith, Obey S	do	April 7, 1864	April 7, 1864	Do.
Skaggs, Benjamin O	do	Mar. 28, 1864	Aug. 29, 1864	Do.
Treat, Andrew J	do	Jan. 17, 1864	Feb. 6, 1864	Do.
Terry, John J	do	Jan. 17, 1864	May 12, 1865	Do.
Tate, Thomas W	do	April 13, 1864	July 25, 1864	Do.
Thurman, Pleasant	do	April 19, 1864	Aug. 20, 1864	Absent, sick at Little Rock, Arkansas; no discharge furnished on muster out of regiment.
Weaver, Alfred G	do	May 25, 1864	July 25, 1864	Mustered out with regiment.
Wadkins, Samuel	do	April 20, 1864	July 25, 1864	Do.
Weeks, James	do	May 13, 1864	July 25, 1864	Do.
Williams, Samuel T	do	April 20, 1864	Aug. 20, 1864	Do.

Second regiment Arkansas infantry volunteers. Mustered into service July 6, 1864, (three years;) mustered out August 8, 1865.

COMPANY I—Continued.

Names.	Rank.	Enlistment.	Muster.	Remarks.
Wooden, James	Private	Jan. 6, 1864	May 18, 1864	Mustered out with regiment.
Ward, William P	do	Jan. 15, 1864	Feb. 6, 1864	Do.
Zackerey, John B	do	Jan. 8, 1864	Feb. 6, 1864	Do.
Missing in action.				
Willis, Carroll	Private	Jan. 20, 1864	Feb. 6, 1864	Missing after battle at Jenkins's Ferry, Arkansas, reported to be alive in general hospital at Pine Bluffs, Arkansas.
Died.				
Arnold, William	Private	Mar. 23, 1864	May 18, 1864	Died at Lewisburg, Arkansas, July 23, 1864.
Bayer, William H	do	Mar. 28, 1864	Aug. 20, 1864	Died at Clarksville, Arkansas, February 16, 1865.
Black, Robert W	do	April 30, 1864	July 25, 1864	Died between Fort Smith and Little Rock, Arkansas, December 29, 1864.
Bowers, John	do	Jan. 5, 1864	Feb. 29, 1864	Died at Little Rock, Arkansas, October 17, 1864.
Capps, William W	do	Jan. 1, 1864	May 18, 1864	Died at Huntersville, Arkansas, July 11, 1864.
Chappel, Littleton	do	Jan. 28, 1864	Feb. 29, 1864	Died at Clarksville, Arkansas, April 11, 1865.
Hinton, William G. M	do	Jan. 29, 1864	Feb. 29, 1864	Died at Lewisburg, Arkansas, December 27, 1864.
Ladd, Thomas	do	Mar. 28, 1864	Aug. 20, 1864	Died at Clarksville, Arkansas, April 3, 1865.
Murphy, William H	do	Feb. 29, 1864	July 25, 1864	Died at Lewisburg, Arkansas, May 21, 1865.
Price, James P	do	Jan. 24, 1864	Feb. 29, 1864	Died at Fort Smith, Arkansas, March 2, 1865.
Rodgers, Jesse	do	Mar. 23, 1864	May 18, 1864	Died at Clarksville, Arkansas, August 23, 1864.
Treat, Jesse	do	Jan. 17, 1864	Feb. 6, 1864	Died at Clarksville, Arkansas, March 11, 1864.
Weaver, James Z. T	do	Jan. 23, 1864	Feb. 29, 1864	Died at Lewisburg, Arkansas, December 22, 1864.
Yarbrough, James	do	April 21, 1864	Aug. 20, 1864	Died at Clarksville, Arkansas, March 26, 1865.
Deserted.				
Allen, Andrew J	Private	Jan. 20, 1864	Feb. 6, 1864	Deserted at Little Rock, Arkansas, May 10, 1864.
Brown, James H	do	Jan. 8, 1864	Feb. 6, 1864	Deserted at Clarksville, Arkansas, February 25, 1864.
Brown, John M	do	Jan. 8, 1864	Feb. 6, 1864	Deserted at Clarksville, Arkansas, May 12, 1864.
Clark, William C	do	Jan. 16, 1864	Feb. 29, 1864	Deserted at Mulberry Creek, Arkansas, January 16, 1865.
Clay, Madison	do	Jan. 8, 1864	Feb. 6, 1864	Deserted at Clarksville, Arkansas, February 28, 1864.
Conger, John D	do	Jan. 25, 1864	Feb. 6, 1864	Deserted at Clarksville, Arkansas, March 24, 1864.
Ford, Washington	do	Jan. 20, 1864	Feb. 6, 1864	Deserted at Lewisburg, Arkansas, August 28, 1864.
Glover, James	do	Mar. 1, 1864	May 18, 1864	Deserted at Lewisburg, Arkansas, December 25, 1864.
Hodges, James J	do	Jan. 8, 1864	Feb. 6, 1864	Deserted at Clarksville, Arkansas, March 10, 1864.
Hill, Henry B. L	do	Jan. 20, 1864	Feb. 6, 1864	Deserted at Lewisburg, Arkansas, August 20, 1864.
Higgs, William B	do	Jan. 8, 1864	Feb. 6, 1864	Deserted at Clarksville, Arkansas, February 10, 1864.
Horn, Nathan F	do	Jan. 8, 1864	Feb. 6, 1864	Deserted at Danville, Arkansas, March 28, 1864.
Hickey, Charles P	do	Jan. 25, 1864	Feb. 6, 1864	Deserted at Clarksville, Arkansas, February 28, 1864.
Isabel, John S	do	Jan. 10, 1864	Feb. 6, 1864	Deserted at Clarksville, Arkansas, May 6, 1864.
	do	Jan. 8, 1864	Feb. 6, 1864	Deserted at Clarksville, Arkansas, February 29, 1864.

REPORT OF THE ADJUTANT GENERAL OF ARKANSAS. 229

Name	Rank	Date	Remarks
Joyner, Thomas L	do	Jan. 30, 1864	Deserted at Clarksville, Arkansas, March 30, 1864.
Jett, William S	do	Jan. 20, 1864	Deserted at Clarksville, Arkansas, February 29, 1864.
Langfield, Robert B	do	Jan. 18, 1864	Do.
McClintock, John	do	Jan. 8, 1864	Do.
Moreland, Linley M	do	Jan. 8, 1864	Do.
Miller, Archibald M	do	Jan. 9, 1864	Deserted at Lewisburg, Arkansas, September 3, 1864.
May, Joseph	do	Jan. 25, 1864	Deserted at Spadra Bluffs, Arkansas, February 29, 1864.
Nard, Joseph J	do	April 21, 1864	Deserted at Spadra Bluffs, Arkansas, June 5, 1864.
Nelson, William R	do	July 25, 1864	Deserted at Clarksville, Arkansas, February 29, 1864.
Overbee, Lawson	do	Jan. 25, 1864	Deserted at Lewisburg, Arkansas, August 3, 1864.
Paylor, William	do	Jan. 10, 1864	Deserted at Clarksville, Arkansas, February 8, 1864.
Redden, John A	do	Jan. 30, 1864	Deserted at Little Rock, Arkansas, September 12, 1864.
Sisemore, Granville	do	Jan. 13, 1864	Deserted at Lewisburg, Arkansas, February 29, 1864.
Smith, Charles B	do	Jan. 25, 1864	Deserted at Clarksville, Arkansas, October 4, 1864.
Underwood, George W	do	Oct. 22, 1863	Deserted at Clarksville, Arkansas, May 18, 1864.
Wages, Jackson J	do	Jan. 20, 1863	Deserted at Clarksville, Arkansas, March 30, 1864.
Whittaker, Robert	do	Jan. 30, 1864	Deserted at Lewisburg, Arkansas, September 20, 1864.
		Jan. 8, 1864	

Discharged.

Name	Rank	Date	Remarks
Briston, Wm. G	Private	Mar. 29, 1864	Discharged at Little Rock, Arkansas, from general hospital, June 17, 1865.
Cox, Allen P	do	April 20, 1864	do.
Hudson, Hiram	do	Mar. 22, 1864	Discharged at Little Rock, Arkansas, from general hospital, June 29, 1865.
Lovel, Andrew	do	Jan. 29, 1864	do.
Potter, Thomas J	do	Feb. 29, 1864	do.
Winchester, Fleming	do	Mar. 31, 1864	do.
Wood, Green	do	April 19, 1864	Discharged at Little Rock, Arkansas, from general hospital, June 17, 1864.

COMPANY K.

Name	Rank	Date of rank.	Remarks
John Boyle	Captain	June 29, 1864	Appointed from civil life; mustered out with regiment.
James M. Bethel	1st lieutenant	June 29, 1864	Appointed from civil life.
Charles O. Kimball	2d lieutenant	June 29, 1864	Appointed from private company E 2d Kansas cavalry volunteers; resigned October 14, 1864.
Howell B. Martindale	Sergeant	Dec. 27, 1863	Appointed from corporal; mustered out with regiment.
William Seaharn	do	Nov. 1, 1863	Appointed from private; mustered out with regiment.
Thomas Anthony	do	Jan. 1, 1864	do.
Green C. Anthony	Corporal	Oct. 15, 1863	Mustered out with regiment.
James J. Martindale	do	Jan. 1, 1864	Do.
William Tucker	do	Oct. 15, 1863	Do.
Benjamin F. Arnold	do	Dec. 24, 1863	Do.
Leonard G. W. Morelock	do	Feb. 25, 1863	Do.
William G. B. Littrell	do	Jan. 1, 1864	Do.
William B. McDaniel	do	Dec. 14, 1863	Do.
Amasa McWilliams	Musician	Feb. 15, 1864	Do.

230 REPORT OF THE ADJUTANT GENERAL OF ARKANSAS.

Second regiment Arkansas infantry volunteers. Mustered into service July 6, 1864, (three years;) mustered out August 8, 1865.

COMPANY K—Continued.

Names.	Rank.	Enlistment.	Muster.	Remarks.
Arnold, James	Private	Dec. 13, 1863	Feb. 19, 1864	Mustered out with regiment.
Baskins, William C	do	Jan. 11, 1864	Feb. 19, 1864	Do.
Bearden, John	do	Jan. 25, 1864	May 14, 1864	Do.
Doves, William F	do	Jan. 15, 1864	Feb. 19, 1864	Do.
Doyle, Sparks	do	Oct. 10, 1863	May 14, 1864	Do.
Glenn, Joseph B	do	Oct. 10, 1863	Oct. 15, 1863	Do.
Haggard, Richard	do	Oct. 10, 1863	Oct. 15, 1863	Do.
Hopkins, James B	do	Feb. 15, 1864	Mar. 8, 1864	Do.
Hampton, Aaron B	do	Feb. 15, 1864	Mar. 8, 1864	Do.
Horner, Lewis C	do	Mar. 28, 1864	June 27, 1864	Do.
Howell, Riley G	do	Dec. 1, 1863	Feb. 19, 1864	Do.
Hairston, David N	do	Mar. 17, 1864	June 27, 1864	Do.
Kirk, Caleb	do	Dec. 7, 1863	Feb. 19, 1864	Do.
Kirk, John W	do	Mar. 10, 1864	May 14, 1864	Do.
Loften, John	do	April 18, 1864	May 14, 1864	Do.
Martindale, Thomas	do	Jan. 1, 1864	May 14, 1864	Do.
Mullin, W. F	do	Jan. 24, 1864	Feb. 19, 1864	Do.
Miller, Burgess G	do	Jan. 10, 1864	Feb. 19, 1864	Do.
Oliver, Thomas	do	Jan. 1, 1864	May 14, 1864	Do.
Pool, John J	do	Nov. 15, 1863	May 26, 1864	Do.
Pool, Oliver	do	Nov. 15, 1863	May 14, 1864	Do.
Pryor, William P	do	Dec. 15, 1863	Feb. 19, 1864	Do.
Richardson, Isaac	do	Jan. 1, 1864	Jan. 1, 1864	Do.
Reddick, James W	do	Jan. 14, 1864	Feb. 19, 1864	Do.
Seahorn, Marmaduke	do	Oct. 15, 1863	May 14, 1864	Do.
Short, Richard T	do	Dec. 18, 1863	Feb. 19, 1864	Do.
Swift, Chester A	do	Mar. 17, 1864	June 27, 1864	Do.
Swift, Andrew J	do	Dec. 14, 1863	Feb. 19, 1864	Do.
Temples, James B	do	Dec. 13, 1863	Feb. 19, 1864	Do.
Tucker, Joseph B	do	Oct. 15, 1863	Oct. 15, 1863	Do.
Vails, John F	do	Oct. 15, 1863	May 14, 1864	Do.
Williams, Robert B	do	Mar. 20, 1864	June 27, 1864	Do.
Williams, Joshua A	do	Mar. 23, 1864	May 14, 1864	Do.
Wilsey, Joseph P	do	Mar. 15, 1864	June 27, 1864	Do.
Yarberry, James A	do	Jan. 20, 1864	Feb. 19, 1864	Do.
Killed in action.				
Hairston, John L	Private	Jan. 13, 1864	Never	Killed in action at Moscow, Arkansas, April 13, 1864.
Died.				
Acord, Francis M	Private	Jan. 14, 1864	Feb. 19, 1864	Died of fever at Lewisburg, Arkansas, July 28, 1864.

REPORT OF THE ADJUTANT GENERAL OF ARKANSAS. 231

Name	Rank	Date	Remarks
Baskins, Abraham L	do	Jan. 11, 1864	Killed by guerillas in Johnson county, Arkansas, January 7, 1865.
Baskins, William M	do	Jan. 11, 1864	Died of chills at Little Rock, Arkansas, September 21, 1864.
Blair, William M	do	Jan. 14, 1864	Died of fever at Lewisburg, Arkansas, August 2, 1864.
Doyle, Robert	do	Dec. 1, 1863	Died of fever at Clarksville, Arkansas, March 15, 1864.
Gibbons, William D	do	June 11, 1864	Died in Johnson county, Arkansas, of poison, January 7, 1865.
Horner, Andrew	do	Mar. 29, 1864	Died of measles at Lewisburg, Arkansas, July 31, 1864.
Horner, William K	do	Dec. 6, 1863	Killed by guerillas in Johnson county, Arkansas, August 10, 1864.
Horner, Pleasant	do	Mar. 29, 1864	Died of fever at Lewisburg, Arkansas, August 4, 1864.
Kirk, Isaac	do	Jan. 1, 1864	Died of chronic diarrhœa, Little Rock, Arkansas, September 10, 1864.
Mullin, Swift S	do	Jan. 24, 1864	Died of fever at Clarksville, Arkansas, April 11, 1864.
Jones, Alyriah D	do	Mar. 24, 1864	Died of measles at Little Rock, Arkansas, June 18, 1864.
Steel, Thomas N	do	Jan. 10, 1864	Died of measles at Lewisburg, Arkansas, July 17, 1864.

Deserted.

Name	Rank	Date	Remarks
Bates, Seaborn	Private	Oct. 15, 1863	Deserted at Fort Smith, Arkansas, April 30, 1865.
Brown, Singleton	do	Dec. 25, 1863	Deserted at Lewisburg, Arkansas, September 12, 1864.
Burris, Wiley A	do	Feb. 18, 1864	Deserted at Clarksville, Arkansas, March 15, 1864.
Cloud, William A	do	Dec. 13, 1863	Deserted at Lewisburg, Arkansas, September 12, 1864.
Campbell, William	do	Dec. 6, 1863	Deserted at Clarksville, Arkansas, February 26, 1864.
Campbell, James	do	Dec. 6, 1863	Do.
Chambers, Francis M	do	Mar. 22, 1864	Deserted at Little Rock, Arkansas, April 30, 1865.
Clark, George T	do	Dec. 16, 1863	Deserted at Clarksville, Arkansas, March 10, 1864.
Dickenson, Nathan B	do	Dec. 18, 1863	Deserted at Little Rock, Arkansas, May 15, 1864.
Everett, James W	do	Feb. 15, 1864	Deserted at Clarksville, Arkansas, March 15, 1864.
Fox, William T	do	Feb. 15, 1864	Deserted at Clarksville, Arkansas, May 20, 1864.
Fritts, William G	do	Jan. 10, 1864	Deserted at Clarksville, Arkansas, March 10, 1864.
Farmer, Thomas B	do	Jan. 14, 1864	Deserted at Clarksville, Arkansas, March 15, 1864.
Frisley, James M	do	Dec. 15, 1863	Deserted at Springfield, Missouri, April 30, 1865.
Guthrie, Calvin P	do	Jan. 1, 1864	Deserted at Lewisburg, Arkansas, September 12, 1864.
Gray, George R	do	Jan. 28, 1864	Deserted at Springfield, Missouri, April 30, 1865.
Gantt, Richard	do	Jan. 14, 1864	Deserted at Clarksville, Arkansas, March 10, 1864.
Hardgraves, John D	do	Jan. 10, 1864	Deserted at Lewisburg, Arkansas, July 27, 1864.
Hill, Needham	do	Feb. 13, 1864	Deserted in Franklin county, Arkansas, February 21, 1864.
Hampton, Thomas M	do	Feb. 15, 1864	Deserted at Clarksville, Arkansas, March 15, 1864.
Killgore, John	do	Jan. 12, 1864	Deserted at Danville, Arkansas, March 26, 1864.
Kirley, James D	do	Dec. 23, 1863	Deserted at Clarksville, Arkansas, March 26, 1864.
McAllister, Edward	do	Jan. 23, 1864	Deserted at Lewisburg, Arkansas, July 27, 1864.
Robertson, Andrew M	do	Dec. 13, 1863	Do.
Smith, Lewis A	do	Jan. 25, 1864	Deserted at Little Rock, Arkansas, May 15, 1864.
Wammack, Charles	do	Dec. 24, 1863	Deserted in Scott county, Arkansas, September 1, 1864.

Discharged.

Name	Rank	Date	Remarks
Hodges, Sterling	Private	Jan. 1, 1864	Discharged for disability April 18, 1865.

Transferred.

Name	Rank	Date	Remarks
Satterfield, Levi M	1st sergeant	Oct. 15, 1863	Appointed from private to 1st sergeant May 14, 1864; transferred to non-commissioned staff as regimental commissary sergeant January 1, 1865.

SECOND ARKANSAS INFANTRY VOLUNTEERS.—HISTORICAL MEMORANDA.

The following communication from Colonel M. L. Stephenson, commanding the regiment, gives an account of its organization and services to a period shortly anterior to its muster out of service:

HEADQUARTERS SECOND ARKANSAS INFANTRY VOLUNTEERS, *Clarksville, Arkansas, June 26, 1865.*

GENERAL: In compliance with your request of the 22d instant, I have the honor to make the following statement regarding the history of my regiment. The authority for organizing the 2d Arkansas infantry volunteers was transmitted by the Secretary of War to Major General J. M. Schofield, commanding the department of the Missouri, some time in the month of August, 1863, precise date unknown. In conformity with that authority, Major General Schofield, in paragraph 5, of Special Order No. 238, dated headquarters department of the Missouri, St. Louis, Missouri, September 1, 1863, delegated the general charge and supervision of the organization of the regiment to Brigadier General John McNeil, commanding the district of southwest Missouri, instructing him to appoint some officer to take the immediate charge of the organization, under the supervision of General McNeil. The order further declared that the regiment should be composed of and organized from all recruits that had already been enlisted, and from all that might thereafter be enlisted, for Arkansas infantry from citizens of Arkansas in southwest Missouri and northwest Arkansas, until the organization of the regiment was completed. The officer taking the immediate supervision of the organization was empowered to recommend, with the concurrence of Brigadier General McNeil, competent and efficient men to fill the positions of company officers, taken, as far as practicable, from the citizens of Arkansas, the recommendations to be sent to headquarters department of the Missouri for reference to the Secretary of War, the field and staff officers to be nominated by the major general commanding the department of the Missouri, "from such reliable, competent, and efficient citizens or officers as, in his opinion, had good claims to the positions to be filled."

In obedience to the above order General McNeil entrusted the organization of the regiment to me by paragraph 1, Special Order No. 170, dated headquarters district of southwest Missouri, Springfield, Missouri, August 31, 1863, directing me to the rendezvous of the regiment, there being at that time no other point possessing the same advantages necessary for a rendezvous. The rendezvous was, however, ultimately changed to Fort Smith, Arkansas, by paragraph 5, Special Order No. 317, dated headquarters department of the Missouri, St. Louis, Missouri, November 20, 1863, Fort Smith having been occupied by the federal troops in September, 1863.

In the month of January, 1864, the organization of four companies having been completed, the lieutenant colonel, adjutant, quartermaster, and officers of companies A, B, C, and D were appointed by the Secretary of War, and orders for their muster issued by Major General Schofield.

The organization of the regiment was completed March 13, 1864, at which time the aggregate enlisted strength was 913; but owing to the impossibility of procuring a mustering officer there were but 11 officers and about 600 men mustered. In this condition the regiment was ordered into the field by Brigadier General J. M. Thayer, commanding district of the frontier, March 20, 1864, to take part in the expedition south, commanded by Major General Steele.

Leaving Clarksville, Arkansas, on the 24th day of March, 1864, with eight companies, the regiment reported to Brigadier General Thayer on the 27th day of March, 1864, fifteen miles west of Danville, Arkansas, and from that time forward moved with the 3d division 7th army corps in that disastrous campaign. The regiment was engaged in the battles of Prairie d'Anne, on the 13th of April, and Jenkins's Ferry on the 30th of the same month, in both of which engagements the regiment lost several men killed and wounded. The losses incurred by these battles, deaths caused by sickness, and desertions so reduced the regiment that upon our arrival at Little Rock, Arkansas, the organization was declared incomplete. The two companies (D and G) which had been left at Clarksville rejoined the regiment at Little Rock, and soon after, with the exception of myself, the officers and enlisted men were all mustered, I being at the time absent with leave, having been wounded at Jenkins's Ferry, but was mustered soon after my return to the regiment, to date from July 6, 1864.

In the month of July, 1864, the regiment was ordered to Lewisburg, Arkansas, where it remained until the 7th day of September, 1864, when it was forced to evacuate the place and return to Little Rock with the 3d Arkansas cavalry on account of the advance north of the enemy under General Price, who crossed the Arkansas river at Dardanelle, thirty miles above Lewisburg. About this time the regiment lost a great many men from desertion and deaths. Reports were continually reaching the regiment that the families of the men were being cruelly treated by the guerillas, and in consequence the regiment became so reduced that we mustered, on arriving at Little Rock, but 450 enlisted men.

We remained at Little Rock until the 18th day of October, 1864, when we received orders to escort a supply train to Fort Smith, Arkansas, with the intention of remaining there. Arriving at Fort Smith I reported the regiment to Brigadier General J. M. Thayer, commanding 3d division 7th army corps, and was ordered by him to report to Brigadier General John Edwards, commanding 1st brigade 3d division 7th army corps, for duty.

On the 31st day of December, 1864, we received orders from General Edwards to proceed to this place immediately, for the purpose of collecting together the Union people in the country with the view of moving them to Little Rock, on account of an order having been issued for the evacuation of Fort Smith and the surrounding country. Upon arriving at Clarksville a large number of the men who had deserted at Little Rock and Lewisburg voluntarily rejoined their regiment, and in view of the facts in their cases, have been since restored to duty with loss of pay and allowances during their unauthorized absence, by order of Brigadier General Bussy, commanding 3d division, 7th army corps.

The order for the evacuation of the country having been countermanded, the regiment has remained at this place and has done good service to the country by ridding it of guerillas. The regiment now numbers 27 commissioned officers and 581 enlisted men.

Very respectfully, your obedient servant,

M. L. STEPHENSON, *Colonel, Commanding Regiment.*

Brig. Gen. A. W. BISHOP, *Adjutant General of Arkansas, Little Rock, Arkansas.*

On the 2d day of October, 1864, Special Order No. 240, headquarters department of Arkansas, was issued, assigning the 4th Arkansas infantry (whose history is elsewhere given) to the 2d Arkansas infantry for duty, and on the 28th day of the same month another order was issued, transferring the enlisted men of the former regiment to the latter for assignment to companies. On the 28th day of March, 1865, this last order was amended by including Ira D. Bronson as captain, and William W. Tibbs as 2d lieutenant, who, together with 73 men, were assigned to company I; the transfer to date from October 25, 1864. From this time onward this detachment constituted a portion of the 2d Arkansas infantry, and served with the regiment at Clarksville, Arkansas, and vicinity, until its muster out on the 8th day of August, 1865.

REPORT OF THE ADJUTANT GENERAL OF ARKANSAS. 233

Roster of officers and men of the fourth regiment Arkansas infantry volunteers who, from death or other causes, were not consolidated.

COMPANY A.

Names.	Rank.	Enlistment.	Muster.	Remarks.
Merton A. Payne	1st sergeant	May 10, 1864	Aug. 1, 1864	Mustered out October 24, 1864.
Died.				
John R. Tate	Sergeant	Dec. 5, 1863	July 25, 1864	Died at Little Rock, Arkansas, September 4, 1864.
Akes, John	Private	Dec. 2, 1863	Feb. 29, 1864	Died at Fort Smith, Arkansas, July 26, 1864.
Bevel, William H.	do	April 7, 1864	Never	Missing after skirmish at Ozark, Arkansas, April 26, 1864; supposed to be dead.
Brown, Benjamin L.	do	April 18, 1864	Feb. 29, 1864	Died at Spadra Bluff, Arkansas, July 17, 1864.
Campbell, Asa	do	Nov. 19, 1863	June 19, 1864	Died at Van Buren, Arkansas, June 19, 1864.
Carpenter, James J.	do	Dec. 2, 1863	Feb. 29, 1864	Died at Clarksville, Arkansas, May 15, 1864.
Frasher, Elijah H.	do	June 30, 1864	July 25, 1864	Died at Little Rock, Arkansas, August 20, 1864.
George, William P.	do	April 13, 1864	July 25, 1864	Died at Lewisburg, Arkansas, October 25, 1864.
Hinton, Nicholas S.	do	Dec. 25, 1863	Feb. 29, 1864	Died at Little Rock, Arkansas, October 15, 1864.
Hudson, Franklin	do	May 13, 1864	July 25, 1864	Died at Little Rock, Arkansas, August 12, 1864.
Johnson, John T.	do	April 21, 1864	Never	Captured near Clarksville, Arkansas, May 10, 1864; supposed to have been killed.
Lovell, George W.	do	April 22, 1864	Feb. 29, 1864	Died at Clarksville, Arkansas, May 1, 1864.
Moody, William H.	do	Mar. 30, 1864	July 25, 1864	Died at Little Rock, Arkansas, August 24, 1864.
Rainey, William	do	Dec. 24, 1863	Feb. 29, 1864	Died at United States hospital, Fort Smith, Arkansas, October 11, 1864.
Smith, Abel S.	do	April 7, 1864	Never	Missing after skirmish at Ozark, Arkansas, April 25, 1864; supposed to have been killed.
Smith, Edmond S.	do	April 19, 1864	Never	Died at Fort Smith, Arkansas, June 4, 1864.
Thomas, James	do	April 15, 1864	Never	Died at Fort Smith, Arkansas, July 15, 1864.
Woll, Jesse C.	do	Mar. 21, 1864	July 25, 1864	Died at Little Rock, Arkansas, October 2, 1864.
Weaver, William H.	do	Dec. 22, 1863	Feb. 29, 1864	Died at Little Rock, Arkansas, August 4, 1864.
Deserted.				
Anderson, Preston	Private	April 7, 1864	Never	Deserted at Ozark, Arkansas, April 10, 1864
Baker, Richard A.	do	April 7, 1864	Never	Do.
Blagg, Jesse	do	Feb. 12, 1864	Feb. 29, 1864	Deserted at Van Buren, Arkansas, June 11, 1864.
Blansel, Henry	do	April 7, 1864	Never	Deserted at Ozark, Arkansas, April 10, 1864.
Barnes, John C.	do	April 7, 1864	Never	Do.
Barnes, Israel S.	do	April 7, 1864	Never	Do.
Barnes, James	do	April 7, 1864	Never	Do.
Bates, John G. A.	do	April 7, 1864	Never	Do.
Carpenter, Elijah	do	Feb. 1, 1864	Feb. 29, 1864	Deserted at Van Buren, Arkansas, June 9, 1864.
Daniel, William	do	Mar. 28, 1864	July 25, 1864	Deserted at Little Rock, Arkansas, September 8, 1864.
Dunn, Thomas	do	April 7, 1864	Never	Deserted at Ozark, Arkansas, April 10, 1864.
Durham, James I.	do	Mar. 14, 1864	Never	Deserted at Roseville, Arkansas, August 1, 1864.
Fleming, Samuel R.	do	April 30, 1864	Never	Deserted at Clarksville, Arkansas, May 5, 1864.
Hill, William S.	do	Mar. 28, 1864	Never	Sent to military prison at Alton, Illinois, August 31, 1864.
Hobbs, George W.	do	Feb. 25, 1864	Feb. 29, 1864	Deserted at Little Rock, Arkansas, October 7, 1864,
Hobbs, John W.	do	Jan. 23, 1864	Feb. 29, 1864	Do.

Roster of officers and men of the fourth regiment Arkansas infantry volunteers who, from death or other causes, were not consolidated.

COMPANY A—Continued.

Names.	Rank.	Enlistment.	Muster.	Remarks.
Henry, Arthur	Private	Jan. 12, 1864	Feb. 29, 1864	Deserted at Van Buren, Arkansas, June 8, 1864.
Horner, Andrew	do	April 27, 1864	Never	Deserted at Clarksville, Arkansas, May 5, 1864.
Horner, Pleasant	do	April 27, 1864	Never	Do.
Hunt, John W	do	Dec. 6, 1863	July 25, 1864	Deserted at Little Rock, Arkansas, September 8, 1864.
James, Daniel	do	Dec. 8, 1863	July 25, 1864	Do.
Johnson, Jordan P	do	April 7, 1864	Never	Deserted at Ozark, Arkansas, April 10, 1864.
Kirby, Henley	do	April 7, 1864	Never	Do.
Martin, Edmund T	do	April 21, 1864	July 25, 1864	Deserted at Little Rock, Arkansas, October 7, 1864.
Maynard, Isaac	do	Dec. 25, 1863	Feb. 29, 1864	Deserted at Fort Smith, Arkansas, July 16, 1864.
May, James	do	Feb. 25, 1864	Feb. 29, 1864	Deserted at Little Rock, Arkansas, September 8, 1864.
Miller, Thomas	do	Feb. 25, 1864	Feb. 29, 1864	Deserted at Little Rock, Arkansas, October 7, 1864.
McWilliams, Guy C	do	April 7, 1864	Never	Deserted at Ozark, Arkansas, April 10, 1864.
Mooney, John H	do	April 22, 1864	Never	Deserted at Fort Smith, Arkansas, June 30, 1864.
Newman, Lemuel	do	Mar. 29, 1864	Never	Do.
Patterson, Jonathan C	do	Jan. 20, 1864	Feb. 29, 1864	Deserted at Fort Smith, Arkansas, July 16, 1864.
Posey, Henry M	do	April 21, 1864	Feb. 29, 1864	Deserted at Clarksville, Arkansas, July 17, 1864.
Quin, John T	do	Jan. 22, 1864	Feb. 29, 1864	Deserted at Van Buren, Arkansas, June 11, 1864.
Sewell, Arrington	do	Feb. 1, 1864	Feb. 29, 1864	Deserted at Van Buren, Arkansas, June 8, 1864.
Sewell, James K	do	Dec. 23, 1863	Feb. 29, 1864	Deserted at Fort Smith, Arkansas, June 30, 1864.
Simpson, George M	do	Dec. 5, 1863	Feb. 29, 1864	Deserted at Fort Smith, Arkansas, July 16 1864.
Skaggs, Thomas M	do	Jan. 25, 1864	Feb. 29, 1864	Deserted at Fort Smith, Arkansas, June 30, 1864.
Small, John	do	Jan. 17, 1864	Feb. 29, 1864	Do.
Stout, Ransom	do	April 20, 1864	July 25, 1864	Deserted at Fort Smith, Arkansas, August 16, 1864.
Stanford, James T	do	April 7, 1864	Never	Deserted at Ozark, Arkansas, April 10, 1864.
Smith, John A	do	April 23, 1864	Never	Deserted at Clarksville, Arkansas, May 10, 1864.
Smith, George W	do	April 23, 1864	Never	Do.
Taylor, William W	do	April 7, 1864	Never	Deserted at Ozark, Arkansas, April 10, 1864.
Taylor, James A. J	do	April 25, 1864	Never	Do.
Titsworth, Spear	do	Jan. 12, 1864	Feb. 29, 1864	Deserted at Van Buren, Arkansas, June 11, 1864.
Williams, John W	do	Jan. 27, 1864	Feb. 29, 1864	Deserted at Van Buren, Arkansas, June 8, 1864.

FOURTH ARKANSAS INFANTRY VOLUNTEERS.—HISTORICAL MEMORANDA.

On the 4th day of October, 1863, authority was given by the commanding general department of the Missouri to Edward J. Brooks, of Fayetteville, Arkansas, to raise a regiment of infantry in this State to be called the 4th Arkansas infantry volunteers, he being appointed provisional colonel of the regiment, with his principal rendezvous at Fayetteville, and branch rendezvous at Fort Smith and such other places in western Arkansas as he might select. The difficulties encountered in recruiting for this regiment, and its services in the field, are detailed in a communication to this office from Ira D. Bronson, formerly captain company A, dated Hickory, Illinois, September 18, 1865, from which the following extracts are made:

"On the 10th of December, 1863, Captain H. S. Greeno, 6th Kansas cavalry, was detailed on recruiting service for the 4th Arkansas infantry, but owing to the fact that the 2d Arkansas infantry was in process of formation, and had nearly exclusive control of recruiting for infantry, and also that the 2d, 3d and 4th Arkansas cavalry, and the 2d Kansas cavalry, were recruiting in the State, and a large portion of those who were disposed to enlist preferred the cavalry arm of the service, recruiting for the 4th Arkansas infantry was very slow and tedious.

"About the middle of March, 1864, I had fifty men recruited and stationed at Fort Smith; Lieutenant Hunter had the same number at Fayetteville; other recruiting officers had a number each, making in all about one hundred and eighty men. Brave and efficient recruiting officers were continually within the rebel lines, and many men were in this way picked up.

"On the 10th of April, 1864, Captain Greeno, with a number of recruiting officers, accompanied General Steel's expedition to Camden, hoping thereby to secure a sufficient number of recruits, with those already raised, to organize a major's command. Captain Greeno succeeded in obtaining a large number of recruits, and forwarded them with a train to Little Rock, but unfortunately they were captured with it before reaching Pine Bluff.

"The headquarters of the regiment remained at Clarksville, Arkansas, until the 18th day of May, 1864, the troops meantime acting a conspicuous part in defending the post against the combined efforts of the guerillas of western Arkansas, aided by a portion of Shelby's command that had returned to the north side of the Arkansas river. My detachment had frequent engagements with them, scarcely a day passing without our taking some prisoners.

"On or about the 20th day of May, 1864, Captain Goss, 6th Kansas cavalry, commanding the post of Clarksville, having ascertained that a large force of rebels had crossed the Arkansas river, and were threatening the post with overwhelming numbers, ordered an abandonment of the place, and fell back on Fort Smith. Upon our arrival there the detachment of the 4th Arkansas infantry was placed on duty as an extreme outpost south.

"While stationed near Fort Smith Captain Greeno received orders to proceed with a portion of his command into southern Arkansas, and move out the families of federal soldiers, who had been plundered and maltreated by the rebel troops, consisting of bushwhackers, Indians, and renegades, prowling about in that portion of the State. Several trips of this description were made, and frequent encounters with the enemy occurred.

"On the 15th day of July we were ordered to Little Rock, and for a time after our arrival did outpost duty. On the 25th day of July my company was mustered in. At this time there were on the regimental rolls two hundred and twenty-three names, a portion of whom were recruited by Lieutenants Hunter and Tennant, and partially so for cavalry—were unwilling to serve as infantry—and were transferred to the 4th Arkansas cavalry. Captain Greeno was also transferred, and on the 16th day of October, 1864, was mustered as a major in that regiment. I was thus left in command of the detachment which, on the 2d day of October, 1864, was assigned to the 2d Arkansas infantry for duty. On the 28th day of the same month all the enlisted men of our regiment were transferred to the 2d Arkansas infantry for assignment to companies. This assignment was afterwards confirmed in orders from the War Department, and the officers of the regiment, though mostly retained in service, were left without a command. Lieutenant R. S. Crampton, regimental quartermaster, resigned prior to the transfer, and Assistant Surgeon B. Blanchard was mustered out, to be mustered in again as surgeon, having received an appointment as such, though he was never in fact re-mustered.

"March 28, 1865, the order of assignment was so amended as to include myself as captain, and William W. Tibbs as second lieutenant, who, with seventy-three men, were formally assigned to company I, 2d Arkansas infantry, the transfer to date from October 25, 1864.

"Out of the number recruited for the 4th Arkansas infantry forty-five (45) deserted, thirty (30) died, thirty (30) were captured, forty-five (45) were transferred to the 4th Arkansas cavalry, and seventy-three (73) as stated above.

"Very respectfully, your obedient servant,

"IRA D. BRONSON,

"*Late Captain Company I, 2d Arkansas Infantry, formerly Captain Company A, 4th Arkansas Infantry.*"

236   REPORT OF THE ADJUTANT GENERAL OF ARKANSAS.

First Arkansas (six months) infantry volunteers. Organized at Helena, Arkansas, July 21, 1862; mustered out December 31, 1862.

FIELD AND STAFF.

Names.	Rank.	Enlistment.	Date of rank.	Remarks.
John C. Bundy	Lieutenant colonel	July 21, 1862		Mustered out with battalion.
Jos. S. Van Sant	Adjutant	Sept. 3, 1862		Do.

COMPANY A.

Names.	Rank.	Enlistment.	Date of rank.	Remarks.
Hiram V. Gray	Captain	June 10, 1862	July 1, 1862	Died at St. Louis, Missouri, December 2, 1862.
Calvin C. Bliss	1st lieutenant	June 10, 1862	July 1, 1862	Mustered out with battalion.
Thomas J. Bruce	2d lieutenant	June 10, 1862	July 1, 1862	Died at Helena, Arkansas, August 19, 1862.
			Muster.	
McKelvey, Elijah	Sergeant	June 10, 1862	July 1, 1862	
Hadler, Charles P	do	June 10, 1862	July 1, 1862	
Pace, A. J	do	June 10, 1862	July 1, 1862	
Williams, J. H	do	June 10, 1862	July 1, 1862	
Miller, John	do	June 10, 1862	July 1, 1862	
Hard, William H	Corporal	June 10, 1862	July 1, 1862	
Cobert, William E	do	June 10, 1862	July 1, 1862	
Brown, William	do	June 10, 1862	July 1, 1862	
Clark, Alexander	do	June 10, 1862	July 1, 1862	
Griscom, Thompson	do	June 10, 1862	July 1, 1862	
Hogan, George B	do	June 10, 1862	July 1, 1862	
Liscomb, William J	do	June 10, 1862	July 1, 1862	
Ray, John S	do	June 10, 1862	July 1, 1862	
Alexander, G. W	Private	June 10, 1862	July 1, 1862	
Alexander, W. C	do	June 10, 1862	July 1, 1862	
Browing, A. A	do	June 10, 1862	July 1, 1862	
Bruce, John	do	June 10, 1862	July 1, 1862	
Burrows, J. R	do	June 10, 1862	July 1, 1862	
Bruce, W. G	do	June 10, 1862	July 1, 1862	
Brown, Lewis	do	June 10, 1862	July 1, 1862	
Bullington, Jesse	do	June 10, 1862	July 1, 1862	
Bullington, J. L	do	June 10, 1862	July 1, 1862	
Bullington, J. M	do	June 10, 1862	July 1, 1862	
Bruce, B. F	do	June 10, 1862	July 1, 1862	
Brady, Clinton	do	June 10, 1862	July 1, 1862	
Brady, P. G	do	June 10, 1862	July 1, 1862	
Bailey, G. P	do	June 10, 1862	July 1, 1862	

REPORT OF THE ADJUTANT GENERAL OF ARKANSAS. 237

Bradley, G. W	do	June 10, 1862	July 1, 1862
Barnes, W. P	do	June 10, 1862	July 1, 1862
Burrows, J. R	do	June 10, 1862	July 1, 1862
Conner, J. E	do	June 10, 1862	July 1, 1862
Copeland, G. W	do	June 10, 1862	July 1, 1862
Crowell, D. R	do	June 10, 1862	July 1, 1862
Casson, J. B., sr	do	June 10, 1862	July 1, 1862
Clark, James	do	June 10, 1862	July 1, 1862
Cash, W. J	do	June 10, 1862	July 1, 1862
Corbett, J. M	do	June 10, 1862	July 1, 1862
Cochrane, W. H	do	June 10, 1862	July 1, 1862
Cochrane, John	do	June 10, 1862	July 1, 1862
Crigler, Nicholson	do	June 10, 1862	July 1, 1862
Crigler, Overton	do	June 10, 1862	July 1, 1862
Corbett, Thomas	do	June 10, 1862	July 1, 1862
Crawson, W. W	do	June 10, 1862	July 1, 1862
Casson, J. B., jr	do	June 10, 1862	July 1, 1862
Drake, Johnson	do	June 10, 1862	July 1, 1862
Douglass, D. L	do	June 10, 1862	July 1, 1862
Daggett, D. R	do	June 10, 1862	July 1, 1862
Evans, D. B	do	June 10, 1862	July 1, 1862
Fowler, Miles	do	June 10, 1862	July 1, 1862
Golden, G. D	do	June 10, 1862	July 1, 1862
Gillam, Harris	do	June 10, 1862	July 1, 1862
Gray, Henry C	do	June 10, 1862	July 1, 1862
Hearlson, N. H	do	June 10, 1862	July 1, 1862
Hearlson, A. B	do	June 10, 1862	July 1, 1862
Hogan, James M	do	June 10, 1862	July 1, 1862
Hour, Albert	do	June 10, 1862	July 1, 1862
Hearlson, Martin	do	June 10, 1862	July 1, 1862
Harper, G. W	do	June 10, 1862	July 1, 1862
Kyle, W. B	do	June 10, 1862	July 1, 1862
King, William	do	June 10, 1862	July 1, 1862
King, James	do	June 10, 1862	July 1, 1862
King, H. C	do	June 10, 1862	July 1, 1862
Lawrence, J. C	do	June 10, 1862	July 1, 1862
Long, B. P	do	June 10, 1862	July 1, 1862
Long, G. W	do	June 10, 1862	July 1, 1862
Lamb, G. W	do	June 10, 1862	July 1, 1862
Lamb, B. F	do	June 10, 1862	July 1, 1862
Long, W. R	do	June 10, 1862	July 1, 1862
Long, H. H	do	June 10, 1862	July 1, 1862
Long, F. M	do	June 10, 1862	July 1, 1862
Martin, William	do	June 10, 1862	July 1, 1862
Mitchell, B. F	do	June 10, 1862	July 1, 1862
McNulty, A. J	do	June 10, 1862	July 1, 1862
McKnight, Benjamin	do	June 10, 1862	July 1, 1862
Means, Samuel	do	June 10, 1862	July 1, 1862
Miller, James	do	June 10, 1862	July 1, 1862
Norrnah, Isaiah	do	June 10, 1862	July 1, 1862
Northram, William	do	June 10, 1862	July 1, 1862
Perkins, Joshua	do	June 10, 1862	July 1, 1862

238   REPORT OF THE ADJUTANT GENERAL OF ARKANSAS.

First Arkansas (six months) infantry volunteers. Organized at Helena, Arkansas, July 21, 1862; mustered out December 31, 1862.

COMPANY A—Continued.

Names.	Rank.	Enlistment.	Muster.	Remarks.
Perkins, D. B	Private	June 10, 1862	July 1, 1862	
Parks, D. W	do	June 10, 1862	July 1, 1862	
Reeves, J. T	do	June 10, 1862	July 1, 1862	
Smart, J. W	do	June 10, 1862	July 1, 1862	
Sexton, Miles	do	June 10, 1862	July 1, 1862	
Sexton, W. A	do	June 10, 1862	July 1, 1862	
Stoner, J. W	do	June 10, 1862	July 1, 1862	
Sanford, Elijah	do	June 10, 1862	July 1, 1862	
Seward, H. M	do	June 10, 1862	July 1, 1862	
Sims, Jacob	do	June 10, 1862	July 1, 1862	
Sealy, William	do	June 10, 1862	July 1, 1862	
Warm, James	do	June 10, 1862	July 1, 1862	
Whiteworth, J. W	do	June 10, 1862	July 1, 1862	
Warm, Nathaniel	do	June 10, 1862	July 1, 1862	
Williams, Wesley	do	June 10, 1862	July 1, 1862	
Willson, J. W	do	June 10, 1862	July 1, 1862	
Willson, R. W	do	June 10, 1862	July 1, 1862	
Weldon, J. W	do	June 10, 1862	July 1, 1862	
Willson, G. W	do	June 10, 1862	July 1, 1862	
Wait, William	do	June 10, 1862	July 1, 1862	
Young, G. W	do	June 10, 1862	July 1, 1862	
Young, John	do	June 10, 1862	July 1, 1862	
Watson, F. S	do	June 10, 1862	July 1, 1862	

NOTE.—Of the further military history of the enlisted men of this and the other companies of the battalion, this office can only give the information contained in the accompanying historical memoranda.

COMPANY B.

Names.	Rank.	Enlistment.	Date of rank.	Remarks.
Thomas J. Williams	Captain	June 10, 1862	July 20, 1862	Mustered out with battalion.
George M. Galloway	1st lieutenant	June 10, 1862	July 20, 1862	Do.
Nathan Williams	2d lieutenant	June 10, 1862	July 20, 1862	Do.

Names.	Rank.	Enlistment.	Muster.	Remarks.
Stesley, James J	Sergeant	June 10, 1862	July 20, 1862	
Prince, Larkin H	do	June 10, 1862	July 20, 1862	
Holbrook, Jeremiah	do	June 10, 1862	July 20, 1862	
Wells, Thomas S	do	June 10, 1862	July 20, 1862	
Wells, David A	do	June 10, 1862	July 20, 1862	

REPORT OF THE ADJUTANT GENERAL OF ARKANSAS 239

Jenkins, John	Corporal	June 10, 1862	July 20, 1862
Holbrook, W. S	do	June 10, 1862	July 20, 1862
Reynolds, H. M	do	June 10, 1862	July 20, 1862
Skipper, Joseph	do	June 10, 1862	July 20, 1862
Goile, Owen	do	June 10, 1862	July 20, 1862
Whitehead, James J	do	June 10, 1862	July 20, 1862
White, Richard	do	June 10, 1862	July 20, 1862
Hovel, Richard	do	June 10, 1862	July 20, 1862
Allen, Isaac	Private	June 10, 1862	July 20, 1862
Atkinson, Gideon P	do	June 10, 1862	July 20, 1862
Barnes, Andrew	do	June 10, 1862	July 20, 1862
Bird, Thomas G	do	June 10, 1862	July 20, 1862
Bigham, Virgil C	do	July 18, 1862	July 20, 1862
Boatman, George	do	June 10, 1862	July 20, 1862
Boatman, Perry	do	June 10, 1862	July 20, 1862
Boatman, Robert	do	June 10, 1862	July 20, 1862
Breeding, Calvin	do	July 18, 1862	July 20, 1862
Can, Vinson	do	July 18, 1862	July 20, 1862
Carpenter, Robert	do	June 10, 1862	July 20, 1862
Carter, Felix	do	June 10, 1862	July 20, 1862
Childers, James J	do	June 10, 1862	July 20, 1862
Cooper, Virgil J	do	June 10, 1862	July 20, 1862
Crane, Martin	do	June 10, 1862	July 20, 1862
Crane, Lewis A	do	June 10, 1862	July 20, 1862
Cunningham, Jonathan	do	June 15, 1862	July 20, 1862
Dunham, Thomas J	do	June 10, 1862	July 20, 1862
Denoy, John	do	June 18, 1862	July 20, 1862
Dickinson, James H	do	June 10, 1862	July 20, 1862
Gilbert, Arthur	do	June 10, 1862	July 20, 1862
Gwinn, Thomas J	do	June 10, 1862	July 20, 1862
Gordon, Joseph	do	June 10, 1862	July 20, 1862
Hill, Anderson	do	June 10, 1862	July 20, 1862
Holland, John	do	July 18, 1862	July 20, 1862
Jenkins, Chesley	do	June 10, 1862	July 20, 1862
Jening, Thomas D	do	July, 1862	July 20, 1862
Kines, Mathias	do	July 18, 1862	July 20, 1862
Lemmas, Young	do	June 10, 1862	July 20, 1862
Lee, William	do	June 10, 1862	July 20, 1862
Lockhart, Andrew J	do	June 10, 1862	July 20, 1862
Lockhart, Charles	do	June 10, 1862	July 20, 1862
Mahan, John	do	June 10, 1862	July 20, 1862
Masson, Alaphil	do	June 10, 1862	July 20, 1862
Maxwell, Bailey, sr	do	June 10, 1862	July 20, 1862
Maxwell, Bailey, jr	do	June 10, 1862	July 20, 1862
Maxwell, G. A	do	June 10, 1862	July 20, 1862
Maxwell, Solomon	do	June 10, 1862	July 20, 1862
McCarley, Thomas J	do	June 10, 1862	July 20, 1862
Melton, Charles C	do	June 10, 1862	July 20, 1862
Middleton, James J	do	June 15, 1862	July 20, 1862
Middleton, Thomas G	do	June 15, 1862	July 20, 1862
Patterson, James	do	July 18, 1862	July 20, 1862
Prince, William J	do	June 10, 1862	July 20, 1862

First Arkansas (six months) infantry volunteers. Organized at Helena, Arkansas, July 21, 1862; mustered out December 31, 1862.

COMPANY B—Continued.

Names.	Rank.	Enlistment.	Muster.	Remarks.
Porterfield, W. R.	Private	June 10, 1862	July 20, 1862	
Reed, Henry	do	June 10, 1862	July 20, 1862	
Scroggins, Green	do	June 10, 1862	July 20, 1862	
Scroggins, Leroy	do	June 10, 1862	July 20, 1862	
Scroggins, Wiley	do	June 10, 1862	July 20, 1862	
Shoemake, James M	do	June 10, 1862	July 20, 1862	
Shoemake, Wilson C	do	June 10, 1862	July 20, 1862	
Stobaugh, Edmund S	do	June 10, 1862	July 20, 1862	
Stobaugh, Ananias	do	June 10, 1862	July 20, 1862	
Stobaugh, James	do	June 10, 1862	July 20, 1862	
Stafford, Edmund P	do	June 10, 1862	July 20, 1862	
Stanfield, John	do	June 10, 1862	July 20, 1862	
Strickland, M. G	do	June 10, 1862	July 20, 1862	
Taylor, Jacob	do	June 10, 1862	July 20, 1862	
Vaun, Joseph	do	June 10, 1862	July 20, 1862	
Withey, Alonzo	do	June 10, 1862	July 20, 1862	
Williams, Nathaniel	do	June 10, 1862	July 20, 1862	
Williams, George	do	June 10, 1862	July 20, 1862	
Williams, Morton	do	June 10, 1862	July 20, 1862	
Williams, John H	do	June 10, 1862	July 20, 1862	
Williams, Riley S	do	June 10, 1862	July 20, 1862	
Williams, John I	do	June 10, 1862	July 20, 1862	
Williams, Leroy	do	June 10, 1862	July 20, 1862	

COMPANY C.

Names.	Rank.	Date of rank.	Muster.	Remarks.
Pleasant Turney	Captain	June 10, 1862	July 20, 1862	Died October 3, 1862, at Helena, Arkansas.
Elijah James	1st Lieutenant	June 10, 1862	July 20, 1862	Died November 14, 1862, at St. Louis, Missouri.
George W. Pool	2d lieutenant	June 10, 1862	July 20, 1862	Mustered out with battalion.
Birdwell, James M	Sergeant	July 7, 1862	July 20, 1862	
Lee, Lindsey R	do	June 10, 1862	July 20, 1862	
Sharp, R. T.	do	June 10, 1862	July 20, 1862	
Sharp, Samuel G	do	June 10, 1862	July 20, 1862	
Wells, William C	do	June 10, 1862	July 20, 1862	
Copeland, R. E	Corporal	June 10, 1862	July 20, 1862	

REPORT OF THE ADJUTANT GENERAL OF ARKANSAS. 241

Name	Rank	Enlisted	Mustered in
Hargriss, H. C		June 10, 1862	July 20, 1862
Morris, Absalom	do	June 10, 1862	July 20, 1862
Reeves, E. T	do	June 10, 1862	July 20, 1862
Sharp, Hiram A	do	June 10, 1862	July 20, 1862
South, Eldridge	do	June 10, 1862	July 20, 1862
Thomas, John H	do	June 10, 1862	July 20, 1862
Winston, Augustus	do	June 10, 1862	July 20, 1862
Watson, J. E. H	Private	June 10, 1862	July 20, 1862
Sharp, Dan. F	do	June 10, 1862	July 20, 1862
Ard, Azariah	do	June 10, 1862	July 20, 1862
Asher, John	do	June 10, 1862	July 20, 1862
Blawins, D. D	do	June 10, 1862	July 20, 1862
Baird, A. C	do	June 10, 1862	July 20, 1862
Baird, John M	do	June 10, 1862	July 20, 1862
Brown, Thomas	do	June 10, 1862	July 20, 1862
Browning, William	do	June 10, 1862	July 20, 1862
Browning, J. P	do	June 10, 1862	July 20, 1862
Browning, Hawkins	do	June 10, 1862	July 20, 1862
Browning, John	do	June 10, 1862	July 20, 1862
Bryant, J. P	do	June 10, 1862	July 20, 1862
Browning, A. J	do	June 10, 1862	July 20, 1862
Carter, J. W	do	June 10, 1862	July 20, 1862
Carter, Samuel	do	June 10, 1862	July 20, 1862
Carter, W. H	do	June 10, 1862	July 20, 1862
Cryles, W. H	do	June 10, 1862	July 20, 1862
Crouch, J. E	do	June 10, 1862	July 20, 1862
Chandion, J. A	do	June 10, 1862	July 20, 1862
Edmund, Anthony	do	June 10, 1862	July 20, 1862
Edmund, Richard	do	June 10, 1862	July 20, 1862
Edwards, Isaac	do	June 10, 1862	July 20, 1862
Endaly, Thomas	do	June 10, 1862	July 20, 1862
Endaly, Robert	do	June 10, 1862	July 20, 1862
Edwards, James M	do	June 10, 1862	July 20, 1862
Edwards, Isaac H	do	June 10, 1862	July 20, 1862
Fitzgerald, Robert	do	June 10, 1862	July 20, 1862
Henley, A. M	do	June 10, 1862	July 20, 1862
Harley, William B	do	June 10, 1862	July 20, 1862
Hearlson, J. A	do	June 10, 1862	July 20, 1862
Hearlson, T. L	do	June 10, 1862	July 20, 1862
Jones, Josiah	do	June 10, 1862	July 20, 1862
Jones, T. J	do	June 10, 1862	July 20, 1862
James, T. J	do	June 10, 1862	July 20, 1862
Kirkpatrick, A. T	do	June 10, 1862	July 20, 1862
Kirkpatrick, C. W	do	June 10, 1862	July 20, 1862
Merritt, Osmor	do	June 10, 1862	July 20, 1862
Mahan, John A	do	June 10, 1862	July 20, 1862
McClan, J. D	do	June 10, 1862	July 20, 1862
McClan, J. A	do	June 10, 1862	July 20, 1862
Maltingly, Asa	do	June 10, 1862	July 20, 1862
McKenney, T. B	do	June 10, 1862	July 20, 1862
Moody, John C	do	June 10, 1862	July 20, 1862
Miliken, A. W	do	June 10, 1862	July 20, 1862

MIS. DOC. 53——16

First Arkansas (six months) infantry volunteers. Organized at Helena, Arkansas, July 21, 1862; mustered out December 31, 1862.

COMPANY C—Continued.

Names.	Rank.	Enlistment.	Muster.	Remarks.
Norman, Richard	Private	June 10, 1862	July 20, 1862	
Pool, R. W	do	June 10, 1862	July 20, 1862	
Parks, William	do	June 10, 1862	July 20, 1862	
Price, J. J	do	June 10, 1862	July 20, 1862	
Pipkin, Calvin	do	June 10, 1862	July 20, 1862	
Quinsley, W. C	do	June 10, 1862	July 20, 1862	
Quinsley, T. S	do	June 10, 1862	July 20, 1865	
Quinsley, James O	do	June 10, 1862	July 20, 1862	
Quinsley, William D	do	June 10, 1862	July 20, 1862	
Robinson, Griffith	do	June 10, 1862	July 20, 1862	
Sharp, W. J	do	June 10, 1862	July 20, 1862	
Smith, J. S	do	June 10, 1862	July 20, 1862	
Smith, W. D	do	June 10, 1862	July 20, 1862	
Stoner, J. M	do	June 10, 1862	July 20, 1862	
Soward, G. M	do	June 10, 1862	July 20, 1862	
Strickler, G. R	do	June 15, 1862	July 20, 1862	
Thomas, H. J	do	June 10, 1862	July 20, 1862	
Tanner, L. R	do	June 10, 1862	July 20, 1862	
Webber, John	do	June 10, 1862	July 20, 1862	
Walker, J. D	do	June 10, 1862	July 20, 1862	
Williams, A. J	do	June 10, 1862	July 20, 1862	
Williams, Thomas	do	June 10, 1862	July 20, 1862	
Williamson, G. M	do	June 10, 1862	July 20, 1862	
Wooldridge, R. W	do	June 10, 1862	July 20, 1862	

COMPANY D.

Names.	Rank.	Enlistment.	Date of rank.	Remarks.
Lorenzo D. Toney	Captain	July 1, 1862	July 14, 1862	Mustered out with battalion.
Johnson Clark	1st lieutenant	July 1, 1862	July 14, 1862	Died November 15, 1862.
Matthew G. McKelvey	2d lieutenant	July 1, 1862	July 14, 1862	Mustered out with battalion.

Names.	Rank.	Enlistment.	Muster.	Remarks.
Ceneyers, W. G	Sergeant	July 1, 1862	July 14, 1862	
Haywood, Edmund R	do	July 1, 1862	July 14, 1862	
Johnson, G. A	do	July 1, 1862	July 14, 1862	
Kipport, W. H	do	July 1, 1862	July 14, 1862	
Kennedy, J. A	do	July 1, 1862	July 14, 1862	

REPORT OF THE ADJUTANT GENERAL OF ARKANSAS. 243

Betts, J. F.	Corporal	July 1, 1862	July 14, 1862
Childers, F. M.	do	July 1, 1862	July 14, 1862
Haines, J. M.	do	July 1, 1862	July 14, 1862
Jones, Willis C.	do	July 1, 1862	July 14, 1862
Lassiter, William	do	July 1, 1862	July 14, 1862
Petrum, A. H.	do	July 1, 1862	July 14, 1862
Shannon, J. B.	do	July 1, 1862	July 14, 1862
Turby, Joseph W.	Private	July 1, 1862	July 14, 1862
Arnold, George	do	July 1, 1862	July 14, 1862
Arnold, James R.	do	July 1, 1862	July 14, 1862
Arnold, Jefferson L.	do	July 1, 1862	July 14, 1862
Atkinson, H. C.	do	July 1, 1862	July 14, 1862
Atkinson, William	do	July 1, 1862	July 14, 1862
Barlow, Alfred	do	July 1, 1862	July 14, 1862
Barlow, J. M.	do	July 1, 1862	July 14, 1862
Barnes, Davis	do	July 1, 1862	July 14, 1862
Barlow, John	do	July 1, 1862	July 14, 1862
Bird, J. W.	do	July 1, 1862	July 14, 1862
Browning, William	do	July 1, 1862	July 14, 1862
Carnes, James	do	July 1, 1862	July 14, 1862
Carney, N. W.	do	July 1, 1862	July 14, 1862
Clark, S. M.	do	July 1, 1862	July 14, 1862
Carney, Thomas	do	July 1, 1862	July 14, 1862
Custer, H. S	do	July 1, 1862	July 14, 1862
Carter, Isaac M	do	July 1, 1862	July 14, 1862
Cane, Elijah	do	July 1, 1862	July 14, 1862
Clark, J. T.	do	July 1, 1862	July 14, 1862
Clark, M	do	July 1, 1862	July 14, 1862
Claxton, W. P.	do	July 1, 1862	July 14, 1862
Claxton, F. M	do	July 1, 1862	July 14, 1862
Claxton, M	do	July 1, 1862	July 14, 1862
Clafton, H. M.	do	July 1, 1862	July 14, 1862
Congers, James M	do	July 1, 1862	July 14, 1862
Colliers, Jr., Alexander	do	July 1, 1862	July 14, 1862
Craven, William S	do	July 1, 1862	July 14, 1862
Crewer, F. R. H. P	do	July 1, 1862	July 14, 1862
Crazen, Z. W	do	July 1, 1862	July 14, 1862
Cuaney, James H	do	July 1, 1862	July 14, 1862
Cudney, Ezekiel	do	July 1, 1862	July 14, 1862
Dew, David	do	July 1, 1862	July 14, 1862
Drumsight, R. S	do	July 1, 1862	July 14, 1862
Dunn, Richard S	do	July 1, 1862	July 14, 1862
Ellis, Jacob W	do	July 1, 1862	July 14, 1862
Ellmore, Benton C	do	July 1, 1862	July 14, 1862
Galloway, Benjamin	do	July 1, 1862	July 14, 1862
Gillmore, William C.	do	July 1, 1862	July 14, 1862
Goodrich, Charles	do	July 1, 1862	July 14, 1862
Gordon, Lewis P	do	July 1, 1862	July 14, 1862
Green, William E	do	July 1, 1862	July 14, 1862
Hays, James B	do	July 1, 1862	Ju y 14, 1862
Haywood, E. M	do	July 1, 1862	July 14, 1862
Hays, W. A.	do	July 1, 1862	July 14, 1862

First Arkansas (six-months) infantry volunteers. Organized at Helena, Arkansas, July 21, 1862; mustered out December 31, 1862.

COMPANY D—Continued.

Names.	Rank.	Enlistment.	Muster.	Remarks.
Hill, Abner	Private	July 1, 1862	July 14, 1862	
Hill, Isaac	...do...	July 1, 1862	July 14, 1862	
Hodges, Amasa	...do...	July 1, 1862	July 14, 1862	
Henderson, Constance	...do...	July 1, 1862	July 14, 1862	
Henderson, Reuben	...do...	July 1, 1862	July 14, 1862	
James, Silas	...do...	July 1, 1862	July 14, 1862	
Kirk, Joseph R. F	...do...	July 1, 1862	July 14, 1862	
Lassiter, Francis M	...do...	July 1, 1862	July 14, 1862	
Lee, William C	...do...	July 1, 1862	July 14, 1862	
Lassiter, Jesse	...do...	July 1, 1862	July 14, 1862	
Lassiter, J. C	...do...	July 1, 1862	July 14, 1862	
Lassiter, John A. T. J	...do...	July 1, 1862	July 14, 1862	
Lassiter, John A	...do...	July 1, 1862	July 14, 1862	
Marchant, J. A. A	...do...	July 1, 1862	July 14, 1862	
Marchant, Thomas J	...do...	July 1, 1862	July 14, 1862	
Marchant, William B	...do...	July 1, 1862	July 14, 1862	
McBride, Francis M	...do...	July 1, 1862	July 14, 1862	
McKee, James M	...do...	July 1, 1862	July 14, 1862	
Miller, G. W	...do...	July 1, 1862	July 14, 1862	
P——, Isaac A	...do...	July 1, 1862	July 14, 1862	
Pittman, Ephraim	...do...	July 1, 1862	July 14, 1862	
Powers, John B	...do...	July 1, 1862	July 14, 1862	
Powers, K. W	...do...	July 1, 1862	July 14, 1862	
Powers, William M	...do...	July 1, 1862	July 14, 1862	
Pratt, John G	...do...	July 1, 1862	July 14, 1862	
Richardson, James T	...do...	July 1, 1862	July 14, 1862	
Ross, William A	...do...	July 1, 1862	July 14, 1862	
Robinson, David	...do...	July 1, 1862	July 14, 1862	
Robinson, Jeremiah	...do...	July 1, 1862	July 14, 1862	
Russell, James C	...do...	July 1, 1862	July 14, 1862	
Shannon, H. C	...do...	July 1, 1862	July 14, 1862	
Smith, John	...do...	July 1, 1862	July 14, 1862	
Southard, Polk D	...do...	July 1, 1862	July 14, 1862	
Steward, John W	...do...	July 1, 1862	July 14, 1862	
Talla, Isam H	...do...	July 1, 1862	July 14, 1862	
Thompson, John C	...do...	July 1, 1862	July 14, 1862	
Tarney, William H	...do...	July 1, 1862	July 14, 1862	
Woodson, John L	...do...	July 1, 1862	July 14, 1862	
Weatherford, David L	...do...	July 1, 1862	July 14, 1862	

FIRST ARKANSAS SIX-MONTHS INFANTRY VOLUNTEERS.—HISTORICAL MEMORANDA.

On the march of General Curtis from northwestern Arkansas to Helena in 1862 several hundred of the loyal citizens of the State joined the army at Batesville. The following extract of a letter from Hon. C. C. Bliss, late lieutenant governor of the State, and who was himself connected with them, gives an account of their organization:

"A few days after the arrival of the federal army in Batesville, in the spring of 1862, H. V. Gray, a loyalist from Black River township, in Independence county, with about forty of his neighbors, who, with others to the number of one hundred or upwards, had previously banded themselves together to resist, by force if need be, attempts to urge them into the rebel service, made their appearance at the headquarters of General Curtis, and tendered their services to the government. Captain Gray requested permission to recruit for a regiment of six-months men. A few months previous to this he came near losing his life at the hands of a mob, but a short distance from where headquarters then were, for saying that if he did any fighting during the contest it would be under the stars and stripes. This circumstance, with others showing the determined bravery and persistent loyalty of himself and associates, so challenged the respect and admiration of the commanding general that he complied with the request, notwithstanding he then had no authority from the War Department to recruit six-months men. Afterwards authority was given to Pleasant Turney, of Independence, and L. D. Toney, of Izard county, to recruit. In June Thomas S. Williams and George Galloway came into the lines from Conway county, each with about thirty men. They had organized some time previously, in like manner with the people of Black River township, for self-defence, and were compelled to flee to the army, be killed, or go into the rebel service. Men recruited under the authority referred to, residing within the lines, remained at home until the last of June, no authority having been given for their muster in.

"On the last day of June, very unexpectedly to the people, General Curtis moved down White river. These recruits, with many other persons obnoxious to those in rebellion, left with the army, and so sudden and unexpected was the leaving that men about their daily avocations a short distance from home, on learning that the army was in motion, left without returning to say farewell to their families or procure a change of clothing. All believed the country was to be held, and that they were not again to be subjected to rebel violence and oppression. In this they were mistaken.

"On the arrival of the army at Helena, these recruits, with others who had been compelled to leave their homes, were mustered and organized into a battalion of infantry, of which J. C. Bundy was appointed lieutenant colonel. They had expected to be permitted to mount themselves, and for this purpose, on leaving, as well as to prevent their rebel neighbors from getting them, had taken their horses. This they were denied, and not being allowed either to forage upon the country or draw forage from the quartermaster's department, some of their animals died, and the remainder were sold for a trifle or given away. Anxiety concerning their families, who were suffering every indignity at the hands of their enemies, and could be heard from only after uncertain and long intervals; inactivity in camp, loss of property, and disappointment in not seeing their State seized and held by the strong arm of military power, so aggravated diseases prevailing in camp that in October there were not sufficient men in health for camp duty. In this condition they were ordered to St. Louis, and sent to Benton barracks, where they remained until their muster out on the 31st day of December, 1862. During the six months nearly one hundred and fifty died from disease, including Captains Gray and Turney and Lieut. Clark.

"It is worthy of note that this battalion was composed mostly of men who had banded themselves together to resist the cause of treason before federal troops entered the State.

"Very truly, your obedient servant,

"C. C. BLISS."

Fourth Arkansas mounted infantry volunteers. *Disbanded June 2, 1864.*

COMPANY A.

Names.	Rank.	Enlistment.	Date of rank.	Remarks.
T. A. Baxter	Captain	Jan. 1, 1864		Commanding regiment since March 25, 1864.
John W. Ayres	1st lieutenant	Jan. 1, 1864		Commanding company since March 25, 1864.
Noel G. Reaves	2d lieutenant	Jan. 1, 1864		
Thos. M. Tyer	1st sergeant	Jan. 1, 1864		
John W. Carter	Sergeant	Jan. 1, 1864		
W. J. Roach	do	Jan. 1, 1864		
C. J. Fuller	do	Jan. 1, 1864		Wounded in skirmish February 19, 1864.
M. J. Bradley	do	Jan. 1, 1864		
W. A. Curtis	Corporal	Jan. 1, 1864		
A. J. Sherrill	do	Jan. 17, 1864		
W. H. Fuller	do	Jan. 15, 1863		
J. C. Reynolds	do	Jan. 1, 1864		
E. E. Rushing	do	Jan. 1, 1864		
J. D. Massey	do	Jan. 1, 1864		
J. M. Freeman	do	Jan. 1, 1864		
Jas. H. Wyatt	do	Jan. 1, 1864		
			Muster.	
Allen, Marcus	Private	April 3, 1864		
Arnold, Ralph	do	Jan. 1, 1864		
Blevins, Alcana	do	Mar. 15, 1864		
Berry, Spencer	do	Jan. 1, 1864		
Bell, Wm. W.	do	Jan. 1, 1864		
Bass, Wm. M.	do	Jan. 4, 1864		
Blevins, Oliver C.	do	Feb. 5, 1864		
Bryant, Wm. H.	do	Jan. 29, 1864		Wounded in skirmish February 19, 1864.
Brown, Grigsby	do	Jan. 1, 1864		
Burgess, Leroy	do	Jan. 1, 1864		
Chastain, Abner	do	April 6, 1864		
Chastain, Joseph	do	April 6, 1864		
Chastain, Berry F.	do	April 6, 1864		
Craven, Jno. M.	do	Mar. 17, 1864		
Chamoress, N. C.	do	Jan. 13, 1864		
Churchwell, Wm. P.	do	Jan. 1, 1864		
Coveston, A. J.	do	Mar. 8, 1864		
Curtis, John	do	Jan. 1, 1864		
Curtis, Wm. R.	do	Jan. 1, 1864		
Davis, Elijah	do	Jan. 8, 1864		
Evans, David T.	do	May 2, 1864		
Evans, John T.	do	May 2, 1864		
Fox, John O.	do	Jan. 30, 1864		
Foust, Ellison	do	Jan. 1, 1864		
Forrester, C. C.	do	Jan. 23, 1864		

REPORT OF THE ADJUTANT GENERAL OF ARKANSAS. 247

Forrester, Robt. C	do	Jan. 23, 1864	
French, Wm	do	Mar. 26, 1864	
Fuller, H. N	do	Jan. 1, 1864	
Furgison, Ellis A	do	Jan. 23, 1864	
Holland, John G	do	Jan. 1, 1864	
Harris, Frank S	do	Jan. 1, 1864	
Holt, Elijah	do	Feb. 18, 1864	
Holt, Pleasant	do	Feb. 18, 1864	
Hughes, F. M	do	Jan. 1, 1864	
Hunt, W. J	do	Jan. 1, 1864	
Hawk, S. M	do	Feb. 17, 1864	
Knight, John	do	Mar. 5, 1864	
Knight, J. J	do	Jan. 1, 1864	
Knight, M. V	do	Mar. 5, 1864	
Knight, M. M	do	Feb. 17, 1864	
Knight, L. T	do	April 8, 1864	
Knight, L. F	do	April 6, 1864	
Lacy, James	do	Jan. 12, 1864	
Liles, Wm. H. H	do	Feb. 4, 1864	
Lemans, John R	do	Mar. 15, 1864	
Lemans, Samuel	do	Jan. 25, 1864	
Markham, Holland	do	Jan. 14, 1864	
Mathis, Wm. J	do	Jan. 1, 1864	
Merritt, John C	do	Jan. 19, 1864	
McCyee, John C	do	Jan. 1, 1864	
Marshall, Wm	do	Jan. 29, 1864	
Meeks, Richard D	do	Feb. 8, 1864	
Nunn, Wm. P	do	Jan. 1, 1864	
Nunnelly, Wm	do	Jan. 30, 1864	
Owen, Thos. R	do	Jan. 1, 1864	
Overstreet. Jas	do	Jan. 1, 1864	
Azement, Wm. L	do	Mar. 15, 1864	
Pool, Robert W	do	Jan. 1, 1864	
Pickel, Joseph	do	Jan. 1, 1864	
Reynolds, George M	do	Jan. 1, 1864	
Rhoades, Jackson	do	Feb. 6, 1864	
Snodgrass, George D	do	Feb. 8, 1864	
Scruggs, W. K. N	do	Jan. 13, 1864	
Scruggs, John B	do	Feb. 4, 1864	
Stephens, Henry M	do	Feb. 18, 1864	
Stone, Jas. A	do	Mar. 1, 1864	Captured in Independence county, Arkansas, March 20, 1864.
Southard, Andrew J	do	Jan. 1, 1864	
Taylor, Robt. A	do	Jan. 14, 1864	
Toney, Wm	do	Jan. 11, 1864	
Twilley, D. L	do	Jan. 16, 1864	
Watson, Benj. L	do	Jan. 1, 1864	
Watson, Jas. A	do	Jan. 1, 1864	Wounded in a skirmish February 19, 1864.
Watson, Samuel W	do	Jan. 1, 1864	
Wilson, G. M. D	do		
Wilson, J. K. P	do		
Wackerly, Henry H	do		
Williams, Granville	do		

Fourth Arkansas mounted infantry volunteers. Disbanded June 2, 1864.

COMPANY A—Continued.

Names.	Rank.	Enlistment.	Muster.	Remarks.
Yates, Watsel A.	Private	Jan. 1, 1864		
Died.				
Mathis, Jesse C	Private	Jan. 30, 1864		Died at Batesville, Arkansas, March 7, 1864.
Evans, Thos J.	do	Jan. 1, 1864		Died at Batesville, Arkansas, May 2, 1864.

COMPANY B.

Names.	Rank.	Date of rank.	Muster.	Remarks.
George W. Robertson	1st lieutenant			Elected lieutenant January 28, 1864.
Solomon K. Chandler	1st sergeant			Appointed 1st sergeant January 30, 1864.
J. H. Jones	Sergeant			Appointed sergeant January 30, 1864.
G. H. Pinkston	Corporal			Appointed corporal January 30, 1864.
G. W. Goad	do			Appointed corporal February 10, 1864.
J. E. Gifford	do			Do.
Adams, B. F	Private	Dec. 1, 1863		
Anderson, Isaac	do	Jan. 18, 1864		
Anderson, J. W	do	Dec. 15, 1863		Captured in skirmish at Holt's Mill, Arkansas, February 10, 1864; clothing, horse, and equipments taken from him.
Bishop, Joseph	do	Jan. 18, 1864		
Bishop, W. A.	do	Jan. 22, 1864		
Bryson, R. J	do	Dec. 1, 1863		
Barber, A. A.	do	Mar. 22, 1864		
Chandler, B. F	do	Dec. 1, 1863		
Cochran, Henry	do	Dec. 15, 1863		
Carter, J. E.	do	Jan. 27, 1864		
Dugger, A. M.	do	Dec. 1, 1863		
Dolin, William	do	Mar. 29, 1864		
Embry, G. M.	do	Mar. 23, 1864		
Embry, W. M.	do	Mar. 23, 1864		
Embry, D. C	do	Jan. 27, 1864		
Ford, B. F.	do	Jan. 27, 1864		
Ford, W. R	do	Jan. 15, 1864		Deserted May 30, 1864, at Jacksonport, Arkansas.
Goad, J. J.	do	Dec. 1, 1863		
Gire, W. H.	do			

REPORT OF THE ADJUTANT GENERAL OF ARKANSAS. 249

Hicks, G. C	do	Mar. 17, 1864	
Hamley, A. R. D	do	Feb. 1, 1864	
Hamley, A. N. M	do	Feb. 1, 1864	
Huff, W. B	do	Dec. 15, 1863	
Hall, E. E	do	Jan. 25, 1864	
Hall, J. A	do	Jan. 25, 1864	
Harris, Simeon	do	Jan. 27, 1864	
Hunt, A. M	do	Mar. 14, 1864	
Hawkins, S. D	do	Mar. 21, 1864	
Johnson, B. D	do	Mar. 22, 1864	
Lane, Bird	do	Jan. 25, 1864	
Lingo, Moses	do	Mar. 9, 1864	
McGee, J. R. P	do	Dec. 15, 1863	
McCrary, F. E	do	Dec. 1, 1863	Captured and his clothing taken from him.
McLeod, Mill	do	Feb. 1, 1864	
Morgan, J. D	do	Jan. 21, 1864	
Massey, Eli	do	Jan. 14, 1864	
Mobley, Calvin	do	Feb. 18, 1864	
Montgomery, James	do	April 12, 1864	Captured and his clothing taken from him.
Norris, W. R	do	Jan. 25, 1864	
Pinkston, Phineas	do	Dec. 15, 1863	
Privett, Jesse	do	Jan. 18, 1864	
Price, J. G	do	Mar. 14, 1864	
Price, L. C	do	Mar. 14, 1864	
Price, William	do	April 1, 1864	Deserted May 30, 1864, at Jacksonport, Arkansas.
Rodgers, G. M. D	do	Dec. 1, 1864	
Renick, Henry	do	Jan. 28, 1864	Lost horse and equipments in action, February 10, 186
Suddith, Gerard	do	Dec. 15, 1863	
Swick, G. W	do	Jan. 27, 1864	
Sarope, John	do	Dec. 15, 1863	
Scoggins, G. W	do	Mar. 14, 1864	
Simpson, A. A	do	Jan. 29, 1864	
Sellers, T. W	do	Jan. 26, 1864	
Smith, J. E	do	Feb. 5, 1864	
Smith, W. T	do	Feb. 18, 1864	
Stout, H. H	do	Mar. 22, 1864	Deserted May 30, 1864, at Jacksonport, Arkansas.
Stevens, G. W	do	April 26, 1864	
Tindle, R. P	do	Jan. 18, 1864	
Wolfe, John	do	Jan. 25, 1864	
Wilson, C. D	do	Dec. 15, 1863	
Wasson, J. B	do	Feb. 5, 1864	
Wilkerson, F. J	do	Feb. 5, 1864	
Whitlaw, S. C	do	Jan. 27, 1864	
Ward, Jasper	do	April 18, 1864	Deserted May 30, 1864, at Jacksonport, Arkansas.
Wolfe, David	do	Jan. 25, 1864	

FOURTH ARKANSAS MOUNTED INFANTRY VOLUNTEERS.—HISTORICAL MEMORANDA.

In November, 1863, authority was given by General Steele, commanding the army of Arkansas, to Elisha Baxter, of Batesville, to raise a regiment of infantry for twelve months. Shortly afterwards verbal permission was given to mount it, and recruiting was immediately proceeded with, especially at Batesville, where regimental headquarters were established. Company "A," organized and commanded by Captain T. A. Baxter, reported for duty on the 1st day of January, 1864, to Colonel Livingston, 1st Nebraska infantry, commanding district of northeastern Arkansas, at Batesville, and continued to do duty under him until the company was disbanded. Company "B" partly organized January 30, 1864, with forty-two men, by the selection of George W. Robertson as 1st lieutenant; was also, to the time of its disbandment, engaged in active service with the 1st Nebraska infantry and the 3d Missouri cavalry in the same section of country. The rolls of no other companies have been received at this office, and not even these organizations were ever mustered into the service, owing to the interruption of communication between Batesville and department headquarters.

In the month of May, 1864, the command of all recruits for the regiment was transferred to Captain T. A. Baxter, for the reason assigned in the following order:

SPECIAL ORDER No. 91.

[Extract.]

HEADQUARTERS DEPARTMENT OF ARKANSAS,
Little Rock, Arkansas, May 3, 1864.

VIII.—Hon. E. Baxter, recruiting officer for the 4th Arkansas mounted infantry, having been elected to the Senate of the United States from the State of Arkansas, is hereby relieved from duty with that regiment, and will turn over his command and all orders and instructions he may have received relating to the organization of the same to Captain T. A. Baxter, 4th Arkansas mounted infantry, subject to the approval of the War Department.

By order of Major General F. STEELE:

W. D. GREEN, *Assistant Adjutant General.*

While Hon. Elisha Baxter was in command of the regiment nearly four hundred recruits were enlisted, and after his relief other accessions were made, but the War Department refusing to confirm the authority for raising the regiment as a twelve-months organization, the following order was issued:

SPECIAL ORDER No. 121.

[Extract.]

HEADQUARTERS DEPARTMENT OF ARKANSAS,
Little Rock, Arkansas, June 2, 1864.

I.—The authority heretofore granted for the enlistment for one year of a regiment of Arkansas troops, to be designated the 4th Arkansas mounted infantry, not having been confirmed by the War Department, the organization is hereby disbanded. All quartermasters' property and ordnance stores in the possession of the battalion will be turned over to the proper staff officers at Duvall's Bluff.

By order of Major General F. STEELE:

W. D. GREEN, *Assistant Adjutant General.*

The regiment was accordingly disbanded.

Battery A, 1st Arkansas light artillery volunteers. Mustered into service August 31, 1863, (three years;) mustered out August 10, 1865.

Names.	Rank.	Enlistment.	Date of rank.	Remarks.
Denton D. Stark	Captain	Aug. 15, 1863	Aug. 31, 1863	Promoted from regimental adjutant, 1st Arkansas cavalry, to fill original vacancy; resigned July 23, 1864.
Henry H. Easter	...do...		Mar. 11, 1865	Appointed from quartermaster sergeant, 5th Ohio battery; mustered out with battery.
Robert Thompson	1st lieutenant	—, 1862	Aug. 31, 1863	Appointed from sergeant major, 1st Arkansas cavalry, to fill original vacancy; mustered out January 11, 1864.
Edward D. Brogan	2d lieutenant	Jan. 8, 1863	Aug. 31, 1863	Promoted from 1st lieutenant from organization of battery; mustered out January 11, 1864.
William Mayes	...do...	Feb. 20, 1863	Sept. 10, 1863	1st lieutenant from organization of battery; mustered out with battery.
Alexander Thompson	1st sergeant	Feb. 13, 1863	Sept. 1, 1863	Appointed from sergeant; mustered out with battery.
John B. Malidon	Quartermaster sergeant	Mar. 4, 1863	June 1, 1864	Appointed from private; mustered out with battery.
Henry Hiatt	Sergeant	Mar. 21, 1863	Sept. 1, 1864	Appointed from corporal; mustered out with battery.
William J. Stuart	...do...	Mar. 21, 1863	Sept. 1, 1863	Do.
William F. Jones	...do...	Nov. 19, 1863	Sept. 1, 1863	Do.
John Mayes	...do...	Feb. 14, 1863	April 1, 1864	Appointed from private; mustered out with battery.
Albert Roberts	...do...	Mar. 21, 1863	Sept. 1, 1863	Do.
James Lemons	...do...	April 14, 1863	Sept. 1, 1864	Do.
James H. Taylor	Corporal	Mar. 21, 1863	Aug. 31, 1863	Corporal from organization of battery; mustered out with battery.
William Hatley	...do...	Feb. 13, 1863	Aug. 31, 1863	Do.
John W. Hutchinson	...do...	Mar. 26, 1863	Aug. 31, 1863	Do.
William J. Stroud	...do...	Mar. 29, 1863	Aug. 31, 1863	Do.
Richard Hood	...do...	Feb. 4, 1863	Sept. 1, 1863	Appointed from private September 1, 1863; mustered out with battery.
Calvin Howell	...do...	Feb. 17, 1863	Sept. 1, 1863	Do.
Richard Dewitt	...do...	Mar. 16, 1863	April 1, 1864	Appointed from private April 1, 1864; mustered out with battery.
Barnhard Preussner	...do...	Mar. 29, 1863	April 1, 1864	Do.
Albert W. Wilmoth	...do...	Oct. 24, 1863	April 1, 1864	Do.
Julius Ellig	...do...	Mar. 29, 1863	April 1, 1864	Do.
William Collins	...do...	Feb. 3, 1863	May 24, 1865	Appointed from private May 24, 1865; mustered out with battery.
Joseph Wilds	...do...	Sept. 15, 1862	May 28, 1865	Appointed from private May 28, 1865; mustered out with battery.
Thomas Towns	Bugler	Feb. 13, 1863	Aug. 31, 1863	Bugler from organization of battery; mustered out with battery.
Robert Edwards	...do...	July 15, 1863	April 1, 1865	Appointed from private; mustered out with battery.
John M. Brinson	Artificer	Feb. 14, 1863	Sept. 1, 1863	Do.
John Mason	...do...	Sept. 17, 1863	April 1, 1865	Do.
			Muster.	
Ash, John L.	Private	Dec. 7, 1863	Dec. 7, 1863	Mustered out with battery.
Amos, Elisha S.	...do...	May 10, 1863	Aug. 31, 1863	Do.
Brewer, Josiah	...do...	Nov. 3, 1863	Dec. 7, 1863	Do.
Brewer, William	...do...	May 10, 1863	Aug. 31, 1863	Do.
Brewer, Zebedee	...do...	May 13, 1863	Aug. 31, 1863	Do.
Boren, John W.	...do...	May 10, 1863	Aug. 31, 1863	Do.
Burlingame, Elvin	...do...	June 10, 1863	Aug. 31, 1863	Do.
Brimley, Andrew J.	...do...	Feb. 17, 1863	Aug. 31, 1863	Do.
Brimley, Thomas H.	...do...	Feb. 23, 1863	Aug. 31, 1863	Do.
Buck, Aaron J.	...do...	Feb. 23, 1863	Aug. 31, 1863	Do.
Barnett, Jacob	...do...	Mar. 2, 1863	Aug. 31, 1863	Do.

252 REPORT OF THE ADJUTANT GENERAL OF ARKANSAS.

Battery A, 1st Arkansas light artillery volunteers—Continued.

Names.	Rank.	Enlistment.	Muster.	Remarks.
Cox, Samuel	Private	Feb. 26, 1863	Aug. 31, 1863	Mustered out with battery.
Clay, George W	...do...	Sept. 12, 1863	Sept. 12, 1863	Do.
Chastain, James	...do...	Feb. 14, 1863	Aug. 31, 1863	Do.
Cox, Franklin	...do...	Feb. 23, 1863	Aug. 31, 1863	Do.
C———, John	...do...	Jan. 26, 1864	Feb. 26, 1864	Do.
Crawford, Andrew P	...do...	Jan. 26, 1864	Feb. 28, 1864	Do.
Dawson, James M	...do...	May 9, 1863	Aug. 31, 1863	Do.
Dougherty, Preston	...do...	May 10, 1863	Aug. 31, 1863	Do.
DeWitt, Francis M	...do...	Feb. 13, 1863	Aug. 31, 1863	Do.
DeWitt, Richard C	...do...	Feb. 17, 1863	Aug. 31, 1863	Do.
Date, Sanford	...do...	Feb. 13, 1863	Aug. 31, 1863	Do.
Fallen, Holmes	...do...	Jan. 8, 1863	Aug. 31, 1863	Do.
Fallen, James M	...do...	Jan. 8, 1863	Aug. 31, 1863	Do.
Frazier, Henderson	...do...	Jan. 8, 1863	Aug. 31, 1863	Do.
Fulks, Samuel	...do...	Jan. 25, 1863	Aug. 31, 1863	Do.
Finton, William	...do...	Feb. 17, 1863	Aug. 31, 1863	Do.
Feaurstan, Jacob	...do...	Mar. 31, 1863	Oct. 31, 1863	Do.
Greenwood, Job	...do...	Feb. 25, 1863	Aug. 31, 1863	Do.
Grady, James F	...do...	Sept. 21, 1863	Dec. 7, 1863	Do.
Hochler, George	...do...	May 4, 1863	Aug. 31, 1863	Do.
Howell, Thomas B	...do...	May 25, 1864	Feb. 24, 1865	Do.
Howell, James R	...do...	Nov. 3, 1863	Dec. 7, 1863	Do.
Harris, Francis	...do...	May 4, 1863	Aug. 31, 1863	Do.
Honk, Lorenzo	...do...	Mar. 31, 1863	Aug. 31, 1863	Do.
Hatley, John	...do...	Feb. 14, 1863	Aug. 31, 1863	Do.
Jones, Laban B	...do...	Jan. 29, 1864	Feb. 28, 1864	Do.
Lewis, Abner	...do...	Mar. 27, 1863	Aug. 31, 1863	Do.
Lewellen, William	...do...	Feb. 12, 1863	Aug. 31, 1863	Do.
Lively, John	...do...	May 10, 1863	Aug. 31, 1863	Do.
Lively, Joseph M	...do...	May 13, 1863	Aug. 31, 1863	Do.
Lively, Solomon	...do...	May 13, 1863	Aug. 31, 1863	Do.
Lock, Charles	...do...	Mar. 28, 1863	Aug. 31, 1863	Do.
Malidon, George J	...do...	Mar. 4, 1863	Aug. 31, 1863	Do.
McGrady, Wellington	...do...	Feb. 23, 1863	Aug. 31, 1863	Do.
Meroe, Wolfgang H	...do...	Feb. 2, 1863	Aug. 31, 1863	Do.
Mayes, Samuel	...do...	Feb. 13, 1863	Aug. 31, 1863	Do.
Mason, Joshua	...do...	Sept. 17, 1863	Oct. 31, 1863	Do.
O'Connor, Peter	...do...	Jan. 8, 1863	Aug. 31, 1863	Do.
Pistol, John	...do...	Feb. 4, 1863	Aug. 31, 1863	Do.
Redman, Benjamin	...do...	Feb. 14, 1863	Aug. 31, 1863	Do.
Ross, Wesley W	...do...	Nov. 3, 1863	Dec. 7, 1863	Do.
Rice, John B	...do...	Mar. 11, 1863	Aug. 31, 1863	Do.
Rogers, William F	...do...	Feb. 4, 1863	Aug. 31, 1863	Do.
Skinner, John R	...do...	Mar. 16, 1863	Aug. 31, 1863	Do.
Shaw, Joseph	...do...	Feb. 13, 1863	Aug. 31, 1863	Do.

REPORT OF THE ADJUTANT GENERAL OF ARKANSAS.   253

Name	Rank	Enlisted	Expiration of service	Remarks
Stifler, George	do	May 9, 1863	Aug. 31, 1863	Do.
Stowers, Albert J	do	May 14, 1863	Aug. 31, 1863	Do.
Stowers, Marion	do	Mar. 4, 1864	Aug. 31, 1863	Do.
Simpkins, Thomas W	do	May 15, 1863	Aug. 31, 1863	Do.
Standberry, William	do	June 10, 1863	Aug. 31, 1863	Do.
Sheidel, Nicholas	do	Mar. 4, 1863	Aug. 31, 1863	Do.
Stewart, William J	do	Aug. 22, 1863	Aug. 31, 1863	Do.
Simpson, Beatty	do	Jan. 8, 1863	Aug. 31, 1863	Do.
Sheeppe, Frederick	do	Mar. 31, 1863	Aug. 31, 1863	Do.
Towns, George M. D	do	Feb. 13, 1863	Aug. 31, 1863	Do.
Towns, William	do	May 1, 1863	Aug. 31, 1863	Do.
Vaughan, William	do	Feb. 11, 1863	Aug. 31, 1863	Do.
Woodruff, Wesley	do	Feb. 12, 1863	Aug. 31, 1863	Do.
Wooten, Jeptha	do	Apr. 27, 1863	Aug. 31, 1863	Do.
Waddle, Young D	do	Apr. 19, 1863	Aug. 31, 1863	Do.
Williams, George W	do	May 10, 1863	Aug. 31, 1863	Do.
Wright, Biljah B	do	Aug. 9, 1863	Aug. 31, 1863	Do.
Walker, Robert L. D	do	Mar. 10, 1863	Aug. 31, 1863	Do.
Wheeler, William P	do	Mar. 29, 1863	Aug. 31, 1863	Do.
Wilson, John	do	Feb. 13, 1863	Aug. 31, 1863	Do.
Wilson, James F	do	Oct. 3, 1863	Oct. 3, 1863	Do.
Waldon, James	do	May 15, 1863	Aug. 31, 1863	Do.
Yates, Newton	do	Mar. 2, 1863	Aug. 31, 1863	Do.

Cooks.

Buchanon, Adam	Under cook	Feb. 26, 1864	Feb. 28, 1864	Mustered out with battery.
Crawford, William H	do	Feb. 26, 1864	Feb. 28, 1864	Do.
Hollan, Jerry	do	Feb. 3, 1864	Feb. 28, 1864	Do.
Spencer, Washington	do	Feb. 26, 1864	Feb. 28, 1864	Do.

Killed in action.

Brewer, Lewis	Private	Apr. 3, 1863	Aug. 31, 1863	Killed by guerillas near Fort Smith, Arkansas, December 16, 1864.
Harris, William C	Sergeant	Feb. 3, 1863	Aug. 31, 1863	Killed by guerillas near Fort Smith, Arkansas, August 13, 1864.
Post, Martin	Private	Feb. 9, 1863	Aug. 31, 1863	Killed by guerillas near Fayetteville, Arkansas, November 3, 1863.
Snow, Henry	do	Jan. 30, 1863	Never	Killed by guerillas near Warsaw, Missouri, June 15, 1863.

Died.

Allen, Zimri B	Private	Feb. 13, 1863	Never	Died of brain fever at Fayetteville, Arkansas, March 12, 1863.
Alfred, Patten	do	Jan. 8, 1863	Never	Died of inflamation of brain at Springfield, Missouri, June 17, 1863.
Brimley, William G	do	Feb. 5, 1863	Never	Died of typhoid fever, Fayetteville, Arkansas, March 12, 1863.
Camp, William	do	Feb. 13, 1863	Never	Died at Fayetteville, Arkansas, March 15, 1863.
Crawford, David	do	Feb. 26, 1864	Feb. 28, 1864	Died at Fort Smith, Arkansas, June 3, 1864.
Edwards, Jesse	do	Feb. 13, 1863	Aug. 31, 1863	Died at Fort Smith, Arkansas, January 25, 1863.
Fyffe, Benjamin	do	Apr. 27, 1863	Aug. 31, 1863	Died of intermittent fever at Fort Smith, Arkansas, August 23, 1864.
Gunter, John B	do	Feb. 13, 1863	Never	Died of typhoid fever, Springfield, Missouri, July 11, 1863.
Holmes, Samuel	do	July 15, 1863	Aug. 31, 1863	Died of pneumonia at Fayetteville, Arkansas, December 12, 1863.
Hall, David L	do	Jan. 15, 1863	Aug. 31, 1863	Died of fever at Fort Smith, Arkansas, July 8, 1864.
Lipscomb, Simpson	do	Feb. 13, 1863	Never	Died at Springfield, Missouri, May 12, 1863.
Little, Asberry	do	Feb. 14, 1863	Aug. 31, 1863	Died of dropsy at Springfield, Missouri, September 22, 1863.

Battery A, 1st Arkansas light artillery volunteers—Continued.

Names.	Rank.	Enlistment.	Muster.	Remarks.
Moore, Nathan W	Private	Jan. 30, 1863	Aug. 31, 1863	Died of dysentery at Springfield, Missouri, September 15, 1863.
Powell, John	do	Feb. 4, 1863	Never	Died at Fayetteville, Arkansas, April 7, 1863.
Powell, Josiah	do	Feb. 4, 1863	Never	Died at Fayetteville, Arkansas, April 16, 1863.
Patrick, John F	do	Mar. 18, 1863	Never	Died of typhoid fever at Fayetteville, Arkansas, April 18, 1863.
Palmer, Thomas	do	Jan. 19, 1864	Never	Died of pneumonia at Fayetteville, Arkansas, January 27, 1864.
Pierce, Benjamin	do	May 14, 1863	Aug. 31, 1863	Died of fever at Fort Smith, Arkansas, August 10, 1864.
Robertson, John W	do	Feb. 3, 1863	Aug. 31, 1863	Died of erysipelas at Fort Smith, Arkansas, June 11, 1865.
Wettig, Christian	do	Mar. 31, 1863	Never	Died at Springfield, Missouri, June 30, 1864.
Wilson, John F	do	Sept. 26, 1863	Oct. 31, 1863	Died of fever at Fort Smith, Arkansas, June 8, 1864.
Deserted.				
Ash, John L	Private	Jan. 8, 1863	Never	Deserted at Springfield, Missouri, August 27, 1863.
Cozins, Daniel	do	May 9, 1863	Aug. 31, 1863	Deserted at Fort Smith, Arkansas, September 25, 1864.
Danozy, Bennett	do	Mar. 1, 1864	April 18, 1864	Do.
Hester, Robert	do	Jan. 8, 1863	Mar. 10, 1864	Deserted at Fayetteville, Arkansas, September 25, 1863.
Harris, John	do	Feb. 12, 1863	Never	Deserted at Fayetteville, Arkansas, April 18, 1863.
Ivens, Wyard	do	Feb. 14, 1863	Never	Do.
Ingram, Isaac	do	June 10, 1863	Never	Do.
Jay, George W	do	Feb. 2, 1863	Never	Deserted at Springfield, Missouri, September 20, 1863.
LeCage, James	do	Jan. 30, 1863	Never	Deserted at Fayetteville, Arkansas, April 18, 1863.
McDonald, Martin	do	Mar. 29, 1863	Never	Deserted at Fort Smith, Arkansas, December 1, 1864.
Newman, Henry M	do	Mar. 3, 1864	Mar. 10, 1864	Deserted at Fort Smith, Arkansas, September 25, 1864.
Stroud, Francis M	do	Jan. 22, 1864	Feb. 28, 1864	Do.
Stanbery, Henry	do	Feb. 13, 1863	Aug. 31, 1863	Deserted at Fort Smith, Arkansas, September 16, 1864.
Sauders, James	do	Feb. 14, 1863	Aug. 31, 1863	Deserted at Fort Smith, Arkansas, September 25, 1864.
Son, James	do	Feb. 9, 1863	Never	Deserted at Springfield, Missouri, June 24, 1863.
Thomas, Benjamin	do	Jan. 26, 1863	Feb. 28, 1864	Deserted at Fayetteville, Arkansas, April 25, 1863.
Watts, Samuel	do	Feb. 3, 1863	Never	Do.
Watts, John B	do	Feb. 13, 1863	Never	Do.
Watts, William	do	Feb. 17, 1863	Never	Do.
Wann, Josiah W	do	Feb. 14, 1863	Never	Do.
Wadkins, McKinney	do	April 27, 1863	Aug. 31, 1863	Deserted at Fort Smith, Arkansas, September 16, 1864.
West, Hamilton B	do	June 1, 1863	Never	Deserted at Springfield, Missouri, May 25, 1863.
Wyatt, Edmund	do	April 28, 1863	Never	Deserted at Springfield, Missouri, August 22, 1863.
Gideon, James J	do	Sept. 6, 1863	Never	Deserted at Springfield, Missouri, September 20, 1863.
Discharged.				
Bentley, Jacob P	Private	Feb. 4, 1863	Aug. 31, 1863	Mustered out from hospital at Fort Smith, Arkansas, June 28, 1865.
Dale, William	do	Feb. 14, 1863	Aug. 31, 1863	Discharged for disability November 17, 1864.
Howell, Benjamin F	do	May 23, 1864	April 18, 1865	Discharged from hospital at Fort Smith, Arkansas, June 28, 1865.
Imber, Peter	do	Aug. 23, 1862	Aug. 31, 1863	Do.
Jamison, Thomas J	do	June 8, 1863	Aug. 31, 1863	Discharged from hospital at Fort Smith, Arkansas, July 7, 1865.
Johnson, James A	do	Aug. 23, 1862	Aug. 31, 1863	Discharged from hospital at Fort Smith, Arkansas, June 28, 1864.

REPORT OF THE ADJUTANT GENERAL OF ARKANSAS. 255

Lively, Joseph	do	May 13, 1863	Aug. 31, 1863	Discharged for disability January 28, 1864.
Hirs, Solomon	do	Sept. 15, 1862	Aug. 31, 1863	Discharged from hospital at Fort Smith, Arkansas, June 28, 1865.
McCormick, Thomas	do	Feb. 17, 1863	Aug. 31, 1863	Discharged for disability May 11, 1865.
Phelps, Calvin	do	May 2, 1863	Aug. 31, 1863	Discharged for disability May 22, 1864.
Pipkins, Daniel W	do	Sept. 6, 1863	Sept. 6, 1863	Discharged from hospital at Fort Smith, Arkansas, June 28, 1865.
Rourk, William	do	Feb. 27, 1863	Aug. 31, 1863	Discharged for disability November 8, 1863.
Reeder, Jasper	do	Feb. 13, 1863	Aug. 31, 1863	Discharged for disability November 17, 1864.
Simpson, John B	do	Feb. 7, 1863	Aug. 31, 1863	Discharged for disability May 22, 1864.
Vaughan, John W	do	Feb. 2, 1863	Aug. 31, 1863	Discharged for disability December 12, 1864.

BATTERY A, FIRST ARKANSAS LIGHT ARTILLERY VOLUNTEERS.—HISTORICAL MEMORANDA.

In January, 1863, Denton D. Stark, then adjutant 1st Arkansas cavalry volunteers, received authority to raise the first battery of Arkansas light artillery. April 1st the battery was full, but was not mustered into the service until August 31, 1863. Meantime and until the 25th of April, of this year, it was stationed at Fayetteville, Arkansas, (though officers and men were absent in Missouri procuring horses when the battle of the 18th of April took place), when, by orders from headquarters of the Department of the Missouri, northwestern Arkansas was evacuated. From May 4 to September 21, 1863, the battery was stationed at Springfield, Missouri, receiving while there guns and equipments. In September, Lieutenant Robert V. Thompson, with one section of the battery, participated in an expedition under the command of Colonel M. Larue Harrison, through southwestern Missouri and northwestern Arkansas, in pursuit of Colonel Coffee's command, then raiding in that section of country, and proceeded thence to Fayetteville, Arkansas. The remaining two sections of the battery, under command of Captain Stark, left Springfield, Missouri, September 21, 1863, for Fayetteville, marching at first, however, as far north as Greenfield, Missouri, under Colonel Harrison, who was then in pursuit of General Shelby. Moving then to Fayetteville, one section of the battery took part, about October 20, in a skirmish with the enemy, under Colonel Brooks, at Cross Timbers, Missouri. The battery remained at Fayetteville until March 19, 1864, when, by order of Brigadier General Thayer, it marched to Fort Smith. On the 22d of March it joined the expedition to Camden, forming a part of Colonel Adams's brigade. It was present in the skirmish at Moscow, on or about the 13th day of April, with four guns in action, and relieved the 2d Indiana battery, under a severe fire from the enemy's artillery. Leaving Camden with the retreating force under General Steele, April 28, it reached Little Rock May 3, 1864, and moved thence with the frontier division of the Army of Arkansas to Fort Smith. In October, 1864, one section of the battery, under Lieutenant Mayes, was sent with other troops in pursuit of Colonel Gano, who had captured a supply train between Fort Scott and Fort Smith, making a forced march to Cabin creek, north of Fort Gibson, where they came up with the enemy retreating, but he escaped.

The battery occupied Fort No. 2, at Fort Smith, until the 30th day of August, 1865, when it was mustered out of the service. The men were principally residents of Benton, Washington, Madison, Crawford, Sebastian, Franklin, Johnson, and Sevier counties; were faithful, brave, and efficient, and reflected great credit upon the battery and the State.

SUMMARY.

Commands.	Mustered out with organizations.		Died.		Discharged.		Deserted.		Total.		Aggregate.
	Officers.	Enlisted men.	Officers.	Enlisted men.	Officers.	Enlisted men.	Officers.	Enlisted men.	Officers.	Enlisted men.	
1st Arkansas cavalry volunteers	57	1,036	8	334	35	184		111	100	1,665	1,765
2d Arkansas cavalry volunteers	33	907	2	157	25	153		117	60	1,334	1,394
3d Arkansas cavalry volunteers	40	585	4	193	23	331		211	67	1,320	1,387
4th Arkansas cavalry volunteers	32	662	3	233	37	97	1	138	73	1,130	1,203
1st Arkansas infantry volunteers	33	786	2	185	23	70		196	58	1,237	1,295
2d Arkansas infantry volunteers	26	560	1	164	12	20		183	39	927	966
* 3d Arkansas infantry											
4th Arkansas infantry volunteers, before consolidation, (losses only)				19	1			45	1	64	65
1st Arkansas six months infantry volunteers	14	360							14	360	374
4th Arkansas mounted infantry	4	160		2					4	162	166
1st Arkansas battery	2	105		25	3	15			5	169	174
Total	241	5,161	20	1,312	159	870	1	1,025	421	8,368	8,789

* In the fall of 1863 effort was made at Little Rock to raise the 3d regiment of infantry volunteers, but without success. About the same time the raising of the 4th infantry was begun, in the western portion of the State, and, though the efforts to raise the 3d were shortly afterwards abandoned, the 4th underwent no change of name, while it remained a separate organization.

APPENDIX B.

DOCUMENTS

RELATING TO

THE COUNTERMAND OF THE ORDER FOR THE EVACUATION OF FORT SMITH AND ITS DEPENDENCIES.

DECEMBER, 1864.

APPENDIX B.

Documents relating to the countermand of the order for the evacuation of Fort Smith and its dependencies, December, 1864.

Advices having been received that the evacuation of Fort Smith and its dependencies had been ordered by the general commanding the division of west Mississippi, and this order being considered by the State authorities as extremely disastrous if executed, the undersigned was directed to proceed at once to Washington to procure, if possible, its countermand, and for this purpose, to act in conjunction with the members of Congress and senators elect from the State, should they be at the capital.

The documents with which he set out on the 15th of December, 1864, and which he was directed to lay before the President, as also the communications sent and received in the progress of the negotiations, are hereinafter set forth as follows:

No. .1

LITTLE ROCK, ARKANSAS, *December* 14, 1864.

To ABRAHAM LINCOLN, *President of the United States:*

The undersigned, officers of the loyal government of the State of Arkansas, have learned with profound solicitude of the promulgation of an order of the commander of the division of west Mississippi, directing the immediate evacuation of Fort Smith and its dependencies, a measure that involves the abandonment of the whole western portion of the State, and our control of the Indian territories, and throws open southwestern Missouri and southern Kansas to the incursions of the enemy.

This blow is disastrous in the extreme to the suffering loyalty of this State, and unless justified by imperative military necessity, we most earnestly and respectfully request that the order in question be revoked. We are loth to believe that you are advised of the consequences of this movement, particularly at a time when the country is freer from guerillas than it has been at any period since the outbreak of the rebellion. Rebel families are almost daily moving south, and the well-nigh crushed Union men of the State were taking heart.

Your re-election, and the consequent increased hope of the recognition of their State government, inspired them, and they will now contemplate with dismay the abandonment of the homes of a large majority of them to the enemies of the government, whose hate, intensified by disaster, will utterly desolate their country.

Meantime hundreds of Union citizens will be powerless to avert this calamity. Their means of transportation are exceedingly limited, and they will be fortunate if they leave the State with their lives alone. Must these things be? General Steele says to his immediate superior that he can supply Fort Smith by the Arkansas river, and there is no difficulty in provisioning Fayetteville from Springfield, Missouri.

Not to be importunate, then, much less unseemly in our application, we again earnestly ask, in behalf of our suffering fellow-citizens, for the maintenance in whose country of the Constitution and laws of the United States armies are sent here, that this step throwing back the section of country evacuated to its condition in 1862 be not taken, or if consummated before our action in the premises and that of the legislature of the State are made known, that the reoccupation of this country be ordered.

With the highest respect, we remain, your obedient servants,

ISAAC MURPHY,
Governor of Arkansas.
ROBERT J. T. WHITE,
Secretary of State.
T. D. W. YONLEY,
Chief Justice Supreme Court.
C. A. HARPER,
Associate Judge Supreme Court.
C. T. JORDAN,
Attorney General of Arkansas.
E. D. AYRES,
Treasurer of Arkansas.
C. C. BLISS,
Lieutenant Governor of Arkansas.
J. R. BERRY,
Auditor of Arkansas.
A. W. BISHOP,
Lieut. Col. First Arkansas Cavalry, Acting Adjutant Gen.

No. 2.

Resolutions of the general assembly of Arkansas, passed at Little Rock, December 14, 1864.

Whereas the general assembly has learned with surprise and regret that despatches have reached this city ordering the United States military forces to evacuate the district of the frontier in this department; and whereas such evacuation will leave the northern and northwestern counties of this State and southwestern Missouri, a country several hundred miles in extent, subject to the merciless ravages of the bushwhackers and robbers, and thus cause the most loyal portion of Arkansas to become a scene of ruin and desolation; and whereas there are large amounts of valuable government and private property at the posts of Fort Smith, Van Buren, and Fayetteville, that for want of transportation will necessarily be destroyed or fall into the hands of the enemy, amounting to many thousands of dollars, without taking into consideration valuable public expenditures that have been made; and whereas, above all other considerations, there are thousands of persons, members of loyal families, now under the protection of federal soldiers of that district who have no means of transportation to remove themselves or effects, who will therefore necessarily be left at the mercy of those who spare neither bedding, food, nor clothing, and thus in the rigors of midwinter will be compelled to travel on foot to the federal lines, or famish for want of the necessaries of life; and whereas the people in common with ourselves have already suffered much for our devotion to the Union of our fathers and have great confidence in the justice, patriotism and humanity of the Executive of the United States, and an abiding faith that he will fulfil his promises to the loyal people of this State, and extend to each of them all the protection in his power, consistent with the common good of the nation: Therefore,

Be it resolved by this general assembly, That in behalf of the hundreds of families of Union soldiers and of many loyal citizens, who are without the means of transportation in this time of dire necessity, we appeal to those in authority not to carry the above order into effect during the severity of winter, and if it must be executed, that this be done at a different season of the year.

Be it further resolved, That in the name of humanity and the loyal people of western and northwestern Arkansas, we appeal to the President to cause said order issued as aforesaid requiring the evacuation of the district of the frontier of this department, to be revoked, and that a sufficient number of troops remain to hold the posts now occupied in said district.

Resolved further, That we call the attention of the government to the propriety of establishing a military post at Jacksonport or Batesville in northeastern Arkansas.

Resolved further, That our delegation at Washington with Lieutenant Colonel Bishop, acting adjutant general of Arkansas, be intrusted with the foregoing resolutions.

Approved December 14, 1864.

ISAAC MURPHY,
Governor of Arkansas.

No. 3.

HEADQUARTERS DEPARTMENT OF ARKANSAS,
Little Rock, Arkansas, November 24, 1864.

GENERAL: It is my opinion that the Arkansas can be relied upon as a means of transportation for supplies to Fort Smith. The river is at present navigable, and supplies have been forwarded by steamers sufficient to last until there shall be another rise, when a year's supply can be sent at once. If there had been a year's supply here for Fort Smith last winter it might have been sent there by steamers. There is every indication now that we shall have a navigable river. It has been cloudy and rainy here for several weeks, which is a sure indication of snow in the mountains. The bayous and sloughs are all full and the streams high. At all events I am opposed to breaking up Fort Smith for the following reasons: It has been strongly fortified at a very considerable expense and can be held against great odds. It is a flanking arrangement to this depot and helps to cover De vall's Bluff as well as Arkansas and Missouri.

To give up the whole northwestern portion of Arkansas would be a breach of good faith on the part of the government towards the loyal citizens of that section, and to the friendly Indians of the Territories. If our troops should evacuate Fort Smith the rebels would at once take possession of it and prepare for raids.

*　　　*　　　*　　　*　　　*　　　*

If Fort Gibson should be given up, which would necessarily follow the evacuation of Fort Smith, we should lose all influence over the friendly Indians, who would be compelled to plunder the settlements of the whites or starve, or they would be plundered and perhaps driven out of their country by the rebels. There are some other considerations that I will not now mention.

Very respectfully, general,

F. STEELE, *Major General.*

Major General J. J. REYNOLDS,
Commanding Military Division West Mississippi.

No. 4.

MARSHAL'S OFFICE, UNITED STATES DISTRICT COURT,
EASTERN DISTRICT OF ARKANSAS,
Little Rock, December 14, 1864.

DEAR SIR: I have just returned from an interview with General Steele, in which he showed me General Canby's order for the abandonment of Fort Smith and all the posts in Arkansas northwest of this. During the afternoon my office was visited by men from Fayetteville, &c., army officers, in deep distress at the ruin entailed upon them, and the danger and suffering in store for their families and neighbors. It is truly a terrible necessity, if it is a necessity at all, that a fortification like Fort Smith, the key of Kansas and Missouri, built at great expense, easily defensible and well garrisoned, not to speak of other posts, must be turned over to rebel occupation without a blow.

I should not write this if I knew that the order was given with your sanction, for I should then have faith that all was well, and that the great present sacrifice was essential to the sure attainment of some greater good to come. Now, I do not so feel, and the trouble of these poor men cuts me to the heart. The order relieving General Steele does not take effect until the 25th instant, and as General Canby's order for the evacuation is dated the 5th, General Steele is compelled to perform, and is promptly now performing, a duty against the imposition of which he has protested in the strongest language.

There will be many loyal men who will be unable to get away, and of these not a man will be left alive upon whom the rebels can lay their hands.

Do not, I beg of you, consider me presumptuous. I am not speaking for myself; but without some great and good reason, something overbearing and imperative, this thing ought not to be done.

With great respect, your obedient servant,

W. O. STODDARD.

President LINCOLN.

No. 5.

EXECUTIVE OFFICE, LITTLE ROCK, ARKANSAS,
December 14, 1864.

A. LINCOLN, *President of the United States:*

The President, we all feel, wishes the loyal people of the rebel States to receive protection. An appeal to him will not be disregarded as we hope and trust. Oppression, wrong, and outrage we have suffered beyond the capability of expression, and now comes General Canby's order to abandon Fort Smith and its dependencies, leaving the loyal portion of the State at the mercy of the Indians and desperadoes of the frontier.

For the sake of humanity and the honor of the government, we beseech you, as President and commander-in-chief of the army, to redeem your pledge of protection. We have done all that could be done on our part. We have been true to the stars and stripes, at the risk of life and property. We ask only protection and that our devotion may meet with some respect. The bearer, Colonel Bishop, has our confidence. Will you listen to him, redress our wrongs, and save your friends from utter ruin.

With high respect,

ISAAC MURPHY,
Governor of Arkansas.

No. 6.

LITTLE ROCK, ARKANSAS, *December* 14, 1864.

ABRAHAM LINCOLN, *President of the United States:*

The undersigned, officers of Arkansas regiments in the service of the United States, beg leave to represent to you some of the effects of the order for the evacuation of Fort Smith, Arkansas. It is now garrisoned in part by these regiments, and the families of the soldiers are living in the country adjacent, and even were they fortunate enough, in the great scarcity of transportation, to get away with their lives, would have to leave all their possessions behind, come to our military posts as beggars, and be the despised and contemned refugees of this war. Those who would be left behind would become the prey of rebel desperadoes.

Fort Smith is the key of Kansas and Missouri and the western frontier of

Arkansas. All here and south would feel that we were losing ground, and the demoralizing effect upon Arkansas troops would be damaging to a great degree. We therefore would respectfully suggest to you the propriety of revoking the order for the abandonment of Fort Smith and its dependencies.

L. GREGG,
Colonel Fourth Arkansas Cavalry.
J. M. JOHNSON,
Colonel First Arkansas Infantry·
A. H. RYAN,
Colonel Third Arkansas Cavalry.

No. 7.

HEADQUARTERS DEP'T OF ARKANSAS AND 7TH ARMY CORPS,
OFFICE PROVOST MARSHAL GENERAL,
Little Rock, Arkansas, December 14, 1864.

GOVERNOR: I have heard with profound regret and surprise of the order of Major General Canby for the abandonment of western Arkansas and the Indian territory. I have been, as you are aware, in the service of the United States since the opening of the war, and on many a hard-fought field have perilled my life to secure the very territory now ordered to be abandoned, and at a time when to me it seemed for the first time firmly secured to the government of the United States. At no time has it been so free from hostile tread, and it can be truly said that no portion of the territory in dispute is so thoroughly regained. I have to-day received my honorable discharge from the service, and I feel at liberty to make some statements to you which I could not so properly have done while in office, that bear directly on this point.

I have filled the office of provost marshal general since the occupation of Little Rock until to-day, and had organized a very thorough system of secret service. The result of the information which has of late been obtained establishes conclusively the fact that since the disastrous failure of General Price's raid, the enemy had resolved on the abandonment of the State of Arkansas, and fixing their line of defence on Red river. General Magruder has ordered the country to be abandoned by the people, and announced that he will leave only thirty day's provisions to any family failing to obey his instructions to move south of Red river.

The entire strength of General Magruder's army, inclusive of the broken remnant of General Price's army, does not exceed twenty thousand men, effectives. I trust that if possible such representations may be made to the President as will induce him to direct the reoccupation of the territory named.

I am, governor, very respectfully, your obedient servant,
J. L. CHANDLER.

His Excellency ISAAC MURPHY,
Governor of Arkansas.

EXECUTIVE OFFICE,
Little Rock, Arkansas, December 14, 1864.

The foregoing communication is respectfully referred to the President of the United States.

ISAAC MURPHY,
Governor of Arkansas.

No 8.

EXECUTIVE OFFICE,
Little Rock, Arkansas, December 14, 1864.

To Lieutenant Colonel A. W. BISHOP, *greeting:*

Reposing especial confidence in your loyalty, patriotism, and zeal for the welfare of the good citizens of Arkansas, and at the instance of the legislature of the State now in session, I, Isaac Murphy, governor of the said State, do, by these presents, commission and appoint you as special agent of the State for the purpose of carrying to the President the remonstrance and protest of the legislature and people thereof against the abandonment of Fort Smith and its dependencies.

You will proceed with all haste to Washington city and urge the impolicy and ruinous consequences that will follow the enforcement of General Canby's order, and will represent to the President of the United States the condition of the western section of this State as it will necessarily and disastrously be affected by the execution of the said order.

In testimony whereof, I have hereunto set my hand and caused the seal of the State of Arkansas to be affixed at Little Rock, Arkansas, the day and year first above written.

[L. S.]
          ISAAC MURPHY,
          Governor of Arkansas.

By the Governor:
 R. J. T. WHITE, *Secretary of State.*

While *en route* to Washington, a letter of which the following is a copy was received by the undersigned, and used with the foregoing communications:

No. 9.

STEAMBOAT WAR EAGLE, MISSISSIPPI RIVER,
December 17, 1864.

DEAR SIR: In reply to your communication asking information with reference to the practical navigation of the Upper Arkansas river with light-draught boats, I respectfully submit the following facts and suggestions:

I commenced steamboating on the Mississippi river July 4, 1834, and since that time have constantly followed this vocation, having at various periods been master of the following named boats, among others the Pulaski, Elizabeth Rialto, Miami, Marietta, Ed. Walsh, Flying Cloud, Wm. H. Langley, Belvidere, J. J. Cadot, and St. Cloud. I also had a license as a first-class pilot issued under an act of Congress, approved August 30, 1852, by the supervising inspector for the fourth supervising district at St. Louis, specially licensing me to act as such pilot on the Arkansas from the mouth up to the head of navigation of said river.

I first went up this river in 1840, going to Fort Smith, and have navigated it since that time at nearly all seasons of the year, going up forty miles above its confluence with Grand river in the Cherokee nation, and up this river to Fort Gibson. I have likewise navigated the Missouri to Council Bluffs; the Black to Pacahontas, in northeastern Arkansas; the White to Batesville; the Ouachita in southern Arkansas to the mouth of the Little Missouri, fifteen miles above Camden, and the Red river to Fulsom's Bluff in the Choctaw nation, seventy-five miles above Fort Towson. My present address is the Lindell Hotel, St. Louis. It is my experience that the Arkansas is navigable nine months in the year to Fort Smith for boats not drawing more than two feet.

For four months in the year there is an average depth of four feet from its mouth to Fort Smith, and during what is called the June rise it is navigable for boats of the largest draught and capacity.

At present there is an average depth of two feet between Little Rock and Fort Smith, and of three and a half feet from the former place to the mouth of the river, and on this stage of water two round trips, and perhaps more, can be made per month. Boats can be procured or constructed that will carry seventy-five tons of freight on two feet of water from Little Rock to Fort Smith, and tow two barges carrying twenty-five tons each; and such boats are now in commission on some of the tributaries of the Mississippi.

Should it be thought desirable to build others, Pittsburg, Pennsylvania, offers the best facilities. These boats should draw from 12 to 15 inches light; have an extreme length of about 140 feet; 36 feet beam; $3\frac{1}{2}$ feet depth of hold; cylinders, 15 inches in diameter, with $3\frac{1}{2}$ feet stroke. Two boilers would be sufficient.

I remain, very respectfully, yours,

J. J. DAVIS.

Lieutenant Colonel A. W. BISHOP.

No. 10.

[Telegram.]

CAIRO, ILLINOIS, *December 20, 1864.*

Colonel M. LA RUE HARRISON, *Comd'g Fayetteville, Ark.:*

General Canby has ordered the evacuation of Fort Smith and dependencies— General Steele protesting. Should you evacuate also, send out Colonel Gregg's family with yours. Am *en route* to Washington to remonstrate against this most disastrous proceeding.

A. W. BISHOP.

No. 11.

[Telegram.]

FAYETTEVILLE, ARKANSAS,
December 22, 1864.

Lieutenant Colonel A. W. BISHOP, *Washington, D. C.:*

You will arrive in a day or two. Exert yourself for northwestern Arkansas. Don't let government leave a thousand Union families to the tender mercies of assassins and robbers.

I write you to-day; await my letter at Washington.

M. LA RUE HARRISON.
Colonel Commanding.

On the evening of the 27th of December, 1864, an interview was had with the President by the Hon. S. C. Pomeroy, United States senator; Hon. John T. Henderson, United States senator; Hons. Henry T. Blow and Joseph W. Mc-Clurg, members of Congress from Missouri; the Commissioner of Indian Affairs; Colonel Weer, 10th Kansas infantry volunteers; Robert McBratney, esq., presidential elector from Kansas, and the undersigned, that resulted, after interviews also with the Secretary of War, in the following telegrams:

No. 12.

WASHINGTON, D. C., *December 31, 1864.*

Governor MURPHY, *Little Rock, and the commanding officer, Fayetteville, Ark.:*

I am told to-day by the highest authority that Fort Smith is not to be evacuated. What are your latest advices from that point? Answer at once.

A. W. BISHOP.

January 1, 1865, the following telegram was received at Washington:

No. 13.

FAYETTEVILLE, ARKANSAS, *December* 31, 1864.

Lieutenant Colonel A. W. BISHOP:

General Thayer will wait till January 5, but must have definite orders. Work fast. Get Fayetteville included. It is the work of humanity. I will hold long as I can, but must hear in a few days. All is lost if order is not revoked.

M. LA RUE HARRISON.

January 2, 1865, the undersigned was requested by the Secretary of War to state what he knew concerning the ordered evacuation of Fort Smith, and how he, an officer, came to be in Washington, whereupon the following communication was transmitted to the Secretary:

No. 14.

WASHINGTON, D. C., *January* 2, 1865.

SIR: I have the honor to submit the following facts in relation to the recently ordered evacuation of Fort Smith and dependencies:

General Canby's order to that effect, dated the 5th December, was received at Little Rock, on or about the 13th ultimo, and on the evening of that day was telegraphed, by order of General Steele, to Lewisburg, 60 miles west of Little Rock, from which place it was to be forwarded by messenger across the country to Fort Smith, a distance of 120 miles. By General Steele this order was interpreted to be peremptory, and such I understood from him personally, to be the character of his order to General Thayer.

On the morning of the 15th, with the knowledge of General Steele, though not at his suggestion, but accredited by the governor of the State, the legislature then in session, and variously otherwise, as will more fully appear from the documents which I had the honor of laying before the President of the United States on the evening of the 27th ultimo, I started from Little Rock for this city *via* Duvall's Bluff, Memphis and Cairo, to respectfully remonstrate against the execution of this order, or at least to insure, if possible, a suspension of proceedings under it until its disastrous effect upon our frontier interests, especially as concerns the Union people of Arkansas and the friendly Indians, should be brought to your notice.

Fayetteville, which controls northwestern Arkansas and aids in protecting southwestern Missouri, though in no sense a dependency of Fort Smith, (always receiving its stores and supplies from Springfield, Missouri,) is in the district of the frontier, and Colonel Harrison, in command, is fully expecting to be compelled to evacuate.

I have been on duty on the frontier since the spring of 1862, and at no time since our occupation of that country has it been so free from the enemy's presence, especially east of the Cherokee line, as since the disastrous termination of General Price's raid into Missouri; and in making this statement allow me to say, that I but simply repeat the declarations of those much higher in authority than myself.

I am here, I am frank to say, without your permission, but entirely upon the business indicated, and coming at a time when, if we acted at all, we must do so promptly. Permit me also and finally to say, that I am on duty with General Steele's consent, as adjutant general of the State, and awaiting, before resigning my position in the army, the action of the present Congress upon the application of the State for the recognition of her government.

I have the honor to remain, very respectfully, your obedient servant,

A. W. BISHOP,
Lieut. Col. First Arkansas Cavalry Volunteers.

Hon. EDWIN M. STANTON,
Secretary of War.

On the same day a communication, of which the following is a copy, was received and placed on file in the War Department:

No. 15.

FAYETTEVILLE, ARK., *December 23, 1864.*

COLONEL : To-day I replied to your telegram of the 21st instant, from Cairo. I write this as a simple memorandum to guide you in your entreaties for the suffering women and children of northwestern Arkansas. There are thousands of old men, women, and children left here yet. You know their condition. I have from time to time worked to assist and protect them. Since you left I have established, at their request, post colonies at Rheas's Mill, Engle's Mill, Bentonville, Pea Ridge, Elm Spring, and Huntsville, and am about organizing others at Mudtown, Mount Comfort, Oxford Bend, Richland, McGuire's, Middle Fork, West Fork, and Hog Eye.

The plan is:

1. Fifty men, capable of bearing arms, unite and ask to be organized into a home guard company, and permission to settle on a large tract of abandoned land, which is all in one body.

2. They are organized, armed, and move their families to the place.

3. They build a block-house or small fort in the best point on the land (selected by me.)

4. They sign articles agreeing to be loyal to the United States authorities; to abide by the laws and orders from the nearest military post; the laws and present constitution of Arkansas; the proclamation of the President, &c., and are mustered in as home guards.

They also agree to parcel out the land by vote, giving to each one all he wants to cultivate, but to have nothing in common, except common defence and obedience to law. Thus all persons within ten miles of these settlements are expected to enroll their names and belong to them, and none but rebels have, so far, objected.

Six of the settlements have made such progress that each will raise large quantities of corn next season, and the Union Valley settlement has agreed to deliver one thousand tons of hay next season, if needed.

Bentonville and Elm Springs are filling with people who have moved in. Winningham is going to settle Mudtown with fifty Arkansas families returned from Missouri.

All this is no chimera; it is half accomplished now, and the other companies are forming and will be at work within ten days. Some of the forts are nearly done. The refugees have nearly all left this place and gone to the colonies.

Bushwhackers' families have, two-thirds of them, been scared to Texas, and the others are fast going. No bushwhacker can exist here next season if government gives these people a little protection. One regiment here is enough. I have excellent winter quarters just about completed for the whole regiment. You know of the warehouses and forts. The latter have been made almost impregnable with scarp, galleries, &c. You know the rest.

Say it to the powers that be—beg for this distressed people, who have so often been committed to our cause and then had their support withdrawn; represent how few troops I have in this district; I don't ask for more; I don't even ask to stay, though I would like to do so for the sake of the people, but at all events have some troops sent here. You can say all that is needed.

Telegraph me the instant the order is revoked, and telegraph if you fail. It must be before January 1, 1865, if possible, or it will not save us.

Yours, for Arkansas,

M. LA RUE HARRISON,
Colonel First Arkansas Cavalry.

Lieut. Colonel A. W. BISHOP,
Acting Adjutant General, Arkansas.

While it was still unknown by the undersigned whether the order of countermand had actually been issued or not, the following telegram was received:

No. 16.

FAYETTEVILLE, ARKANSAS, *January 7, 1865.*

Lieut. Col. A. W. BISHOP, *Washington, D. C.*

You will please see that the order revoking the order for abandonment of this district, if one has been issued, is sent to Fayetteville, directed to care of Colonel Harrison.

I cannot be ready to leave Fort Smith before 15th instant.

By order of General Thayer:

M. LA RUE HARRISON,
Colonel First Arkansas Cavalry.

To which the following reply was sent:

No. 17.

WASHINGTON, *January 8, 1865.*

General THAYER, *Fort Smith,*
(care Colonel Harrison, Fayetteville,) Ark.:

Order of countermand sent to General Reynolds *via* Cairo, 30th ultimo. Secretary of War away, but department assures me that General Halleck will be requested in morning to telegraph to you to await receipt of this order.

A. W. BISHOP.

No. 18.

In answer to this last despatch the following was received:

FAYETTEVILLE, ARK., *January 9, 1865.*

Lieutenant Colonel A. W. BISHOP, *Washington, D. C.:*

General Thayer says: "Get War Department to telegraph to him at once to this place, *via* St. Louis, that order has been revoked. He must have it immediately or leave in a few days."

M. LA RUE HARRISON,
Colonel First Arkansas Cavalry.

Reply.

No. 19.

WASHINGTON, D. C., *January 10, 1865.*

Colonel M. LA RUE HARRISON, *Fayetteville, Ark.:*

Your despatch of 9th submitted to War Department. Colonel Hardee in charge will see General Halleck to-day. General Thayer will be justified in holding on.

A. W. BISHOP.

On the following afternoon the following closing despatch was forwarded:

No. 20.

WASHINGTON, *January* 10, 1865—4 p. m.

General THAYER, *Fort Smith,*
(care Colonel Harrison, Fayetteville,) Ark.:

The War Department have just assured me that General Halleck will telegraph you to-day the order to General Reynolds.

A. W. BISHOP.

The same day the following telegraphic order was issued:

U. S. MILITARY TELEGRAPH,
Washington, D. C., January 10, 1865.

To COMMANDING OFFCERS *Fort Smith and Fayetteville:*

Lieutenant General Grant has directed that Fort Smith and adjacent posts be not evacuated if they can be supplied, and if they be already abandoned that they be reoccupied as early as supplies can be furnished to them.

These orders have been sent to Major General J. J. Reynolds.

H. W. HALLECK,
Major General and Chief of Staff.

A partial evacuation had taken place before this order was received at Fort Smith, but the troops were recalled and the disasters feared mainly avoided.

The undersigned, by direction of the governor of the State, then remained in Washington until the close of the second session of the thirty-eighth Congress, co-operating with the members elect from Arkansas in endeavoring to secure the recognition of the State government.

A. W. BISHOP,
Adjutant General Arkansas.

APPENDIX C.

ROSTER

OF ARKANSAS MILITIA, ORGANIZED WITH THE APPROVAL OF MAJOR
GENERAL J. J. REYNOLDS, COMMANDING THE
DEPARTMENT OF THE ARKANSAS.

1865-'66.

272   REPORT OF THE ADJUTANT GENERAL OF ARKANSAS.

APPENDIX C.—*Roster of Arkansas militia, organized with the approval of Maj. Gen. J. J. Reynolds, commanding the department of the Arkansas, 1865–'66.*

Names.	Rank.	Date of commission.	Date of approval by department commander.	County organized for.	Remarks.
Nathan Williams	Captain	Feb. 22, 1865	Feb. 22, 1865	Conway	NOTE.—These commissions were all given for a term not exceeding one year from the date of the organization of companies, and, unless revived, ceased from that time to be operative. But a very few reissues have taken place. The commissions issued to subaltern officers it was not considered necessary to have approved by the commander of the department.
T. H. Boyd	do	Feb. 29, 1865	Feb. 29, 1865	Crawford	
Christopher Denton	do	March 27, 1865	March 27, 1865	Van Buren	
George A. Cline	do	March 27, 1865	March 27, 1865	Washington	
John M. Rivers	do	March 27, 1865	March 27, 1865	Madison	
Absalom H. Alfrey	do	March 27, 1865	March 27, 1865	Benton	
Anthony Hinkle	do	April 5, 1865	April 5, 1865	Conway	
A. D. Napier	do	April 8, 1865	April 8, 1865	Pope	
J. B. R. Holleman	do	April 11, 1865	April 11, 1865	Sebastian	
Milton Aldridge	do	April 11, 1865	April 11, 1865	...do...	
James Kennedy, jr	do	April 12, 1865	April 12, 1865	Dallas and Jefferson	
William W. Allen	do	April 13, 1865	April 13, 1865	Madison	
George W. Seamans	do	April 18, 1865	April 18, 1865	Washington	
Joseph R. Rutherford	do	April 18, 1865	April 18, 1865	...do...	
James Carney	do	April 18, 1865	April 18, 1865	...do...	
Bracken Lewis	do	April 18, 1865	April 18, 1865	...do...	
John O. Stockburger	do	April 18, 1865	April 18, 1865	Benton	
William Shreve	do	April 18, 1865	April 18, 1865	Benton	
Elijah H. Butram	do	April 18, 1865	April 18, 1865	Madison	
Elitle Haynes	do	April 18, 1865	April 18, 1865	...do...	
John Wilkinson	do	April 18, 1865	April 18, 1865	...do...	
Bethel Counts	do	April 20, 1865	April 20, 1865	...do...	
Elijah Drake	1st lieutenant	April 20, 1865		...do...	
John A. McCurry	2d lieutenant	April 21, 1865		Polk	
Addison D. Flynn	Captain	April 21, 1865	April 21, 1865	Polk	
George M. Galloway	do	April 22, 1865	April 22, 1865	Conway	
Simpson Mason	do	April 24, 1865	April 24, 1865	Fulton	
William P. Wyatt	1st lieutenant	July 1, 1865		...do...	
John F. Crafton	2d lieutenant	July 1, 1865		...do...	
John B. Brown	Captain	April 24, 1865	April 24, 1865	Izard	
Jesse Shortess	do	April 24, 1865	April 24, 1865	Benton	
John Gillcoat	do	April 24, 1865	April 24, 1865	Sevier	
Jonas B. Spivey	do	April 25, 1865	April 26, 1865	Montgomery	
P. R. Miller	1st lieutenant	April 25, 1865		...do...	
Ezekiel Golden	2d lieutenant	April 25, 1865		...do...	
Graphen H. Greene	Captain	April 26, 1865	April 26, 1865	Clark	
Samuel G. Weaver	1st lieutenant	April 26, 1865		...do...	
William B. Lack	Captain	April 26, 1865	April 26, 1865	Searcy	
Peter Moseley	do	May 1, 1865	May 1, 1865	Bradley	
George A. Rice	1st lieutenant	May 11, 1865		...do...	
A. P. Knight	2d lieutenant	May 11, 1865		...do...	
Thomas Quinn	Captain	May 3, 1865	May 3, 1865	Arkansas	
A. Rlansett	do	May 2, 1865	May 3, 1865	Benton	
Philip Gregory	do	May 2, 1865	May 3, 1865	Washington	

REPORT OF THE ADJUTANT GENERAL OF ARKANSAS. 273

Name	Rank	Date	Date	County	Remarks
William B. Paggett	....do......	May 6, 1865		Independence	
Daniel W. Wilson	....do......	May 6, 1865		Van Buren	
James H. Greer	....do......	May 8, 1865		Calhoun	
James Boren	....do......	May 10, 1865	May 6, 1865	Hempstead	Resigned June 12, 1865.
George Sutton	....do......	Nov. 27, 1865	May 6, 1865	...do......	Appointed vice Boren, resigned.
Jesse Sewell	1st lieutenant	May 11, 1865	May 8, 1865	...do......	
William W. Ridgeway	2d lieutenant	May 11, 1865	May 11, 1865	...do......	Resigned June 12, 1865.
Harvey Sutton	........do........	Nov. 27, 1865	Nov. 27, 1865	...do......	Appointed vice Ridgeway, resigned.
James H. Reynolds	Captain	May 10, 1865		Conway	
James R. Laffery	....do......	May 12, 1865	May 11, 1865	Yell	
L. A. Reich	....do......	May 14, 1865	May 13, 1865	Perry	
Elijah Rogers	....do......	May 14, 1865	May 14, 1865	Independence	
James Craig	....do......	May 25, 1865	May 15, 1865	Pulaski	
Robert C. Wall	....do......	May 28, 1865	May 25, 1865	...do......	
Warren Drake	1st lieutenant	May 31, 1866	May 28, 1865	...do......	Appointed vice Craig, on expiration of service.
William H. Pennington	....do......	May 28, 1865		...do......	Appointed vice Drake, on expiration of service.
John M. Paty	2d lieutenant	May 31, 1865		...do......	
John P. Sanders	....do........	May 28, 1866		...do......	Appointed vice Paty, on expiration of service.
Carroll Davis	Captain	May 20, 1865		Crawford	
Thomas Whitten	....do......	May 25, 1865	May 25, 1865	Hot Spring	
George W. Jobe	....do......	May 21, 1865	May 25, 1865	Carroll	
Uriah Dowthit	....do......	May 25, 1865	May 26, 1865	Lawrence	
Daniel Yager	1st lieutenant	Aug. 30, 1865		...do......	
John Wanright	2d lieutenant	Aug. 30, 1865		...do......	
James P. Dial	........do........	March 27, 1866		...do......	Appointed vice Wanright, left the State.
William G. Dossey	Captain	May 29, 1865	May 29, 1865	Pike	
M. G. McBay	1st lieutenant	May 29, 1865		...do......	
William M. Kimbro	2d lieutenant	May 29, 1865		...do......	
William W. Frazier	Captain	May 29, 1865		Ouachita	
Russel B. Chitwood	....do......	June 2, 1865	May 29, 1865	Johnson	
Alexander C. Stephenson	....do......	June 2, 1865	June 2, 1865	Searcy	
William K. Bradford	....do......	June 15, 1865	June 2, 1865	Van Buren	
Conway Scott	....do......	June 17, 1865	June 15, 1865	Pulaski	
James M. Greene	....do......	July 26, 1865	June 17, 1865	Independence	
Benton Jones	....do......	Dec. 26, 1865	July 27, 1865	Scott	
John Mouser	1st lieutenant	Dec. 26, 1865	Dec. 27, 1865	Hempstead	
John Galloway	2d lieutenant	Dec. 26, 1865		...do......	
James Cantley	1st lieutenant	Feb. 19, 1866		...do......	
Jesse Payne	Captain	Feb. 21, 1866	Feb. 21, 1866	...do......	
W. B. Morgan	1st lieutenant	Feb. 21, 1866		...do......	
W. A. Curtis	2d lieutenant	Feb. 21, 1866		...do......	
M. C. Duggan	Captain	March 9, 1866	March 9, 1866	Polk	
Anthony W. Davis	1st lieutenant	March 9, 1866		...do......	
Moses Morris	2d lieutenant	March 9, 1866		...do......	
Jacob Hufsteadler	Captain	April 2, 1866	April 2, 1866	Randolph	
John M. Eaton	1st lieutenant	April 2, 1866		...do......	
John D. Dunn	2d lieutenant	April 2, 1866		...do......	
D. L. Downs	Captain	April 6, 1866		...do......	
James F. Clure	....do......	Sept. 13, 1866	Sept. 13, 1866	Jefferson	
Jesse Crits	1st lieutenant	Sept. 21, 1866	Sept. 13, 1866	Pope	
William Stout	2d lieutenant	Sept. 21, 1866		...do......	
Simpson Mason	Captain	Sept. 21, 1866	Sept. 21, 1866	Fulton	

Mis. Doc. 53——18

HISTORICAL MEMORANDA.

Prior to the organization of this militia the Union citizens of various portions of the State had acted together for their mutual defence. In the autumn of 1863, in accordance with orders from Major General Schofield, then commanding the department of the Missouri, several companies of Union men were organized in northwestern Arkansas, the general government issuing arms and ammunition, and when on active service furnishing them with subsistence. These companies were commanded as follows: In Washington county by Captains Bracken Lewis and Mackey; Benton county. Captain Mizer; Carroll county, Captains Gaddy and Walker, and in Madison county by Captain John W. Bivens. There was also a very efficient company organized in West Fork township, Washington county, whose population were pre-eminently loyal, and where, perhaps, to a greater extent than in any other single locality in northwestern Arkansas, outside of a military post, rebellion was made odious and bushwhackers received severe and sudden punishment.

Captain Bivens's company was in active service more than a year, participating frequently in raids upon the enemy and in skirmishes without number.

Captains Lewis and Mackey's companies took part in the defence of Fayetteville on the 3d of November, 1864; and all of these organizations rendered valuable aid to the government, for which they have received no compensation.

In the spring of 1864, while the frontier division of the 7th army corps were in the field, co-operating with General Steele, it became necessary for the defence of Fort Smith, and the Union men living in the vicinity, to organize there also a local militia. Four companies were thus formed to do duty in the surrounding country, commanded respectively by Captains Turner, Smith, Gibbons, and Thomas, the battalion by Major Charles C. Reid. Companies were also organized at Ozark and other points on the Arkansas river. At that time guerillas were unusually troublesome in this portion of the State, and in warfare with them, which was actively waged by this militia, Captains Turner, Gibbons, and Thomas, and many of their men, were killed. These companies likewise have never received pay for their services. At the same time the citizens of Fort Smith were partially organized and drilled, and precautions were taken against an attack upon the town, which was somewhat apprehended when the news reached it of the failure of the Red River expedition, and General Thayer, with the frontier division, was stubbornly falling back with General Steele to Little Rock.

Under the following circumstances the militia, the roster of whose officers is published, next arose:

After the unsuccessful attack upon Fayetteville, and the retreat of the rebel army south of the Arkansas river, in November, 1864, large numbers of the Union people, who had during the fall campaign fled to Fayetteville for protection, were left entirely destitute of the means of subsistence. In addition to this, the order for the abandonment of western Arkansas was issued in the December following, and caused until its revocation the stopping of southward-bound trains and the further importation of provisions by citizens. To prevent utter desititution and wretchedness, the danger of which was exceedingly imminent, several armed colonies were organized by Colonel M. La Rue Harrison, then commanding the post of Fayetteville, and shortly afterwards a general system, similar in character, was inaugurated by the governor of the State, with the approval of the commander of the department of the Arkansas. The object of these companies is elsewhere more specifically set forth, and occasion will only be taken here to allude briefly to results. In northwestern Arkansas, where Colonel Harrison supervised their organization, colonies were established at various places in Washington, Madison, and Benton counties, and preparations were made by him to organize similar ones in the counties of Carroll, Marion, Newton, and Searcy, when the close of the war rendered their establishment unnecessary.

The "Union Valley Post Colony"—a type of them all—located near Rhea's mill, in Washington county, elected J. R. Rutherford, an old citizen of the county, as their captain, built a strong earthwork and stockade redoubt, erected temporary buildings for their families, and went to work earnestly to cultivate the soil. Religious services were observed; a Sabbath and a day school were established, and a blacksmith and wagon shop, and various other appurtenances of a peaceful community, soon sprung up.

As indicative also of the same spirit and necessity in another portion of the State, the following report is presented:

"WHITE OAK COLONY, *Arkansas, May 20, 1865.*

"SIR: I beg leave to submit to you the following report of the White Oak colony. On the 25th of April, 1865, by Special Order No. 105, I was assigned to take charge of this colony. I entered upon my duties the same date, and brought down sixteen government teams freighted with families, and organized the colony on what is known as the "Fish Farm," five miles below Pine Bluff, on the bank of the Arkansas river. Since then, and up to the present date, I have the honor to report the present strength of the colony ninety-six men, home guard militia, (under command of Captain James Kennedy,) forty-nine women, and sixty-two children. I have a day school in operation, with fifty scholars, under a male teacher. I have drawn forty-eight unserviceable government horses for the use of the colony. Notwithstanding the lateness of the season when I organized the colony, and laboring under great disadvantages in procuring farming implements, I have progressed well with corn crops. At this date I have 250 acres of corn planted, and by the 10th of June we will have between five and six hundred acres planted in corn and potatoes. The gardens are also late, but looking well. This colony is composed of loyal, peaceable citizens, and the home guard do their duty as soldiers on guard and picket. This colony is a success, with no expense to the government except rations.

"Very respectfully, your obedient servant,

"WILLIAM LARIMER, JR., *Captain Company A, 14th Kansas Cavalry.*

"Brigadier General POWELL CLAYTON, *Commander United States Forces, Pine Bluff, Arkansas.*"

APPENDIX D.

DISBURSEMENTS

OF

ADJUTANT GENERAL'S OFFICE,

FROM

ORGANIZATION OF PRESENT STATE GOVERNMENT

TO NOVEMBER 1, 1866.

APPENDIX D.—*Disbursements of Adjutant General's Office, from organization of present State government to November 1, 1866.*

1865.			
Jan.	14	For printing letter heads and envelopes...	$21 00
June	13	For warrants drawn to pay expenses of adjutant general in going to and returning from adjutant generals' convention at Boston, Massachusetts, July, 1865............	300 00
Aug.	26	For R. P. Studley & Co.'s bill (St. Louis) for office books............................	311 00
Aug.	26	For office expenses (lights, stationery, postage, &c.) from April 1, 1865, to date.......	50 00
Oct.	3	For office expenses for September, 1865...	13 00
Oct.	31	For stationery...	11 06
Nov.	1	For office expenses for October, 1865...	5 55
1866.			
May	29	For R. P. Studley & Co.'s bill for muster-out roll book and express charges...........	39 25
June	18	For stationery...	2 50
July	23	......do...	7 70
Aug.	25	For postage stamps..	1 00
Aug.	25	For express charges on rolls from St. Louis	2 00
Oct.	31	For postage stamps and box rent	4 03
Oct.	31	For George H. Gibbs's bill for stationery, books, &c.................................	32 00
		Total..	800 09

INDEX.

	Page.
PREFATORY NOTE	1
REPORT OF ADJUTANT GENERAL	2
APPENDIX A.—Roster of Arkansas volunteers	9
First regiment Arkansas cavalry volunteers	10
Field and staff	10
Non-commissioned staff	11
Company A	12
Company B	15
Company C	19
Company D	23
Company E	26
Company F	30
Company G	34
Company H	37
Company I	41
Company K	45
Company L	48
Company M	51
Historical memoranda	55
Second regiment Arkansas cavalry volunteers	57
Field and staff	57
Non-commissioned staff	57
Company A	58
Company B	61
Company C	63
Company D	67
Company E	70
Company F	73
Company G	76
Company H	79
Company I	82
Company K	85
Company L	88
Company M	91
Historical memoranda	93
Third regiment Arkansas cavalry volunteers	96
Field and staff	96
Non-commissioned staff	96
Company A	97
Company B	99
Company C	103
Company D	106
Company E	109
Company F	112
Company G	115
Company H	118
Company I	121
Company K	124
Company L	128
Company M	131
Historical memoranda	134
Fourth regiment Arkansas cavalry volunteers	135
Field and staff	135
Non-commissioned staff	135
Company A	136
Company B	139
Company C	141
Company D	144
Company E	147
Company F	149
Company G	152
Company H	155

	Page.
Company I	158
Company K	161
Company L	163
Company M	166
Historical memoranda	168
First regiment Arkansas infantry volunteers	169
Field and staff	169
Non-commissioned staff	169
Company A	170
Company B	173
Company C	176
Company D	180
Company E	183
Company F	186
Company G	189
Company H	192
Company I	196
Company K	199
Historical memoranda	203
Second regiment Arkansas infantry volunteers	205
Field and staff	205
Non-commissioned staff	205
Company A	205
Company B	208
Company C	211
Company D	213
Company E	216
Company F	218
Company G	221
Company H	223
Company I	225
Company K	229
Historical memoranda	232
Fourth regiment Arkansas infantry volunteers	233
Company A	233
Historical memoranda	235
First Arkansas (six months') infantry volunteers	236
Field and staff	236
Company A	236
Company B	238
Company C	240
Company D	242
Historical memoranda	245
Fourth Arkansas mounted infantry volunteers	246
Company A	246
Company B	248
Historical memoranda	250
First Arkansas light artillery volunteers	251
Battery A	251
Historical memoranda	255
Summary	256
APPENDIX B.—Documents relating to countermand of order for evacuation of Fort Smith and dependencies	257
APPENDIX C.—Roster of Arkansas militia	271
Historical memoranda	274
APPENDIX D.—Office disbursements	275

www.ingramcontent.com/pod-product-compliance
Lightning Source LLC
Chambersburg PA
CBHW060339170426
43202CB00014B/2819